Ch. 647

VISUAL PERCEPTION OF FORM

Visual Perception of Form

LEONARD ZUSNE

Department of Psychology
University of Tulsa
Tulsa, Oklahoma

 ACADEMIC PRESS 1970 New York and London

ACADEMIC PRESS, INC.
111 Fifth Avenue, New York, New York 10003

United Kingdom Edition published by
ACADEMIC PRESS, INC. (LONDON) LTD.
Berkeley Square House, London W1X 6BA

LIBRARY OF CONGRESS CATALOG CARD NUMBER: 70-117111

PRINTED IN THE UNITED STATES OF AMERICA

CONTENTS

10. Applications and Aesthetics

INTRODUCTION

It has been said that the literature on visual form perception is relatively small. It may be small in certain areas or if visual form perception is considered from some narrow point of view. Thus, one annotated bibliography of form perception (Sleight & Duvoisin, 1952) lists only 40 references. The comprehensive bibliography appended to this volume contains, on the other hand, over 2500 items. The impression of paucity in the output of visual-form-perception literature may arise because there is no major work that presents a comprehensive survey of the field. A 1957 symposium publication on form discrimination (Wulfeck & Taylor, 1957) relates it to military problems only. Harold Hake's 1957 study of the contributions of psychology to the study of pattern vision in humans is an excellent contribution itself, and its organization and coverage comes closest to the present volume. Unfortunately, this brief offset publication was also designed for military needs, left substantial areas untouched, and, having gone out of print, has become a rarity. Shape discrimination by animals was reviewed by N. S. Sutherland in a 70-page monograph published in 1961. Finally, a 1966 collection of papers edited by Leonard Uhr deals mostly with pattern recognition by computers. Thus, anyone interested in visual perception of form must work his way through the original papers, review articles on specific topics, and textbook chapters on visual perception of form.

It could be speculated that no comprehensive survey of the field has been attempted because of a lack of agreement on what form is. Looking back through the history of the study of visual form, it is quite clear that form has meant many different things to the many investigators who have chosen to speak about it. A lack of agreement on the definition of crucial concepts, however, has not prevented the publication of comprehensive surveys in other fields, e.g., the field of personality. It could have been one of the reasons, nevertheless. An additional reason could have been the extreme variety of concepts and phenomena associated with visual form, a variety that seems to militate against their integration into any kind of coherent whole. Gestalt psychology did make some lasting contributions in the direction of integration; much of what can be found today in a textbook chapter on visual form is a discussion of it in Gestalt terms. The theory itself was incomplete, however, and the work on visual perception of form that has accumulated since the Gestalt period appears in such books appended to the Gestalt discussion as unrelated sections.

As late as 1965, Clarence Graham, in a handbook on vision and visual perception confessed that, "The field of form perception consists of relatively disjointed areas rather than firmly joined segments [p. 569]." I do not presume to have joined the segments in this volume; it simply appeared to me that, because of the amount of experimental and theoretical work that had accumulated in this field, it was ripe for a comprehensive survey. The possibility of "joining the segments" in the process of preparing such a survey seemed real. The reader needs only to examine the table of contents of this book, however, to see that some degree of joining has occurred only within these "segments." As I struggled with the organization of this volume, it soon became apparent that it probably would not be possible to provide an integrative viewpoint to the mass of material with which I was dealing. The reason for this had already been suggested some 20 years ago. Starting with the publication in 1950 of *The Perception of the Visual World* and in subsequent papers, J. J. Gibson has expounded the idea that, since the concept of visual form was so heterogeneous, it could not be treated on a single level of discourse, let alone encompassed in a single theory. I feel that the reason why the material presented here fails, as a whole, to fall into a single mold is a direct consequence of its heterogeneity.

It therefore seems likely that because the concept of visual form will crumble of its own weight, it will not be possible to write a volume quite like the present one in the future. Form will be considered separately as contour on the psycho-physiological level; as a property of three-dimensional objects in the real world, and hence studied in natural and quasinatural settings and in terms of ecological optics; and as image in the Gibsonian sense, i.e., representations of real objects in photographs, drawings, etc. Whatever the shape of things to come, visual form will lose not only its philosophical antecedents and the Gestalt association of a thing in disembodied space, but also its present (and already weak) conceptual unity. At a time when the field of visual perception of form appears to be approaching a crossroads, this reference volume is offered to those students and researchers who have a need for a systematic source of information on all aspects of perception of static, two-dimensional visual form as it has been conceptualized historically and until the recent past.

The organization of this book reflects both the centripetal forces of theory and broad, integrative concepts and the centrifugal forces of the sheer mass of the material as well as of its heterogeneity. The three chapters following Chap. 1, which surveys the history of the investigation of visual form, are concerned with theoretical formulations. The first of these three chapters talks of the psychophysiology of contour perception, the second considers theories of discrimination and recognition of pictorial form, while the third one discusses more comprehensive theories of form perception. Each of these chapters also discusses the relevant empirical work.

There is also a large body of experiments which have not been performed in order to confirm or refute a particular theory but which are exploratory in nature or center on some specific problem or hypothesis that is unrelated or only loosely related to a theory. I felt that to force all of these experiments into some theoretical mold was unjustifiable. I had also become convinced that the nature of the perceptual task in a given experiment was a most important variable which modified the effects of all others. Detection, discrimination, scaling, recognition, identification, and reproduction became therefore the major headings under which these experiments are discussed in Chaps. 6 and 7. In addition to the more general and preliminary matters concerning perceptual tasks and response variables discussed in these chapters, the entire Chap. 5 concerning the distal stimulus serves as an introduction to Chaps. 6 and 7. Most of Chap. 5 is about the parameters of the single stimulus and their measurement. That portion of Chap. 5 is organized according to my conceptualization of single form parameters, i.e., as being either transpositional, informational, configurational, or relational. Where the amount of experimentation justifies it, work on visual perception of form in animals (Chap. 8) is also analyzed under these headings, the only type of perceptual task given an animal being discrimination. In Chap. 9, developmental studies are likewise discussed, first, in terms of the perceptual task involved, and second, in terms of the form parameters investigated. Chapter 10 concerns applied form-perception research and discusses experimental findings in the aesthetics of simple forms.

REFERENCES

Gibson, J. J. *The perception of the visual world.* Boston, Massachusetts: Houghton-Mifflin, 1950.

Graham, C. H. (Ed.) *Vision and visual perception.* New York: Wiley, 1965.

Hake, H. W. Contributions of psychology to the study of pattern vision. WADC Tech. Rep., 57-621, 1957.

Sleight, R. B., & Duvoisin, G. An annotated bibliography of form perception. Office of Naval Research, 1952.

Sutherland, N. S. *The methods and findings of experiments on the visual discrimination of shape by animals.* Oxford, England: Experimental Psychology Society, 1961.

Uhr, L. (Ed.) *Pattern recognition.* New York: Wiley, 1966.

Wulfeck, J. W., & Taylor, J. H. (Eds.) *Form discrimination as related to military problems.* Washington, D.C.: Nat. Acad. Sci.-Nat. Res. Coun., Publ. No. 561, 1957.

Chapter 1 / A HISTORICAL PERSPECTIVE ON VISUAL FORM

Form, like love, is a many-splendored thing. Pitrim Sorokin, who studied love so passionately, counts scores of ways in which love has been defined. There are at least as many ways in which form has been described. They range from the shape of a solid object to the values of coordinates in objectless space; from a synonym for the manner in which some event takes place to the philosophical notion of form as opposed to substance. The realm of visual forms proper shows further complexities.

In the area of visual form research, there is no agreement on what is meant by form, in spite of the tacit assumption that there is. In each case, one needs to know what specific operations were performed that led the investigator to use the term "form" before it may be decided whether form was (a) the corporeal quality of an object in three-dimensional space, (b) the projection of such an object on a two-dimensional surface, (c) a flat, two-dimensional pictorial representation, (d) a nonrepresentational distribution of contours in a plane, or (e) the values of coordinates in Euclidean space. Within each of these broad classes of form, several more specific types may be listed.

In this volume, visual form is all those things that psychologists have been calling visual form in their books and research papers. The specific meaning in each case should become clear from the context. In addition to "form," the terms "figure," "shape," and "pattern" are found in the literature. The term "figure" presents no special problems. Its use has no theoretical implications, but it does have a technical connotation: its most specific use is found in the distinction that is made between figure and ground. Otherwise, it is usually applied to a visual stimulus when the emphasis is on the physical properties of the stimulus, as in the phrase, "The figures were cut from black construction paper." Attempts have been made to associate the terms "form" and "shape" with the physical and psychological dimensions of form. Thus, Bartley (1958, p. 92) uses "form" to designate the visual target and "shape" to designate its perception. Alluisi (1960), on the other hand, uses "form" for the response dimension and "shape" for the stimulus dimension. Earlier, Bingham (1914) had applied the term "form" to the physical contour of a stimulus and "shape" to the way it looked when rotated. Most other psychologists have used "form" and "shape" interchangeably. There is no uniform use of these two terms, and the preference for one or the other among those who do not feel there is a need for special terms to designate the stimulus-response dichotomy seems to be dictated largely by the degree of generality that inheres in these terms in common usage: "form" seems to be the most general term, and combinations like "form perception" and references to "form as such" are indicative of this; "figure" is intermediate in generality: it is something more concrete than form, yet not as specific as shape. "Shape" is usually applied to the specific instance of a visual configuration: one cuts out shapes, constructs random shapes, recognizes and identifies them.

The term "pattern" has two major connotations. One is that the configuration consists of several elements, such as dots, lines, or small shapes which somehow belong together. "Pattern" in this sense is sometimes contrasted with "form," which then means a single closed contour. Among those working in the area of artificial intelligence and computer simulation of form perception, the term "pattern" is used almost exclusively to denote both single, closed contours and configurations composed of several separate elements. This usage stems from the broader connotation that the word "pattern" has, namely patterned physical energy of any kind. In computer science, "pattern recognition" usually means not just the recognition of patterned light energy, but also of sound patterns and the like. In this book, the term "pattern" is used either to designate visual targets consisting of several elements or where form is discussed in connection with computer work.

1. Philosophical Antecedents and the Nineteenth Century

Before visual form and its perception entered the domain of psychological inquiry, it was mainly the occasional concern of artists and philosophers, and long before there appeared the first treatise on form in art, artists were making practical application of some of the aspects of form perception that still engage the attention of the experimental psychologist. The ancient Greek architects were familiar with some of the geometric illusions and corrected for them in the larger structures, such as the Parthenon, where the magnitude of the illusion would be considerable. For instance, the long architraves were made to curve upward in the middle to appear straight to the ground observer, and vertical features, such as columns, were made to incline inward in order to correct for the apparent leaning outward of such features if they were perfectly straight physically. The antique world has also provided us with certain canons of beauty, such as the ideal proportions of a human body, yet neither the Greeks nor the Romans, nor the Renaissance artists contributed much to the understanding of the perception of visual form.

The issue of form and content or matter is as old as philosophy, but the philosophical use of the term "form" is considerably broader than that of the common language. It includes the notion of figure or shape, i.e., sensible, visually or tactually perceptible form, but also an abstract aspect. "That which in the phenomenon corresponds to the sensation, I term its *matter,* that which effects that the content of the phenomenon can be arranged under certain relations, I call its form," said Kant. In saying so, he was only echoing the great controversy over whether objects "imitated" ideal forms or not. It started between Plato and Aristotle, has been repeatedly engaged in by philosophers and theologians through the Middle Ages (e.g., Thomas Aquinas), and has continued in some fashion or another in the writings of Hobbes, Bacon, Descartes, Spinoza, Locke, and others. This continuing discussion has made little if any difference as far as the perception of sensible form is concerned.

Since space is a fundamental concept in philosophy, space perception has entered the discussions of philosophers as well, but with equally meager results as far as psychology is concerned. In psychology, space perception is a subject with its own peculiar problems and has merited a number of treatments in book form. Since the perception of form is predicated on the perception of space, the high points in the development of philosophical and scientific thought in this area will be touched upon briefly.

James (1890) has an extensive chapter (Chap. 20) on space perception in *The Principles of Psychology.* It brings together the knowledge of the subject as it existed in James' time. It is disheartening to note that, save for shifts in emphasis on this or that factor in space perception, the only significant and influential contribution to the problem since James' time has been Gibson's gradient theory (Gibson, 1950). James' chapter, with a few changes, can still be used today. It has a 13-page historical survey of the problem of space perception at the end. James notes that the first significant contribution to the study of space perception was made by Berkeley. Berkeley attempted to establish the basis of space perception in the touch modality, not in vision. In fact, he insisted that there were no common qualities between vision and touch, an idea that has been since shown to be erroneous. Berkeley's thinking, however, agreed well with James' concept of the "blooming, buzzing confusion" in the visually and otherwise inexperienced neonate. How coherence and coordination of the different sense modalities and therefore space perception emerges was never explained by Berkeley. The British associationists' various attempts at such an explanation did not satisfy James, and it is not necessary to discuss them here.

As James states, there are but three possible kinds of theory concerning space: (a) sensations have no spatial quality, and space is merely a symbol of succession, i.e., a derivative of time; (b) in certain sensations, an extensive quality is given immediately; and (c) space is an inborn, intuitive category, which is imposed upon sensations from within. The latter is the Kantian view. Space and time are transcendental forms of intuition. In this sense, form is pure order, organization, structure having no sensory content. Because of his influence, Kant, by taking space out of the realm of the physical, observable, and measurable world, rendered a disservice to psychology, and the scientific study of form perception could not begin until some time later. James, though, dismissed the Kantian position as "mythological," along with those who in some way subscribed to it (Brown, the Mills, Bain, Sully, Schopenhauer, Herbart). To quote from James: "I have no introspective experience of mentally producing or creating space. My space-intuitions occur not in two times but in one. There is not one moment of passive inextensive sensation, succeeded by another of active extensive perception, but the form I see is as immediately felt as the color which fills it out." (James, 1890, p. 275.)

James, the sensationalist, having discovered internal contradictions in Wundt's theory of space perception, dismissed it as "the flimsiest thing in the world" (James, 1890, p. 277). In form perception, Wundt and the school of structuralism represented the last and most refined statement of a position that had prevailed for some time. It was based on the dichotomy between sensation and perception. Sensations were elementary processes and perceptions were more complex ones made up of sensational elements. One wondered, though, what the sensations were for the obviously complex experience of seeing form, that is, visual form perception. One of the answers given, which was also Wundt's (Wundt, 1880-1883, II, p. 457-460), was that the elementary sensations underlying form perception were the sensations of points of light. A line was composed of such points of light, and lines made up the contour of a form. What constituted a point of light was a question never answered satisfactorily. Referring to the mosaic of points formed on the retina due to the existence of discrete retinal elements did not provide a solution either, but the greatest difficulty arose in attempts to explain how the points of light became connected together to produce the perception of a continuous, unitary contour. It was this notion that James objected to. The Gestalt psychologists, who came later, took more time working over Wundt's theory than James did.

In James' hands, Helmholtz fared no better, for unconscious inference (Helmholtz, 1924) cannot produce space quality in the mind unless it is in some way already given in the sensations from which the inference is made. James could have criticized Lotze on the same grounds, for Lotze postulated an inherent capacity of the mind to derive space from nonspatial sensations. The springboard for theories such as Lotze's, and there were a number of them, was the physicists' (originally Newton's) concept of space as a geometric extent in which every point could be determined by means of the Cartesian coordinates.

Since spatial coordinates could not be perceived directly, psychologists had to develop a theory that would attribute to each spatial point a unique characteristic that distinguished it from every other point. It was a matter of simple observation to note that a person could point to and distinguish spatial points. This, it was decided, was possible because each point had its locality characteristic or "local sign." There was controversy, of course, as to whether local signs were something given at birth or learned, but since the local-signs theory has passed from the scene, it is a matter of historical interest only.

To return to James, he chose to dispose of Lotze's theory in these words: "[Lotze] insisted that space could not emigrate directly into the mind from without, but must be reconstructed by the soul; and he seemed to think that the first reconstructions of it by the soul must be super-sensational. But why sensations themselves might not be the soul's original spatial reconstructive acts Lotze fails to explain." (James, 1890, p. 276.)

Psychologists seem to agree that the scientific study of visual form perception started with Ernest Mach. Like Helmholtz and other great German scientists who influenced psychology, Mach was well versed in a number of disciplines: physics, mathematics, physiology, philosophy, and psychology. Mach did not develop a well-formulated theory of form perception or even of perception. His chief contribution, as far as form perception is concerned, is that he corrected the Kantean disservice to psychology by making space and time *sensations* that were correlated with the physical world, hence amenable to scientific study.

His most important book, *The Analysis of Sensations,* first appeared in 1886. While it contains the most complete and latest exposition of Mach's ideas on form perception, the basic concepts appeared both in print and in oral presentations to learned societies in the 1860s, which was about 60 years after Kant's death.

Mach did not break with Kant completely. While it is true that he started a school of positivistic thinking, reducing all phenomena, both physical and psychological, to sensations, he was as nativistic as Kant. Mach, the philosopher, agreed with Kant; Mach, the scientist, by resorting to psychophysical parallelism and the positivistic approach, found a method for bringing space perception out into the arena of scientific inquiry and experimentation. Mach was thus a most important member in the line of descent that links Kant with the Gestalt school by way of the form-quality theorists.

What were Mach's specific contributions to visual form perception? First, he demonstrated that form is experienced independently of other attributes: a melody is experienced immediately as a whole, as a tonal form; a tree is sensed as a whole, not as a composite of leaves, branches, etc.; two differently colored objects are recognized as identical regardless of the difference in color sensations produced by them; recognition and, more generally, experience, is sensation, hence there are sensations of form.

Second, he analyzed the physical form parameters that determine the recognition of a shape. His main thesis was that there is no one-to-one relationship between perception and the geometric properties of form. Mach appears to be the first one to have demonstrated the different precepts elicited by the square and by the same square rotated 45 degrees. It became a favorite demonstration of the Gestalt psychologists to illustrate the importance of central factors in visual perception. He further demonstrated that the same form is more or less readily recognized when compared with itself, depending on the type of symmetry operation performed on it: translation, rotation, reflection, or change in area.

Third, Mach made a contribution to the aesthetics of visual form. Briefly, he attempted to explain the aesthetic preference for straight lines, regularities, and different types of symmetry in terms of the space sensations that such configurations elicit in the perceiver. Finally, based on his discovery of the phenomenon now known as the Mach bands (see Chap. 2), he made an attempt at a mathematical analysis of the appearance of contours where none existed physically. It was based on a principle used by Mach to explain other form-perception phenomena, namely an early form of the adaptation level concept. Mach spoke of the effect of deviations from the mean of the environment and what occurred in instances where such deviations did not form part of a continuum but differed markedly from the surrounding milieu: abrupt changes in a contour are perceptually emphasized and appear as contours themselves; acute angles are magnified and obtuse angles are diminished, hence all angles tend to become right angles, etc.

The above-mentioned Mach's contributions are only those that are directly relevant to visual form perception. Mach spoke of space perception as well, analyzing, e.g., the effect of intersections in a plane figure on the likelihood of its being perceived as a three-dimensional solid, as well as the phenomenon of three-dimensional vision in general. Thus, Mach anticipated a number of very recent research efforts in the psychophysics of visual form.

Mach spent 28 years at the University of Prague, where he did most of his important work. Prague at that time was in the Austro-Hungarian empire. Mach also spoke of space sensations, thus establishing a link between himself and the Austrian school of act psychology, specifically the school of form-quality *(Gestaltqualitaet)*. The doctrine of form quality did not arise because its proponents had special interest in form perception. That they spoke of form is rather incidental to the main point, which was a critique of Wundt's elementism.

Mach's thoughts on space, time, and sensations were anything but a systematic theory. In addition, he had never stated clearly whether he thought form sensations were simply combinations of elements or something not contained in the elements. Christian von Ehrenfels not only systematized Mach's concepts but presented the whole subject of form in such a way that psychologists' interest was attracted to it. In his important 1890 paper, he introduced the concept of form quality. The burden of the paper was to determine whether form was a combination of other qualities or something new. It must be remembered, though, that when Ehrenfels spoke of form quality, he did not have just visual stimuli in mind. Any change occurring in a definite direction was a form quality to Ehrenfels, such as change in color or temperature. Relations were also form qualities. Form quality, in modern terms, was a hypothetical construct of considerable generality. As to visual form, squareness, e.g., argued Ehrenfels, is not inherent to any of the four straight lines that make up a square. When they are brought together, a square appears and is immediately and directly experienced, hence it must be a new element. Form is something more than the sum of its elements. A square emerges as four lines are brought together in a certain relationship.

The elements that made up a form were the *Fundamente* (each separately) or *Grundlage* (if taken together). Form quality emerges as a secondary phenomenon from a *Grundlage*. Making a fine distinction, Ehrenfels saw form quality as something that is independent of the *Grundlage,* yet not given independently. Most psychologists, however, while granting the reality of form, failed to agree with Ehrenfels that it was a new, albeit superior, "element," and used the concept of "parts in relation" to explain form; this, of course, was a more parsimonious approach not requiring the introduction of new concepts.

As a result of Ehrenfels' paper, a large literature arose that discussed the status of form quality. As Helson and Fehrer (1932) have it, "The controversy . . . involved almost every psychologist of the time and contains almost every argument, pro and con, advanced today with regard to the importance of *Gestalt*" (p. 80). Bentley (1902) wrote an ample review and critique of the ideas of the various workers in the school of form quality.

Alexius Meinong, leader of the Austrian school at the University of Graz, elaborated on Ehrenfels' theory, introduced the terms founding contents (*fundierende Inhalte*) and founded contents (*fundierte Inhalte*) for Ehrenfels' *Fundamente* and *Gestaltqualitaet* (Meinong, 1891, 1899), but added little that was useful to the study of visual form perception. In fact, his thinking, more than that of Ehrenfels, drifted even more into the philosophical. To explain how sensory elements are combined to form unitary wholes, he introduced the notion of a higher psychic process, the production process (*Produktionsvorgang*), a concept severely criticized by the founders of the Gestalt school, who saw no need for such a process, since form to them was a given and not something synthesized from simpler elements.

Hans Cornelius, a philosopher, joined the discussion, and proposed that form quality was not a founded content but a founded attribute; more importantly, while founded attributes were given in experience as wholes, they could be destroyed through analysis if attention was paid to the parts (Cornelius, 1892,

1893). The point was that attributes and attention had been dealt with by the elementists–they were contents. Yet act psychologists considered attention an act and the act of founding led easily to attributes. Obviously, the form-quality doctrine had many loopholes, if not worse.

An empirical fact which helped in the development of thinking about form in the form-quality school was the constancy phenomenon. It was noted that a melody sounds the same regardless of where on the scale one begins to play it. Transposed to a different scale, a melody sounds the same. Likewise, a retinal image, when transposed to a different locus on the retina will not produce a different percept but the same form will be seen. It was therefore reasoned, and correctly, that form, lines, and surfaces did not consist of points of light sensations which together resulted in the perception of form, but that form must be something separate and independent that could not be analyzed into more elementary sensations. In terms of the dichotomy then held between sensation and perception, form was neither. At the same time, none of the psychologists of the Austrian school were able to even suggest what the stimulus parameters of visual form could possibly be. Since they were neither points, geometric or actual, nor the form of these points, it constituted a real problem. Gestalt psychologists attempted to solve this problem by resorting to the concept of wholes and the organization of the visual field. It was not a complete success, since the hypothesized process of sensory organization in the brain was a difficult one to demonstrate. It was not until many years later that Gibson arrived at a more felicitous solution.

While the theoretical and philosophical arguments in and around the form-quality doctrine were going on, Friedrich Schumann was carefully observing form. While not shunning theoretical discussion, he also conducted a large number of experiments that now belong to the classical experimental literature (Schumann, 1900a, 1900b, 1902, 1904). Schumann's experiments would not be considered bona fide experiments today. His approach was closer to the Gestalt psychologists' 'crucial experiments,' i.e., demonstrations, and are perhaps best designated as experimental phenomenology. In doing anything experimental at all and in rejecting elementism, Schumann clearly represented a break away from the form-quality school.

Always relating his results to the physical properties of the stimuli and to the factor of attention, Schumann arrived at a number of conclusions that later became basic Gestalt laws. First, he observed that attention may either join the parts of a figure into a whole or else emphasize a part so that the perception of the whole becomes secondary. For example, in the Mueller-Lyer illusion, perception is determined by the impression of the line and the wings taken as a whole; in Mach's rotated square, the impression of angularity and larger size comes from paying attention to the four corners of the diamond and the prominence of the longer distances between the corners along the diagonals.

Here not only attention, a central factor, but also the stimulus properties are important: in the 45-degree-rotated square corners, the most conspicuous portions of the square are located on the vertical and horizontal axes of the visual field. That stimulus properties are not to be neglected was shown by Schumann time and again in dot pattern demonstrations, which anticipated the perceptual grouping demonstrations of the Gestalt psychologists.

There can be no doubt that Schumann was the immediate and direct precursor of the founders of Gestalt psychology, as can be seen from the following partial list of his findings and conclusions: incomplete figures tend to be perceived as complete; nearness as well as equal distances among components make for grouping of components into larger wholes; vertical symmetry favors perceptual connectedness; ambiguous figures have a tendency to be seen as 'good' figures; properties of figures, such as grouping or organization, have their origin in both central and stimulus factors. While there is nothing incompatible with act psychology in Schumann's work, his relatively neutral theoretical attitude contributed to his findings being used as an argument against the doctrine of form quality.

The 1890s and the years around 1900 saw the experimental work of a number of psychologists who did not necessarily belong to any particular school of thought and who concentrated more on empirical findings. Among the names that are still cited in contemporary literature are those of Stratton and Dodge. Stratton is best known for his experiments with inverted vision, but he also studied the role of eye movements in form perception. He showed, e.g., that the aesthetic effect of symmetry had no relation to eye movements, as had been theretofore supposed (Stratton, 1902). Dodge (Dodge & Cline, 1901) invented a useful device for the recording of horizontal and vertical eye movements that was subsequently used in the study of form perception, including the study of visual illusions. It was in the 1890s that interest in visual illusions mounted, on the supposition that a satisfactory explanation of the illusions would provide the key to the understanding of "normal" perception. The volume of literature on perceptual illusions equals only that on three-dimensional vision, but in neither area has the effort expended produced commensurate results.

While most of the important work of the form-quality school was done during the 1890s, Stephan Witasek (1910), Vittorio Benussi (1904, 1914), Theodor Lipps (1900), and others experimented and wrote for some time afterward, until the doctrine of form-quality faded away. It did so for several reasons, the main ones being that act psychologists began to be occupied with matters other than form quality and also because it had failed as a criticism of elementism. As Boring (1950) points out, instead of offering a new point of view, it merely added a new element. The criticism offered by act psychology, however, was taken up shortly by the Gestalt school. This initiated a second period in the history of the psychology of visual form perception, one that was characterized by the dominance of the Gestalt viewpoint.

2. The Gestalt School

The clearest demonstration of Gestalt principles is to be found in the area of visual form perception, and Gestalt psychologists have made full use of this circumstance. The largest number of chapters in Koffka's textbook of Gestalt psychology (Koffka, 1935) are devoted to the perception of two-dimensional visual forms. For this reason, Gestalt psychology is often identified with form perception, even by those who are familiar with the school as a whole.

In spite of the very close connection that Schumann's work had with Gestalt psychology, Schumann himself is not "officially" counted among the founders of that school. There is, however, little conceptual and temporal distance between him and Wertheimer, Koehler, and Koffka, the trio of founding fathers of Gestalt psychology. Edgar Rubin, a Danish psychologist, must be mentioned here as one who made a direct contribution to the raw material of which Gestalt psychology was made. Rubin's name is associated with the figure-ground phenomenon. He started his research on this phenomenon in 1912, the same year in which Wertheimer published the paper on movement that is taken as the official birth of the Gestalt school. Rubin (1914) analyzed visual perception in terms of its two basic components, figure and ground. Figure is that which one pays attention to, which has a "thingness" about it, while the ground is that formless, less conspicuous extent upon which the figure is seen. Rubin's phenomenological analysis of figure-ground relationships and his demonstrations, the phenomenologists' *experimenta crucis,* of the role of attention in the perception of ambiguous, figure-ground reversal pictures made his work made-to-order Gestalt material.

Max Wertheimer was the originator and the 'brain' of the Gestalt school. His 1912 paper that started the Gestalt school was concerned with visually perceived movement and not so much with form perception. Wolfgang Koehler wrote considerably more than Wertheimer. Because of his articulateness, he became the 'front man' of the school, expounding its tenets to all who would listen. His most important, oft-cited, but little-read 1920 book on physical Gestalten deals with fields and systems, including the possibility of the existence of electric fields in the brain. The existence or nonexistence of such fields and how they would account for the existence and perception of Gestalten, contours, and forms have been widely debated and tested experimentally. In 1929, Koehler published *Gestalt Psychology,* the most important general statement of the Gestalt position. The investigation of the phenomenon of figural aftereffects started when Koehler, rather late in the development of the Gestalt school, published a paper on the subject (Koehler & Wallach, 1944). Kurt Koffka, the most prolific of the three men, while not contributing as much in terms of originality as the other two, wrote an encyclopaedic treatise on Gestalt psychology in 1935. It is the most often cited (and read) Gestalt reference. All that the Gestalt school had to say about form and form perception is contained in that volume.

The theory about the fundamental nature of visual form changed a great deal in the Gestalt school as compared with the form-quality school. Elements that combined to produce form were replaced by whole forms, wholes, and dynamic substructures that were, if not greater than, at least different from the sum of any elements that they could be analyzed into. Form perception in the Gestalt school became a less speculative enterprise than it had been before: crucial 'experiments,' i.e., demonstrations were used, specific, demonstrable 'laws' were formulated. While basically phenomenological, the school was friendly to experimentation. However, many aspects of form perception in the Gestalt school lacked precision and clarity, either because the concepts had not been unequivocally defined or because the physical stimulus characteristics of form had not been specified or quantified. Schumann was perhaps first to note that the concept of "form" was not as clear and unequivocal as it appeared; this fact was largely ignored by the Gestalt psychologists. Many years later, J. J. Gibson asked the question "What is form?" again, and found that there were many answers. The concept of Gestalt, as Helson (1925, 1926) pointed out quite early, suffers from all sorts of ambiguity. Gestalt psychologists seemed to know what a 'good' figure was: the circle, the square, the equilateral triangle, and other regular and symmetric figures. Symmetry and other kinds of regularity appeared to be involved, but no one could spell out exactly the common denominator of figural 'goodness' in general terms.

Gestalt psychologists themselves never solved the problem. They remained satisfied that perceptual organization was an incontrovertible fact, but their emphasis eventually shifted to the underlying physiological processes. While Koehler had provided a physiological explanation of form-perception phenomena, it no doubt occurred under the pressure of the *Zeitgeist*. This pressure coincided with the second world war.

World War II marked a period of transition for psychology in many ways. In the United States, the study of the perception of form was given strong impetus by the practical requirements of the Armed Forces. Many psychologists were called upon to do research for the Armed Forces. In the area of form perception, what started out as a number of isolated, little-publicized pieces of military research, turned into important trends of thought in the post-war years. The period of history of the study of visual form that started with World War II is characterized by a decline in the amount of work associated with the Gestalt point of view. The reasons for this decline have been analyzed by the historians of psychology (see Boring, 1950, p. 600). One of them was the great success of the Gestalt viewpoint: much of it became incorporated in general psychology and lost its particular "school" label. As far as form perception is concerned, shortcomings in the Gestalt formulation led to attempts to overcome them. These attempts were successful. The most important development in the study of visual form perception during this last period has been the quantification of form. Since ways were found of relating perception and form in more precise, measurable ways than it had been possible before, the phenomenological Gestalt approach had to recede into background. It did not disappear entirely, but it did become secondary.

3. Contemporary Psychophysics of Form

The first milestone in the quantification of form was the formulation of a theory of information by workers in nonbehavioral fields: communications (Shannon, 1948) and cybernetics (Wiener, 1948). Psychologists adopted the concepts of information theory and applied them to psychological problems immediately; within a year, a paper (Miller & Frick, 1949) had been published showing how informational concepts could be applied to psychology. The authors showed, e.g., that organization or patterning could be quantified. Since form can be looked upon as a set of discrete elements that are organized or patterned in a certain way, the idea was applied in form-perception studies.

Visual patterns consisting of small squares, points of light, etc. are easily quantified. Before information measures could be applied to regular polygons or Rorschach inkblots, however, someone had to point out what the stimulus elements of such configurations were. The credit for having done so goes to Fred Attneave, who published the results of his preliminary work in 1951, then wrote an article (Attneave & Arnoult, 1956) on the quantitative study of shape and pattern perception that is probably the most often cited paper in today's form-perception literature. The contribution of these papers was twofold. First, they showed that information in a two-dimensional shape is contained in its contour, specifically at any point of change in the gradient of the contour, that is, mainly at the vertices, corners, or curves. The "vertices" of a curved shape could be obtained by approximating its contours by means of straight-line segments. Thus, information carried by a two-dimensional shape could be easily assessed. Second, Attneave and Arnoult proposed a number of methods for constructing random two-dimensional shapes that would be more generalizable than any stimuli used theretofore. The significance of this contribution is comparable to that of the introduction, by Ebbinghaus, of the nonsense syllable as a means of studying the learning process.

As has been pointed out by a number of authors, one of the very attractive aspects of information theory is that it makes possible the quantification of organization or patterning. This was first shown by Miller and Frick in 1949. Hochberg and McAllister in 1953 and Attneave in 1954 showed independently the importance of this for Gestalt psychology:

"Gestalt psychologists have been vigorously attacked in the past for assigning a major importance to these concepts, on the ground that they are subjective, unquantifiable, perhaps even a trifle ghostly. Such arguments no longer have much weight, since organization is demonstrably measurable in informational terms: roughly speaking, organization and redundancy are the same. On the other hand, gestalt psychologists must now be prepared to see their most cherished principles subjected to experimental tests which have hitherto been impossible, and perhaps modified as a result . . . . I used the guessing-game technique of Shannon to demonstrate that principles of perceptual grouping such as similarity and good continuation refer to various types of redundancy . . . . I suggested that perception might be conceived as a set of preliminary 'data-reduction' operations, whereby sensory information is described, or encoded, in a form more economical than that in which it impinges on the receptors. Hochberg and McAllister discussed the gestalt organizational principles in somewhat similar terms, giving particular attention to cases of ambiguous organization. (Attneave, 1959, p. 82.)

The breakthrough that was achieved in the field of visual form perception through the application of information theory is best exemplified by the subjection to quantified experimental tests of the Gestalt concept of figural goodness. Gestalt psychologists have insisted, for instance, that 'good' figures are remembered better than 'poor' ones. If figural goodness is the same as organization, and organization is redundancy, i.e., repetition of the same information, then one may suspect that good figures are remembered better because they contain less independent information. Attneave tested this hypothesis experimentally and was able to confirm it. Another "cherished principle" of Gestalt psychology had been that the circle is the "best" possible figure. It should, among other things, possess the lowest detection threshold. Even before the advent of information theory, experimental tests of this idea were inconsistent. What has been learned since about human information-processing capacity suggests that information processing is not a linear function of information content. For optimum performance, a certain amount of stimulus information is necessary, not the least possible amount, which is what the circle presents. While information theory gave impetus to the quantification of visual form, such quantification has not been exclusively in terms of bits of information. In fact, the bit measure has turned out to be a useful measure in certain specific instances only. It did, however, encourage the search for additional measures, and researchers in the 1950s and 1960s have been very diligent in defining numerous configurational measures of visual form. The plethora of such measures is one of the characteristics of present-day form-perception research. It also marks the beginning of a true psychophysics of visual form.

REFERENCES

Alluisi, E. A. On the use of information measures in studies of form perception. *Percept. mot. Skills,* 1960, **11**, 195-203.

Attneave, F. The relative importance of parts of a contour. US Human Resources Res. Center, Res. Note P&MS No. 51-8, 1951.

Attneave, F. Some informational aspects of visual perception. *Psychol. Rev.,* 1954, **61**, 183-193.

Attneave, F. *Applications of information theory to psychology.* New York: Holt, 1959.

Attneave, F., & Arnoult, M. D. The quantitative study of shape and pattern perception. *Psychol. Bull.,* 1956, **53**, 452-471.

Bartley, S. H. *Principles of perception.* New York: Harper, 1958.

Bentley, I. M. The psychology of mental arrangement. *Amer. J. Psychol.,* 1902, **13**, 269-293.

Benussi, V. Zur Psychologie des Gestalterfassens. In A. Meinong (Herausg.), *Untersuchungen zur Gegenstandstheorie und Psychologie.* Leipzig: Barth, 1904.

Benussi, V. Die Gestaltwahrnehmungen. *Z. Psychol.,* 1914, **69**, 256-292.

Bingham, H. C. A definition of form. *J. Anim. Behav.,* 1914, **4**, 136-141.

Boring, E. G. *A history of experimental psychology.* New York: Appleton, 1950.

Cornelius, H. Ueber Verschmelzung und Analyse. *Vtljsch wiss. Phil.,* 1892, **16**, 404-446.

Cornelius, H. Ueber Verschmelzung und Analyse. *Vtljsch. wiss. Phil.,* 1893, **17**, 30-75.

Dodge, R., & Cline, T. S. The angle velocity of eye-movements. *Psychol. Rev.,* 1901, **8**, 145-157.

Ehrenfels, C. V. Ueber Gestaltqualitaeten. *Vtljsch. wiss. Phil.,* 1890, **14**, 249-292.

Gibson, J. J. *The perception of the visual world.* Boston, Massachusetts: Houghton, 1950.

Helmholtz, H. v. *Physiological optics* (Transl. by J. P. C. Southall). Rochester, New York: Optical Society of America, 1924-25.

Helson, H. H. The psychology of Gestalt. *Amer. J. Psychol.,* 1925, **36**, 342-370; 494-526.

Helson, H. H. The psychology of Gestalt. *Amer. J. Psychol.,* 1926, **37**, 25-62; 189-216.

Helson, H. H., & Fehrer, Elizabeth. The role of form in perception. *Amer. J. Psychol.,* 1932, **44**, 79-102.

Hochberg, J. E., & McAlister, E. A quantitative approach to figural "goodness." *J. exp. Psychol.,* 1953, **46**, 361-364.

James, W. *The principles of psychology.* New York: Holt, 1890. (Republished: New York, Dover, 1950.)

Koehler, W. *Die physischen Gestalten in Ruhe und im stationaeren Zustand.* Erlangen: Philosophische Akademie, 1920.

Koehler, W. *Gestalt psychology.* New York: Liveright, 1929.

Koehler, W., & Wallach, H. Figural after-effects; an investigation of visual processes. *Proc. Amer. Phil. Soc.,* 1944, **88**, 269-357.

Koffka, K. *Principles of Gestalt psychology.* New York: Harcourt, Brace, 1935.

Lipps, T. Zu den" Gestaltqualitaeten." *Z. Psychol.,* 1900, **22**, 383-385.

Mach, E. *The analysis of sensations.* Transl. from 5th German ed. Chicago: Open Court, 1914. (Republished: New York, Dover, 1959.)

Meinong, A. Zur Psychologie der Komplexionen und Relationen. *Z. Psychol.,* 1891, **2**, 245-265.

Meinong, A. Ueber Gengenstaende hoeherer Ordnung und deren Verhaeltnis zur inneren Wahrnehmung. *Z. Psvchol.*, 1899, **11**, 180-272.

Miller, G. A., & Frick, F. C. Statistical behavioristics and sequences of responses. *Psychol. Rev.*, 1949, **56**, 311-324.

Rubin, E. Die visuelle Wahrnehmung von Figuren. In F. Schumann (Ed.), *Ber. u. d. VI. Kongress f. exper. Psychol.* Leipzig: Barth, 1914. Pp. 60-63.

Schumann, F. Beitraege zur Analyse der Gesichtswahrnehmungen. I. *Z. Psychol.*, 1900, **23**, 1-32. (a)

Schumann, F. Beitraege zur Analyse der Gesichtswahrnehmungen. II. *Z. Psychol.*, 1900, **24**, 1-33. (b)

Schumann, F. Beitraege zur Analyse der Gesichtswahrnehmungen. III. *Z. Psychol.*, 1902, **30**, 241-291.

Schumann, F. Beitraege zur Analyse der Gesichtswahrnehmungen. IV. *Z. Psychol.*, 1904, **36**, 161-185.

Shannon, C. E. A mathematical theory of communication. *Bell Syst. Tech. J.*, 1948, **27**, 379-423; 623-656.

Stratton, G. M. Eye-movements and the aesthetics of visual form. *Phil. Studien*, 1902, **20**, 336-359.

Wertheimer, M. Experimentelle Studien ueber das Sehen von Bewegungen. *Z. Psychol.*, 1912, **61**, 161-265.

Wiener, N. *Cybernetics.* New York: Wiley, 1948.

Witasek, S. *Psychologie der Raumwahrnehmung des Auges.* Heidelberg: Winter, 1910.

Wundt, W. M. *Logik.* Stuttgart: Enke, 1880-1883.

Chapter 2 / CONTEMPORARY THEORY OF VISUAL FORM PERCEPTION: I. THE PSYCHOPHYSIOLOGY OF CONTOUR PERCEPTION

The term "theory" in this and the next two chapters is used in the sense of all active theorizing about form in any of its aspects rather than in the sense that there might be a single theory of visual form perception. Strictly speaking, we do not even have different theories of visual form perception, because theories that in some way concern themselves with the problem of visual form are so incomplete that they can be labeled "form-perception theories" in the sense only that they all talk about visual form and its perception.

There are, first of all, theories that explain why contours are perceived, as well as how various spatial and temporal factors affect contour perception. These are, by and large, formulations at the neurophysiological and neuroanatomical levels and could be labeled theories of contour detection. Detection theories treat the detecting organism largely as an entity that possesses certain sense organs that respond to light, and concern themselves with the anatomical and physiological properties of these organs and how they respond to variations in photic energy.

Once contour is perceived, it becomes possible for the organism to perform additional operations on it, e.g., to compare two contours present in the visual field (to discriminate between them) or a contour and its memory trace (to recognize it). Discrimination and recognition shift the emphasis to the *experiencing* organism, the organism that learns, compares, and makes decisions; hence, discrimination and recognition theories, of necessity, must concern themselves also with the phenomenon of learning.

Finally, there are a few comprehensive theories of behavior or of perception that deal with the perception of form. These theories do not ask how contours are detected or how they are recognized, but rather, what form is, be it from a physiological, physical, or phenomenological point of view. The present and the following two chapters describe the more important theories in the order just given.

1. Contours and Edges

As far as their effects on the perceiving organism are concerned, in the following, no distinction is made between the terms contour and outline on the one hand, and edge, on the other, save for the not-too-consistent or clear distinction found in common language that associates contour and outlines more frequently with two-dimensional forms or objects that look two-dimensional, such as a silhouette, and edges with three-dimensional objects. It seems that Gibson (see Chap. 5) follows this usage. Contours form where there are sudden changes in some gradient: color, shadow, parallel lines seen in perspective, or texture. A contour is the one-dimensional interface between figure and ground. An object's edge has the same nature: it is a sudden change in color, texture, or the direction of lines, except that an edge here signifies the end of a surface, hence passage to another surface or simply the end of an object. An edge stands out against another surface of some other color, texture, etc., or simply the air. There is no difference between the contours or outlines of a two-dimensional form and the edges of an object when both are projected through the lens onto the surface of the retina.

There is one material difference between a hairline and an edge, though. The two produce unequal distributions of excitation in the nervous system. As a result, the subjective edge does not coincide with the geometric edge, while the perceived hairline does coincide with the geometric hairline, but this is a phenomenon of a different order and is discussed elsewhere in this chapter.

Following this line of reasoning, it is hard to see why some psychologists have found it necessary to compare contours and edges and to point out their similarities and differences. They seem to arise when reversible figure-ground configurations are considered, such as Rubin's vase-face figure. Forgus (1966) and Hochberg (1964) point out that, while both a contour and an edge can delineate only one of two adjacent areas to which they are common, a contour may shift its "allegiance" quite easily, delineating now one, now the other area, if the conditions favor both areas as figure, but that an edge does not do this. That this is true is due to no particular property of edges, however, and it does not make them a different class of phenomenan. Consider Escher's woodcut in Fig. 2-1. It is a partially reversible figure-ground configuration. It differs from Rubin's figure in that, at least in the middle portion, both the dark and the light birds have full contours and both can be seen clearly at the same time if attention is paid to only a pair of them. In Rubin's figure, the faces are at a disadvantage because the eyes are missing, for instance, and the backs of the heads are not complete, while the vase is complete. Anyway, even in Escher's woodcut, if the whole group of birds is looked at at once, attention must be shifted in order to see just the dark or just the light birds. The important point is that "Day and Night" is only a picture, and a labile configuration like this may be produced without too much effort. What would it take to see the same thing in nature, i.e., a labile figure-ground combination among actual birds in flight? It is not an impossibility, but the odds against anyone actually observing such a situation are astronomical. Natural objects simply do not behave in this way. The difference between Escher's woodcut and actual birds in the sky is the difference between thought and actuality. Thought can produce possible, probable, improbable, and plainly impossible ideas and images. Some of the impossible thoughts occasionally acquire thing-like quality, such as in science-fiction films, but they are never real things. It is incomparably easier to think than to make thought reality; likewise, it is incomparably easier to produce a reversible figure-ground configuration than to obtain such a configuration among surfaces and edges, i.e., real objects. When military experts use camouflage, however, edges do shift allegiance between two objects, hence there is no reason to assume that edges are any different from contours.

Hochberg (1964), in addition to using a version of Escher's birds to illustrate the supposed difference between contours and edges, also uses a drawing of one of the so-called impossible objects for the same purpose. A similar object is shown in Fig. 2-2a. If it is assumed, and the drawing certainly is made to suggest it, that the frame is made of four four-sided bars, the drawing does represent an

Fig. 2-1. M. C. Escher's 1938 woodcut "Day and Night." Reproduced by permission of the Escher Foundation.

impossible object. It is more parsimonious, however, to assume that the draftsman made a mistake, hence the drawing is really meaningless. Another parsimonious approach is to assume that the frame bars have not four, but only three sides and that at least two of the bars are twisted along their longitudinal axes. By introducing some shading in the original figure and remembering that if we looked at the other side of the frame we would see only two edges of each bar, the "impossible" object no longer looks impossible (Fig. 2-2b). The often-reproduced three-stick clevis (Schuster, 1964) shown in Fig. 2-2c is another such "impossible" object. It is only impossible if it is assumed that it is a representation of an actual object. Again, a more parsimonious approach, because it involves fewer and simpler assumptions, is to consider it either a mistake or a joke in two dimensions. It is quite possible that the original drawing was an honest draftsman's mistake. Penrose and Penrose (1958) were first to present some examples of these "impossible" objects, e.g., the ever-ascending-descending closed staircase. They inspired some of Escher's (see Escher, 1960)

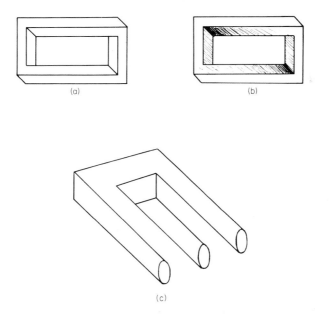

Fig. 2-2. "Impossible objects." (b) is from J. Hochberg. The Psychophysics of pictorial perception. *Audio Vis. Comm. Rev.*, 1962, **10**(5), 22–54. Reproduced by permission. A drawing similar to (c) appeared in an advertisement in *Aviat. Week Space Technol.*, 1964, **80**(12), 5.

art, but their statement that the objects represented a new kind of visual illusion was unfortunate. For one thing, it attached to these drawings a label that belongs to an already hopelessly heterogeneous group of phenomena and therefore suggested that they should be studied with the same degree of seriousness and assiduity as the illusions have been studied. They certainly do not belong with the Mueller-Lyer and other classical geometric illusions. I doubt whether they even merit being called illusions since there is no disparity between the stimulus and the percept, only between the percept and the perceiver's assumption that the drawing represents a real object. The realization of the paradox that such an object cannot really exist produces a feeling of ill ease or amusement. The latter is the more realistic response, since a *jeu d'esprit,* intellectual or visual, is to be enjoyed and not taken seriously.

2. Neuroanatomy and Neurophysiology of Form Perception

A. THE ANATOMY OF THE VISUAL PATHWAY

The anatomy of the mammalian eye and of the nerve pathway between the receptors in the retina and the cortical cells in the visual projection area is now well understood. What surprises at first is that, in man and many mammals at least, the stimulus is usually perceived just as it is despite the tremendous number of deformations and transformations undergone by the light rays and the electrical impulses produced by them.

The optical system of the eye, which consists of the cornea, the lens, the vitreous humor, and the associated fluids, is incredibly poor when compared with man-made optical systems. It is flexible, hence it distorts; it contains gross impurities which obstruct and distort light; and it is not corrected for either chromatic or spheric aberrations; to name just a few of its faults. It does project a recognizable but imperfect image on the retina. The image is further distorted by the physical properties of the retina: the retina is not flat, but concave; it has an excentric blind spot where no reception takes place; and there is a tremendous difference in sensitivity between its center and its periphery. The image itself is not two-, but three-dimensional since, before it falls on the receptor elements proper, it is partially intercepted by the ganglion and bipolar cells of the retina as well as a net of retinal blood vessels. The cones and the rods, in addition to being illogically the deepest, instead of the uppermost, cell layer in the retina, are also oriented with their vertical axes parallel to the light rays.

The receptor elements immediately converge upon the bipolar and ganglion cells, so that only about one million neurons form the optic nerve of one eye instead of more than 100 million, which is the number of single receptor cells in one eye. While foveal cones each synapse with a bipolar cell and these in turn with single ganglion cells (no convergence or divergence), the peripheral receptors show increasing convergence with increasing peripherality: several peripheral receptors converge upon a single bipolar and several bipolar cells converge upon a single ganglion cell. Thus, there is no one-to-one mapping of retinal receptors in the visual cortex. Further decrease in the size of the visual pathway occurs beyond the optic chiasma (Fig. 2-3). Twenty to thirty percent of the fibers do not synapse at the next relay station in the thalamus, but pass on to the superior colliculi and from there to the pretectal region. These last two

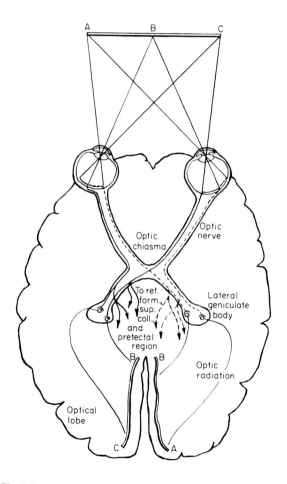

Fig. 2-3. A diagram of the visual pathway in the human brain.

structures mediate eye movements and the pupillary reflex, respectively. Some collaterals also enter the reticular formation without passing through the lateral geniculate bodies of the thalamus. All remaining optic-tract fibers synapse here. In man, there are only about 570,000 cells in each geniculate body, however, which suggests even further compression of information into fewer channels. From the geniculate bodies onward, the fibers continue in a well-defined pathway called the optic-radiation or geniculo-calcarine tract, terminating along the upper and lower lips of the calcarine fissure in that portion of the occipital lobe called the striate cortex (Brodmann's area 17), seat of the visual primary cortical projection area.

The striate cortex is only partially visible from the outside since a portion of it continues on the inside of the longitudinal fissure that separates the two hemispheres of the brain. Like every other region in the brain, it is represented in both hemispheres, each of which receives impulses from one-half of the visual field but originating in both eyes.

The striate area sends axons only into the immediately adjacent prestriate area (Brodmann's area 18), a second visual area which is even more directly involved in pattern vision.

While retinal receptors do not have individual representation in the visual cortex, points of light do map one-to-one on the contralateral occipital lobe (Fig. 2-4). Recordings made from the visual cortex of responses to light stimuli reveal that the foveal region of the retina is overrepresented in comparison with its periphery. Thus, while the topological relationships of a stimulus pattern are preserved in the cortex, this representation is distorted because of the convoluted and curved surface of the cortex as well as the compression of the regions of the pattern whose image falls on the periphery of the retina.

It appears that the striate cortex serves primarily for the perception of light and color while the parastriate is the visual association area and serves the function of form perception. In the conscious human subject, electrical stimulation of area 17 produces sensations of points of light located in space, while such stimulation applied to area 18 gives rise to the perception of forms that have no specific spatial localization. Lesions in this area severely affect pattern recognition.

Most visual stimuli are perceived veridically on the basis of a pattern of electrical impulses which, after having been generated by a distorted retinal image and having themselves undergone a series of recoding processes, produce in the visual cortex only an extremely vague correlate of the physical object. That visual perception under these conditions should remain veridical and, in

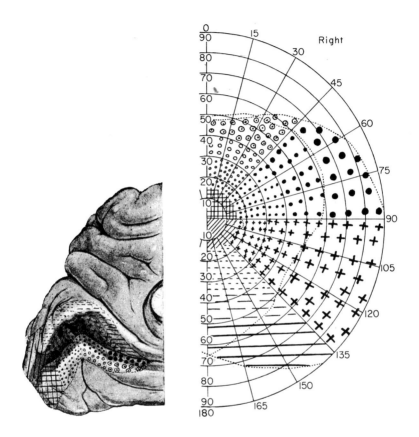

Fig. 2-4. Projection of the retina on the visual cortex. From G. Holmes. The organization of the visual cortex in man. *Proc. Roy. Soc. (London),* 1945, **132B**, 348–361. Reproduced by permission of the Royal Society.

addition, show almost unbelievable sensitivity, far beyond that which could be predicted on the basis of the finest structure of the system, has been considered by many essentially a mystery that demands an explanation. Some attempts at unraveling this mystery are described below. Others have decided that distortion and recoding are nothing peculiar to the visual system but that they are the rule rather than exception in every sense modality, hence perceptual veridicality in spite of a lack of one-to-one correspondence between peripheral and central events in the nervous system is a pseudoproblem. This view is also considered.

B. BRAIN LESIONS AND FORM PERCEPTION

Human Data. Clinical cases of brain injury in humans do not offer much by way of a basis for theorizing about form perception. In fact, the picture of visual information processing in the brain is considerably complicated by certain clinical observations. One such observation is that the perception of embedded figures is affected by lesions not just in the visual area or the visual pathway, but by lesions almost anywhere in the cortex. Aphasic patients with lesions in the speech-association areas do worst on embedded-figure tests (Teuber & Weinstein, 1956), being unable to separate perceptually the figure just seen in isolation from the embedding context (Fig. 2-5). Copying of designs is also disturbed by lesions anywhere in the cortex. In addition, any deficit or incompleteness of the cortex, such as may be found in cases involving low I.Q., immaturity (under age six), senility, or mental disorders, leads to imperfect perception and reproduction of designs. One quantified and standardized test that is usually employed to test for brain damage as well as mental disorder is the Bender-Gestalt Test (Bender, 1938). The nine designs that are presented to the testee for copying incorporate the Gestalt principles of organization, and their reproduction presupposes the ability of the brain to be similarly organized. Two designs of the type used in the Bender-Gestalt Test are shown in Fig. 2-6.

The test is not too sensitive, and significant deviation scores are obtained only with patients with fairly severe brain damage. The specific deviations from

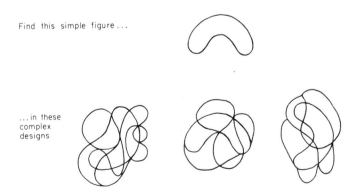

Find this simple figure...

...in these complex designs

Fig. 2-5. A problem from an embedded-figure test.

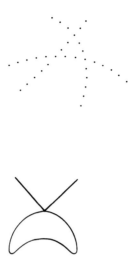

Fig. 2-6. Designs whose reproduction may reveal brain damage.

normal reproduction are numerous. Scoring details for the Bender-Gestalt Test may be found in a 1951 monograph by Pascal and Suttell in which these authors quantify and standardize the test for adults. In general, with increasing cortical damage, disturbance in reproduction increases, resulting in simpler, more primitive versions of the originals and the breaking down of "good" forms and designs. When the lesion is in the striate cortex or elsewhere in the visual pathway, difficulty with the Bender-Gestalt may be accompanied by other visual defects. When no such defects are seen and the Bender-Gestalt scores indicate lesion, it may be inferred that it is not in the visual pathway. The important conclusion is that some aspects of pattern perception in man depend on brain areas other than the striate cortex.

Even when a lesion is in the striate cortex or the geniculo-calcarine tract, the changes which occur in pattern vision are not always those that could be predicted from our knowledge of the topographical projection of retinal points onto the visual cortex. While total destruction of the striate cortex or the interruption of the geniculo-calcarine tract leads to total loss of pattern vision (Teuber, Battersby, & Bender, 1960), partial destruction leaves some pattern vision intact while scotomata or areas of visual loss of smaller or greater extent and shape blanket the rest of the visual field. The scotomata are homonymous but only similar, not congruent, in the two visual fields. This suggests that the two retinas are represented by two overlapping, yet distinct populations of cells in the visual cortex. The scotomata do not affect vision in an all-or-none fashion. That contours are completed over the blind spot has been known for some time, and Gestalt psychologists made quite a point of the phenomenon since it appeared to confirm their notion of the holistic nature of percepts (e.g., Feinberg & Koffka, 1925). Sometimes, scotomata due to brain lesions may be quite large, covering more than one-half of the visual field, yet it is not unusual to find completion of figures taking place when objectively the contours are interrupted to a large extent by the blind areas (Fuchs, 1920, 1921, 1922, 1923; Teuber et al., 1960). This is difficult to reconcile with theories of form perception that postulate a scanning of the visual projection areas (e.g., Pitts & McCulloch, 1947), and even the Gestalt field theory, which emphasizes the phenomenon so much, because it does not fit the assumption of isomorphism between stimulation and cortical events.

In addition to the completion phenomenon, the so-called extinction phenomenon (Bender, 1952) shows that the functional and nonfunctional areas of the retina may interact to produce still another effect not predictable from neuroanatomy alone. When the visual defect in a particular area of the visual field is not too pronounced, objects may be perceived normally as long as they are on a homogeneous background. When another object is introduced in an unaffected portion of the visual field, the object seen first fades or even completely disappears. As soon as the second object is removed, vision of the object in the defective portion returns.

The nonstriate protions of the occipital cortex do not appear to be involved in vision. The removal of these portions in one hemisphere does not produce visual defects either in man (Penfield & Jasper, 1954) or monkey (Ades & Raab, 1949; Lashley, 1948).

Teuber *et al.* (1960) summarize findings regarding defects in form vision due to occipital-lobe lesions by saying that such lesions produce two kinds of effects: focal (such as scotomata) and nonfocal, involving visual functions over the entire field and many aspects of visual performance (difficulty with embededness, right-left discriminations, etc.), and that the presence of the one or the other depends on the nature of the task that the subject is given to perform.

Unilateral temporal-lobe lesions appear to interfere with the understanding of complex pictorial material. In epileptic patients with lesions in the temporal lobes and accompanying visual deficit, the epileptic focus is usually in the inferior and mesial portions of the temporal lobes, but it makes a difference which of the two hemispheres is actually involved. Thus, it is lesions in the right lobe that lead to deficits of space perception. The role of the temporal lobes in form perception is not, however, entirely clear. As a matter of fact, a case may be made either against the involvement of the temporal lobes in pattern vision (e.g., Brindley, 1960) or for it (e.g., Milner, 1954), depending on which studies are taken into account and which are ignored.

There are no reliable reports indicating that visual or form-vision defects have resulted from lesions in the frontal lobes. The parietal lobes, however, do play a considerable role in the perception of form. While there is a large clinical literature on the effects of parietal lobe lesions, the true state of affairs is obscured by the uncontrolled nature and extent of the lesions. Six cases of right-parietal-lobe ablations which come closest to an actual experiment have been described by Hécaen, Penfield, Bertrand, and Malmo (1956). Among the various disturbances in visually guided behavior, such as disorientation in the left portion of the visual field, the most conspicuous one consisted in an extremely poor performance in figure drawing, both when copying and when drawing from memory. Typically, the left side of the drawing was left incomplete, the whole drawing was distorted, and right-left reversals were frequent.

Animal Data. Since in the case of animal subjects the researcher does not depend on the accumulation of clinical cases over the extent and type of which he has no control, it could be expected that animal data would produce a more definitive and complete picture regarding the role that the various portions of the brain play in the perception of visual form. This is true only to some extent: to a large degree, the state of our knowledge here is as incomplete as in the case of humans. For one thing, the greater precision acquired through controlled lesions is offset by the inability of the subjects to produce verbal reports or to perform such tasks as drawing. For another, the ablation of homologous structures in different species does not guarantee that functions will be affected in a homologous fashion. This may be due either to phyletic differences in visual organization or in the localization of visual functions. It has been generally agreed and it is still a tenable assumption that the corticalization of visual functions is directly related to phylogenetic level. The relationship, however, may not be a linear one. The removal of the entire forebrain in fish appears to have little if any effect on visual discriminations (Herter, 1953). The same appears to be true for birds, but there the findings are quite contradictory and puzzling, and a great deal more research is needed. In man, visual functions do depend on the visual cortex to a greater extent than in other mammals. Our data on interspecies differences among infrahuman mammals, however, are so scarce that even tentative conclusions have not been drawn.

Since detailed reviews of the effects of central-nervous-system lesions on form perception in animals are found elsewhere (e.g., Milner, 1954; Morgan, 1965; Teuber et al., 1960), only a summary of the better-established findings will be presented here.

As in man, the destruction of the visual cortex in adult mammals leads to the complete loss of pattern vision. This, however, is not true for young animals.

Young cats, for instance, in whom the striate cortex is completely destroyed, as evidenced by postmortem histological examinations, show unimpaired perform-ance on all tasks involving vision, including the retention of postoperatively acquired discriminations. It is obvious that some other portion of the brain outside the geniculostriate system must take over the visual functions completely.

Incomplete ablation of the visual cortex leads to visual impairment along the lines found in man, although the absence of verbal reports makes it difficult sometimes to know exactly how vision has been affected. There is, e.g., no way of telling whether there is any completion over scotomata, although there is indirect evidence that this phenomenon may take place. Damage short of ablation, such as the horizontal and vertical shorting of the occipital cortex with gold foil and pins, or the isolation of portions of the visual cortex from each other by means of mica plates (Sperry & Miner, 1955; Sperry, Miner, & Myers, 1955) does not seem to have any effect at all on pattern vision in the monkey.

Incomplete ablation of the visual cortex in the rat has never led to a complete loss of the ability to learn pattern discrimination or to retain learned discriminations, as attested by the many studies done by Karl Lashley. Since all visual functioning in the rat appears to be concentrated in the sensory cortex, lesions in any other part of the brain have failed to produce any effect on pattern discrimination whatsoever. Between the rat and the monkey there occurs, however, a gradual spreading of the visual functions into other brain areas. In the monkey, subtotal destruction of considerable areas of the striate cortex leads to some loss in the retention of learned pattern discriminations. The loss, however, may be redressed through retraining. It is difficult to demonstrate that the loss is due to the loss of memory alone since scotomata and other visual defects produced by lesions necessitate new visual adaptations, so that a delay is introduced between stimulus and response until such adaptations have been completed.

In monkeys, the prestriate area covers portions of the occipital, temporal, and parietal lobes. Extensive lesions in this area lead to a loss of memory for learned visual discriminations; in addition, relearning of such discriminations takes more trials than the original preoperative learning. The effects of smaller lesions, however, vary from experimenter to experimenter, and the question of whether such lesions have a definite effect on form perception is yet to be answered.

Frontal-lobe lesions in monkeys have only weak and transitive effects. They are due to factors other than a direct impairment of visual functions. The temporal lobes, however, play an important part in pattern vision, especially visual discrimination. It is the temporal lobe that plays the role in vision formerly assigned the visual "association" area in the prestriate cortex. The most important portion of this lobe as far as pattern vision in monkeys is concerned is the ventral or inferotemporal one. Extirpation of this portion of the temporal

Riggs and Ratliff (1951) were able to show that the tremor is not coordinated between the two eyes, which somewhat undermines the idea of "corresponding points" on the two retinas. This is one effect of the tremor. The other effect, to which the other involuntary eye movements also contribute, is to keep the retinal image in constant motion. It has been calculated (Riggs, Armington, and Ratliff, 1954) that, on the average, a contour will traverse about 10 retinal receptors in 1 sec. With briefer exposures, there is less and less relative movement, until, with exposure times of .01 sec., the retinal image is virtually stationary. This is one way to stop the retinal image. Yet, because of the extremely short duration of the stimulus, no particular phenomenon is observed. A way to stop the retinal image for prolonged periods of time was discovered independently by Lorrin A. Riggs of Brown University (Riggs, Ratliff, Cornsweet, & Cornsweet, 1953) and R. W. Ditchburn of the University of Reading in England (Ditchburn & Ginsborg, 1952). Among the phenomena observed by Riggs and Ditchburn, the most striking was the rapid disappearance of patterns whose retinal image was stabilized, which suggested that physiological tremor played a direct role in form perception. The moving moiré patterns just described are not seen when the image of the stimulus pattern is stabilized (MacKay, 1958).

Prolonged stabilization of the retinal image may be achieved in a number of ways. One is to observe the internal structure of the eye. The retinal capillaries, for instance, are not seen because they cast perfectly stabilized images on the receptors. They may be made visible, however, by rapidly moving a pinhole back and forth in front of the eye and by looking through it at a brightly illuminated surface. This method has been known for a long time. Cornsweet (1962) has suggested a modification of the pinhole method which allows for better control over the stimulus characteristics. The subject is shown a drawing of the gross anatomical features of his retina. At the proper distance and when properly aligned, the visual field appears blank. The variety of stimuli that can be stabilized in this manner is, of course, very limited, and little or no control is afforded over the stimulus. Evans (1966) has proposed a stabilization method that eliminates any kind of attachment or apparatus to the subject's eye and provides maximal stabilization. A powerful flash behind the stimulus pattern leaves a long-lasting, clear, and intense afterimage whose fading, fragmentation, etc. can be conveniently studied and measured. While an afterimage is not an entoptical phenomenon, its image is stable with regard to the retina.

Optical lever systems were the earliest type of device used to stabilize the retinal image. They vary in design and degree of complexity. The basic component of such a system is a small first-surface mirror attached to a contact lens worn by the subject. The stimulus is projected upon this mirror, which reflects it either upon a screen or else into the subject's eye by way of a mirror and lens system. In either case, the effect is to stabilize the retinal image. While the variety of stimuli that can be stabilized is unlimited, the slippage of the contact lens is a problem. Also, additional mirrors, lenses, and prisms must be introduced to compensate for the irregularities of the eye, and the subject's head must be immobilized through the use of a bite board.

A later development in stabilization methodology was the attachment of the target directly to the eye. Pritchard (1961), for instance, has used a miniature slide projector attached to a stalk which sits on a contact lens. The entire optical system weighs only one-quarter of a gram. While slippage of the contact lens may still be a problem, it may be overcome by the subject's lying on a couch or by using a suction-type contact lens.

One of the first findings was that the role of eye movements, including tremor, was not to increase visual acuity but mainly to prevent loss of vision due to invariance of stimulation. This conclusion was confirmed using flickering light to illuminate the target whose image was stabilized. At a rate of about 1 cps., the target remains visible practically all the time (Cornsweet, 1956).

The disappearance of stabilized visual targets is not, however, entirely a matter of local retinal adaptation. Pritchard (1958), for instance, reports that the portions of a target that a subject is paying attention to remains visible for longer periods of time, and that stimulation of other sense modalities, such as a sudden noise, makes faded images reappear. Other nonretinal factors also play a role: Krauskopf and Riggs (1959), for instance, demonstrated interocular transfer of the disappearance of a stabilized retinal image.

Stabilized and faded images reappear if stabilization is not total. Contact-lens slippage makes total stabilization impossible. Yarbus (1957) was able to obtain permanent disappearance after an initial visibility period of only 3 sec. by using a special suction-type contact lens. Otherwise, complete stabilization is possible only when the target is some internal structure of the eye (e.g., Campbell & Robson, 1961; Doeschate, 1954). Such targets disappear in a few seconds and never return.

Using any other method of stabilization leads to an interaction between stabilization and the type of target presented for viewing. Most of the relevant work comes from Pritchard (1961) and others in the McGill group (e.g., Pritchard, Heron, & Hebb, 1960). One interesting finding is that the length of time an image persists is a function of, among other things, its complexity. While a single line may remain visible during one-tenth of the total viewing time, a more complex target may be visible, in whole or partially, up to 80% of the time. Others have made related observations on the disappearance phenomenon. Cohen (1961), for instance, reports that variations in the distance between two parallel lines, one of which is stabilized while the other is not, affects the visibility of the stabilized line: its duration increases with increasing distance between the lines, i.e., a kind of field phenomenon is observed. Tees (1961), however, reports that when the two parallel lines are connected by an additional, stabilized diagonal line, the two parallel lines are seen together much more frequently than the unstablized line and the stabilized diagonal line, so that the field effect is not the only factor involved. That it may have something to do with similarity has been demonstrated by Donderi (1966): when pairs of random shapes are fixated for a relatively long period of time (5 min.), one of them or both tend to disappear. The duration of total disappearances increases with increased scaled similarity of the forms. Donderi hypothesizes that this disappearance may be due to cell fatigue at some higher level of the visual system.

Evans (Bennet-Clark & Evans, 1963; Evans, 1965, 1966), using hundreds of subjects, has confirmed the finding of Pritchard that the primary form unit is the straight line. In a pattern such as a cross in a circle, the horizontal and vertical bars of the cross disappear as units. This finding is of considerable importance to some of the theories of form perception that are discussed in more detail in Chap. 5.

The significance of the Ditchburn-Riggs effect for form perception is that it shows that eye movements are an absolute necessity for the perception of contours. The underlying physiological mechanism is not completely understood, however. The exhaustion of photopigments in retinal cells is obviously responsible for the cessation of electrical impulses transmitted from the retina to the visual cortex. Krauskopf and Riggs (1959) suggest that at least two additional mechanisms may be involved: centrifugal control of retinal processes and some sort of neural adaptation in addition to the photochemical adaptation in the retina. Clarke and Evans (1964) think that either the lateral geniculate or the cortex may contribute to the phenomenon also.

The Ditchburn-Riggs phenomenon is unique only in that the technique of stabilizing the retinal image produces a dramatically rapid and complete effect. Basically, it it closely related to several other phenomena of subjective disappearance of visual targets. These phenomena have been known for a long time. In 1804, Troxler described the disappearance of objects in peripheral vision when the observer fixated a point, a phenomenon that now bears his name. Pirenne, Marriott, & O'Doherty (1957), using a 5-degree test field 20 degrees away from the fixation point, found that when the subject fixated a red point, the test field disappeared within 5-10 sec. after the test field was turned on. This time interval remained invariant for luminances slightly above threshold to 1000 times this. At threshold levels, the test field disappears even before all of the rods covered by the image of the target have had a chance to be stimulated, hence the disappearance phenomenon must originate at some level in the visual pathway above that of the photoreceptors (Pirenne, 1962). A similar conclusion has also been reached with regard to stabilized retinal images. A further similarity is that, with stabilized retinal images, the disappearance latency is also in the order of from 3 to 6 sec. (Clarke, 1957), regardless of retinal illumination.

Since the stabilized retinal image is in the fovea, there seems to be no basic difference between these two phenomena.

That even a bright visual field becomes obscured by a dark fog creeping in from the periphery was observed as early as 1865 by Aubert. Test fields under normal illumination tend to disappear under steady fixation if their borders are blurred. Early investigators, such as Ferree (1906) attributed the disappearance of blurred images to the fatigue of retinal receptors and their reappearance to the periodical fluctuation of attention which reestablished the excitation of these receptors. Fry and Robertson (1935), on the basis of a series of experiments, removed the origin of the effect to the retinal synapses, showing that the fatigue of receptors and eye movements were not primarily involved and that the length of disappearances varied directly with the degree of blurredness of the borders of the target. As Dember (1960) points out, the disappearance of blurred images fits well with the Ditchburn-Riggs effect. When the border of a target is narrow, small eye movements cause frequent and large changes in illumination in the area of the border, which in turn keeps the receptors firing actively. When the border is blurred, changes in illumination are small, neural activity in the border region decreases, and the target disappears, which is to say that it is the border which maintains the inside of the target. Without a border, there can be no inside of a target.

The most recently observed related phenomenon is that of luminous figures that when viewed in the dark, undergo fragmentation comparable to that observed with stabilized retinal images (McKinney, 1963). McKinney points out that this and the Ditchburn-Riggs and Troxler effects are all closely related.

3. The Cortical Correlates of Contour

A. CONTOUR AS INTERFERENCE PATTERNS

Karl Lashley advanced the idea that the cortical counterpart of a contour was an interference pattern. Form perception was to Lashley only one aspect of brain functioning. It had to be considered for a complete exposition of how the brain worked, hence what he said about contours cannot be separated from his fundamental notions concerning the functioning of the brain, namely stimulus equivalence, equipotentiality, and mass action.

Starting with a hypothesized memory trace, Lashley stressed that after a first stimulation the stimulus is recognized regardless of whether the same neurons are involved in perception or an entirely different set of them, and that a memory trace cannot be associated with any restricted set of neurons. Lashley believed that memory somehow became a property of the entire brain. Among the basic characteristics of cerebral activity postulated by Lashley were the following: (1) Each stimulus activates millions of neurons in the nervous system, hence the contribution of a single neuron is small; the memory traces that are the basis of stimulus equivalence are the result of changes in a large number of neurons. (2) The memory trace is reduplicated throughout the system in which stimulus equivalence holds (e.g., the striate area). What, then, is the mechanism that leads from a single stimulus exciting a restricted group of cells to the reproduction of this stimulus in the form of a memory trace that establishes itself in all areas of the brain that these cells are connected to? Based on Lorente de Nó's findings of cross-connections and closed neuron loops in the cortex, Lashley assumed that such a system of neurons provides for the spread of nervous excitation from one point along the surface of the system. If there are several points of excitation, interference patterns will form:

Disregarding for the moment the effect of return circuits in order to get a simplified picture, the action should be somewhat analogous to the transmission of waves on the surface of a fluid medium. Interference of waves in such a system produces a pattern of crests and troughs which is characteristic for each spatial distribution of the sources of wave motion and which is reduplicated roughly over the entire surface. A somewhat similar patterning of excitation in the plane of the cortex is to be expected. Spatially distributed impulses reaching the cortex from the retina will not reproduce the retinal pattern of excitation in the cortex but will give rise to a different and characteristic pattern of standing waves, reduplicated throughout the extent of the functional area. An immediate objection is that the excitation of one part of the field may render that part refractory to impulses coming from other parts, and so block the formation of a uniform pattern. However, if the transcortical paths or reverberatory circuits are of random length, as they apparently are, not all in any region will be simultaneously in a refractory state and blocking will not occur. (Lashley, 1942, pp. 313-314.)

This idea had already been adumbrated in a paper on migraine scotomata published a year earlier (Lashley, 1941). The effective stimuli, thought Lashley, must be boundary lines. A linear stimulus should produce parallel waves which, in turn, should lead to a kind of polarization of the neurons lying in these parallel rows, hence simultaneously excited rows of neurons will acquire functional connections. Lashley pointed out that lower animals readily learn the direction of lines, and primitive visual memory rests on the fixation of a direction or directions in visual space. He suggested, in effect, that the organization of the visual field is the same for birds, rodents, man, and probably even the invertebrates, in spite of tremendous differences in brain structure, for the functioning of the brain occurs according to the same plan in all cases. Others have subsequently confirmed some of Lashley's ideas in this respect, even while undermining the idea of nonspecificity.

As to Lashley's main hypothesis that, in the brain, contours are interference patterns created by standing waves of electrical excitation, it did not find much favor among psychologists. The reason for this was the uncertain state of Lashley's more basic notions about how the brain functions, and the interference-pattern hypothesis was based on them. In addition, the hypothesis rested on a fieldlike concept that resembled too much the Gestalt hypothesis of electrical fields in the brain, another controversial issue. While Lashley did not produce any evidence for the actual existence of interference patterns in the brain, Pribram's (1969) current theorizing about memory storage using the hologram analogy removes the "of historical interest only" label from Lashley's hypothesis.

B. HOW WE SEE STRAIGHT LINES

The fact that the cortical representation of a visual pattern is neither a coded message, nonisomorphic with the stimulus, nor like a projected image cast on a screen, but something in between is a clue to the mystery of the true and undistorted perception of contours. If the cortical representation can be that poor and still present no problem to the perceiver, then perhaps the fact that it bears some resemblance to the physical counterpart is purely incidental and is not an essential feature of form perception at all. How something that distorted is restored to perfection remains a mystery only as long as we keep looking at the microstructure of the retinal image, or assume that the brain does it somehow, as suggested by Helmholtz long ago in his "local-signs" theory of form vision. Platt (1960) has called this the "microscope fallacy." At the microscopic level, the proximal stimulus is, of course, a grossly inadequate counterpart of the physical object. A fine line, for instance, is not at all like the image of a line drawn in India ink and cast upon a screen by a slide projector: the latter is wiggly, irregular, discontinuous, and exists in more planes than one. But at this level of observation, another thing becomes evident: if the smallest receptive unit in the retina is the cone or the rod, how is it possible that we see a break in a line whose width is only about one-thirtieth of the width of a cone cell? The explanation of the amazing acuity of vision and perceptual veridicality must be sought, it seems, on a level that is different from the molecular, microscopic, and strictly anatomical and physical level. One such explanation is given by Platt (1960). The explanatory concept invoked by Platt is functional geometry, which is a set of spatial relations that arise in the course of eye movements and are used by the brain to make decisions relative to the straightness of lines and pattern perception in general. Eye movements—physiological tremor, saccades, or scanning movements—have a horizontal, a vertical, and a circular component. If the eye moves parallel to a line, the same retinal elements are stimulated. This self-congruence of electrical impulses in the neurons from one moment to the next indicates to the brain that the line is straight, regardless of exactly which retinal receptors are stimulated, whether there are any gaps in the string of receptors stimulated, such as the blind spot, and regardless of any other distortions in the retinal image as compared with the physical object, i.e., the line. Eye movements perpendicular to the line also convey information about the degree of its straightness: since different receptors are stimulated from one moment to the next, judgments of straightness may be made on the basis of the time lag between signals that come from receptors at the extremes of the excursion of the image of the line on the retina. The circular movements of the eye serve to scan curves, and, if the curve has constant curvature, the same receptors will be stimulated and the principle of self-congruence will lead to the judgment of the existence of arcs of a circle, concentric circles, etc. A straight line is distinguished from a curved one because the brain probably responds to the difference in kinesthetic feedback from the eye muscles produced by rectilinear and torsional movements of the eye.

Platt suggests that learning takes place in the retinal receptors, so that the adult organism requires few or no scanning movements at all to see straight lines as straight. To support his theory, Platt refers to Hebb's work (see Chap. 4) and the prolonged visual learning observed in dark-reared animals and adult humans who see for the first time. The implication is that vision in lower animals whose learning capacity is limited should depend largely on the performance of specific visual receptors that respond to the geometric features of the environment. That such is the case has been demonstrated by the investigators whose work is discussed in the next chapter.

Regardless of whether one agrees with Platt's views or not, and there are many points left unclarified in his theory, the "microscope fallacy" is just that—a fallacy—and for the reasons suggested by Platt. From that point of view, attempts to find patterns of excited cells in the visual cortex that correspond to a physical configuration, electrical fields that are isomorphous with the stimulus, or EEG patterns that suggest inflections along the contours of a polygon are misplaced and irrelevant if the purpose of such efforts is to explain how form happens to be perceived just the way it is. To quote B. F. Skinner on the subject:

Suppose someone were to coat the occipital lobes of the brain with a special photographic emulsion which, when developed, yielded a reasonable copy of a current visual stimulus. In many quarters, this would be regarded as a triumph in the physiology of vision. Yet nothing could be more disastrous, for we should have to start all over again and ask how the organism sees a picture in its occipital cortex, and we should now have much less of a brain available in which to seek an answer. (Skinner, 1962, p. 954. Copyright 1962 by the American Association for the Advancement of Science.)

The EEG experiments reported by Koehler and Held (1949), inspired by the Gestalt concept of isomorphism, are one example of efforts of this type. Bok's

(1959) demonstration that in spite of the convolutions, furrows, grooves, and fissures found in the striate cortex it is essentially a flat surface is another example of the unnecessary assumption that cortical projection needs, like optical projection, a flat screen. While the cortical response does suggest certain correspondence to physical stimulus characteristics, this correspondence is only incidental. In addition, the relationship between the physical characteristics of form and cortical response may be further distorted and complicated by the processes which, in humans at least, intervene between stimulus and response. Thus, John, Herrington, and Sutton (1967) found that evoked EEG potentials differed depending on whether human subjects saw a blank visual field or one containing a geometric form. They also differed depending on the kind of form presented as long as the forms did not differ in area. Two different words equated for total letter area also produced different response patterns, while similar patterns were produced by two similar forms of unequal areas. In other words, the shape of the evoked wave does not depend solely on the set of retinal cells stimulated but also on the perceived content of the stimulus.

4. Neural Interaction and Contour Perception

A. HOW WE SEE SHARP CONTOURS

Mach's Bands. The discussion of the possible mechanisms that underlie the fact that sharp contours are seen as sharp despite a blurred retinal image may be started advantageously with the consideration of the so-called Mach's bands. When a pattern like the one shown in Fig. 2-8 is rotated on a color wheel at a rate sufficient to eliminate flicker, the appearance of the disk is not what one would expect: there is no annulus of width a-b gradually growing lighter from its black core to the point a; rather, the gray is homogeneous throughout the width of the annulus. Two more uniformly gray annuli of widths b-c and c-d are seen surrounding the first one. In addition, a dark circle or band appears at point b and a light circle at point c, i.e., contours appear where physically there are none. Mach, who first described this phenomenon in 1886 (Mach, 1914), used a rectangular strip of paper which rotated on a cylinder instead of a disk, hence the term bands rather than rings. Movement is not a necessary condition for the effect: they appear in photographs and are seen when the retinal image is stabilized (Riggs, Ratliff, & Keesey, 1961).

Mach's explanation of the bands and the uniformity of the gray areas was as follows. The visual system is so organized that deviations from the mean stimulation are emphasized. Points c, for instance, are no more luminous than the neighboring parts, but their luminance is higher than the mean luminance of the immediately adjacent parts. The visual process emphasizes these deviations. At the same time, a homogeneous gradient of gray is hardly perceived as such as

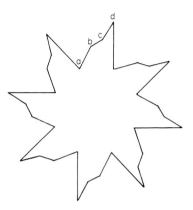

Fig. 2-8. A pattern for the production of Mach's bands. See text for explanation.

long as the luminance of each point equals the average luminance of adjacent points, i.e., a point above the one in question will have a slightly higher luminance and the one immediately below it will be lower in luminance by that same amount. The bands are perceived where there is a change in the rate of change in the gradient. Such significant deviations from the mean luminance are accentuated and contours are perceived where none exist in reality. Making a mathematical generalization of the phenomenon, Mach stated that brightness perception depends on the second derivative of the spatial luminance distribution, or the change in the rate of change of this distribution. Eighty-seven years later, Kovaszany and Joseph (1953) were able to abstract contours in ordinary photographs using an electrooptical scanner. The essence of the process of contour enhancement that results in the conversion of shades of gray into contour lines on a homogeneous background is the formation of the second derivative of light intensity in time, d^2I/dt^2.

   The phenomenon of Mach's bands is related to the phenomenon of assimilation in a *Ganzfeld*. When a uniform gradient of luminance is introduced in the Ganzfeld so that at any one point the gradient is below threshold, the gradient is not perceived by the observer, who continues to see a uniformly illuminated field. However, when a thin vertical line is introduced in the middle of the Ganzfeld, it suddenly reorganizes itself into a darker half-field of uniform luminance and a brighter half-field, also of uniform brightness (Fig. 2-9).

   Mach's conclusion was that "Small differences are slurred over by the retina, and larger differences stand out with disproportionate clearness. The retina schematizes and caricatures." (Mach, 1914, p. 217.) Even though the retinal image is imperfect, a sharp edge is seen as sharp because the blur in the image is

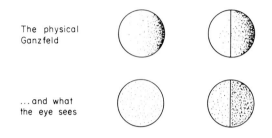

The physical
Ganzfeld

...and what
the eye sees

Fig. 2-9. Assimilation in *Ganzfeld.* See text for explanation.

eliminated through the border-contrast-enhancement effect that gives rise to Mach's bands. It has been found since Mach that the physiological basis for this phenomenon is the well-known process of neural inhibition and facilitation. Hartline (1940) must be credited with the first experiments on the physiology of inhibition in the visual system. He found that, while ganglion cells in the retina summed their respective excitations if stimulated with very small spots of light, increasing the area of the spot actually increased the brightness threshold, which indicated that some inhibitory mechanism was at work. Kuffler (1953) showed that the same cell would act as an on- or off-cell, depending on where the stimulating light spot was or which of two light spots was the strongest. Barlow (1953) produced similar and additional related results in his study of the frog's retina. While the literature on the physiology of the inhibitory mechanism in the visual system is fairly ample, disappointingly little has been added to Mach's original observation on the mode of operation of the retina in this respect. A detailed treatise on Mach's bands, along with translations of pertinent passages from Mach's original writings, may be found in Ratliff (1965), the only complete treatment of the subject.

Statistical Theory of Contour Perception. Marshall and Talbot (1942) have considered in detail the problem of how contours are perceived as sharp and exact in spite of the tremendous amount of diffusion, blur, and distortion produced by the eye, as well as the reduction in the number of elements in the visual nerve from millions to thousands.

The mechanisms that Marshall and Talbot consider in their theory are the following: (a) light diffraction produced by the pupil, which leads to a bell-shaped distribution of intensity along any contour; (b) eye tremor, which distributes the graded intensity among retinal receptors in a nearly statistical fashion; (c) reciprocal overlap between visual pathways, which leads to an enhancement of excitation and its stabilization because of peaking in the distribution of neuronal contacts; (d) neural recovery cycle, which either facilitates or inhibits synaptic transmission, depending on the rate of neuronal firing; (e) the increase in the fineness of grain of the retinal mosaic between the retina and the visual cortex; (f) threshold mechanisms which pass more or less of neural activity; (g) the range of neural activity, which covers about two logarithmic units of stimulus intensity.

Research done by Marshall and Talbot as well as others suggests that the mechanisms of reciprocal overlap and neural recovery cycle produce a summation effect in the nervous system. Neural summation due to reciprocal overlap of neural connection has a vertical and a lateral component. Lateral summation occurs if, e.g., a cell may be fired by the simultaneous action of five synapses, but only three happen to be fired at a time. If these three fire again within a few milliseconds, their action may be added to the residual effect of the preceding firing and the cell in question may now fire, spreading excitation among fringe (submaximally stimulated) neurons. Lateral summation also has a vertical component: maximal response in a group of cells will occur in the center of that group because of the large number of connections involved there. Vertical summation manifests itself as lower synaptic thresholds or faster transmission. The lateral type of summation predominates in the periphery of the retina and the associated afferent neurons, while vertical summation predominates in the fovea and the associated ascending pathways. The lateral component in the foveal system, according to Marshall and Talbot, plays a role in the integration of lines and patterns; the lateral component in the periphery serves to sum intensity from a larger number of receptors; the vertical component, or the peaking effect, aids in preserving pattern vision.

Marshall and Talbot consider the neural summation mechanism as a sort of flexible regulator: it amplifies weak responses and fails to amplify stronger responses. This mechanism is superimposed upon the adaptive mechanism of the receptors. As a result, there is a sliding scale of sensitivity that permits the perception of brightness levels covering a range of 12 logarithmic units.

Reciprocal overlap and neural recovery cycle are two mechanisms of statistical averaging of stimulation in which the time factor is important. Statistical averaging also occurs spatially. Anatomical evidence shows that there is a one-hundredfold increase in neuronal representation between the retina and the cortex:

...Each active retinal cell projects *functionally* to a probability distribution of cortical cells, *not always by the same paths, nor to the same cells.* The peak of this functional cortical distribution from a foveal cone is indeterminate and tends to lie within a small circle, about ¼ mm. in diameter at the cortex. Perhaps only a small fraction of the cells are responding at any instant, but they still conform to this distribution. (Marshall & Talbot, 1942, p. 135.)

The vision of hairlines (minimum visible acuity) where the line subtends a visual angle that is smaller than the width of a single receptor is explained by Marshall and Talbot in terms of the summation effect and of eye tremor: as the image of the line moves back and forth across several receptors, their separate subliminal excitations sum to produce a center of gravity of excitation. There is a further peak in this center of excitation produced by overlapping neuronal connections. The trembling image is further modified by the neural recovery cycle, as is the distribution of intensity. Near an edge, light intensity drops, as does nerve impulse frequency.

Both factors cause neural amplification for impulses within the facilitation period, and neural subnormality for longer periods. For both reasons, propagated activity at an edge is peaked at the bright side and depressed at the dim side, while gradient is enhanced. For the different neurons near a point in a synaptic field will be at various stages of recovery when a burst of activity arrives. This distribution of relative thresholds may be regarded as another statistical mechanism in the transmission, which insures the continual availability of pathway for vision. (Marshall & Talbot, 1942, p. 140-141.)

The cortical activity involved in the perception of edges and hairlines is illustrated schematically in Fig. 2-10.

The overall picture, then, is one of rapidly fluttering retinal image, summation of subliminal stimulation, and the enhancement and stabilization of contours by means of a number of physiological mechanisms whose operation can be best described as massive statistical averaging in a complexly interacting system of neural mechanisms.

As is apparent from Fig. 2-10, Marshall and Talbot predict that the perceived contour of an edge, i.e., the subjective edge, should lie toward the darker of the two areas between which the edge exists, while the perceived hairline should coincide with its physical position. In addition, because of the S-shaped distribution of excitation along an edge and the normal distribution of excitation along a hairline there will be more fluctuation in the position of the subjective edge than the perceived position of the hairline. This prediction may be easily verified by having subjects align two hairlines or two edges, yet it was not until two decades later that such an experiment was actually performed. Springbett (1961) confirmed the prediction of Marshall and Talbot experimentally.

B. INTERACTION BETWEEN CONTOURS

Facilitation, Inhibition, Irradiation. Light falling upon the retina from two adjacent stimulus areas that differ in intensity will activate two sets of neurons in the visual system, one of which will fire more frequently than the other. As a

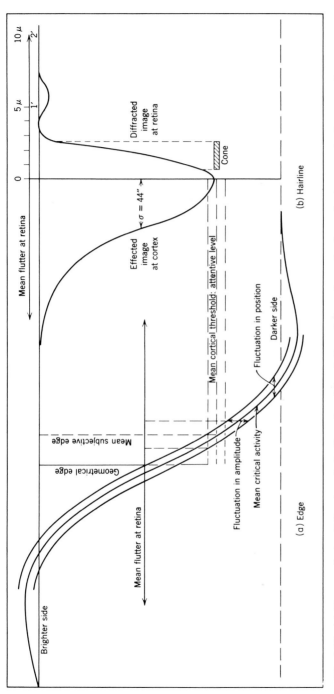

Fig. 2-10. (a) Mean cortical activity at an "edge," produced by static and dynamic mechanisms of primary projection, operating statistically on the (similar) diffraction image. Showing mean "subjective edge" resulting from residual fluctuation at cortex, at a threshold level determined by attention. (b) Optical intensity on retina (due to diffraction) from a line element of bright object. Showing relation to a probability distribution nearly fitting the subjective effect of same. σ is the half-width to inflection. (Arrow shows mean amplitude of physiological nystagmus.) From Marshal and Talbot (1942).

result, a contour between the two areas will be seen. Its sharpness varies directly with the intensity difference. Two factors work toward the enhancement of intensity differences: one is the lateral reciprocal overlap of neural connections (in the retina), the other is the statistical peaking of excitation due to vertical facilitation (further down the visual pathway) of neuronal impulses. Closely associated with the latter phenomenon is neural inhibition on both sides of such ridges of excitation. This results in a decrease in the rate of firing in neurons, hence further accentuation of perceived brightness differentials, i.e., contours. The basic mechanism underlying these phenomena appears to rest mainly on the on-off characteristic of receptive fields in the retina. As these are continually stimulated due to eye movements, sharp, nonfading contours are perceived.

Neural facilitation and inhibition are at work not only in connection with a single contour, but also affect the relationship between two nearby contours and the fields demarcated by them. Bartley (1941, Chap. 10) described amply how contour formation is governed in part by already existing contours in the visual field. Brightness-difference threshold between a circle and a surrounding annulus (i.e., visibility of the contour that separates them) decreases as the area of the annulus is increased. Fry and Bartley (1935) demonstrated that the lowering of the threshold is not due to a summation process brought about by the increased area of the annulus, but that it was effected by the outer contour of the annulus. Using a stimulus configuration such as is shown in Fig. 2-11, Fry and Bartley kept the total area of B and C constant but varied the distance of the B-C contour from circle A. The difference threshold varied inversely with this distance, thus demonstrating the effect of contour B-C and negating the effect of

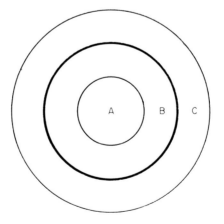

Fig. 2-11. Pattern used by Fry and Bartley (1935) to demonstrate the functional dependence of the visibility of a contour upon the presence of another nearby contour.

area. Other similar experiments led to the conclusion that an existing contour inhibits the formation of other contours nearby.

A related phenomenon is found in visual acuity tests in which parallel light bars on a dark background are used. Wilcox (1932) found that, while the visibility of dark bars on light background increased steadily with increased retinal illumination, the visibility of light bars on a dark background increased up to a certain point, then decreased sharply. This cannot be explained by anything that is known about the anatomy of the visual system. Kravkov (1938) offered the following explanation in terms of contour interaction. As the intensity of the bars is changed, their subjective width also changes: due to the phenomenon of irradiation, a light object on a dark background will appear larger than a dark object of the same size on a light background. This, however, does not explain why, under some conditions, the bars expand, contract, then expand again as their intensity is increased. In addition, the phenomenon is also a function of the width of the bars: when wide (e.g., 6 min. of arc) bars are used, irradiation increases with increasing intensity, whereas it decreases to a minimum, then increases, if the bars are narrow (e.g., 3 min. of arc). Kravkov combined the irradiation and contour-interaction phenomena to explain the observed reversal in the following manner. One border depresses another if it acts upon it at right angles, i.e., when they are both parallel, as in the case of the two longer sides of a bar. The mutual depressing action of the two sides of a bar will cause it to appear narrower; this effect is greater, the narrower the bar. Kravkov called this the "contrast of perceptibility." Increased intensity, which increases the perceptibility of borders, tends to increase the depressant effect still further. Increased intensity, however, also steepens the blur gradient between tthe contours of the bar and the dark background, hence increases irradiation. Thus, net irradiation is the result of two sources of irradiation: "contrast of perceptibility" and stimulus intensity. Kravkov showed how net irradiation first decreases, then increases as intensity increases. Wide bars show no "contrast of perceptibility," hence there is no reversal in the curve of difference thresholds.

Marshall and Talbot (1942) provide a similar explanation of the phenomenon as it takes place in visual acuity tests where two parallel light bars are used as test stimuli:

Irradiation . . . varies with brightness in a way that completely agrees with the observed resolution of two such bars, with a variety of backgrounds, provided the bar is less than 3' wide. But observed irradiation effects for a 6' bar are completely opposed to the observed resolution of such bars. We wish to point out that 4' is approximately the mean nystagmic fluctuation, and that acuity test-bars narrower than this, never expose the retina to uniform intensity within the image. For low intensities, this would result in a neural image like [Fig. 2-12] .... At medium brightness, the bars develop edges; that is, local

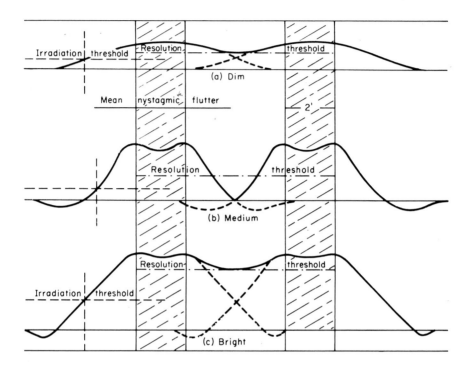

Fig. 2-12. Narrow bars: Single-bar irradiation agrees with double-bar resolution. From Marshall and Talbot (1942)

depression and facilitation bounding the amplified gradient becomes prominent [Fig. 2-12b]. The center is slightly depressed by neural saturation which does not affect the edges. The acuity is greatest because the formed edges attract the threshold of attention away from the interspace and background. At high brightness, the resolution of two narrow bright (or dark) bars is poorer, in agreement with the behavior of single irradiating bars. We attribute this to not one, but several physiological changes. The physical scatter *inside the retina* becomes significant; it moves nystagmically with the diffracted edge, effectively widening the latter. The original edge-gradient is thus reduced, and with it the close external depression [Fig. 2-12c]. The edges are now well peaked, because, though *saturated* in the center, the random flutter prevents *equilibration* there. Hence, the depression of the center is not marked. (Pp. 145-146.)

Metacontrast. Contour interaction that involves the factor of time is found in the phenomenon called metacontrast. Metacontrast, the Broca-Sulzer effect, and the Crawford effect are three forms of visual backward masking. The reduction in the brightness of a light flash when followed by an adjacent second flash was termed *Metakontrast* by Stigler (1910). He and Baroncz (1911) were first to investigate the phenomenon. Fry (1934) rediscovered metacontrast when he found that the center one of three rectangular forms would be masked if it was flashed shortly before the two flanking rectangles. Alpern, who did some work in this area himself, has reviewed (Alpern, 1952) the earlier studies of metacontrast, visual masking, and related matters. The whole field of backward visual masking, including metacontrast, has been reviewed recently by Raab (1963).

If a circle (Fig. 2-13a) is presented for observation first, followed in about 150 msec. by an annulus whose lumen has the same diameter as the circle, only the annulus will be seen if both figures are concentric, i.e., the annulus will produce backward masking of the circle. Longer interstimulus intervals result in either complete visibility and sequential perception of the circle and the annulus or in the darkening of the lumen of the annulus. Shorter intervals may result in considerable brightening of the lumen. First to use such a setup was Werner (1935), who explained it in terms of the time required for the formation of the outside contour of the circle and the inside contour of the annulus. The 150-msec. interval is not long enough for the contour of the circle to be formed

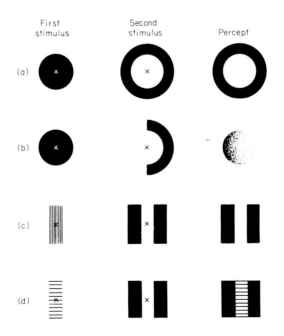

Fig. 2-13. Stimuli and percepts in metacontrast experiments. See text for explanation.

completely. Thus, when a second contour, that which belongs to the annulus, begins to form in the exact same position, its formation is furthered, while the circle, not having a contour, is not seen at all. When the sequence of presentation of the two figures is reversed, however, both the annulus and the circle are seen. Werner, not too clearly, suggested that this result was due to the fact that the circle had only one contour while the annulus had two, and that the outer contour of the annulus was responsible for the visibility of the annulus. The size of the effect of one contour on another depends on their proximity. Werner showed that, when the circle was smaller than the lumen of the annulus, no masking occurred. Thus, one would not expect that the contour of the circle would affect the outer contour of the annulus. At the same time, the visibility of the enclosed area of a figure depends entirely on whether the contour which separates it from the ground is actually perceived. If the contour is not perceived, the entire figure is invisible. Thus, there is still the question of whether the larger solid circle that the observer sees when the annulus is followed by the circle is actually the two figures together (i.e., no masking), or the filling-in of the lumen of the annulus by its unaffected outer contour because the formation of the inner contour has been inhibited by the circle.

Other experiments of Werner's suggest that the phenomenon of metacontrast is not entirely a retinal or neural one but depends on events that take place in the brain. Figure 2-13b shows that, when the masking figure is a semiannulus, about one-half of the circle only is masked while the rest is still seen as a gradient of gray. The vertical stripes in Fig. 2-13c will be masked by two adjacent dark bars, but not the horizontal stripes in Fig. 2-13d. Finally, when the circle is presented to one eye and the annulus to the other, the phenomenon is still obtained.

Considerable literature has accumulated on metacontrast since Werner. These studies have investigated the factors of luminance, duration of the stimuli, interstimulus interval, spatial separation of the stimuli, information content of the stimuli, shape of the stimuli, age and intelligence of subjects, instructions to the subjects, and other factors. An interesting finding is that there is a proactive effect of the shape of the stimulus presented first even when it is not actually seen, i.e., masked by a second stimulus. Smith and Henriksson (1955) presented the fan of lines and the square of the Ehrenstein figure (Fig. 4-16d) in succession. While the fan was not seen by the observers, they did see the square, but it was distorted in the shape of a trapezoid, i.e., the usual illusory effect obtained when the square is seen on the background of the fan of lines. There are other similar reports, but since they actually form part of the literature on discrimination without awareness, they are not further discussed here.

Figural Aftereffects. After looking steadily at the cross of the *I* figure in Fig. 2-14 for about 60 sec., the right-hand set of parallel lines in the *T* figure will

Fig. 2-14. Test (*T*) and inspection (*I*) figures for observing figural aftereffect.

appear to be further apart than the left-hand set of lines. This is the phenomenon of figural aftereffects, first described by Koehler and Wallach in 1944. It plays a prominent role in contemporary Gestalt psychology since it is thought to demonstrate the principle of isomorphism and the existance of electrical brain fields that correspond to the stimulus configuration (cf. Chap. 4). The phenomenon, while weak and undramatic—in one experiment, maximum displacement was found to be of the order of 2 min. of arc—undoubtedly exists and is intimately related to the question of how contours are perceived.

The phenomenon of figural aftereffects is not to be confused with another phenomenon which has often borne the same name. This was first described by Gibson (1933) and hence has sometimes been called the Gibson phenomenon, although Gibson himself called it "negative aftereffect." Hochberg (1964) calls it shape aftereffects. Either visual or tactual inspection of, say, a curved line or surface will produce the perception of a curved line or surface that curves in the opposite direction if the test line or surface is straight. It was Koehler who saw the possibility of utilizing the Gibson phenomenon to produce experimental evidence for cortical electrical fields, hence the connection between it and figural aftereffects.

As Hochberg points out, figural aftereffects and shape aftereffects are at least operationally different phenomena. Figural aftereffects require steady fixation; in fact, the effect may be obtained with stabilized retinal image. Shape aftereffects, by contrast, require active eye or hand movements and cannot be obtained without them. The figural aftereffect implies some sort of fatigue or satiation and a resulting interaction between contours. By the very nature of the operations involved in obtaining shape aftereffects, the satiation and contour- -repulsion explanations are inapplicable here. Since shape aftereffects are only tangentially relevant to the problem of the visual perception of contours, they are not considered here.

The shift in the respective apparent locations of contours that are close together may be called, in general, the displacement effect. Typically, the contours of the test figure are displaced away from the contours of the inspection figure. The effect is maximal, not when the contours of the inspection and test figures abut, but when they are separated. Koehler and Wallach called this the paradoxical distance effect. In addition to the displacement effect, other phenomena may be observed when contours are close together. If a circle is the inspection figure (Fig. 2-15), fixated at a point on its circumference, and if the test figure is a rectangle fixated at the same point, observers report that the portion of the rectangle inside the circle looks smaller (the size effect), paler (color effect), and further back in space (depth effect).

The literature on the figural aftereffect is extensive. A large portion of it is concerned with theoretical issues, some of which are discussed below. The rest is experimental work on the various factors that affect the phenomenon: distance between the inspection and test figures, temporal factors, contrast, area, luminance, and color. Several authors have reviewed this work as well as the entire field of figural aftereffects, e.g., Graham, Bartlett, Brown, Hsia, Mueller, & Riggs (1965) and Malhotra (1966).

Koehler and Wallach explained the figural aftereffect in terms of flow of direct currents in the visual cortex, chemical changes produced in cell membranes by constant stimulation (electrotonus), and the inhibition to further spreading of electrical current due to these changes: a steadily fixated contour produces polarization in brain tissue, so that, when another contour is fixated subsequently and happens to coincide with the first, it will be perceptually (and physically, in the brain) displaced toward a less-polarized region of the brain. The theory, while ingenious, has been criticized on a number of counts. For one, the spreading of currents laterally through the visual cortex can be helped or hindered without any accompanying perceptual changes, e.g., by shorting adjacent cortical areas or isolating them from each other (Lashley, Chow, & Semmes, 1951; Sperry & Miner, 1955; Sperry *et al.*, 1955). A number of investigators have also shown that the apparent displacement of contours sometimes occurs toward the presumably satiated cortical area, not away from it as the theory predicts. The time element is probably the most problematic one.

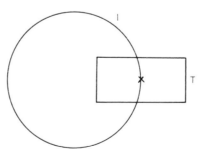

Fig. 2-15. Test (*T*) and inspection (*I*) figures which, in addition to figural aftereffect, produce size, color, and depth effects. See text for explanation.

As the term figural aftereffects implies, the effect takes some time to build up and occurs after the inspection figure has been fixated for some time. Yet there are several studies showing an instantaneous or almost instantaneous effect.

For a while, the most successful competitor of the satiation theory was the statistical theory of Osgood and Heyer (1952). Osgood and Heyer rejected the existence of electrical fields in the brain and based their explanation of the various phenomena associated with the figural aftereffect on the work of Marshall and Talbot, discussed above. The basic feature of the theory of Marshall and Talbot is the statistical distribution or gradient of excitation around the cortical counterpart of a contour. To oversimplify, there is already a peak of excitation occurring along an I-contour. When a T-contour falls next to it, its peak will be displaced because of differential excitability of nervous tissue due to previous stimulation. It is, in short, a fatigue effect. The principle is illustrated in Fig. 2-16.

Since the theory is a fatigue theory, the criticisms that have been brought up against the satiation theory apply here as well. In addition, the Marshall and Talbot theory is based on the existence of the physiological tremor of the eyes, hence the Osgood and Heyer explanation of the figural aftereffect rests basically

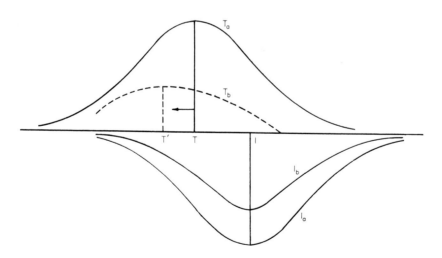

Fig. 2-16. Osgood and Heyer's (1952) theory of figural aftereffects. I_a is the excitation produced by the inspection figure I; after removal of I and before test figure T is presented, differential recovery flattens I_a to I_b; T_a is the excitation produced by T alone; since T falls to one side of I, the bilaterally symmetric distribution of excitation T_a is modified to produce T_b. Since the apparent localization of a contour coincides with the maximum of excitation, the perceived contour of the T figure is now shifted to T'. Copyright 1952 by the American Psychological Association. Reproduced by permission.

on this mechanism. If it could be shown that the effect does not occur in the absence of eye tremor, the theory would receive very strong support. This, however, is not the case. Several investigators (e.g., Hochberg & Hay, 1956) have shown that the effect is observed even when the retinal images of the *I* and *T* figures are stabilized. As these investigators have pointed out, this of itself does not destroy the Osgood-Heyer theory. More importantly, if the physiological assumptions of the satiation and statistical theories are ignored, essentially the same predictions are derived from either one, so that a test of them is not actually possible (Gardner, 1960). The argument around these two explanations of the figural aftereffect is by no means finished. The original articles have produced a discussion that continues even now.

Ganz (1966b) has presented a theory of figural aftereffects based entirely on available psychological and physiological evidence without postulating either the existance of electrical fields, fatigue, satiation, or other problematic factors. Neither are eye movements necessary for the operation of the figural-aftereffect mechanism proposed in this theory. To Ganz, the displacement effect and the proactive nature of the effect appear to be due to two independent mechanisms, and Ganz considers them separately. The mechanism responsible for the displacement effect is lateral inhibition. Ganz shows mathematically why the inhibition of the *I* figure should produce a displacement in the apparent position of the *T* figure. He believes that all contour displacements, whether those observed in a figural-aftereffect situation or those seen in certain geometric illusions, are due to the operation of lateral inhibition. In humans, it is effective in neighboring figures and restricted to about 10 to 20 min. of arc. The idea, as Ganz points out, is nothing new. It was previously suggested by Day (1962) and Deutsch (1964). The reason why the figural aftereffect works in time is simply that the *I* figure leaves an afterimage whose contours continue to interact with the *T* figure after the observer shifts his gaze. For all practical purposes, it does not matter whether the inducing contour belongs to a black or a white figure. Since afterimages decay with time, so does the aftereffect.

Ganz (1966a) has examined the question of whether the temporal sequence of *I* and *T* figures is an essential characteristic of the phenomenon, and has arrived at the conclusion that it is not. In fact, Ganz has marshalled evidence that it is just another instance of simultaneous illusion:

> The inspection of a figure, even momentarily, induces retinal processes which decay exponentially in time as the eye recovers. These residual processes . . . account for light adaptation, the loss of sensitivity which follows exposure to light. It is known . . . that these are in large measure *neural processes involving inhibition* and *not* simply the photochemical bleaching of retinal pigment, although some bleaching is involved. This residual process establishes contours of neural activity at multiple levels of the visual system. These ridges of activity in turn exert lateral inhibitory effects (evidenced by the Mach bands in afterimages,

for example). When a test contour-process is brought close to this inhibition, displacement ensues . . . . In a monocular presentation, such a juxtaposition can occur at the retina, superior colliculus, lateral geniculate nucleus, or visual cortex. In an interocular presentation, the juxtaposition of the ridge of inhibition and the test contour-process can *only* occur at the visual cortex. Color effects (e.g., fading of contrast) and displacement effects can be dissociated (the latter can be obtained without the former) in the interocular presentation because the color effects are predominantly retinal in origin while the displacement effects clearly are not. Therefore, the figural aftereffect is simply another member of the class of geometric illusions. (Ganz, 1966a, p. 163.)

This, again, is not an entirely new idea. About 10 years earlier, Japanese investigators (Ikeda & Obonai, 1955a, 1955b) who, incidentally, have done a considerable amount of work in this field, noted a similarity between the concentric circles (Delboeuf) illusion and the figural aftereffect: as the time interval between inspection and test is reduced, the size of the aftereffect approaches the illusory (simultaneous) effect.

Ganz's views have been recently challenged from two quarters. Pollack (1967) has offered developmental data which show that afterimages and figural aftereffect are due to two different processes. Immergluck (1968a) has offered further evidence that optical illusions and figural aftereffect are different processes by relating both of them to individual differences in field dependence. If the field-dependent person's perceptions are determined by the nature of the immediately present stimulus situation, he would be less affected by the memory trace of an absent stimulus when viewing the test figure in a figural-aftereffect experiment, whereas a field-independent person would show a stronger figural aftereffect. One of Immergluck's (1966b) studies demonstrated this difference. By the same token, a field-dependent person would show stronger illusional responses, while a field-independent person would be able to counteract the classical geometric illusions. This prediction has been also verified by Immergluck (1966a). In still another study, Immergluck (1968b) pitted figural aftereffect against illusory effects in the same stimulus context and measured the responses of field-dependent and field-independent subjects to it. Subjects first looked at the single curved inspection line, then at the modified Hering illusion shown in Fig. 2-17. Immergluck's results were that field-independent subjects saw the seemingly curved line in Hering's illusion as straight, whereas field-dependent subjects continued to see it as curved. If Ganz is correct and the memory trace from the curved inspection line acts in essentially the same way as an immediately present, illusion-producing stimulus, then both field-dependent and field-independent subjects should have continued to see the appropriate line in the Hering illusion as curved. The fact that the field-independent subjects saw it as being straight is explained by Immergluck as the result of the stronger figural aftereffect in this type of subject, which

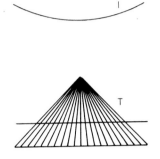

Fig. 2-17. Inspection (*I*) and test (*T*) figures from Immergluck's (1968b) study of figural aftereffects and geometric illusions. Reproduced by permission.

counteracted the illusory effects of the radiating lines in the Hering illusion to "straighten out" the horizontal line which is normally seen as curved.

The evidence suggests ... that the temporal differences between optical illusions and figural aftereffects are much more than incidental and irrelevant differences, and that optical illusions depend primarily on the degree to which a subject is perceptually bound to whatever external stimuli impinge on him, simultaneously and presently, while figural-aftereffect phenomena are locked to as-yet little-understood and temporarily surviving inner trace residues, which in turn appear to be related systematically to a wider and more complex gammut of behavioral and perceptual response categories. (Immergluck, 1968a, p. 200.)

REFERENCES

Ades, H. W., & Raab, D. H. Effect of preoccipital and temporal decortication on learned visual discrimination in monkeys. *J. Neurophysiol.,* 1949, **12**, 101-103.

Alpern, M. Metacontrast; historical introduction. *Amer. J. Optom.,* 1952, **29**, 631-646.

Aubert, H. *Physiologie der Netzhaut.* Breslau: Morgenstern, 1865.

Barlow, H. B. Summation and inhibition in the frog's retina. *J. Physiol.,* 1953, **119**, 69–88.

Baroncz, Z. Versuche ueber den sogenannten Metakontrast. *Pflueg. Arch. ges. Physiol.,* 1911, **140**, 491-508.

Bartley, S. H. *Vision.* Princeton, New Jersey: Van Nostrand, 1941.

Bender, Lauretta. A visual motor Gestalt test and its clinical use. *Amer. Orthophychiat. Ass. Res. Monog.,* No. 3, 1938.

Bender, M. B. *Disorders of perception* Springfield, Illinois: Thomas, 1952.

Bennet-Clark, H. C., & Evans, C. R. Fragmentation of patterned targets when viewed as prolonged after-images. *Nature,* 1963, **199**, 1215-1216.

Bok, S. T. *Histonomy of the cerebral cortex.* Princeton, New Jersey: Van Nostrand, 1959.

References   55

Brindley, G. S. *Physiology of the retina and the visual pathway.* London: Arnold, 1960.

Campbell, F. W., & Robson, J. G. A fresh approach to stabilized retinal images. *J. Physiol.,* 1961, **158**, 1-11.

Clarke, F. J. J. Rapid light adaptation of localized areas of the extrafoveal retina. *Opt. Acta,* 1957, **4**, 69-77.

Clarke, F. J. J., & Evans, C. R. Luminous design phenomena. *Science,* 1964, **144**, 1359.

Cohen, H. B. The effect of contralateral visual stimulation on visibility with stabilized retinal images. *Can. J. Psychol.,* 1961, **15**, 212-219.

Cornsweet, T. N. Determination of the stimuli for involuntary drifts and saccadic eye movements. *J. Opt. Soc. Amer.,* 1956, **46**, 987-993.

Cornsweet, T. N. A stabilized image requiring no attachments to the eye. *Amer. J. Psychol.,* 1962, **75**, 653-656.

Day, R. H. Excitatory and inhibitory processes as the basis of contour shift and negative after-effect. *Psychologia,* 1962, **5**(4), 185-193.

Dember, W. N. *The psychology of perception.* New York: Holt, 1960.

Deutsch, J. A. Neurophysiological contrast phenomena and figural aftereffects. *Psychol. Rev.,* 1964, **71**, 19-26.

Ditchburn, R. W., & Ginsborg, B. L. Vision with a stabilized retinal image. *Nature,* 1952, **170**, 36-37.

Doesschate, J. T. A new form of physiological nystagmus. *Ophthalmologica,* 1954, **127**, 65-73.

Donderi, D. C. Visual disappearances caused by form similarity.*Science,* 1966, **152**, 99-100.

Escher, M. C. *The graphic work of M. C. Escher.* New York: Duell, 1960.

Evans, C. R. Some studies of pattern perception using a stabilized retinal image. *Brit. J. Psychol.,* 1965, **56**, 121-133.

Evans, C. R. Studies of pattern perception using an afterimage as the method of retinal stabilization. *Amer. Psychologist,* 1966, **21**, 646. (Abstract)

Feinberg, N., & Koffka, K. Experimentelle Untersuchungen ueber die Wahrnehmung im Gebiet des blinden Flecks. *Psychol. Forsch.,* 1925, **7**, 16.

Ferree, C. E. An experimental examination of the phenomenon usually attributed to fluctuation of attention. *Amer. J. Psychol.,* 1906, **17**, 81-120.

Forgus, R. H. *Perception.* New York: McGraw-Hill, 1966.

Fry, G. A. Depression of the activity aroused by a flash of light by applying a second flash immediately afterwards to adjacent areas of the retina. *Amer. J. Physiol.,* 1934, **108**, 701-707.

Fry, G. A., & Bartley, S. H. The effect of one border in the visual field upon the threshold of another. *Amer. J. Physiol.,* 1935, **112**, 414-421.

Fry, G. A., & Robertson, V. M. The physiological basis of the periodic merging of area into background. *Amer. J. Physiol.,* 1935, **47**, 644-655.

Fuchs, W. Untersuchungen ueber das Sehen der Hemianopiker und Hemiamblyopiker. I: Verlagerungserscheinungen. *Z. Psychol.,* 1920, **84**, 67-169.

Fuchs, W. Untersuchungen ueber das Sehen der Hemianopiker und Hemiamblyopiker. II: Die totalisierende Gestaltauffassung. *Z. Psychol.,* 1921, **86**, 1-143.

Fuchs, W. Eine Pseudofovea bei Hemianopikern. *Psychol. Forsch.,* 1922, **1**, 157-186.

Fuchs, W. Experimentelle Untersuchungen ueber das Hintereinandersehen auf derselben Sehrichtung. *Z. Psychol.,* 1923, **91**, 145-235.

Ganz, L. Is the figural aftereffect an *after*effect? *Psychol. Bull.,* 1966, **66**, 151-165. (a)

Ganz, L. Mechanism of the figural aftereffects. *Psychol. Rev.,* 1966, **73**, 128-150. (b)

Gardner, R. A. A note on theory and methodology in the study of figural aftereffects. *Psychol. Rev.,* 1960, **67**, 272-276.

Gibson, J. J. Adaptation, after-effect, and contrast in the perception of curved lines. *J. exp. Psychol.*, 1933, 16, 1-31.

Gippenreiter, Y. B., Vergiles, H. Y., & Schedrovitskii, L. P. Novoe o metodike registratsii tremora glaz. *Vop. Psikhologii*, 1964, 10(5), 118-121.

Graham, C. H., Bartlett, N. R., Brown, J. L., Hsia, Y., Mueller, C. G., & Riggs, L. A. *Vision and visual perception.* New York: Wiley, 1965.

Hartline, H. K. The effects of spatial summation in the retina on the excitation of the fibers of the optic nerve. *Amer. J. Physiol.*, 1940, 130, 700-711.

Hécaen, H., Penfield, W., Bertrand, C., & Malmo, R. The syndrome of apractognosia due to lesions of the minor cerebral hemispheres. *Arch. Neurol. Psychiat.*, 1956, 75, 400-434.

Helmholtz, H. von. *Physiological optics.* (Transl. by J. P. C. Southall). Rochester, New York: Optical Society of America, 1924-1925.

Herter, K. *Die Fischdressuren und ihre sinnesphysiologische Grundlagen.* Berlin: Akademie-Verlag, 1953.

Hochberg, J. E. *Perception.* Englewood Cliffs, New Jersey: Prentice-Hall, 1964.

Hochberg, J. E., & Hay, J. Figural after-effect, after-image, and physiological nystagmus. *Amer. J. Psychol.*, 1956, 69, 480-482.

Ikeda, H., & Obonai, T. Figural after-effect, retroactive effect, and simultaneous illusion. *Jap. J. Psychol.*, 1955, 26, 235-246. (a)

Ikeda, H., & Obonai, T. The studies of figural after-effects: IV. The contrast-confluence illusion of concentric circles and the figural after-effect. *Jap. psychol. Res.*, 1955, 2, 17-23. (b)

Immergluck, L. Resistance to an optical illusion, figural aftereffects, and field-dependence. *Psychon. Sci.*, 1966, 6, 281-282. (a)

Immergluck, L. Visual figural aftereffects and field-dependence. *Psychon. Sci.*, 1966, 4, 219-220. (b)

Immergluck, L. Further comments on "Is the figural aftereffect an *after*effect?" *Psychol. Bull.*, 1968, 70, 198-200. (a)

Immergluck, L. Individual differences in figural aftereffect potency: Aftereffect trace versus immediate stimulus context as a determiner of perception. *Psychon. Sci.*, 1968, 10, 203-204. (b)

John, R. E., Herrington, R. N., & Sutton, S. Effects of visual form on the evoked response. *Science*, 1967, 155, 1439-1442.

Junge, K. The moving radii illusion. *Scand. J. Psychol.*, 1963, 4, 14-16. (a)

Junge, K. Final note on the moving radii illusion. *Scand. J. Psychol.*, 1963, 4, 134. (b)

Koehler, W. & Wallach, H. Figural after-effects; an investigation of visual processes. *Proc. Amer. Phil. Soc.*, 1944, 88, 269-357.

Koehler, W., & Held, R. The cortical correlate of pattern vision. *Science*, 1949, 110, 414-419.

Kovasznay, L. S. G., & Joseph, H. M. Processing of two-dimensional patterns by scanning techniques. *Science*, 1953, 118, 475-477.

Krauskopf, J., & Riggs, L. A. Interocular transfer in the disappearance of stabilized images. *Amer. J. Psychol.*, 1959, 72, 248-252.

Kravkov, S. V. Illumination and visual acuity. *Acta Ophthal.*, 1938, 16, 385-395.

Kuffler, S. W. Discharge patterns and functional organization of mammalian retina. *J. Neurophysiol.*, 1953, 16, 37-68.

Lashley, K. S. The problem of cerebral organization in vision. In J. Cattell (Ed.), *Biological symposia.* Vol. VII: Visual mechanisms, edited by Heinrich Kluever. Copyright 1942, Ronald Press, New York. Pp. 301-322.

Lashley, K. S. Patterns of cerebral integration indicated by the scotomas of migraine. *Arch. Neurol. Psychiat.,* 1941, **46**, 331-339.

Lashley, K. S. The mechanism of vision: XVIII. Effects of destroying the visual "associative areas" of the monkey. *Genet. Psychol. Monog.,* 1948, **37**, 107-166.

Lashley, K. S., Chow, K. L., & Semmes, J. An examination of the electrical field theory of cerebral integration. *Psychol. Rev.* 1951, **58**, 123-136.

Mach, E. *The analysis of sensations.* Chicago: Open Court, 1914. (Republished: New York, Dover, 1959.)

MacKay, D. M. Moving visual images produced by regular stationary patterns. II. *Nature,* 1958, **181**, 362-363.

MacKay, D. M. Interactive processes in visual perception. In W. A. Rosenblith (Ed.), *Sensory communication.* Cambridge, Massachusetts: M.I.T. Press, 1961. Pp. 339-355.

Malhotra, M. K. Figurale Nachwirkungen. *Psychol. Forsch.,* 1966, **30**, 1-104.

Marshall, W. H., & Talbot, S. A. Recent evidence for neural mechanisms in vision leading to a general theory of sensory acuity. In J. Cattell (Ed.), *Biological symposia.* Vol. VII: Visual mechanisms, edited by Heinrich Kluever. Copyright 1942, Ronald Press, New York. Pp. 117-164.

McKinney, J. P. Disappearance of luminous designs. *Science,* 1963, **140**,403-404.

Milner, B. Intellectual function of the temporal lobes. *Psychol. Bull.,* 1954, **51**, 42-62.

Mishkin, M. Visual discrimination performance following partial abalations of the temporal lobe: II. Ventral surface vs. Hipocampus. *J. comp. physiol. Psychol.,* 1954, **47** 187-193.

Morgan, C. T. *Physiological psychology.* New York: Mc-Graw-Hill, 1965.

Osgood, C. E., & Heyer, A. W., Jr. A new interpretation of figural after-effects. *Psychol. Rev.,* 1952, **59**, 98-118.

Pascal, G. R., & Suttell, Barbara J. *The Bender-Gestalt test.* New York: Grune and Stratton, 1951.

Penfield, W., & Jasper, H. *Epilepsy and the functional anatomy of the brain.* London: Churchill, 1954.

Penrose, L., & Penrose, R. Impossible objects: a special type of visual illusion. *Brit. J. Psychol.,* 1958, **49**, 31-33.

Pirenne, M. H. Light-adaptation. In H. Davson (Ed.), *The eye.* Vol. 2. New York: Academic Press, 1962. Pp. 197-204.

Pirenne, M. H., Marriott, F. M. C., & O'Doherty, E. F. Individual differences in night-vision efficiency. *Spec. Rep. Ser. Med. Res. Coun., London,* 1957, 294.

Pitts, W., & McCulloch, W. S. How we know universals; the perception of auditory and visual forms *Bull. Math. Biophys.,* 1947, **9**, 127-147.

Platt, J. R. How we see straight lines. *Sci. Amer.,* 1960, **202**(6), 121-129.

Pollack, R. H. Comment on "Is the figural aftereffect an *after*effect?" *Psychol. Bull.,* 1967, **68**, 59-61.

Pribram, K. H. The neurophysiology of remembering. *Sci. Amer.,* 1969, **220**(1).

Pritchard, R. M. Visual illusions viewed as stabilized retinal images. *Quart. J. exp. Psychol.,* 1958, **10**, 77-81.

Pritchard, R. M. Stabilized images on the retina. *Sci. Amer.,* 1961, **204**(6).

Pritchard, R. M., Heron, W., & Hebb, D. Visual perception approached by the method of stabilized images. *Can. J. Psychol.,* 1960, **14**, 67-77.

Raab, D. H. Backward masking. *Psychol. Bull.,* 1963, **60**, 118-129.

Ratliff, F. *Mach bands.* San Francisco, California: Holden-Day, 1965.

Riggs, L. A., & Ratliff, F. Visual acuity and the normal tremor of the eyes. *Science,* 1951, **114**, 17-18.

Riggs, L. A., Ratliff, F., Cornsweet, J. C., & Cornsweet, T. N. The disappearance of steadily fixated visual test objects. *J. Opt. Soc. Amer.,* 1953, **43**, 495-501.

Riggs, L. A., Armington, J. C., & Ratliff, F. Motions of the retinal image during fixation. *J. Opt. Soc. Amer.,* 1954, **44**, 315-321.

Riggs, L. A., Ratliff, F., & Keesey, U. T. Appearance of Mach bands with a motionless retinal image. *J. Opt. Soc. Amer.,* 1961, **51**, 702-703.

Schuster, D. H. A new ambiguous figure: A three-stick clevis. *Amer. J. Psychol.,* 1964, **77**, 673.

Skinner, B. F. Behaviorism at fifty. *Science,* 1962, **140**, 951-958.

Smith, G. J. W., & Henriksson, M. The effect on an established percept of a perceptual process beyond awareness. *Acta Psychologica,* 1955, **11**, 346-355.

Sperry, R. W., & Miner, Nancy. Pattern perception following insertion of mica plates into visual cortex. *J. comp. physiol. Psychol.,* 1955, **48**, 463-469.

Sperry, R. W., Miner, Nancy, & Myers, R. E. Visual pattern perception following subplial slicing and tantalum wire implantations in the visual cortex. *J. comp. physiol. Psychol.,* 1955, **48**, 50-58.

Springbett, B. M. The subjective edge. *Amer. J. Psychol.,* 1961, **74**, 101-103.

Stigler, R. Chronophotische Studien ueber den Umgebungskontrast. *Pflueg. Arch. ges. Physiol.,* 1910, **134**, 365-435.

Tees, R. C. The role of field effects in visual perception. *Undergrad. Res. Proj. in Psychol., McGill Univ.,* 1961, **3**, 87-96.

Teuber, H.-L., & Weinstein, S. Ability to discover hidden figures after cerebral lesions. *A.M.A. Arch. Neurol. Psychiat.,* 1956, **76**, 369-379.

Teuber, H.-L., Battersby, W. S., & Bender, M. B. *Visual field defects after penetrating missile wounds of the brain.* Cambridge, Massachusetts: Harvard Univ. Press, 1960.

Thompson, S. P. Optical illusions of motion. *Brain,* 1880, **3**, 289-298.

Troxler. Ueber das Verschwinden gegebener Gegenstaende innerhalb unsers Gesichtskreises, In K. Himly & J. A. Schmidt (Herausg.), *Ophthalmologische Bibliothek.* Vol. 2., 1804. Pp. 51-53.

Werner, H. Studies on contour: I. Qualitative analyses. *Amer. J. Psychol.,* 1935, **47**, 40-64.

Wilcox, W. W. The basis of the dependence of visual acuity on illumination. *Proc. Nat. Acad. Sci.,* 1932, **18**, 47-56.

Yarbus, A. L. Novyǐ metod izucheniya deyatel'nosti razlichnykh chasteǐ setchatki. *Biofizika,* 1957, **2**, 165-167.

Chapter 3 / **CONTEMPORARY THEORY OF VISUAL FORM PERCEPTION: II. DISCRIMINATION AND RECOGNITION**

The emphasis in Chap. 2 was on the contour and not so much on form. When forms are discriminated or recognized, contour perception is taken for granted, the emphasis shifts to shape, and the description and measurement of the physical properties of the distal stimulus become the keynote.

1. The Algebra and Geometry of the Physical Form

A. INFORMATION THEORY AND FORM PERCEPTION

Information is not only that which travels along a wire, a radio channel, or a sound wave; anything that reduces uncertainty is information. When uncertainty is reduced, information is gained, something is learned. Information theory provided a basis for an entirely new look at behavior: an organism could be conceived of as an information-handling channel that receives inputs (stimuli) and produces output (responses). Norbert Wiener related perception and information theory, devoting a whole chapter of *Cybernetics* to the consideration of "Gestalt and Universals." In psychology, the main role of information measurement has been to "put the old, seemingly stale problems into a new, and sometimes exciting light" (Alluisi, 1960). Psychologists did arrive at new insights on old problems, without necessarily producing specific new theories of form perception.

The first step in applying information theory to the measurement of form was to show where information was contained in a form. It was demonstrated (Attneave, 1951, 1954) that information is concentrated at points where there is a change in an otherwise continuous gradient: at the contours of a form, which mark the change from ground to figure; and at any inflection along the contour where the direction of the contour changes most rapidly. The latter principle is used to represent forms of curved contours with a few rectilinear strokes by marking the points of sharpest gradient change and then connecting these points with straight lines (Fig. 3-1). The recognizability of the object indicates that most of the important information has been retained. If one were to use *every* point of sharp gradient change, one would have to connect with straight lines every pen stroke in the original drawing that represents individual hairs. In this procedure, the very fine detail is ignored or, rather, averaged out in the interest of a more economical representation of the object. This averaging over *texture* of the figure is analogous to what happens when a halftone photograph is recopied several times on high-contrast paper. In the final version of the photograph, most of the texture redundancy has been eliminated, i.e., encoded in a more economical fashion without impairing the recognizability of the main features (Fig. 3-2).

Homogeneity of color, of contour, of uniform direction, and homogeneity resulting from repetition, such as the mirror image of a form, represents, in informational terms, redundancy. As one tries to guess the outline of a form without actually seeing it, one makes most errors at the points of gradient change, i.e., where information is concentrated, whereas errors decrease below chance level when redundancy is present. Suppose a subject is given a blank 50 by 50 matrix of cells and told to guess the contour of the shape shown in Fig. 3-3 proceeding cell by cell and row by row. Although 2500 cells and therefore 2500 guesses are involved, resulting in a maximum possible 2500 erroneous guesses, it is clear that most errors will be made at points *a, b, c, d, e, f, g,* and *h,* i.e., where there are inflections in the contour. Since few inflections are present, the form conveys little information, is highly redundant, hence admits of few errors.

Attneave and Arnoult (1956) report an experiment in which 80 subjects were asked to approximate curved shapes by placing 10 points on their

Fig. 3-1. A curvilinear object represented by straight lines.

Fig. 3-2. Economical representation of objects through photographic reduction of texture redundancy.

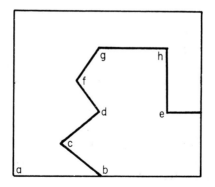

Fig. 3-3. Contour for a contour-guessing task. See text for explanation.

contours and connecting them with straight lines. The results showed a great deal of agreement among subjects in the placement of the points: most of them coincided with the points of greatest change in the degree of curvature in the form.

It is reasonable to expect that different types of perceptual tasks will be made more difficult where forms with many turns, i.e., much information, are used. Forms may be made simpler by reducing the number of turns or by increasing their regularity or symmetry, i.e., increasing their redundancy. Since simpler (more redundant) forms contain less information, they should be easier to process, and they are. This is a well-established principle. Information theory provides a common basis for the explanation of the various instances of "simplicity:" simplicity is inversely related to the "uncertainty" of a stimulus and therefore to its information content, measurable in binary digits.

One measure of the ease of a perceptual task is reaction time. Hick (1952) was first to relate reaction time and the information content of visual stimuli. Using both older data and his own experimental results, he concluded that reaction time was linearly related to the average amount of information transmitted as the subject performed a task, regardless of whether uncertainty was related to the stimulus or to the response. Since that time, a large number of experiments have been performed using either reaction time or other response measures indicative of information processing, with shapes and other visual displays as stimuli.

Simplicity leads to the consideration of certain Gestalt concepts. Simplicity plays an important role in that theory since the simple figure is also a "good" Gestalt. The precision that the Gestalt notions of simplicity, good form, and other principles of organization lacked was provided by information theory. Better still, it furnished the means by which to quantify the even more fundamental notion of organization. Organization implies patterning, patterning involves repetition and symmetry; these are forms of redundancy, hence organization and redundancy are approximately the same. Since redundancy is the complement of uncertainty (Chap. 5) and uncertainty can be quantified, so can organization. If a "good" figure is one that is organized, therefore simpler, more symmetric, showing closure, good continuation, etc., then all these concepts may be reformulated in information terms, and hence also be quantified. The Gestalt principles of organization refer to the distribution of information in a form. Those portions of a pattern showing symmetry, good continuation, similarity, proximity, common fate, and closure have less uncertainty, less information associated with them than others. Information in them is repeated and is redundant, hence it stands to reason that the nervous system would tend to summarize or group such information. The economical processing of redundant information by any system requires it. Hochberg and McAlister (1953) and Attneave (1954) conceived of this idea independently. Paul Fitts and George Miller were thinking along the same lines at about the same time.

The idea was not altogether new since Wiener had already pointed out in *Cybernetics* that the amount of information in a system is a measure of its degree of organization (Wiener, 1948, p. 18). Historically, the idea that the different Gestalt laws of organization might reflect a single principle may be found as early as the 1930s. To Musatti (1931), it was homogeneity: proximity is homogeneity with regard to space, similarity with regard to quality, common fate with regard to movement or change, good continuation with respect to direction. But homogeneity is measured in terms of variance, and variance and information measures can be translated directly into each other. Thus, homogeneity, variation, uncertainty, redundancy, organization, and the Gestalt principles of organization are brought under one roof.

As already mentioned, the rate of errors in guessing the outline of a form varies depending on the amount of information contained in any particular portion of the outline. Using such a guessing technique, Attneave demonstrated that "principles of perceptual grouping such as *similarity* and *good continuation* refer to various types of redundancy which may exist within a static visual field, enabling an observer to 'predict' portions of the field with great accuracy from a knowledge of other portions" (Attneave, 1954, p. 82). Attneave suggested that the number of errors made in guessing the outline of a form could be used as a measure of figural "goodness." Hochberg and McAllister analyzed the organization of the set of ambiguous figures known as Kopfermann cubes. They are ambiguous in that they can be seen as either two-dimensional forms or as perspective drawings of three-dimensional objects. The prediction that the percept of a three-dimensional object would be more frequent the greater the amount of information (number of lines, angles, and points of intersection) contained in a figure was confirmed.

A specific prediction found in Gestalt psychology of form is that 'good' figures will be better remembered than 'poor' ones. Attneave (1955) reasoned that if figural goodness is equivalent to redundancy then perhaps 'good' figures are remembered better because they contain less information. Using both immediate reproduction, delayed reproduction, and identification tasks and symmetric and asymmetric metric patterns containing the same number of cells (same information content), Attneave showed that symmetric patterns were not remembered any better than asymmetric ones; in the two reproduction tasks, they were recalled less accurately than asymmetric patterns. This brings up an important question in the investigation of form perception, namely the role of redundancy in general and the role of specific forms of redundancy, such as symmetry. This is an active area of investigation with no firmly established findings. It is discussed in more detail in Chap. 5.

While concepts from information theory were accepted in psychology readily enough, including the introduction of a more general "new look" at organisms as information-processing systems, it cannot be said that the acceptance of information theory in psychology has been overenthusiastic, indiscriminate, or premature. It is possible, though, to point out instances where practitioners in other disciplines have been guilty of applying it to behavioral problems, especially form perception, in an overly sanguine and rash manner. This moderation among psychologists perhaps accounts for the relative lack of adverse criticism of information-theory applications in psychology. One recent instance of a rather devastating kind of criticism, addressed specifically to the application of information theory to form perception, is for this reason an interesting case to cite.

Green and Courtis (1966) point out that at least four fundamental requirements for the application of information theory are not met when it is applied to visual form perception. They also show with their own experiments that some of the specific predictions from information theory made by Attneave do not come true, at least not always. The four requirements are: (1) that there be an alphabet of signs with known and constant probabilities of occurrence; (2) that these probabilities be objective; (3) that the grain of the matrix within which the form has been constructed be known; and (4) that the sequence of scanning the elements carrying information be linear. These requirements are obviously met in a speech sequence transmitted over a communications channel, but, argue Green and Courtis, they are not met in the case of visual form. They fail to demonstrate this, however, since each of the experiments they present in support of their argument is open to alternative interpretations.

One of the problems stressed by Green and Courtis is that of the place of meaning in information theory. Shannon had said at the very outset that meaning could not be quantified in informational terms. MacKay (1950, 1956) appears to have been one of the very few individuals to ever grapple with this problem. MacKay's (1950) distinction between the metron and the logon contents of information, translated in terms of visual form and simplified somewhat, is as follows: The *amount* of information contained in, say, an eight-sided polygon is fixed and measurable in bits. This number says nothing, however, about *how* this information is encoded in this particular polygon, and there are a very large number of ways in which the points of a given polygon may be arranged. The particular way in which the vertices of a polygon are arranged also caries information, but its measurement is very problematic—too much depends on the perceiver, such as whether he will see a particular arrangement of the eight vertices and sides as an animal or a pine tree.

In this connection, Green and Courtis discuss cartoon-drawing techniques. Some cartoonists convey full information about their subject by suggesting it rather than stating it explicitly, such as by the clever use of blank spaces or gaps in the contour that normally would contain some angle, i.e., change in a homogeneous contour. This, to Green and Courtis, is a clear demonstration of the failure of the information-theoretic approach to visual form perception. This may not be necessarily so, but it does require an explanation. An explanation in terms of closure would be incomplete since, even if it is assumed that already the newborn infant has some rudimentary ability to close gaps perceptually, it is unlikely that he would be able to do so when confronted with an incomplete drawing of an unfamiliar object, a drawing in which the missing portions can be supplied only from one's previous experience with the kind of object depicted. There *is* less measurable information in this drawing as compared with a complete one. As development progresses, however, the missing metron content becomes logon content as it is now supplied from an *internal* source in the observer, namely his past experience: one *knows* that the gap is usually filled with a certain type of contour or angle. For the still older individual, the incomplete figure may actually contain more information than a complete one: the artist's craftsmanship as well as the moment of surprise at the unexpected lack of completeness clashing with the perfect intelligibility of the shape, convey additional information that is not given in the complete drawing. The work of Berlyne (cf. Berlyne, 1966) is relevant here, but already tangential to the central topic of form perception.

Be it as it may, whether information comes from an external or an internal source, it is at least in principle measurable. A satisfactory solution of the problem of meaning and past experience in informational terms and its application to visual form perception is still a task for the future.

B. THE MARGINAL DISTRIBUTION APPROACH TO VISUAL FORM PERCEPTION

Working independently, a number of researchers have formulated a practically identical approach to form discrimination. With the exception of N. S. Sutherland, none of them has attempted to state a formal theory. The approach, nevertheless, amounts to a theoretical position of certain scope.

The basic idea of these formulations, however stated, is that discrimination between two forms occurs when the observer projects or collapses each form on a vertical and/or horizontal axis and then compares the shapes of the corresponding marginal distributions. It is as if a form were divided into a large number of small units and these units rearranged to form a frequency distribution for statistical analysis. Discrimination occurs if there are discriminable differences between the marginal distributions. The idea is presented graphically in Fig. 3-4.

Years of work with the octopus led Sutherland (1957) to formulate the theory that there is a possible neural analyzing mechanism in the octopus which operates by dividing shapes into their vertical and horizontal projections and combining the vertical and horizontal projections of different shapes. Histology points to retinal receptors in the eye of the octopus that favor discrimination along the two major spatial axes. Thus, the octopus learns to discriminate relatively easily between a vertical and a horizontal rectangle but finds it very

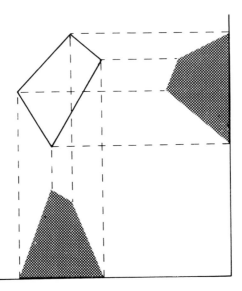

Fig. 3-4. Two one-dimensional projections of a two-dimensional shape.

difficult to learn the difference between two rectangles, one of which is tilted 45 degrees to the left and the other 45 degrees to the right. Sutherland's theory is discussed in more detail in another section of this chapter.

It is not difficult to imagine that, faced with a pair of forms and the task of deciding how similar they are, an observer may mentally slide one form on top of the other to obtain maximum overlap and then judge the similarity of the two forms in terms of the portions that fail to overlap. Since more overlapping may be produced by translating *and* rotating one of the forms, mental rotation may be an additional operation that the observer performs to arrive at more correct judgments. This idea has been advanced by Boynton (Boynton, Elworth, Onley, & Klingberg, 1960; Boynton, Elworth, Monty, Onley, & Klingberg, 1961; Monty & Boynton, 1962). Since maximum overlap, with or without rotation, can be obtained only if the centers of gravity of the two forms are made to coincide, the use of *T*-overlap (maximum overlap obtained by translation alone) or *TR*-overlap (maximum overlap obtained by translation and rotation) criteria by an observer imply that he is able to estimate the coordinates of the centers of gravity of the two forms. The estimation of the center of gravity of a regular ("geometric") polygon is a fairly easy task for most observers; irregularity in the contours of a polygon leads to greater variability in estimates of the location of the centroid, and is most difficult with complicated, irregular polygons in which the centroid lies outside the contours. This may be one reason why Boynton's overlap measures are less than perfect predictors of discrimination performance. Of the two methods of comparing forms, observers seem to be better able simply to translate a form than to rotate it mentally as well. When knowledge of results is given, however, observers perform better by the TR-overlap than the T-overlap criterion (Monty & Boynton, 1962).

That human observers are able to evaluate statistical properties of collections of elements without actually performing the necessary mathematical computations has been shown by Hofstaetter (1939). Using bundles of wooden sticks tied together with rubber bands, Hofstaetter asked his subjects to select from a number of such bundles the one that most resembled a standard. The bundles varied in the mean length and variance of lengths of the sticks. Even though the subjects had no means of measuring or even counting the sticks, their performance appeared to be based on the statistical properties of the bundles. A factor analysis revealed two factors: deviations of the individual sticks from the mean of the bundle, and numerosity. Hofstaetter's conclusion was that the mean, variation, and other moments were direct objects of perception and not the result of conscious calculations performed by the subject.

My own ideas have been developing along the following lines. In statistics, a one-dimensional sampling distribution is specified by stating its mean, variance, skewness, kurtosis, and other higher moments about the mean, or central moments. In physics and engineering, the term moment denotes the product of a quantity and a distance to some significant point connected with that quantity. One such moment is the moment of area, where the quantity is a fractional area and the significant point is the centroid. The area of a shape may be thought of as a two-dimensional distribution of its elements, i.e., small units of area. Such a distribution may be specified by stating its moments of area. Two shapes having identical moments will be identical, at least for the most common types of shapes.

The first moment of area is the center of gravity or, more exactly, the two coordinates that specify its location. Likewise, all higher moments have two values. To compute them, a shape is collapsed one-dimensionally on the two axes of Cartesian coordinates (Fig. 3-4). These collapses are actually frequency distributions or histograms of the unit areas. It is therefore possible to compute their variance, skewness, kurtosis, and other higher moments. As a shape is rotated about a point, the shape of the two marginal distributions change constantly, hence there are two values for every moment in each position of the shape.

In general, the second moment of area measures the overall dispersion or compactness of the shape. It correlates about .67 with Boynton's T-overlap measure. The third moment measures the symmetry of the shape about a given axis, and the fourth moment its elongation, or what has usually been described in terms of some height-to-length ratio. Compactness, symmetry, and elongation have repeatedly turned out to be good predictors of discrimination performance. The use of moments of area provides a common denominator for all of these measures.

The direct estimation of moments of area appears to be no more difficult than the estimation of moments of one-dimensional distributions, as in Hofstaetter's (1939) experiments. On the average, the estimation of the location of the center of gravity of shapes is fairly accurate; subjects will also draw, without too much hesitation, an "axis of symmetry" through the centers of gravity of asymmetric random shapes (Zusne, 1965). It turns out that they draw it in such a way that it corresponds with either the minimum value of the third moment of area or its maximum. When subjects are presented with discrimination problems, differences in the second and third moments of area are significant predictors of reaction time, but not the fourth moment (Zusne, 1965). It appears that with increasing order of moments their value as predictors of discrimination performance decreases.

Moments of area are rather insensitive to small but perceptually conspicuous protrusions of shape. Such a protrusion may be the only but quite obvious difference between two otherwise identical shapes. What this means is that information is contained in the perimeter of a shape (Attneave & Arnoult, 1956), and not in the enclosed area (Zusne & Michels, 1964). When moments are computed, the sheer size of the enclosed area obscures small perimetric differences. Moments, however, may be computed on the contours of a shape alone (moments of the perimeter). In a discrimination task, moments of the perimeter are somewhat better predictors of performance than are moments of area (Zusne, 1965), including the fourth moment.

Given enough moments, every variable of contour distribution in two-dimensional space may be specified. Thus, moments basically describe the distribution of the area or perimeter of a single shape, and the differences in the same moment between two shapes is a derived measure. For this reason, ulike Boynton's overlap measures, some order and type of moment could be used as predictor of performance with single shapes, as in a detection task. To date, no such attempt has been made. It may be mentioned at this point that the moment approach has also been used in the area of pattern recognition by machines (Alt, 1962; Guiliano, Jones, Kimball, Meyer, & Stein, 1961; Hu, 1961) but without any reference to behavioral data.

With certain types of visual patterns, the marginal distribution approach suggests itself easily. If the pattern is constructed by filling in or by lighting square cells in a matrix of low order (e.g., a 3 × 3, or 4 × 4 matrix), two patterns may be compared by examining, row by row, each pair of corresponding cells to see if both are in the same state or not. The number of cells in disparate states can then be used as a measure of difference between the two shapes. Polidora (1966) calls this measure "unique elements." Not only does it reflect any difference whatsoever between two shapes constructed in the same matrix, but also vertical and horizontal displacement of one of two identical shapes, i.e., a figure-ground difference. While this measure is practical only with patterns containing a relatively small number of elements, Boynton's T-overlap measure, if applied to such patterns, would be the exact complement of unique elements. Since T-overlap and the second moment of area are also correlated, unique elements and the second moment of area must correlate also—provided the number of pattern elements is sufficiently large. This problem is discussed further in Chap. 5.

Whether one talks of marginal distributions, stimulus overlap, or the variance of fractional areas, the underlying idea seems to have wide appeal. Between 1956 and 1962, a number of other, related, but simpler measures were proposed by other investigators. Because some of them were too coarse, they did not predict discrimination performance, while others did so only weakly or inconsistently. These measures are mentioned in Chap. 5.

2. The Theoretical Brain

Efforts to formulate mathematical models for the functioning of the brain have come from individuals with varied backgrounds: electrical engineering, mathematics, and physiology; yet, they all share a common language, orientation, and goals, namely those of the interdisciplinary field of cybernetics.

Wiener's *Cybernetics* was the first summary statement of a way of thinking held by an initially small group of scientists as well as a programmatic statement for the future that had considerable latitude: in his book, Wiener makes excursions into the fields of protheses, the translation of Braille into sound patterns, the mode of operation of digital computers, the measurement of information in communications, form perception, psychopathology, social psychology, statistical mechanics, and the problem of time in relation to subatomic particles. The chapter on "Gestalt and Universals" concerns the perception of form, with particular emphasis on how invariance in form may be represented in the brain and the computer. This, as well as the chapters on "Time Series, Information, and Communication" and "Computing Machines and the Nervous System" were propadeutic to the blossoming of the field of pattern recognition by machines. From the very beginning, however, the field was marked by a glaring discrepancy between the sophisticated mathematical descriptions of neural and behavioral events and the cavalier treatment of the actual behavior of organisms. This is quite evident in Wiener's *Cybernetics*. What Wiener lacked in depth and detail of treatment of behavioral phenomena he compensated for by the brilliance of his insights and prophetic vision. Such redeeming qualities are sadly lacking in the works of Wiener's epigones.

The mathematical description of brain processes has found a number of different avenues. Topology and set theory have been very much on the map recently and have found their way into psychology. Lewin's use of topological concepts was an isolated instance of its allegoric application. That Piaget turned to lattices, groups, and sets in talking about intelligence, however, was no longer such an isolated instance but part of a general trend. The pressure comes from outside the field of psychology. There are relatively more electrical engineers, mathematicians, and physiologists who work with "artificial intelligence" and pattern-recognition computer programs than there are psychologists who do this kind of work. It is among these professionals that we find instances of application of the concepts of sets and groups and of topological concepts to behavioral physiology.

A. 2- AND 3-MANIFOLDS

In mathematical terms, the retinal image is a 2-manifold. It is a surface and it is two-dimensional. This surface Hoffman (1966) calls the visual manifold. Hoffman does not concern himself with color and brightness, but deals only with contours and textures, that is, figure-ground relationships, and specifically those figure-ground relationships that are called perceptual constancies. These invariances can be formulated exactly as Lie groups of transformations over the visual manifold. A series of visual transformations, such as occur when a shape is rotated or translated, is characterized by closure, the existence of identity and inverse elements, and associativity, hence form a mathematical group. A Lie group of transformations is a group of the "continuous" or "infinitesimal" kind, hence capable of differentiation. Starting from this premise, Hoffman develops the mathematical expressions, in Lie algebra, of the various perceptual invariances. One is tempted to speculate that J. J. Gibson's psychophysical theory (see Chap. 4) might have suffered less criticism and enjoyed greater precision had the textured optical array of the retina been described in terms of Lie transformation groups back in 1950.

If the retinal image is a 2-manifold, the visual cortex is a 3-manifold, and its functions may be described in the language of topology. This has been done, e.g., by Zeeman (1962). His starting point is the following: "A mathematical explanation of how the brain works should be as follows: First, develop a piece of mathematics X that describes the permanent structure (memory) and the working (thinking) of the *mind,* and another piece of mathematics Y that describes the permanent structure (anatomy) and working (electrochemical) of the *brain*; then, from hypotheses based on experimental evidence, prove an isomorphism $X = Y$." (Zeeman, 1962, p. 240.) Should this be a preamble to a complete treatment of behavior in mathematical terms, the psychologist would be immediately alarmed by the implied assumptions of the statement. As it turns out, in his paper, Zeeman does justice to neither mind nor body, leaving the psychology of visual form perception where it was before. Zeeman does bring out a point which is important for the problem of constancy. Since the retinal image and the cortical projection have only a topological correspondence, we can perceive, globally, only the topological relations among elements of the stimulus, the linearity of contours, and the symmetry of a shape, but not its metric. "The whole difficulty in explaining the phenomenon of constancy lies in assuming that we have built in a metric; if we assume the opposite, there is nothing to explain" (Zeeman, 1962, p. 245/6). While this is not as simple as Zeeman puts it, the fact is that a visual percept by itself has no definite size, for instance. An afterimage acquires size only in relation to the distance of the background upon which it is projected, according to Emmert's law. This still calls for an explanation of how distance is perceived. When this is explained, then size constancy needs no further explanation.

Others who have described the brain mathematically have followed other lines of reasoning. The Pitts and McCulloch theory, for instance, takes as its major task to explain constancy, as do most cybernetically oriented theories. The decisive point is whether a brain analog needs programmed constancy or not. Zeeman does not seem to be concerned about how well a computer might be able to show constancy. Those who have written pattern-recognition programs inevitably find that special provisions must be made for the recognition of a shape in different sizes, orientations, and other distortions. The explanation may be that the computer is infinitely simpler than the brain and needs these special features to show constancy. No one has been able yet to build a computer in which a metricfree image of a form floats freely in the computer's "mind," to be given a metric depending on the particular circumstances in which the form is to be used.

B. THE PITTS AND McCULLOCH MODEL FOR THE PERCEPTION OF INVARIANTS

In 1947, Walter Pitts and Warren McCulloch published an article in which certain nervous mechanisms were postulated to account for invariance in the perception of auditory and visual stimuli. It was an intellectual exercise of high caliber which, however, failed to produce any research or to receive empirical support for the nervous mechanisms postulated. The theory has now mostly historical interest, but it is instructive to examine it because it is a good example of the type of theorizing concerning form perception that prevails in cybernetics.

Wiener (1948) in *Cybernetics* tells us about the antecedents of the theory:

In the spring of 1947, Dr. McCulloch and Mr. Pitts did a piece of work of considerable cybernetic importance. Dr. McCulloch had been given the problem of designing an apparatus to enable the blind to read the printed page by ear. The production of variable tones by type through the agency of a photocell is an old story, and can be effected by a number of methods; the difficult point is to make the pattern of the sound substantially the same when the pattern of the letters is given, whatever the size. This is a definite analogue of the problem of the perception of form, of *Gestalt,* which allows us to recognize a square as a square through a large number of changes of size and of orientation. Dr. McCulloch's device involved a selective reading of the type imprint for a set of different magnifications. Such a selective reading can be performed automatically as a scanning process. This scanning, to allow a comparison between a figure and a given standard figure of fixed but different size, was a device which I had already suggested at one of the Macy meetings. A diagram of the apparatus by which the selective reading was done came to the attention of Dr. von Bonin, who immediately asked, 'Is this a diagram of the fourth layer of the visual cortex of the brain?' Acting on this suggestion, Dr. McCulloch, with the assistance of Mr. Pitts, produced a theory tying up the anatomy and the physiology of visual cortex, and in this theory the operation of scanning over a set of transformations plays an important part. (Pp. 31/2.)

The mechanism whereby two identical forms having different areas are perceived as being the same is one that translates space into time, so goes the theory. A form is projected onto the brain in some fashion that preserves the order of adjacent points, although not the configuration itself. The spatial order of points is translated into time by means of a scanning mechanism which, somewhat like the scanning beam of a television camera, converts distance into temporal sequences of nerve impulses. This mechanism is a "sheet of negativity" which sweeps the cortex, namely the neural correlate of the alpha rhythm.

Figure 3-5 shows diagramatically a cross section of the cortex in area 17 whose structure conforms with the proposed mode of action of the brain in form perception. The multiplicative and divisive factors of $\times 3$, $\div 3$, etc. are hypothetical factors of enlargement and reduction of the form produced in the afferent cells of layer III by the sweeping of the alpha rhythm through the upper three layers of the cortex.

Unlike the Gestalt theory of electrical brain fields, which requires at least a topological projection of the form on the cortex, Pitts and McCulloch did not assume that the cortical counterpart of a figure would resemble it in any simple way.

Thus . . . we might suppose that the efferent pyramids in the layer III of our diagram project topographically another cortical mosaic, which only responds to corners, and accumulates over a cycle of scansion. A square in the visual field, as it moved in and out in successive constrictions and dilations in Area 17, would trace out four spokes radiating from a common center upon the recipient mosaic. This four-spoked form, not at all like a square, would then be the size-invariant figure of square. (Pitts & McCulloch, 1947, p. 136.)

Since area 18 does not behave in this way—patients in whom it is stimulated perceive well-defined objects but without a determinate size or position, like afterimages—the mechanism shown in Fig. 3-5 is placed by Pitts and McCulloch in area 17.

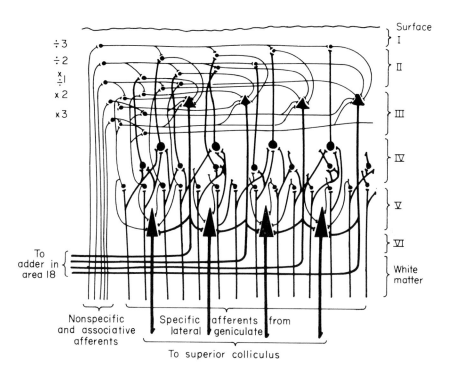

Fig. 3-5. Semischematic cross section through area 17 of the cortex taken radially outward from that cortical point to which the center of the fovea projects. Impulses relayed by the lateral geniculate from the eyes ascend in specific afferents to layer IV, where they branch laterally, exciting small cells singly and larger cells only by summation. Large cells thus represent larger visual areas. From layer IV, impulses impinge on higher layers, where summation is required from nonspecific thalamic afferents or associative fibers. From there, they converge on large cells of the third layer, which relay impulses to the parastriate area 18 for addition. On their way down, they contribute to summation on the large pyramids of layer V, which relays them to the superior colliculus. From Pitts and McCulloch (1947). Reproduced by permission.

The second mechanism postulated is one for the invariant perception of form over a translation group. Whenever a form appears anywhere in the visual field, the center of gravity of that form is computed by the superior colliculus. Using double integration, the colliculus, like a computer, computes the x and y coordinates of the centroid. These coordinates are referred to the zero-value coordinates of the fovea, which serves as the origin of a Cartesian coordinate system in the retina, and signals issue from the colliculus to the eye muscles to contract and move the eyes so that the differences between the two sets of coordinates are decreased. As the eyes move and the size of the differences dwindles, the eyes slow down and eventually stop when the center of gravity of the form is fixated, i.e., the differences are reduced to zero.

In this, as in other cybernetically oriented theories, the brain is viewed as a computing mechanism, and computer-like processes are postulated for it. The question, of course, is whether the hypothesized mechanisms exist in reality. It is well known that the alpha rhythm may be altered by the subject consciously without thereby affecting perception or memory in any way. Paying attention or engaging in mental activity also blocks the alpha rhythm without affecting form perception in the slightest. This leaves the mechanism of size invariance without an essential component.

The second mechanism implies that an individual is able to determine the exact location of the center of gravity of a two-dimensional form. While Pitts and McCulloch do not mention the work of Walker and Weaver (1940), they may have been aware of the finding of these investigators that peripheral stimulation of the monkey's brain produced eye movements in such a direction that the eyes would have fixated the light source, had there been one, in the peripheral location of the visual field corresponding to the cortical point stimulated. At any rate, the implication may be easily tested. I have found that the estimation of the centers of gravity of shapes is relatively easy if the shapes are regular geometric forms. As irregularity increases, so does the difficulty of the task. Forms having the centroid outside the contours present the greatest difficulty, showing the widest variation in estimates among subjects. Eye-movement records of subjects scanning such shapes (Zusne & Michels, 1964) show that the eye seldom dwells anywhere near the center of gravity. Fixations and scanning movements are concentrated largely along the contours and points of the contours, which, because of their complexity, attract attention.

Thus, relatively easily obtainable evidence, including some that has come from McCulloch's own laboratory, has left the theory with little leg to stand on. As Pribram (1966), who enjoyed a long period of association with McCulloch, put it, the conception was "brilliant, lively, productive, and wrong."

C. MACHINE MODELS OF FORM PERCEPTION

Machines that recognize patterns are of interest to the psychologist only to the extent that they are intended to represent some analog of the structural and functional characteristics of an actual nervous system. The majority of such machines are not simulated nervous systems and are better included in the class of "artificial intelligences," i.e., devices which perform human tasks that, in humans, require some amount of intelligence, but which do not simulate any known nervous system. The end result of processing a pattern by such a machine may be the same as when it is done by a human being, yet the processes involved are entirely different. Machine models have heuristic value for the psychologist only as long as it is assumed that the model reflects some aspect of the functioning of the nervous system or when its relevance to such functioning is unknown. When it is known beforehand that nothing in the model resembles any nervous structures or processes, the machine remains just that—a machine that is of no interest to the behaviorist. This position is not, however, shared by everybody (cf. Uhr, 1965).

Thus, pattern-recognition machines range from those in which only one predetermined type font may be recognized by some optical or mechanical device, such as an IBM sorter or a check-reading machine, to those that represent serious attempts to duplicate both the structure of a nerve net and the learning process that is inherent in pattern recognition. Transforming a pattern so that it may be handled by a computer is not a problem: there are a number of ways of doing it, e.g., by punching the contour or the enclosed area of a shape with one-punches into punched cards. The problem, and it remains *the* crucial problem, is to formulate rules of decision in the *comparison* of the input information with some existing standards in the machine's memory. This involves (a) the specification of the structural elements in the pattern that must be used in the comparison, (b) the specification of how the comparison is to be done, and (c) the incorporation of learning rules to allow for the variations that are always encountered in a given pattern, as, e.g., a letter, and for the accumulation of a store of memories of past "experiences" by the computer itself.

Since the information that is fed into a computer must be exact and specific, the programmer must have an exact idea of the nature of discrimination and recognition processes, including the principle of invariance. Whether his ideas are right or wrong makes no difference to the computer, as long as they are exactly specified. When, in such circumstances, the computer shows a high degree of correct recognitions under conditions resembling pattern-recognition tasks as they present themselves to humans, such a result is very exciting to the researcher since it confirms not only stimulus-response relationships which obtain in the human being, but also has a direct bearing on the nature of the intervening variable, perception, which in the case of a human subject can be only surmised and theorized about on the basis of externally observable behavior but cannot be manipulated in quite the same way as when a computer program is written.

Form can be handled by both the analog and the digital computer. Since the human nervous system has the characteristics of both types of computer, it stands to reason that the simulation of form perception in humans should be modeled using them in combination. In practice, either type is used alone, and most of the psychologically interesting work has involved the use of digital computers. In the following description of machine models, Uhr's (1965) categorization of computer programs for form perception is followed. There are, however, a number of ways of classifying such programs, and Uhr himself has changed his at least once (cf. Uhr, 1963, 1965).

General Characteristics of Pattern-Recognition Programs. The majority of computer programs written to date have been programs for the recognition of digits and the letters of the alphabet, although some have been written for more general kinds of patterns. There are now programs that recognize even sloppy handwritten characters. The problem of recognizing individual letters when they are linked in ordinary script has not been solved, however. One program that has attempted to divide a continuous pattern of letters into individual characters (Uhr & Vossler, 1961b) shows only about 50 to 60% success, i.e., correct recognition.

Regardless of what the discrimination and recognition rules of the program are, in virtually every case the pattern is represented within some matrix of a certain grain and by means of some discrete symbol, distinct from that which characterizes ground, such as 1- and 0-punches in punched cards. While there is no problem in representing shades of gray or texture, such as by using the digits 1·5 to denote five shades of gray, this technique is seldom resorted to (cf. Ledley & Ruddle, 1966).

The first step of a program in processing a pattern is to direct the computer to measure certain predetermined portions of the pattern. Since the number of part configurations that can be obtained from a pattern is extremely large, any pattern-recognition program is essentially an instance in the search for the smallest possible set of convenient and efficient descriptions of the pattern that the computer is to recognize. This first step may consist of a preliminary operation in which the area of the pattern is adjusted to a standard size or its edges smoothed, gaps filled, etc., plus the subsequent operations that involve actual measurement. The latter produce a new set of units, e.g., subpatterns with names attached to them, upon which additional measurements may be performed. The exact number of sets of measurements and the order in which they are taken vary considerably from program to program. Two main types may be distinguished nevertheless: the program proceeds in a sequential order, from measurement to measurement, each step depending on the preceding one; or, several measurements are made simultaneously.

A sequential processing program written to discriminate, e.g., the letters *A, H, V,* and *Y* may ask questions about such features as the presence or absence of concavities at the top of the letter, crossbars, and vertical lines. In parallel processing programs, the same questions may be asked, but they are asked at once. The sequential processing system has the main advantage of being faster than the parallel processing system and the main disadvantage of carrying with it any errors introduced anywhere along the line. Most programs follow either the sequential or the parallel processing principles, although it would seem that some combination of the two would make for a more powerful pattern-recognition program:

> What we would really like a program to do, then, is to make a few 'first glance' measurements of a sensed pattern, decide on the basis of these measurements what to look for next and where, and continue this process until it is sufficiently certain to make a decision. There should also be general expectations, from long-term and immediate past experience, as to what general type of pattern to expect, and there should be flexible costs and values attached (again depending upon past experience which has shown what each pattern implies) that will affect how careful the program is in choosing to decide upon less-than-certain evidence. (Uhr, 1966, p. 369.)

Such a complete program, however, is very difficult to write and often exceeds the capacity of existing computers.

That the choice of the particular measurements a computer is to make is a crucial problem in pattern-recognition work sounds like a familiar problem to the experimental psychologist who works in the field of form perception. The question of which stimulus parameters are predictors of response in various tasks in visual perception is still one that has received only partial and incomplete answers. Both in computer work and experimentation with human and animal subjects, the method of approaching this problem has been largely pragmatic: one has a hunch as to what features of a pattern an organism pays attention to, the appropriate measurements are taken, and a test—an experiment or a computer run—is made to see if they predict response.

One group of pattern-recognition machines may be called *template-matching* machines. In this type of machine [for a collection of papers, see Fischer, 1962; Broido (1958) describes several machines of this type; good single examples are described by Anonymous (1960b, 1961) and Fitzmaurice, Sabbagh, and Elliott (1959)], there is typically a set of templates for the letters of the alphabet or the ten digits, and the pattern to be recognized is compared with all templates on a one-trial basis. The comparison is usually accomplished by optical means: the amount of light reflected from the pattern is compared with that which, for a given character, would be present if the character and its corresponding template would be perfectly aligned, i.e., some maximum. When this "correlation" is 1.00, the machine indicates the name of the template.

The chief drawback of such a machine is, of course, that it will recognize only one specially designed font of letters or digits. While performing at the 99.5%-plus accuracy level on such a font, it is not usable with any other kind of pattern and fails whenever a character suffers even the slightest imperfection. Even so, it finds ample practical use in check reading and similar areas. Since even the specially designed and invariant characters may show slight variations from time to time, the template-matching machine may have an optical sharpening or blurring device built into it which may increase its accuracy to 100%. Such "cleaning-up" is a first step toward solving the problem of invariance. Otherwise, the straightforward template-matching machine offers little that is of interest in terms of a pattern-perception model. In spite of the seeming simplicity of the operation, the process of one-trial, whole-pattern matching and the upgrading or degrading of patterns is actually so complex that, when written for a digital computer, it results in an extremely time-consuming and awkward program of one-by-one matching of the cells of pattern and template and the solution of exceedingly complex equations.

To make the template-matching machine somewhat more flexible, it has been attempted to use templates, not for whole patterns, but for components of patterns, such as the component strokes of the letters of the alphabet. While the number of basic strokes may be smaller than the total number of letters in the alphabet, a decision-making process must be incorporated to attach the appropriate label to a character after its component strokes have been identified. This makes a program (e.g., Anonymous, 1960a; Diamond, 1957; Eldredge, Kamhoefner, & Wendt, 1957; Rabinow, 1954a, 1954b, 1962; Shepard, Bargh, & Heasley, 1957; Stearns, 1960; Wada, Takahashi, Iijima, Okumuru, & Imoto, 1960) not much different from a characteristic-features program described below.

Some of the template-matching programs convert space into time, an idea that appears in some of the psychophysiological theories of form discrimination, such as Deutsch's (1955) and Pitts and McCulloch's (1947). Singer (1961) has described curves by measuring distances between points on the curve and the center of gravity, suggesting that the varying distances may be converted into temporal patterns in nerve conduction. Harmon's (1960) machine makes concentric circular scans of a shape and is able to discriminate simple geometric figures.

While no one has seriously suggested that anything like template-matching in a machine also occurs in the brain, the more general proposition that in discrimination something like matching may be done by an organism has some support. Uhr (1965) points out that it is easy to ask, via a computer, "Are these two patterns identical?" but that it is extremely difficult to ask, "Are these two patterns similar?" The problem is that any deviation from identity is nonidentity and only dichotomized response is required, while deviations from similarity are continuous, and to specify a point on a continuum of similarity, the parameters of similarity must be known. It is not an insuperable problem if one is content with a simple statement of the amount of dissimilarity without regard to dimensions. The method of measuring similarity between two shapes devised by Boynton (Boynton *et al.*, 1960) entails the use of an apparatus that is analogous to certain optical character-recognition devices. The differences are that Boynton's device assesses the similarity of any pair of shapes instead of only a specific font of type (there are no templates), any form serving as "template" when it is compared with another form, and that it is manually controlled. As already mentioned, both the translation-overlap and rotation-overlap measures of similarity predict how well a subject will be able to tell the difference between two random shapes.

Another group of programs is characterized by the use of what may be called the *1-tuple* method. In a sense, this method is the exact opposite of the template-matching method: instead of processing the entire pattern at once, programs written for this method examine the individual cells that make up a pattern. Typically a program of this type performs statistical tests on the distribution of pattern elements in a sample taken from the pattern and compares the results with the probability characteristics of patterns stored in memory. An extension of this method provides for the elimination of redundant cells and the examination of only those cells that make for good discrimination. The 1-tuple method is not as powerful a method as some of the others, mainly because the characterization of a pattern that is supplied by the interaction of portions of a pattern is not taken into account. However, all other programs may be looked at as extremes of this very simple principle, e.g., the template-matching method may be said to use only one element, namely the entire pattern. Examples of programs in this group are those of Highleyman and Kamentsky (1960) and Baran and Estrin (1960).

Characterizers involving more than one element extend the 1-tuple method to account for the interaction factor among portions of a pattern. The program written by Bledsoe and Browning (1959) is representative of the *N-tuple* method. Randomly generated 1-, 2-, 3-, 5-, and 9-tuples are the characterizers in this program. Cells are combined only once, e.g., in a 10×15 matrix, seventy-five 2-tuples are possible. In the case of 2-tuples, each can be in one of four states: both cells filled or excited, one filled and the other unfilled, etc. The statements corresponding to each 2-tuple of a pattern are then matched against those stored in the memory of the computer. Bledsoe and Browning found that increasing N beyond 7 did not bring about a corresponding increase in performance, which has some interesting implications about the limits of interaction and the size of a Gestalt. The one conspicuous fault of both the 1-tuple and N-tuple methods is that there does not seem to exist a physiological analog of this process.

The problem of interacting segments of a pattern is tackled every time the relationships among portions of a pattern are examined. When the emphasis is on larger portions of the pattern or the pattern as a whole and the organization of the pattern in terms of Gestalt principles is stressed as well, we may speak of the *Gestalt method* of pattern recognition (e.g., Guiliano *et al.*, 1961). This term, however, is somewhat vague since it presupposes exact knowledge of what the Gestalt principles are and how they are quantified, which is not quite the case. The uncertainty surrounding the Gestalt principles is reflected by the writers of computer programs of this kind, who may refer to them as Gestalt programs even when the elements related are single cells, the only reason for using that term being that these elements are looked at and summed over the entire pattern (e.g., Nieder, 1960).

The modified template-matching approach described above underlies the group of programs sometimes called "characteristic-feature" or "plausible-properties" programs. The computer "looks" at a few or many features of the pattern that the programmer has decided may be important in the recognition process, such as straight-line segments, curves, angles, and intersections, measures them, and makes recognition decisions on that basis. Examples of this type of program are found in Alt (1962), Bomba (1959), Doyle (1960), Grimsdale, Sumner, Tunis, and Kilburn (1959), Uhr (1959), and Unger (1958, 1959). The program proposed by Grimsdale and collaborators is recognized as the most successful of its kind. The elements upon which the computer performs its measurements are the basic strokes that make up the letters of the alphabet, i.e., lines of different lengths, curvatures, and slopes. These are geometric properties. Some programs, such as Sherman's (1960), assess the topological features of patterns, but topology alone is often not enough since, for instance, no difference would be detected by the computer between an 8 and a *B,* or a *W* and an *M.* Hence, topological programs are usually supplemented with geometric operators.

It may be satisfying to know that the visual systems of certain animals, such as the frog and the cat, contain receptors that are sensitive to just such elements of visual patterns, and also that humans seem to use curves, angles, and slopes of lines to identify patterns. It is less satisfying to know that no such receptors have been discovered in the human visual system so far. That programs of this type work may be an indication that neuronal specificity with regard to form may still be encountered in the human visual system some day.

Programs within this category differ in sophistication. It is this type of program that has been used most often to analyze more complex patterns, such as handwriting (e.g., Frishkopf & Harmon, 1961; Harmon, 1960) and pictorial material (e.g., Joseph & Feller, 1958; Wholey, 1961). The best example of the more powerful kind of program is that of Selfridge (Doyle, 1960; Selfridge & Neisser, 1960), although the work of Bomba (1959) and Unger (1958, 1959) could be cited as well. The term "powerful" is used here in the sense that the "plausible properties" are on a high level of complexity (e.g., curves and areas as contrasted with cells or points) and that the operators process pattern elements over a certain range of displacement, such as detecting right angles anywhere in the pattern and regardless of orientation. Selfridge and Neisser stress the advantages of parallel processing as contrasted with sequential processing (e.g., Booth, 1956; Unger, 1959). In addition to the advantages already mentioned, parallel processing allows for the differential weighting of the features that make up a pattern. Injecting a droll kind of life into the program, Selfridge has facetiously reified the parallel-decision-making process as so many little demons who inspect the various features of the pattern and shout their answers simultaneously to a supervising decision-making demon. The name for the program, "Pandemonium," derives from this analogy. It is possible, with this program, to introduce variability in the intensity of shouting of the demons. One could, e.g., make the presence of a vertical line twice as important as the absence of an acute angle, something that is impossible to incorporate in a sequential processing program. The weights to be given the various features may be assigned by the program writer, as was done in the earlier stages of development of this program, or it may be done by the program itself on the basis of backward probabilities, i.e., the probabilities of successful recognition with different weights in the past are compared and the more successful weighting scheme is eventually selected by the computer. This is something akin to a learning feature. Doyle's (1960) program showed only 10% error on a test set of handwritten letters as compared with a 3% error made by human subjects. The program used Bayesian probabilities determined on "training" trials, and its demons examined 28 different features of the characters. These features, however, were predetermined by the program writer.

One comes much closer to what actually happens in human pattern recognition by incorporating into a program a decision-making process that allows the computer itself to extract those features from the patterns that eventually result in the best possible recognition scheme. Uhr and Vossler (1961a) have written such a program. It performs very well on a much larger variety of patterns than most computers do. The patterns, in addition, are not found originally in the computer's memory. A pattern is first presented to a 20 × 20 array of photocells which simulate the retina. Each of the cells of the pattern either excites or does not excite one of the photocells. The program then sets in motion a process whereby an operator is generated. The operator is a 5 × 5 matrix in which randomly selected n cells having the values of 1 or 0 (excited or not excited) form what amounts to a template. The center of this operator moves across the pattern that has been presented to the "retina." At each point, a match between the pattern and the template is made and the hits recorded. A number of such operators is generated. Following the various matches, a recognition decision is made based on the information provided by the operators. The decision is then compared with the correct answer. Operators that produce more hits are given more weight, while poorer operators decrease in importance or may be entirely eliminated from the set of operators. Eventually, the machine winds up with a very successful set of operators. The process apparently has all the learning features, including "reinforcement," i.e., the selection of operators based on their performance, yet it is not at all certain that it represents the learning process in a nervous system. Still, Uhr and Vossler contend, for instance, that the 5×5 operator may have an analog in the living retina in the form of functionally and structurally connected cell groups, such as apparently exist in the retina of the frog. The program, however, does not extract the same features from a pattern that humans do, and the fact that it performs successfully is not a guaranty that it is a successful model of nervous functions in form perception.

Random Nets. A nervous system is a neural network. Events in electrical networks may be calculated, thus one of the important concerns of cyberneticists has been the calculation of events in theoretical networks of neurons after making certain assumptions that tend to simplify the system. A convenient starting point is a "random net," a collection of neurons among which synaptic connections may be formed with equal probabilities. Such a net is suggested by the seemingly random cortical connections found in mammals. Statistical computations then establish such values as the expected number of pathways between two randomly chosen neurons, the expected number of neurons a given number of synaptic connections away from a given neuron, etc. The simplifying assumptions made may be as follows: complete synchronization of all neurons; synaptic thresholds are fixed; the effects of drugs and hormones are ignored; interaction between neurons is ignored; glial cells are ignored. These assumptions were actually made by McCulloch and Pitts (1943). Given these data and assumptions, it is possible, e.g., to compute whether an input of certain intensity will spread excitation throughout the net or die out. On this basis, one can proceed to study the properties of "biased" nets, i.e., nets where the synaptic connections are not equiprobable, where synaptic thresholds change, etc. The mathematics of biased nets become extremely unwieldy, however, even though a biased net represents more closely the activity of an actual nervous system.

The problem of complete randomness vs. bias in simulated nerve nets has been at the center of the work associated with the more complex but also more interesting pattern-recognition programs. Both theoretical considerations (e.g., Kalin, 1961) and actual performance of completely random machines have suggested that random organization is not practical in its pure form. The "Perceptron" program is a good example of a development in this area.

The Perceptron is a mathematical model of visual perception as well as a piece of actual hardware developed by F. Rosenblatt and his co-workers at Cornell University (Rosenblatt, 1958, 1960). The Perceptron is not built to recognize any particular patterns, but to "learn" to recognize patterns from a set after a number of trials. A pattern is presented to a mosaic of photocells, which are activated or not depending on how much light is received from the stimulus pattern. The Mark I Perceptron had a 20 X 20 matrix of photocells. At the output end of the machine are some response units or effector counterparts of an organism. The connection between the sensory and response units, however, is not a direct one, but is mediated by association units, which represent the nervous system proper. The number of sensory units is small, as is the number of response units, but the number of association units is much larger. The interconnections of the association units are random. Originally, the entire system was randomly connected and the connections were of the many-to-many type. This model exhibited only a slight degree of learning and was not an effective pattern recognizer. By shifting to converging and diverging connections, by introducing restraints in the form of, e.g., subnets for line recognition, and by building in provisions for reinforcement, an incomparably better preformance has been achieved.

The Perceptron has long-term memory. This memory is a function of the past activity of the system and works through changes effected at junction points between elements. These affect the magnitude of the impulse carried by these junctions. Feedback from performance determines the weights that are eventually given the individual association units. Since the physiological counterparts of reinforcement are practically unknown, the Perceptron group simply incorporated reinforcement rules that made theoretical or practical sense.

How Successful Are Pattern-Recognition Programs? For almost every program of pattern recognition, a success rate of 90% or more has been claimed on at least one occasion. Success in recognition depends almost entirely on the type of form that is presented for recognition. With an appropriately small, invariant, and simple set of stimuli, most programs will register near-100% success. Differences between programs begin to show up when nontrivial sets of forms are presented for recognition, but here it is difficult to make comparisons because no two researchers have used exactly the same forms or have varied them in exactly the same way. A comparison of the success figures of a large number of pattern-recognition programs has been made by Uhr (1963). It serves the purpose of illustrating the lack of systematicity that exists in the field.

Indirectly, the success figures, which are seldom below 50% and are much higher in most cases, tell us that the main reason for the success is the careful selection of a limited, preselected set of patterns and the ignoring of some substantial problems, so that success is assured beforehand. The most important problem is the problem of invariance. It has not been solved for pattern perception by machines, although the theoretical problems associated with it have been handled since the birth of cybernetics. If it had, there would be no need to write more programs or to fail to follow up an initial report of a surprisingly high success rate demonstrated by a particular program. The reason is that the problem of how invariance is achieved in a living organism is still unsolved. Indications are that much more than repeated visual experience of the same pattern under different conditions is involved. A most important factor is kinesthetic feedback, as well as inputs from other sense modalities, as is the fact that form in everyday life is not a two-dimensional array of points but a surface or object and is perceived under continuous series of transformations as the perceiver moves in three-dimensional space. Reafference, to use this term in von Holst's sense, but applying it to cover other similar concepts, including Gibson's, is most certainly an essential variable contributing to the existence of perceptual invariance. Reafference, except perhaps only in the sense of experimenter-provided feedback to the machine about its performance, has not been incorporated in pattern-recognition programs in any important sense. This problem has been discussed in detail by Gyr, Brown, Willey, and Zivian (1966), who have also provided some suggestions for a remedy, including a computer program based on the idea of an active, rather than passive, process of form perception. The program still appears to be in the developmental stage.

The basic weakness of pattern-recognition programs is that the problem of pattern recognition has not yet been solved on the psychological level. The physical dimensions of form that determine recognition and the range of their variability have not been specified yet; neither have the populations of patterns that a computer may be expected to recognize. The "learning" computer, in spite of appearances, does not start from scratch, since it is the programmer who provides criteria of correct performance to the computer, based upon which the computer makes decisions about the goodness of its operators.

At this point in the history of modeling pattern perception on the computer, the task is really one of modeling discrimination rather than recognition. Recognition in a computer is recognition only in a trivial sense. Recognition by organisms implies previous experience, and with experience there accrue meanings to patterns that are uncorrelated in any important way with the physical dimensions of patterns. Whether a machine will ever be able to cope with this problem is uncertain. The issue here is analogous to that encountered in computer translation of foreign languages. It is no particular problem to have a computer "translate" single words where synonymity is not involved and words have no excessive surplus meaning. Synonymity and context, however, introduce problems which at the present time are insuperable. The fundamental problem in both translation and form-perception programs is the same: no computer can generate its own criteria of performance. "The effectiveness of all of them is forever restricted by the ingenuity or arbitrariness of their programmers. We can barely guess how this restriction might be overcome. Until it is, 'artificial intelligence' will remain tainted with artifice." (Selfridge and Neisser, 1960, p. 68.)

3. Comparative Theories of the Physiology and Psychology of Contour Perception and Form Discrimination

While the most common term used by comparative theorists is discrimination, some use recognition instead, while still others use both terms interchangeably when referring to their theories of how shapes may be discriminated by animals and man. The use of two different terms to designate the same thing is confusing and requires clarification.

In terms of complexity and the amount of time that goes by before the task may be performed, it is possible to distinguish (1) discrimination pure and simple, (2) discrimination learning, and (3) recognition. In simple discriminations, the organism's capacity to distinguish relatively small differences in shape parameters is called upon. In an n-choice oddity problem, the organism's capacity to distinguish degrees of compactness, symmetry, etc. is tested. The test may also involve the investigation of preferences for or the salience of cues, but this is a secondary aspect of the task. Essentially, the difference thresholds for curvature, angularity, symmetry, or any other form parameter are involved. For this reason, no previous learning except that of mastering the oddity task itself is involved.

While oddity is not a form parameter, learning based on the discrimination of a particular form parameter may be made the basis of the task. Thus, if the rat is required to learn that the vertical striations rather than the horizontal ones are rewarded, he is also engaged in a discrimination learning task, i.e., a simple concept is learned. This kind of task is already to a large extent removed from the area of form discrimination as such—the emphasis is on the learning ability of the organism, especially the ability to form concepts, such as that of triangularity, elongation, color, or position. Theories which explain this process belong in the domain of learning and are not considered here.

Recognition implies previous learning and the fact that some concept or identity scheme has already been formed. There is some memory trace which enables the organism to make the decision that the shape in question has been seen before and signifies either reward or punishment. This is not what so-called theories of shape recognition in animals are about. If they are, they are then no different from discrimination learning theories, except perhaps that they deal with processes which presuppose already-formed concepts. The shape-recognition theories labeled as such by the authors discussed below deal instead with the recognition of shapes as being the same when they are presented in a different size, in a different retinal locus, rotated, or reflected, i.e., recognition over transformation groups. Strictly speaking, no recognition is involved. The term is actually used in a figurative sense: it appears as if the organism had learned that, e.g., all squares regardless of size are the same, and that when one is presented that differs in size from another presented previously, the organism "recognizes" it as being the same. The question these theories attempt to answer is, "What shapes produce equivalent neural signals and are therefore responded to in the same fashion by the organism?" No previous learning is involved or necessary here, hence this sort of "recognition" is very similar to the simple type of discrimination defined above. The difference consists in the type of parameters that are involved. Changes in curvature, elongation, or compactness produce a differently configurated shape. In simple discrimination tasks, the questions asked concern the size of the difference thresholds for these continua. Changes in size or orientation do not produce different configurations, yet something changes. Theories of shape "recognition" ask why response remains the same in spite of these changes, and mechanisms are proposed to account for this. Size, nevertheless, may be made a discriminative cue, as in pairs of otherwise identical figures. While animals show, e.g., size constancy, they are also able to discriminate on the basis of size. The theoretical problem then becomes to postulate another mechanism or make provision in the same mechanism to account for this behavior as well.

As will be seen from the following discussion, Sutherland (1961b) was quite right when he said that, "Until the late 1930's, it could be said that there were too many experiments insufficiently guided by theory; since that date, there have been too many theories insufficiently based on experimental evidence" (p. 1). Lashley's and Fields' visual discrimination experiments with the rat must be counted with the early corpus of experimental work. While the strategy of these investigators was to formulate a neurophysiological theory of form perception based on observable shape-classification behavior in the rat, the theoretical stage was never actually reached.

A. FORM PERCEPTION IN LOWER ANIMALS

Deutsch (1955) was first to formulate a theory of shape discrimination, which became related to but competitive with the theories of Dodwell (1957b) and Sutherland (1957).

The original version of Deutsch's theory was purely speculative, yet specific enough to permit at least one attempt at its programming for the digital computer, as disclosed by Uhr (1966, p. 175). The theory applies mainly to a single species, the octopus, even though Deutsch repeatedly refers also to the rat and, by suggesting some additional assumptions, attempts to extend it to man. The problem that Deutsch sets himself is to postulate a shape-discrimination mechanism which (1) would not be hampered by the problems arising out of symmetry operations that can be performed on form (rotation, reflection, translation) as well as area differences in the same shape; (2) would account for the inability (according to Deutsch) of primitive organisms to discriminate between a circle and a square; and (3) would eliminate the need for either scanning the form or fixating its center in order to perceive it correctly. The first and third requirements mean that the mechanism should permit discrimination of form unrelated to any external or internal frames of reference, while the second requirement tends to remove the theory from the consideration of the geometric properties of form, such as angularity.

The neural events which, according to Deutsch, occur in perception are as follows:

> Let us assume that there is an array of . . . cells arranged in two dimensions . . . . This plane composed of cells has messages arriving on it from . . . the retina. Each group of cells is joined to a particular retinal element in such a way that neighboring retinal elements also excite neighboring groups of cells . . . . When [excitation from contours falling on the retina] arrives, each unit will pass on a pulse down what will be called a final common cable. It will also excite its neighbor. This neighbor will pass it on in its turn. Therefore, when a contour is projected on the two-dimensional array, two things will occur: a message consisting of one pulse will be passed down the final common cable by each cell or unit on which that contour lies. Thus, a measure of the total number of cells stimulated will be passed down. Second, the contour will excite all the cells which lie next to it on the two-dimensional array. These will pass the excitation on to their neighbors but not down the final common cable. The assumption is made that a cell will pass on its excitation at right angles to the contour of which it happens to be a component . . . . As such lateral excitation from a point in a contour advances, another message will be sent down the final common cable as soon as it coincides with another point in a contour imposed on the two-dimensional array. (Deutsch, 1955, p. 31/2.)

The message sent down the "final common cable" by a rectangle will be three volleys: one corresponding to the total number of cells excited by the contour, and two indicating the lengths of the two sides. The message generated by a square would be two volleys, as would be the message sent by a circle, both equal in magnitude. This, reasons Deutsch, is the main cause of why a circle and a square are indistinguishable to primitive organisms, such as the octopus. Since the message corresponding to a figure depends entirely on the properties of the figure itself without any reference to external frames or axes, rotated, translated, and reflected figures will generate the same message as the untransposed figure. Identical figures of different areas will produce identical messages differing in strength. The important feature of these messages is the ratio of the first volley, indicating the total length of the contour, to the subsequent volleys. This ratio, regardless of the area of the figure, remains the same, and the two figures are recognized as identical.

Deutsch makes a number of very specific predictions from his theory. For instance, he predicts that it will be easier to discriminate a square and a rectangle than a square and a rectangle both with one side missing; that there will be perfect transfer from an equilateral triangle to another with one side missing; that shallow curves will be indistinguishable from straight lines in the absence of other contours in the vicinity, etc. At the time of its publication, none of these predictions from the theory had been tested experimentally. Nevertheless, Deutsch extended the theory from octopus to man by postulating for man an unspecified mechanism sensitive not merely to absolute differences in the height of the nerve impulses but also to their spacing in time, so that the easy discrimination that humans make between a circle and a square could be accounted for.

Having performed an interesting experiment with ten rats, Dodwell (1957b) published a paper which bore both on Deutsch's theory and a number of Lashley's (1938) experiments on visual discrimination in rats. In this paper, Dodwell offered an amended version of Deutsch's theory.

One of Lashley's findings was that rats, instead of discriminating between the entire shapes of two stimulus figures, were actually doing so on the basis of part-figures or elements present in one of the shapes but not in the other. Also, they appeared to use the relationship of this part figure to the borders of the stimulus card rather than paying attention to the figure alone. Dodwell attributed the first finding to the size of Lashley's shapes: they were too large for the rat to look at and to process in their entirety. He attributed the second finding to the proximity of the contours of the figure to the edges of the card as well as to the fact that many of Lashley's stimuli were solid rather than outline figures: the rats could have conceivably responded to the brightness distribution on the card rather than to shape per se. The interpretation of Lashley's findings is further complicated by pretraining on vertical and horizontal striations that his rats were exposed to prior to the experiments. Dodwell's own experiment was designed to test the boundary effect by eliminating boundaries, to test the effect of pretraining, and to test the effect of the size of the stimulus figures. According to Deutsch, a shape, to be recognized, must be seen in its entirety at once, so that his postulated mechanism could not have been operating in Lashley's experiments, hence the rat's inability to discriminate circles from squares must stem from another source. Using Lashley's experimental procedure but with the above modifications, Dodwell was able to conclude (tentatively, because of the small number of subjects) that (a) pretraining on horizontal and vertical striations makes a difference in whether a rat can subsequently discriminate a circle from a square; (b) the rat can learn to discriminate a circle from a square quite rapidly (when the border effect is absent) by isolating an element in one of the shapes; (3) rats transfer learned discriminations to other shapes that have the isolated element in common, including smaller shapes; (4) the square and the diamond are not confused with one another, nor is either with the circle. Based on these findings, Dodwell proposed the following modified version of Deutsch's theory that would accord better with the fact that recognition of shapes in any orientation is not a property of primitive visual systems, and that the rat (who, to Dodwell at least, has a primitive visual system) does isolate part figures and react to them. Deutsch's theory was made to fit just the opposite assumptions. Like Deutsch, Dodwell assumes:

> . . . a two-dimensional array of units (or cells) arranged in chains, in such a way that each unit is connected to two neighbors, except for the end units of each chain, each of which has only one neighbor. Each chain is functionally separate from every other chain, except in two important respects: one set of end units (set A) is so arranged that if one fires, they all fire simultaneously, and the other set of end units (set B) discharges into a common channel, which, following Deutsch's terminology, is called the final common cable . . . . Any unit of the array can pass excitation from itself to a neighboring unit in the same chain: this excitation originates in the firing of the end-set A, and is not to be confused with activation by stimulation of receptors to which the unit is connected. The passing of this excitation from one unit to another involves a small delay, the length of which is determined by whether the unit transmitting excitation is active or passive. (Dodwell, 1957b, p. 226.)

Dodwell assumes that the array's chains represent functionally one of the two main spatial axes. Thus, e.g., a horizontal line will fire all units in a chain. Which chain it will be is immaterial as far as the signal in the final common cable is concerned. If the contour deviates from the horizontal, more chains will be involved but fewer units in each chain. Such a contour will produce a large first discharge (yet smaller than in the first case), followed by another volley produced by the simultaneous firing of several chains of units. A square and a triangle, seen separately, will both produce three volleys: one from all chains of units on which the contours of the figure do not fall; the second from the nonhorizontal sides of the figure, caused by a few active units on a large number of chains; and the third produced by the horizontal contours. The difference between the two figures is that the square will produce a third volley about twice as strong as that produced by the triangle since the square has two horizontal sides while the triangle has only one. To eliminate the difficulty that the system would have in discriminating between two figures neither one of which has horizontal sides, Dodwell assumes that there is another identical system which functions perpendicularly to the first one. This double system has the interesting property that two lines perpendicular to each other are more easily discriminated if they coincide with the vertical and horizontal spatial axes but not when they are tilted 45 degrees to the horizontal. This has been a frequent finding in the octopus.

This system explains both Dodwell's own experimental results mentioned above as well as many of Lashley's findings. The system has the advantage over Deutsch's in that it accounts for discrimination based either on part figures or whole figures since the signal set up in the final common cable would be the same in Dodwell's but not in Deutsch's system. In the latter, the signal is changed radically even if only a small portion of the figure falls outside the field of vision. At the time, though, Dodwell was rather tentative on several important points, including the discrimination of small shapes: his own experiment was not sufficient to provide a firm answer to all questions.

Deutsch (1958) answered Dodwell's criticisms of his theory in a brief note, whereupon Dodwell (1958) wrote an equally brief refutation. This exchange dealt mainly with the problem of shape recognition under conditions of tilt. The argument is not repeated here since the exchange ended right then and both theorists have since written a number of papers in which both theories are considerably modified on the basis of further theorizing and additional experimental evidence. The fact is that at the time the original papers were written both theories were only half-baked.

In 1960, making no mention of his 1955 theory, Deutsch offered a new one. This time, it was clearly spelled out that the theory applied only to the octopus, although Deutsch did not exclude the possibility that a system similar to the one proposed for the octopus could be operative in higher organisms as well. An important difference between this and the 1955 version of Deutsch's theory was that this time he tried to explain observed behavior in terms of neural structures, also observed. Neither kind of observation had been done by Deutsch himself. The behavioral data were Sutherland's, who by that time had accumulated as much data on visual shape discrimination in the octopus as Lashley had previously done on the rat. The neural structures had been observed and drawn by Ramón y Cajal in 1917. The feature of the plexiform layer of the retina of the octopus that had attracted Deutsch's attention was that receptor fibers appeared to connect with, and penetrate to, various depths, but perpendicularly to a layer of parallel fibers from another set of cells in the plexiform layer.

Deutsch's shape-discrimination system converts space into neural output whose magnitude varies inversely with distance. The farther apart are any two points on two contours to be compared, the weaker is the neural signal. He describes the assumed mode of functioning of the system as follows:

There is a set of lines running parallel to each other. Each line is interrupted at randomly chosen points, so that each line is divided into a number of segments of varying size. Into this set of parallel segments enter at right angles a set of other lines (to be called retinal receptor fibres). These enter the layer of segmented lines at equally spaced intervals and penetrate the layer of the segmented lines to its other boundary. Now let us assume that the retinal receptor fibres become active when they have been stimulated by a boundary discontinuity. The distance between two retinal receptor fibres reflects the distance between two points on a boundary. Let us also assume that the line segments in the parallel line layer also become active only when two or more than two simultaneously active retinal receptor fibres cross them. It will then follow that the closer together the two active retinal receptor fibres are, the greater the number of line segments that will become active. The sum of active line segments in the parallel line layer will correspond in inverse ratio with the distance apart of the active incoming retinal receptor fibres .... The arrangement described would transform the distance between a pair of points into an amount of neural activity. The shapes to be discriminated, however, are composed of a great number of pairs of points. It is assumed that these pairs lie on lines parallel to each other and that each pair is measured by an arrangement such as was described above. This is done by having many such arrangements side by side, parallel to each other, running in the vertical visual axis. It is assumed that the total amount of excitation generated by the whole set of these arrangements gives the octopus its chief cue to the discrimination of shape. Different shapes are in this way translated into a single continuum of amount of activity. The problem of discriminating between them becomes one of differentiating between various levels of activity in a single channel. (Deutsch, 1960, p. 444.)

Deutsch makes two additional assumptions necessary for the theory: (1) vertical lines produce little or no output because excitations on the same vertical arrangement inhibit each other, and (2) the octopus can discriminate relative vertical positions. This system accounts easily for size constancy, but not in all cases. Thus, when a square is increased in area, its sides move apart, thereby reducing the magnitude of neural output. At the same time, however, the length of the sides increases proportionately, so that two squares of different areas produce signals of identical strength. This process will or will not occur depending on (1) the shape used, and (2) the other member of the pair which the octopus has learned to discriminate. Thus, a small $<$ and a scaled enlargement of it will produce different outputs, since the small $<$ is part of the larger figure. The same holds for diamonds and triangles. Careful consideration of these relatively simple principles allows one to make a considerable number of specific predictions. For instance, discrimination between two different shapes may improve or worsen depending on which of the two shapes is changed in area and whether area is increased or decreased. If the pair of shapes is a square and a triangle, increasing the size of the triangle will improve discrimination, since a triangle that has the same area as a square produces a larger output than the square, while neither an increase nor a decrease in the area of the square will affect discrimination since it is assumed that vertical lines produce little or no output. Some of Sutherland's (1958) data actually show this to be the case. The theory explains neatly many other instances of shape discrimination by the octopus, but not all.

Deutsch did not attempt to fill in the gaps in the 1960 theory, but proceeded to formulate still another two years later (Deutsch, 1962). It is not too dissimilar, in principle, from the one formulated for the octopus, which is one of the reasons why it is not described here any further. The other reason is that its bases are even less firm than those of Deutsch's two preceding theories. The starting point for the theory is the structure of the optic lobe of the bee as drawn by Ramón y Cajal in 1915, which shows incoming fibers from the bee's eye entering a number of horizontal layers in the optic lobe. The number of fibers decreases with increasing depth of the layers. Deutsch, while admitting that such a structure may not actually exist in vertebrate brains, uses it as a demonstration that a mechanism of this sort is biologically possible. Deutsch describes two alternative mechanisms of this type, both of which provide for discrimination over transformation groups and yield discrimination of distance and angle between points. The correlate of distance between two points is the number of impulses which arrive at the various horizontal layers in the optic lobe. Unfortunately, Deutsch never states what other species besides the bee could posses this type of mechanism, although the impression is given that it could exist in other animals, including the vertebrates. These ambiguities are compounded by the use of many auxiliary assumptions to make the system work. There is the additional defect that Deutsch adduces practically no behavioral or supporting physiological data to lend some measure of validity to the theoretical structure.

Dodwell waited until 1964 before publishing another version of his 1957 theory, although he did propose a theory of discrimination learning in 1961 (Dodwell, 1961a). The impetus for proposing an amplified version of the theory appears to have come from the neurophysiological investigations of Hubel and Wiesel, which are discussed at the end of this chapter. The system consists of two coupled subsystems: a coding and a recognition system. The coding system is identical to the one proposed by Dodwell in 1957. This system translates space into neural signals spaced in time and differing in amplitude. The "recognition" system is coupled to the coding system in order to allow for the classification of stimuli into equivalent and non equivalent ones. Since the need for a special recognition system was not brought up in Dodwell's 1957 paper and its utility is not made too clear in the 1964 paper either, it is hard to see exactly what purpose it serves, especially since Dodwell defines recognition as the "registration of some constant pattern of activity at some constant locus, for a given input pattern or class of input patterns." The recognition system is one that Dodwell borrows almost intact from Uttley (1954). As it turns out, Uttley's cybernetically oriented system of signal classification in the nervous system has been criticized on the grounds that, in order to process all possible combinations of signals arising in the receptors, the system, as proposed, would need an astronomical number of units. This difficulty is solved if a coding system is introduced between the receptors and the recognizer. Looking at it this way, Dodwell's proposal is actually one designed to salvage Uttley's recognizer.

Since Uttley's recognizer handles only discrete signals of equal amplitude and the output of Dodwell's coding system represents analogs of the shapes, Uttley's recognizer, as modified by Dodwell, also performs the task of converting analog into digital signals. A schematic of the recognizer is shown in Fig. 3-6. It works as follows:

Each volley in the coder output gives rise to a 'unit' impulse in one of the inputs to the recognizer . . . . For the simplest case, where only two different amplitudes are recognized, two inputs to the recognizer are required, inputs j and k, say. These two inputs are connected to counters which register either (a) the initial arrival of unit impulses in either input, or (b) the temporal patterns of impulses on either or on both inputs. This is achieved by feeding each input into a series of delay units, and then to the counters . . . . Except for the first two counters (j and k), a counter will only register when two impulses arrive at it simultaneously or within an arbitrarily small interval of time. To see how this works, consider the counter labeled jj'' [Fig. 3-6]. It will register if, and only if, an impulse in the j input is followed by a second impulse in the same input after time τ where τ is the delay induced by the first delay line on input j. Similarly, the adjacent counter jk' registers only when an impulse on j is followed by an impulse on k after time τ. (The primes refer to the number of delay units separating a pair of impulses.) Assuming $\tau = h\,\Delta T$, where h is an integer, the time intervals required to activate different counters will be simply related to the output from the coder. It can be seen that the recognizer of [Fig. 3-6] will discriminate all possible patterns for the two inputs j and k, up to time delays of 3τ. For patterns involving more than two impulses, more than one counter (excluding the initial j and k counters) will register. A simple higher-order type of recognition can easily be added . . . . This hierarchical system of classification can be continued to any desired level of complexity, according to the number of

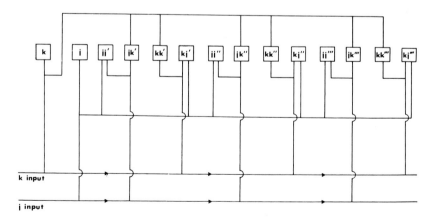

Fig. 3-6. Recognizer for outputs from a shape-coding system. From Dodwell (1964). See text for explanation. Copyright 1964 by the American Psychological Association. Reproduced by permission.

inputs, and the number and complexity of pattern to be classified. The only restriction required is that $u\tau < n\,\Delta T$, where u is the number of delay units in the recognizer, and n, as before, is the number of units per chain in the array. 'Equivalent stimuli' can now be defined as inputs from the receptors which give rise to the activation of the same set of counters in the recognizer. (Dodwell, 1964, pp. 152/3.)

In order to account for perceptual learning and other processes that presuppose information storage, Dodwell suggests that each counter in the system just described may also act as a storage unit for information, such that with each count its state is altered, but that time without counts would tend to make it revert to its initial state, something like a leaky electrical condenser. Dodwell then envisages two types of stimulus equivalence. One is due to the fact that some outputs of the coder are identical or very similar, the other is due to a prolonged output of a regular sequence of signals from the coder. This latter sequence would tend to build up higher levels of equivalence in the recognizer and would be the counterpart of perceptual learning.

At just about the same time as Deutsch and Dodwell were publishing their respective views on shape perception in lower animals, Sutherland formulated another such theory. In contrast to those of Deutsch and of Dodwell, Sutherland's theory was based primarily on his own experiments with the octopus. The papers that Sutherland has published on form vision in the octopus constitute the largest single body of information on the subject.

The first theory (Sutherland, 1957) was rather simple. The octopus classifies shapes using the following mechanism:

The excitation produced by the shapes on the retina is relayed to an array of nerve cells representing a projection of the retina in the optic lobes. The outputs from this array are so arranged that the cells of each column and each row have connexions to further cells specific to each column and row. The amount of firing in the output from the cells connected with the columns will now represent the height of the figure, and the amount of firing in the output from the rows will represent the lateral extent of the figure .... On this system, discrimination can be performed by comparing two quantities in the nervous system. A further analysing mechanism is needed to analyse and compare the size of outputs on rows and columns; such a mechanism presents no difficulty in principle, but . . . no suggestions about it are made here. (P. 12.)

The net result of the operation of the suggested mechanism is the projection of the shape on the axes of a Cartesian coordinate system so that two one-dimensional distributions of the area of the shape (or patterns of neuronal firing) are obtained. Some of the shapes used by Sutherland in his 1957 experiments and later, as well as the corresponding patterns of neuronal excitation predicted from the theory are shown in Fig. 3-7. Since the system works by comparing the respective magnitudes of neural excitation, Sutherland postulated no memory mechanism and pointed out that no specific nerve pathways were necessary and that transpositions to a different retinal locus or to a different size did not affect the working of the mechanism.

Support for the first version of the theory could be found in Sutherland's own experimental results. When differently oriented rectangles are used, discrimination is easiest when one of them is oriented vertically, the other horizontally. Such a configuration, as may be inferred from Fig. 3-7, should produce the largest difference between the outputs of the discrimination system. Discrimination is not as good when a horizontal rectangle is to be distinguished from an oblique one, while two oblique rectangles positioned at 90 degrees to each other are not discriminated at all, again as predicted by the theory. Similar results are obtained with squares, diamonds, triangles, and circles. Thus, e.g.,

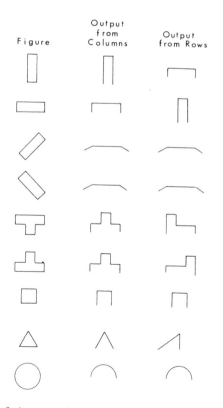

Fig. 3-7. Examples of shapes used by N. S. Sutherland in his form-discrimination experiments with the octopus, with their predicted patterns of neuronal excitation.

discrimination is very poor when the figures to be discriminated are a diamond and a triangle. These, as Fig. 3-7 indicates, should produce almost identical signals in the nervous system.

While admitting that the proposed mechanism was probably an oversimplification of the true state of affairs, the agreement between predicted and obtained data led Sutherland to suggest that something roughly resembling the hypothesized mechanism might exist not only in the octopus but also in man. In the latter case, however, such a mechanism would be only one of a number of mechanisms used in form discrimination.

Dodwell, whose first version of his own theory was in the press at the time Sutherland's was published, immediately wrote a note (Dodwell, 1957a) contesting some aspects of Sutherland's theory, such as his failure to postulate a mechanism for the discrimination between the outputs of two different shapes. Since Dodwell's own theory, which he offered as a substitute for Sutherland's, underwent the modifications already mentioned, these criticisms are not further discussed here. In his subsequent experiments, Sutherland (1959a, 1959b), without stating explicitly the nature of the discriminative mechanism, suggested that discrimination between two different shapes occurs as the animal combines the vertical and horizontal projections of these shapes. More detail was offered in a 1960 paper. Further analysis of the projections proceeds, in Sutherland's words, in the following manner:

(a) The ratios maximum horizontal extent to square root of area, and maximum vertical extent to square root of area are computed. (b) The two projections obtained may be differentiated so that they are analysed in terms of the direction and size of changes. This means that octopuses will be able to discriminate between shapes which yield a different distribution of vertical extent along the horizontal axis, or a different distribution of horizontal extent along the vertical axis .... It is further hypothesized that behaviour is more readily controlled by differences in the horizontal projections than by differences in the vertical projections, possibly because horizontal projections of shapes are more accurately represented in the nervous system. Therefore, the discriminability of shapes will be more determined by the similarity of their horizontal projections than the similarity of their vertical projections. In general, the theory makes three types of prediction: (1) Shapes having large differences in relative horizontal or vertical extents will be more readily discriminable than shapes having small differences. (2) Shapes which have the same horizontal projections as one another and the same vertical projections will be indiscriminable. (3) Shapes differing only in their horizontal projections will be more readily discriminable than shapes differing only in their vertical projections. (Sutherland, 1960a, p. 841.)

Since by this time Sutherland had accumulated more than a dozen published and unpublished studies on form discrimination in the octopus, he was well prepared to undertake a comparison between his theory, the 1957 version of Dodwell's theory, and the 1960 version of Deutsch's theory. While in some respects the theories were rather similar, Sutherland insisted that octopuses used horizontal and vertical projections as clues in discrimination, Dodwell thought it was deviations from the horizontal and vertical axes, while Deutsch maintained it was distances between contours in the vertical direction. Of 12 predictions about the relative discriminability of specific pairs of shapes, the projection theory was supported by experimental results in 10 of them; the distance theory in no instance yielded a correct prediction where the projection theory failed, and yielded several incorrect predictions where the projection theory was successful; the inclination theory yielded practically no correct predictions.

Dodwell's objections to Sutherland's theory continued after he read Sutherland's comparison (Dodwell, 1961b, 1962). He was joined by Deutsch (1960) who, like Dodwell, suggested his own theory was better than Sutherland's. This led to replies by Sutherland (1960b, 1961a) and a revision of his original model of form perception in the octopus. The revision draws upon Young's (1962) evidence of the existence of receptive fields in the optic lobe of the octopus. Most of the fields appear to be oriented in a plane corresponding to the visual horizontal, a smaller number being oriented vertically, and a smaller number still being oriented obliquely. Assuming an excitatory area about the longitudinal axis of a receptive field flanked by two inhibitory areas, Sutherland (1963) shows how different combinations of the orientation of the receptive field and of the shape, together with the particular configuration of the shape, will modify the number of neurons firing when the contours of a shape fall upon a receptive field. The revised version of the theory explains some of the exceptions and contradictory findings that have accumulated since 1957, but not all.

It is clear from Sutherland's 1964 review article on visual discrimination in animals that he as well as Deutsch and Dodwell have remained convinced of the virtues of their respective theories. As Sutherland (1961a) has justly observed, the disagreement arose because none of the theories was complete and because none had received sufficient systematic testing. It must be said, though, that of all three theorists Sutherland has provided by far the amplest range and amount of experimental evidence in support of his theory. Neither did he commit the error of generalizing findings on visual form discrimination in the octopus to species far removed from it.

B. CATS, FROGS, RECEPTIVE FIELDS, AND CYTOARCHITECTURE

The latest development in research on contour perception and form discrimination in animals offers what would seem as the best opportunity so far to clarify and to specify exactly the nature of these processes and to relate them to observable neural structures on the one hand, and to eliminate the necessity for calculus and neural network theories in their description on the other. This development is the discovery and investigation of functionally related groups of cells, the receptive fields, in the retinas, geniculate bodies, and the visual cortices of animals belonging to a variety of species.

Hartline (1940) discovered that the mammalian retina possessed a higher degree of functional organization than had been surmised. He observed that retinal elements feeding into single visual cells constituted "fields," the receptive fields, which acted as functional units, and that some visual fibers would fire at the onset of a light stimulus, while others would fire only when light was turned off. Kuffler (1953) extended these observations, showing that the receptive fields consisted of a center and a surrounding annulus and were of two types: when a small light spot illuminated the center of one type of receptive field, the ganglion cell that the field fed into would fire, while illumination of the annulus would suppress firing until stimulation ceased, which event triggered a discharge from the field. Another type acted in just the opposite way, having an "off" center and an "on" periphery. This is the basic mechanism that underlies the recent discoveries of specialized cells in mammalian visual systems that respond to movement, direction of movement, and the shape and size of contours. Movement and contour detectors have been discovered in the rabbit (Barlow & Hill, 1963; Oyster & Barlow, 1967), cat (Baumgartner, Brown, & Schulz, 1964; Hubel & Wiesel, 1959, 1962; Rodieck, 1967; Spinelli, 1966; Stone & Fabian, 1966), spider monkey (Hubel & Wiesel, 1960), frog (Lettvin, Maturana, McCulloch, & Pitts, 1959; Lettvin, Maturana, Pitts, & McCulloch, 1961; Maturana, Lettvin, McCulloch, & Pitts, 1960), pigeon (Maturana & Frenk, 1963), and the ground squirrel (Michael, 1966). The best-known representative work has been originated by Hubel and Wiesel, who have used the cat as subject, and from Lettvin and his group of researchers at MIT, whose principal subject has been the frog.

Hubel and Wiesel (1959, 1960, 1962) found that individual cells in the cat's geniculate body were also activated by receptive fields in the cat's retina. These fields have the same on-off functional structure as the fields which feed into ganglion cells, except that the difference between an "on" and an "off" response when either the center or the periphery of a receptive field is stimulated is much more pronounced in the geniculate cells than in ganglion cells. Thus, specialization with regard to intensity differentials in the retina begins to shift toward spatial differentials in the geniculate. Cells in the cat's visual cortex, however, are driven by receptive fields that do not possess the concentric structure of fields associated with the ganglion or geniculate cells. Hubel and Wiesel divide the cat's cortical cells into two large groups, the "simple" and the "complex" cells. The "simple" cells respond to slits, dark bars, and edges, i.e., linear stimuli. Response, however, is a function of the orientation of the stimulus and its location in the receptive field. The "complex" cells respond to the same type of linear stimuli. The difference between the two types of cell is that the complex cells are less sensitive to the location of the stimulus in the receptive field and that they keep firing as long as the stimulus keeps moving.

Since cortical cells respond to highly specific orientations of line stimuli, it follows that there must be a very large number of cells, each responding to a particular orientation. Hubel and Wiesel have indeed found a large variety of responses in the cat's cortical cells, even though they have examined only a few hundred of them. The structure of the cortical receptive fields is not circular but may be described as that of adjacent narrow strips of "on" and "off" cells. A field may, e.g., consist of a narrow "on" strip with two adjacent, somewhat wider "off" areas, or two equally wide adjacent "on" and "off" strips. A narrow, linear stimulus, such as an illuminated slit, coinciding exactly with the "on" region of the field, produces maximum response in the cortical cell. Other orientations produce diminished response, and a stimulus oriented perpendicularly to the field evokes no response at all. While the receptive fields differ in orientation, Hubel and Wiesel find no predominance of one orientation over others, such as the horizontal or the vertical.

Hubel and Wiesel believe that the specificity of the simple cells may be explained by the fact that they receive their inputs directly from the geniculate bodies. They assume that a simple cortical cell synapses with many geniculate cells whose "on" centers, for instance, are all arranged along the same straight line. Stimulation of any of these centers will produce a response in the simple cell; if all are stimulated at the same time, their effect on firing the simple cell is at a maximum.

The complex cells, on the other hand, behave in a way that cannot be explained if it is assumed that they are connected directly to the geniculate bodies. Rather, Hubel and Wiesel believe that each of them receives its inputs from a large number of simple cells, each having the same orientation. This explains why the complex cells, while not showing anything like an organization into "on" and "off" regions, fire or fail to fire in response to the direction of the movement of an edge. For instance, a typical complex cell fires when the moving edge has light on the right, but does not fire if the light is on the left. At the same time, this type of response can be elicited anywhere in the receptive field. Exploration with small spots of light reveals no specific "on" or "off" regions in the receptive fields of the complex cortical cells.

The assumption that the simple cells that send their messages to a single complex cell all respond to the same orientation of line stimuli presupposes a highly structured organization of the cortex, and this is precisely what Hubel and Wiesel have demonstrated. Exploration of the cortex with microelectrodes shows that the cat's cortical cells are not distributed randomly but are arranged in a highly organized manner. It is a columnar arrangement: cells with the same receptive field orientation extend in a thin column downward toward the center of the brain, perpendicularly to the surface. This columnar structure is not visible under a microscope, and appears only in electrical recordings. As long as the electrode penetrates the brain in a direction perpendicular to the surface of the brain segment under investigation, it records a response to the same stimulus orientation from all cells that it encounters in its path. If the direction changes, other cells are encountered whose response is to other stimulus orientations and which belong to other adjacent columns. Thus, the columns may be considered the functional units of the cat's visual cortex.

More recently, Hubel and Wiesel (1965) have obtained additional evidence for the surprisingly high level of cytoarchitectonic and functional organization in the cat's brain. Whereas the simple cells are found mostly in visual projection area I (corresponding to area 19 in humans) and the complex cells in visual area II (area 18 in humans), there appears to exist a third area in the cat's brain, corresponding to area 17 in the human visual cortex. Two additional types of cell have been found here, the lower- and higher-order hypercomplex cells. The lower-order hypercomplex cell responds to slits, bars, and edges, but the stimulus must have an end at least in one of its extremities. A stimulus which will evoke optimum response in this type of cell is a right-angle corner. Hubel and Wiesel show evidence that this type of cell may be receiving its input from two complex cells, one excitatory, the other inhibitory. The higher-order hypercomplex cells are similar to the lower-order ones in most respects except that they respond to a line in eithei one of two orientations 90 degrees apart. Their action seems to indicate that their input originates in a large number of lower-order hypercomplex cells.

Since exploration with microelectrodes cannot be done in humans, there is no evidence at the present time that the human visual cortex is organized on the same principles of cytoarchitecture as the cat's. Nor, for that matter, is there any evidence against this possibility. Hubel and Wiesel actually assume that man and cat share the same principle of organization in their visual brains. Evans (1966) submits indirect evidence for the existence of receptive fields in the human retina. Assuming that there is a large number of receptive fields in the human retina, eye movements in normal vision would result in the sampling of many receptive fields, and some mean signal would indicate the size and shape of the stimulus. When the retinal image is stabilized, only the orientation of the axis of the receptive fields would count. The nature of unitary and fragmentary disappearance of single lines described by Evans may well be explained in such terms as the number of receptive fields with the same orientation that the stimulus line covers, and the size of the stimulus. Using the afterimage method of obtaining stabilization of retinal images, as described earlier in this chapter, Evans makes his subjects press one key when a stimulus line vanishes as a whole and another key when it breaks up into one or more fragments. Subjects are given a large number of trials with each line length, so that a plot can be made of changes from unitary to fragmentary disappearance as a function of stimulus size. It turns out that with increasing stimulus size unitary disappearances decrease in frequency while fragmentary disappearances increase. The point of intersection of the two curves gives the size of the hypothetical receptive fields. Evans has found that they are of the order of about 1 degree of visual angle in the fovea, but increase in size toward the periphery of the retina. As in the cat, they appear to show different orientations of their main axes.

Receptive fields are found in the retina of the frog as well, and their study has led the MIT group of researchers headed by J. Y. Lettvin to conclusions similar to those of Hubel and Wiesel: specificity of response of these receptive fields accounts for much of the behavior of the frog when faced with significant visual stimuli of a specific form.

Five types of ganglion cells are found in the frog's retina, distinguished by the shape and size of their dendritic trees (Lettvin *et al.*, 1961). Having found five types of receptive fields in the frog's optic nerve, it was reasonable for the MIT group to assume that structure and function were correlated along these lines.

The experimental procedure consisted of recording nerve fiber responses as the frog was exposed to stimuli of different shapes and figure-ground contrasts that were moved on a vertical screen by means of magnets located on the other side of the screen. One group of fibers, having receptive fields 2-4 degrees in diameter, was found to respond to any sharp boundary between two shades of gray. The response is not affected by the degree of contrast between the two fields, although it is enhanced if the boundary is set in motion. Another group of fibers, having receptive fields 3-5 degrees in diameter, responds also to sharp boundaries only, but the boundary must be convex, the darker area must be inside the convex contour, and the boundary must either move or have been in movement. It may be safe to assume that these cells act something like "bug detectors" and must therefore be of great importance to the frog. A third group of fibers has receptive fields whose diameter is considerably larger, namely 7-11 degrees. A response is observed in these cells only if an edge is moved across the visual field. The response lasts only as long as there is movement. Lettvin calls these the moving-edge or contrast detectors. A fourth group of cells responds to the dimming of light in the whole receptive field, boundaries playing no role in the response pattern of this type of cell. The diameter of the fields is about 15 degrees. The third and fourth types of cell may conceivably be involved in the detection of large moving objects, such as would signify an enemy to the frog. Cells in the fifth group fire at a rate that is inversely related to the average illumination of the visual field, and this rate changes slowly with changing illumination. Lettvin has not been able to measure the boundaries of the receptive fields that set off the activity of this type of cell, and it is not found with any frequency.

In addition to these five types of cell in the optic nerve, Lettvin and his group have found two additional types of cell in the frog's colliculus. One type has receptive fields about 30 degrees in diameter and is triggered by the appearance of novel stimuli in the visual field. Movement of a stimulus along any path will elicit a response, while movement along the same path 5-10 sec. later produces no response, the refractory period lasting anywhere from 10 to 20 sec. Refractoriness is observed only with regard to the same path of the stimulus, however. No delay is needed to produce a response in the same cell if the object is moved along a different path. This type of neuron was dubbed the "newness" neuron. The other type acts in an opposite fashion: the response lasts as long as the stimulus is present in the visual field. It is as if the neuron "latched" onto the stimulus and followed it as long as it remained in the visual field. When the object is stationary, the response is at a low level, but shows a burst of renewed activity whenever there is new movement of the object. This type of neuron has been called the "sameness" neuron.

Lettvin, Maturana, Pitts, and McCulloch make no attempt to generalize these findings to other species. They emphasize that the anatomy of the visual system of the frog is not the same as that of the mammals or even other amphibians. As compared with the cat, the frog's visual system is more specifically adapted to the needs of the species. In fact, it would seem that, as we descend the phylogenetic scale, the specificity of adaptation increases. One only has to think, e.g., of the moth's auditory system, which in its entirety appears to serve only one purpose—to enable the moth to respond to the cries of the bat, its natural enemy. While some of this specificity of function and structure of the visual system may have been preserved even in man, its degree here is incomparably lower than in any other animal.

While there is no doubt that animals possess structures which respond to specific form parameters as well as directionality of movement, the question of the degree of specificity with increasing complexity of form stimuli is an open one. Ethologists and comparative psychologists have described the characteristics of natural stimulus objects that elicit, without learning, specific responses in many species of animals (cf. Hinde, 1966, pp. 49-50). It is noteworthy that form is not found among the physical dimensions of major importance that elicit species-characteristic responses, although movement, size, texture, and particularly color are some of the visual stimulus dimensions that do play such a role. Shape is sometimes a dimension of minor importance, but here the investigator runs into the major problem of separating the effects of heredity and the environment, a problem that the field of ethology has had and still has to contend with. For instance, Tinbergen's (1948) finding that turkeys which had lived in the open fled when the silhouette of a hawk was moved overhead but did not flee when the same silhouette was moved in the opposite direction and resembled a goose or duck in flight has been vitiated by the preexperimental visual experience of the subjects with geese. It does not seem likely that any animal, regardless of phylogenetic level, would possess the extremely specific templates of the shapes of all predators (as well as harmless animals) and other significant objects built into its nervous system for immediate, unlearned recognition. On the other hand, it is easily demonstrated (see Section 3 on J. J. Gibson in Chap. 4) that certain higher-order visual stimuli that at first appear quite complex may be perceived for what they are, without learning, on the basis of the various visual gradients, such as those of texture, perspective, and shading. Here would belong such findings as that of Tinbergen (1951) that nestling thrushes respond to relational properties of stimuli: if two cardboard circles of different sizes are used to represent the bodies of the mother thrush and two smaller circles are used to represent her head and are attached to these "bodies," the nestling will always respond to that circle as the "head" which bears a constant size relationship to the body. While the experimental work is yet to be performed, it is not unreasonable to assume that many if not all of the seemingly inborn responses to complex visual stimuli could be explained in terms of the specific responses of neurons and groups of neurons to the orientation, curvature, size, movement, and the direction of movement of contours. Combined with the built-in perceptual ability of the organism to extract information about the three-dimensionality of space directly from the stimulus as well as its colors, these items provide the organism with most of the basic information necessary for survival.

While the template idea is attractive, it is not parsimonious, and, on closer examination of behavior, is usually found to be untenable. The idea of a template for the human face, for instance, has been applied to the human infant. The most recent investigator in this area, R. L. Fantz, who originally opted for that idea (Fantz, 1961), has found that, when the elements of a stylized human-face pattern are scrambled, the infant still prefers it to other stimuli, the principal determinant of preference being stimulus complexity, not its specific organization.

REFERENCES

———. Machine reading. *Data Processing,* 1960, **2**, 208-223. (a)

———. Reading machines. *Data Processing,* 1960, **2**, 184-185. (b)

———. Articles on optical reading machines. *Datamation,* 1961, 7(3), 22-32.

Alluisi, E. A. On the use of information measures in studies of form perception. *Percept. mot. Skills,* 1960, 11, 195-203.

Alt, F. L. Digital pattern recognition by moments. In G. L. Fischer, Jr. *et al.* (Eds.), *Optical character recognition.* Washington: Spartan Books, 1962.

Attneave, F. The relative importance of parts of a contour. *US Human Resources Res. Center, Res. Note P&MS* No. 51-8, 1951.

Attneave, F. Some informational aspects of visual perception. *Psychol. Rev.,* 1954, **61**, 183-193.

Attneave, F. Symmetry, information, and memory for patterns. *Amer. J. Psychol.,* 1955, **68**, 209-222.

Attneave, F., & Arnoult, M. D. The quantitative study of shape and pattern perception. *Psychol. Bull.,* 1956, **53**, 452-471.

Baran, P., & Estrin, G. An adaptive character reader. *IRE WESCON Conv. Rec.,* 1960, **4**(Pt. 4), 29-36.

Barlow, H. B., & Hill, R. M. Selective sensitivity to direction of movement in ganglion cells of the rabbit retina. *Science,* 1963, **139**, 412-414.

Baumgartner, G., Brown, J. L., & Schulz, A. Visual motion detection in the cat. *Science,* 1964, **146**, 1070-1071.

Berlyne, D. E. Curiosity and exploration. *Science,* 1966, **153**, 25-33.

Bledsoe, W. W., & Browning, I. Pattern recognition and reading by machine. *Proc. East. Joint Comp. Conf.,* 1959, **16**, 225-232.

Bomba, J. S. Alpha-numeric character recognition using local operations. *Proc. East. Joint Comp. Conf.,* 1959, **16**, 218-224.

Booth, A. D. Session on the computer in a non-arithmetic role. *Proc. IEE,* 1956, **103**(Pt. B, Suppl. No. 3), 450-451.

Boynton, R. M., Elworth, C. L., Onley, J. W., & Klingberg, C. L. Form discrimination as predicted by overlap and area. USAF RADC TR 60-158, 1960.

Boynton, R. M., Elworth, C. L., Monty, R. A., Onley, J. W., & Klingberg, C. L. Overlap as a predictor of form discrimination under suprathreshold conditions. USAF RADC TR 61-99, 1961.

Broido, D. Recent work on reading machines for data processing. *Automat. Progr.,* 1958, **4**, 183-185, 224-226.

Deutsch, J. A. A theory of shape recognition. *Brit. J. Psychol.,* 1955, **46**, 30-37.

Deutsch, J. A. Shape recognition: A reply to Dodwell. *Brit. J. Psychol.,* 1958, **49**, 70-71.

Deutsch, J. A. The plexiform zone and shape recognition in the octopus. *Nature,* 1960, **188**, 443-446.

Deutsch, J. A. A system for shape recognition. *Psychol. Rev.,* 1962, **69**, 492-500.

Diamond, T. L. Devices for reading handwritten characters. *Proc. East. Joint Comp. Conf.,* 1957, No. T-92, 232-237.

Dodwell, P. C. Shape discrimination in the octopus and the rat. *Nature,* 1957, **179**, 1088. (a)

Dodwell, P. C. Shape recognition in rats. *Brit. J. Psychol.,* 1957, **48**, 221-229. (b)

Dodwell, P. C. Shape recognition: A reply to Deutsch. *Brit. J. Psychol.,* 1958, **49**, 158-159.

Dodwell, P. C. Coding and learning in shape discrimination. *Psychol. Rev.,* 1961, **68**, 373-382. (a)

Dodwell, P. C. Facts and theories in shape discrimination. *Nature,* 1961, **191**, 578-581. (b)

Dodwell, P. C. A test of two theories of shape discrimination. *Quart. J. exp. Psychol.,* 1962, **14**, 65-70.

Dodwell, P. C. A coupled system for coding and learning in shape discrimination. *Psychol. Rev.,* 1964, **71**, 148-159.

Doyle, W. Recognition of sloppy hand-printed characters. *Proc. West. Joint Comp. Conf.,* 1960, **17**, 133-142.

Eldredge, K. R., Kamhoefner, F. J., & Wendt, P. H. Teaching machines to read. *Stanford Res. Inst. J.,* 1957, **1**, 18-23.

Evans, C. R. Studies of pattern perception using an afterimage as the method of retinal stabilization. *Proc. 74th ann. Conv. Amer. Psychol. Assoc.* 1966, 65-66.

Fantz, R. L. The origin of form perception. *Sci. Amer.,* 1961, **204**(5).

Fischer, G. L., et al. (Eds.) *Optical character recognition.* Washington, D.C.: Spartan Books, 1962.

Fitzmaurice, J. A., Sabbagh, E. N., & Elliott, W. G. Optical reader text filter study. *USAF RADC Tech. Rep.,* 1959, No. 59-95.

Frishkopf, L. S., & Harmon, L. D. Machine-reading of cursive script. In C. Cherry, (Ed.), *Fourth London Symposium on Information Theory.* London and Washington, D.C.: Butterworth, 1961. Pp. 300-316.

Green, R. T., & Courtis, M. C. Information theory and figure perception: The metaphor that failed. *Acta Psychologica,* 1966, **25**(1), 12-35.

Grimsdale, R. L., Sumner, F. H., Tunis, C. J., & Kilburn, T. A system for the automatic recognition of patterns. *Proc. IEE,* 1959, **106**(3B), No. 26, 210-221.

Guiliano, V. E., Jones, P. E., Kimball, G. E., Meyer, R. F., & Stein, B. A. Automatic pattern recognition by a Gestalt method. *Inform. Control,* 1961, **4**, 332-345.

Gyr, J. W., Brown, J. S., Willey, R., & Zivian, A. Computer simulation and psychological theories of perception. *Psychol. Bull.,* 1966, **65**, 174-192.

Harmon, L. D. A line-drawing pattern recognizer. *Proc. West. Joint Comp. Conf.,* 1960, **17**, 351-364.

Hartline, H. K. The receptive fields of optic nerve fibers. *Amer. J. Physiol.,* 1940, **130**, 690-699.

Hick, W. E. On the rate of gain of information. *Quart. J. Psychol.,* 1952, **4**, 11-26.

Highleyman, W. H., & Kamentsky, L. A. Comments on a character recognition method of Bledsoe and Browning. *IRE Trans. Electron. Comput.,* 1960, **EC-9**, 263.

Hinde, R. A. *Animal behaviour.* New York: McGraw-Hill, 1966.

Hochberg, J. E., & McAlister, E. A quantitative approach to figural "goodness." *J. exp. Psychol.,* 1953, **46**, 361-364.

Hoffman, W. C. The Lie algebra of visual perception. *J. Math. Psychol.,* 1966, **3**, 65.

Hofstaetter, P. R. Ueber die Schaetzung von Gruppeneigenschaften. *Z. Psychol.,* 1939, **145**, 1-44.

Hu, Ming-Kuei. Pattern recognition by moment invariants. *Proc. IRE,* 1961, **49**(9), 1428.

Hubel, D. H., & Wiesel, T. N. Receptive fields of single neurones in the cat's striate cortex. *J. Physiol.,* 1959, **148**, 574-591.

Hubel, D. H., & Wiesel, T. N. Receptive fields of optic nerve fibres in the spider monkey. *J. Physiol.,* 1960, **154**, 572-580.

Hubel, D. H., & Wiesel, T. N. Receptive fields, binocular interaction, and functional architecture in the cat's visual cortex. *J. Physiol.,* 1962, **160**, 106-123.

Hubel, D. H., & Wiesel, T. N. Receptive fields and functional architecture in two non-striate visual areas (18 and 19) of the cat. *J. Neurophysiol.,* 1965, **28**, 229-289.

Joseph, H. M., & Feller, D. Final engineering report for electrophotographic viewer AN/GSQ-14-(XW-1): Shape detection phase. *USAF RADC Tech. Rep.,* 1958, No. 58-103.

Kalin, T. A. Some metric considerations in pattern recognition. *AFCRL* 327, 1961.

Kuffler, S. W. Discharge patterns and functional organization of mammalian retina. *J. Neurophysiol.,* 1953, **16**, 37-68.

Lashley, K. S. The mechanism of vision: XV. Preliminary studies of the rat's capacity for detail vision. *J. gen. Psychol.,* 1938, **18**, 123-193.

Ledley, R. S., & Ruddle, F. H. Chromosome analysis by computer. *Sci. Amer.,* 1966, **214**(4).

Lettvin, J. Y., Maturana, H. R., McCulloch, W. S., & Pitts, W. H. What the frog's eye tells the frog's brain. *Proc. IRE,* 1959, **47**, 1940-1951.

Lettvin, J. Y., Maturana, H. R., Pitts, W. H., & McCulloch, W. S. Two remarks on the visual system of the frog. In W. A. Rosenblith (Ed.), *Sensory communication.* Cambridge, Massachusetts: M.I.T. Press, 1961, Pp. 757-776.

MacKay, D. M. Quantal aspects of scientific information. *Phil. Mag.,* 1950, 41, 289-311.

MacKay, D. M. The place of meaning in the theory of information. In C. Cherry (Ed.) *Information theory.* London and Washington, D.C.: Butterworth, 1956. Pp. 215-255.

Maturana, H. R., Lettvin, J. Y., McCulloch, W. S., & Pitts, W. H. Anatomy and physiology of vision in the frog *(Rana pipiens). J. gen. Physiol.,* 1960, 43, Part 2, 129-176.

Maturana, H. R., & Frenk, S. Directional movement and horizontal edge detectors in the pigeon retina. *Science,* 1963, 142, 977-979.

McCulloch, W. S., & Pitts, W. A logical calculus of the ideas immanent in nervous activity. *Bull. Math. Biophys.,* 1943, 5, 115-133.

Michael, C. R. Receptive fields of directionally selective units in the optic nerve of the ground squirrel. *Science,* 1966, 152, 1092-1095.

Monty, R. A., & Boynton, R. M. Stimulus overlap and form similarity under suprathreshold conditions. *Percept. mot. Skills,* 1962, 14, 487-498.

Musatti, C. L. Forma e assimilazione. *Arch. Ital. Psicol.,* 1931, 9, 61-155.

Nieder, P. Statistical codes for geometrical figures. *Science,* 1960, 131, 934-935.

Oyster, C. W., & Barlow, H. B. Direction-selective units in rabbit retina: Distribution of preferred directions. *Science,* 1967, 155, 841-842.

Pitts, W., & McCulloch, W. S. How we know universals; the perception of auditory and visual forms. *Bull. Math. Biophys.,* 1947, 9, 127-147.

Polidora, V. J. Stimulus correlates of visual pattern discrimination by monkeys: Multidimensional analyses. *Percept. Psychophys.,* 1966, 1 405-414.

Pribram, K. Brilliant, lively, productive and wrong. *Contemp. Psychol.,* 1966, 11, 580-581.

Rabinow, J. Standardization of the 5 X 7 font. *Diamond Ordnance Fuze Labs. Tech. Rep.* No. TR-39, 1954. (a)

Rabinow, J. DOFL first reader. *Diamond Ordnance Fuze Labs. Tech. Rep.* No. TR-128, 1954. (b)

Rabinow, J. Developments in character recognition machines at Rabinow Engineering Company. In G. L. Fischer, Jr. *et al.* (Eds.), *Optical character recognition.* Washington, D.C.: Spartan Books, 1962. Pp. 27-50.

Rodieck, R. W. Receptive fields in the cat retina: A new type. *Science,* 1967, 157, 90-92.

Rosenblatt, F. The perceptron: A probabilistic model for information storage and organization in the brain. *Psychol. Rev.,* 1958, 65, 386-408.

Rosenblatt, F. Perceptron simulation experiments. *Proc. IRE,* 1960, 48, 301-309.

Selfridge, O. G., & Neisser, U. Pattern recognition by machines. *Sci. Amer.,* 1960, 203(8).

Shepard, D. H., Bargh, P. F., & Heasley, C. C., Jr. A reliable character sensing system for documents prepared on conventional business devices. *IRE WESCON Conv. Rec.,* 1957, 1(Pt. 4), 111-120.

Sherman, H. A quasi-topological method for the recognition of line patterns. In *Information processing.* Paris: UNESCO, 1960. Pp. 232-238.

Singer, J. R. Electronic analog of the human recognition system. *J. Opt. Soc. Amer.,* 1961, 51, 61-69.

Spinelli, D. N. Visual receptive fields in the cat's retina: Complications. *Science,* 1966, 152, 1768-1769.

Stearns, S. D. Method for design of pattern recognition logic. *IRE Trans. Electron. Comput.,* 1960, EC-9, 48-53.

Stone, J., & Fabian, Miriam. Specialized receptive fields of the cat's retina. *Science,* 1966, 152, 1277-1279.

Sutherland, N. S. Visual discrimination of orientation and shape by *Octopus. Nature,* 1957, **179**, 11-13.

Sutherland, N. S. Visual discrimination of shape by *Octopus.* Squares and triangles. *Quart. J. exp. Psychol.,* 1958, **10**, 40-47.

Sutherland, N. S. A test of a theory of shape discrimination in Octopus vulgaris Lamarck. *J. comp. physiol. Psychol.,* 1959, **52**, 135-141. (a)

Sutherland, N. S. Visual discrimination of shape by *Octopus:* circles and squares, and circles and triangles. *Quart. J. exp. Psychol.,* 1959, **11**, 24-32. (b)

Sutherland, N. S. Theories of shape discrimination in *Octopus. Nature,*1960,**186**,840-844.(a)

Sutherland, N. S. Theories of shape discrimination in the *Octopus. Nature,* 1960, **188**, 1092-1094. (b)

Sutherland, N. S. Facts and theories of shape discrimination. *Nature,*1961,**191**,581-583. (a)

Sutherland, N. S. *The methods and findings of experiments on the visual discrimination of shape by animals.* Oxford, England: Experimental Psychology Society, 1961. (b)

Sutherland, N. S. Shape discrimination and receptive fields, *Nature,* 1963, **197**, 118-122.

Sutherland, N. S. Visual discrimination in animals. *Brit. Med. Bull.,* 1964, **20**(1), 54-59.

Tinbergen, N. Social releasers and the experimental method required for their study. *Wilson Bull.,* 1948, **60**, 6-51.

Tinbergen, N. *The study of instinct.* London and New York: Oxford Univ. Press (Clarendon), 1951.

Uhr, L. Machine perception of forms by means of assessment and recognition of gestalts. Preprint No. 34. Ann Arbor, Michigan: Univ. Michigan, 1959.

Uhr, L. "Pattern recognition" computers as models for form perception. *Psychol. Bull.,* 1963, **60**, 40-73.

Uhr, L. Pattern recognition. In A. Kent & O. E. Taulbee (Eds.), *Electronic information handling.* Washington, D.C.: Spartan Books, 1965. Pp. 51-72.

Uhr, L. (Ed.) *Pattern recognition.* New York: Wiley, 1966.

Uhr, L., & Vossler, C. Suggestions for self-adapting computer model of brain functions. *Behav. Sci.,* 1961, **6**, 91-97. (a)

Uhr, L., & Vossler, C. A pattern recognition program that generates, evaluates, and adjusts its own operators. In *1961 Proc. West. Joint Comp. Conf.,* 555-569. (b)

Unger, S. H. A computer oriented toward spatial problems. *Proc. IRE,* 1958, **46**, 1744-1750.

Unger, S. H. Pattern detection and recognition. *Proc. IRE,* 1959, **47**, 1737-1752.

Uttley, A. M. The classification of signals in the nervous system. *EEG clin. Neurophysiol.,* 1954, **6**, 479-494.

Wada, H., Takahashi, S., Iijima, T., Okumuru, Y., & Imoto, K. An electronic reading machine. In *Information processing.* Paris: UNESCO, 1960. Pp. 227-232.

Walker, A. E., & Weaver, T. A. Ocular movements from the occipital lobe in the monkey. *J. Neurophysiol.,* 1940, **3**, 353-357.

Wholey, J. S. The coding of pictorial data. *IRE Trans.: Information Theory,* 1961, **7**, 99-104.

Wiener, N. *Cybernetics.* New York: Wiley, 1948.

Young, J. Z. The visual system of *Octopus:* 1. Regularities in the retina and optic lobes of *Octopus* in relation to form discrimination. *Nature,* 1960, **186**, 836-839.

Zeeman, E. C. The topology of the brain and visual perception. In M. K. Fort, Jr. (Ed.), *Topology of 3-manifolds.* Englewood Cliffs, New Jersey: Prentice-Hall, 1962. Pp. 240-256.

Zusne, L. Moments of area and of the perimeter of visual form as predictors of discrimination performance. *J. exp. Psychol.,* 1965, **69**, 213-220.

Zusne, L., & Michels, K. M. Nonrepresentational shapes and eye movements. *Percept. mot. Skills,* 1964, **18**, 11-20.

Chapter 4 / CONTEMPORARY THEORY OF VISUAL FORM PERCEPTION: III. THE GLOBAL THEORIES

1. The Gestalt Viewpoint

The Gestalt theory is still the only theory to deal with visual form in a comprehensive fashion. The Gestalt theory is, of course, more than a theory of form perception. It is a theory of behavior. I shall examine here only the viewpoint of the Gestalt theory regarding visual form.

The central concept of the theory is the concept of Gestalt—form or configuration. As mentioned in Chap. 1, even before Wertheimer began to use the term Gestalt, some of the workers of the form-quality school had already dropped "quality" from *Gestaltqualitaet* and spoke of *Gestalt* only. The Gestalt of Wertheimer, Koehler, and Koffka, while in some respects similar to form quality, was a different concept. It meant more than simply visual form, but a definition of Gestalt was not immediately given by the founders of the Gestalt school, until Koehler said that it was "any segregated whole or unit." This was an improvement, but hardly a precise, unequivocal definition. The question of what Gestalten are and are not has since occupied the minds of many psychologists and the pages of many publications. Helson and Fehrer (1932), for instance, were able to arrive at the following list of definitions of Gestalt: (1) the form of an apprehended whole; (2) some factor within a group that dominates the whole; (3) the totality of conditions determining a perception, memory, or behavior pattern; (4) physical structures; (5) physiological structures; (6) biological structures; (7) logical structures; (8) psychological structures; (9) purpose; (10) necessary and sufficient conditions. Of these definitions, the first, fourth, fifth, and eighth concern visual form. Specifically, they refer to (a) the visible form of an object in general, (b) the physical parameters of visual form; (c) the neurophysiological counterpart of form in the brain, and (d) the structuring or restructuring of a form as a result of the activity of the central nervous system.

Thus, Gestalt psychology looked at form from the physical, physiological, and behavioral points of view. The emphasis, however, was always on the dynamic properties of perception. Whatever Gestalten were, they were never static, but dynamic entities. Wertheimer's first Gestalt article was on apparent movement; Koehler's 1920 book, which may be taken as the publication which launched Gestalt psychology as a school of psychological thought, is a treatise on the general dynamics of the formation of Gestalten. By demonstrating form dynamism in purely physical systems first, then in perception, Koehler was able to establish a relationship between physical and psychological systems, as formulated in the principle of isomorphism: the dynamic events that occur in a physical configuration, such as a physical form, are paralleled by the dynamic events of the brain and in perception.

While experimental introspection led to the formulation of most of the Gestalt principles concerning form, sheer logical analysis led Koehler from known physical phenomena to the postulation of physiological brain processes underlying the perception of contour (Koehler, 1920). Since the brain is a physical system, it can be expected to show phenomena similar to those found in the rest of nature. Thus, if physical phenomena show configurations, so should the brain. This is the Gestalt principle of isomorphism. As Boring (1950) points out, isomorphism is not projection, but implies it. Before there was any evidence for it, Gestalt psychologists argued that visual form is represented in the brain, not symbolically, but directly in terms of corresponding points of excitation. The correspondence is not topographical and cannot be topographical. It is topological, that is, order and relationships are preserved, even though distances, angles, and curvature are not.

Specifically, how do Gestalten that are the counterparts of visual form arise in the brain? The electrochemical events in the nervous system, so goes the argument, are similar to such events as they occur in solutions, i.e., to ionic reactions. Constant excitation at the receptors will produce a constant ionic state in the nervous system, specifically the cortical projection areas. There arise, as a result of excitation, ionic fields in the brain whose strength depends on the concentration of ions. The perceived form is brain-form: at the retina, there are only excited neurons which fire messages to the visual cortex. It is only in the visual cortex that the electrical field forces begin to operate, leading to the formation of Gestalten.

Even before Koehler's formulation, Rubin (1921) had pointed out that contours are not geometric lines but boundaries formed by two adjacent fields. A figure will be seen upon ground if there is some difference in the properties of the fields along the boundary that defines form, such as differences in color or reflectance. A contour runs between figure and ground; it is, as we would say today, the figure-ground interface. Two adjacent fields differing in color will produce two adjacent electrical fields in the brain that will differ in ionic concentration or electrical potential. In other words, there will be a gradient of excitation.

Given the electrical fields in the brain that correspond to the fields occupied by figure and ground and the facts that electrical potentials grow and wane and electrical fields shift their positions, a flexible basis is given for explaining both static and dynamic aspects of form perception. The phenomenal fact that the figure is more impressive and predominates over ground is explained in terms of different electrical potentials in the two fields: the figure is smaller than ground, hence more energy will be concentrated in a white spot, for instance, than in the larger gray background on which it lies. The color of the figure is immaterial, as long as there is a difference between it and that of ground. Thus, a gray patch will be also more impressive than ground even though the latter may be white.

A deduction from the cortical field theory is that, as a current passes through a medium, it creates an obstruction to its own passage, called electrotonus. Koehler dubbed it "satiation" and used it as the explanatory principle for the figural aftereffect phenomenon. Prolonged visual inspection of a configuration changes it, and this change affects the appearance of other figures: test figures appear displaced or they change their shape as a result of gazing at an inspection figure for some time.

The cortical field theory provides for the physiological explanation of many visual phenomena, including the various principles of organization of the visual field. Thus, the tendency of a form to become as good as possible, i.e., as simple, symmetric, and regular as possible, is directly related to such tendency existing in electrical fields outside the organism. The strength of 'good' configurations is directly related to the strong cohesive forces that exist in electrical fields organized according to the principles of simplicity, symmetry, etc. Constancy and transposition can be explained in terms of changes in the intensity or the location of the electrical field corresponding to a figure, without changes in the gradients of electromotor forces that correspond to slopes, angles, etc.

The theory is ingenious, elegant, and parsimonious, and Gestalt psychologists have been able to produce some evidence for the actual existence of the postulated electrical fields in the brain. Others have been equally successful in showing that such fields could not possibly exist. It is not enough to show, as Koehler and Held (1949), for instance, did, that there is peaking of electrical potentials in the occipital cortex as visual stimulation occurs. This is no evidence for the existence of electrical fields in the brain. The experiment done by Lashley, Chow, and Semmes (1951) was quite damaging to the theory. Memory for form implies that electrical fields in the brain are formed not only during perception, but that they persist after stimulation has ceased. Furthermore, they should persist essentially undisturbed if comparison with other stimuli is to take place. Since the brain fields are assumed to be relatively large, it should be possible, so argued Lashley, *et al.,* to distort the flow of current in a cortical field by short-circuiting it. This was accomplished in one monkey by placing gold foil on the surface of the occipital lobe and in another by inserting gold pins vertically into the same cortical area. Both monkeys, previously trained to discriminate between two geometric figures, showed no loss of discrimination when tested 24 hr. after the operation. While arguments have been raised against the possibility of shorting or breaking up cortical fields, the evidence weighs against the cortical field theory.

Before Gestalt psychology became involved in experiments on brain fields, demonstrations with simple drawings were the main tool for establishing the various 'laws' of visual form. The Gestalt position is that, to answer the question of why things look as they do, one must study the laws of organization. "Things look as they do because of the field organization to which the proximal stimulus distribution gives rise" (Koffka, 1935, p. 98), and not because they are what they are, or because the proximal stimulus is what it is, or because that is the way we have learned they are. To answer the question of why forms look as they do, one must study the laws of visual organization.

The literature on Gestalt laws (more correctly, principles) is ample. By 1933, Helson was able to extract and state 114 such 'laws.' While relatively few of them mention visual form specifically, all but very few are applicable to visual form. Boring (1942) was able to summarize them in 14 major principles. Allport (1955) tried to reduce them to a mere six, producing, however, more of a summative whole than a good configuration. I shall attempt another, somewhat ampler summary of Helson's 114 laws, with the additional change that, where applicable, the term 'visual form' or 'visual pattern' will be used instead of 'configuration' or 'Gestalt.' It will also be taken for granted that visual form is a unitary whole, hence the numerous statements which in different ways reiterate this truth will not be considered. As Koffka (1935) put it, "A shape is itself and nothing else" (p. 175), meaning that it is not made up of simpler elements but is an autonomous entity, a whole.

1. *"In some respects, form is the most important property a configuration may have."* (Koehler, 1929, p. 219.) This is an arguable statement, but when Koehler said that the most primitive phenomena are figural and other Gestaltists used words to the same effect, they were stating a testable hypothesis that others did not leave unchallenged. Evidence to the contrary was presented early, even before Koehler had made the above statement. Gelb and Goldstein (1920) and Poppelreuther (1923) discussed clinical cases in which form perception had been lost while brightness and color vision remained. In intact subjects, forms presented either in the periphery of the visual field or at threshold intensity do not show contours. Only a contourless, diffuse patch of light is seen, more definite contours appearing only gradually as the stimulus is moved toward the point of fixation or light intensity is increased above threshold level. Earliest

such reports came from Helson and Fehrer (1932), Kleitman and Blier (1928), and Zigler, Cook, Miller, & Wemple (1930). Most subsequent workers have confirmed their findings (see Chap. 6 on this subject).

Shape is the result of the same process that produces figure-ground segregation. However, having demonstrated that the perceived shape of a figure varies with its orientation, Koffka (1935, p. 129 ff.) concluded that unification and segregation as such do not explain shape. He proceeded to show the "reality" of shape by demonstrating that shape as such influences other processes, such as critical fusion frequency. There is no doubt that shape is an important determiner of other psychological processes: detection threshold, hue, size contrast, shape discrimination and recognition, to mention a few. The problem that Gestalt psychology faced all along was the failure of its proponents and supporters to specify clearly what the "forces" that organized the visual field into separate objects were exactly, and, therefore, how they affected other processes. In other words, the theory has continuously lacked exact specification and quantification of the parameters of visual form. When others outside the school eventually devised them, it became easy to check on the validity of the demonstrations of the Gestaltists that form was of prime importance in perception.

2. *Visual forms are either dynamic or the outcome of dynamic processes which underlie them.* The basis for this statement is the principle of isomorphism and the theory of electrical brain fields. Because forms are brain forms having the nature of electrical fields, they are of necessity dynamic, not static entities. The reversible figure phenomenon is one demonstration of the dynamic nature of forms. Each reversal means that a new figure is seen, a figure with new properties, not that change in attention has merely altered the degree of clarity with which the two figures are perceived. Fuchs (1922) has shown that patients suffering from hemianopsia will tend to shift, perceptually, the visual form as a whole to a new center of clarity which is not the anatomical center (the fovea). From an investigation of either the fovea or the stimulus alone it cannot be predicted that such a change will occur.

The dynamic nature of form will not necessarily show itself immediately. If sufficient time is allowed, however, the dynamic nature of visual form may be revealed. One of the examples that used to be given by Gestaltists was the gradual desaturation of colors if gazed at steadily. The disappearance of stopped retinal images (Chap. 2) is a more direct and convincing demonstration of the dynamic nature of form. Rothschild (1923) anticipated the very recent use of negative afterimages in lieu of the optically produced stoppage of the retinal image. While the stopping of the retinal image was not Rothschild's intent, he did demonstrate phenomena similar to those obtained under this condition. They bear witness to the dynamic nature of form. For instance, the afterimages of configurations made of white threads on a black background that were not unitary did not appear at once; rather, parts would appear in rivalry. Thus, the head of an arrow would alternate with its tail. Little irregularities in the form were corrected in the afterimage to produce a "better" figure, and incomplete figures were completed in the afterimage.

3. *The first and simplest configurations are qualities on a ground. All visual forms possess at least two distinguishable aspects, a figured portion called figure and a background called ground.* "If the proximal stimulation is such that it consists of several areas of different homogeneous stimulation, then the areas which receive the same stimulation will organize unitary field parts segregated from others by the difference between the stimulations. In other words, the equality of stimulation produces forces of cohesion, inequality of stimulation forces of segregation, provided that the inequality entails an abrupt change." (Koffka, 1935, p. 126.) An abrupt change, however, does not ensure clear segregation of figure and ground. In the Liebmann effect (Liebmann, 1927), a chromatic figure on an achromatic background will look blurred and appear simpler, if complex, when the luminances of figure and ground are made equal. In fact, the figure may disappear completely for short periods of time.

Figure and ground have certain contrasting properties: figure occupies an area that is smaller than that of ground; figure has distinguishable parts, ground has none; figure has contours, ground is boundless; figure appears to be nearer to the observer, ground appears to extend behind figure, unbroken by it; figure has thinglike quality, ground is formless, diffuse, indefinite. In short, figure is more strongly organized than ground. Because of this, extraneous elements are more difficult to perceive when they appear within the figure. Thus, a spot of colored light has a higher threshold when projected inside a figure than when projected upon adjacent ground (Gelb & Granit, 1923; Granit, 1924).

Rubin, who originated the figure-ground concept, and others did considerable early work on the various factors that influence figure-ground relations, especially when these factors are in equilibrium and the resulting percept is ambiguous. Thus, of two configurations, the smaller-size configuration will be seen as figure (Fig. 4-1a), but if the smaller configuration happens to enclose the larger one, it will appear as ground nevertheless, as illustrated in Fig. 4-1b. If the areas of the two configurations are approximately equal, other things being equal, one may be seen as figure, producing the so-called reversible figure, such as Rubin's vase-profile demonstration (Fig. 4-1c). One of the other things that must be equal is the degree of figural 'goodness,' otherwise the less-articulated, less-enclosed, or more-homogeneous figure will be seen as ground more often (Fig. 4-1d). Symmetric figures are 'better' figures than asymmetric ones. In Fig. 4-1e, the contours of the vertical configuration are identical, but in one case the observer sees the white columns as figures, in the other the black ones, both of which are symmetric. Symmetry, however, may be overcome by area. In Fig. 4-1f, the asymmetric columns were made narrower than the symmetric ones, which makes them appear as figure rather than ground. The closing of contours may also override the effect of symmetry, as shown in Fig. 4-1g. In Fig. 4-1h, black stripes on white background are seen because the black stripes have uniform width, a type of regularity, hence 'goodness' as compared with the white area.

Another stimulus parameter that has been found to determine figure-ground relationship is the coincidence with, or deviation from, a configuration's main axis and the horizontal or vertical axes of space. Of two identical configurations,

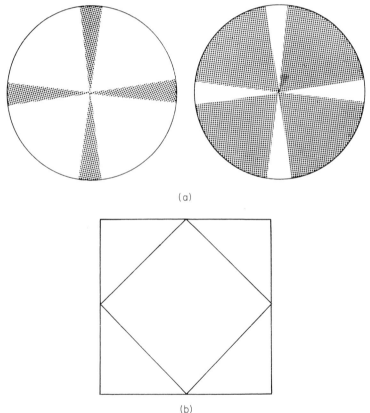

(a)

(b)

Fig. 4-1. Factors that influence figure-ground relationship. See text for explanation. (d) is M. C. Escher's 1960 woodcut "Heaven and Hell." Reproduced by permission of the Escher Foundation.

Fig. 4-1.

(c)

(d)

Fig. 4-1.

(e)

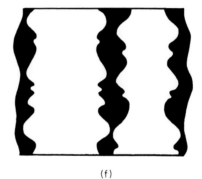

(f)

Fig. 4-1.

the one whose axis coincides with either one of these main spatial directions will be seen as figure (Fig. 4-1i).

There is a large but heterogenous group of more or less complex two-dimensional visual configurations that, at one time or another, have been called puzzle, reversible, or ambiguous figures. The so-called impossible objects belong here. They were discussed in Chap. 2. The reversible-perspective figures constitute another type. These were also dealt with in Chap. 2. Here, it is appropriate to discuss another group of puzzle pictures, one that is intimately related to the figure-ground phenomenon. The classical example of this type of puzzle picture is Rubin's vase-profile picture (Fig. 4-2e). Because here both ground and figure are equally strong in organization, either one may be seen as figure or ground, hence alternation between the two percepts results. The

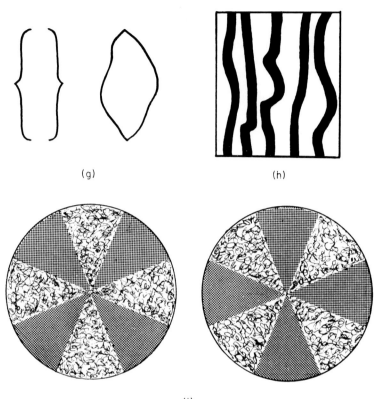

(g)   (h)

(i)

Fig. 4-1.

reversible figure-ground, however, cannot be considered an isolated phenomenon. Rather, it belongs with other related configurations, all of which are
characterized by two parameters: the intensity and quality of visual noise. At
one end of the continuum, there is the clearly delineated figure on homogeneous
ground, figure-ground contrast being optimum (Fig. 4-2f). By increasing the
interfering effect of ground as noise, the perception (detection) of figure (signal)
becomes increasingly more difficult, until a point is reached where detection is
very difficult or impossible (Fig. 4-2a). This is the intensity dimension of ground
as random noise. Noise, however, may be also organized noise, in which case the
figure, instead of being obscured by the noise, is embedded in the ground. The
perceptual task here is not detection, but discrimination. Cases of organized

ground where ground does not particularly interfere with clear perception may be placed close to the apex of the triangular array in Fig. 4-2. When the degree of organization in ground is about the same as that of the figure, the reversible figure-ground configuration results (Fig. 4-2c, d, e). Increasing the degree of organization of ground still more results in the camouflage or embedding of the figure in ground. Gottschaldt's (1926) embedded figure (Fig. 4-2b) is embedded

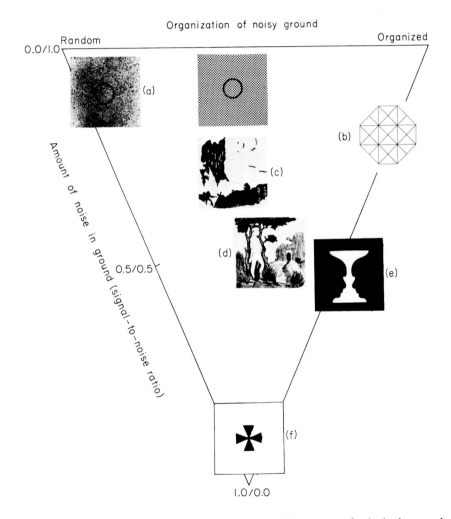

Fig. 4-2. Figure-ground relationships as functions of the amount of noise in the ground and the degree of organization in the noise.

are not discussed here. A full discussion of the topic may be found in Solley and Murphy (1960) and Epstein (1967).

Individual differences play an important role in the perception of labile figure-ground patterns. Porter (1938), for instance, found that subjects showing a more rapid rate of fluctuation between the two percepts tend to be more socially introverted and that each individual has a characteristic rate of fluctuation. The same results were obtained when other types of perceptually fluctuating figures were used, such as the reversible-perspective figures and polyfigurations.

Sex is a factor in the perception of embedded figures, females ordinarily taking more time to search for them (Witkin, Lewis, Hertzman, Machover, Meissner, & Wapner, 1954). This phenomenon, however, does not seem to be biologically determined, since it has been found (Goldstein & Chance, 1965) that at the end of an extended series of tests with embedded figures the initial significant differences between the sexes is reduced to almost zero.

Practically no attempts have been made to explain in physiological terms the periodic merging of figure into ground in reversible configurations (cf. Fry & Robertson, 1935; Hochberg, 1950). Because of the manifold stimulus and subject variables, the Gestalt theory of electrical fields in the brain and the satiation process is not a very good candidate to provide an explanation. Actually, one may wonder whether a special explanation is called for. Hebb's (1949) theory has no difficulty in accounting for the phenomenon: if two cell assemblies correspond to the two configurations and both are equivalent in

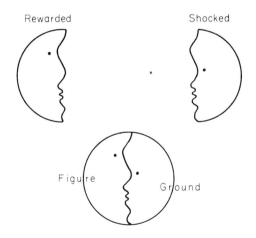

Fig. 4-5. In a labile figure-ground, motivation may determine which portion of the configuration will be perceived as figure and which will be perceived as ground. After Schafer and Murphy (1943).

terms of the strength of the nervous processes, the fluctuation is due either to built-in oscillations in the level of functioning of the nervous system or to the operation of other cell assemblies or phase sequences, which manifest themselves as selective attention, set, etc.

Kuennapas (1961), without attempting to explain the phenomenon, has introduced a method which, instead of simple enumeration of reversals as a function of time, enables the experimenter to measure the intensity of the neural process which underlies observable fluctuations. Kuennapas has produced experimental data which agree exceedingly well with his theoretical model. The operator of the model is that of a damped harmonic vibration.

4. *Visual forms may possess one or several centers of gravity about which the form is organized. The center of gravity exercises an inordinate influence upon the form.* The shifting of forms to new centers of clarity or pseudofoveas has already been mentioned (Fuchs, 1922). The same investigator also produced the following demonstration. If a circle and a dot outside it but still within the visual field are exposed tachistoscopically, only the circle is seen; if the dot is moved toward the center of the circle, it too may be seen. This, according to the Gestalt viewpoint, occurs because the dot, having been moved into the circle so as to form an integral part of it, is perceived as such, whereas before it was a separate configuration.

Whether Wertheimer's *Schwerpunkt* is identical with the center of gravity of physics or is something more than that is hard to say. A two-dimensional form has only one point upon which it will balance. The reference to multiple centers of gravity suggests that what is actually meant is points which attract attention, of which, of course, there may be several, especially in more complex forms. I have mentioned an unpublished experiment of mine on the estimation of centers of gravity of two-dimensional shapes. The estimates vary from almost complete accuracy in the case of simple, regular figures to no agreement at all among subjects when the shapes are highly irregular. The different portions of the contours of even relatively simple two-dimensional nonrepresentational shapes, however, are not equivalent in terms of their ability to attract attention, and eye movements are certainly determined by the existence of such foci of attention (Zusne & Michels, 1964).

5. *Visual forms are transposable—to a different locus in the visual field, to a different size, to a different orientation, to a different color—without loss of identity.* The principle of transposition was formulated as such by the Gestalt school, but its origins are older. When Mach spoke of space-form, he implied that it was something over and above and independent of the constituent elements; Ehrenfels' *Gestaltqualitaet* meant the same thing.

This is an important principle in form perception: it states that under certain transformations form remains itself. The transformations are those that leave the relationship between the original and the transformed states of form unchanged.

It follows that only changes in *form* parameters may alter this relationship. Since color is not a form parameter, it should not have been included in the transposition principle. Color does not affect contours, only the area enclosed within the contours. Wavelength, intensity, and purity are energetic, not form parameters. Of the actual form parameters, only changes in those classified as transpositional will leave form unaffected: changes in area, and the three symmetry operations of translation, rotation, and reflection. Assuming that both rotation and reflection are included under "orientation," these variables account for the other transpositions mentioned in the statement of the transposition principle. All other changes in form alter the identity relationship.

6. *Visual forms tend to resist change. They tend to maintain their structure against disturbing forces.* This is the law of constancy as applied to visual form, i.e., shape constancy. A form tends to be perceived as being the same in spite of changes in the angle by which it deviates from the frontoparallel plane. When objects are seen incompletely, that is, when some of the usually available information is missing, constancy breaks down. Thus, if the gradual tilting of a circle is not observed from the very beginning but only at some intermediate stage and clues as to the degree of tilt are absent, there is no reason to suppose that what is seen is an inclined circle rather than an ellipse.

That objects are seen the way we know them to be had been known to psychologists before the advent of the Gestalt school, but in the 1920s the law of constancy became one of its fundamental laws. In the 1930s, Thouless, as well as Brunswick, conducted many experiments on shape and other constancies and quantified the law of constancy.

Constancy, Gestalt psychologists claimed, is innate; it is not an interpretation of present experience in terms of past experience. It is directly given, arising from the organization imposed upon perception by the central nervous system. The clue to shape constancy is the relation between the shape of the retinal image and the slant of the object. Because the object deviates from its normal position, it creates a field of stress. The perceiver tends to right the object; this tendency, in combination with the actual retinal image of the object, produces the perception of the shape in its normal position. The problem inherent in this explanation is, of course, that field forces are not defined, and the whole process, including the supposed tendency to right tilted objects, is a purely assumed one with no empirical evidence for it.

It is clear that the laws of transposition and constancy are closely related, to the point of being sometimes practically indistinguishable. Transposition implies relations, constancy of relations, and constancy implies that a perception is compared with another, i.e., a relation is being established. In both cases, the parameters of the proximal stimulus (the retinal image) are ignored in favor of a decision that establishes the identity of all members of the transformation group on the basis of past experience.

7. *Form will always be as 'good' as the prevailing conditions allow.* This is a paraphrase of Koffka's (1935, p. 110) famous 'law' of *Praegnanz.* 'Good' here means regular, symmetric, simple, uniform, closed, showing uniform direction— in short, exhibiting the minimum possible amount of stress. "Prevailing conditions" refer to the stimulus pattern. This is the best known and most important of the Gestalt principles, having a number of corollaries and subsidiary principles.

One corollary is that *visual forms possess different degrees of accentuation or articulation (Praegnanz).* For instance, visual forms may be strong or weak. Their strength is determined by the degree of cohesiveness among the members.

Having rejected the notion that space perception is based on the perception of its elements (points of light), Gestalt psychologists (e.g., Metzger, 1930) demonstrated that no definite spatial perception was possible in a field lacking any kind of heterogeneity (a *Ganzfeld*). Heterogenity had to be introduced before any perception of spatial relations could begin. This is a viewpoint that leads directly to Gibson's theory of space perception. In the Gestalt theory, a surface is a product of inhomogeneity, but not just any inhomogeneity, since even in the Ganzfeld, the fog that filled the observer's field of vision grew denser with distance. Inhomogeneity implies forces, and a surface is the effect of a degree of organization. A portion of a surface surrounded by a sharp line of inhomogeneity or contour is a form. Forms, therefore, vary in the degree of their strength or cohesiveness among the members that make them up.

Points, as figures having no phenomenal shape, are considered to be a special case of figure-on-ground rather than an elementary building block for all forms. As a structure, a point is very unstable, weak, and tends to disappear because the cohesive forces in the field upon which the point is found are stronger than the single point of inhomogeneity.

Lines, while they lack an inside and an outside, are stronger configurations. A closed or almost closed line is a still better configuration. It is seen as a shape rather than a line on ground because it is a better, stabler way of organizing the visual field.

A second corollary is that *if not 'good,' visual forms will tend to become 'better.'* Under conditions such as short exposure time, low intensity, small size, in afterimages, and reproduction of form from memory, (1) irregular forms tend to appear as regular, (2) complex forms as simple, (3) asymmetric forms as symmetric, (4) interrupted contours as continuous; furthermore, (5) random patterns tend to be organized or grouped, (6) disconnected pattern elements tend to become connected, and (7) groups of elements tend to become organized into larger whole forms. In general, the visual field tends to become organized and take form.

Visual forms may be 'good' or 'bad.' There are degrees of goodness: configurational concepts do not represent absolutes. Perceptual organization will go in a direction that secures a minimum of change and differences. Thus, Fig. 4-6a is seen as one figure because the circle is a better figure than either Fig. 4-6b or 4-6c. The configuration in Fig. 4-6d, however, is seen as two because each part separately is a better (simpler) figure than the two together. Whether one or two shapes will be seen can always be explained in terms of figural goodness and the law of good continuation.

Whether a plane figure will be seen as two- or three-dimensional depends on the goodness of both shape and contour continuation. If both shape and continuation are good, a two-dimensional figure will be seen, as in Fig. 4-7a. If not, a three-dimensional shape will be seen, as in Fig. 4-7b. More exactly, the first figure is seen as a two-dimensional configuration because it is simpler as a two-dimensional shape, whereas the second one is seen as having depth because it is simpler when seen in three dimensions.

Gestalt psychologists insisted that it was possible to specify the physical parameters of figural 'goodness.' Figural goodness, however, proved to be an elusive entity. If goodness was articulation, what precisely constituted articulation? If symmetric figures were good, was a just slightly asymmetric figure still good? Were there degrees of symmetry? The quantification of goodness, in spite of promise, never arose out of the ranks of Gestalt psychologists. Others (e.g., Hochberg & McAlister, 1953), using the new tool of information measurement, showed how figural goodness could be quantified.

Since, according to the Gestalt theory, organization exists not only in the stimulus, but just as much in the nervous system, an attractive alternative to measuring Gestalt strength in the distal stimulus is to measure it in terms of differences in some global response that is mostly biologically determined and not subject too much to cognitive processes. Two promising approaches along these lines have been reported. Clement (1964) hypothesized that ratings of pattern goodness, uncertainties of verbal naming responses, and latencies of these responses were highly correlated. The hypothesis was confirmed when simple dot patterns, rated on goodness by one group of subjects, were presented to another group with the instructions to name them. All correlations were found to be significant and a single factor was found to underlie the correlations. Thus, reaction time is one candidate for ranking patterns on figural goodness. Cowan and Bliss (1967) presented different patterns in a stereoscope and gradually increased the separation of the two images. The point at which binocular fusion broke down varied with pattern goodness: patterns constructed to reflect the Gestalt principles of a good figure were more resistant to the effects of separation than were poorer patterns.

As to the above example of two- and three-dimensional polygons/cubes, with the appearance of information theory, it became possible to show (Hochberg & Brooks, 1960) that an increase in the likelihood of seeing a three-dimensional object went with increased complexity (information content)

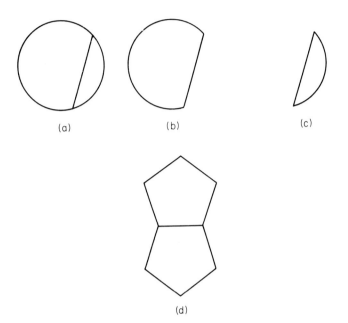

(a)   (b)   (c)

(d)

Fig. 4-6. Degrees of configurational 'goodness.'

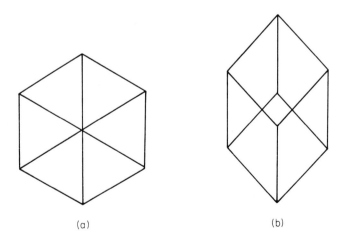

(a)   (b)

Fig. 4-7. Three-dimensionality as a function of configurational 'goodness.'

of the two-dimensional representation. There were suggestions to that effect already in the investigations of Kopferman (1930), who designed the cubes that bear his name, but the exact hypothesis and experimental proof of it did not come until 30 years later.

Visual pattern elements that are alike tend to form groups (law of similarity). This and the following few statements under the law of *Praegnanz* are the principles that are usually found in psychology textbooks. They are quite specific, easily demonstrated, and of considerable practical importance. Similarity, proximity, and good continuation are configurational properties that are closely related in that they may either enhance each other's effect or cancel it. The relative strengths of these factors determine which one will prevail. This is a crucial variable in such phenomena as embeddedness and its practical application, camouflage.

As to the law of similarity, it applies not only to similarity in shape among visual pattern elements, but also to similarity in color, position, and other variables. The pattern shown in Fig. 4-8 illustrates a simple case of grouping due to similarity of shape.

Visual pattern elements having smaller distances between them tend to group together rather than elements separated by larger distances (law of proximity). This principle is illustrated in the pattern shown in Fig. 4-9a. In Fig. 4-9b, the principle of proximity holds and dominates over the principle of similarity.

If there are several alternate ways in which a pattern element may be included in the total pattern, the simpler and more regular way will be chosen (law of good continuation). In Fig. 4-10a, a Maltese cross is seen in spite of the irregular subdividing lines; in Fig. 4-10b, four separate triangles are seen instead because these are simpler figures showing better continuation. The experiential argument (we see good shapes because we have been exposed to them more frequently) is countered by Gestalt psychologists by presenting a 'crucial' demonstration, such as is shown in Fig. 4-11, where two vertical parallel lines and a diamond are seen rather than the letters *W* and *M,* which should have been seen according to the empiricist argument.

Sometimes a law of common fate is distinguished, which states that any change in a pattern element which runs contrary to the overall tendency of the total pattern will be resisted. A corollary of this principle is that, if the parts of a visual pattern are strongly directed toward each other, a strongly configurated form will result. It would seem that these are not separate principles, but rather restatements of the more general principle of good continuation.

Symmetrically located pattern elements will tend to organize themselves and associated elements into groups. This principle is related to that aspect of the figure-ground phenomenon that leads to the perception of the symmetric configuration as figure and the asymmetric configuration as ground, as illustrated in Fig. 4-12. In Fig. 4-13, the principle of proximity is counteracted by the principle of symmetry.

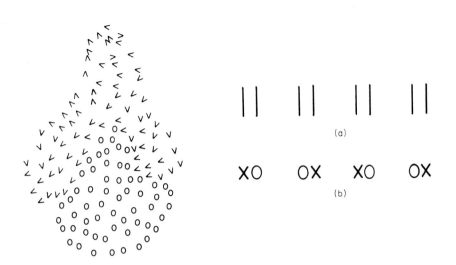

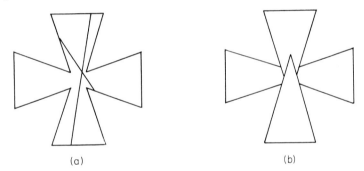

Fig. 4-8. Left: Segregation in the visual field produced by the law of similarity.

Fig. 4-9. Right: Organization of the visual field produced by the law of proximity.

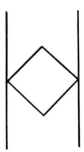

Fig. 4-10. Perceptual cohesiveness and organization as a function of the law of good continuation.

Fig. 4-11. A Gestalt demonstration of the predominance of the law of good continuation over the effects of past experience.

|)   C| |)   C|

Fig. 4-12. Left: Of two groups of perceptual elements, the symmetric group will be seen as figure, the asymmetric one as ground.

Fig. 4-13. Right: The law of symmetry may sometimes supersede the law of proximity in organizing the visual field.

Visual forms may be open or closed, complete or incomplete. An open form tends to change toward a 'better' form. When a stable point of equilibrium is reached, the form has achieved closure. A common illustration of the principle of closure is the perception of a circle with a gap in it as a complete circle, especially under conditions of impaired visibility. Incomplete letters, numbers, and other familiar forms tend to be seen as complete in spite of severe discontinuities (Fig. 4-14). Various visual phenomena observed by Fuchs (1920, 1921, 1922, 1923) in patients suffering from hemianopsia were widely used by Gestalt psychologists to show the importance of closure in form perception. Fuchs found that, if an incomplete circle is presented tachistoscopically to these patients so that the gap falls on the blind portion of the retina, the circle is still seen as complete. The completion is thought to be a central process and a function of the Gestalt qualities of the circle, the 'best' possible figure. More recent work, however, suggests that factors other than goodness of form may be operating in such cases, such as familiarity with the form, the ability to name it, and the expectation of seeing it complete (Postman & Bruner, 1952). Forms possessing these qualities may be quite complex and show neither symmetry nor any other kind of goodness (Warrington, 1965). Forms in which closure is more frequently achieved are the simpler geometric forms, but these are also more familiar and more readily named than others.

When several configurational forces are in conflict, the stronger one will predominate, leading to the perception of that form in which it predominates. The phenomena of embedded figures, camouflage, and shifts in the grouping of

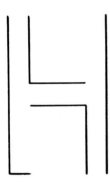

Fig. 4-14. Because of closure, forms may be seen as complete in spite of severe discontinuities.

pattern elements as the values of proximity, similarity, symmetry, and good continuation are changed are examples of this principle. It means that the five preceding principles should by modified by the statement, "Other things being equal, ..."

The 'law' of *Praegnanz*, just as the rest of the Gestalt 'laws,' by itself is not sufficiently precise to qualify even as a principle. It begins to take shape only as its various corollaries are examined. Such examination brings up again the possibility, mentioned earlier, that figural goodness, which is what Praegnanz is mostly about, is a multidimensional variable. While all of its aspects may be measurable in bits of information, the more specific aspects of figural goodness may be sufficiently independent to warrant their separate treatment.

8. *Visual forms may fuse to produce new ones; simple forms fuse more easily than complex ones; forms of the same strength fuse more easily than forms of different strengths.* In Fig. 4-15a, the two triangles fuse to form a six-pointed star, a new form. The two triangles have the same strength. In Fig. 4-15b, the square and the irregular quadrilateral do not fuse, since they exhibit different configurational strengths.

9. *A change in one part or aspect of a visual form affects other parts or aspects of the form* (law of compensation). *Alteration of one part of a visual form alters the whole form. The 'better' the form, the greater the effect.* This principle should be considered in conjunction with the principle of transposition and be supplemented by what is now known about the differences between types of form parameters and their effects on form (Chap. 5). Changes in the transpositional parameters, such as changes in area, rotation, reflection, or translation, do not affect the identity of form or any of its parts. Changes in complexity or linearity (transitive parameters) and changes in contours (intransitive parameters) affect form. It is clear, e.g., that changing a polygon

from a four-sided to a five-sided one will change not only its complexity, but also its compactness, elongation, and, usually, symmetry. A change in compactness will also affect the elongation of form and, often, its symmetry. Deviations from a 'good' form are more noticeable because regular forms mark one end of the continua of symmetry, compactness, etc. Because of the extreme values of their various parameters, such forms are well known and used as standards of comparison, hence small deviations from these standards are more noticeable than larger differences between two forms somewhere else on the continuum.

10. *Visual forms tend to appear and disappear as wholes.* As early as 1901, McDougall observed the operation of this principle in afterimages. Later workers (e.g., Rothschild, 1923) repeated his observation. The stopped-retinal-image technique was discovered too late for the observed phenomena to become incorporated into the body of evidence supporting the Gestalt theory. It is, of course, a beautiful illustration of this principle, but can also be used to support the Hebbian position. This subject is discussed in more detail in the next section of this chapter.

11. *Visual forms leave aftereffects that make them easier to remember than other, nonconfigurated wholes. If only a part of a form reappears, having appeared before together with the rest of the whole form, it will tend to reinstate the whole form* (law of reproduction). There is a large body of research relevant to this statement. It concerns the learning, memory for, and reproduction of form. Since it is difficult to summarize, the reader is referred to Chap. 7 for a full discussion of memory for form.

12. *Phenomenal space is anisotropic, it has different properties in different directions.* While this principle does not speak of form as such, these spatial inequalities affect every form since form is a space form. Anisotropy is observed when the organization of figures affects the surrounding field. Some geometric illusions, such as Jastrow's and Zoellner's, are taken by Gestalt psychologists to illustrate this aspect of the principle of anisotropy. In addition, space as a framework is anisotropic. There are main directions in space, the horizontal and the vertical, and these main directions influence organization. The vertical dimension is overestimated, which produces the horizontal-vertical illusion. The detection and discrimination of figures is also a function of their location along these main spatial axes. The subject of geometric illusions and spatial anisotropy is discussed more fully at the end of this chapter.

The fullest statement on visual form is found in Gestalt psychology. There are, however, some serious omissions. A metric analysis of the stimulus is almost completely lacking. Being phenomenological, the Gestalt theory perhaps could not be expected to deliver on this score. The effects of internal states of the observer on the perception of form are taken into consideration, but their role is

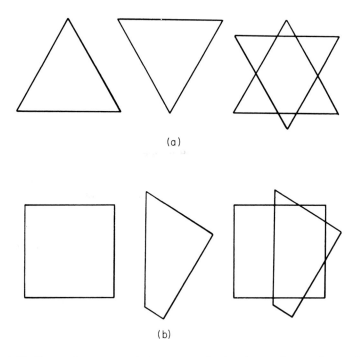

(a)

(b)

Fig. 4-15. Forms of same strength fuse more easily than forms of unequal strengths.

minimized. It is admitted that attention and set may affect the organization of the visual field, but such states are not very well integrated with the theory.

While Koffka (1927) wrote a text dealing with development, there is not too much that is explicit in Gestalt psychology regarding the role of development in form perception. The formation of electrical brain fields, hence of form, is a property of the nervous system. In this sense, form perception is innate. At the same time, it cannot be truly said that form perception in Gestalt psychology is regarded as an innate behavior. It would be if the theory insisted on the idea of inborn perceptual templates that allow the infant to discriminate specific forms from the outset. Although Koffka (1927, p. 133) hints that very young infants do discriminate biologically significant patterns, such as the human face, the position taken is actually an intermediate one between nativism and empiricism (Koffka, 1927, p. 297/8).

Although the amount of research done on the development of the role of configurational laws is not very large, it does show that these laws are not as potent in early childhood as they are in later life (e.g., Rush, 1937; Shroff, 1928;

Usnadze, 1929), and that some of the Gestalt predictions for development do not hold up (e.g., Elkind & Scott, 1962). Shape and size constancies, as Koffka himself shows, are at least incompletely developed in the infant. While late appearance of a function is not in itself an argument against its innateness, it does present the problem of determining the degree of contribution of postnatal learning that influences the development of any function.

2. Form in Hebb's Neuropsychological Theory

Hebb's theory, presented in *The Organization of Behavior* in 1949, is a comprehensive theory of behavior. As such, it encompasses form perception. Hebb takes definite issue with the Gestalt point of view, and there are substantial differences in the two ways of looking at behavior in general. At the same time, both theories share one common characteristic: they start out with, and use as illustrations, instances from form perception, then develop a basic concept into a wide-ranging behavioral theory.

The general features of Hebb's theory are sufficiently well known not to need a recapitulation here. As neurological and behavioral evidence accumulated, Hebb had to make certain revisions, which he presented in 1959 in an article describing the status of the theory at that time. The basic line of thought, however, has not suffered major alteration.

Hebb's first step is to show that the Gestalt assumption that form is perceived as a distinct, unitary whole, without the need for learning or the recognition and summation of its component parts, is not valid. He proceeds to demonstrate that such seemingly simple percepts as those of a triangle or a square are in fact complex, that they are additive, that the apparent simplicity results from a long learning process, and that learning to perceive is based on motor activity.

The only instance where a figure acts as a unit innately is where a figure is distinguished from ground upon which it finds itself. This percept is determined by the simple operation of the neurons involved in vision. The perception of a figure whose shape is determined by past experience and is not simply something that differs from ground is a function of learning, as is the perception of a figure as something that has identity.

The primitive unity of form is perceived without the necessity for learning, as evidenced in case histories of patients who, having been blind from birth due to cataracts, see for the first time as adults (von Senden, 1932). Hebb reared rats in darkness, and observed that the ability to distinguish figures from ground was present in the animals upon first vision. In humans, the ability to perceive nonbounded portions of objects (the "middle" of a stick, for instance) as figures, areas between moving objects as figures, and either one of the two possible percepts in reversible figures as figure is something that must be learned, however. But even the primitive distinction between figure and ground is not as stable and constant as presented by the Gestalt theory. In ordinary perception, figure-ground organization shifts very easily, even when the perceptual setting is not at all ambiguous. The fluctuation of attention points out the role of nonsensory factors in any kind of perception.

The identity of figures, even of simple figures, is learned. The recognition of a shape as belonging with other, similar shapes, or the ability to attach verbal labels to shapes are the result of learning. von Senden's cases all had good figure-ground discrimination, but learning to identify even the simplest forms by name took weeks, even months. Initially, identification of shapes was done by resorting to such devices as counting the number of angles in a figure. Even after some learning had taken place, the simple transposition of a figure to a different color or orientation interfered with identification. Tactual recognition of the same figures, however, was prompt and accurate. The same slowness in perceptual learning after visual deprivation had been shown in primates (Riesen, 1947). In constructing his theory, Hebb drew heavily on both von Senden and Riesen.

Based on evidence from human patients and visually deprived primates, Hebb suggests that learning is probably also involved in the development of perception in a newborn infant. Since the perception of such figures as a triangle or a circle is so direct and simple in adults, the notion sounds unlikely, yet Hebb shows that even in normal perception in the adult there are traces of the original learning process left, such as the imaginary or actual eye movements in the visualization of a form. Eye movements are to Hebb the essential factor that produces the integration of simpler perceptual elements, such as angles and lines, into more complex forms, such as a triangle. While in the adult, eye movements are not necessary for perception—forms are clearly perceived even when there is no time to make a single scanning movement of the eyes (e.g., Battro & Fraisse, 1961; Mooney, 1957, 1958, 1959, 1960)—they are essential in the initial piecing together of the perceptual constituents at the outset of the perceptual learning process.

While rejecting the notions of electrical brain fields and of equipotentiality, Hebb does not deny the positive contributions of both Koehler and Lashley. He only points out that their positions were almost as radical in their rejection of elementism and behaviorism as these earlier schools were themselves. Hebb seeks an intermediate position.

The evidence that leads Hebb to reject both the field theory and equipotentiality comes from both animal and human studies. Birds, in which there is a complete crossover in the chiasma, transfer pattern elements found in the lower portion of the stimulus but not in the upper portion (Levine, 1945a, b). Errors made in tachistoscopic recognition suggest that the perception of patterns is originally learned. What the subject perceives is the slope of lines and their distance from each other. The complete pattern as perceived is something reconstituted in accordance with previous experience, and does not reflect the actual stimulus properties faithfully. Thus, in order to recognize pattern without eye movements, all that is needed is the ability to recognize the slopes of lines and the degree of separation of points.

The development of reading skills also points up equipotentiality as an inadequate explanation of form perception. For instance, it would require the immediate recognition of words regardless of their orientation, which is obviously not the case. In addition, the development of reading skill involves the gradual extension of the visual field to encompass stimulus portions that project on the periphery of the retina. Reading does not train all parts of the retina equally. For instance, English readers recognize two and three times as many words to the right of the fixation point than to the left of it, whereas the reverse is true for persons who read Hebrew.

von Senden's patients took a long time to learn to recognize simple forms without first counting the number of corners; neither were they able to recognize them, once learned, if the forms were transposed to a different color or presented in a different setting, all of which contradicts the thesis of equipotentiality. Some of the clinical evidence used by Gestalt psychologists to support the theory of field forces (e.g., Fuchs, 1920) is used by Hebb to prove just the contrary: a bullet wound that destroys part of the visual cortex would preclude the experienced completeness of form because it is there that the dynamic completion of forms would have to occur. Likewise, in Lashley's (1941) migraine patient with a scotoma, the symptoms indicate the existence of a nonfunctional visual area during the attack, an area in which, according to Lashley, interference patterns originate to produce the physiological counterpart of perceived form.

In spite of his criticism of Lashley's theory, a comparison of Hebb's ideas and those of Lashley cannot fail to impress one with the degree of similarity. I think one is justified in adding the name of Lashley to those of von Senden and Riesen as one of the major shapers of Hebb's ideas.

What events, then, are involved in the perception of a form? While there is topological correspondence between the retina and Brodmann's area 17, there is such a diffusion and spread of excitation from area 17 to areas 18, 19, and 20 that the correspondence disappears completely. One must conclude that different aspects of the perceptual process would be mediated by area 17 and the areas beyond it. The identity of form is one aspect of form perception that cannot be mediated by area 17, since even the same form will produce different topological projections depending on where it is fixated, not to speak of transpositions in area and rotation. Since the neuronal excitation that arrives in area 18 is essentially randomly distributed in that area, it appears that it would be even more difficult to locate form identification and nonsensory figure-ground organization there, but that is precisely what Hebb does.

The basis for identification is the formation of functional groups of cells that Hebb calls "cell assemblies." Cell assemblies consist of interconnected groups of cells that may fire together when stimulated by an afferent impulse. The reason why a particular group of cells will fire together is that they are near enough to each other to be mutually excited and that repeated firing will produce metabolic changes resulting in the development of synaptic knobs and an increase in the area of contact between the afferent axon and efferent soma. As a result, synaptic resistance is lowered and a number of cells become functionally associated. Since closed loops of cells are frequent structural elements, in the cortex, cell assemblies are thought to be these loops. In them, a nerve impulse will continue to circulate for some time even after the initial stimulation has ceased. Thus, the nature of cell assemblies is that of reverberatory circuits. They are not necessarily all closed rings or loops, but most likely three-dimensional lattices in which reverberations may alter among its subordinate units. Be this as it may, the basic mode of functioning of cells in the visual area is as follows: because of repeated firing in the past, a number of cells in area 17 will be able to excite the same cell assembly in area 18. If, because of damage or transpositional shifts in the stimulus, one will not fire, another area-17 cell will take over and fire the same assembly. Thus, a degree of equipotentiality is provided in spite of the basic specificity of neuronal activity as envisioned in the formation of superordinate functional units, the phase sequences, that correspond to the perception of form.

The stimulus elements that make up more complex percepts are, in Hebb's view, angles and lines. Angles and lines are not, however, the same as the punctate sensory elements of Wundt, and their perception is not fully innate. Compared with normal rats, dark-reared rats take, on the average, six times as long to learn to discriminate vertical from horizontal striations (Hebb, 1937). Some dark-reared rats, however, learn as rapidly as normal rats. Animal and human data agree in that crude differentiation between horizontal and vertical lines exists from the outset, but that the identification of the vertical and the horizontal is immensely improved through learning.

In discussing the mechanism of summation of excitation along the borders of a projected contour in area 17, Marshall and Talbot (1942) suggest that there would be a tendency to fixate the different portions of a contour successively. Hebb uses this notion to link up eye movements to contours, and the repeated stimulation provided thereby to the formation of cell assemblies:

It is important to observe that the figure made up of straight lines, instead of irregular curves, has special physiological properties. When one point of a straight line is fixated, every point to one side of the fixation tends to arouse exactly the same direction of eye movement, and every point in the line on the other side exactly the opposite direction. At times the two vectors may balance, but often they will not. It follows that there is a strong tendency for the eye to make a sweep along the line, in one direction or the other; and, as the sweep is made, at the moment when a corner is reached the stimulation of the intersection line is at the maximum, since at this moment every point in the second line has the same vector, for a new direction of eye movement. It appears from these considerations that the eye would tend to seek out the contours of a figure and follow them—irregularly and with reversals, it is true, and subject to disturbance by other events, but it seems that such a tendency must exist. (Hebb, 1949, p. 82.)

If angles and lines are the building bricks and primitive figure-ground organization the mortar, then eye movements are the mason's hand that builds the perceptual house. The recognition of members of a transformation group is thus provided for: regardless of the size of the angles of a triangle and regardless of its area, all triangles contain identical elements, three angles and three straight lines connecting them, so that all such shapes will be recognized as belonging to the same class of percepts, the class of triangles.

Suppose now that an organism that has had no previous visual experience is looking for the first time at a triangle. Whenever one of the vertices is fixated it will fall within the area of the macula, but not the whole triangle. One side of the triangle (chance factors determine which one), falling as it does on the peripheral retina, will evoke the tendency in the eye to follow it. In doing so, the next vertex is fixated, and so the eye keeps scanning the figure along its contours. Corresponding to the three corners of the triangle, three cell assemblies will eventually form in area 18 of the cortex. After a sufficient number of scannings of the triangle, the stimulation of any of the three cell assemblies, such as fixating only one corner of a triangle, will produce the integrated activity of all three cell assemblies and a triangle will be seen without the necessity of scanning the entire contour. Such a "phase sequence," then, would correspond to the idea or concept of "triangle," and any size or shape of stimulation containing the same elements would produce the experience of triangularity. If we designate by a, b, and c the cell assemblies corresponding to vertices A, B, and C, the percept of the triangle will not be the only percept: as one looks at a triangle, one alternately sees it as a whole and also its parts separately, so that the sequence of events may be designated as a-b-t-c-a-b-t-t-a-c, and so on.

Such, in brief, is Hebb's theory of form perception. It comprises, with the Gestalt and Gibson theories, a triad of the more comprehensive form-perception theories. What constitutes form is clearly defined: it is, like the Gestalt form, a brain-form, although the brain processes involved are interpreted in a different fashion. In 1949, Hebb's theorizing beyond the level of the cell assemblies was largely speculative. It still is, and direct physiological evidence may be long in coming.

Whatever evidence Hebb had about events past the cell assembly level was behavioral. Additional experimental data that have been accumulated since the writing of *The Organization of Behavior* have been in no instance directly contradictory to Hebb's theory. The aspect of Hebb's theory that is most readily tested is the role of eye movements in perception. That the eyes do follow the contours of a shape has been demonstrated (e.g., Zusne & Michels, 1964). The disappearance of contours in stabilized retinal images was not discovered until 1952, so Hebb did not know about it. The technique of stabilizing the retinal image allows for a comparison of some of the propositions made by the Gestalt school and Hebb. The evidence, it turns out, favors both theories. Pritchard (1961), one of Hebb's co-workers, has described the evidence. Simple contours, such as lines, disappear and reappear as complete images. More-complex patterns may disappear and reappear as wholes or in fragments, and the manner of their fading and regeneration would support the notion that pattern perception is learned. While the drawing of a human profile fades and regenerates in meaningful units, such as the nose, the eyes, hair, etc., the elements of a random collection of curved lines appear and disappear to form any pattern that is possible to make up from the original set of elements. Prolonged viewing, however, leads to the formation of stabler subpatterns which tend to come and go as units. Monograms disappear and reappear as the component letters or as any other letter or number that can be formed from them, with periods of complete fadeout interspersed between moments of vision. A word like BEER may become PEER, PEEP, BEE, or BE, all of which are other meaningful words. The letters never disintegrate into meaningless component strokes.

All such phenomena show too much structure and organization to attribute pattern fluctuations to temporary fluctuations of threshold in the various portions of the retina. They are definitely in line with the cell-assembly interpretation of pattern vision and point to the role of learning in seeing patterns. Lines, angles, portions of a profile, groups of curlicues, all these are "perceptual elements" for which cell assemblies already exist in the brain or are formed during prolonged inspection. The eye movements necessary for the maintenance of the entire pattern are absent, however, and the entire pattern is seldom seen.

Pritchard points out, though, that the same phenomena may be explained in Gestalt terms. If the stimulus is a letter on a cross-hatched background, what is seen is either the letter or the hatching lines. Sometimes, the two are seen together, but the letter appears to be floating in the foreground. If the letter is replaced by some nonrepresentational shape, the same phenomenon is observed, which means that it is not necessarily the meaning attached to a letter that makes it appear and disappear as a whole. Rather, it may be argued that it is the whole-character of both the shape and the hatching lines that produce the phenomenon. A more frequently observed effect is that some parts of both the nonrepresentational shape and the lines disappear together while the rest is seen as a new figure which is a 'better' figure, a better Gestalt. Nonrepresentational figures presented alone undergo a process of change, the end result of which is a smoothing of the contours and a stabler configuration. A square matrix of rows and columns of little squares, a figure often used to demonstrate Gestalt principles of organization, tends to disappear so that only a row or a column or a diagonal of the square elements is left. A random collection of dots fades in such a way that only a line of dots showing best continuation remains visible. All such units, segregated from the larger, undifferentiated whole, then disappear and reappear as wholes. Pritchard emphasizes that the cell-assembly theory and the Gestalt theory, considered to be mutually exclusive, are really complementary. In the stabilized retinal image, lines behave highly independently. They come and go as indivisible units. More-complex figures made up of lines are broken at intersections. Solid figures begin to fade from the middle of a side; fading then spreads toward the middle of the figure. The last to go are corners. When the figure reappears, it is the corners that appear first. When it comes to the perception of detail, the cell-assembly theory appears to be the most useful one in analyzing pattern perception. To interpret perception in a broad sense, the Gestalt approach is best used. At some intermediate point, both theories work equally well. For instance, when a circle and a triangle are presented close together, one will fade, leaving the other visible. This may be interpreted either as the result of learning or the effect of Gestalten acting as units.

Some phenomena observed with a stabilized retinal image cannot be explained satisfactorily by either the Gestalt or the cell-assembly theories. Tees (1961), for instance, found that the Gestalt field does not completely account for the interaction observed between certain line patterns, while the breaking up of lines at intersections, i.e., the failure of angles to act as perceptual units, and the completion of incomplete figures run against the cell-assembly theory.

In terms of the relative contributions of innate and experiential factors to form perception, Hebb's theory presents a thoroughly integrated picture: given a normal visual system, stimulation cannot help but lead to the formation of cell assemblies; functional connections between cell assemblies (phase sequences), however, are produced by experience. Parks (1965) and Hochberg (1968), who studied the perception of form when it is presented sequentially (moved) behind a narrow slit, found that form is perceived as usual under these conditions, even though it is never seen in its entirety. Hochberg concludes that "The perceived structure of an object may consist of two separable components: (a) the features glimpsed in momentary glances, and (b) the integrative schematic map into which those features are fitted" (Hochberg, 1968, p. 330). It is the "schematic map" or storage structure which is affected by past experience, whereas the briefly glimpsed contour features are relatively immune to it. Although it is in Helmholtz, Wundt, and Titchener that Hochberg finds the greatest similarity with his views, the theoretical position that Parks' and Hochberg's findings seem to confirm most readily is that of Hebb's.

Additional supporting evidence for the Hebbian viewpoint comes from the work of McFarland (1965a, 1965b). McFarland measured thresholds of simultaneity-succession in the perception of figures whose sides or angles were presented not at the same time but one after another, thus simulating the hypothesized sequential, analytic process that precedes the integration of these elements into the percept of a whole form. It was found that the perception of parts as simultaneous and joined took place at longer intervals when the elements used were the sides of a triangle than when they were angles. Sequence thresholds were also lower when the sides were presented clockwise and, with words as stimuli, when the individual letters of a word were presented from left to right. These findings point up the role of past experience in pattern perception.

Hebb's theory is mostly qualitative and the visual stimulus is not analyzed quantitatively. In his original statement, Hebb relied chiefly on available physiological evidence and clinical and developmental data. The purpose was to provide a revision of perceptual theory and to deal with the physiological basis of form perception. The relationship between the distal stimulus and response was to a large extent neglected. For the same reason, Hebb fails to mention the phenomenon of geometric illusions and the problem of fidelity in vision in general.

The developmental aspect of form perception is, of course, basic to Hebb's reasoning. Although it is not spelled out, there is the implication that the concept of cell assemblies could be applied to any phyletic level, and that form perception is essentially the same process in all animals. A discordant note has been recently introduced by Ganz and Wilson (1967), though. Monkeys raised from birth without experience with visual patterns were trained to discriminate a horizontal from a vertical line. An optical system was used to prevent the subjects from contouring the edges of the figures with their eyes. Even though, according to Hebb, learning should not have occurred under these conditions, the monkeys did generalize to a variety of other forms in a manner that was no different from normal monkeys.

3. The Perception of Visual Form in J. J. Gibson's Theory

William James (1890) classified theories of space in terms of whether the theorist believed space perception was innate, given in sensations as a special attribute, or was only a derivative of time. Sixty years later, Gibson (1951) was able to add a fourth position on this matter, namely that retinal excitation is converted into a brain-form due to processes of organization inherent in the brain. This, the Gestalt position, may be considered as neither nativistic nor empiricist, but one based on a more general property of all matter. Gibson's own theory would appear to fall in the same broad category.

The Perception of the Visual World (Gibson, 1950b) spells out a unique theory of space perception in that it has no direct antecedents and no direct derivative theories. It is principally a theory of how we see the three-dimensional world and not a theory of behavior in general. It is not primarily a theory of form perception either, yet Gibson is very specific, perhaps more specific than anyone else, on what form is and what it is not and how it should be studied.

While Gibson's pervasive concern is with the perception of the real, physical, three-dimensional visual world, two-dimensional shapes also occupy an important place in his theory, albeit in a somewhat negative fashion. In order to understand Gibson's particular point of view regarding two-dimensional form, it is necessary to understand his basic theory concerning the perception of three-dimensional space.

First, Gibson rejects the notion that one must start out with the concept of an abstract, geometric space describable only in terms of a system of coordinates. The space that is perceived is *visual* space, and it is perceived only by virtue of what fills it, namely things or, more generally, surfaces and edges. Surfaces and edges make up any and all objects. If a surface is continuous and its edges are not clearly delineated, it may be perceived as background. A seen edge may produce the contour of a figure. Together with the surface enclosed by the contour, they constitute the figure-ground phenomenon.

Second, Gibson believes that both simple and complex visual perceptions have some stimulus counterpart in the physical world. The stimulus is some gradient. The gradient is some property of a visual surface. Phenomenally, a visual surface possesses the properties of being visually resistant or 'hard,' having color and some degree of brightness, having a degree of slant, being at some distance from the observer, having a closed contour and the contour having a certain shape, and having a certain size. The physical gradients that give rise to the perception of these properties are the following.

Assuming a more or less homogeneous texture and a discernible grain of texture, it will be the gradually decreasing size of texture elements which, other things being equal, will inform the observer of a receding surface, i.e., surface in the third dimension. Lacking a gradient in texture, the observer may see a tilted surface on the basis of the degree of convergence of the edges of the surface, such as the two lateral edges of an inclined sheet of smooth white paper and, in general, from the gradient of width of parallel lines in surface as it extends in the third dimension. A sudden change in either texture or line-width gradients indicates the presence of an edge, as do other discontinuities in continuous gradients. Lacking gradients of texture or perspective, gradients of hue, such as the desaturation of colors with increasing distance (aerial perspective), and gradients of shading that give shape are the effective stimuli at the retina that inform of the existence of objects in the third dimension.

These are some of the psychological or pictorial distance or depth cues. They are used deliberately by the artist to produce the impression of depth in a flat, two-dimensional picture. For moving objects and for a moving observer, the gradients are gradients of deformation of the retinal image as objects actually move past one another or move apparently as the observer moves (motion parallax). If to these is added the gradient of differences between the two images formed on the two retinas, a gradient which corresponds to the various distances at which an object may be located, the list constitutes the entirety of information that one needs to locate objects in space.

At the retina, gradients of texture, movement, and retinal disparity produce a textured optical array. Gradients imply change, and change in energy constitutes stimulation, hence if the retinal image lacks texture and change, clues to the true state of affairs in the three-dimensional world are lacking and the perception of spatial relations is ambiguous. The role of central factors is minimized by Gibson. To him, agreement among observers as to how things really look and the accuracy and precision with which we all respond to the spatial environment are so overwhelming that cases of nonveridical perception, such as optical illusions and distortions introduced by the observer's set, are dismissed as mere exceptions. In addition, most of the illusions, including the geometric illusions, may be described in Gibsonian terms quite adequately. Gibson has done that briefly in his latest book (Gibson, 1966) for the classical illusions.

The physiological processes underlying perception get little attention from Gibson. They can be safely bypassed, he says, as they have been bypassed by the psychologists who for the past century have been concerned only with the correspondence between stimulus and response. He takes some pains, however, to demonstrate that the idea of the retinal image as a picture is highly inappropriate and leads to erroneous views of perception. If the retinal image were a picture, it would be necessary to have another eye behind it to perceive the picture, etc. The retinal image is nothing but the projection of edges and surfaces of the visual world onto a flat retina, a pattern of gradients of edges and gradients of surface textures and shadows. The visual field corresponds with the anatomical pattern of excitation on the retina; the visual world, however, corresponds to successive patterns of excitation. The order of excitation counts here, the structure of excitation in the case of the visual field. As a result, the field shifts with eye movements, the world does not.

Gibson's theory is based on the proposition that abstract points, lines, and planes are a poor basis for analyzing how we see, because no one has ever seen them; hence, points and lines drawn on a sheet of paper to represent surfaces are poor material to use in form-perception studies. Gibson chooses to study objects with surfaces and edges rather than geometric forms. In *The Perception of the Visual World,* form is projected form, such as would be obtained if the silhouette of an object were cast on a screen. But in the process of projecting, we have already abstracted something from the real object: its form. Form is never experienced alone, in two dimensions. It is objects that have form, and objects are three-dimensional, hence form is always form-in-depth.

The historically determined tendency to think of form as two-dimensional only is, to Gibson, a major obstacle to the correct understanding of visual perception. The main historical reason is that two-dimensional vision has always been thought of as the more primitive sort of vision and that some higher process or processes were required to make three dimensions out of the two only given in the retinal image. How the flat retinal image becomes a three-dimensional percept has always been something of a mystery. Gibson's contention is that three-dimensional vision, i.e., vision of the visual world, is more primitive because all the necessary information to see the world in three dimensions is given in the retinal image, and that it takes a special attitude to see things in two dimensions only. Gibson implies that, since Gestalt psychologists were mostly concerned with the projected form and developed their principles of organization using two-dimensional shapes, their understanding of form perception was not quite correct. He suggests that the 'laws' of form proposed by the Gestalt school might not be laws of form as such but laws that relate projected forms to the objects that project them. Conceived in this way, form is a resultant of an object, a variable whose value is entirely determined by the three-dimensional object, not an independent entity. Form is merely another parameter of a perceived object, just like its size, color, or some other variable whose values change along a continuum. The dynamism of form as presented by the Gestaltists reflects no more than the instability of the percept of a two-dimensional shape that has been abstracted away from the cause of its being, the three-dimensional object. Form in the visual world is a stable affair.

As far as rejecting the use of "geometric" shapes in form-perception studies goes, there can be no argument with Gibson. Such shapes represent the extremes of continua of innumerable transformations: the equilateral triangle is just a single instance among all possible discriminable triangles. For this reason, any conclusions from studies in which "geometric" shapes alone are used have extremely limited generality. Some passages in Gibson, however, read like wholesale condemnation of any and all two-dimensional shapes as stimuli in perceptual studies. This is an untenable position, and it mellowed considerably between the writing of *The Perception of the Visual World* in 1950 and *The Senses Considered as Perceptual Systems* in 1966. To establish what kinds of forms are acceptable for psychological study, one needs to examine Gibson's list of definitions of the term "form." Such a list is found in Gibson's 1951 article on form. The following meanings of the term are listed there.

1. *Solid form.* This is the physical surface that constitutes the interface between one mass of substance and another, usually air. Seeing an object means seeing a solid form, a form in depth.

2. *Surface form.* Optically, objects are masses of substance enclosed by surfaces that have edges. Surface form is one such surface with its edges. But since surfaces always belong to some object and objects are located in three-dimensional space, surface forms must be forms in a certain spatial orientation—they have slant. The percept of a surface form includes both the slant and the edges of the surface.

3. *Outline form.* Representations, in ink, pencil, paint, etc., and on a surface, of the edges of solid form are outline forms. The lines which stand for edges are actually very thin shapes—they have two sides—whereas an edge has only one dimension and no thickness. This, however, presents no difficulty to the observer, who usually sees an object and not simply traces of some darker substance on a lighter background. The observer is aware, though, that what he sees is not an object but only a picture of it.

4. *Pictorial form.* This group includes representations of objects on some surface: representations drawn, photographed, painted, projected, etc. When the representation has contour, color, texture, perspective, and is viewed through a small aperture so that no visible frame is present, it may be mistaken for reality.

5. *Plan form.* A plan form is the plan projection of the edges of a surface form, such as the plan of the foundations of a building. To obtain a plan form, the object is projected geometrically and perpendicularly on a flat surface. The projection involves no distortion due to slant or distance (i.e., perspective).

6. *Perspective form.* A perspective view of an object in which only the edges and surfaces are indicated, such as a line drawing of a cube in perspective, is a perspective form.

7. *Nonsense form.* A nonsense form is made up of tracings on a surface which do not represent a recognizable object, either because of the inability of the tracer to represent objects recognizably, because the tracing is made nonrepresentational intentionally, or because, while the form may be a correct representation of an object, it is not readily recognized as such.

8. *Plane geometric form.* This is the abstract geometric form, such as a triangle, trapezoid, circle, or square, which is not to be confused with an outline form, which is an attempt to make a geometric form visible. A plane geometric form is best represented by a mathematical equation, not by deposits of ink or pencil on a sheet of paper.

9. *"Solid" geometric form.* This is the abstract or imaginary portion of imaginary three-dimensional space enclosed by imaginary surfaces. Such a form can be imagined but not actually seen.

10. *Projected form.* This is a plane geometric form that is in a point-to-point correspondence with a form on another plane. It may be larger or smaller than, or some transformation of, the latter, but there is a one-to-one correspondence between them. The silhouette of an object on a screen illustrates this relationship, but a silhouette is a pictorial form, not a projected form.

The above ten kinds of form are grouped by Gibson into three major classes: solid form and surface form constitute one class; outline, pictorial, plan, perspective, and nonsense forms constitute another; and plane and solid geometric forms, together with the projected form, constitute a third class. The first class of forms is the most "real" kind, since they belong to the real, three-dimensional, visual world. The second class of what may be called pictorial forms represents some degree of abstraction, hence irreality, of solid or surface form. The third class of forms is pure mathematical abstraction, a "ghost" of a real form, as Gibson has it. These three classes of form are so different that the question of how we perceive form must be asked for each class of form separately.

The question of how we perceive solid and surface forms has already been answered in the preceding discussion of how Gibson explains three-dimensional vision. As compared with the perception of pictures, the perception of objects is a simple matter. Pictures are not only objects themselves, but they also stand for other objects. A landscape, for instance, stands for the real, three-dimensional world that it depicts. The fact that pictorial forms are representations constitutes a special problem in their perception. Gibson reports the results of having shown observers a number of outline forms and having asked them to describe what they saw. No observer reported seeing spots of ink or pencil marks. Very few observers reported seeing angles, lines, or geometric figures. Rather, the reports were either of plan forms or perspective forms, and for each outline drawing, both of these reports were given. Thus, an arrow of the kind that is used in the Mueller-Lyer illusion would be reported as either an arrow (plan form) or the top of a tent (perspective form). This, to Gibson, makes outline forms, the most frequently used kind of stimulus in studies of form perception, inappropriate stimulus objects because they are not taken by observers to be themselves but to stand for something else. Not only do they stand for something else, but the same outline form may stand for two or more quite different objects. "If it be granted that these are actually *pictures of forms,* the research is irrelevant to the problem. A genuine psychophysics of form perception will have to deal with 'shape-slant,' i.e., with transformations of form which co-vary with degrees of slant." (Gibson, 1951, p. 410.) This statement is acceptable only with regard to a very narrow area of research in the field of space perception, namely shape constancy. Modern literature in the field of psychophysics of form shows quite clearly that in many instances the slant variable is irrelevant. Researchers in the area of psychophysics of form no longer use the classical geometric outline forms. Neither do they use representations of objects. Rather, randomly constructed polygons and curved nonrepresentational shapes are used. Meaning possessed by these forms can be equated by using their association values.

More importantly, however, it may be objected that while Gibson correctly emphasized the existence of different classes of form and clarified our thinking in regard to the consequences of these differences, he failed to show that the different types of perceptual tasks are of equal importance. If there are different kinds of form, there are also different ways of perceiving form, but the way in which we perceive form depends also on what we *do* as we comply with instructions, from an experimenter or ourselves, to "perceive form." For instance, the use of a pictorial representation of an arrow as a stimulus in an experiment can be appropriate or inappropriate depending on whether (a) the subject's occipital cortex is being mapped as the arrow is moved in front of the subject's eye; (b) a series of arrows of different lengths, color, etc. are compared to test their usefulness as highway markers; (c) the effect of acute and obtuse angles on the perception of alphanumeric characters is studied; (d) the arrow is a projection of an actual object and the subject is judging the "real" shape of the object; (e) the arrow is one among a dozen other redundant shapes, such as crosses, stars, and triangles, used in an experiment on peripheral vision; (f) the arrow is one among a fairly large number of other simple pictorial representations of objects used to study changes occurring in memory images; (g) the arrow is a stimulus, among a number of other similar stimuli, in a verbal association experiment. In some of these instances, the arrow would be an inappropriate stimulus; in others, there can be no objection to it; and in still others, its use would depend on one or several additional variables and whether these are or are not involved in the experiment. All of these types of experiment have been named, at one time or another, form-perception experiments, yet it is clear that what the subject does in each case is different, and the nature of the task is as important as the nature of the stimulus in determining the content of "form perception."

Geometric forms, plane, solid, or projected, have no stimulus correlates in the visual world, hence they cannot be seen. The illustrations found in geometry textbooks are simply symbols. Not only do they approximate the abstract form through the use of lines of certain thickness, but they are also pictorially represented concepts, ideas based on numerous prior experiences of solid and surface forms as well as pictorial representations of them. Unless some indication is given of the kind of object that such a drawing stands for, it is everything but the simple stimulus that it is often assumed to be.

What, then, are Gibson's suggestions for the psychophysicist of form as to how he should proceed in his work?

The primary problem for psychologists is to isolate the invariant properties in visual stimulation which are in physical correspondence with constant phenomenal objects. According to the proposed definitions, *solid* forms and *surface* forms are realities. *Outline*-forms and also *pictorial-, plan-, perspective-,* and *nonsense*-forms are representations which the perceiver takes to stand for realities. For these, a special theory of picture-perception is required. *Geometrical* forms, both *plane* and *solid,* are abstractions which cannot even be represented, strictly speaking, but can only be specified by symbols . . . . At least three separate levels of theory will be required: first, a theory of how we perceive the surface of objects—a theory of slant-shape or, in older words, of shape-constancy; second, a theory of how we perceive representations, pictures, displays, and diagrams; and third, a theory of how we apprehend symbols. (Gibson, 1951, pp. 411/2.)

Gibson himself took care of the first level of theory, rejecting both the learning and sensory organization explanations and substituting the notion that the perception of solid and surface forms is given in the proximal stimulus.

As far as outline forms in the frontoparallel plane are concerned, Gibson's suggestion is that to classify forms into groups (square, triangle, etc.) is a barren approach since single instances of form only represent either the extremes of continua of endless variation or else they are pictorial symbols of abstractions for which there is no stimulus counterpart. What is needed to investigate is serial transformations of form. Certain transformations leave the percept of shape identity unaltered. Others affect only a portion of a shape at a time, but as a result, the nature of the entire shape is changed and identity is not preserved. Any shape can be changed into any other by gradual and continuous transformation. The problem is to establish how perception changes with systematic and gradual changes along a continuum of transformations: transformations of complexity, curvature, elongation, symmetry, or any other form parameter. Gibson himself has studied some of these variables, both with simple line stimuli and more complex ones, even constructing an apparatus, the shadow transformer, to study the perception of continuous optical motions and transformations (Gibson, 1937; Gibson & Gibson, 1957). While it is fairly easy to establish that the direction or slope of a curve (first differential) and its curvature (second differential) account for the entirety of the experience of a line segment, Gibson admits that, when a line becomes a closed contour, "the variations of shape appear to jump to a higher level" (Gibson, 1950, p. 196). This, however, is to him no reason why the stimulus-analysis approach to the perception of pictorial form cannot be applied.

After Gibson's influential criticism of the idea of form-in-general, it is unlikely that an attempt will again be made to state a theory of form perception in the manner of Koehler or even Hebb. The theories considered here each attempt to identify some process, structure, or mechanism responsible for the perception of form, elements of form, or contours. The postulated processes, structures, and mechanisms are different for each theory. The reason for this may be, as Gibson has suggested, that there are several different brain mechanisms involved in form perception depending on whether the form perceived is that of a natural object, that of a picture, or that of a symbol. In each case, a different theory of form perception is needed. It is quite possible, as Gibson thinks it is, that the category of "form perception" will evaporate when these theories are developed.

4. The Fidelity of Contour Perception

If a visual stimulus and the response to it are measurable, then fidelity of vision may be defined as the correlation between stimulus and response (Hake, 1957). Neither in vision nor in any other sense modality is this correlation perfect. This is particularly true for that aspect of vision that concerns the perception of form. There are many reasons why physical form and the response to it should not correlate perfectly. As common everyday experience shows, however, the degree of imperfection in correspondence between stimulus and response is not too gross. Form and its cortical counterpart also show certain correspondence, and this is the same kind of correspondence that we find at all levels of investigation: behavioral, phenomenological, or physiological; it is topological but not topographical correspondence. As Hake (1957) puts it, the visual system can show coherence but not fidelity.

While the assumption that there is no fidelity in form perception may be made almost on an *a priori* basis, and while there is considerable empirical evidence in favor of that assumption, there has been no systematic treatment of the problem. It may be said that the basic cause of the lack of fidelity in form perception is interaction—interaction between stimulus parameters themselves and interaction between stimulus parameters and observer variables. The number of stimulus and subject variables in the field of form perception is very large, and the number and complexity of interactive processes increases as some power function of the complexity of form. It is for this reason that only the simplest kinds of configurations have been used in the study of the fidelity of form perception. This has limited the generalizability of the findings enormously, so that it is possible to talk only of sporadic, incomplete, and unsystematic attempts to study this problem. Specifically, these attempts have been directed toward the various forms of visual illusions.

A. GEOMETRIC ILLUSIONS

In terms of publications, the single most populated area in visual perception is that of illusions, especially the geometric illusions. The term "geometrical optical illusions" was coined by Oppel in 1854. Since these illusions have been found to exist in the haptic perceptual system also, the term "optical" is no longer appropriate. By 1901, Titchener was able to show dozens of examples of such illusions in his *Experimental Psychology,* and only very few new ones have been added since that time.

While modern texts still talk about geometric illusions and provide graphic illustrations cf them, the topic has receded into background without having

(s)

(t)

Fig. 4-16.

Experiments have been performed, however, which indicate that fatigue-type processes in the nervous system cannot account for the geometric illusions. In spite of the difficulties associated with the field-theoretic concept when it is transferred from the field of physics to psychology, both Gestalt-oriented investigators and others have turned to this concept repeatedly. Lately, mathematically exact predictions have been made of illusory effects on the basis of the field theory and with surprising success. Orbison's (1939a, 1939b) work was the first pioneering instance. Brown and Voth (1937) saw the visual field, as represented in the nervous system, as a vector field, each vector having certain magnitude and direction. These vectors are of two kinds, cohesive and restraining. The cohesive forces attract points, but their confluence is prevented by the restraining forces. The reason why a visual field appears as it does is because the interaction of the cohesive and restraining forces is what it is for a given configuration.

This explanation did not quite pinpoint what the force vectors were exactly. Orbison showed that the vector concept could be applied to static events as well and not only to the apparent movement that the work of Brown and Voth was concerned with. Orbison's contribution was the systematic production of visual "force fields" and the prediction and quantification of the distortion of contours when introduced in these force fields. Orbison predicted that, when the restraining and cohesive forces were equal, the illusion figure would be distorted in the direction of the position of cohesive equilibrium. For the circular field containing regularly spaced radii, e.g., the position of cohesive equilibrium would be circles concentric with the circumference of the field. Berliner and Berliner (1948) argued that Orbison's statements concerning various types of equilibrium between cohesive and restraining forces were not specific enough. Based on earlier work by Hofman and Bielschowsky (1909), they suggested the substitution of the following principle of distortion for Orbison's: "A geometrical figure superposed on a geometrical field will be distorted at each crossing point in accordance with the formula $c \sin 4\alpha$," where α is the size of the angle of intersection.

A few years after Orbison's publications appeared, Marshall and Talbot (1942) provided a neurophysiological explanation of the distortions occurring when two lines cross at some acute angle:

Experimentally, the activity from two borders crossing at right angles seems not to interfere. Physiologically, this could mean that, in a field of incoming teledendrons, excitation moving parallel to a 'line' is prevented (possibly by phase opposition of electric fields), leaving these pathways open. But perpendicular to the 'ridge' or 'cliff' of activity, most of the branches would be activated subthreshold, to a state of subnormality. Hence, when a line is imposed on a grid [Fig. 4-17] its field activity F finds its component (y) precluded but (x) free. The line (A) therefore acquires the subvisual surround pertaining to line (B). This would be one physiological basis for the 'pattern' type of illusion sometimes explained by vector 'forces' . . . . There are other factors operating even above threshold levels which partially account for this illusion without using a remote field structure. Specifically, at any junction of two excitation ridges, the acute angle is the site of mutual depressive activity, while the obtuse angle allows fuller development at the bases of the activity distribution. This results in skewing the ridges of activity at an intersection toward perpendicularity. The tendency of higher levels to maintain 'straightness' would cause the observed illusion of general twist. (Pp. 152/3.)

Sickles (1942) applied the field concept to the Ponzo illusion by treating the area between the two converging lines as an electromagnetic field, distorted by

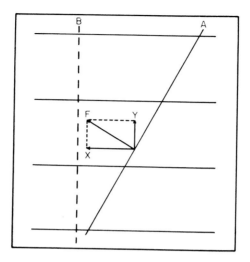

Fig. 4-17. Grid illusion. From Marshall and Talbot (1942).

the line within it, which is perpendicular to the bisectrix of the angle. Since an electromagnetic field can be calculated, so can the effects of the line in the field as well as the change in its apparent length as a function of its proximity to the vertex of the angle. A very good correlation between predicted and observed changes in the length of the illusion was obtained by Sickles.

Yakose (e.g., Yakose, 1954) applied Savart's law of electromagnetism to a variety of shapes and constructed equal-force contours within and without them. The apparent displacement of points in the vicinity of the shapes could be predicted with considerable success on the basis of the equal-force contours.

Tests favorable to the field theory have been conducted using a very different approach. A small point of light is presented at various distances in and around a figure and its brightness threshold measured. Investigators like Craik and Zangwill (1939), Kaneko and Obonai (1952), and Yakose and Uchiyama (1952) have found that the threshold for a small patch of light or a small figure within a larger figure is higher than when the same patch or figure is presented outsid the contours of the larger figure. While the larger figure does not need to closed, the threshold of the test stimulus is related to the completeness c effect-producing figure as well as to the distance of the test stimulus f   e figure. Critical fusion frequency measures produce contours that are ve   lar to Yakose's equal-force contours (Ohkawa, 1954).

Motokawa's (1950) method of mapping the "field of induction" surrounding a figure is rather unique. The field of induction is the field in the retina produced by the retinal image and whose origin is the discontinuities in the activity of the retinal elements due to differentials in retinal illumination. Intense yellow contours are used for the inducing figure, which is presented to the eye for 2 sec. This is followed by a small white test light presented at various sites in the vicinity of the inducing figure. Then a 100-msec. electric pulse is applied to the eye and the phosphene threshold measured. The inducing effect of the yellow figure is measured by the difference between the thresholds for white light alone and white light followed by the electric pulse. The shape, size, and discontinuities in the force fields mapped by this method are thought by Motokawa to explain a number of different geometric illusions. One problem with Motokawa's approach is that it is not a theory: to predict a specific illusion, one needs to plot the induction field for each figure separately (Ogasawara, 1958). Another problem is that, while supporting evidence for Motokawa's explanation has been provided (e.g., Day, 1961; Ohwaki, 1960; Springbett, 1961), evidence that central processes are responsible for illusions rather than retinal induction has also been presented (e.g., Boring, 1961; Schiller & Wiener, 1962).

Information-Sampling Theories. One of the earliest theories of geometric illusions attributed the illusory effects to bias in information-sampling produced by adjacent contours as the eye explored the illusion figure. For instance, differences in effort in eye movements along lines varying in directionality were said to produce incorrect judgments of their length. Both tachistoscopic presentation of geometric illusions, which allows no eye movements (Helmholtz, 1924; Hicks & Rivers, 1908; Lewis, 1908; Piaget, Bang, & Matalon, 1958), and the viewing of geometric illusions with stabilized retinal image (Pritchard, 1958) have disposed of this theory, since the illusory effect is still present under these conditions.

Piaget's theory of geometric illusions is based on central processes and not specifically on eye movements, although it may appear so from a description of his theory. Piaget obtained his data from developmental studies and compared the performance of adults and children instead of limiting himself to adult subjects alone. Since all illusions undergo changes in their magnitude as a function of age, a theory of illusions must contend with this fact, which most of them do not. The latest summary statements of Piaget's theory of geometric illusions may be found in Piaget (1961) and Piaget (1967).

Piaget's basic assumption is that the perceptual process is not like that of copying or taking exact measurements. Rather, it is a sampling process in which only some elements of the stimulus are sampled while others are not. The size of the elements that are sampled will be overestimated in comparison with those that are not. The phenomenon of overestimation is more complex than that, however, and the following factors play a role, regardless of the observer's age: (a) the overestimation of stimulus elements that are being fixated (i.e.. upon which the observer's attention centers); (b) intensity of the attentional process; (c) duration of the fixation period; (d) the sequence in which stimulus elements are fixated, the last one in the sequence being overestimated (i.e., the classical time error); and (e) clarity of perception, which is determined by such factors as the visual angle, level of illumination, etc. An optimum combination of these factors leads to a "centering" of perception and results in the overestimation of the stimulus elements involved, i.e., illusory perception.

The magnitude of overestimation of stimulus elements fixated increases with time, following the course of an exponential curve. Piaget explains this particular relationship by resorting to the concepts of "encounters" and " pairings." Line segments that are fixated in the fovea "encounter" receptor elements in the retina during visual exploration. Assuming that stimulus elements, once "encountered," play no role when encountered again, after the jth instance of n encounters, during time t, of αN elements, N being the total of elements that can be "encountered," the number of elements that remain to be "encountered" is $N_j = N(1 - \alpha)^j$. Thus, the sum of elements "encountered" after each new set of n "encounters," $\alpha N + \alpha N_1 + \alpha N_2 + \cdots$, grows in an exponential fashion. Since geometric illusions are due to interaction between contours, Piaget introduces a further concept, "pairings," defined as the association of "encounters" in two line segments. "Complete pairing" occurs if the number of "encounters" in one line is equal to that in the other, while "incomplete pairing" occurs if these two quantities are dissimilar. On this basis, two types of error are distinguished: "elementary error I" is the absolute overestimation of a line as a function of the number of "encounters"; "elementary error II" is the relative overestimation of one line with respect to another as a result of "incomplete pairing." In the case of "complete pairing," "elementary error II" is equal to zero, regardless of the size of error I. If an unbalanced process of centering produces "incomplete pairing," coordinated or compensatory centration should produce "complete pairing," hence a reduction in "elementary error II" through the process of "decentering."

The following formula has been proposed by Piaget to predict the size of illusory distortion on the basis of physical measurements taken on illusion-producing contexts that Piaget calls primary (those that depend directly on the effects of an inducing field): the illusion of rectangles (whose longest side is overestimated), of half-rectangles, of the angles of a diamond, of curves, of parallelograms, of trapezoids, and of the Mueller-Lyer illusion (which Piaget considers to be an instance of two double trapezoids), of interrupted extent, and others:

$$P = \left[\frac{(L_1 - L_2)L_2}{S} \right] \left[\frac{nL}{L_{\max}} \right] = \frac{nL(L_1 - L_2)L_2}{(S)(L_{\max})},$$

where P is the amount of overestimation or underestimation of one of the extents of the illusion figure; L_1 is the longer of two extents that are being compared (e.g., the long side of a rectangle); L_2 is the shorter of the two extents being compared; L_{max} is the longest extent of the figure; S is the area of the field of comparison between L_1 and L_2 (which, in the case of line patterns, is equal to L_{max}^2); n is the number of comparisons made between L_1 and L_2 (e.g., two in the case of the Delboeuf illusion); and L is the length of that line segment that is used as reference. The formula is the mathematical expression of what Piaget calls the "law of relative centrations."

Judgmental Theories. The judgmental-type theories invoke some form of learning to explain geometric illusions, e.g., the learning of size relationships as a function of distance, i.e., perspective. In the Ponzo illusion, e.g., distance is suggested by the barest minimum of information, namely the convergence of two straight lines. The Ponzo illusion may be considered a case of size constancy misapplied (cf. Tausch, 1954): since the retinal images of the two short lines are equal in length and the two converging lines are assumed to represent the parallel sides of a road, railroad tracks, or the like, the line closer to the point of their convergence appears longer, i.e., inappropriate compensation is made.

The Mueller-Lyer illusion can also be considered a two-dimensional representation of three-dimensional objects. The line with the inward pointing wings could be the contours of a corner of a room, whereas the line with the outward pointing wings could be the corner of a building seen from the outside. In the first figure, two walls receding from the observer are suggested, whereas in the second, the suggestion is that of two walls converging toward the observer. One explanation of the Mueller-Lyer illusion is that one of the two lines appears to be longer than the other because it is seen as the representation of a contour that is nearer to the observer. This is the perspective theory of geometric illusions attributed to Thiery (1895, 1896). There are two difficulties with this theory. First, it must be explained why the illusion looks flat in spite of its features that suggest perspective. Second, it must be explained why size constancy is at work at all since, according to Emmert's law, constancy is a function of apparent distance. Gregory (1963, 1965, 1966) has undertaken to furnish these explanations and to advance a more complete perspective theory as an explanation of the Mueller-Lyer illusion.

The reason why the illusion figure looks flat is that the surface (usually paper) on which the illusion figure is presented has the homogeneous texture of a flat surface. If, however, the Mueller-Lyer figures are made of wire, painted with luminous paint, suspended in a dark room, and observed with one eye, they look three-dimensional—like a corner of a room and like the outside corner of a building. In other words, the cues for flatness of the paper or cardboard surface normally dominate and counteract the depth cues of linear perspective of the illusion figures.

The second difficulty is harder to overcome since it must be shown that the observer responds to the figure as if it had depth, even though it lies in a plane. Gregory (1966) has used a specially designed apparatus to show that subjects indeed see the illusion figure in depth. The strength of the impression of depth varies with the degree of strength of the perspective clues: for instance, lengthening the inward-pointing wings will both make the straight line look shorter and increase the apparent distance between the tips of the wings and the middle of the straight line.

Kristof (1961) has offered a similar theory, based on the phenomenon of size constancy, but without any empirical support. The misplaced-constancy-scaling theory has not found support among all investigators. Thus, Carlson (1966) and Hamilton (1966) report results that weaken Gregory's proposition, while Balser (1963) presents findings that undermine Kristof's. The field theory (Motokawa, 1950) and other global theories (e.g., Cleary, 1966) discount this approach.

Previous experience is an important aspect of the problem of geometric illusions. It has a direct bearing on the adequacy of any theory. It has been shown beyond doubt that previous experience does affect the magnitude and direction of geometric illusions. The pertinent studies are reviewed here briefly.

The effect of previous experience on geometric illusions has been studied in the form of prolonged experimental exposure to the illusions, the lack of visual experience in congenitally blind subjects, and culturally determined differences in lifelong experience. It may be said, in general, that repeated exposure to the geometric illusions produces a decrement in the magnitude of these illusions. The most frequently studied illusion in this connection has been the Mueller-Lyer illusion (e.g., Azuna, 1952; Day, 1962; Koehler & Fischback, 1950a; Parker & Newbigging, 1963) but others, such as the Poggendorff and Zoellner illusions, show similar decrements (e.g., Judd, 1902). The effect is apparently not one of practice (learning), but a habituational one: the effect is greater when massed trials are used as against spaced trials (Mountjoy, 1957); there is spontaneous recovery of the illusion after a 24-hr. interval (Mountjoy, 1958), and the decrement occurs regardless of whether the subject is informed of the accuracy of his settings or not (Mountjoy, 1958). When the Mueller-Lyer pattern is turned around end to end after a series of trials, the decrement in the illusion disappears. This is similar to the figural aftereffect phenomenon, which is maximal when the inspection pattern is associated with a specific site in the visual field. Koehler and Fischback (1950a, 1950b) have therefore proposed that the illusion decrement phenomenon is due to the operation of the same factor that produces figural aftereffects. The explanation of figural aftereffects in terms of the satiation theory, however, is open to serious criticism, which has been already mentioned. Such criticism would also apply to the explanation of the decrement in the Mueller-Lyer illusion in terms of satiation. Mountjoy (e.g.,

1957, 1958, 1963, 1965) has produced considerable evidence in favor of a perceptual habituation hypothesis as against the satiation hypothesis.

The effects of culture on the perception of illusions have been studied as early as the turn of the century when Rivers (1901a, 1901b, 1905) presented data on certain native populations in southeast Asia and India, showing considerable differences between them and Europeans in susceptibility to geometric illusions.Rivers collected quantitative data showing that non-European groups were more susceptible to the vertical-horizontal illusion but less susceptible to the Mueller-Lyer illusion than English subjects. In addition to this difference, the significant finding was the difference between these two types of illusion. It suggested that the differences between types of subjects were real and that the two types of illusion were different in nature.

Segall, Campbell, and Herskovitz (1966) present the amplest and most recent data on the subject, along with some hypotheses as to the cause of the differences in susceptibility, which Rivers did not do. *The Influence of Culture on Visual Perception* summarizes some six years of data collection in 14 non-Western cultures as well as in the United States and among South African whites. The data are responses of 1878 subjects to the Mueller-Lyer illusion, the Sanders parallelogram, the Ponzo illusion, and the *T* and *L* versions of the horizontal-vertical illusion. These illusions were chosen because of ease of measurement of the illusion and also because the investigators accepted one explanation for all of these illusions, namely the perspective theory. More specifically, it was predicted that:

> For figures constructed of lines meeting in nonrectangular junctions, there will be a learned tendency among persons dwelling in carpentered environments to rectangularize these junctures, to perceive the figures in perspective, and to interpret them as two-dimensional representations of three-dimensional objects . . . . It is predicted that Western peoples will be more susceptible to [the Mueller-Lyer, the Sanders parallelogram, and the Ponzo] illusions than people dwelling in uncarpentered environments. The horizontal-vertical illusion results from a tendency to counter the foreshortening of lines extending into space away from the viewer, so that the vertical in the drawing that is the stimulus for the illusion is interpreted as representing a longer line. Since the tendency has more ecological validity for peoples living mostly outdoors in open, spacious environments, it is predicted that such peoples will be more susceptible than Western peoples in urban environments. On the other hand, some non-Western groups should be less susceptible to the illusion, e.g., rain-forest or canyon dwellers. (From pp. 96/7 of *The Influence of Culture on Visual Perception* by Marshall H. Segall, Donald T. Campbell, and Melville J. Herskovits. Copyright 1966, by The Bobbs-Merrill Company, Inc. Reprinted by permission of the publishers.)

Like Rivers, these investigators found that Westerners were significantly more susceptible to the Mueller-Lyer and Sanders illusions than were non-Western subjects. Many, but not all, of the non-Western subject samples scored higher on the two forms of the horizontal-vertical illusion, a finding also obtained by Rivers. As predicted, rain-forest dwellers in Africa were the least susceptible group. The Ponzo illusion did not produce significant differences between Westerners and non-Westerners. What the results of this study imply is that the physical features of an individual's habitat affect his perceptions. The particular illusions chosen for study were of the kind that can be explained in terms of learning. The Wundt, Poggendorff, or Zoellner illusions, as well as any other illusion involving apparent changes in the size of angles or direction of lines, are much more difficult to measure, especially when it comes to communicating the intent of the experimenter to subjects whose experience contains nothing related to science or experimentation. Thus, the question of whether this type of illusion is less susceptible to modifications through learning, because it is based directly on neural interaction, still remains to be answered.

It may be mentioned here that the carpentered-world hypothesis by itself has not been always confirmed by other investigators. Thus, Gregor and McPherson (1965), who tested it among Australian aborigines, found no difference between two groups of aborigines who lived under two conditions, a "carpentered" and an "uncarpentered" one.

The perception of geometric illusions by congenitally blind individuals who see for the first time tends to support the general proposition that learning plays a very large role here. The number of well-documented cases, however, is very small. The most recent one has been described by Gregory and Wallace (1963). Among the numerous vision tests given the patient were several geometric illusions. They were administered during the second month after the corneal transplant that restored the patient's vision, thus allowing for some minimal learning between the time that the bandages were removed and the tests were administered. Even so, the patient showed either no susceptibility to the Hering, Zoellner, Poggendorff, and Mueller-Lyer illusions or a degree of susceptibility far below average. As evidenced by a number of other tests, constancy scaling was not present in this individual. Thus, the theory that at least the Mueller-Lyer illusion is explicable in terms of misapplied constancy scaling receives support from these observations.

B. ANISOTROPY OF SPACE

A pole looks considerably taller when erect than when lying on the ground; the silk hat in Fig. 4-18a appears taller than it is wide; and of the two perpendicular lines in Figs. 4-18b and 4-18c, the vertical one invariably looks longer than the horizontal one. This is the so-called horizontal-vertical illusion. Its first mention has been attributed to both Oppel (1854) (by Ritter, 1917) and Wundt (1862) (by Boring, 1942). It has tempted psychologists to explain it in terms of the assumed difference in the effort involved in moving the eyes vertically as compared with horizontal movements: the greater effort needed to move the eyes vertically (to overcome gravitational force) was for some time assumed to suggest greater distance. As in the case of other illusions, here, too, the illusion persists when eye movements are eliminated. Additional characteristics of the illusion set it apart from the geometric illusions described above. In its pure form, no context is involved, no contour interaction, no contrast, no suggestion of perspective, nothing to refer the two lines to except themselves, and yet judgment errs here. We experience and judge horizontal and vertical extents every day, but the illusion persists: there is no adaptation to the distorting factors. And yet it is known that the human visual system makes adjustments to very severe kinds of distortion, such as the complete inversion of the visual field. It would seem that the illusion is due to a fundamental property of perceived space itself, namely anisotropy. Space appears to have different properties in different directions. It is well known that because of the imperfections of the optics of the eye constant errors are built into the visual system. The observation of these distortions takes some effort, though, and they are not noticeable during the everyday activities that a person is engaged in. The visual system adequately compensates for these distortions. Anisotropy of space is a principle, however, which has to do with the non-Euclidean properties of behavioral space and not with the distortions due to the inadequacies of the visual system. The metric along the vertical axis of space, for instance, differs from the metric along the horizontal axis. Gestalt psychologists (Koffka, 1935, p. 275 ff.) made anisotropy of space one of their explanatory principles for visual phenomena, without explaining what it really was. Koffka stated that it had two aspects: one was that the organization of figures and things created stresses which affected the field they were in and therefore other figures and things in it. This aspect of anisotropy is equivalent to forces, force fields, and vectors in the visual field. Some of the efforts to explain geometric illusions in these terms have already been described. According to Koffka (1935, p. 275), both the Zoellner and the Jastrow illusions are due to this aspect of anisotropy. In other words, both contrast and contour interaction are subsumed under the heading of anisotropy. As a figure of speech for other, operationally definable concepts, this use of the term anisotropy may be ignored. Space as a framework, in addition, is itself anisotropic, according to Koffka. There are main directions in space and these directions exert an influence upon organization, specifically upon the organization of visual form. Attneave (1955) has supplied evidence that human observers do indeed use an imagined coordinate system when locating points in a circular field. However, while the idea of a coordinate system is clear enough, to speak of the main directions of space as exerting an influence upon visual form can be tolerated only if it is understood that "main directions" is a short-hand expression to designate the actual factor responsible for the phenomenon that, for instance, vertical lines look longer than horizontal ones.

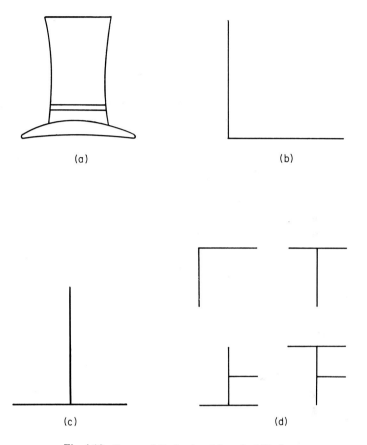

(a)   (b)

(c)   (d)

Fig. 4-18. Forms of the horizontal-vertical illusion.

Koffka, however, states outright that it is this second aspect of anisotropy itself that is responsible for the horizontal-vertical illusion, as well as a large number of other spatial phenomena that need not be mentioned here. Space, it turns out, is somehow "flattish."

Many researchers have investigated the horizontal-vertical illusion. The use of the term anisotropy may be justified in this connection in order to describe an observable behavioral fact, namely that different metrics apply to the different directions in space, if by space is meant the imagined Cartesian coordinate system in the frontoparallel plane and whose origin coincides with the point of fixation. The use of the term "space," i.e., a geometric abstraction, as if it were reality, however, is not a happy one, certainly not from the Gibsonian point of view. Nevertheless, since anisotropy is a behavioral fact, it must be explained in some fashion. Since neither the visual world nor the visual field are "flat" in the anisotropic sense, it must be some aspect of the functioning of the visual system which makes them appear so. At the present time, it is not clear which aspect it is exactly, but the recent discoveries in the area of histology of the retinas of animals point to an answer to this question. As was mentioned in Chap. 3, it is not inconceivable that even in man there may be retinal cells that respond to direction. It is just possible that the organization of the retina goes even as far as producing biases in favor of certain spatial directions.

Kuennapas has probably the largest number of publications on the horizontal-vertical illusion to his credit. In a summary of four years of investigation of this particular illusion, Kuennapas (1959b) arrives at the conclusion that the horizontal-vertical illusion is actually a composite illusion, consisting of the overestimation of the vertical and the illusion of interrupted extent (or the filled-unfilled illusion). Some of the versions of the horizontal-vertical illusion used by Kuennapas (and others) to separate the effects of orientation and interruption of extent are shown in Fig. 4-18d. The overestimation of the vertical is due, according to Kuennapas, to the anisotropy of visual space which, as Koffka had noted, is flattish or elliptical in the horizontal direction. Kuennapas predicted that, under conditions where the visual field had no clear boundary, as in complete darkness, the magnitude of the horizontal-vertical illusion would be reduced. This prediction was confirmed experimentally (Kuennapas, 1957). In another experiment (Kuennapas, 1958), it was found that, when the observer's head was in a horizontal position, the vertical was underestimated rather than overestimated, which again confirms the hypothesis about the oval shape of the visual field. No amount of optical distortion of the visual field produces an overestimation of the horizontal (Kuennapas, 1959).

A fact that was not known while the major works of the Gestalt school were being published was that the illusion is not strongest when the two lines intersect at 90 degrees. Pollack and Chapanis (1952), e.g., found that the illusion reaches a maximum when the upright line is tilted 20-30 degrees to the left instead of being perpendicular to the horizontal. Lines tilted to the right did not look as long, however, as those tilted to the left. This appears to be related to the fact that the size of objects in the nasal region of the visual field is overestimated.

When geometric figures instead of simple lines are used, the evidence for the overestimation of the vertical is not as clear. Overestimation of geometric figures with their main axes vertical has been reported by Sleight and Austin (1952), Stavrianos (1945), and Veniar (1948), while Sleight and Mowbray (1951) have reported that the horizontal dimensions of rectangles were judged longer than their actual dimensions. The estimation of the horizontal and vertical dimensions of natural objects in a natural setting (Chapanis & Mankin, 1967), however, is quite in accord with findings based on the use of only two straight lines on a piece of paper.

Spatial anisotropy is not limited to the horizontal and vertical axes of the visual field. Objects presented to one side of a fixation point are distorted in shape. The central portion of straight lines is seen as bowed-out and reduced in length (Ames, Proctor, & Ames, 1923), giving rise to the so-called "barrel distortion." This type of distortion was described very early (Helmholtz, 1924). Collier's (1931) finding was essentially the same: small forms, exposed in the periphery of the visual field, appear compressed with the major axis at right angles to the plane of the quadrant of the field. Collier was also one of the first to report a reduction in apparent size of forms seen peripherally as well as a decrease in their size with increasing eccentricity. Brown (1953) extended Collier's work, finding that objectively equal targets, when presented at the same distance away on both sides of the fixation point, did not appear equal. Brown, who called these differences "half-meridional differences," found their size to be quite substantial. Other investigators have similarly established that objects in the temporal and lower portions of the visual field appear smaller. It is for this reason that photographed objects look smaller when presented in the left portion of the visual field (Bartley & Thompson, 1959) and breaks in the Landolt ring are harder to detect (Carlson & Tinker, 1946). This aspect of anisotropy is easily demonstrated using the bisection of lines as the perceptual task. In such a task, the nasal and upper portions of the lines are made shorter than the temporal and lower portions. This finding can and has been explained in terms of misapplied constancy: since targets in the nasal and upper portions of the visual field are usually farther away from the observer (nearer the vanishing point), correction for constancy would tend to lead to an overestimation of these targets.

REFERENCES

Allport, F. H. *Theories of perception and the concept of structure.* New York: Wiley, 1955.
Ames, A. J., Proctor, C. A., & Ames, B. Vision and the techniques of art. *Proc. Amer. Acad. Arts Sci.,* 1923, **58**, 36.
Ammons, R., Ammons, C., Dubbe, A., Techida, A., & Preuninger, C. Preliminary report of studies of perspective and figure-ground reversals as learned responses to depth perception. *Proc. Montana Acad. Sci.,* 1958, **18**, 81.
Attneave, F. Perception of place in a circular field. *Amer. J. Psychol.,* 1955, **68**, 69-82.
Azuna, H. [The effect of experience on the amount of the Mueller-Lyer illusion.] *Jap. J. Psychol.,* 1952, **22**, 111-123.
Baldwin, J. M. An optical illusion. *Science,* 1896, **4**, 774.
Balser, M. Untersuchungen zu Kristofs Zweikomponententheorie der geometrischoptischen Taeuschungen. *Arch. ges. Psychol.,* 1963, **115**, 307-329.
Bartley, S. H., & Thompson, R. A further study of horizontal symmetry in the perception of pictures. *Percept. mot. Skills,* 1959, **9**, 135-138.

Battro, A. M., & Fraisse, P. Y a-t-il une relation entre la capacité d'appréhension visuelle et les mouvements des yeux? *Année Psychol.*, 1961, **61**, 313-324.

Berliner, A., & Berliner, S. The distortion of straight and curved lines in geometrical fields. *Amer. J. Psychol.*, 1948,**61**, 153-166.

Boring, E. G. *Sensation and perception in the history of experimental psychology.* New York: Appleton, 1942.

Boring E. G. *A history of experimental psychology.* New York: Appleton, 1950.

Boring, E. G. Letter to editor. *Sci. Amer.*, 1961, **204**(6), 18-19.

Botha, E. Past experience and figure-ground perception. *Percept. mot. Skills.*, 1963, **16**, 283-288. (a)

Botha, E. Practice without reward and figure-ground perception of adults and children. *Percept. mot. Skills*, 1963, **16**, 271-273. (b)

Braly, K. W. The influence of past experience in visual perception. *J. exp. Psychol.*, 1933, **16**, 613-643.

Brown, J. F., & Voth, A. C. The path of seen movement as a function of the vector field. *Amer. J. Psychol.*, 1937, **49**, 543-563.

Brown, K. T. Factors affecting differences in apparent size between opposite halves of a visual meridian. *J. Opt. Soc. Amer.*, 1953, **43**, 464-472.

Carlson, Julia A. Effect of instructions and perspective-drawing ability on perceptual constancies and geometrical illusions. *J. exp. Psychol.*, 1966, **72**, 874-879.

Carlson, W. S., & Tinker, M. A. Visual reaction-time as a function of variations in the stimulus-figure. *Amer. J. Psychol.*, 1946, **59**, 450-457.

Cesarec, Z. Figure-ground reversal as related to stimulus exposure, observation time, and some personality dimensions. *Psychol. Res. Bull.*, 1963, **3**(5), 1-17.

Chapanis, A., & Mankin, D. A. The horizontal-vertical illusion in a visually-rich environment. *Percept. Psychophys.*, 1967, **2**, 249-255.

Chiang, C. A new theory to explain geometrical illusions produced by crossing lines. *Percept. Psychophys.*, 1968, **3**, 174-176.

Cleary, A. A binocular parallax theory of the geometric illusions. *Psychon. Sci.*, 1966, **5**, 241-242.

Clement, D. E. Uncertainty and latency of verbal naming responses as correlates of pattern goodness. *J. Verb. Lrng. Verb. Behav.*, 1964, **3**, 150-157.

Collier, R. M. An experimental study of form perception in indirect vision. *J. comp. Psychol.*, 1931, **11**, 281-289.

Cornwell, H. G. Prior experience as a determinant of figure-ground organization. *J. exp. Psychol.*, 1963, **65**, 156-162.

Cowan, R. F., & Bliss, W. D. Resistance to distortion as a metric for pattern goodness. *Psychon. Sci.*, 1967, **9**, 481-482.

Craik, K. J. W., & Zangwill, O. L. Observations relating to the threshold of a small figure within the contour of a closed-line figure. *Brit. J. Psychol.*, 1939-40, **30**, 139-149.

Crowley, M. E. A puzzle-picture in silhouette. *Amer. J. Psychol.*, 1952, **65**, 302-304.

Day, R. H. On the steroscopic observation of geometric illusions. *Percept. mot. Skills.*, 1961, **13**, 247-258.

Day, R. H. The effect of repeated trails and prolonged fixation on error in the Mueller-Lyer figure. *Psychol. Monogr.*, 1962, **76**, (14, Whole No. 533).

Delboeuf, J. L. Sur une nouvelle illusion d'optique. *Bull. Acad. Roy. Belg.*, 1893, **24**, 545-558.

Djang, S. The role of past experience in the visual perception of masked forms. *J. exp. Psychol.*, 1937, **20**, 29-59.

Dreistadt, R. The effect of figural after-effects on geometrical illusions. *J. Psychol.*, 1968, **69**, 63-73.

Dutton, M. B., & Traill, P. M. A repetition of Rubin's figure-ground experiment. *Brit. J. Psychol.*, 1933, **23**, 389-400.

Ehrenstein, W. Versuche ueber die Beziehungen zwischen Bewegungs- und Gestaltwahrnehmung. *Z. Psychol.*, 1924, **95**, 305-352.

Elkind, D., & Scott, L. Studies in perceptual development: I. The decentering of perception. *Child Develop.*, 1962, **33**, 619-630.

Epstein, W. *Varieties of perceptual learning.* New York: McGraw-Hill, 1967.

Epstein, W., & Rock, I. Perceptual set as an artifact of recency. *Amer. J. Psychol.*, 1960, **73**, 214-228.

Festinger, L., White, C. W., & Allyn, M. R. Eye movements and decrement in the Mueller-Lyer illusion. *Percept. Psychophys.*, 1968, **3**, 376-382.

Fisher, G. H. Preparation of ambiguous stimulus materials. *Percept. Psychophys.*, 1967, **2**, 421-422.

Fisher, G. H. Gradients of distortion seen in the context of the Ponzo illusion and other contours. *Quart. J. exp. Psychol.*, 1968, **20**, 212-217.

Francès, R. L'apprentisage de la segregation perceptive. *Psychol. Franç.*, 1963, **8**, 16-27.

Fraser, J. A new visual illusion of direction. *Brit. J. Psychol.*, 1908, **2**, 297-320.

Fry, G. A., & Robertson, V. M. The physiological basis of the periodic merging of area into background. *Amer. J. Psychol.*, 1935, **47**, 644-655.

Fuchs, W. Untersuchungen ueber das Sehen der Hemianopiker und Hemiamblyopiker: I: Verlagerungserscheinungen. *Z. Psychol.*, 1920, **84**, 67-169.

Fuchs, W. Untersuchungen ueber das Sehen der Hemianopiker und Hemiamblyopiker. II: Die totalisierende Gestaltauffassung. *Z. Psychol.*, 1921, **86**, 1-143.

Fuchs, W. Eine Pseudofovea bei Hemianopikern. *Psychol. Forsch.*, 1922, **1**, 157-186.

Fuchs, W. Experimentelle Untersuchungen ueber das Hintereinandersehen auf derselben Sehrichtung. *Z. Psychol.*, 1923, **91**, 145-235.

Ganz, L., & Wilson, P. D. Innate generalization of a form discrimination without contouring eye movements. *J. comp. physiol. Psychol.*, 1967, **63**, 258-269.

Gatti, A. Di alcune nuove illusioni ottiche in rapporto alla percezione dei complessi rapprasentativi. *Arch. Ital. Psicol.*, 1926, **4**, 208-225.

Gelb, A., & Goldstein, K. *Psychologische Analysen hirnpathologischer Faelle.* Leipzig: 1920.

Gelb, A., & Granit, R. Farbenpsychologische Untersuchungen: I. Die Bedeutung von "Figur" und "Grund" fuer die Farbenschwelle. *Z. Psychol.*, 1923, **93**, 83-118.

Gibson, J. J. Adaptation with negative after-effect. *Psychol. Rev.*, 1937, **44**, 222-244.

Gibson, J. J. *The perception of the visual world.* Boston, Massachusetts: Houghton, 1950.

Gibson, J. J. What is form? *Psychol. Rev.*, 1951, **58**, 403-412.

Gibson, J. J. *The senses considered as perceptual systems.* Boston, Massachusetts: Houghton, 1966.

Gibson, J. J., & Gibson, Eleanor J. Continuous perspective transformations and the perception of rigid motion. *J. exp. Psychol.*, 1957, **54**, 129-138.

Goldstein, A. G., & Chance, J. E. Effects of practice on sex-related differences in performance on Embedded Figures. *Psychon. Sci.*, 1965, **3**, 361-362.

Gottschaldt, K. Ueber den Einfluss der Erfahrung auf die Wahrnehmung von Figuren. *Psychol. Forsch.*, 1926, **8**, 261-317.

Gottschaldt, K. Ueber den Einfluss der Erfahrung auf die Wahrnehmung von Figuren. II. Vergleichende Untersuchungen ueber die Wirkung figuraler Einpraegung und den Einfluss spezifischer Geschehensverlaeufe auf die Auffassung optischer Komplexe. *Psychol. Forsch.*, 1929, **12**, 1-87.

Granit, R. Die Bedeutung von Figur und Grund fuer bei unveraenderter Schwarz-Induktion bestimmte Helligkeitsschwellen. *Skand. Arch. Physiol.*, 1924, 43-57.

Gregor, A. J., & McPherson, D. A. A study of susceptibility to geometric illusion among cultural subgroups of Australian aborigines. *Psychologia Africana*, 1965, 11, 1-13.

Gregory, R. L. Distortion of visual space as inappropriate constancy scaling. *Nature*, 1963, 199, 678-680.

Gregory, R. L. Inappropriate constancy explanation of spatial distortions. *Nature*, 1965, 207, 891-893.

Gregory, R. L. *Eye and brain.* New York: McGraw-Hill, 1966.

Gregory, R. L., & Wallace, J. G. Recovery from early blindness. *Exp. Psychol. Soc. Monogr.*, 1963, No. 2.

Hake, H. W. Contributions of psychology to the study of pattern vision. *WADC Tech. Rep.* 57-621, 1957.

Hamilton, V. Susceptibility to the Mueller-Lyer illusion and its relationship to differences in size constancy. *Quart. J. exp. Psychol.*, 1966, 18, 63-72.

Hanawalt, N. G. The effect of practice upon the perception of simple designs masked by more complex designs. *J. exp. Psychol.*, 1942, 31, 134-148.

Hebb, D. O. The innate organization of visual activity: I. Perception of figures by rats reared in total darkness. *J. genet. Psychol.*, 1937, 51, 101-126.

Hebb, D. O. *The organization of behavior.* New York: Wiley, 1949.

Hebb, D. O. A neuropsychological theory. In S. Koch (Ed.), *Psychology: A study of a science.* Vol. I. New York: McGraw-Hill, 1959. Pp. 622-643.

Helmholtz, H. von. *Handbuch der physiologischen Optik.* Leipzig: Voss, 1867.

Helmholtz, H. von. *Physiological optics.* Rochester, New York: Optical Soc. Amer., 1924-25.

Helson, H. The fundamental propositions of Gestalt psychology. *Psychol. Rev.*, 1933, 40, 13-32.

Helson, H., & Fehrer, E. V. The role of form in perception. *Amer. J. Psychol.*, 1932, 44, 79-102.

Henle, M. An experimental investigation of past experience as a determinant of visual form perception. *J. exp. Psychol.*, 1942, 30, 1-22.

Hering, E. *Beitraege zur Physiologie.* I. Leipzig: Engelmann, 1861.

Hicks, G. D., & Rivers, W. H. R. The illusion of compared horizontal and vertical lines. *Brit. J. Psychol.*, 1908, 2, 243-260.

Hochberg, J. E. Figure-ground reversal as a function of visual satiation. *J. exp. Psychol.*, 1950, 40, 682-686.

Hochberg, J. E. In the mind's eye. In R. N. Haber (Ed.), *Contemporary theory and research in visual perception.* New York: Holt, 1968. Pp. 309-331

Hochberg, J. E., & McAlister, E. A quantitative approach to figural "goodness." *J. exp. Psychol.*, 1953, 46, 361-364.

Hochberg, J. E., & Brooks, Virginia. The psychophysics of form: Reversible-perspective drawings of spatial objects. *Amer. J. Psychol.*, 1960, 73, 337-354.

Hoffmann, F. B., & Bielschowsky, A. Ueber die Einstellung der scheinbaren Horizontalen und Vertikalen bei Betrachtung eines von schraegen Konturen erfuellten Gesichtsfeldes. *Pflueg. Arch. ges. Physiol.*, 1909, 126, 453-475.

James, W. *The principles of psychology.* New York: Holt, 1890. (Republished: New York: Dover, 1950.)

Jastrow, J., & West, H. A study of Zoellner's figures and other related illusions. *Amer. J. Psychol.*, 1892, 4, 382-398.

Judd, C. H. Practice and its effects on the perception of illusions. *Psychol. Rev.*, 1902, 9, 27-39.

Kaneko, T., & Obonai, T. [Factors of intensity, quantity, and distance in psychophysiological induction.] *Jap. J. Psychol.*, 1952, 23, 73-79.

Kleitman, N., & Blier, Z. A. Color and form discrimination in the periphery of the retina. *Amer. J. Physiol.*, 1928, **85**, 178-190.

Koehler, W. *Die physischen Gestalten in Ruhe und im stationaeren Zustand.* Erlangen: Philosophische Akademie, 1920.

Koehler, W. *Gestalt psychology.* New York: Liveright, 1929.

Koehler, W., & Fishback, Julia. The destruction of the Mueller-Lyer illusion in repeated trials: I. An examination of two theories. *J. exp. Psychol.*, 1950, **40**, 267-281. (a)

Koehler, W., & Fishback, Julia. The destruction of the Mueller-Lyer illusion in repeated trials: II. Satiation patterns and memory traces. *J. exp. Psychol.*, 1950, **40**, 398-410. (b)

Koehler, W., & Held, R. The cortical correlate of pattern vision. *Science*, 1949, **110**, 414-419.

Koehler, W., & Wallach, H. Figural after-effects: An investigation of visual processes. *Proc. Amer. Phil. Assoc.*, 1944, **88**, 269-357.

Koffka, K. *The growth of mind.* New York: Harcourt, Brace, 1927.

Koffka, K. *Principles of Gestalt psychology.* New York: Harcourt, Brace, 1935.

Kopfermann, H. Psychologische Untersuchungen ueber die Wirkung zweidimensionaler Darstellungen Koerperlicher Gebilde. *Psychol. Forsch.*, 1930, **13**, 293-364.

Kristof, W. Ueber die Einordnung geometrisch-optischer Taeuschungen in die Gesetzmaesigkeiten der visuellen Wahrnehmung. Teil I. *Arch. ges. Psychol.*, 1961, **113**, 1-48.

Kristof, W. Eine Faktorenanalyse geometrisch-optischer Taeuschungen. *Z. exp. u. ang. Psychol.*, 1963, **10**, 583-596.

Kuennapas, T. M. The vertical-horizontal illusion and the visual field. *J. exp. Psychol.*, 1957, **53**, 405-407.

Kuennapas, T. M. Influence of head inclination on the vertical-horizontal illusion. *J. Psychol.*, 1958, **46**, 179-185.

Kuennapas, T. M. The vertical-horizontal illusion in artificial visual fields. *J. Psychol.*, 1959, **47**, 41-48. (a)

Kuennapas, T. M. *Visual field as a frame of reference: With special regard to the vertical-horizontal illusion.* Uppsala: Almquist & Wiksell, 1959. (b)

Kuennapas, T. M. Measurement of the intensity of an underlying figural process: A methodological study. *Scand. J. Psychol.*, 1961, **2**, 174-184.

Lashley, K. S. Patterns of cerebral integration indicated by the scotomas of migraine. *Arch. Neurol. Psychiat.*, 1941, **46**, 331-339.

Lashley, K. S., Chow, K. L., & Semmes, J. An examination of the electrical field theory of cerebral integration. *Psychol. Rev.*, 1951, **58**, 123-136.

Leeper, R. A study of a neglected portion of the field of learning–the development of sensory organization. *J. genet. Psychol.*, 1935, **46**, 42-75.

Lehmann, G. Die Analyse geometrisch-optischer Taeuschungen durch Vektorfelder. *Z. exp. u. angew. Psychol.*, 1967, **14**, 442-462.

Levine, J. Studies in the interrelations of central nervous structures in binocular vision: I. The lack of bilateral transfer of visual discriminative habits acquired monocularly by the pigeon. *J. genet. Psychol.*, 1945, **67**, 105-129. (a)

Levine, J. Studies in the interrelations of central nervous structures in binocular vision: II. The conditions under which interocular transfer of discriminative habits takes place in the pigeon. *J. genet. Psychol.*, 1945, **67**, 131-142. (b)

Lewis, E. O. The effect of practice on the perception of the Mueller-Lyer illusion. *Brit. J. Psychol.*, 1908, **2**, 294-306.

Liebmann, S. Ueber das Verhalten farbiger Formen bei Helligkeitsgleichheit von Figur und Grund. *Psychol. Forsch.*, 1927, **9** 300-353.

Lipps, T. Aesthetische Faktoren der Raumanschauung. *Helmholtz-Festschrift*, 1891, p. 217.

Marshall, W. H., & Talbot, S. A. Recent evidence for neural mechanisms in vision leading to a general theory of sensory acuity. In J. Cattell (Ed.), *Biological Symposia.* Vol. VII: Visual mechanisms, edited by Heinrich Kluever. Copyright 1942 The Ronald Press Company, New York. Pp. 117-164.

McDougall, W. Some new observations in support of Thomas Young's theory of light and colour-vision. *Mind,* 1901, **10**, 52-97, 210-245, 347-382.

McFarland, J. H. The effect of different sequences of part presentation on perception of a form's parts as simultaneous. *Proc. 73rd Ann. Conv. Amer. Psychol. Assoc.,* 1965, 43-44. (a)

McFarland, J. H. Sequential part presentation: A method of studying visual form perception. *Brit. J. Psychol.,* 1965, **56**, 439-446. (b)

Metzger, W. Optische Untersuchungen am Ganzfeld. II. Zur Phaenomenologie des homogenen Ganzfelds. *Psychol. Forsch.,* 1930, **13**, 6-29.

Mooney, C. M. Closure as affected by viewing time and multiple visual fixations. *Can. J. Psychol.,* 1957, **11**, 21-29.

Mooney, C. M. Recognition of novel visual configurations with and without eye movements. *J. exp. Psychol.,* 1958, **56**, 133-138.

Mooney, C. M. Recognition of symmetrical and non-symmetrical ink-blots with and without eye movements. *Can. J. Psychol.,* 1959, **13**, 11-19.

Mooney, C. M. Recognition of ambiguous and unambiguous visual configurations with short and longer exposures. *Brit. J. Psychol.,* 1960, **51**, 119-125.

Motokawa, K. Field of retinal induction and optical illusion. *J. Neurophysiol.,* 1950, **13**, 413-426.

Mountjoy, P. T. Spontaneous recovery following response decrement to the Mueller-Lyer illusion. *J. Sci. Labs. Denison Univ.,* 1957-58, **44**, 229-238.

Mountjoy, P. T. The effect of exposure time and intertrial interval upon rates of decrement in the Mueller-Lyer illusion. Unpublished doctoral dissertation, Denison Univ., 1958.

Mountjoy, P. T. Mueller-Lyer decrement as a function of number of adjustment trials and configurations of the illusion figure. *Psychol. Rec.,* 1963, **13**, 471-481.

Mountjoy, P. T. Effects of self-instruction, information, and misinformation upon decrement to the Mueller-Lyer figure. *Psychol. Rec.,* 1965, **15**, 7-14.

Mueller-Lyer, F. C. Optische Urteilstaeuschungen. *Arch. Physiol., Suppl. Ed.,* 1889, 263-270.

Ogasawara, J. Motokawa's induction-field theory and form perception. *Psychologia,* 1958, **1**, 182-183.

Ohkawa, N. [The effect of various figures upon critical fusion frequency, of a flickering small patch.] *Jap. Psychol. Res.,* 1954, No. 1.

Ohwaki, S. On the destruction of geometrical illusions in steroscopic observation. *Tohoku Psychologica Folia,* 1960, **19**, 30-36.

Oppel, J. J. Ueber geometrisch-optische Taeuschungen. *Jber. phys. Ver. Frankfurt,* 1854-55, 37-47.

Orbison, W. D. Shape as a function of the vector field. *Amer. J. Psychol.,* 1939, **52**, 31-45. (a)

Orbison, W. D. The correction of an omission in *Shape as a Function of the Vector-Field. Amer. J. Psychol.,* 1939, **52**, 309. (b)

Over, R. Explanations of geometrical illusions. *Psychol. Bull.,* 1968, **70**, 545-562.

Parker, Nora L., & Newbigging, P. L. Magnitude and decrement of the Mueller-Lyer illusion as a function of pre-training. *Can. J. Psychol.,* 1963, **17**, 134-140.

Parks, A. Post-retinal visual storage. *Amer. J. Psychol.,* 1965, **78**, 145-147.

Pauli, R. Eine neue geometrisch-optische Taeuschung (Sektorentaeuschung). *Arch. ges. Psychol.,* 1939, **103**, 151-159.

Piaget, J. *Les mécanismes perceptifs.* Paris: Presses Universitaires de France, 1961.

Piaget, J. Le dévelopement des perceptions en fonction de l'âge. In J. Piaget, P. Fraisse, E. Vurpillot, & R. Francès, *Traité de psychologie expérimentale.* Paris: Presses Universitaires de France, 1967. Pp. 1-62.

Piaget, J., Vinh-Bang, & Matalon, B. Note on the law of the temporal maximum of some optico-geometric illusions. *Amer. J. Psychol.,* 1958, 71, 277-282.

Pollack, W. T., & Chapanis, A. The apparent length of a line as a function of its inclination. *Quart. J. exp. Psychol.,* 1952, 4, 170-178.

Ponzo, M. Rapports de contraste angulaire et l'appreciation de grandeur des astres a l'horizon. *Arch. Ital. Biol.,* 1912, 58, 327-329.

Poppelreuther, W. Zur Psychologie der optischen Wahrnehmung. *Z. ges. Neurol. Psychiatrie,* 1923, 83, 26.

Porter, E. L. H. Factors in the fluctuation of fifteen ambiguous phenomena. *Psychol. Record.,* 1938, 2, 231-253.

Postman, L., & Bruner, J. S. Hypothesis and the principle of closure: the effect of frequency and recency. *J. Psychol.,* 1952, 33, 113-125.

Pressey, A. W. A theory of the Mueller-Lyer illusion. *Percept. mot. Skills,* 1967, 25, 569-572.

Pritchard, R. M. Visual illusions viewed as stabilized retinal images. *Quart. J. exp. Psychol.,* 1958, 10, 77-81.

Pritchard, R. M. Stabilized images on the retina. *Sci. Amer.,* 1961, 204(6), 72-77.

Riesen, A. H. The development of visual perception in man and chimpanzee. *Science,* 1947, 106, 107-108.

Ritter, S. M. The vertical-horizontal illusion; an experimental study of meridional disparities in the visual field. *Psychol. Monogr.,* 1917, 23, (4, Whole No. 101).

Rivers, W. H. R. Introduction and vision. In A. C. Haddon, (Ed.), *Reports of the Cambridge anthropological expedition to the Torres Straits.* Vol. II, Pt. I. London and New York: Cambridge Univ. Press, 1901. (a)

Rivers, W. H. R. Primitive color vision. *Pop. Sci. Monthly,* 1901, 59, 44-58. (b)

Rivers, W. H. R. Observations on the senses of the Todas. *Brit. J. Psychol.,* 1905, 1, 321-396.

Rock, I., & Kremen, I. A re-examination of Rubin's figural aftereffect. *J. exp. Psychol.,* 1957, 53, 23-30.

Rothschild, H. Ueber den Einfluss der Gestalt auf das negative Nachbild ruhender visueller Figuren. *Arch. Ophthalmol.,* 1923, 112, 1-128.

Rubin, E. *Visuell wahrgenommene Figuren.* Kobenhavn: Gyldendalske Boghandel, 1921.

Rush, G. P. Visual grouping in relation to age. *Arch. Psychol.,* 1937, No. 217.

Schafer, R., & Murphy, G. The role of autism in a visual figure-ground relationship. *J. exp. Psychol.,* 1943, 32, 335-343.

Schiller, P., & Wiener, M. Binocular and stereoscopic viewing of geometric illusions. *Percept. mot. Skills,* 1962, 15, 739-747.

Schwartz, C. B. Visual discrimination of camouflaged figures. Unpublished doctoral dissertation, Univ. of California at Berkeley, 1961.

Segall, M. H., Campbell, D. T., & Herskovits, M. J. *The influence of culture on visual perception.* Indianapolis, Indiana: Bobbs-Merrill, 1966.

Senden, M. von. *Raum- und Gestaltauffassung bei operierten Blindgeborenen vor und nach der Operation.* Leipzig: Barth, 1932.

Shroff, E. Ueber Gestaltauffassung bei Kindern im Alter von 6 bis 14 Jahren. *Psychol. Forsch.,* 1928-29, 11-12, 235-267.

Sickles, W. R. Experimental evidence for the electrical character of visual fields derived from a quantitative analysis of the Ponzo illusion. *J. exp. Psychol.*, 1942, **30**, 84-91.

Sleight, R. B., & Mowbray, G. H. Discriminability between geometric figures under complex conditions. *J. Psychol.*, 1951, **31**, 121-127.

Sleight, R. B., & Austin, T. R. The horizontal-vertical illusion in plane geometric figures. *J. Psychol.*, 1952, **33**, 279-287.

Solley, C. M., & Murphy, G. *Development of the perceptual world.* New York: Basic Books, 1960.

Springbett, B. M. Some stereoscopic phenomena and their implications. *Brit. J. Psychol.*, 1961, **52**, 105-109.

Stavrianos, B. K. Relation of shape perception to explicit judgments of inclination. *Arch. Psychol.*, 1945, **42**, 1-94.

Tausch, R. Optische Taeuschungen als artifizielle Effekte der Gestaltungsprozesse von Groessen- und Formenkonstanz in der natuerlichen Raumwahrnehmung. *Psychol. Forsch.*, 1954, **24**, 299-348.

Tees, R. C. The role of field effects in visual perception. *Undergrad. Res. Proj. in Psychol.*, *McGill Univ.*, 1961, **3**, 87-96.

Thiery, A. Ueber geometrisch-optische Taeuschungen. *Phil. Stud.*, 1895, **11**, 307-370.

Thiery, A. Ueber geometrisch-optische Taeuschungen. *Phil. Stud.*, 1896, **12**, 67-126.

Titchener, E. B. *Experimental psychology.* Vol. 1, Pts. 1 & 2. New York: Macmillan, 1901.

Usnadze, D. Gruppenbildungsversuche bei vorschulpflichtigen Kindern. *Arch. ges. Psychol.*, 1929, **73**, 216-248.

Veniar, F. A. Difference thresholds for shape distortion of geometrical squares. *J. Psychol.*, 1948, **26**, 461-476.

Vetter, R. J. Perception of ambiguous figure-ground patterns as a function of past experience. *Percept. mot. Skills*, 1965, **20**, 183-188.

Warrington, Elizabeth K. The effect of stimulus configuration on the incidence of the completion phenomenon. *Brit. J. Psychol.*, 1965, **56**, 447-454.

Witkin, H. A., Lewis, H. B., Hertzman, M., Machover, K., Meissner, P. B., & Wapner, S. *Personality through perception.* New York: Harper, 1954.

Woodworth, R. S., & Schlosberg, H. *Experimental psychology.* New York: Holt, 1954.

Wundt, W. *Beitraege zur Theorie der Sinneswahrnehmungen.* Leipzig: Winter, 1862.

Wundt, W. Die geometrisch-optischen Taeuschungen. *Abh. saechs. Ges. Wiss., Math.-phys. Cl.*, 1898, **24**, 53-178.

Yakose, Z. The law of the "field" in visual form perception (I). A theoretical formula to seek the field strength of the form and its experimental proof. *Jap. Psychol. Res.*, 1954, No. 1, 55-64.

Yakose, Z., & Uchiyama, M. [The measurement of the field forces in visual perception.] *Jap. J. Psychol.*, 1952, **22**, 41-56.

Zigler, M. J., Cook, B., Miller, D., & Wemple, L. The perception of form in peripheral vision. *Amer. J. Psychol.*, 1930, **42**, 246-259.

Zoellner, F. Ueber eine neue Art von Pseudoskopie und ihre Beziehungen zu den von Plateau und Oppel beschriebenen Bewegungsphaenomenen. *Ann. Phys. Chem.*, 1860, **186**, 500-520.

Zusne, L. Visual illusions: publication trends. *Percept. mot. Skills*, 1968, **27**, 175-177.

Zusne, L., & Michels, K. M. Nonrepresentational shapes and eye movements. *Percept. mot. Skills*, 1964, **18**, 11-20.

Chapter 5 / VARIABLES OF THE DISTAL STIMULUS

The form of a two-dimensional stimulus object may be considered either a one-dimensional or a multidimensional attribute. Form remains invariant under transformations of area and the symmetry operations of rotation, reflection, and translation. It is also usually perceived as a whole rather than in terms of its separate aspects or dimensions, so that it may be considered a one-dimensional variable, along with color and movement. On the other hand, form does present, upon closer examination, many different aspects or dimensions. When these change, form changes. Any form may be made into any other form by introducing gradual changes in its contour. These changes are changes in complexity, linearity of the contour, angularity or compactness, symmetry, and elongation. It is possible to vary these dimensions independently, but not always, because they are interrelated. The degree of correlation depends on the dimensions being considered and the characteristics of the population of shapes of which the shapes under consideration are a sample.

Thus, form may be considered both a one-dimensional emergent of its physical dimensions and a multidimensional variable. Although the idea is a simple one, it was not explicitly stated until the late 1950s. The effect of this failure to realize the nature of the physical form was that the results of experiments performed before 1950 or so could not be generalized to anything but the exact stimuli employed in these experiments. In a typical experiment, visual stimuli were said to vary along the dimension of form, yet every stimulus was so different from every other that each was actually a representative of a different stimulus domain. In 1956, Attneave and Arnoult laid the groundwork for wider generalization from stimulus samples to populations. The relationship between stimulus sampling and stimulus parameters was not spelled out until the late 1960s (Brown & Michels, 1966; Brown & Owen, 1967).

Until the early 1950s, the situation was further aggravated by the almost complete absence of any physical form measures. A psychophysics of form presupposes both the ability to identify form dimensions and the ability to measure them. The definition of form as a stimulus began in the 1950s under the influence of information theory. Its impetus has carried the quantification of form beyond the limits of information measurement, producing a veritable plethora of physical form measures. Only lately have attempts been made to reduce them to a smaller number and to relate them to some theory.

1. Types of Experimental Forms and Their Construction

A. GEOMETRIC AND OTHER ARBITRARILY CONSTRAINED FORMS

Before 1956, when Attneave and Arnoult proposed methods for constructing "random" shapes, "geometric" shapes were the most widely used type of stimuli in form-perception experiments. Since these shapes are commonly found in geometry texts, it has been somehow assumed that they belong together, constituting a well-defined taxonomic unit. If one compares a sample of geometric shapes with a sample of random shapes, it indeed appears that these are two distinct populations of shapes. The physical characteristics that would define all geometric shapes, however, are somewhat elusive. It is possible, for instance, to go from a strictly geometric form to one that is not by changing the former by very small steps, such as decreasing one of the four 90-degree angles in a square by steps of 1 degree or even 30 minutes. When a systematic sample of such transformations of the square or of the regular pentagon is presented to subjects for rating on a scale of "geometricity" (Zusne & Michels, 1962a, 1962b), the sample may be seen consisting of two independent samples: all bilaterally symmetric shapes are judged to be more geometric than asymmetric shapes. This result cannot be predicted on the basis of physical measures taken on the forms. However, the ratings of the asymmetric shapes can be well predicted on the basis of a weighted sum of the measures of asymmetry, compactness, and elongation, the extreme values of which determine the two ends of the continuum of geometricity. Thus, while any rectilinear polygon, symmetric or asymmetric, may occasionally be called "geometric," linguistic convention more often reserves the term for those shapes that represent the very end of this continuum. At this end point, shapes have either 90-degree angles or angles of equal size, and the shapes are symmetric at least about one axis. Even here, there appears to be a hierarchical ordering of shapes. For instance, symmetric four-sided shapes are ranked from most to least geometric as follows: the square, rectangles, diamonds and parallelograms, and other bilaterally symmetric shapes.

While shapes differing only in complexity have not been rated on geometricity, regular (geometric) and irregular (random) polygons differ radically in appearance as the number of sides is increased. If the polygon is irregular, increasing the number of sides from three, which is the minimum number of sides necessary to enclose an area, to some very large number will lead from the equilateral triangle, through the square, the regular pentagon, etc.

to the circle. The triangle and the circle, while quite different in other respects, are actually not too different in complexity. As a matter of fact, the circle is simpler than the triangle. If we start with an irregular triangle, however, adding sides of random lengths would keep increasing the complexity of the polygon almost indefinitely. If the area of the polygon is fixed, at least, the sides of the irregular polygon, while short, will be clearly perceptible, while those of the regular polygon will have long merged into the continuous contour of a circle.

In a typical form-perception experiment of the past, the usual series of geometric shapes employed as stimuli has consisted of something like the equilateral triangle, the square, perhaps a rectangle or a trapezoid, a regular pentagon, a six-pointed star, a cross, the circle, and the ellipse. Each shape in such a series represents not only a different level of complexity, but also a different form of regularity, different degrees of compactness, and different types and degrees of symmetry. The only communality that could be attributed to these shapes would be redundancy, but this is not a simple, unitary concept either (see the section on redundancy in this chapter). Since the size of the sample of geometric shapes has been usually limited to a dozen or less, it cannot be said that the results of an experiment in which they are used may be generalized even to other redundant figures. In fact, the results can be generalized only to other identical samples or samples showing very limited variation upon the prototypes.

Thus, stimulus generalizability in a large portion of the older experimental literature on form perception has been extremely limited. What has been said about geometric forms applies to a large extent to any other sample of shapes that, while arbitrarily constructed, show a high degree of redundancy—generalization from such stimuli to other stimuli is always difficult, sometimes impossible, and always suspect. It is for this reason that the methods of stimulus construction described in the following sections were proposed. Using these methods, samples of forms may be constructed that are representative of large populations of forms. For this reason, results obtained from experiments in which samples of forms so constructed are used may be generalized to these populations. The degree to which any sample represents any population of forms depends, of course, on the particular method of construction used. Since the number of different two-dimensional shapes is practically infinite, any finite set of rules will produce samples that represent only larger or smaller subpopulations or domains of shapes. There is no truly random sample of shape in general, only random samples of particular types, populations, subpopulations, or domains of shapes.

B. RANDOM SHAPES: METHOD 1

In one respect, the methods for constructing random shapes proposed by Attneave and Arnoult (1956) have had the same significance for form-perception studies as Ebbinghaus' nonsense syllables have had for the study of verbal learning. Because randomly constructed forms are shorn of meaning (although not totally, just as Ebbinghaus' syllables are not), they do not offer differential advantages to subjects depending on each subject's previous experience with forms. The basic idea, namely that of stimulus sampling or situation sampling, originated with Egon Brunswik. To obtain "ecological validity" in form-perception experiments, Attneave and Arnoult proposed a number of methods for generating samples of forms whose statistical characteristics would be representative of the statistical parameters of the parent population of stimuli or stimulus domain. Basic to all of these methods is the use of tables of random numbers in the selection of points to be connected to form the contours of a shape.

Method 1 of Attneave and Arnoult is the most commonly used method. The rules of method 1 (Attneave & Arnoult, 1956, pp. 454-455) are as follows. A square grid of, say, 100×100 cells is used. The complexity level (number of points of inflection) of the shape is determined beforehand. The location of the points to be used as vertices is determined by entering a table of random numbers and selecting pairs of numbers having values of between 00 and 99. After plotting the points, they are connected with a ruler. First, the most peripheral points are connected to each other to form a polygon with convex angles only. Almost invariably, this will leave some of the points unconnected and inside the polygon. A check is now made for unconnected points that are very close to the contour of the polygon. Points which are at some arbitrarily determined small distance from the contour are included in the contour even though this produces a shallow concave angle, as, for instance, the point between sides 2 and 3 in Fig. 5-1a. While this procedure introduces an amount of uncertainty, it prevents the possibility that the shape might be divided into two halves later. The sides of the polygon are then assigned numbers, as are unconnected points. Which point will be connected to which side is then determined by using a table of random numbers. Since the polygon must remain whole and no two connecting lines may cross (thus forming more points of inflection than originally plotted), the number of remaining possibilities, after the first choice has been made, is automatically restricted. This is evident in Fig. 5-1b. If several possibilities of connection still remain, random pairing of points and sides is again resorted to until for any point only one possible side remains to which it may be connected. As the polygon acquires new sides, these are also numbered, so that an unconnected point will find itself opposite some numbered side at all times.

The amount of work involved in the construction of fairly large samples (50 or more) of random polygons having six sides or more is considerable. It is possible to have a computer do all the work, beginning with the selection of

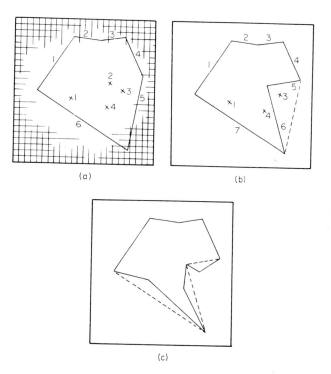

Fig. 5-1. Stages in the construction of a random shape according to method 1 of Attneave and Arnoult (1956).

pairs of random numbers through the final step of printing out the actual contours of the finished shape. A program for the construction of random shapes has been written, for instance, by Brown and Owen (1967). Using this program, even a digital computer needs relatively huge (for a computer) amounts of time to design a shape. Because of the cost factor, Brown has returned to the use of student assistants who, as he calculates, construct shapes at the average cost of only 17 cents per shape.

Knoll and Stenson (1968) made a considerable advance by writing a program which not only constructs more interesting forms (method 4 of Attneave and Arnoult, which involves both straight-line segments and arcs of a circle), but also computes 20 important physical form parameters and four sets of descriptors sufficient to draw the form. Since some of the measures are moments of area, manual computation of these would involve prohibitive amounts of time. The

IBM 7044/7094 system, however, constructs and measures 82 forms, starting with about 19 points, at the rate of approximately 63 sec. per form. While the cost per form is measurable not in cents but dollars, it still represents tremendous savings in time as compared with the manual method.

C. RANDOM SHAPES: METHOD 2

This method was also originated by Attneave and Arnoult (1956). It represents a variation on method 1. Here, too, points are plotted using pairs of random numbers. Each point is given an order number as it is plotted. The points are then connected in the order in which their numbers are found in a table of random numbers (Fig. 5-2). Certain connections, however, are not permitted: (1) a line may not be drawn twice, i.e., if the number of a point is found twice or more, the second and all subsequent occurrences are rejected; (2) no line may be drawn if that line, in conjunction with lines already drawn, encloses a point; (3) no two points may be connected directly if they are already connected by a line that is part of the perimeter of the shape and does not pass through any other plotted points. To complete a shape, each point must be connected to at least two other points. If the point-selection procedure leads to a point that already has all the permissible connections made, some other point is chosen randomly as the new origin and the process is continued. As in the case of method 1, two persons, given the same coordinates of points and the same sequences of numbers used in connecting the points, will produce identical shapes. The two methods differ in that method 2 may generate angles in the perimeter of the shape where none are plotted originally. Thus, if it is decided to

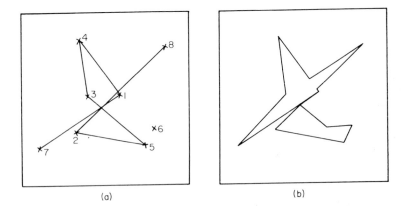

(a)   (b)

Fig. 5-2. Stages in the construction of a random shape according to method 2 of Attneave and Arnoult (1956).

generate shapes of only one level of complexity, more than the minimum number of shapes required would have to be constructed. Shapes generated by method 2 also seem to represent a population of shapes that differs somewhat from that of method 1. Attneave and Arnoult point out that method 2 shapes are characterized by "good continuation," hence given the same number of points, their information content may be lower than that of a method 1 shape. The number of studies in which shapes generated by the two methods have been compared is not large enough, though, to allow a more precise statement.

D. METRIC HISTOFORMS

A method for generating representative samples of measurable visual forms originated in the Laboratory of Aviation Psychology of Ohio State University during the 1950s. Working under the direction of Paul M. Fitts, a group of investigators (O. S. Adams, N. S. Anderson, J. A. Leonard, M. Rappaport, and M. Weinstein) produced a series of papers on the processing of visual information (for a summary of the project, see Fitts and Leonard, 1957). Since the main orientation of these studies was toward the practical aspects of visual information processing by human operators, the need arose to employ standard visual stimuli that could be easily and exactly quantified as to their information content. Because there was also some interest in the visual perception of electronically generated signals, the type of visual shape that was selected bore some resemblance to the one-dimensional patterns produced by amplitude-modulated potentials over time, e.g., those of an oscilloscope, EEG recorder, etc. One-dimensional distributions, in addition, can be analyzed by standard statistical procedures. To avoid problems associated with curved contours, the Ohio group simplified the patterns using discrete, uniform pattern elements. The construction method was to fill a predetermined number of the cells of a relatively small ($3 \times 3, 4 \times 4, 6 \times 6$) square matrix, the position of a cell to be filled being determined by the use of a table of random numbers. Since this procedure usually results in a pattern of unconnected or only partly connected cells, the restriction is introduced that all cells in a given column are put together, with the first cell resting on the horizontal axis of the matrix. What this amounts to is the random selection of the height of each column of the matrix, with the resulting shape looking like a bar graph or histogram (Fig. 5-3). Variations may be introduced in the shapes by applying certain restrictions, e.g., by introducing the rule that no two columns may be of the same height, by adding to a shape its mirror reflection, etc. Some of these more redundant variants of metric histoforms are illustrated in Fig. 5-4.

The characteristic that distinguishes the Ohio metric shapes from all others is not so much their appearance, as the basic approach to stimulus representativeness taken by their originators. Most other shape-construction proposals start with a sample of shapes and then state that the sample represents a certain

stimulus population. The characteristics of the population, however, are not spelled out. Rather, they are pointed at by pointing at the sample. While the estimation of population parameters from sample statistics is a routine matter, this is never done with visual forms. The Ohio group, by contrast, started out with the parameters of the entire population of metric figures of a certain type and then proceeded to construct more limited, representative samples of that population. Given a matrix of a certain size and the further specification that a cell may be only either black or white, the exact size of the entire population of unrestricted patterns that may be generated in this matrix may be calculated. In the case of a 4×4 matrix, for instance, it would be 2^{16} patterns. Any restriction in the pattern-construction procedure will reduce the number of patterns that may be constructed, and also increase their redundancy. Thus, only eight squares of different sizes may be constructed in an 8×8 matrix, and the information conveyed by any of these squares will be very small as compared with an unrestricted pattern. The measurement of the information content of metric patterns is discussed elsewhere in this chapter.

While the quantification of metric histoforms is convenient and simple, one of their drawbacks is that they are not common in everyday experience. Even when it is assumed that they are related to the patterns that may be seen in recorders of electrical potentials, the fact remains that such patterns are in the experience of relatively few people. While the quantification of random polygons is more problematic, they obviously represent populations of shapes that are much more frequent in nature.

E. METRIC POLYGONS

The metric polygon has the appearance of method 1 shape and the metric properties of the Ohio histoforms. Thurmond (1966) has proposed the following method for constructing this type of shape. A circular matrix is used, which is analogous to the square matrix. Instead of filling in, say, 4 cells in a given column of an 8×8 matrix, a point on a radius 4 distance units away from the center is marked. The polygon is completed by connecting the points marked on adjacent radii (Fig. 5-5). Since the construction rules are analogous to those of the metric histoforms, any histoform has its polygonal counterpart, as illustrated in Fig. 5-6.

Whether histoforms and metric polygons can be substituted for each other is a question that still awaits an answer. Thurmond's own preliminary experiments seem to indicate that, while in some respects there is no difference, in others there is. The type of constraint used, for instance, interacts with the type of shape. This is another instance of the limitations of informational measures: they indicate how *much* information there is, but not *how* this information is encoded—which may be just as important a factor to consider.

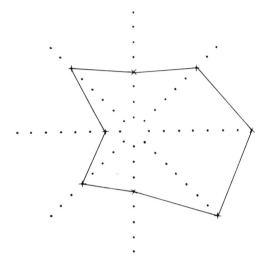

Fig. 5-5. Construction of a metric polygon.

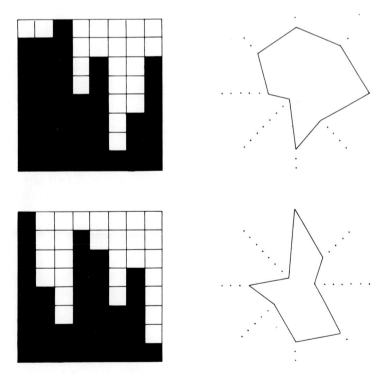

Fig. 5-6. Two histoforms with their corresponding metric polygons.

While the examples in Fig. 5-6 look like some of the eight-sided shapes that can be obtained by method 1 of Attneave and Arnoult, eight-sided shapes constructed in a 100 × 100 square matrix will be much more variable than eight-sided shapes constructed in an eight-point circular matrix. It is, however, the grain of the matrix used to construct the histoform that determines the number of vertices in a metric polygon, so that a 100 × 100 square matrix should yield a 100-pointed polygon. Thurmond has not proposed, however, a method for constructing, say, an eight-sided metric polygon in a 100-point circular matrix.

F. CELLULAR POLYGONS

The cellular polygon (Smith, 1964) resembles the metric histoform but is quantified more like a random polygon. It has the advantage of easy measurability that the histoform enjoys, but represents a somewhat larger population of figures, of which the histoforms are a subsample. The cells of a cross-ruled sheet of paper are the basic units or cells of the polygon. One such cell is outlined in the middle of the sheet. The next cell to make up the form is one of the four cells adjacent to the original one (Fig. 5-7a). It is selected by drawing lots or using a table of random numbers. The three cells adjacent to cell 2 may be placed in three different ways, depending on where cell 2 was attached to cell 1 (Fig. 5-7b). Which of these becomes cell 3 is again determined by some random procedure. Additional cells are attached to the core in the same manner until the required number of cells is reached. The resulting shape may look something like Fig. 5-7c. Since the total number of cells to be used may be predetermined, samples of figures of equal areas may be constructed without further processing. The fact that all angles in such a polygon are right angles reduces measurement to the simple counting of cells.

G. OPEN CONTOURS

The most frequently used shape is one that has closed contours. Occassionally, shapes with open contours are used, constructed according to the arbitrary rules of the researcher. The construction of open contour shapes is more indeterminate than the construction of closed-contour polygons. Any of several different methods may be used, and the resulting patterns may be said to be representative of certain populations of open contour shapes as long as the selection of the elements that make up the shape is made randomly. Attneave and Arnoult (1956) describe one such method. A square grid of convenient size is used. A point (grid intersection) near the center of the grid is connected to one of the adjacent eight points by means of a straight or curved line. This latter point then becomes the starting point for drawing another line to another point, and the process is continued until some predetermined number of line segments has been drawn. At each point, the point to which it is to be connected is determined by random selection of a number between one and eight. Many

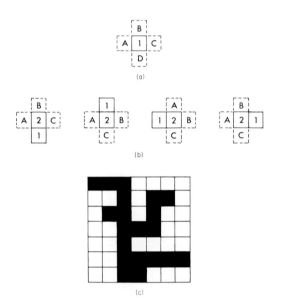

Fig. 5-7. Construction of a cellular polygon. See text for explanation.

variations of this basic technique are possible, such as reducing the number of available points from eight to four, varying the length of the line segments, using straight and curved line segments, varying the radius of the curved segments, etc. This type of pattern has not had much appeal in the past, and few studies can be found in which it has been used.

H. CURVED SHAPES

Given any closed or open shape whose sides are rectilinear, these may be replaced, totally or in part, by curved lines. The curved lines may be regular or irregular. If the former, it is usually arcs of a circle that are used, although there is nothing against using parabolic arcs or some other form of regular curvature. The measurement of irregular curves is so complex that, as a rule, no attempt is made to quantify irregularly curved shapes. Even when arcs of circles are used, the closest that anyone has ever come to quantifying curvature has been to state the length of the perimeter, in percent, that is occupied by curves.

Irregularly shaped, totally curved forms are usually constructed by the simple expedient of drawing them on a piece of paper as they occur to the researcher. Thus, Boynton (1957), for instance, describes how he happened to use a particular sample of 16 curved shapes or "struniforms" in an experiment:

"Where did these forms come from? They came from a larger population of 240 forms. The latter came out of me. I just sat down one night and drew them. There were implicit ground rules that I followed, but I couldn't say with any certainty what they were." (Page 176). It can be safely assumed that the "implicit ground rules" that Boynton refers to were something like the reverse of the process of approximating curved shapes with rectilinear segments (Attneave, 1951, 1954). Whether Boynton actually started with an imagined polygon and then drew curves at the vertices is not important, although his struniforms may be obtained by following this procedure. Since the details of the procedure to draw struniforms or similar curved shapes are not spelled out, the degree of randomness and therefore of representativeness of a sample of such shapes is not known.

Attneave and Arnoult (1956) have suggested a method for introducing regular curves in a random polygon that affords better control over the quantitative aspects of the shapes. First, a decision is made with respect to how many and which of the angles of the polygon are to be rounded. The radius of the circle whose arc will replace a given angle is then determined in the following fashion. Suppose the angle is the angle *ABC* in Fig. 5-8. A bisector of the angle, *Bp*, is constructed first. Then, the shorter of the two sides of angle *ABC* is divided into equal units, starting from the apex. The length of the unit may be the length of the side of one of the cells of the grid in which the polygon has been constructed. The divisions are numbered, assigning 0 to the apex, 1 to the first division, etc. One of these divisions is chosen at random, point 3 for instance,

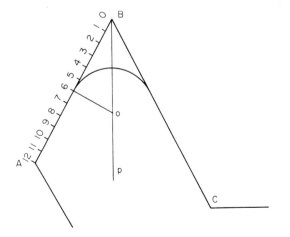

Fig. 5-8. Introducing curves in a random polygon. After Attneave and Arnoult (1956).

and a perpendicular is erected at this point. The point where the perpendicular crosses the bisector becomes the center of the circle, i.e., the line 3-o is the radius of the arc that rounds off vertex *B*. Knoll and Stenson (1968) have written a computer program for the construction of shapes by this method.

Attneave and Arnoult describe still another method of obtaining rounded-off shapes. A transparency or a negative of the polygon is printed out of focus on high-contrast paper. Since the contours here are not only rounded but also blurred, the image is photographed again and recopied a number of times on high-contrast paper until the contours are both rounded and sharp. There are no instances described in the literature of the use of this method—probably because of the cost, time, and effort involved. While it is possible to obtain a graded series of curved shapes by this procedure, the method described in the preceding paragraph may also be used for the same effect. It is also cheaper and faster.

I. PATTERNS

In this section, the term "pattern" is used to designate visual displays consisting of several unconnected elements or elements connected at some points only and not forming a continuous contour. The variables that must be considered when several shapes are in a spatial relationship to each other are discussed in Section 5C of this chapter. When visual displays of more than just, say, six or seven individual shapes are used in an experiment, it is likely that the experiment deals with visual search. In visual search tasks, the emphasis is more on information processing than form perception, hence the particular configuration of any of the elements in the pattern is of secondary importance. In patterns that can be considered simply a "noisy" ground, the particular configuration of the noise elements is of no importance whatsoever. The consideration of visual search has been deliberately omitted from this book. Visual noise is discussed elsewhere in this chapter (Section 5C). At this point, only certain configurations will be mentioned which, while representing true patterns, are usually treated in an experiment as unitary form stimuli.

The initial step in the construction of a metric histoform is the random filling of some of the cells in a square matrix. If these cells are not translated toward the baseline so as to form solid columns but are allowed to remain as originally located, the result is a metric pattern. In such patterns, some of the cells share a corner, some may form a system of two or three cells that touch along an edge, but in general each cell forms an independent element in the square array. Polidora (e.g., 1966) is one researcher who has used such patterns extensively. If the filled-in cells are represented by small bulbs placed behind transparent square windows, a system may be devised whereby different patterns are produced rapidly on the same screen. Such patterns have the advantages of the metric histoforms, of being easily and exactly quantified. Their disadvantage is obvious: their validity with respect to everyday experience is limited to similar patterns produced in a laboratory, since the normal physical environment of neither man nor animal is likely to produce such patterns very often, unless one considers them, e.g., as schematized approximations of blips on a radar screen. In addition, if it is assumed, as Polidora does, that a sequential cell-by-cell scanning and comparison of pattern elements is done by the subject, such patterns begin to remind one all too uncomfortably of the defunct Wundtian notion of form as a punctiform distribution of light.

2. Enclosed Area and Grain

A. SOLID AND OUTLINE SHAPES

Whether "solid" or outline shapes are used in an experiment is largely a matter of preference or convenience: if a set of forms is to be presented to a group of subjects, it is easier to draw them in outline on a duplicator master and then reproduce the required number. If slides are to be prepared of the same shape in various orientations, it is easier to cut the shapes from construction paper. While there are practically no studies comparing solid and outline shapes, the evidence that is available seems to indicate that no significant differences exist between the two types (e.g., Baughman, 1954). *A priori* considerations as well as eye-movement studies suggest as much: in a black-and-white polygon or nonrepresentational curved shape, all information is contained in its contour, and the interior of the shape is "empty," informationwise (Attneave & Arnoult, 1956; Brandt, 1945; Buswell, 1935; Zusne & Michels, 1964).

B. BLACK, WHITE, AND TRANSLUCENT SHAPES

It makes a difference whether black or dark shapes are presented on white background or white shapes on black background. In the latter case, one can distinguish white (reflecting) shapes from translucent (radiating) shapes. When white or translucent shapes are presented on a dark background, the phenomenon known as irradiation takes place. The white or radiant area "spills over" its excitation into adjacent regions of the retina, so that the area appears larger than an identical area in black.

In some experiments, this phenomenon has affected the results in an uncontrolled fashion. It also has an additional practical consequence: black characters on white background are, in general, more legible than white characters on black background (e.g., Holmes, 1931; Taylor, 1933). When the level of luminance over the area of a transilluminated shape is low or moderate, the dark surround which, on occasion, may be so large as to occupy the rest of the visual field, induces white in the shape, but not in a uniform manner throughout its interior: only a narrow band along its contour is affected. This has two consequences: one is that, of two shapes equal in area, the one with the longer perimeter will appear brighter; the other is the "puckering" out of narrow angles in the shape. Wherever two opposed contours of the shape come close together, their brighter marginal bands will tend to merge, so that the area below the vertex of a narrow angle will appear brighter throughout in comparison with the rest of the shape. Since irradiation is also at work simultaneously, the contours of transilluminated shapes are not as sharp as those of dark figures on a light background. All this introduces practical difficulties in the study of such phenomena as the detection of forms in the periphery of the retina. In this type of experiment, the preferred stimulus type has been transilluminated shapes, and some of the contradictory findings in this area may be attributed to the combined effect of irradiation and brightness contrast in figures having one or more narrow angles.

C. GRAIN

Typically, shapes are constructed in matrices of a certain grain. Whether a matrix is explicitly used or not, some degree of graininess is implied. It becomes explicit when, e.g., the shape is measured—in inches, millimeters, etc.

The order of the grain has two related consequences. One affects the end result of any calculation performed on the shape. The coarser the grain, the more difficult it is to represent and to calculate fine differences between two shapes, and the greater are the relative changes in any measure produced by the displacement or removal of an increasingly smaller number of "cells" in the shape. The implication is that, whenever measurements on a shape call for the multiplication of numbers or their raising to a power, the grain of the matrix must be sufficiently fine to absorb the impact of these operations.

The second consequence is the divergence between physical and psychological complexities in random cell matrices with increasing fineness of the grain. Beginning with very few cells and up to some indeterminate point, an increase in the number of filled cells will result in an increase in the perceived complexity of the pattern. Further increase in the number of cells that constitute the pattern, however, will not result in further increase in the perceived complexity of the pattern. Rather, the pattern gradually ceases to be perceived as a pattern and is more readily seen as a homogeneous field having a homogeneous texture, as illustrated in Fig. 5-9. It is not simply a matter of visual acuity, for deliberate search and concentration of attention on isolated portions of the field permit the discrimination of smaller subpatterns without any particular difficulty. As Attneave (1954) points out, it is a matter of how the organism processes information: when the amount of information to be processed is grossly in excess of the organism's capacity to do so, it begins to treat information something like statistical error variance—averaging is resorted to and certain other descriptive statistics are abstracted to describe the visual field in terms that are much more economical than the sheer number of bits of information.

Fig. 5-9. Increasing physical complexity leads to an increase in psychological complexity up to a point only. Beyond that point, it is perceived as increasing homogeneity of the pattern since the area of the pattern cannot be increased indefinitely.

Because of its random construction, the matrix contains, mathematically speaking, a near-maximum amount of information. The perceptual system, however, treats it as a highly redundant system containing very little information. The point at which a complex pattern becomes homogeneous texture is indeterminate: in a matrix whose cells may be only black or white, it varies with the number of cells in the pattern and the visual angle subtended by the pattern. The latter factor is related to the organism's visual acuity.

3. The Description of Contours

Attneave and Arnoult (1956) distinguish between description of the contours of a form and measurement of what they call the "Gestalt-variables." Contours may be described in terms of the course that they follow in space. For most purposes, these terms must be independent of the size, place, and orientation of the form. This is contrasted with measures that do not permit reconstruction but that abstract important properties of the shape instead, namely the variables that describe different aspects of the distribution of the contours of a shape in space. The purpose of describing the course of a contour is a practical one: a set of numbers is conveniently transmitted, stored, and utilized by different devices, be it a mailed message or a punched card. Also, a dimensionless set of numbers is needed to compare an original with its reproduction. There are several satisfactory methods of shape description available, yet instances of their actual use are few.

Without actually specifying a system for contour description, Gibson (1950, p. 195) has stated the bases for the description of straight and curved lines. After stating its length, a line is completely specified by stating its direction (left slant, right slant, zero slant) and curvature (convex, straight, concave). The slant or slope of a curve and the direction in which the slope is changing can be measured exactly: they are the first and second derivatives of the curve. A line is completely specified, both physically and perceptually, by specifying its direction and curvature. Without resorting to calculus, the methods of contour description mentioned below are different ways of specifying these two variables.

If the coordinates of each of the vertices of a polygon are specified, it is possible to reconstruct the polygon from them, provided that the pairs of coordinates are given in order. If the points are connected with straight lines in the same order as they are plotted, a duplicate of the original form is obtained. If the scales used in the original construction and in reproduction are the same, the two forms will also have identical areas.

Curves, in general, present problems that are not solved by any of the methods here described. Some regular curves have fairly simple equations. The polar coordinate system is more convenient for plotting such curves than the Cartesian system. The contour of the shape shown in Fig. 5-10 is given by the equation $r = 1 + \sin \theta$, where r is the length of the radius vector and θ is the value of the vectorial angle. While it is still necessary to prepare a table of values of r for the range of the values of θ and to make a free-hand drawing of the

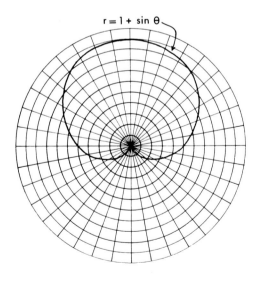

Fig. 5-10. A mathematically simple curve.

curved segments corresponding to these intervals, the resulting contour is quite close to being an exact duplicate of the original figure.

Equations for irregular curvilinear contours, however, are extremely unwieldy and difficult to obtain. It is more practical to use any of the following three methods to reproduce irregular contours. They are described by Attneave and Arnoult (1956), where the details may be found. Only the main features will be given here.

One of the methods consists of plotting the reciprocal of the radius of curvature against distance along the contour. This yields a periodic function that can be made independent of the scale of the original shape. In this function, an angle is represented by a vertical line that rises or falls to infinity. Although these spikes may be treated mathematically, it is not very practical to do so.

In another method, a three-wheeled device is used. If this device is equipped with recorders for recording the deviations of the front wheel from a forward position and of the distance traveled by the front wheel, plotting deviations against distance will yield a periodic function that will describe the contour.

In the third method, instead of describing a contour as a continuous function, the contour is analyzed into parts that are individually homogeneous. The method represents a reversal of methods 1 or 2 of constructing random shapes, and the system of coordinates used in describing a contour is based on the possibility of approximating a curved contour with straight-line segments by drawing tangents at points of zero curvature, at points of minimal curvature, and at discontinuities of slope, i.e., angles. The entire contour is therefore described in terms of successive sets of tri-coordinates. These coordinates give, for each pair of adjacent segments, (a) the change in direction (in degrees), (b) the change in the logarithm of length, and (c) the proportion of the distance between the apex of the angle and the end of the shorter segment at which the arc best approximating the curve is tangent.

The description of the contours of a complex curvilinear shape using manual methods is very laborious, and computer techniques are available to perform this task. While the details vary, the basic idea is the same: either a light or cathode-ray spot moves rapidly across or along the contour and the resulting feedback signal is converted into a digital or analog output. Examples of such devices, too numerous to mention, may be found in connection with computer pattern-recognition programs.

Blum (1967) has offered a rather unique way of describing shape. It is based on the Gibsonian proposition that shape cannot be isolated and normalized without introducing too much artificiality. Blum rejects attempts to geometrize shape in Euclidean terms. His geometry is not topological, however. It is a geometry based on the interaction of shape with itself. This is not an entirely new notion, but the specific application is. Blum obtains his descriptors of shape as he considers what happens when a contour falls upon an isotropic plane—a granular surface or network where each point can be in a state of excitation or nonexcitation, which propagates excitation (with a delay proportional to distance), and which possesses the property of refractoriness, in other words, the retina. As a contour falls upon this plane, excitation is propagated uniformly in all directions but in such a way that the waves of excitation do not flow through each other (something like grass fire). Corners in contours and colliding wavefronts, however, produce cancellation of excitation. These points of cancellation constitute the "medial axis"; when the time of corner occurrence on the medial axis is included, it is referred to as the "medial axis function."

Some examples of wavefronts and "corners" produced by simple patterns are shown in Fig. 5-11a-c. Figure 5-11d shows how a medial-axis function may be generated in a simple symmetric form. Since Blum applies the model to form discrimination (medial-axis functions are unique), the explanation of closure, geometric illusions, and cortical cell responses to contours, it is actually a type of theory of form discrimination.

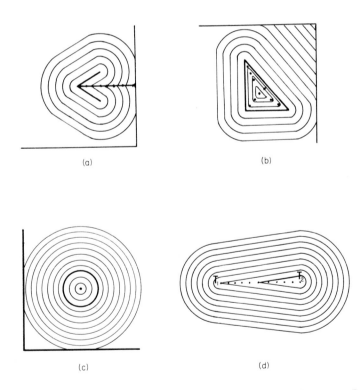

(a)

(b)

(c)

(d)

Fig. 5-11. Examples of wavefronts and "corners" produced by simple patterns. In (d) T_1 is the appearance of a corner, T_2 its disappearance. From Blum (1967).

4. Parameters of the Single Stimulus and Their Measurement

At one time, it was acceptable to state that the independent variable in a form-perception experiment was "form." By that was meant that a sample of different geometric figures was being used. How they were different was not spelled out. In this section, the numerous measures that have been developed since the days of no quantification are described. The extent to which these measures have been found to correlate with behavior is the subject matter of Chap. 6.

Until very recently, form was measured with no reference to any theory. A free-wheeling, "cut-and-try" approach has produced a veritable plethora of form measures. Shapes have been cut from construction paper (or drawn in pencil or India ink) and various measures taken on them, measures whose selection has depended on their past usage as well as the researcher's preferences and hunches. If a given measure did not work in an experiment, it was discarded and replaced by another. This approach, while not very efficient, has had a heuristic value: it has been possible to detect certain communalities in these measures, classify them, and to theorize, in turn, about what might be a more systematic and theory-based set of form parameters. Brown's (1964) list of variables, intended to describe visual patterns completely and quantitatively, fails in this respect. The division of all variables into component (i.e., form in itself) variables and pattern (several forms in a field) variables is sound enough. The further subdivision of the component variables into structural, nonstructural, and ground variables, however, suffers from too much overlap and vagueness of definition. Since, in addition, Brown lists such variables as color and blur under the heading of nonstructural component variables, his list is actually a partial list of variables for the description, not of form, but of any distal visual stimulus, including its immediate surround. As such, this list is incomplete since it should but does not include such variables as movement and its parameters, and exposure time. In short, it is a beginning of an algorithm for the complete specification of an experimental situation where forms are used as stimuli. As such, it can never be complete. Being nontheoretical, it is also only descriptive, not explanatory.

The classification of form parameters proposed by Michels and Zusne (1965) is an attempt to introduce some degree of order in this area, and this classification, with slight modifications, is presented here.

Gibson (1950) has pointed out that it is possible to transform any closed form into any other closed form by gradual changes: a polygon with a few sides into one of many, a rectilinear figure into a curvilinear one, or a form into its mirror image. Thus, all ordinary closed-contour forms would appear to be on the same continuum or, to be mathematically exact, to constitute a transformation group. The universe of forms, however, is so large that it is not inappropriate to talk of different types or classes of form, though not in terms of the formerly accepted phenotypes, such as geometric and nongeometric forms, but in terms of form genotypes defined by the type of geometric operation performed on a configuration to produce the whole range of instances of that genotype. These operations appear to be sufficiently orthogonal to each other on logical, physical, and psychological grounds. The latter are presented in Chap. 6, where experimental work in form perception is discussed. The logical and physical grounds are presented here.

Let us assume that we are dealing with a single two-dimensional form of closed contours, and that when any type of transformation is performed on this form it will either affect or fail to affect (1) the amount of measured information contained in this form, and (2) the way in which this information is distributed along the contours of the form. Physically and as far as form itself, i.e., contour is concerned there is nothing else that can be affected. Form, of course, carries information in addition to that which can be measured by the Wiener-Shannon formula, but this information, meaning, is something that can be ascertained only in relation to the observer and his past experience. Thus, while the approach taken here is not necessarily an informational one, the first criterion used to classify physical form parameters is change in the calculated number of bits of information in the outline of the form as it undergoes a transformation. Psychologically, it is the change in the perceived complexity of the shape.

The second criterion is that of self-congruence. The question is asked, "Is the form, after the transformation operations have been performed, still congruent with itself?" A form is judged to be incongruent with itself only if it fails to show geometric congruence with itself after all four symmetry operations—translation, enlargment or reduction, rotation, and reflection—have been performed (Yaglom, 1962).

These four symmetry operations themselves form the first group of parameters, here called the transpositional parameters, since they only transpose form to another locus or area. Changes in these parameters affect neither the information content of the shape nor its self-congruence. The transitive parameters constitute a second major class of form parameters. The term transitive stems from the fact that changes in these parameters affect, in every case, the distribution of the contour of the shape, hence its self-congruence. The form goes on to become a different kind of form, however slightly. This class is broken down into two major types. Changes in one type of parameter affect, in addition to the contour of the shape, its information content, while changes in the other do not. The characteristics of the three main types of single form parameters are summarized in Table 5-1. It should be explained here why the fourth logical possibility, namely that of a type of parameter that would change the information content of a shape without affecting its contour, has not been

TABLE 5-1
Categories of Parameters of the Single Form Stimulus

Changes in the values of the following parameters	Produce changes in:	
	Measured information content	Self-congruence
A. Transpositional parameters		
1. Translation	No	No
2. Transposition to different size	No	No
3. Rotation	No	No
4. Reflection	No	No
B. Transitive parameters		
1. Informational		
a. Number of turns	Yes	Yes
b. Linearity of contour	No/yes	No/yes
2. Configurational		
a. Moments of distribution of contours	No	Yes

included. It has been proposed (Alluisi & Hall, 1965) that it should, and the label of "transphenomenal parameter" has been attached to it. Basically, it is impossible to change the information content of a shape without also changing the way in which this information is distributed along the contour. The transpositional and transitive parameters are single form parameters. What Alluisi and Hall call a transphenomenal parameter is not a parameter at all, in the sense that it is not a variable whose value changes with the circumstances of its application. Rather, what they mean is any of a set or the whole set of sampling rules for the selection of a sample from a population of shapes. The use of such a rule produces a sample of shapes that share a certain common characteristic which may be described by a statistic. At best, it is this statistic that is the parameter, but it always refers to a sample of shapes, hence describes the relation of any given shape to other shapes, not a property of a shape in isolation. The subject of relational parameters is treated in Section 5 of this chapter.

A. TRANSPOSITIONAL PARAMETERS

The transpositional parameters are identical with the four so-called symmetry operations. These are the geometric operations that must be performed on a form before deciding whether it is congruent or incongruent with another form.

Translation. To superimpose one form upon another in order to make this decision, the only necessary operation may be that of translation, i.e., one of the forms is moved horizontally or vertically until every point of its contour coincides with every point on the contour of the second form. In form-perception experiments, this operation would correspond to the presentation of a form in peripheral vision. Presenting a form in loci other than the fixation point affects neither the information content nor the contour of the form, save for extreme cases of peripherality when distortions due to the imperfect optics of the eye may occur. Since the visual field lends itself easily to a representation in a system of polar coordinates, the measurement of peripherality presents no particular problem, and is usually expressed in terms of the location of the shape in one of the four quadrants of the visual field, degrees of deviation from the two main axes of the coordinate system, visual angle of the space between the object and the fixation point, etc.

Area. Transposing a form to a larger or smaller size affects the size of the visual angle subtended by the form at the eye of the observer and therefore the observer's ability to discriminate details of the form (if the form is reduced in size) or to attend to and perceive the form as a whole (if the form is enlarged), but not its information content or the distribution of its contours in space. When the form is that of a familiar object, size constancy is at work and the absolute size of the form is immaterial, as long as it does not affect the clear perception of the form adversely. While size constancy may not be operating with unfamiliar or nonrepresentational silhouettes, these shapes, because of their unfamiliarity, may be presented in different absolute sizes consistent with a clear and unitary perception of the shapes.

Since it is only the contours of a shape that convey information about it, area as a form parameter is of secondary importance only: a change in the area of a shape affects the length of the different portions of the contour of the shape. For this reason, if shapes of unequal areas are to be compared on sides, total perimeter, or any other linear measure, these must be normalized by dividing them by some function of the area. This is the function of A in the often-used measure of jaggedness of form, P^2/A. The length of the perimeter is squared only because area is essentially a quadratic measure. If the areas of two forms are identical, a comparison of their untransformed perimeters is all that is necessary to compare their respective degrees of jaggedness, since of two perimeters enclosing the same area, the longer one will belong to the more jagged form. The square-root and logarithmic transformations of area that are sometimes employed only serve to make the distribution of the values of area for a series of shapes more symmetric, hence more amenable to statistical treatment.

There are a number of measures that include some function of either the total area of a shape or partial areas, such as moments of area or measures of areal asymmetry in the four quadrants of a shape. These cannot be considered transpositional measures, and they are discussed below under the heading of measures of areal and perimetric variability.

There are well-known formulas for the computation of the areas of the simplest types of regular, geometric forms. The general formula for the computation of the area of a regular polygon is

$$A = \tfrac{1}{4} N L^2 \cot 180/N,$$

where N is the number of sides of the polygon and L the length of the side. The measurement of the areas of irregular polygons would be very time-consuming and the measurement of curved shapes virtually an impossibility if it were not for the existence of a simple measuring device, the planimeter: As the contour of a shape is traced with one of its arms (Fig. 5-12), the distance traveled by that arm is converted into a measure of area, which can be read off directly from a dial. It is an indispensable tool for anyone working in the area of form perception.

The measurement of area by means of a planimeter is the first step in the process of equating a sample of shapes on area. Such equation is necessary if area is to be eliminated as a cue in discrimination. In the construction of random shapes, the 100 X 100 cell matrix with .10 sq. in. or 4 mm^2 cells has often been used because it fits a letter-size sheet of paper, providing at the same time a fine enough grain. Most shapes constructed in such a matrix are of a size that can be

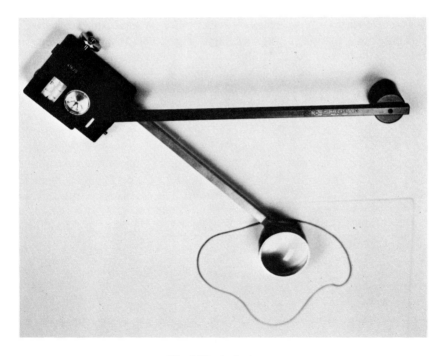

Fig. 5-12. A planimeter.

used immediately, e.g., in sorting tasks. If the sample of shapes constructed is of any magnitude, there will be considerable variation in the degree of compactness of the shapes, which presents a problem when it comes to equating the shapes on area. When the area of shapes is equated to that of the most compact shape in the sample, the dimensions of the thinner, more jagged shapes become inconveniently large. If, however, the area of the most compact shapes is adjusted to that of the more jagged shapes, they become too small. It is more convenient, therefore, to make the area of every shape equal to that of some middle-sized shape, which means a reduction in the area of some shapes and the enlargment of others. Unfortunately, there is no single device that will perform both tasks satisfactorily. Such a device has to contain a lens, and the use of a lens means that one has to contend with two parameters: distance (object-lens of lens-screen distance) and blur. Changing the size of the image and keeping the image in focus simultaneously is possible in an autofocus enlarger, but this device requires the use of transparencies; in addition, to achieve reduction in size requires a modification in its construction.

Most of the time, it is possible to get by using enlargement alone: that shape in the sample is selected that has the largest area and all other shapes are enlarged to match it. A simple shadow-casting device working on Emmert's principle performs this task very well and eliminates the need for a costly optical device. The shape to be enlarged is cut from a piece of paper and attached vertically to a transparent holding frame (Fig. 5-13). The frame and a point source of light, such as a flashlight bulb, are mounted on a platform. The distance between the platform and the screen on which the enlarged shadow of the shape is projected may be varied. The track along which this platform moves

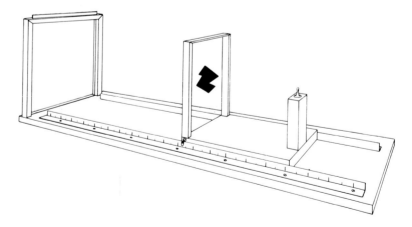

Fig. 5-13. A shadow-casting device for enlarging silhouetted shapes.

is marked off in millimeters. To use this device, it is necessary to prepare a table for the conversion of enlargement factors into millimeters (the distance of the platform from the screen). The shadow enlarger can also be used to produce continuous changes in the area of a shape, e.g., in psychophysical judgment experiments. Since any shape may be used in this device, it is less restricted than the device described by Haralson (1965), which produces continuous changes in the area of rectangles only.

Rotation. The orientation of a shape does not affect its structure. Unlike transposition to a different locus or a different area, however, transposition to a different orientation affects perception of the shape: it looks different as compared with its original orientation. If the shape is originally familiar to the observer, in other orientations, the same shape may look less familiar or entirely unfamiliar, e.g., an upside-down face. Even when familiarity is not involved, as in the case of nonrepresentational shapes seen for the first time, each different orientation presents a different aspect of a shape, so that one may even get the impression that one is dealing with a series of unrelated shapes.

To place a shape in a different orientation, the symmetry operation of rotation is resorted to: with only one point, the rotation point, immobile, all other points of the shape are made to describe arcs of concentric circles whose centers are the immobile point. Which point is used as the center of rotation is immaterial, only the degrees of arc through which rotation takes place and the direction of rotation are the pertinent variables.

The amount of rotation is usually determined by the size of the angle that is formed between a vertical axis and a straight line that passes through the point of rotation, the latter being common to both the vertical and the straight line. The straight line is sometimes inappropriately called the axis of rotation. It is an inappropriate term since rotation in a plane requires only a reference point, the rotation point, and an axis is needed only to effect rotation in the third dimension.

An axis is not an inherent characteristic of shapes unless they are perfectly symmetric, in which case they may have one or more axes of symmetry. The relative rotation of a symmetric shape is usually determined in terms of degrees of deviation of its axis of symmetry from the vertical. Using their respective axes of symmetry, the orientations of two symmetric shapes with regard to each other can be determined without difficulty even when the shapes are different. A difficulty arises with asymmetric shapes since these do not possess anything like a predetermined axis. A nonrepresentational shape is not oriented in any particular way since there is no axis of reference that may be said to deviate so many degrees from the vertical. A nonrepresentational, asymmetric shape can be rotated meaningfully only when each different position of such a shape is compared with some initial position, but not otherwise. Two random shapes seen together cannot be said to be rotated in any particular way with respect to each other unless some reference axis is drawn through them. It is the drawing of a reference axis that presents a problem. Several different approaches have been used to solve it. One approach has been to define the vertical or the horizontal axis of the shape-construction matrix as the reference axis and to talk of rotation in terms of deviation of this axis from the vertical. The position of such an axis has, of course, nothing to do with any other physical properties of the shape.

Another solution has been to draw the reference axis to coincide with the longest extent of the shape. This axis would correspond to something like the dominant direction of the shape, but since the longest extent of a complex shape may be determined in a number of ways, the exact placement of such an axis varies from researcher to researcher.

Smith (1964) has introduced an "angle of tilt" measure which, while quite complex to calculate, amounts to a measure of inclination of the longest axis of a shape with regard to the horizontal when the thickness or thinness (elongation) of the shape is also taken into account. Thus, of two shapes showing the same inclination of their longest axis, the thinner one would have a greater angle of tilt than the more compact one. In Smith's own experiment, this measure did not affect judgments of area, and it has not been used by other investigators.

Brown, Hitchcock, and Michels (1962) describe the following method of drawing a "rotation axis" in random polygons. The polygon, in any given orientation, is divided into an upper and a lower half by drawing a horizontal line through its geometric center. (The geometric center is determined by enclosing the shape in a rectangle and finding the midpoint of that rectangle.) The two most distant points in each half are connected with straight lines, the lines bisected, and a "rotation axis" drawn through the two points of bisection. Rotation is then defined as the deviation of this axis from the vertical. This axis, however, when drawn systematically through 180 degrees of rotation of a shape, shows an unpredictable pattern of change, including reversals. It has been used in only one or two experiments, and its usefulness, while largely unexplored, is doubtful.

Chou (1935) has suggested that nonrepresentational shapes may have certain inherent characteristics, seen everywhere in nature, which may make their "upright" position less than indeterminate. Chou had a large number of American subjects judge the orientation of Chinese characters presented in several positions. Chou's subjects did correctly identify 48% of the rotated characters as rotated. Chinese ideograms are not quite comparable, though, to random shapes since the former, in spite of a great amount of formalization and transformation, still bear traces of the concrete objects that they originally were pictures of. Because of this factor, their upright position is more easily recognized, even when they have no other meaning to the subject.

Ghent's (1961) work with children suggests that certain features, present in all forms, are used to determine which is the right-side-up position of nonrepresentational forms: the focal point of a shape is usually placed in an upper position and the longest axis in a vertical orientation. In an unpublished study, I had a large number of observers draw an "axis of symmetry" through asymmetric random shapes. To anchor judgments, it has to be assumed that such an axis would pass through the center of gravity of the shape, and this center must be marked on it. Under these conditions, individuals draw the required "axis of symmetry" with considerable confidence, showing a relatively high degree of agreement. There is less agreement in the case of shapes that show no dominant direction and tend toward roundness. In other words, in these shapes, the placement of the reference axis is unimportant. The subjective axes of symmetry have one important property that makes them perhaps the most meaningful of all reference axes: their placement coincides with the measured maximum and minimum values of the second and third moments of area (cf. p. 219). Goldstein and Andrews (1962) have reported analogous results: given random shapes and asked to put them in "right-side-up" position, subjects can actually do it, which suggests that these shapes tend to have a certain position which may be called "upright."

Reflection. The operation of reflection may appear to be an either-or operation, i.e., a shape is either itself or its mirror image. Still, it is possible to conceive of reflection as a series of gradual transformations, as when a shape is rotated about an axis that passes through two of its vertices and the shadow of the shape is projected upon a screen. The shadow becomes more and more "compressed" in one direction, turning into a single straight line, then expanding again, but so that the final shape is a mirror image of itself as it was before this transformation.

Like rotation, reflection affects the familiarity of shapes, although not to the same extent as rotation. Mirror images of faces, profiles, paintings, etc. do look somewhat different at first, although the nature of the difference cannot be easily stated. Reflected images of meaningful objects can be identified without difficulty. Less complex and less meaningful shapes are more difficult to recognize, while nonrepresentational shapes are even more so. Still, the effect is much less pronounced than in the case of rotation.

The term inversion has a number of different but related meanings in geometry. It is sometimes used to describe the combined operations of rotation and reflection. As such, inversion cannot be considered an independent transpositional parameter.

B. TRANSITIVE PARAMETERS

Informational Parameters. A transition from one population of shapes to another is achieved when (a) the number of inflections in the contour of a shape is changed or (b) when the type of contour (rectilinear or curvilinear) is changed. Changing the number of inflections or vertices cannot be accomplished without affecting the arrangement of contours in space at the same time. Thus, while a change in the information content is the primary result of a change in an informational transitive parameter, an intransitive, noninformational or simply configurational change will be the inevitable secondary consequence.

Measurement of the information content of a form is based on the principle established by Attneave (Attneave, 1951; Attneave & Arnoult, 1956) that, in a two-dimensional shape, information is concentrated along its contours, namely at points where changes in the direction of the contour are sharpest. In a polygon, information measurement thus reduces to the counting of the number of its turns. Since, as shown by Attneave and others, curvilinear shapes can be approximated by rectilinear transformations without a substantial loss of information, information measurement in these forms does not present any special problem. Since polygons are the most frequently used type of form stimuli, number of turns has been the most frequently used information measure. For purposes of comparison, it would be convenient to measure the information content of a form in terms of bits, i.e., the binary logarithm of the number of turns. This has actually been done; most researchers, however, have abstained from doing this. A $\log_2$ measure of the number of turns in a regular polygon is justifiable in that the equal spacing of the vertices of such polygons gives each vertex an equal chance of being perceived, and equiprobability of events underlies the use of the simple $\log_2$ measure. In irregular polygons, all vertices do not have the same chance of being perceived. To measure the information content of such polygons, each event (the perception of a vertex) must be weighed by the probability of its occurrence. But probability of occurrence in this instance must be inferred from some response measure, such as the judged complexity of polygons having different numbers of turns. The use of the Wiener-Shannon formula involves more than that, since it must be determined not only that, say, a 16-sided shape is perceived, on the average, as having only 12 sides, but also how, on the average, all vertices rank in terms of their perceptibility. Preliminary studies to determine the actual perceived complexity of a sample of shapes to be used in an experiment have never been made. While it is not absolutely necessary that they be made whenever shapes are used, it is worth remembering that the differences between actual and judged number of turns in shapes are not trivial and that the psychophysical relationship is not rectilinear (Seiler & Zusne, 1966). There is therefore a justification for distinguishing information content, as measured in terms of turns or bits, from complexity, or judged information content.

To visual stimuli other than closed, two-dimensional shapes, somewhat different measures of information content have been applied. For dot patterns, both the number of dots and the binary logarithm of the number of dots have been used. Since in dot patterns the dots are usually equally spaced and unconnected, the use of the latter measure may be justified.

Fitts and Leonard (1957) define the information content of metric figures as "the size of the total population of figures that can be constructed in a matrix of a given size" (p. 17). This is a statistical approach to the measurement of the information content of a form, so that the resulting measure has reference to the statistical characteristics of the population and the sample of figures involved rather than single figures. For this reason, the measurement of metric figures is discussed more fully in Section 5 of this chapter on relational parameters.

If changes in the direction of a line are informative, so are points of intersection of two or more line segments as well as the segments themselves. This extension of the rationale for information measurement in polygons can be applied to line patterns, both closed and open. Hochberg and Brooks (1960), for instance, measured the information content of such closed patterns as the Kopferman cube by counting, among other things, the number of line segments, points of intersection of two and three lines, and the number of closed subfigures within the exterior contours.

While exact methods have been proposed for the description of the course of a curvilinear contour, the quantification of the Gestalt properties of curved shapes has not progressed beyond the crude index of the percentage of the total perimeter length made up of curved segments. There are very few investigations of the effect of curvature on the perception of form. They differ so much in methodology that only a few tentative conclusions have been reached regarding this question.

What the introduction of curves in, say, a polygon, does to it is a more difficult matter to determine as compared with the effects of a change in the number of inflections in a polygon. While it is true that a curved shape may be approximated with straight-line segments without loss of too much information, some information is inevitably lost, depending on how crude or fine the approximation is. How such approximation affects perceived complexity is not known. Self-congruence between a curvilinear form and its rectilinear approximation is also a matter of degree. Strictly speaking, as long as the approximation is only an approximation, there can be no congruence.

The most important effect of curvature shows up in an observer's response. Data are sparse here, but it does appear that, while in the case of representations of well-known objects "a cat is a cat is a cat," regardless of whether it is represented with straight or curved lines, a nonrepresentational shape, such as an inkblot, may appear to belong to two entirely different form worlds, depending on whether its contours are curved or approximated with straight lines. Whether only associative responses are affected (Edelman, 1960) or this is a phenomenon found with any perceptual task is, again, not known.

Configurational Parameters. The last group of form measures to be discussed is by far the most populous. Here are concentrated the numerous attempts to measure distances, angles, and areas. In essence, these are the various parameters that in a more or less complete way describe the relatively few major dimensions along which the distribution of contours of a shape may vary: how variable are the distances of its contour segments from a central reference point, how symmetrically distributed are the contours about some axis, and how thin or thick it is. Variations in the value of any of these measures do not affect the measured information content of the shape, but they may, as already indicated, affect its perceived complexity—e.g., by making the same form increasingly flatter, some of the vertices may come so close together that they are difficult to discriminate, hence lose their role as information bearers.

Most numerous in this group are measures of distances between various points within a shape, of the length of its sides, and of the size of its angles. These measures, as a rule, reflect some limited aspect of the total configuration, in contrast, e.g., to a measure of overall dispersion. While most of these measures have been taken on single forms, in some cases distances between corresponding features in two different but adjacent forms have been measured. For this purpose, one of the forms is usually translated laterally until the centers of gravity of the two forms coincide, and the difference measures then taken. Since this amounts to measuring the same configuration, the corresponding measures do not constitute a different class.

Among the distance measures used, the following may be mentioned. Apical deviation was defined by Chambliss (1957) as the sum of all distances between the corresponding vertices of two shapes when their respective coordinate axes were superimposed. Paired points were defined by the same author by measuring distances between all pairs of points in a figure, then taking the absolute sum of the differences between the corresponding distances in a pair of polygons. The same author also measured the length of vectors ("polar vectors") drawn from the origin of the coordinate system in which the shape was constructed to any of its vertices.

Another distance that has been measured in forms is the distance from the center of gravity to any point on the contour. Such distances may be designated as radii. If a sufficient number of equal intervals is laid off on the contour, adjacent radii can be plotted as a one-dimensional frequency distribution. The ends of the radii, when connected, form a curve (Fig. 5-14). Such an expansion of the contour was first used by Barskiĭ and Guzeva (1962) for the purpose of computing the information content of shapes. What the graph in Fig. 5-14 suggests is that this distribution should reflect the degree of compactness of the shape. Brown and Owen (1967), having computed the second, third, and fourth moments of radial lengths of a large sample of random shapes and having factored a large matrix of intercorrelations between form measures, found that

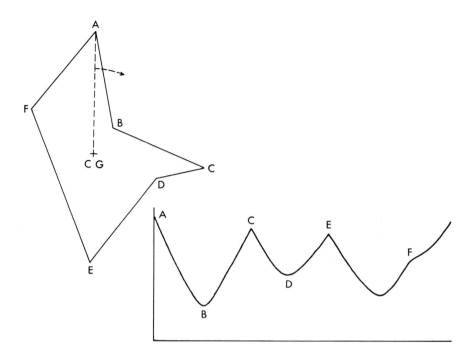

Fig. 5-14. One-dimensional expansion of the contour of a closed, two-dimensional shape.

all of these moments loaded heavily on the factor of compactness. In the shape shown in Fig. 5-14, none of the radii are interrupted by the contours. In the case of deep invaginations, some of the radii may be interrupted once or even twice. The decision must then be made whether to use the total length of the segments of the radius within the contours only, to include the segments outside the contours, or to take some other measure of the radius. At the present time, no data are available to help the researcher make this decision.

The most frequently taken measure is some measure on the sides of a polygon. Stilson (1956), using pairs of triangles in a task of similarity judgment, measured the length of each of the three sides of a triangle, variation in the lengths of the sides, and the variation of ratios of pairs of sides. Small (1961) measured the lengths of the sides of a polygon that enclosed the largest angle, the length of the longest side, the ratio of this side to the perimeter, and the standard deviation of the lengths of sides. Other investigators have used one or several of these measures in their experiments. Other measures on sides, such as the total length of the perimeter and its derivatives, are not included here since they reflect other form properties yet to be discussed.

Simple measures on angles are not found too frequently in the literature. Stilson (1956) measured all angles in the triangles used in his experiment, the variation in the size of the angles (which is identical to "angular variability," discussed below), variation of the ratios of pairs of angles, and the ratio of largest to smallest angle. Chambliss (1957) introduced a measure on angles in which the absolute sum of the differences between corresponding angles in each pair of shapes was taken. Chambliss used the exterior angles of the polygon, assigning positive value to clockwise turns in the perimeter and negative values to counterclockwise turns. Small (1961) added the size of the largest angle (using random polygons as stimuli), the ratio of the largest angle to the total degrees of interior angles, and the standard deviation of angle size.

In anticipation of the discussion of the experimental results obtained with these measures, it must be said that none of them has turned out to be a useful predictor of performance, regardless of the type of task used. Neither have the logarithmic and trigonometric transformations of these measures. The first four moments of distribution of side lengths or of angles appear to have more promise, although they have not been used in actual experiments. Both Vanderplas, Sanderson, and Vanderplas (1965) and Brown and Owen (1967) have included these measures in matrices of correlations among a large number of other form measures and have factored these matrices. Brown and Owen compute the first four moments of interior angles by the formula

$$IA_k = \sum_{i=1}^{n} (a_i - \bar{a})^k / n,$$

where K is the power of the moment, $\bar{a}$ is the arithmetic mean of the interior angles, a_i is the size of angle i, and n is the total number of interior angles. An analogous formula is used to compute the first four moments of side lengths as well as of radii. Vanderplas' sample of 1000 random shapes constructed by method 1 of Attneave and Arnoult (1956), measured on 12 parameters, yielded four factors. Three of them correlated highly with the standard deviation of side length and of angular variability, the third moment of interior angles, and the fourth moment of interior angles, respectively. The 80 × 80 correlation matrix of form measures factored by Brown and Owen yielded 12 factors, 5 of which could be labeled. Some of the measures that correlated highly with these factors were the first four moments of radial length, the second moment of side length, and the first four moments of interior angles. These results in themselves are not a sufficient reason for deciding upon the use of these measures, because other considerations, theoretical and practical, must be taken into account. Some of them are presented in Section 5 of this chapter.

A measure related to the total configuration of a shape that readily suggests itself is a measure of the degree of its jaggedness, angularity, or dispersion. The term compactness will be reserved to describe the response to dispersion. A simple way to measure dispersion is to compare the length of the perimeter of a shape with the area it encloses. Given a constant area, the shape with the longest perimeter will appear to be the least-compact shape. If the shapes to be compared have equal areas, the comparison reduces itself to a comparison of the lengths of the perimeters. Otherwise, the perimeters must be divided by the respective areas and, since area is a quadratic measure, the perimeter must be squared. In most experiments where this measure has been used, it has been found to be quite useful as a predictor of performance in some perceptual tasks.

One disadvantage of the P^2/A measure is that it breaks down at both the upper and lower ends of the continuum. Thus, while the difference between P^2/A for the equilateral triangle and the square is only about 4 units, the two shapes are highly discriminable, while a difference in dispersion between two shapes measuring, say, 400 and 450 units is hardly noticeable. It can readily be seen that very long perimeters do not necessarily produce a corresponding increase in the degree of dispersion of the area of the shape; hence, in general, the longer the perimeter, the larger will be the discrepancy between measured dispersion and judged compactness.

Brown, Hitchcock, and Michels (1962) have suggested another measure of dispersion: the sum of deviations in line length from the length of a side of a regular polygon of the same number of sides. Calculations show that this measure does not correlate very highly with P^2/A, but since it depends on the length of the perimeter, it suffers from the same disadvantage as the latter measure, namely it breaks down at the low and high ends of the continuum. So far, this measure has been used in one experiment only and its usefulness therefore cannot be properly evaluated.

Of other measures of dispersion mention may be made of a measure of "regularity," defined as the ratio of the standard deviation of side lengths and the standard deviation of all angles (Small, 1961), and "angular variability" (Attneave, 1957). The former measure was used only once, without success; the latter, by various other investigators besides Attneave, with some success. As defined by Attneave, angular variability is the arithmetic mean (sign ignored) of algebraic differences in degrees of slope change (sign observed) between all successive or adjacent angles taken in overlapping pairs about the contour, convex angles being considered positive and concave angles negative. According to Attneave, angular variability measures something like "goood continuation." Attneave found that, although this measure correlated with the P^2/A measure, it accounted for 7% of the total variance of judgments of complexity of random shapes. Results by other investigators indicate that angular variability as a predictor of performance varies in its utility, hence its status is not quite clear as yet.

Symmetry is another form parameter of the total configuration. Geometrically, a figure is symmetric if it remains unchanged after a symmetry operation has been performed on it. The two principal symmetry operations that are relevant to the study of the physical properties of form are rotation and reflection. A form may be "richer" or "poorer" in symmetry depending on how many types of symmetry operations may be performed on it without affecting it. Reflection may take place along any number of axes. Some shapes, when a mirror is placed vertically to the plane in which they lie, will remain unchanged in only one position of the mirror, i.e., they will be symmetric only about one axis. The letter *A* is an example. The letter *B*, on the other hand, remains unchanged only if reflected in a mirror placed above or below it. It thus shows horizontal symmetry. In terms of rotation, the letters *S, H, I, O,* and *X* possess twofold symmetry because they appear the same after a 180-degree rotation. An equal-arm cross shows fourfold symmetry because it appears identical in four different rotations, whereas a circle remains symmetric regardless of orientation of the axis about which it is reflected, thus representing the richest kind of symmetry.

The types of symmetry just described are still conceivable in dichotomous terms: a figure is either symmetric or asymmetric regardless of how many symmetry operations may be performed on it. Symmetry, nevertheless, is a continuous variable—there are degrees of symmetry—hence it is measurable on a continuum. Until recently, however, measurement of symmetry had not advanced beyond the stage of the simple symmetry-asymmetry dichotomy. In statistics, the skewness of a one-dimensional distribution is measured, but skewness means some degree of deviation from symmetry. In other words, skewness measures symmetry. The same concept may be applied to two-dimensional distributions, and the asymmetry of a shape may also be measured on a continuum. This measure is related to a number of other measures and is discussed more fully below.

A third intrinsic parameter of a global character is elongation, i.e., the overall "thinness" or "thickness" of a shape. Since thin shapes have more of their area removed from the center of gravity, elongation is clearly a measure related to dispersion. The ratio of the length and width of rectangles has been used as an independent variable as far back as 1876, when Fechner did his work in experimental aesthetics. The width-height ratio, occasionally applied to figures other than rectangles, has been used by a number of other experimenters since Fechner. These workers, however, have been chiefly concerned with experimental aesthetics (e.g., the role of the "golden section"), and their efforts do not shed too much light on the problem of physical form parameters.

The longest extent of a shape is occasionally used as a measure of elongation (Casperson, 1950). The diameter of the smallest circle that can be described around a shape without crossing its contours at any point provides this measure also. Thus, Small's (1961) "covering circle" is identical to the longest-extent measure. Both Casperson and Small have found this measure of some predictive value. Regardless of which measure of elongation is used, for purposes of comparison, shapes must be first equated on area.

Neither the width-height ratio nor the longest extent of a shape depend on any particular orientation of the shape. Brown, Hitchcock, and Michels (1962), however, introduced the factor of rotation in their definition of elongation: elongation was defined as the ratio of the horizontal and vertical extents of a shape in a given rotation. In this and two other experiments (Zusne & Michels, 1962a, 1962b), this measure was found to be of only limited value. Small (1961) used the horizontal and vertical extents separately, obtaining negative results in a judgmental task. This brings up the question of whether form parameters should be measured in a particular orientation of the shape or absolutely. Although the evidence is not plentiful, it seems to indicate that, in the case of elongation at least, the latter choice is to be preferred. For instance, the elongations of shapes used by Zusne and Michels (1962a, 1962b) were recomputed using the longest extent of the shape as the baseline (width) and averaging the overall elongation and the elongations of those parts of the shape that exceeded the overall elongation of the shape. This resulted in a substantial increase in the correlations between the new measure of elongation and the previously obtained response measures.

Measures of Areal and Perimetric Variability. In any study where an attempt is made to predict perceptual response from physical form measures, the implicit question asked is this: "How can we arrive at an index or a set of related indices that would completely describe the way a shape, i.e., its area or its perimeter, is distributed in space?" The key concept here is distribution. In the following, various attempts to describe the distribution of the area of two-dimensional shapes are presented.

Stilson (1956) defined a measure, called "overlapping areas," as the sum of the areas that overlap when a triangle is folded along each of its medians. Boynton (Boynton, Elworth, Onley, & Klingberg, 1960; Boynton, Elworth, Monty, Onley, & Klingberg, 1961; Monty & Boynton, 1962) have used "stimulus overlap" in a fashion that is related to, yet different from, Stilson's. The maximum value of overlapping areas of two random polygons obtained by translation alone is called T overlap, and the maximum value of overlapping area obtained by translation and rotation is called TR overlap. To measure overlap, Boynton and his co-workers built an optical device called an overlap analyzer (Fig. 5-15). A similar device was built earlier by Kretzmer (1952) and its use was analyzed by Horowitz (1957). Its main component is an autofocus enlarger. A transparency of one of the two forms (A) to be compared on overlap is inserted in the enlarger and its image projected on a glass plate located on the table that

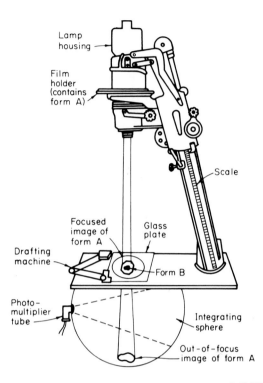

Fig. 5-15. The overlap analyzer. From Boynton *et al.* (1961).

supports the enlarger. In this transparency, the form is a clear area on black background. The other form (B) is also prepared as a transparency, but it is black on clear background. This transparency has an octogonal shape. It is positioned on the glass plate and may be rotated to any of eight equally spaced positions. The glass plate itself is attached to the rule-supports of a drafting machine. This permits horizontal and vertical translational movements of the second shape. There is a hole in the table under the glass plate. An 18-in.-diameter integrating sphere painted flat white on the inside is mounted beneath the table. The sphere has two apertures: one to admit the light from the first form not blocked by the second; the other for mounting a photomultiplier pickup. The photocell picks up the light coming from the opposite side of the sphere. The luminance of this area is proportionate to the total amount of luminous flux entering the sphere. The readings on the scale of a photometer attached to the photomultiplier indicate the amount of nonoverlap between the two forms. Four types of overlap comparison between forms of equal areas are shown in Fig. 5-16.

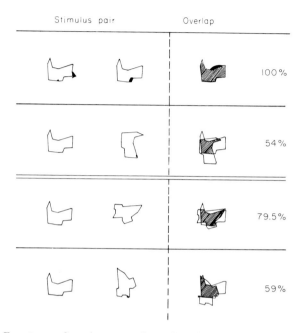

Fig. 5-16. Four types of overlap comparison of equal-area forms. From top to bottom: (1) *T*- and *TR*-same forms with 100%. *T*-overlap; (2) *T*-different but *TR*-same forms with 54% *T*-overlap; (3) *T*- and *TR*-different forms with 79.5% overlap (the maximum for these forms); (4) the same *T*- and *TR*-different forms in position of minimum overlap (59%). From Boynton *et al.* (1961).

Boynton's experiments show that, when no further information is given, subjects judge the similarity of pairs of shapes using *T* overlap as a clue. With repeated practice, however, subjects seem to be more capable of utilizing the *TR* criterion than the *T* criterion in making judgments. Translation and rotation (along with reflection) are the appropriate geometric transformations used to test the congruence of figures. Only when all three operations have been performed does it become certain whether two figures are congruent or not and to what extent. Translation alone is the weakest test. Assuming that a sample of forms contains no mirror images of some of them, rotation must be used in addition to check for the amount of overlap between two forms, but to visualize rotation is more difficult than to visualize translation.

Polidora has used a similar approach in comparing the disparity between two patterns of lighted square cells. Since the unit of measurement is a cell in a matrix, Polidora measures the amount of similarity between two patterns by overlapping them and counting the number of elements that do not have a matching counterpart in the other pattern (Polidora, 1966). It is not difficult to visualize a pattern of partially connected elements collapsed on one axis, as in the case of the Ohio metric histoforms. The variance of this distribution of pattern elements would be the second moment of area of the pattern along one axis. The difference between the two second moments of area of two patterns would then reflect the amount of overlap that can be obtained between the two frequency distributions if one is superimposed upon the other so that their midpoints (means) coincide. One would expect this difference to be closely related to Boynton's T overlap, although not perfectly, because the shape of a pattern changes as it is projected one-dimensionally upon an axis. I have computed T overlap for 99 pairs of eight-sided random shapes by superimposing each pair so that their centers of gravity coincided as well as the axes about which their second moments of area had been computed. The value of Pearson's r between T overlap and the second moment of area was $-.67$, a correlation of the expected order of magnitude and in the expected direction.

In a number of studies (Brown, Hitchcock, & Michels, 1962; Hitchcock, Michels, & Brown, 1963; Small, 1961; Zusne & Michels, 1962a, 1962b), a measure called areal asymmetry has been used. It is defined as the variance of the portions of the total area of the shape enclosed by each of the four quadrants when, in a given rotation, a horizontal and a vertical axis are passed through the geometric center of the shape. Thus defined, the measure is more properly called areal variance since its relationship to figural symmetry is indeterminate. Perfect symmetry calls for the equality of the areas and the congruence of the contours of the symmetric halves of a shape, and the areal asymmetry measure takes account of area only. By chance alone, a symmetric and an asymmetric figure may have exactly the same value of this measure if the corresponding four quadrant areas of the two figures happen to be equal. In spite of this and the fact that the measure is rotation-dependent, it has accounted for some variance in discrimination response in some of the above-mentioned studies, although not in a clear-cut fashion. When subjects are allowed to turn the stimuli around so that they are not bound to any external frame of reference, areal asymmetry does not contribute anything to response variance (Zusne & Michels, 1962b).

Small (1961) used three related but simpler measures: horizontal balance, defined as the ratio of the area of the shape lying in the upper half of the smallest enclosing rectangle and that lying in the lower half; vertical balance, defined analogously but relative to the right and left halves of the shape; and quadrant balance, defined as the ratio of vertical balance to horizontal balance. These measures did not turn out to be useful predictors in a similarity judgment task.

Guiliano, Jones, Kimball, Meyer, and Stein (1961) have used several measures, which they call central moments, to specify letters of the alphabet. These moments describe the location of the center of gravity of a letter with respect to its geometric center (hence "central"), hence the relative balance of the portions of the letter in the right and left halves of the letter and the upper and lower halves of the letter (hence "moments").

What the areal overlap, areal variance, and similar measures have in common is that they tap some aspect of variability or some moment of the statistical distribution of fractional areas of the shape. In this respect, they come close to the moment approach to the measurement of visual form of the author (Zusne, 1965). In this approach, the parameters of dispersion, symmetry, and elongation are considered to be analogs of the second, third, and fourth moments of distribution of the area of a shape. In statistics, a one-dimensional sampling distribution is specified by stating its mean, variance, skewness, kurtosis, and other higher moments. The area of a shape may be thought of as two one-dimensional distributions of its elements, i.e., small units of area. Figure 5-17 shows the two one-dimensional collapses of a nonrepresentational shape.

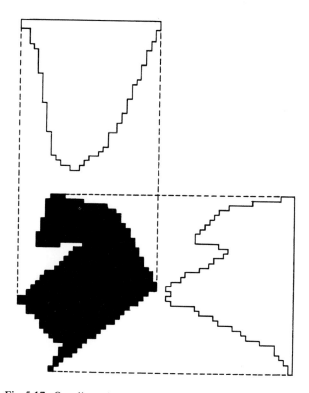

Fig. 5-17. One-dimensional collapses of a two-dimensional shape.

Such a distribution may also be specified by stating its moments of area about the centroid of the shape and along the two axes of the coordinate system in which it is placed.

Years of work with the octopus has led Sutherland (1957) to formulate the theory that there is a possible neural analyzing mechanism in the octopus which operates by dividing shapes into their vertical and horizontal projections and combining the horizontal and vertical projections of different shapes. This is almost literally the definition of what I have called the second-moment constant (p. 218). Alt (1962) and Hu (1962) have used moments of area to specify two-dimensional distributions (letters and numbers for the purpose of their optical recognition by computer), but their work does not deal with the behavioral correlates of moments.

The first moment of area or the centroid can be determined in several ways. The mechanical method consists in cutting the shape out of some homogeneous material, suspending it from some point on its periphery, dropping a vertical from that point, then suspending the form from some other point on the contour and dropping another vertical. The point of intersection of the two verticals is the center of gravity. This is a fast, easy method, and precise enough for all practical purposes.

Another method consists in placing the form in a coordinate system and, taking its vertices as data points, computing the best-fitting straight line for these points, first in one position of the form, then in another. These two lines will cross in the centroid. This is a more laborious method than the mechanical one. If mathematical precision is desired and the coordinates of the centroid are needed, it is better to use the computer, which, for the computation of higher-order moments, must be used anyway.

The computation of higher-order moments is extremely time-consuming, so that the use of a computer is mandatory. In one computer program, written by Knoll and Stenson (1968), the shape is divided into triangles, using the vertices of the shape as reference points. What moments really are is more evident in another method in which the shape is divided into smaller incremental areas (Fig. 5-18). Assuming that the form has been so divided, the operations performed by a computer in computing the first moment of area are based on the following. The product of the distance of the centroid from the Y reference axis, $\bar{y}$ (Fig. 5-19), and the total area A, equals the sum of all the elementary moments ay:

$$\bar{y} = \sum_{j=1}^{n} ay/A .$$

Similarly,

$$\bar{x} = \sum_{i=1}^{n} ax/A .$$

The numbers $\bar{y}$ and $\bar{x}$ are the coordinates of the centroid.

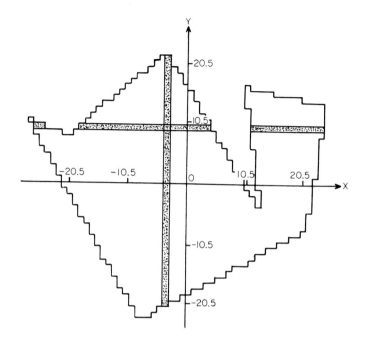

Fig. 5-18. An irregular polygon laid out for the computation of moments of area by means of a desk calculator.

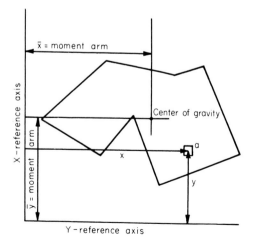

Fig. 5-19. Determination of the coordinates of the centroid of an irregular polygon.

Regardless of how a shape is presented to the computer, the computer sums the unit areas vertically and horizontally and multiplies each such row and column by its distance from the point of origin. Once these elementary moments have been stored, it is relatively easy to perform the various operations required to compute the higher-order moments of area. This computation amounts to double integration over the rectangle containing the shape where area units are represented by, say, 1-punches and nonarea by 0-punches in the data cards. It is convenient to make the origin of the coordinate system coincide with the centroid, so that $\bar{x} = \bar{y} = 0$.

It is known from physics and engineering that, for one variable x, moments are defined as

$$U_k = \iint_R (x - \bar{x})^k dF(x, y) ,$$

where k is the order of the moment, R is the region within the boundary of the form, and $F(x, y)$ is the distribution function. Specifically, the second moment of area computed along the x axis is

$$U_{2x} = (x - \bar{x})^2 dA ,$$

where x is the distance of an incremental area dA from the origin and x the distance of the centroid from the origin. If the centroid is made to coincide with the origin, $\bar{x} = 0$, and the formula, when expanded, reduces to

$$U_{2x} = \int x^2 \, dA - [(\int x \, dA)^2 / A] ,$$

or, in terms of discrete quantities,

$$U_{2x} = \sum_{i,j=1}^{n,m} i^2 a_{ij} - [(\sum_{i,j=1}^{n,m} i a_{ij})^2 / A] ,$$

where i and j are the values of the coordinates along the x and y axes, respectively, a the smallest discrete unit of area used, and A the total area. Similarly, for the second moment along the y axis, the quantity is

$$U_{2y} = \sum_{i,j=1}^{n,m} j^2 a_{ji} - [(\sum_{i,j=1}^{n,m} j a_{ji})^2 / A] .$$

The U_{2x} and U_{2y} functions are mirror images of each other; in addition, each of them is also symmetric about its single maximum (or minimum), which occurs every 90 degrees of rotation of the shape. Thus, since the two functions are complementary, they sum to a constant in any rotation:

$$U_{2x} + U_{2y} = c.$$

This sum, then, may be used as the rotation-independent value of the second moment of area. Since compactness is a variable judged without regard to orientation, the second moment constant makes psychological sense.

Expanding the expression

$$U_{3x} = (x - \bar{x})^3 dA ,$$

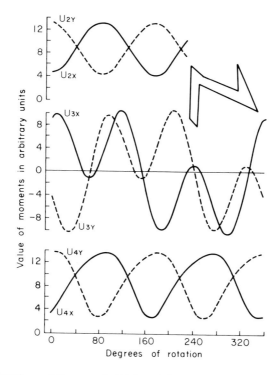

Fig. 5-20. Functions of the second, third, and fourth moments of area of a random shape rotated through 360 degrees. From top to bottom, the three vertical scales are in the ratio of 1 : 10 : 100.

we obtain, if $\bar{x} = 0$,

$$U_{3x} = \int x^3 \, dA - 3 \int x^2 \, dA \, (\int x \, dA/A) + 2[(\int x \, dA)^3/A] \, .$$

The formula for U_{3y} is analogous.

Since the two third-moment functions are neither symmetric nor complementary, but identical, having a phase difference of 90 degrees (Fig. 5-20), no simple additive relationship obtains here. The function is congruent to itself about the 180-degree point, but only after a reflection operation (i.e., reversal of the algebraic sign) and a 180-degree translation along the x axis of the plot are performed. Actually, as in the case with the second moment, all information about the basic cycle of change in the third moment is obtained by rotating the shape through 90 degrees only. The only difference is that in the case of the third moment the algebraic sign of the function changes in the four quadrants of rotation, hence the appearance of the plotted function changes.

The absence of a rotation-independent value of the third moment leaves the experimenter with the choice of which value of the third moment to use in a particular situation. Since symmetry judgments are made with respect to some axis of symmetry, the orientation of this axis is important, hence a rotation-independent value of the third moment would not be psychologically meaningful, although it is mathematically possible to obtain it (Hu, 1962).

Again assuming that $\bar{x} = 0$, for the fourth moment, the expression

$$U_{4x} = \int (x - \bar{x})^4 \, dA$$

is expanded to

$$U_{4x} = \int x^4 \, dA - 4\int x^3 \, dA(\int x \, dA/A) + 6\int x^2 dA \, [(\int x \, dA)^2/A^2] - 3[(\int x \, dA)^4/A^3].$$

Similar to the third moment, the x and y functions are identical here except for a 90-degree phase difference (Fig. 5-20). Unlike the third moment, however,

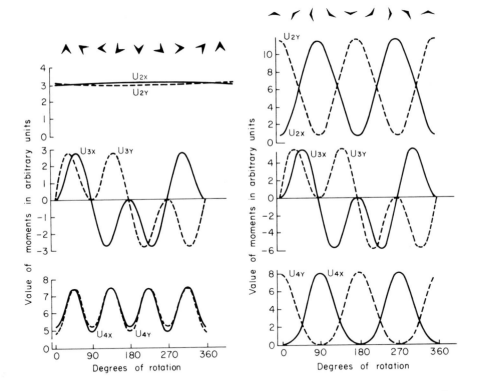

Fig. 5-21. Left: Functions of the second, third, and fourth moments of area of a compact, symmetric shape rotated through 360 degrees. From top to bottom the three vertical scales are in the ratio of 1 : 10 : 100.

Fig. 5-22. Right: Functions of the second, third, and fourth moments of area of an elongated, symmetric shape rotated through 360 degrees. From top to bottom the three vertical scales are in the ratio of 1 : 10 : 100.

the fourth-moment function can be brought to congruence with itself through a simple 180-degree translation along the x axis of the plot, without reflection. While the general configuration of the function is similar to that of the second moment, its properties differ: the fourth-moment function, e.g., is not symmetric about its point of maximum/minimum. Here, too, it is up to the experimenter to choose the rotation in which to compute the fourth moment. Since elongation is also judged with respect to some axis, the fourth moment computed about the longest axis of the shape, e.g., is a psychologically meaningful measure. A rotation-independent measure of the fourth moment has been discovered though (Hu, 1962).

The way moment values change with rotation is more clearly illustrated in Figs. 5-21 and 5-22. In Fig. 5-21; the rotations of a compact, symmetric, V-shaped figure are shown at the top. Figure 5-22 shows essentially the same figure except that it is considerably more elongated, hence less compact. This factor affects the shape of the function of the second moment while leaving the third moment unaffected. It may be noted here that the moment subscripts x and y mean a moment *along* the particular axis and *about* the axis orthogonal to it.

Moments of area are rather insensitive to small but perceptually conspicuous protrusions from a shape. Such a protrusion may be the only, but quite obvious difference between two otherwise identical shapes. When moments of area are computed, the sheer size of the area enclosed by the contour obscures small perimetric differences.

The computation of moments of the perimeter is identical to that of areal moments, except that the shape is represented on cards by punching only the contour of the shape. An experiment (Zusne, 1965) in which the task was the discrimination of pairs of shapes showed that not only the second and third moments but also the fourth moment of the perimeter were significant and somewhat better predictors of performance than moments of area. The two kinds of moments appear to describe somewhat different configurational properties of form, and it appears almost certain that their effectiveness as predictors of performance depends on the type of perceptual task.

In spite of the small amount of work done with moments, they show several important advantages as compared to other form measures: they constitute a few basic form measures having the same mathematical basis; they probably provide uniqueness in form specification; and they make possible the quantification of configurational properties of shapes on continua rather than dichotomously. It remains to be seen how well these measures will stand the test of time.

Although it does not involve behavior, one such test has recently been performed. Brown and Owen (1967) performed factor analyses of five 80×80 correlation matrices of single form parameters measured in five samples of 200 random shapes each, where each sample contained shapes of one complexity level only. Shapes of 4, 8, 12, 16, and 20 sides were used, i.e., the extracted factors may be considered a function of complexity. Twelve factors were extracted, but only five of them could be interpreted meaningfully. In addition, these five accounted for a relatively large proportion of matrix variance while the other seven each accounted for small, approximately equal proportions of the remainder of the variance. The five factors and the measures that were most highly correlated with each of them are given in Table 5-2. The table shows that moment measures were highly correlated with all five factors. Since moments may be computed on any set of measures, this in itself is not a significant fact. What is significant is that, first, some of these moments were the areal and perimetric moments just discussed; second, the names given by Brown and Owen to the five factors also suggest moment characteristics. The first factor was called "compactness," the second "jaggedness." Since compactness (or better, dispersion) and jaggedness are the two ends of the same continuum, it appears that these two factors represent two aspects of the same property. When the examples of shapes shown by Brown and Owen are examined, it is evident that the first factor should have been labeled "elongation." At least the examples of four-sided shapes shown by these authors vary only in elongation, while the examples shown under the jaggedness factor differ in the degree of dispersion of their contours around the center of gravity instead. The examples of 12-sided shapes shown appear, on the other hand, to have been interchanged between the two factors. The second and fourth moments of areal and perimetic distributions are, of course, highly correlated and the confusion is understandable. One measure that would have permitted to decide which of these two factors represents elongation and which jaggedness, namely the second-moment constant, was not included in the correlation matrix. This is one measure which describes the jaggedness continuum and is a better predictor of performance than the second moment of x or the second moment of y alone.

Factors III and IV reflected the third moment of areal or perimetric distribution, namely symmetry. Since no psychologically meaningful rotation-independent measure of symmetry is available, it is understandable that this property was eventually represented by two factors rather than one and that the separate x and y measures of the third moment correlated highly with these factors. The fifth factor, which Brown and Owen label the "dominant-axis" factor, appears to be an artifactual one. In a random sample of 200 shapes, the number of compact, rounded shapes or even jagged shapes that have their most peripheral points about the same distance removed from their centers of gravity is quite small. Most shapes are longer in one direction than in others. If the position of the longest axis varies randomly, a sample of shapes will be characterized by the deviation of this axis from the vertical, for instance. A number of measures that are otherwise quite unrelated to direction, axes, or

TABLE 5-2

Five Major Factors Extracted and Physical Form Measures Most Highly Correlated with These Factors in a Study by Brown and Owen (1967)

Name of factor	Measures correlating highly with factor
"Compactness" (I)	Largest complementary radial pair
	Area of enclosing rectangle
	First four moments of radial lengths
	Second moment of side lengths
	Second areal moment of x
	Second perimetric moment of x
	Maximum second areal moment of x
	Maximum second perimetric moment of x
"Jaggedness" (II)	All measures based on angles
"Skewness" (of contours relative to the y axis) (III)	Mean of the y coordinates
	The y coordinate of first moment of area
	Third moment of area of y
	Third moment of perimeter of y
"Skewness" (of contours relative to the x axis) (IV)	Mean of the x coordinates
	The x coordinate of first moment of area
	Third moment of area of x
	Third moment of perimeter of x
"Dominant axis" (V)	Ratio between vertical and horizontal extents
	Second moment of area of x
	Second moment of perimeter of x
	Second moment of area of y
	Second moment of perimeter of y
	Variance of x coordinates
	Variance of y coordinates

rotation reflect this property of a shape, such as the second and third moments of area about an axis.

5. Relational Parameters

Every form belongs to a population of forms as well as to some sample of forms that is actually being used in an experiment. This sample, however, may represent several different populations of forms. For this reason, the dimensions of relationship between a given form and potential or actual other forms are a factor which it is just as important to consider as the physical dimensions of a single form. "How the single stimulus is perceived is a function not so much of what it is, but is rather a function of what the total set and the particular subset are. The properties of the total set and the subset are also the properties of the single stimulus, so we cannot understand the knowing of the single stimulus without understanding the properties of the sets within which it is contained." (Garner, 1966, p. 11.)

A. SAMPLING

The problems implied in the above quotation have received surprisingly little attention. A beginning was made by Vanderplas (Vanderplas *et al.*, 1965), who performed a factor analysis of 13 form measures taken on 1100 random shapes, and by Brown and Michels (1966), who in a brief note suggested that a discrepancy observed between the results of two groups of researchers could have been due to the fact that the two kinds of stimuli used by them could have belonged to two different stimulus domains differing in both the number of attributes and the range of values of each attribute. An article by Brown and Owen (1967) is the only one dedicated entirely to the importance of studying the statistical characteristics of the populations of shapes from which samples are selected for behavioral studies. The conclusions reached by Brown and Owen are based on factor-analytic study of a very large number of form parameters measured in five samples of random shapes, each sample consisting of 200 shapes of a given level of complexity. While the major factors were the same for all levels of complexity, differences were found to exist across levels of complexity. These differences have an important bearing on form-perception research.

One difference consisted in the distribution of the attributes represented by the factors. For instance, it was found that the modal shape is more jagged when it has 12 sides than when it has only four sides. The practical consequence of this phenomenon is that a random sample of 12-sided shapes will tend to be more jagged than a similar sample of four-sided shapes. If this factor needs to be kept constant, contrained rather than random samples of shapes would have to be used. There is, however, a certain amount of artifactuality in this situation which arises whenever the extremes of a variable are sampled. The variable in this case is complexity. Most older studies and many current studies have employed samples of shapes in which the complexity variable has been represented by instances from its lowest extreme, such as four- and six-sided polygons. Triangles are also frequently used, and three sides is the smallest number of sides that a polygon can have. Relationships that obtain for the middle range of values break down at the extremes. Even a superficial comparison of 3-, 4-, and 5-sided shapes reveals large, quantal jumps in an attribute from one complexity level to the next. The simpler the shapes, the larger are these differences. For instance, a triangle can have only one right angle, whereas, by adding only one side, it is possible for the resulting polygon to have four such angles. A triangle can have no concave angles, a quadrilateral can have one, a 5-sided shape two, an 8-sided shape five. In general, there are $n - 3$ concave angles, where n is the total number of sides or vertices. The presence or absence of a concave angle at low levels of complexity makes a very striking difference perceptually. Concave angles also quite naturally increase the jaggedness of the more complex shapes: while the expected frequency of four-sided shapes with one concave angle is 50%, the expected frequencies of shapes with one or more concave angles are 75, 87, 93, and 97% for shapes of 5, 6, 7, and 8 sides, respectively. At the same time, with increasing complexity, differences in jaggedness between any two adjacent levels of complexity become increasingly smaller. Thus, while with respect to jaggedness, shapes with up to about seven or eight sides each can be put in a separate category, there is practically no difference in this variable between, say, 24-, 25-, and 26-sided shapes. Regardless of what the basic cause of the differences in the distribution of attribute between shapes of different complexities might be, these differences are real and must be taken into account in the design of experiments.

A second variable to be considered in form-perception experiments is the number of dimensions needed to describe a shape. Attneave and Arnoult (1956)

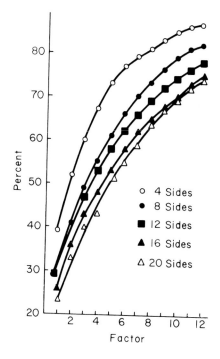

Fig. 5-23. Percentage of communality accounted for by 12 factors for shapes with 4, 8, 12, 16, and 20 sides. From Brown and Owen (1967). Copyright 1967 by the American Psychological Association. Reproduced by permission.

stated some time ago that this number would vary with the complexity of the shape. Brown and Owen confirm this statement. As may be seen from Fig. 5-23, the percentage of communality accounted for by 12 factors for shapes of different levels of complexity decreases with increasing complexity, albeit in a negatively accelerated fashion. Thus, while 5 factors will account for just about 75% of the communality in four-sided shapes, 12 are necessary to account for the same amount of communality in 20-sided polygons.

Brown and Owen also tested the reliability of the factorial results in two samples of 500 shapes each (100 at each level of complexity). It was found that stability of sampling decreased as the number of factors extracted at a given complexity level increased and as complexity itself increased. Brown and Owen favor the explanation that, as the number of sides increases the degree to which a shape is free to vary increases. The consequences of this are a decrease in linear dependence among measures and decreased stability. For these reasons, with increased complexity, representativeness in a sample of shapes can be maintained only by increasing sample size or by using stratified samples of shapes. Both approaches have their own problems. Since even the simplest shapes vary along several dimensions simultaneously and since many of these dimensions are correlated, it is actually impossible to obtain large random samples of shapes in which these dimensions are orthogonal to each other. The usual procedure is to construct small samples of shapes by selecting them from larger pools in such a way that orthogonality is assured. In factorial studies, this procedure theoretically decreases the generalizability of findings to other random samples from the same population to zero since the factors have been made fixed rather than allowed to remain random. The only other alternative, as Brown and Owen point out, is to use stratified samples. Stratification, however, requires that information be available on the sampling characteristics of the parameters studied for the shape population sampled. This information is only now being made available on a limited scale.

B. REDUNDANCY

Applying the informational concept of redundancy to visual form has turned out to be one of the most difficult tasks in the quantification of form. In common language redundancy means surplus or unneeded information. A form whose two halves are congruent after reflection is said to be symmetric. Since one of its halves repeats exactly the same information that is contained in its other half, it is a redundant form or, more exactly, it contains redundant information. But symmetry is only one way in which information may be repeated. The presence of right angles in a form would constitute redundancy. So would the repetition of the same pattern in a series, as in a wallpaper border, in short, any kind of homogeneity. There are "as many kinds of redundancy in the visual field as there are kinds of regularity or lawfulness" (Attneave, 1954, p.

192), and it is reasonable to assume that the perceptual response would differ depending on the kind of redundancy that an observer faces.

Then there is the considerable problem of measuring the amount of redundancy. Not that it is particularly difficult to do so or that there is a dearth of measures. On the contrary, there are several simple and exact measures of redundancy available. One problem is that they measure different aspects of redundancy. Another problem is that of matching type and amount of redundancy. This is directly related to the problem of the concept of redundancy as applied to single stimuli and as a statistical concept. Since redundancy is an informational term and information theory is statistical in nature, redundancy is handled appropriately only when it is applied to sets of stimuli and not to single stimuli. Symmetry is one property of shape that raises a problem in this respect. Earlier in this chapter, symmetry was identified with the third moment of areal or contour distribution in a one-dimensional collapse of a shape. The third moment of distribution may be computed meaningfully for a single form without reference to any sample statistics or population parameters. The third moment, however, is not a measure of redundancy. Redundancy has to do with stimulus uncertainty, which cannot be specified except with reference to sets of stimuli. Redundancy, and therefore symmetry, as a statistical concept refers to the extent to which a stimulus sample is smaller than the total population that could exist. "Amount of redundancy is determined by how many stimuli are selected, and form of redundancy is determined by which particular ones are selected" (Garner, 1962, p. 184). Thus conceptualized, redundancy offers a way for fitting statements about single forms into the statistical framework of information theory, which deals with sets of elements and their probabilities. Garner suggests that when a figure is judged to be redundant it is not actually the figury itself that is judged to be redundant but the sample of figures from which it is presumed to have come. When this sample is very small, the redundancy of a particular figure from this sample is judged to be high. Thus, the circle is judged to be the most symmetric, regular, "best" figure because it represents a very small inferred sample of figures characterized by a set of certain variables. From this point of view, a symmetric figure is judged to be symmetric, regular, a good Gestalt, etc. because there are relatively few symmetric figures in a population of figures of a certain level of complexity, compactness, and elongation. To use the third moment of area as a measure of a certain aspect of the distribution of the area of a single shape and to call this measure the third moment of area is quite appropriate; to refer to the third moment of area as a measure of symmetry means taking a certain amount of liberty, however, or at least suddenly switching one's viewpoint: the reference is not to the degree of asymmetry of the shape itself, but of the shape of a particular one-dimensional projection of its area. It is the shape of this distribution whose redundancy is judged with respect to the size of the total population of such projections from which this particular one is presumed to have come.

Not infrequently, amount and form of redundancy become imperceptibly intertwined. Fitts and Leonard (1957), two investigators who were among the first to introduce information measures in the field of form perception, computed form redundancy in the following manner. If a 4×4 matrix is used to construct metric figures as described earlier in this chapter, 4^4 or 256 different random metric figures may be constructed, as compared with a total of 2^{16} or 65,536 different cell patterns. The sample of metric figures is considered to be constrained with regard to the total number of patterns possible. Similarly, if further restrictions are introduced in the construction of the metric figures, the smaller sample would be constrained or redundant with regard to the total of 256 metric figures that are possible. For instance, by introducing the rule that no two columns may be of the same height in the same figure (called Redundancy I by Fitts and Leonard) the total number of such figures is reduced to 4! or 24. In terms of identifying any one of the cell patterns, the random metric figures, and the Redundancy-I metric figures, 16, 8, and 4.6 bits of information are obtained, respectively. Thus, the smaller the amount of information obtained upon identification, the more redundant is the figure. In addition to Redundancy I, Fitts and Leonard have used other types of constraints, illustrated in Fig. 5-4. The amount of redundancy in these figures cannot be specified, however, without reference to the asymmetric, non-reflected, or nonrepeated figure, hence the relationship between these figures and the Redundancy-I type of figure is an indirect one since two different bases for computing redundancy are used, namely sample size and a single form. This intertwining of the quantitative, qualitative, statistical, and determinate aspects of redundancy has occurred with other researchers who have emphasized the use of information measures in the study of visual form. Attneave (1954) was among the first to point out that, since organization and redundancy were roughly the same and redundancy could be measured, so could organization. This, of course, had an important consequence for the Gestalt theory because now the different aspects of organization, including symmetry, could be subjected to quantitative study. Attneave at first did not distinguish the two aspects of symmetry discussed above, for which he, in retrospect, has been criticized (e.g., Staniland, 1966).

Another example comes from Alluisi and Hall (1965). These researchers have suggested that, in addition to the three classes of form parameter proposed by Michels and Zusne (1965), a fourth one should be added. While a fourth one is a logical possibility, it is a physical impossibility (cf. pp. 196/7). Furthermore, the "transphenomenal parameter" proposed by Alluisi and Hall is not a single form parameter, which the other three classes are, but a sampling rule for the selection of samples of forms from a population. It is identical with Redundancy I of Fitts and Leonard (1957), and is therefore a relational parameter.

Within the confines of the technical or informational meaning of redundancy, there are also problems since it presents several different aspects, each of which has its separate consequences when used in the quantification of the redundancy of visual form. The reconciliation of contradictory experimental results depends on the clarification of the definition and measurement problems. The major works that tackle this problem stem from Evans (1967), Garner (1962), and Staniland (1966). Evans' paper clarifies terms, concepts, and complexities associated with redundancy, offers solutions for measuring redundancy in metric patterns, and summarizes and reconciles the often confusing statements on the subject made by earlier investigators.

C. CONTEXT

Form is perceived not only in terms of its own unique characteristics and its belonging to an inferred, but physically absent, set of forms, but also in relation to other forms that are actually present in the visual field. The physical characteristics of these other forms have an effect on response to a particular form. This effect is absent when the other forms are absent. In this situation must be included the separate or sequential presentation of form stimuli that make up the sample used in an experiment where eventually a subject is exposed to the entire sample, such as in discrimination or paired comparison tasks. While statistical considerations are also of importance here, such as the total number of forms that is presented for discrimination or recognition, the probability with which each stimulus is presented, etc., these are considerations pertinent to the experimental design and a matter of empirical investigation. In this section, the more general matters of stimulus properties that pertain to similarity and visual noise are considered.

Similarity. To establish functional relationships, three or more data points are needed. Such forms as are found in textbooks of geometry are useless for this purpose: each of them is practically an invariant configuration at the very end of a continuum, so that no information about the effects of changes in these forms can be obtained. Even random forms present difficulties. Since most physical form measures are to a lesser or greater extent correlated, the selection of stimuli for parametric studies, especially of evenly spaced stimuli, is a major problem in the design of form-perception experiments.

Among J. J. Gibson's programmatic statements regarding the psychophysics of form was the suggestion that a form should be studied in its continuous transformations, such as occur, e.g., during the motion of the observer: one-way compression, change in area, etc. (Gibson, 1950, pp. 192/6). To take a simple example, the entire range of possible transformations in the rectangle could be

Fig. 5-24. Matrix of similarity
transformations of the rectangle.

represented in a chart like the one shown in Fig. 5-24. Since only two
transformations are possible, namely the extension or contraction of the two
sides of the rectangle, the entire population of rectangles can be presented in a
two-dimensional array.

In simple forms, such as triangles, quadrilaterals, and five-sided polygons, the
entire range of all possible transformations along any and all dimensions may be
obtained fairly easily since the number of degrees of freedom to vary is relatively
small in these shapes. Beginning with six-sided figures, however, the task of
sampling systematically every possible transformation becomes increasingly
unwieldy. The only resort is to use samples of random shapes. Given a random
shape, though, it is possible to vary it systematically along a given continuum
and thus sample it for purposes of parametric studies. Method 8 of Attneave and
Arnoult (1956) is one method for the production of systematic variation in a
shape, i.e., of a family of shapes having a specifiable relationship among them.
By this method, a prototype shape is constructed first, then each of its points is
moved some distance and reconnected as before. The prototype may be
constructed using any of the methods described earlier in this chapter. The new
locations of the points of the prototype are determined by holding constant or
varying randomly the number of points moved, the particular points moved, the
distance through which a point is moved, and the direction of movement.
Variations produced in this manner will constitute a family of related shapes. A
prototype and a related family of shapes constructed by this method are shown
in Fig. 5-25.

LaBerge and Lawrence (1957) have presented two methods for generating
families of related shapes that differ somewhat from that of Attneave and
Arnoult. The first method leads to a series of shapes of graded similarity that

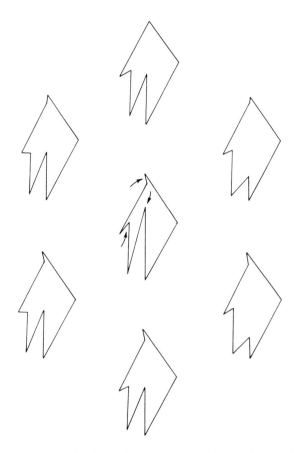

Fig. 5-25. Prototype and related shapes constructed by method 8 of Attneave and Arnoult (1956).

"connect" any two randomly chosen shapes of the same level of complexity. Given two polygons, their centers of gravity are made to coincide, then each vertex in one form is connected to a vertex in the other. These lines are divided into an equal number of units of equal length. By moving all points of the first form one unit along the connecting lines toward the second form and by connecting the new points, a new form, intermediate between the two forms, is obtained. All points of the first form are then moved two units and a second intermediate form is obtained, etc. If the forms have n vertices, these vertices may be connected in $n!$ different ways. To decide which way of connecting is to be used, LaBerge and Lawrence measure the length of all n^n connecting lines and

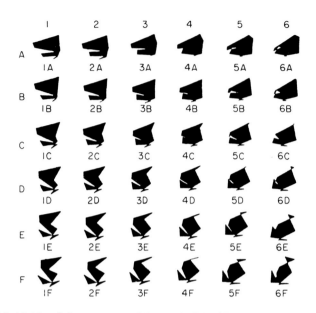

Fig. 5-26. Matrix of forms generated by method I of LaBerge and Lawrence (1957). Reproduced by permission.

decide upon that combination that yields the smallest sum of squared distances between paired points. The drawing of the outlines of an intermediate form is determined by the rule that, if points *a* and *b* are joined in the outline of the original form, then the points paired with them in the intermediate form are also joined. This last rule, however, creates situations where two sides may cross each other or where a piece of ground may appear inside a form.

The above method produces a line or row of forms which relates the two originally constructed forms. A related set of columns of forms may be produced by rotating the *n* lines that connect the two prototypes 90 degrees counterclockwise and proceeding as before. This procedure creates new forms; it does not rotate the prototype. In general, LaBerge and Lawrence's first method generates a matrix of forms where any two adjacent forms are equally spaced in terms of the physical dimensions of distortion. An example of such a matrix is shown in Fig. 5-26.

The second method is more general than the first. Only one form is constructed originally. By gradually changing the location of its points, it is possible to arrive at any other form of the same level of complexity if a sufficient number of intermediate forms is created. The first variant of the original form is produced by selecting, at random, as many pairs of coordinates as there are vertices and by moving each vertex to its new position. For the x coordinates, a range of values is selected, say, from $-.6$ in. to $+.6$ in. and as many values from this range are selected as there are vertices. One of these coordinates is then randomly assigned to each vertex. A second assignment produces the y coordinates. If the initial selection of the values of x (and, of course, the y) coordinates is such that they sum to zero, the center of gravity of the form remains unchanged. To obtain the second variant, the same coordinate increments are added to the coordinates of the vertices of the first variant, etc. The columns of the form matrix are obtained in the same way as in the first method, namely by rotating 90 degrees counterclockwise the paths along which the vertices are moved.

In tests of the subjective distances between forms generated by these two methods, LaBerge and Lawrence found that, while the ordering of the forms corresponded, on the average, exactly to the order in which they were generated, the perceived distances between forms varied depending on whether comparisons were made with a column or a row of the matrix as reference and, in large matrices, on which partial matrix was used, i.e., subjective distances varied as a function of the physical characteristics of a particular set of forms. It is clear that the two methods would produce forms which differed, on occasion, in orientation only or in configuration. In addition, since serial transformations are involved, one type of change in configuration that is of importance here is compression or expansion, i.e., perspective transformations that one might observe in the shape of the projection of a rotating three-dimensional object. LaBerge and Lawrence suggest that, if the purely orientational component as well as the compression-expansion component were eliminated and only the purely configurational changes remained, the subjective spacing of the forms would correspond more closely to their objective spacing. One way of accomplishing this would be by subtracting, from the response obtained by LaBerge and Lawrence, the effects obtained by only rotating the individual shapes as well as the effects obtained with perspective transformations only. Continuous perspective transformations may be obtained by projecting the shadow of a rotating shape unto a screen. Gibson and Gibson (1957) have described such a shadow transformer to be used in the study of response to objects in motion.

When forms are complex representations of real objects, the exact approach to gradual transformations, while not an impossibility, is not very practical. Also, the principle of moving some or all points of the form in randomly determined directions through a randomly determined distance cannot be applied here, unless a distortion is desired that would decrease the resemblance to the real object. In the case of pictures, variation along some logical or psychological continuum must be resorted to. While the distance between any two adjacent picture variants may not be measurable physically, it can be measured in terms of subjectively perceived distance, i.e., scaled. This procedure has been used, e.g., by Fisher (1967), who produced two-dimensional matrices of polyfigurations of the kind typified by Boring's (1930) wife-mother-in-law picture. The two alternative percepts are the basis for producing a graded matrix of variants of the same figure.

Visual Noise. When a single form is presented in the visual field and the boundaries of the field are indefinite or so far removed from the figure that they are not brought into relationship with the figure, only the properties of the figure need to be considered. More frequently, however, figures are presented in a field which may or may not be perceived as ground: if the field has contours and they are near the figure, either the intended figure or the ground upon which it lies may be perceived as figure. This happens if the conditions that favor the perception of a figure are nearly in balance in the two portions of the visual field. These conditions were discussed in Chap. 4. This situation is of particular importance in animal studies where a form presented for discrimination appears on a square or round window that the animal pushes back in search of the reward. The windows are usually small enough for the space between the contours of the figure and the edges of the window to be perceived also as figure, at least occasionally. This has been one of the problems that has made the interpretation of a number of Karl Lashley's experiments ambiguous. Unless the window is made to blend with the surrounding wall in which it is suspended, the figure must be made small enough to be clearly perceived as figure rather than a hole in another figure whose outside contours are those of the window.

When forms are presented in pairs in the same visual field, as is done in various discrimination and scaling tasks, it cannot be assumed that the contours of each figure are perceived separately and then compared without regard to the mutual orientation of the contours of the two figures. Since they are in close proximity, they are also, to some extent at least, perceived as portions of the same configuration. It therefore makes a difference whether a form appears to the right or to the left of another figure, for instance. How the relative positions of the two shapes may affect judgments of similarity in a pair comparison task, for instance, is illustrated in Fig. 5-27. When forms are presented in pairs repeatedly, care is usually taken to randomize the left-right positions of the figures, so that the influence of the relative orientation of the portions of the contours in the two figures is reduced to something close to zero. If a pair of figures is presented only once, and especially if the two figures are relatively simple, the possibility of how this might affect the observer's response must be considered.

As the number of other forms presented in the visual field is increased, the factor of the relative orientation of shape contours decreases in importance

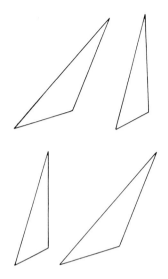

Fig. 5-27. The relative positions of two shapes presented for discrimination may affect the appearance of the visual field drastically and, as a consequence, the relative discriminability of the shapes.

while other factors assume increasing importance. The number and type of the forms in the visual field and their location with regard to the critical shape are some of these factors. In an n-choice oddity-type discrimination problem, for instance, there are n forms in the visual field, one of which differs from the rest, the rest $(n - 1)$ of the forms being identical. Unless $n = 2$, the relative orientation of the contours of the shapes is of lesser importance here than is the distribution of the contours of the shapes taken separately. The other important factor is the way in which the n shapes are arrayed in the visual field. It is common to arrange them so that no shape is favored in terms of attracting more attention than the others. Three shapes are usually arranged as the vertices of an equilateral triangle, and four as the corners of a square or a diamond. With five or six shapes, which is about the maximum number of shapes used in a discrimination problem, different arrangements are possible. One arrangement that seems attractive but which cannot be recommended is a circular one: the odd shape, because it acts as a gap in a form of extremely good continuation, is bound to attract immediate attention, hence decrease the variability in the dependent variable (reaction time, errors).

While it is important that under tachistoscopic conditions the subject's attention be directed toward the general area where the stimulus display is to appear, it is not desirable to have a fixation point in, say, the middle of the area occupied by the display because it will bias the perception of the odd shape on trials in which it happens to be located in the center. The randomness of eye movements prior to exposure, while confined to the display area, will ensure random distribution of fixations throughout the display area in the long run.

As the number of forms in the visual field is increased further, additional factors need to be considered. These have already been discussed in Chap. 4, Section 1 in the consideration of figure-ground phenomena. As illustrated in Fig. 4-2, a figure can become increasingly obscured by visual noise in the ground, but in two different ways: in one, the noise makes detection more difficult, in the other, it is discrimination that is interfered with. In the former case, noise is a large number of shapes more or less randomly distributed throughout the visual field. An organized ground becomes noisy when it begins to penetrate the figure. Organization of the ground is a relative matter here since the degree of organization in the ground necessary to produce good continuation with the figure depends on the degree to which the figure itself is organized. For instance, a pattern consisting of a cluster of dots needs little organization in the ground to be obscured, only sufficiently intense noise. Instances of such penetration of the figure by the ground would be found toward the upper left corner of the triangle in Fig. 4-2.

The matter of quantification of figure-ground organization has not been really tackled by psychologists, although the concepts involved are clear enough to be operationally defined. The quantification of the figure has been the subject of the bulk of this chapter. The quantification of the number, shape, size, orientation, and spatial dispersion of several but not too numerous forms does not represent any problems, and the ordinary geometric and mathematical tools can be and have been applied here. Visual noise comes in different modes, and its quantification depends on the way a researcher defines it. Visual noise can be, for one thing, a "within-figure" noise. This usage comes primarily from the Ohio State group of researchers. Anderson (1957), for instance, describes two types of visual noise. In one, the figure is degraded in a way that resembles the physical shattering or crumbling of a shape made of thin, brittle material. The second type consists in right-left translations of one or more of the bars of a horizontal metric histoform. These two types of visual noise are illustrated in Fig. 5-28. Strictly speaking, visual noise is not involved here at all. Rather, the shapes in Fig. 5-28 belong in some matrix of gradual transformations of a shape of the type illustrated in Fig. 5-26.

If noise is something extraneous to the signal and the figure is a "signal," then noise must be something that, of necessity, pertains to ground. Two situations may be distinguished here. In one situation, a "noisy" condition is obtained by degrading the contours of the figure, e.g., by introducing blur. Since blurred contours tend to merge with the ground, the latter is involved, but indirectly. Blurring of contours may be achieved in several different ways, such as by rubbing the contours if these are drawn in pencil, using an air brush, etc. These

Fig. 5-28. Two types of visual noise. The first figure in rows (a) and (b) is undistorted or noisefree. In the remaining figures of row (a) three levels of visual noise (6.25%, 12.5%, and 25%) have perturbed the cells adjacent to the contour lines; in the remaining figures of row (b) three comparable noise levels have affected all cells of the matrix. Noise level is defined here as the probability that the brightness of a given cell will be reversed. From Anderson (1957).

methods, however, make it impossible to attach any numerical values to the degree of blur, hence some blur-generating device must be used if blur is to be quantified. Green (1957) describes a computer system for generating very large matrices of dots. These are displayed on an oscilloscope screen and photographed. By programming different probabilities of appearance of the dots for different areas on the screen, it is possible to generate displays of figures with blurred contours. Figure 5-29 shows an indistinct square generated by this method. In this display, the probabilities of occurrence of the dots in both figure and ground may be quantified exactly. In Fig. 5-30, the transition between the lighter and the darker bars is not abrupt. While the probabilities for a dot in the middle row of the light bar and for no dot in the middle row of the dark bar are 1.0, the probability for no dot and for a dot in the two bars, respectively, increases by increments of .06 in each successive row.

Fry (1957) has described an optical device for generating blurred edges. A diagram of the apparatus is shown in Fig. 5-31. The opal flashed glass A is illuminated by light sources C and D. The edge of screen H is projected on A by a projector which, instead of a slide, contains a screen with an aperture G. The aperture may have different shapes, each of which produces a different gradient of blur. M is a piece of ground glass inserted between the two lenses of the condenser. The degree of blur may be varied (and measured) by varying the distance of H from A. One advantage of this method of blurring is that, unlike simple defocusing of an image projected on a screen by a projector, it does not

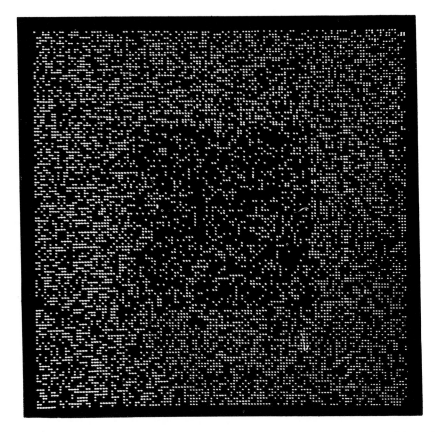

Fig. 5-29. A blurred square generated in a large computer-produced matrix of dots of varying probability of appearance. From Green (1957).

produce additional images, which may be bothersome in some cases. When multiple images are not a problem, simply throwing a slide out of focus will produce degrees of blur that can be quantified by taking readings of the setting of the lens. Still another simple method of blurring contours is described by Fry. It consists in interposing a piece of ground glass between the object and the eye. Varying the distance of the piece of glass will vary the degree of blur. The nature of the blur is, of course, determined by the scattering characteristics of the particular piece of glass used, and only one type of blur gradient may be obtained.

A genuine noisy condition results from a noisy ground rather than from changes in the figure. It is a condition which veils or masks the figure, thus

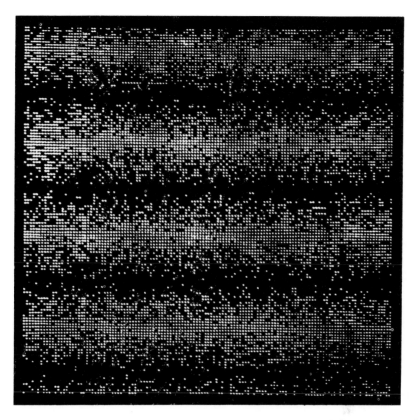

Fig. 5-30. Computer-generated sequence of light and dark bars with fuzzy outlines of determined probabilities of occurrence of dots. From Green (1957).

reducing the contrast between figure and ground. When the figure is a pattern made up of dots, squares, etc., noise is introduced simply by increasing the number of identical elements in the ground. When closed contours characterize the figure, noise is a large number of unrelated visual elements, such as lines, specks, dots, small closed contours, and such in the ground alone or covering or veiling the figure as well. Weisz (1957) and Crook (1957) describe the use of facsimile equipment to generate different degrees of a quantified "veil" that masks a configuration. If the ground is white and the figure is black, the veil introduces black specks in the ground and white ones in the figure, so that veiling is actually accompanied by the blurring of the contours and the degradation of the interior of the figure as well. It is, of course, possible to increase noise in the background only, leaving the interior of the figure intact.

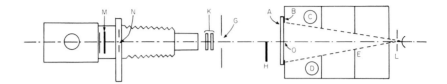

Fig. 5-31. Optical device for generating blurred contours. From Fry (1957).

Commercially available overlay sheets (e.g., Zip-a-Tone) with many different kinds and degrees of fine dot, speck, etc. patterns provide a much simpler, faster, and less expensive way of introducing noise in a visual display, e.g., in conjunction with transparencies used in an overhead projector. While the quantification of the patterns does not go beyond a simple noise density statement in terms of percentage of grayness and the grain size of the pattern, in many actual instances this may be all that is needed. An example of a figure obscured by two complementary types and amounts of regular visual noise using Zip-a-Tone overlays is shown in Fig. 5-32.

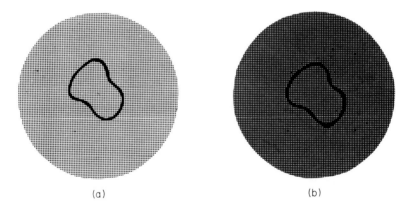

(a)   (b)

Fig. 5-32. Figures on background of redundant noise. In (a) black dots cover 40% of area (40% gray); in (b) white dots leave 40% of the area uncovered (60% gray). Superimposed upon each other and in register, the two overlays would yield a totally black surface.

6. The Material Form

In a form-perception experiment, the form that the subject perceives is some kind of a physical object. While different kinds of objects have been used, their number has been comparatively small.

The most obvious object is ink or pencil deposited on a piece of paper, i.e., a "picture" of a shape. Whether the shape is drawn in outline or is "solid," i.e., filled in, makes no difference. If the position of the shape is to be changed a number of times, it is preferable to cut it out from construction paper and reposition it according to need.

In their original state, drawn or paper cut-out forms may be presented on rectangular sheets of paper bound in booklets if the task is, e.g., a scaling task; on separate pieces of cardboard if the task is sorting; or in a tachistoscope if the task is detection or discrimination under less than optimum viewing conditions. There are a fairly large variety of tachistoscopes available commercially; more are put together from some basic component parts by researchers as the need arises. They all operate on the same basic principle, namely presenting a visual display for a very brief period of time, usually some fraction of a second. A mirror tachistoscope is shown in Fig. 5-33. Since ordinary incandescent light sources have considerable time lag in reaching a point of full intensity and in ceasing to emit light, exposure time cannot be controlled by simply turning the light source on and off. The exact control of stimulus duration may be accomplished in a number of ways. One is to use a light source with little or no inertia, such as a gas discharge tube. Ordinary white neon light tubes can be wired so that the onset and cessation of light are almost instantaneous (Behar, 1960). Another method is to have the light on constantly but to admit it to the stimulus by means of a mechanical device, such as a large photographic shutter. This last method may be used with stimuli presented in the form of projector transparencies. The light source is the projector bulb, but a slide is projected only when the shutter attached in from of the lens is operated (Fig. 5-34). The projection of slides is the most frequently employed method of stimulus presentation in form-perception studies since it offers several advantages over other methods: the exposure control is exact; stimulus presentation is not only rapid but can be automated; and the sequence in which stimuli are presented can be made random (in random-access slide projectors).

Although slides are transparent, forms projected on a screen using slides do not differ essentially from forms drawn on paper or cut from cardboard. Transilluminated openings in opaque materials, however, present problems when used as visual stimuli, such as simultaneous brightness contrast and the apparent enlargement of corners and narrow slits. They may present problems in applied studies, such as the study of visibility and legibility of transilluminated signs and alphanumeric characters used in control panels, airplane cockpits, etc.

Self-luminance in itself does not constitute a problem. For instance, the use of small light bulbs to form patterns will not present a problem unless the bulbs are too bright. Arranging such bulbs in a square matrix, each bulb behind a small translucent window, and by arranging for electronic programming of the patterns to be presented offers an attractive possibility, and several investigators have availed themselves of this method.

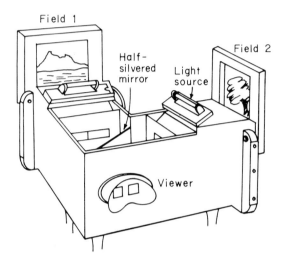

Fig. 5-33. A mirror tachistoscope.

Fig. 5-34. A projection tachistoscope (Lafayette Instrument Co.).

The ultimate in speed, convenience, and degree of automation is offered by electronics, either in the form of oscilloscopes or analog computers in which an electronic picture tube is an integral part of the device. Tape-generated oscilloscope patterns were used as early as the 1950s (e.g., Archer, 1954). Lately, configurations of all degrees of complexity have been generated electronically. While there can be no doubt that the future will see an increased use of computers in the study of form perception, it is also clear that in terms of cost and simplicity nothing at the present time comes near the humble polygon, cut from black construction paper or drawn on a white sheet of paper.

Form may be presented not only to human and animal subjects but also computer "subjects," albeit for different purposes. When form is presented to a computer for computation or recognition, its contour must be broken down into discrete elements. This is done either by the operator, who may, e.g., punch the contour of a shape in IBM cards, or by the computer itself: when appropriately programmed, a computer will represent the contours of a shape in discrete terms when only the coordinates of the vertices of the shape are given. This procedure has been touched upon in this chapter in connection with the computation of moments, and in Chap. 3 in connection with pattern recognition by computers. The breakdown into discrete elements takes place even in analog computers where, e.g., the contours of a cardboard figure are intercepted and broken down by photocells or where seemingly continuous contours are painted on a fluorescent screen by an electron beam.

When computations must be performed by the digital computer on complex shapes that have an internal structure as well as external contours, such as photographs, more-complex preprocessing is necessary. Kovaszany and Joseph (1953) describe an electronic device in which a scanning beam reduces photographs to outlines. Computations on the external and internal structures of complex patterns are not performed very frequently. One case where they are is the mathematical analysis and comparison of the structure of chromosomes in photomicrographs, where large numbers of similar patterns must be examined for small differences. Ledley and Ruddle (1966) describe a process whereby a scanning device (called the FIDAC) reduces shades of gray in the micrograph to six discrete levels. In the computer printout of the chromosome, shades of gray appear as areas filled with the digits 0 through 6.

REFERENCES

Alluisi, E. A., & Hall, T. J. Effects of a transphenomenal parameter on the visual perception of form. *Psychonomic Sci.,* 1965, 3, 543-544.
Alt, F. L. Digital pattern recognition by moments. In G. L. Fischer, Jr. *et al.* (Eds.), *Optical character recognition.* Washington, D.C.: Spartan Books, 1962. Pp. 153-179.

Anderson, N. S. Pattern recognition: A probability approach. In J. W. Wulfeck & J. H. Taylor (Eds.), *Form discrimination as related to military problems*. Washington, D.C.: Nat. Acad. Sci.-Nat. Res. Coun., 1957. Pp. 45-49.

Archer, E. J. Identification of visual patterns as a function of information load. *J. exp. Psychol.*, 1954, **48**, 313-317.

Attneave, F. The relative importance of parts of a contour. *US Human Resources Res. Center, Res. Note P&MS* No. 51-8, 1951.

Attneave, F. Some informational aspects of visual perception. *Psychol. Rev.*, 1954, **61**, 183-193.

Attneave, F. Physical determinants of the judged complexity of shapes. *J. exp. Psychol.*, 1957, **53**, 221-227.

Attneave, F., & Arnoult, M. D. The quantitative study of shape and pattern perception. *Psychol. Bull.*, 1956, **53**, 452-471.

Barskiĭ, B. V., & Guzeva, M. A. O zavisimosti prostranstvennykh porogov zreniya ot kharaktera vosprinimaemogo kontura. *Voprosy Psikhol.*, 1962, **8**(2) 101-114.

Baughman, E. E. A comparative analysis of Rorschach forms with altered stimulus characteristics. *J. proj. Tech.*, 1954, **18**, 151-164.

Behar, I. A new tachistoscope for animals and man. *Amer. J. Psychol.*, 1960, **73**, 305-306.

Blum, H. A transformation for extracting new descriptors of shape. In W. Wathen-Dunn (Ed.), *Models for the perception of speech and visual forms*. Cambridge, Massachusetts: M.I.T. Press, 1967. Pp. 362-380.

Boring, E. G. A new ambiguous figure. *Amer. J. Psychol.*, 1930, **42**, 444-445.

Boynton, R. M. Recognition of critical targets among irrelevant forms. In J. W. Wulfeck & J. H. Taylor (Eds.), *Form discrimination as related to military problems*. Publ. 561, Armed Forces—NRC Committee on Vision, National Academy of Science—National Research Council, Washington, D. C., 1957. Pp. 175-184.

Boynton, R. M., Elworth, C. L., Onley, J. W., & Klingberg, C. L. Form discrimination as predicted by overlap and area. *USAF RADC TR* 60-158, 1960.

Boynton, R. M., Elworth, C. L., Monty, R. A., Onley, J. W., & Klingberg, C. L. Overlap as a predictor of form discrimination under suprathreshold conditions. *USAF RADC TR* 61-99, June 1961.

Brandt, H. F. *The psychology of seeing*. New York: Philosophical Library, 1945.

Brown, D. R., & Michels, K. M. Quantification procedures, stimulus domains, and discrimination difficulty. *Percept. mot. Skills*, 1966, **22**, 421-422.

Brown D. R., & Owen, D. H. The metrics of visual form: Methodological dyspepsia. *Psychol. Bull.*, 1967, **68**, 243-259.

Brown, D. R., Hitchcock, L. Jr., & Michels, K. M. Quantitative studies in form perception: An evaluation of the role of selected stimulus parameters in the visual discrimination performance of human subjects. *Percept. mot. Skills*, 1962, **14**, 519-529.

Brown, L. T. Quantitative description of visual pattern: Some methodological suggestions. *Percept. mot. Skills*, 1964, **19**, 771-774.

Buswell, G. T. *How people look at pictures*. Chicago, Illinois: Univ. of Chicago Press, 1935.

Casperson, R. C. The visual discrimination of geometric form. *J. exp. Psychol.* 1950, **40**, 668-686.

Chambliss, D. J. The relation between judged similarity and the physical properties of plane figures. Unpublished doctoral dissertation, Univ. of Wisconsin, 1957.

Chou, S. K. Reading and legibility of Chinese characters: IV. An analysis of judgments of position of Chinese characters by American subjects. *J. exp. Psychol.*, 1935, **18**, 318-347.

Crook, M. Facsimile-generated analogues for instrumental form displays. In J. W. Wulfeck & J. H. Taylor (Eds.), *Form discrimination as related to military problems.* Washington, D. C.: Nat. Acad. Sci.-Nat. Res. Coun, 1957. Pp. 85-98.

Edelman, S. K. Analysis of some stimulus factors involved in the associative response. Unpublished doctoral dissertation, Purdue Univ., 1960.

Evans, S. H. Redundancy as a variable in pattern perception. *Psychol. Bull.,* 1967, **67,** 104-113.

Fisher, G. H. Preparation of ambiguous stimulus materials. *Percept. Psychophys.,* 1967, **2,** 421-422.

Fitts, P. M., & Leonard, J. A. Stimulus correlates of visual pattern recognition: A probability approach. Columbus, Ohio: Ohio State Univ., 1957.

Fry, G. A. Blur as a factor in form discrimination. In J. W. Wulfeck & J. H. Taylor (Eds.), *Form discrimination as related to military problems.* Publ. 561, Armed Forces–NRC Committee on Vision, National Academy of Sciences–National Research Council, Washington, D.C.: 1957. Pp. 75-82.

Garner, W. R. *Uncertainty and structure as psychological concepts.* New York: Wiley, 1962.

Garner, W. R. To perceive is to know. *Amer. Psychologist,* 1966, **21,** 11-19.

Ghent, L. Form and its orientation: A child's eye view. *Amer. J. Psychol.,* 1961, **74,** 177-190.

Gibson, J. J. *The perception of the visual world.* Boston, Massachusetts: Houghton, 1950.

Gibson, J. J., & Gibson, E. J. Continuous perspective transformations and the perception of rigid motion. *J. exp. Psychol.,* 1957, **54,** 129-138.

Goldstein, A. G., & Andrews, J. Perceptual uprightness and complexity of random shapes. *Amer. J. Psychol.,* 1962, **75,** 667-669.

Green, B. F. Jr. The use of high-speed digital computers in studies of form perception. In J. W. Wulfeck & J. H. Taylor (Eds.), *Form discrimination as related to military problems.* Publ. 561, Armed Forces–NRC Committee on Vision, Nat. Acad. Sci.–Nat. Res. Coun., Washington, D. C., 1957. Pp. 65-75.

Guiliano, V. E., Jones, P. E., Kimball, G. E., Meyer, R. F., & Stein, B. A. Automatic pattern recognition by a Gestalt method. *Inform. Control,* 1961, **4,** 332-345.

Haralson, J. V. An apparatus for varying size of rectangles continuously and proportionally. *Percept. mot. Skills,* 1965, **21,** 313-314.

Hitchcock, L. Jr., Michels, K. M., & Brown, D. R. Discrimination learning: Squirrels vs. raccoons. *Percept. mot. Skills,* 1963, **16,** 405-414.

Hochberg, J. E., & Brooks, V. The psychophysics of form: Reversible-perspective drawings of spatial objects. *Amer. J. Psychol.,* 1960, **73,** 337-354.

Holmes, G. The relative legibility of black print and white print. *J. appl. Psychol.,* 1931, **15,** 248-251.

Horowitz, M. Efficient use of a picture correlator. *J. Opt. Soc. Amer.,* 1957, **47,** 327.

Hu, M-K. Visual pattern recognition by moment invariants. *IRE Trans.,* 1962, **IT-8,** 179-187.

Knoll, R. L., & Stenson, H. H. A computer program to generate and measure random forms. *Percept. Psychophys.,* 1968, **3,** 311-316.

Kovaszany, L. S. G., & Joseph, H. M. Processing of two-dimensional patterns by scanning techniques. *Science,* 1953, **118,** 475-477.

Kretzmer, E. R. Statistics of television signals. *Bell Syst. Tech. J.,* 1952, **31,** 751-763.

LaBerge, D. L., & Lawrence, D. H. Two methods for generating matrices of forms of graded similarity. *J. Psychol.,* 1957, **43,** 77-100.

Ledley, R. S., & Ruddle, F. H. Chromosome analysis by computer. *Sci. Amer.,* 1966, **214**(4), 40-46.

Michels, K. M., & Zusne, L. Metrics of visual form. *Psychol. Bull.,* 1965, **63**, 74-86.

Monty, R. A., & Boynton, R. M. Stimulus overlap and form similarity under suprathreshold conditions. *Percept. mot. Skills,* 1962, **14**, 487-498.

Polidora, V. J. Stimulus correlates of visual pattern discrimination by monkeys: Multidimensional analyses. *Percept. Psychophys.,* 1966, **1**, 405-414.

Seiler, D. A., & Zusne, L. Judged complexity of tachistoscopically viewed random shapes. *Percept. mot. Skills,* 1967. **24,** 884-886.

Small, V. H. Judged similarity of visual forms as functions of selected stimulus dimensions. Unpublished doctoral dissertation, Purdue Univ., 1961.

Smith, J. P. The effects of figural shape on the perception of area. Unpublished doctoral dissertation, Fordham Univ., 1964. *Diss. Abstr.,* 1964, **25**(6), 3712.

Staniland, A. C. *Patterns of redundancy.* London and New York: Cambridge Univ. Press, 1966.

Stilson, D. W. A psychophysical investigation of triangular shape. Unpublished doctoral dissertation, Univ. of Illinois, 1956.

Sutherland, N. S. Visual discrimination of orientation and shape by *Octopus. Nature,* 1957, **179**, 11-13.

Taylor, C. D. The perception of black and white symbols. *Psychol. Bull.,* 1933, **30**, 699-670.

Thurmond, J. B. Extensions of an informational deductive analysis of form. Paper read at a symposium on Analyses of the Metrics of Form, held at the meeting of Southern Society for Philosophy and Psychology, New Orleans, April 1966.

Vanderplas, J. M., Sanderson, W. A., & Vanderplas, J. N. Statistical and associational characteristics of 1100 random shapes. *Percept. mot. Skills,* 1965, **21**, 414.

Weisz, A. The use of facsimile equipment and controlled visual noise in form research. In J. W. Wulfeck & J. H. Taylor (Eds.), *Form discrimination as related to military problems.* Washington, D. C.: Nat. Acad. Sci.-Nat. Res. Coun., 1957. Pp. 83-84.

Yaglom, I. M. *Geometric transformations.* New York: Random House, 1962.

Zusne, L. Moments of area and of the perimeter of visual form as predictors of discrimination performance. *J. exp. Psychol.,* 1965, **69**, 213-220.

Zusne, L., & Michels, K. M. Geometricity of visual form. *Percept. mot. Skills,* 1962, **14**, 147-154. (a)

Zusne, L., & Michels, K. M. More on the geometricity of visual form. *Percept. mot. Skills,* 1962, **15**, 55-58. (b)

Zusne, L., & Michels, K. M. Nonrepresentational shapes and eye movements. *Percept. mot. Skills,* 1964, **18**, 11-20.

Chapter 6 / **THE PERCEPTUAL TASKS**

In addition to the physical characteristics of the form, a major determinant of response to it is the type of perceptual task that the observer is given to perform. After a discussion of the nature of the major type of overt response that is specifically associated with form-perception tasks, namely eye movements, and of perceptual tasks in general, empirical findings concerning form perception, which constitute the bulk of the present chapter, are further discussed under the headings of detection, discrimination, and scaling.

1. Form Perception and Eye Movements

With one exception, namely that of eye movements, the different types of overt response that subjects in visual form-perception experiments produce will be mentioned here very briefly. The reason is that these responses are not specific to form perception but may be found in many other different kinds of experiments. As such, their characteristics and associated problems have been treated extensively and repeatedly elsewhere. Eye movements, on the other hand, while not a response to form alone, are mainly a response to visual stimulation, and will be given more attention here for that reason.

The verbal or written responses given by subjects to form vary largely as a function of the perceptual task that the subject faces. In form detection, discrimination, and recognition experiments, it is a yes-no or forced-choice response. If the latter, the subject indicates whether the crucial form is on the right, left, up, down, different, identical, and the like. In the identification task, it is a labeling response: a previously learned label is attached to the form. The scaling or judgmental task is characterized by the "x-ier than " type of response or the placement of forms on a scale. The associative response to form is no different, in principle, from associative responses to any other kind of stimulus.

The motor responses include sorting or arrangement of forms into bins or in a certain sequence according to some criterion; reproduction or drawing of forms;

motor responses to apparatus, such as button and lever pressing, turning of dials or wheels; and eye movements.

The role of the eye tremor has already been considered. It is to make the perception of contours possible in the first place. Our concern here is with the grosser eye movements that serve to scan the different portions of contours that cannot be encompassed by the visual angle subtended by the macula. The role of eye movements in a special type of performance, namely reading, has been studied very extensively. The subject of reading is of somewhat marginal relevance to form perception, and is discussed in the last chapter. Because of their emphasis on information processing rather than form perception, studies of visual search and the associated eye movements are also omitted.

The literature on eye movements is extensive. Eye movements have been observed at least since the times of Johannes Mueller, and have been recorded since the turn of the century. *Experimental Psychology* of Woodworth and Schlosberg (1954) contains a chapter on the history of the study of eye movements, their measurement, and applications. There are several overlapping bibliographies of eye-movement literature containing hundreds of items: Carmichael and Dearborne (1947) cover it through 1947, Scott (1962) covers the period 1932-1961, while Grunin and Mostofsky (1968) list all references dated 1950-1967.

A. EYE-MOVEMENT RECORDERS

Eye-movement recorders have been built mainly for the recording of eye movements of human subjects, although it is not impossible to obtain eye-movement records from animals (Wendt & Dodge, 1938). At the present time, there are three main types of eye-movement recorders: recorders that utilize light reflected from the cornea, cameras for filming eye movements, and electrooculographic recorders.

The photographic corneal reflection recorder has the longest history, dating back to 1901, when Dodge described how to take still photographs of corneal light reflections (Dodge & Cline, 1901). This is still the basic principle on which photographic recorders of eye movements are based: a small spot of light is reflected from the eye onto a photographic plate or a moving film. Plates are used if the fixation pattern is of interest; a relatively slow-moving film is employed if the sequence of fixations and their exact number are of interest. As the eye moves in exploring a visual display, the surface of the cornea acts as a mirror and reflects the spot of light onto corresponding loci on the light-sensitive surface. Fixations record as spots, movements record as fainter thin lines between fixation points.

Dodge's method was constantly improved upon until both vertical and horizontal movements could be recorded, at first on two separate films moving perpendicularly to each other. In the 1930s, it was chiefly G. T. Buswell's name that was associated with the development of several eye-movement cameras: the Minnesota eye camera (Tinker, 1931), the Iowa eye-movement camera (Jasper & Walker, 1931), and his own eye-movement camera (Buswell, 1935). Buswell's camera was very bulky, but did its job well.

As he was working on his doctoral dissertation (Brandt, 1937), H. F. Brandt developed an eye camera (Brandt, 1940, 1945) that had several advantages over other cameras: it had a fairly good accuracy, it could be adapted for use with moving stimuli, tachistoscopic exposures, and other special viewing conditions, and it was relatively inexpensive. It is still available commercially (Fig. 6-1).

The various ophthalmographs used by optometrists and reading researchers record only horizontal eye movements. Dr. Fry of the School of Optometry of Ohio State University has developed a modified version of the Ophthalmograph made by the American Optical Company (Enoch, 1960). It records both vertical and horizontal eye movements and appears to be the most accurate of all photographic eye-movement recorders made in the United States: its accuracy is better than the ability of the eye to focus on a given point, the accuracy of fixation being approximately .37 degrees standard deviation in the vertical meridian for 5-degree movements of the eye between two points.

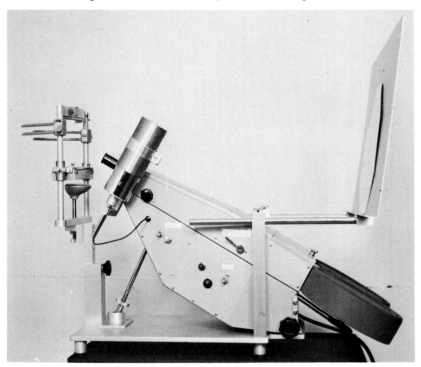

Fig. 6-1. A photographic corneal reflection eye-movement recorder (C. H. Stoelting Co.).

Most eye-movement recorders are rather bulky, stationary precision instruments that necessitate the fixation of the head of the observer and hence his exposure only to pictorial or film materials. To record eye movements that take place as the observer moves freely through the environment or where the laboratory equipment cannot be used (e.g., airplane cockpits), portable eye-movement recording systems have been developed. They consist of a crash helmet with a light 8-mm. movie camera mounted on top of it. The observer's eye movements are picked up by an optical system suspended from the helmet in front of the observer's face and conducted to the camera (e.g., Mackworth & Thomas, 1962). In addition to being less accurate than laboratory recorders, portable eye-movement recorders are also much more expensive.

The cornea is not a very good reflector. A silvered surface on a contact lens is a material improvement, except for the problem of contact-lens slippage and the resulting inaccuracy in the recording. This inaccuracy must be added to the distortions that are being produced anyway by the inherent imperfections in the curvature of the surface of the cornea as well as the marked individual differences in this curvature. The problems of reflection, slippage, and, to a large extent, of the individualities of different corneas have been reduced or eliminated by Yarbus (1967), the most productive investigator of eye movements in the Soviet Union. Yarbus uses a suction cup attachment which is applied to the cornea. The attachment weighs only a fraction of a gram and adheres rigidly to the eye (Fig. 6-2). Different types of suction cup with different combinations of miniature lenses, mirrors, etc. permit considerable latitude in the phenomena that can be investigated, including the perception of stabilized retinal images. The drawback is the necessity of anesthetizing the cornea and the eyelids and of having to keep the latter retracted so as to prevent blinking.

If, instead of using the corneal reflection directly to affect photographic emulsion, the reflection is directed to a photocell and the resulting electric current amplified, analyzed, and displayed on an oscilloscope or channeled to an ink pen recorder, the resulting device is apt to be called a photoelectric recorder. Since the cause of the recording is the same as in the case of a photographic record, namely light reflected from the cornea, this type of device is no different in principle from the one just described. While it may be more convenient for some purposes, it does require considerable additional apparatus. No photoelectric recorders are available commercially. Examples of such recorders built by individual researchers are those of Lord and Wright (1948), Rashbass (1960), Smith and Warter (1960), and Vladimirov and Khomskaya (1961, 1962).

The idea of taking a film of the movements of the eyes is a simple one and is easily accomplished. The problem is one of relating the movements of the eyes to the physical features of the display. The Purdue Eye Camera (Karlslake, 1940), for instance, consists of a 16-mm. movie camera, a half-silvered mirror,

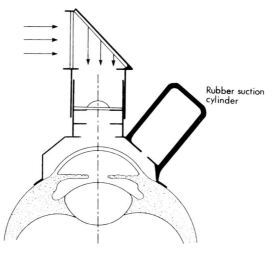

Rubber suction
cylinder

Fig. 6-2. Suction cup device for stabilizing the entire visual field. From A. L. Yarbus, *Rol' dvizheniĭ glaz v protsesse zreniya.* Moscow: Izdatel'stvo "Nauka," 1965.

and two lamps for illuminating the display and the subject. The device discriminates fixations in adjacent areas that are at least 2 in. square (at normal reading distance), and judges are needed to determine where the eye has been. For greater precision, some mark must be placed on the cornea, the head fixated, and the subject's eye movements in a standard pattern established. Narrow beams of infrared light used in conjunction with infrared-light-sensitive film have been used successfully. This method also avoids the necessity of having bright lights illuminating the subject's face. In fact, eye-movement recording with infrared light can be performed in total darkness.

The electrooculographic (EOG) recorders record changes in surface dc potentials around the eyes as the eye muscles move. These recorders have been in use since the 1930s (for a review, see Marg, 1951). While this method is about as accurate as the corneal reflection method, it does have its drawbacks. For one, the method calls for several expensive pieces of apparatus [amplifiers, rectifiers, oscilloscopes, etc. (cf. Ford & Leonard, 1958; and Ford, White, & Lichtenstein, 1959)]. The application of electrodes to the subject's skin is a job in itself. In addition, the system must be calibrated anew for each subject, and it must be very well grounded. The records are not free from artifacts, such as preexcitatory potentials, discrepancies between vertical and horizontal movements, and others. The installation and proper functioning of a satisfactory EOG system are subject to all the difficulties that beset any electrophysiological investigation. It is still the preferred method used with infant subjects in cases where precision of the recordings is essential.

B. CHARACTERISTICS OF EYE-MOVEMENT RESPONSE TO FORM

In addition to the physiological tremor of the eyes, there are two other types of involuntary eye movement: drifts (saccades), which occur during fixation, and the rapid, jerky movements that correct for the saccades and bring the eye back to the point of fixation. When an immobile point is fixated, the amount of drift and corrective moments is considerable, although the observer is usually unable to report any subjective feelings of movement. Figure 6-3 shows a photographic record of eye movements that occurred in one subject during an observation period of 30 sec. while fixating a point. While the number of fixations and saccades is large, the area covered by the excursions of the eye is well within the fovea.

The fact that the eyes do not scan a smooth contour smoothly but do so in jumps and, as well, deviate from the contour was known to nineteenth century investigators. To the observer himself, though, it appears that his eyes move smoothly along the contours of a smoothly shaped object. Figure 6-4 shows that, when instructed to follow a contour as smoothly as possible, the observer's eye movements do produce a recognizable replica of the object. The noteworthy fact, though, is the multitude of fixations and deviations away from the exact contour. Stratton (1902) undermined the notion that positive aesthetic sensations in the perception of graceful forms derive from the smooth and unimpeded action of the eye muscles. His photographic records showed that this could not have possibly been the case since the eyes are unable to follow smoothly even simple, short lines. Rather, jerkiness and deviations away from the true course of the contour were the rule.

So that, on the whole, it seems probable that the motor and tactual sensations obtained during the vision of a beautiful outline are no more intimately connected with the final aesthetic effect than are the sensations from our leg-muscles with our pleasure as we walk through the gallery at Dresden. The external apparatus of the eye merely brings the retina to such points of vantage as will permit various views of the more significant details, and out of the series of snapshots obtained during these stops in the eye's course the mind constructs its object into a clearer whole. (Stratton, 1902, p. 352.)

The above quotation adumbrates what Hebb stated with greater emphasis almost half a century later and what Hochberg (1968) has restated even more recently, namely that eye movements, brief glimpses of fractions of the total configuration, are only the lowly gatherers of information about the physical form, and that the final form percept emerges as a result of past experience and thinking.

The role that Hebb assigned to eye movements was discussed in Chap. 4. Briefly, it is to piece together form elements, such as angles and straight lines, into larger wholes in the process of learning visual identifications. Thus, eye

Fig. 6-3. Eye movements (drifts) during fixation of a stationary point. From A. L. Yarbus, *Rol' dvizheniĭ glaz v protsesse zreniya.* Moscow: Izdatel'stvo "Nauka," 1965.

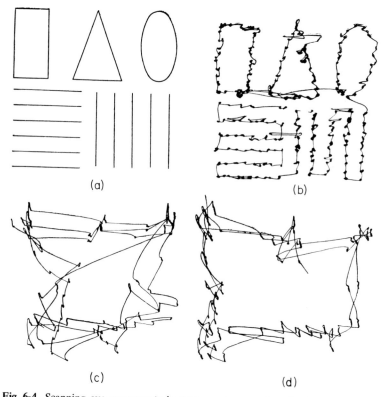

Fig. 6-4. Scanning eye movements in response to a regular visual pattern (a), under instructions to follow its contour with smooth eye movements (b), when inspecting it freely for 20 sec. (c), and when instructed to count the number of straight-line segments (d). From A. L. Yarbus, *Rol' dvizheniĭ glaz v protsesse zreniya.* Moscow: Izdatel'stvo "Nauka," 1965.

movements would be essential in a newborn or naive organism but not in the experienced adult. There is now sufficient evidence that adults need not move their eyes in order to perceive clearly the total configuration of a familiar or meaningful form. When exposure times are long enough for the form to be clearly perceived but not long enough to make even a single scanning movement, recognition, identification, and scaling of the form still take place, regardless of whether it is the form of letters, numbers, or nonsense syllables (Battro & Fraisse, 1961), random shapes (Hayes, 1962; Zusne & Michels, 1964), complex configurations (Mooney, 1957a, 1957b, 1958, 1960), or inkblots (Mooney, 1959). The elementary role of eye movements is further emphasized by the finding that they are not the cause of optical illusions (Yarbus, 1967), and are the result rather than the cause of reversals in reversible-perspective figures (Pheiffer, Eure, & Hamilton, 1956).

What, then, are the characteristics of eye movements of infants when they look at forms? While infants' eye movements have been observed, counted, and described by quite a number of investigators, eye-movement recordings have been made by very few (Dayton & Jones, 1964; Salapatek & Kessen, 1966). Salapatek and Kessen showed a solid black triangle to infants under 8 days of age and recorded their eye movements using a still camera which, through the middle of the triangle, took a picture, one every second, of the reflection from the infant's eye of three spots of infrared light placed at each of the vertices of the triangle. For control, a homogeneous black field was presented. Scanning eye movements in response to the black field were widely dispersed. They also suggested that horizontal eye movements are easier for an infant to make than vertical ones. The response to the triangle was to concentrate fixations at one of the vertices. The middle of the triangle was hardly ever fixated. On the other hand, it was usually only one of the vertices that was fixated, not two or all three. Salapatek and Kessen interpret these findings in the light of Hebb's theory in three different ways:

1. The newborn Ss, either because of lack of maturation or of experience, were at a 'pre-linkage' stage, capable of responding to elements but incapable of linking the elements through scanning. 2. A *solid* triangular form is defined by contour and may not be analyzed by the visual system into elements—sides and angles—that are fundamental to Hebb's theory. 3. The figure used . . . was too large to permit the integration of the elements. (Salapatek & Kessen, 1966, p. 167.)

Thus, different interpretations may be attached to the fact that the very young infants eyes do not appear to "piece together" lines and angles. That the adult's eye needs no such piecing together may also be interpreted in at least two different ways. One is that, in Hebbian terminology, the phase sequence for, say, a triangle, is already well established, so that only a momentary and partial stimulus will elicit the activity of the phase sequence. The other is that, while eye movements may not be necessary for the detection or even the recognition of a shape, the memory trace that the brief stimulation lays down in the nervous system (or reactivates one that is already established) is available for some time after the distal stimulus has disappeared and that scanning of the memory trace is done subjectively. Since the eye continues to perform scanning movements after a tachistoscopic exposure, it is plausible that these movements might be the overt counterpart of subjective postexposural scanning of the visualized shape. Experimental evidence bearing on this hypothesis is scarce and mostly negative. Bryden (1961) found that there was a significant relation between eye movements and the site in a horizontal row where a letter or a geometric figure had been recognized. Bryden, however, recorded only horizontal eye movements, and his evidence is tenuous, at best. Zusne and Michels (1964) were unable to relate postexposural eye-movement patterns to any physical characteristics of shapes when these were presented tachistoscopically and observers were to make symmetry judgments in the absence of the distal stimulus.

Scanning eye movements recorded during relatively prolonged inspection of simple and complex visual displays, however, are closely related to specific stimulus characteristics. Pictorial materials have been used most frequently, geometric and nonsense forms less often. The use of pictures and other complex displays has been due mostly to the interest of the investigators in aesthetics and the attention-getting value of posters, advertisements, and the like. Brandt's (1945) book on the psychology of seeing is concerned with the latter topic. Of interest to the investigation of the relationship between eye movements and form perception are Brandt's findings regarding the perception of a relatively "empty" but symmetric field, similar to the one shown in Fig. 6-5a. Figure 6-5b shows the distribution of time spent by subjects looking at the major divisions of the display. The asymmetric distribution of fixations is quite marked, the left and top positions of the display being the preferred ones. Brandt reports that the tendency for the eye to move toward the left from the initial point of fixation is one of the strongest tendencies in ocular performance. In addition, more horizontal excursions are made than vertical ones; there are more eye movements when displays are presented horizontally than when they are presented vertically. The first few fixations are, in addition to being directed to the left, also directed toward the top portion of the display. On the first exploratory trip, there is the tendency for the eyes to move clockwise. These findings have, of course, important bearing on the design of advertising copy. They are also important to form perception in general, since it cannot be assumed that presenting definite contours in the visual field will necessarily overcome the "naturally" asymmetric tendencies of the eye.

The relationship between form dimensions and eye movements has been

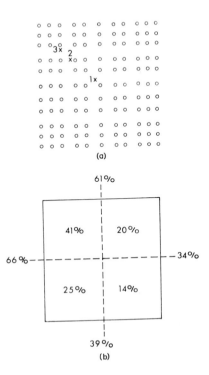

Fig. 6-5. Distribution of fixations (b) in an "empty" but symmetric visual field (a). The three points marked in (a) are the sites where the first three fixations occur most frequently. From Brandt (1945).

investigated only with regard to symmetry. Even here, the amount of data is very small. Stratton (1906) showed his subjects squares, rectangles, and circles, as well as more complex figures, such as the outlines of Greek vases. He observed that there was little correspondence between the symmetry of a shape and eye movements. The subjects' eyes simply rested on points of interest, and the connecting movements could not have supplied much information about the shape of the contour. Symmetric shapes did not produce symmetric eye movements. When looking at a vase, for instance, a subject would examine one of its symmetric halves, glance at the other half and, seeing that it was identical, cease his explorations. Paradoxically, it was the less symmetric figures that produced more symmetric patterns of eye movements. Stratton suggests that the reason for this is an attempt of the subject to make sure about the state of symmetry in the figure, for which the subject needs to cross the axis of symmetry repeatedly. The enjoyment of symmetry, as Stratton emphasizes, lies not with the physical properties of the figure. At least eye movements suggest anything but symmetry, balance, or rest.

Buswell (1935), who had his subjects look mostly at paintings and drawings, had them also look at a figure resembling a symmetric metric histoform and at two asymmetric versions of it. Since only three stimuli and few subjects were involved, Buswell's results were inconclusive. Zusne and Michels (1964) recorded eye movements of subjects as they judged the degree of symmetry of random shapes, singly or in pairs, and both while the stimuli were in view and after a tachistoscopic exposure. As in Stratton's study, eye movements could not be related to symmetry. In simple forms, subjects typically scanned the outlines of the figure. In complex shapes, fixations were concentrated on the outlines or the more intricate or significant portions of the shape.

The last-mentioned finding is confirmed by studies in which subjects have looked at two-dimensional art work. The books written by Buswell (1935) and Yarbus (1967) are the best known in this area. The results of their work may be summarized very briefly: when looking at pictures, the observer's eyes fixate more frequently those features which are actual or potential carriers of information. Information here is not information measured in bits or physically the most complex portions of the picture. It is rather the meaning and significance of a particular portion of the picture to the observer that attracts his attention and, consequently, his eyes. Thus, in a painting of a hunter in a forest, it is not the (physically) very complex branches, bushes, and grass that attract attention. Rather, it is the very small, detailless, inconspicuous figure of the hunter that most fixations center upon. Human figures, regardless of how simple or complex they are, attract most of the fixations in any painting or drawing. In paintings or photographs of faces, eyes attract most of the attention. Two typical visual scanning patterns for two human faces are shown in Fig. 6-6.

Given a painting, the distribution of fixations for a subject does not remain the same under any and all conditions, though. Both Buswell and Yarbus have found that instructions may markedly influence the distribution of fixations, depending on the kind of information that the observer is asked to extract from the picture.

2. Response versus Perception

To bring up the question of the relationship between overt motor response, such as eye movements, and form perception as an intervening variable or the phenomenology of form would mean no less than branching out into a discussion of behaviorism, introspection, and the philosophy of science in general. In a volume like the present one, such a discussion is out of place. Let it

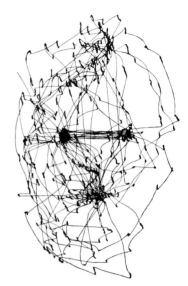

(a)

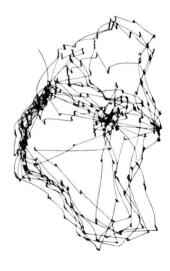

(b)

Fig. 6-6. Patterns of eye movements during a 2–3 min. free inspection of a photograph (a) and a sculpture (b). From A. L. Yarbus. *Rol' dvizhenii̯ glaz v protsesse zreniya.* Moscow: Izdatel'stvo "Nauka," 1965.

only be pointed out that it is easy to give many examples of a distinction between form perception and overt response to form. For instance, a different response may be given where the subjective experience of form remains the same, or identical responses may be given even though phenomenally the form has changed. The difference between perception and response has been demonstrated experimentally with visual stimuli (words, light patches) by a fairly large number of investigators. The concept of convergent operations (Garner, Hake, & Eriksen, 1956) implies this difference, as does the theory of signal detection in its application to the study of psychophysical thresholds (it is the response which is affected by the probability of stimulus presentation and the payoff function, while perception may or may not change). Still, the degree of theoretical development regarding this question is such at the present time that no one has attempted anything approaching a final formulation.

3. Varieties of Perceptual Tasks

   Agreement among psychologists on the distinctions or relationships among the various perceptual tasks involving visual form is not very good. Inconsistent terminology is one result of this disagreement. Nonpsychologists (electrical engineers, cyberneticists) have preferred the term recognition to denote any process in form perception, since it can and has been argued (e.g., Hake, 1957) that even detection implies recognition and that no detection can take place without recognition. Some psychologists have identified form perception with detection only, equating form perception with the bare perception of contours and considering all other tasks as belonging to a different class. This approach may be justified considering the differences in stimulus characteristics that exist between a form presented for detection and one presented for discrimination or recognition. For detection, a contour must be only minimally separable from another contour or from ground, have a minimal size, or show some minimal discontinuity along its course. For recognition to take place, the stimulus must be fully available to the observer, providing more information than a stimulus that is barely detectable (Morris, 1957).
   More typically, several perceptual tasks are differentiated, the usual ones being detection, discrimination, recognition, identification, and judgment. Hake (1957), whose classification is followed by a number of others, distinguishes among these five tasks on the basis of the kind of judgment that the observer makes. In a detection task, the subject judges whether a stimulus is present or not. In a discrimination task, he judges whether a form is different from some other form or a set of forms. In recognition, the observer judges whether he has seen the form previously. In identification, judgment is about whether a specific stimulus is present or not, i.e., the form is named; and in the judgmental task,

judgment is made regarding a specific point on a continuum that a form should be assigned to. Hake does not place the five tasks in any hierarchical order.

While recognizing the same five tasks, Dember (1960) places them in a hierarchy which, from low to high, runs like this: detection, discrimination, recognition, and identification, with the position of judgment being somewhat indeterminate, but presumably located between discrimination and recognition. Dember speaks alternately of the simplicity of the tasks and of the amount of information involved as the criteria for ordering the tasks. This, however, leads to an inconsistency. If by information is meant the amount of information available to the observer about the stimulus under the conditions of the task (and not necessarily the absolute amount of measured information contained in the stimulus), then detection, discrimination, and comparative judgment are appropriately ordered by the criterion of available information as well as the perceptual complexity of the tasks. With recognition and identification, however, there is a problem. While it is true, as Dember points out, that recognition is a much more complex task than detection or discrimination, it is not just because more information must be available in order to perform these tasks. It is also because these tasks involve learning and memory, which detection, discrimination, and judgment do not, at least they need not. For instance, once an animal has learned what to do, which is not the same as learning associations between forms and other stimuli or responses, it can scale stimuli on attributes under conditions not involving learning (during the task), hence no memory. In addition, identification is considered to be on a higher hierarchical level: It is a more difficult task than recognition because it requires recall; yet, at the same time, more information is available (alternatives to choose from) to the observer in recognition than in identification. The key to this problem is that in the two tasks information is provided by two different sources: in recognition, it comes mainly from an external source, while in identification, the observer has to rely chiefly on his memory. Which situation provides more total information is a question which in most cases it is impossible to answer.

Dember's classification of perceptual tasks is not too different from that of Hake's. Using Dember's terminology, detection involves the mere perception of change, with the amount, direction, and the attribute in which the change occurs left unspecified. If the attribute, amount, and direction are left unspecified, discrimination differs from detection only in that the latter occurs with stimuli at suprathreshold levels. Usually information about the attribute, the amount of change, or its direction or any combination of these is available in a discrimination task. A difference that Dember does not stress is that, in detection, response is to single stimuli, while in discrimination, it is to two or more stimuli. If it is considered that the response in either task is one to a relationship, then in detection the relationship is that of figure-ground and in discrimination it is a figure-figure relationship. While these may lie on the same continuum, in most concrete instances it is a material difference that serves to distinguish the two tasks operationally.

If the observer perceives, however grossly, the amount of change, he is able to compare two changes, hence judge similarity. This forms the basis for locating stimuli on an attribute, which is stimulus scaling. Scaling, however, requires the perception not only of the amount of change, but also of its direction and, of course, of the attribute involved (which need not be a conscious or verbalized process).

In addition to the tasks discussed so far, reproduction is sometimes added as a separate task. Like recognition and identification, it is a task involving learning and memory. Unlike these, however, reproduction is a task of unaided recall (rather than recognition) involving a motor response quite unlike any of those required in a recognition or identification task.

While most investigators accept some sort of a hierarchy among the perceptual tasks, the position of the transactionalists is that there is no such hierarchy (Ittelson, 1960, pp. 170-171). Without going into the argument for this particular position, which is based chiefly on the denial of stimulus-response predictability in principle, suffice it to say that it is a view not normally shared by psychologists engaged in the quantitative study of form perception.

The rest of this chapter reviews experiments in form detection and discrimination. Recognition, identification, reproduction, and the associative response are covered in Chap. 7.

Because of the decisive influence that the task exercises upon the response, other factors that also influence response, such as set and past experience, are considered repeatedly under each task. The number of these additional factors, while not inconsiderable, is not too large in comparison with the number of stimulus variables that have been used in form-perception experiments. In Chap. 5, the study by Brown and Owen (1967) was referred to in which an 80 × 80 matrix of physical form measures had been factored. Even this number of entries would not prevent the preparation of a chart in which every form-perception experiment could be accommodated in terms of the variables of the stimulus, the response, the task, the organism, and the stimulus presentation method (Table 6-1). What effectively precludes the preparation of such a chart is the way in which form dimensions have been used as independent variables in form-perception experiments. First, there are the experiments in which "form" has been the independent variable, i.e., where informational, configurational, and transpositional parameters have been unsystematically varied, singly or in some combination. The results of such experiments cannot be compared with the results of experiments in which form parameters have been controlled. Other experiments in which form parameters have been controlled to some extent are not much better in terms of comparability. The main problem is that of

TABLE 6-1
Stimulus, Response, Task, and Organism Variables in Visual Form Perception Experiments

Stimulus variables			Response variables	Perceptual task	Organism variables
Stimulus dimensions	Sampling	Presentation			
(1) 7 major types of form parameter (Table 5-1); (2) controlled (varied systematically or randomized) or uncontrolled; and (3) presented singly or in various combinations of (a) types and (b) conditions of control.	Constrained Random	At threshold intensity At suprathreshold intensity In the fovea Peripherally Tachistoscopically Blurred or noisy By the method of limits By the constant stimuli method In one of *n* time intervals	Forced-choice response Yes-no response Eye movements Critical fusion frequency Reaction time Number of errors Phenomenal reports Looking time	Detection: light; pattern; location; acuity Discrimination Comparative judgment Recognition Identification Associative response	Normal state Past experience that results in differential set, familiarity, meaning, or anxiety level Chronological age Mental age Drugs Sensory deprivation Sex Perceptual type (personality) Phylogenetic level Lesions

nonorthogonal form parameters. While the transpositional parameters (area, rotation, reflection) are orthogonal to the informational and configurational parameters, the latter two are not to each other, nor are the many measures within the class of configurational parameters. Thus, while an investigator may report manipulating one parameter only, several others may be varying along and affecting the results. Since the three classes of form parameter affect response differentially, the various combinations of controlled and uncontrolled form parameters, shown in Table 6-1, mean that very few form-perception experiments can be actually compared with each other. These are mostly experiments in which the independent variable is one of the transpositional parameters, or some measure of compactness taken on a large sample of random shapes of the same level of complexity. When it comes to multivariate designs, the situation becomes hopeless because of the inevitable interactive effects among form parameters. The nature and magnitude of interaction depends on the particular combination of parameters used in an experiment. There are hardly any two experiments in which they have been identical. If they have been, either the perceptual task, or response measure, or some other experimental condition has not. A detailed comparison of single experiments is therefore a rather frustrating enterprise. This is not to say that no consistent, meaningful relationships ever emerge from these experiments. They become apparent, however, only when a bird's-eye view is taken of groups of experiments that have attempted to solve the same problem. Because the number of form-perception experiments is very large, occasionally and accidentally groups of experiments characterized by something like convergent operations may be delineated. This is the basis on which the reviews of detection, discrimination, and memory for form experiments have been written.

4. Detection

The detection of form is a concept that merges imperceptibly with other, related concepts. There is, first of all, the concept of the brightness threshold. The psychophysics of light detection does not immediately involve the question of how form is perceived. The stimuli used in light-threshold determinations, however, have a certain shape. The usual shape has been a circular one. As soon as it was discovered that light patches of a different shape yielded brightness-threshold values that were different from those obtained with circular openings, the question of the relevance of target shape to brightness thresholds arose.

One may be quite satisfied with comparing just the circle with the rectangle since these are the two most practical shapes that one can give a target when the main concern is other variables, such as area, intensity, and duration. From here, however, it is only a short step to a more general investigation of the question of how form affects brightness thresholds. Since threshold conditions obtain not only at low levels of light intensity but also when targets are presented in the periphery of the visual field, when the contours of the target are blurred, when exposure time is very brief, and when the target moves at a rate too great for clear perception, the field of investigation is widened once again, and once again the investigator is one more step removed from the original question about brightness thresholds. As long as the response required of the subject is only some indication that light is being perceived, it is appropriate to talk of detection. To rank forms with regard to visibility requires that the subject describe the form as soon as it becomes perceptible. Whether the forms used are well-known geometric figures, such as circles, triangles, and squares, or nonrepresentational shapes that the observer has previously learned to identify by name, the task is no longer one of detection but of identification.

A related concept is that of visual acuity. The ability to perceive fine detail is only incidental to the question of form perception. The targets used in acuity tests have, by definition, some form, and form does affect acuity. Not only do different forms produce different measures of acuity, the different acuity tests cannot be subsumed under a single heading in terms of the type of perceptual task that is involved. While the minimum visible measure does involve detection, the minimum separable and vernier acuity are measures of contour discrimination. There is evidence (Rabideau, 1955) that the various acuity measures may be related to different processes. A complete review of theories of visual acuity and their physiological bases may be found in Falk (1956).

A. LIGHT-DETECTION THRESHOLDS

Since the perception of form implies the perception of light, the psychophysical variables affecting light thresholds will be briefly discussed here. The most important stimulus variables that affect brightness threshold are the following.

1. *Background intensity.* This refers to Weber's law, $\Delta I/I = k$, which says that the amount of barely perceptible change is a function of the intensity of the stimulus that this change is compared with. In other words, the size of the threshold increases with increasing background intensity. When stimuli are presented on very bright backgrounds, such as in glare experiments, it must be remembered that the Weber-Fechner law does not hold for high intensities.

2. *Target area.* The second most important variable is target area: the greater the area, the lower the threshold (e.g., Graham & Bartlett, 1939). This relationship, like the Weber-Fechner law, holds up to a certain point only, namely about .75 log minutes of arc for circular targets, in which range it is

known as Ricco's law: $\Delta I/I \times A = k$. For larger target sizes, the relationship becomes curvilinear (Kristofferson, 1954).

3. *Target duration.* Since the amount of luminous energy that enters the eye increases with increasing duration of the visual stimulus and since vision starts with a photochemical process, the Bunsen-Roscoe law, $I \times t = k$, may be applied to brightness thresholds when target duration is also a factor. For circular targets, this rectilinear relationship holds for durations up to about .02 sec. When duration is increased from .02 to .08 sec., it continues to contribute to a decrease in threshold level, but at a decreasing rate. From .08 sec. to about .17 sec. the relationship flattens to a horizontal line, but beyond the .17-sec. point the relationship resumes (Clark, 1958).

4. *Wavelength.* Most psychophysical experiments on brightness thresholds employ white light. The distribution of energy throughout the spectrum is not even, most of it being concentrated in the green-yellow region, while the red and blue ends of the spectrum contain amounts that are considerably smaller. Thus, a red patch of light must be much more intense in order to appear as bright as a patch of green or yellow, which is to say that brightness threshold is also a function of wavelength. While monochromatic light at threshold levels appears achromatic and more energy is needed for color to be perceived, the functional relationship between threshold levels and wavelength remains about the same regardless of whether the stimulus is presented at threshold or suprathreshold levels of intensity.

5. *Retinal locus.* Because of the dual structure of the retina, its sensitivity is not uniform throughout. By far the lowest thresholds are obtained in the periphery of the retina, due to the spatial summation feature of the rods. In addition to the foveal-peripheral differential, brightness threshold is also a function of whether the stimulus is presented on the vertical, the horizontal, or any of the oblique axes of the visual field. This phenomenon was discussed in Chap. 4.

6. *Adaptation state.* Brightness threshold is a function of the state of adaptation of the retina. The dark-adapted eye is incomparably more sensitive than the light-adapted eye and therefore yields a very different order of light threshold.

7. *Target shape.* While it would seem a relatively simple matter to investigate and decide upon the question of whether circular or rectangular targets have the lower light threshold, it is still a subject of theoretical controversy. Helson and Fehrer (1932), in testing the Gestalt proposition of the primacy of form in perception, decided that, "So far as the light sense goes, form is not a constitutive factor and plays no part in determining the value of the lower

threshold" (p. 101): 25% more light was needed to see form than to detect light. Helson and Fehrer used only six simple geometric figures in their experiment, which is rather typical for this type of study. Those concerned more with light detection than form perception have used variously shaped narrow slits, which complicates matters because of the irradiation phenomenon that takes place in narrow, transilluminated slits. While Brown and Niven (1944) found that long, illuminated slits have lower thresholds than short slits, Fry (1947) established that the longer the rectangle, the lower the brightness threshold regardless of width or area, and Lamar's (Lamar, Hecht, Shlaer, & Hendley, 1947, 1948) data are similar. Blackwell and Kristofferson (Kincaid, Blackwell, & Kristofferson, 1960; Kristofferson, 1957; Blackwell, 1957) predict just the opposite relationship from their theory. They also predict, again in contrast to most researchers, that circular targets will have the lowest threshold. A very brief, simplified outline of Kristofferson's "element contribution" theory, which is one of the most sophisticated theories in this area, is presented here. It is an elaboration of the basic ideas formulated by Graham, Brown, and Mote in 1939. According to these researchers, brightness thresholds of symmetric targets are a function of the amount of neural excitation produced at the center of the neural representation of the stimulus. Since it is assumed that every unit area of the target contributes excitation to the center of the target in proportion to a power function of its distance from that center, the amount of excitation is maximal at the center of the cortical representation of the target. The level of excitation at each maximum for any target depends on the shape of the target, and since detectability depends on a state of excitation that is above a certain criterion level, detection thresholds will vary with the shape of the target. The exact numerical value of the function that relates the distance of a target point and its contribution to cortical excitation is determined empirically for classes of targets. Once this coefficient is determined, predictions regarding detection thresholds for different shapes of the same class can be made. Predictions made from this theory have found experimental support, although not in an unequivocal manner. Narrow slits, for instance, actually have lower thresholds than predicted by the theory, probably because of the irradiation effect referred to in Chap. 2, which the theory does not take into account. Cross-shaped slits, on the other hand, have thresholds higher than predicted by the theory. Also, some noncircular targets have been found to have lower thresholds than the circle, and geometric forms as varied as the diamond, square, hexagon, cross, and the triangle have been found by Blackwell and Kristofferson to have identical brightness thresholds.

Much of this work merges imperceptibly into the more traditional work on form thresholds that had its origin in the Gestalt theory, which is discussed in Chap. 7.

B. FORM BETWEEN BRIGHTNESS-DETECTION AND FORM-RECOGNITION THRESHOLDS

If the detection of light that shines through an aperture of a certain shape and the identification of this shape constitute two different processes, form between these two points goes through a process of development in which additional intermediate stages may be discerned. They occur regardless of whether the threshold conditions are produced by reduced brightness contrast, tachistoscopic exposure, or the blurring of contours.

The inquiry concerning the temporal development of percepts started with a group of Gestalt psychologists in Leipzig who centered around the figure of Felix Krueger. Krueger's associate Sander (1928, 1930) developed a theory of *Aktualgenese* or microgenesis. The microgenetic theory of perception was tested by Sanders and his students in a number of experimental studies. These studies, while sorely lacking in scientific exactness, did offer evidence against the position of post-Wundtian structuralists. The experimental procedures used were quite varied; still, a remarkable agreement was achieved among the investigators of the Leipzig group. According to Undeutsch (1942), one of Sander's students, the initial perception of form under threshold conditions is one of a diffuse, undifferentiated whole. This is followed by a stage in which figure and ground become differentiated to some degree. The exact configuration of the form, however, is still vague. A third stage intervenes between this and the final stage of a clear percept, namely one in which the observer begins to formulate a tentative hypothesis as to the identity of the form, called the *Vorgestalt* or preconfigurational phase.

While other researchers carried out the same type of work elsewhere, there was curiously little exchange of ideas between them and the Krueger group. In spite of this and the marked differences in theory and experimental design, these groups have produced a rather homogeneous set of data.

Galli (1931), by analyzing the subjective experience of form as it was moved from some extreme point in the periphery of vision toward a fixation point, found five phases of the microgenetic experience: a vague impression of something indefinite in the field of vision, the impression of the presence of an indefinite object, the perception of rudimentary forms that resembled some of the simpler, well-known geometric forms, the perception of the form, and its identification. Freeman (1929) and Bridgen (1933) were satisfied with only three stages. According to Freeman, in the preperceptive determination stage, the observer perceives only the general extent of stimulation. The reports specify only whether the stimulus is one that is scattered over the visual field or one that is compact. In the stage of "perceptive particularity," the observer is aware that he is looking at a thing. The contours become clearer and some of its points become important in determining recognition or identification. In the stage of perceptive familiarity, the form is identified. Zigler, Cook, Miller, and Wemple (1930), in an otherwise poorly controlled experiment, found four stages of perceptual development of form: no figure, formless figure, formlike figure, and clear figure. Hayami (1935) confirmed some of the Gestalt predictions about the primacy of form in the emergence of a visual stimulus, such as closure, hence subjective elongation of unclosed contours. He also observed that longer lines are perceived before shorter ones, and horizontal and vertical lines before oblique ones. The issue of primacy of form, postulated by the Gestalt school, became the center of a small controversy at about this time. It is touched upon in Chap. 7.

Tomoda (1937), using 9-msec. exposures, found essentially the same stages as Zigler *et al.* (1930). An additional finding was that increasing the area of the stimulus changed the relative incidence of the stages: the frequency of occurrence of the second and third stages increases at the expense of the first stage, but it asymptoted with still larger areas. Tanaka (1939) repeated Tomoda's experiment, but increased the exposure time from a minimum of 6 msec. to 8 and 10 msec., and further added multiples of 2 msec., finding the same stages as Tomoda.

In addition to low luminance levels and brief exposure times, blur (e.g., Andresen, 1941) and combination blur and tachistoscopic exposure (Douglas, 1947) have been used to produce threshold conditions. In these last two studies, the perception of Rorschach inkblots was emphasized, but the data are relevant. Douglas' findings especially strike a contemporary note when she refers to the first stage of perception as the sensory stage, the second as the exploratory stage, and the third as the interpretative stage. The most recent work in this area comes from Russia, where one of the findings of one experiment (Barskii & Guzeva, 1962) was that four types of threshold could be established for the perception of form: the threshold of intensity when light but not form is seen; the threshold of incomplete form perception; the threshold of adequate form perception; and the threshold of optimum form perception.

Thus, many investigators from different countries, at different times, and using different methods of achieving threshold conditions find essentially the same three to five stages in the development of a clear percept of form.

A contour may be blurred not only by defocusing an optical device or by interposing diffusing media but also by setting it in motion. The perception of apparent and real movement is a large area of investigation, having much relevance to the Gestalt theory of perception. The perception of contours in movement is a related but somewhat different event. Curiously, the perception of moving contours has received practically no attention. William M. Smith has made a contribution in this area (e.g., Smith & Gulick, 1962), relating his theory of dynamic contour perception to the theory of Marshall and Talbot.

As is apparent from the preceding chapters, Marshall and Talbot have influenced a number of other investigators in the area of form perception. Day (1956) has applied the statistical theory to the phenomenological reports of form perception at threshold levels:

During the first perceptual stage, that of awareness of light, where contrast is low . . ., lateral summation would predominate and vertical summation would be at a minimum . . . . In the absence of a strong vertical component statistical peaking of the excitation of distribution will be less marked than under conditions of greater brightness contrast. In consequence, the normal distribution of activity in area 17 will be flattened or platykurtic, since both the slope of the excitation gradient and the height of the distribution representing rate of excitation about the cortical locus of the contour edge will be slight . . . . [It is assumed that] the apparent localization of a contour in subjective visual space coincides with the location of maximal excitation in area 17 when the slope and height of the excitation gradient exceeds a certain minimum value . . . . Thus there is a stage (light threshold) in form perception . . . at which borders and edges are not perceived . . . . Increasing the brightness of a figure to about 15 times that required for the perception of light results in the impression of a vague and indefinite form . . . . The final phase of form perception is the emergence of clear outlines and definite shapes. This stage is represented cortically by a further development of those processes occurring during the second stage. The slope of the excitation gradient and the height of the distribution of activity will increase still more, and further peaking of the distribution will be revealed in greater sharpening of the activity peak. The sharpness of the edges of the figure concomitant upon still greater figure-ground contrast will lead to more nystagmic oscillation, and the activity of the 'on-off type' fibers will increase. (Day, 1956, pp. 141/3 passim.)

Figure 6-7 shows the hypothesized distribution of cortical excitation about the edge between stimulus figure and ground at the three stages of form perception.

5. Discrimination

A. ACUITY

Visual acuity tests involve the discrimination of simple contours that subtend visual angles at the limits of the resolving power of the visual system. The power of resolution of the visual system is also tested when an observer is required to discriminate, e.g., between two complex shapes that differ only in some significant but fine detail. The optometrist's office is not too far removed from the psychological vision laboratory: when the optometrist uses the Snellen chart

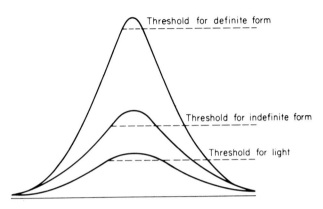

Fig. 6-7. Hypothetical distribution of cortical excitation about the edge between a figure and ground at the three stages of form perception. From Day (1956). Copyright 1956 by the American Psychological Association. Reproduced by permission.

as test object, he is in essence conducting a poorly controlled form-recognition experiment under threshold conditions for detail resolution.

The different types of test object used in acuity tests are not interchangeable. The simplest such object is a fine line or a dot, and the test establishes whether the testee is or is not able to report that the object is visible. The *minimum visible* test involves little more than visual detection since only the lowest level of discrimination is involved, namely figure-ground discrimination. The contours are so simple that the problem of recognition or naming does not arise.

In a *minimum separable* test, two identical objects are used, such as two lines or two dots, and the task is to discriminate between them when they are minimally separated. The target may be a multiple of such double objects, such as a grating or a checkerboard. Because the grating and the checkerboard appear to be more informative than just two lines or two squares, these targets have been preferred by investigators (e.g., Fantz, Hershenson) who study perception in infants: they produce easily observed orienting responses.

The third major type of acuity test object is a line one-half of which is displaced laterally through the width of the line. *Vernier acuity* is measured in terms of whether the displacement is detected or not. The task is one of discrimination.

The Snellen chart is the well-known table of letters of the alphabet of different sizes that is widely used by optometrists. Since letters are complex forms, they vary with regard to recognition thresholds, are more or less confounded with each other (e.g., *C* with *G* versus *X* with *O*), and comprise at least two of the three types of acuity test objects (e.g., *I* and *O* as examples of minimum visible, H and B as examples of minimum separable). An additional complication is the requirement that the testee be familiar with the letters of the Latin alphabet. To avoid these problems, charts with only one form of different sizes have been constructed, such as an E or a circle with a gap. These forms require only that their position (opening right, left, up, down) be correctly stated. The use of the circle with a gap, the Landolt C, was introduced by E. Landolt around the turn of the century (e.g., Landolt, 1906), but it is yet to displace the Snellen chart.

In addition to stimulus characteristics, acuity is determined by a number of other factors. One of them is light intensity. In general, as intensity increases, acuity improves. The relationship has the shape of an ogive, except in the case of two light bars on a dark background. Increasing intensity improves the visibility of these objects only up to a certain point, after which it decreases. This anomalous phenomenon was discussed in Chap. 2. Acuity also increases as the duration of the stimulus increases. An explanation of this phenomenon by Marshall and Talbot in terms of eye movements was presented in Chap. 2. The third major factor affecting acuity is the retinal locus. Since the electrical impulses emanating from the cones are less likely to converge than are messages emanating from the rods, the retinal distribution of light is represented by the cones more faithfully than by the rods. While the periphery of the retina with its predominantly rod population is more sensitive to light energy, visual acuity is much superior in the fovea, which is made up almost exclusively of cones.

B. RESPONSE VARIABLES

Most of the factors that affect perceptual response affect the responses given in form-discrimination experiments. Works such as Dember's (1960) *Psychology of Perception* give full account of the problems and issues associated with perceptual responses. Mention will be made here only of a few of the factors specific to form-discrimination experiments.

If viewing conditions are optimum, discrimination performance is usually perfect or near-perfect. Even under conditions of tachistoscopic exposure, there may not be enough variation in error scores for these to be used as an index of discriminability. Reaction time, on the other hand, has been found to be a satisfactory dependent variable where error scores fail. The usefulness of error measures is a matter of the particular experimental design, procedure, stimuli, etc. used. In a study by Arnoult, Gagne, and Vanderplas (1951), four different measures of visual discrimination of shapes were tested. One was the latency of "same" or "different" responses; in another, the number of .02-sec. intervals needed to elicit a correct response was counted; a third one was reaction time when the subject himself terminated the exposure of the stimulus; and the fourth was a measure of correct similarity judgment responses under conditions of tachistoscopic exposure. All four methods turned out to be equally good measures of discrimination, producing very similar rank orders of stimulus discriminability and similar variances of response scores.

In animals, discrimination learning does not occur as fast as it could because of certain behavioral tendencies that are not related to the task. A learning theory (Harlow, 1959) is based on the proposition that learning occurs as the animal gradually eliminates these "error factors," such as alternation, perseveration, and right-left preferences. There is no reason to suppose that there are no such error factors in human behavior, especially in tasks involving choice, such as a discrimination task. These tendencies have received practically no attention, although there is evidence that, if left uncontrolled, they could seriously affect experimental results. Thus, Winters and Gerjuoy (1966) report that, when making size discriminations between two identical and equal-size geometric forms presented tachistoscopically, normal subjects choose the right-side stimulus more often when the instructions call for reporting which of the two stimuli is the "larger." When a 30-sec. intertrial interval is introduced, the left side is chosen more often under "smaller" instructions; under these instructions, perceptual and motor preferences cancel each other out when the intertrial interval is reduced to 10 sec. Retardates, however, do not behave in the same way as normals (Gerjuoy & Winters, 1966): they show no side preference under tachistoscopic conditions. When exposure is unlimited, they show a strong preference to choose the right-side stimulus as the larger.

C. FORM PARAMETERS AS PREDICTORS OF DISCRIMINATIVE RESPONSE

The most frequently asked question regarding form discrimination is, "Which form parameters or combination of parameters will best predict discrimination," that is, "Which cues do subjects utilize to discriminate between two shapes?" Some of the better established answers to this question follow.

1. The number and kind of stimulus variables that are varied simultaneously affect discriminability. There are several studies (e.g., Eriksen & Hake, 1955) that show that when stimuli vary simultaneously on several dimensions they are discriminated better than when they vary on any one of these dimensions alone. Eriksen and Hake, however, assert further that, if it is assumed that the judgments of magnitude on two or more dimensions are independent, discrimination accuracy for a multidimensional series of stimuli can be predicted with reasonable precision if the discrimination accuracy of the compounding dimensions is known. This could have been true for their particular experiment, where the dimensions were the size, hue, and brightness of squares. When it comes to form parameters, there is no way of predicting the net result of the interaction of these parameters if several of them are varied simultaneously. Several form parameters varying together may interfere with each other and

hence lower discriminability, or potentiate the effect of one another and thus facilitate discrimination (e.g., Zusne, 1965).

2. The number of turns in random polygons and errors in discrimination (or reaction time) are related by a U-shaped function having a minimum between six and eight turns. This function has been obtained by Brown, Hitchcock, and Michels (1962), Coules and Lekarczyk (1963), and Crook (1957), tachistoscopic presentation being used in the first study and visual noise in the last two. The same function has been obtained with squirrels (Michels, Pittman, Hitchcock, & Brown, 1962), with trials to criterion discrimination performance as the dependent variable. In the case of humans, the explanation of this particular relationship has been sought in the information-processing capabilities of the visual system: the less complex shapes have fewer degrees of freedom to vary, hence are not as discriminable as the more complex shapes. The very complex shapes, on the other hand, contain too much information to be processed in a limited time period, hence subjects commit errors or take longer to make the necessary discriminations. While the same kind of logic could be applied to animals, the coincidence of the optimum complexity level in humans and squirrels found by Michels *et al.* is rather curious. Since it is only one such study, further accumulation of data is needed to interpret this phenomenon. French (1953b) also found a curvilinear relationship using 2-, 3-, 4-, 5-, 6-, and 7-dot patterns, but with a minimum at the 3-dot level.

3. Rotating a figure affects its discriminability adversely. The concept of rotation is properly applied to the recognition and identification tasks only. The relationship of rotation and familiarity was discussed in Chap. 5: familiarity of meaningful or familiar forms decreases with rotation. Recognition of non-representational forms never seen before is a contradiction in terms, and the rotation concept is inapplicable here. In the few discrimination studies in which rotation has been an independent variable, the purpose has been simply to study the effect of rotation on "same" and "different" judgments when two identical shapes are presented together but one of them is rotated with regard to the other. Both metric figures (Woodring & Alluisi, 1966) and dot patterns (French, 1953a) are made more difficult to discriminate from their twins if rotated.

4. The effects of reflection on discrimination have been studied more in children and animals than in human adults. As will be seen in Chaps. 8 and 9, in both animals and children, discrimination between a form and its mirror image produced by reflection about its vertical axis (right-left reflection) is more difficult than when the reflection is about a horizontal axis (up-down reflection). The few existing studies with human adults have produced similar results (e.g., Butler, 1964; Sekuler & Houlihan, 1968). For an explanation of this difference, one may look to Sutherland's theory of shape discrimination (Chap. 3). Another possibility is as follows: since, in a two-choice discrimination

problem the two shapes are placed side by side, a right-left reflection leaves the original shape and its reflection in the positions in which they are presented for discrimination. In the case of up-down reflection, however, the mirror-image shape must be moved to this position. Hence, while in the former case there is perfect reciprocity of every shape element, the reciprocal relation of shape parts of up-down reflected shapes is lost, the two shapes appear more different and are more easily told apart.

5. Of the configurational parameters, those that measure the major dimensions along which the total area or the contours of a shape vary, namely dispersion, symmetry, and elongation, are good predictors of discrimination performance (Andrews & Brown, 1967; Boynton, Elworth, Onley, & Klingberg, 1960; Boynton, Elworth, Monty, Onley & Klingberg, 1961; Brown et al., 1962; Brown & LoSasso, 1967; Monty & Boynton, 1962; Zusne, 1965). The relative contributions of these parameters to discriminability are, of course, a function of each particular experimental design. Because of their interactive effects, predictions of the utilization of these parameters as discriminative clues cannot be made in the case of a given experiment.

With the exception of Goodrick (1962), the few investigators who have measured form-discrimination thresholds have done so only with the square-rectangle and the circle-ellipse. Since, in addition, some of their data are quite disparate, no generalizations can be made in this area. Buehler (1913) found a Weber's ratio of .013 for the rectangle, which is very close to that found by Veniar (1948) 35 years later, namely .014. Among the five subjects used by Veniar, individual difference thresholds varied from .009 to .021. The findings of Sleight and Mowbray (1951), however, were quite different: they had to elongate the side of a 1-in. square by 27% before it began to appear as a rectangle, and the major axis of the ellipse had to be 20% longer than the minor axis before the ellipse could be distinguished from a circle. Goodrick's (1962) is the only study in which form difference thresholds have been measured as a function of complexity. Goodrick used 4-, 8-, and 16-sided random polygons and calculated difference thresholds from "same" and "different" judgments of pairs of shapes. Distortions in the stimuli were achieved by moving all vertices a fixed distance in randomly determined directions. Goodrick found that the magnitude of the difference threshold was inversely related to shape complexity. If the size of the difference threshold is related to discriminability, then the results of Goodrick's experiment are inconsistent with those just discussed, at least as far as 16-sided polygons are concerned.

D. ESTIMATION OF AREA, LINE LENGTH, SIZE OF ANGLES, CURVATURE, AND COMPLEXITY

The estimation of such basic magnitudes as the area of a shape, the length of lines, the size of angles, the degree of curvature, and the number of sides or inflections in a contour partakes of all the characteristics of a discrimination task. At the same time, it constitutes the simplest kind of scaling task. Researchers have concentrated on the ability of subjects to judge the magnitude of these simple characteristics because they enter into judgments of more-complex form attributes, so that any constant error in their judgment would affect the scaling of forms, their reproduction, recognition, and identification. The over-estimation and underestimation of areas, lengths, angles, and directions also characterize the geometric illusions.

The *area* of a form may be overestimated or underestimated depending on its configuration. There are several studies of the effect of shape on judgments of area. While it is certain that shape does affect estimates of area, the various researchers do not agree on what kinds of configuration lead to overestimation or underestimation of area. The data came mostly from several older studies in which just a few of the standard geometric forms have been employed. While Mansvelt (1928) and Bolton (1897) agree that the circle is overestimated, Peters (1933) finds that it is underestimated, along with the square and the rectangle. Bolton (1897) is in agreement with Peters (1933) and Warren and Pinneau (1955) that the square is underestimated. Pfeiffer (1932) and Warren and Pinneau (1955) find that the largest amount of overestimation occurs in the equilateral triangle situated on its base, with which Peters (1933) agrees, followed by the equilateral triangle on its vertex, the diamond, the square, and the circle. While Anastasi (1936) also finds that the square and the circle suffer the least amount of overestimation, she disagrees with Pfeiffer (1932) on the place of the equilateral triangle, while agreeing with Peters (1933) that the star is overestimated. To add to the confusion, Wagner (1931) finds that the square and the rectangle are judged more accurately than the triangle and the circle. The picture is further complicated by considerable individual differences found by almost all investigators.

The area of small figures is underestimated while the area of large figures is overestimated. While Mansvelt (1928) finds this to be true for the square and the triangle, the only two shapes used by him, Anastasi (1936) finds that this relationship obtains for all seven of the geometric shapes used by her.

The color of the form also affects the estimation of its area, light forms being judged larger than dark forms of the same area (Gundlach & Macoubry, 1931; Pfeiffer, 1932). While area is the main parameter that affects judgments of size, informational and configurational parameters affect them also. While it is true that the main variable affecting judgments of size is area, it is not true, as it has been asserted (Arnoult, 1957, 1960), that other form characteristics have no effect on such judgments. Thus, it has been found that the length of the perimeter (Anastasi, 1936; Pfeiffer, 1932) and the greatest linear dimension of the figure (Anastasi, 1936; Pfeiffer, 1932; Warren & Pinneau, 1955) are also cues used by subjects in estimating the area of a figure. If the standards for comparison are as different as the square and the triangle, being guided by the vertical extents of these two figures may affect area judgments considerably (Anastasi, 1936). Hitchcock, Brown, Michels, & Spiritoso (1962) have found that errors in judgments of area increase with increased complexity of the figures judged, and Smith's (1964) finding was that compactness is the main factor that determines how shapes will be ranked on area: the more compact shapes are judged to be larger than thin, stretched-out shapes. Smith's study is perhaps the most generalizable of all the studies mentioned in connection with area judgments since a fairly large number of randomly constructed shapes were used and several parameters of these shapes measured to predict judgments.

The amount of work done on the estimation of the *length of straight and curved lines* is considerably less than in the case of area. Of interest is the finding by Fried (1964) that length is underestimated when the stimulus object is viewed monocularly. Takagi (1926) has reported that, while the estimation of the length of curved-line segments is almost as good as that of straight lines, the amount of overestimation of arcs increases with increased curvature. Gaito (1959) reported that curved lines have significantly larger difference thresholds than single straight lines (i.e., curved lines are seen as straight lines more often than the other way around) and that obtuse angles between two straight-line segments were preceived more readily than curves. Kiesow (1926) found that the Weber fraction for the straight line varies from .0105 if the line is 10 mm. long to .0066 if it is 300 mm. long. Della Valle, Andrews, and Ross (1956) have shown that the accuracy of judgment of curvature or of discontinuity in straight lines is a function of the length of the chord and the base length for angles: the perception of curvilinearity and angularity is superior for greater chord and base lengths.

As to *angles,* their overestimation or underestimation is a function of their absolute size. Barden (1927), e.g., found that, while acute angles were overestimated and obtuse angles up to 135 degrees were underestimated, angles between 135 and 150 degrees were overestimated. Beyond 150 degrees, however, they were underestimated again. The greatest amount of over-estimation occurred at 50 degrees and the greatest amount of underestimation at 120 degrees. These results, as well as the finding that subjects had the greatest certainty about their judgments for angles close to 45, 90, and 135 degrees, indicate that the estimation of angle size occurs not so much on the basis of the distance between the two arms of the angle as with reference to an imaginary rectangular coordinate system and the two main diagonal axes, a conclusion also reached by Pratt (1926).

While a correspondence undoubtedly exists between *complexity* of a shape in the information-theoretic sense and perceived complexity, the relationship does not appear to be a one-to-one relationship or even a rectilinear one. As shapes increase in complexity, more of the inflections or vertices have a chance of having a very obtuse angle, and more of the sides have a chance of being very short, so that the discriminability of the sides and vertices should decrease with increasing complexity, especially under conditions of limited viewing time. Seiler and Zusne (1967) have shown that the degree of underestimation of the complexity of polygons does increase monotonically with increasing stimulus complexity and decreasing exposure time.

D. E. Berlyne is noted for his work on the relationship between stimulus properties, such as complexity, and their arousal effects: the experience of novelty, surprise, incongruity, and the like has been shown to vary directly with stimulus complexity. A finding of Berlyne's that regular (more redundant, hence informationally less complex) stimuli are sometimes preferred to informationally more complex stimuli produced a small controversy, in the course of which it was suggested (Heckhausen, 1964) that a definition of complexity in purely informational terms is insufficient and that phenomenal complexity must be taken into account. Heckhausen has argued that Berlyne's more regular figures are phenomenally more complex than they are in informational terms, hence Berlyne's original proposition regarding the relationship between arousal and stimulus complexity still holds. Day's (1965) subjects, however, have ranked Berlyne's stimuli on complexity in the same order in which they were ranked in terms of physical complexity. This discussion again touches upon the place of meaning in information theory. When the task is a straightforward task of judging complexity, a typical psychophysical function is the result. Physiological arousal and preference statements, however, are dependent variables that are affected by past experience, set, meaning, and emotional significance, hence cannot be expected to vary in a rectilinear fashion with measured complexity.

E. VISUAL NOISE AND DISCRIMINABILITY

Visual noise affects the discriminability of random cell patterns adversely: given a constant complexity level, increased noise level increases errors and decreases the rate of information processing; given a constant noise level, increased complexity improves discrimination. Such are the findings of Arnoult and Price (1961), French (1954), Hillix (1960), Pollack and Klemmer (1954), and Webster (1966). In these studies, the stimuli were square cell patterns. Noise in these patterns is defined as additional filled cells that do not belong to the original pattern, and distortion is achieved by displacing cells or cell rows in the pattern.

6. Scaling

Scaling is a somewhat more complex task than discrimination; still, they are basically similar. In scaling, instead of a simple decision in favor of one of two alternatives, the decision must be made as to where a stimulus belongs on a continuum where there are more than two equally spaced points to which stimuli must be assigned.

While form may be scaled with regard to a large number of different variables, the number of variables with regard to which forms have been actually scaled is not too large. They include similarity, complexity, preference, Gestalt goodness (including geometricity and regularity), familiarity, meaningfulness, pleasantness, interest, scaling on a large number of scales that are eventually factor-analyzed (semantic differential technique), as well as a number of others. With the exception of the first four variables mentioned, however, only one or two studies have dealt with each of the others, so that only these four are discussed here.

A. SIMILARITY

The studies in this area may be divided into those that are concerned with the dimensionality of the psychophysical space in which the judging of similarities of shapes occurs, and those in which physical shape properties have been used to predict similarity judgments. In the first type of study, the emphasis is not so much on form as on judgment, psychophysical problems, and perception in general. Such was Attneave's (1950) study, whose purpose was "to determine the way in which several stimulus dimensions are integrated into a single judgment." The stimuli were parallelograms varying in area and the size of angles, squares varying in area and reflectance, and isosceles triangles varying in size of the apex angle. Attneave's conclusion was that psychological distances could not be fitted in a Euclidean space since the psychological difference between any two stimuli was approximately equal to the sum of their differences with respect to the physical variables, not to the square root of the sum of the squared differences as demanded by a Euclidean space. In such a non-Euclidean space, the observer has to "go around the corner" to get from one scaled object to another.

Stilson (1956) factor-analyzed the scaled similarity values of triangles and decided that the psychological space involved was five-dimensional. The proportion of variation in this space which was common to the variance of the several physical measures taken on the triangles was about 60%.

McCullough (1957), also using triangles but a different scaling technique, found two psychological dimensions of similarity: one corresponding to the physical variations in area, configuration, and rotation, and an unidentified dimension. McCullough's data suggest further that stimuli differing physically on one dimension only may differ psychologically in more than one dimension, and that the continuum of psychological similarity has both qualitative and quantitative (metathetic and prothetic) characteristics.

Thomas (1967), using random shapes that varied in complexity from 3 to 40 turns and a still different scaling procedure, decided that the data could be adequately handled by a one- or two-dimensional space, one dimension being complexity, the other tentatively identified as symmetry.

Behrman and Brown (1967) obtained highly correlated results in a similarity scaling experiment using three different scaling techniques. The stimuli were 16 quadrilaterals. The psychological space of similarity had three dimensions: dispersion, jaggedness, and elongation.

The above studies differ so much in the complexity of the shapes used, the physical dimensions analyzed, and the scaling procedures employed that it is no wonder that they yield little by way of any firm conclusions. The few studies in which it has been attempted to account for judged similarity in terms of specific physical form parameters fare no better. Chambliss (1957) found, on the basis of his factor analysis of similarity ratings of five- and ten-sided random polygons on a seven-point scale, that there was only one psychological dimension of similarity. Chambliss used eight basic form measures and the logarithmic, square-root, and squared transformations of them, but only measures of angles and vertices turned out to be useful predictors of response, accounting for most of the variance in the dependent variable.

Small (1961) had his subjects judge the similarity of 4-, 5-, 6-, and 7-sided random polygons on a five-point scale. Of the 21 measures taken on the forms, 8 nonorthogonal measures correlated significantly with the criterion. Best single predictor was complexity, accounting for about 83% of the variance in response.

Attempts have also been made to account for similarity judgments in Gestalt terms, but the two existing studies yield no firm conclusions either. Sleight (1952) had his subjects put into the same bin the six identical copies that had been prepared of each of 21 different geometric shapes. Sorting-time analysis permitted the division of the 21 shapes into four groups of about the same size, within each of which shapes differed little in terms of discriminability. The group of most-discriminable shapes (swastika, circle, crescent, airplane, cross, six-pointed star) differed markedly in appearance from the other three, being noticeably more complex and jagged. Shapes in the remaining three groups, however, did not show any apparent differences among themselves that would distinguish them as homogeneous groups and account for the differences in sorting time. Royer (1966), using simple five-dot patterns, found that sets of patterns consisting of good or simple items were easier to sort.

The possibility that individual differences may play a major role in similarity judgments has been suggested by Silver, Landis, and Messick (1966). When subjects were asked to sort all forms into two groups, then each group into two groups again, etc., five distinct viewpoints emerged, none of which produced the same stimulus space as was obtained by analyzing the average ratings. The problem here was that the investigators gave their subjects three samples of shapes each belonging to a different population. The multidimensional model of successive interval scaling used by these investigators has not been applied to the similarity scaling of forms by others, which makes comparison even more difficult.

B. COMPLEXITY

The scaling of complexity of visual forms has been fairly popular, and the results are more definite here than in the case of similarity. One of the reasons is the lesser amount of simpler dimensions or aspects involved in the concept of complexity. Subjective complexity, however, is not one-dimensional even though it might be physically.

It is fairly well established that the judged complexity of random polygons varies directly with the number of independent turns in the contour, which is the main determinant of perceived complexity. This is one of the main findings reported by a number of investigators (Attneave, 1957; Day, 1967; Edelman, Karas, & Cohen, 1961; Goldstein, 1961), and an indirect result in experiments performed by a number of others. The most complex polygon ever used has been a 160-sided one (Day, 1967). The term "independent turns" refers to the total number of turns counted in an asymmetric shape and about one-half of the total turns in a symmetric shape. [The number of independent turns that a symmetric shape divided along its axis of symmetry will have is $(n + 2)/2$, where n is the number of total turns in the symmetric shape. For shapes with an odd number of sides, the physically impossible half-turn obtained by means of this formula means that the division creates an additional point. Thus, both a ten-sided symmetric shape and a nine-sided symmetric shape will yield asymmetric half-shapes of six turns each.]

Compactness, variability of internal angles, and symmetry are the most important secondary variables that affect judged complexity. In Arnoult's (1960) study, perimeter-squared/area, angular variability, and symmetry (dichotomized), along with independent sides accounted for 87% of response variance in one sample of shapes (method 1) and 82% of response variance in another sample (method 2). Attneave's (1957) data are comparable: independent sides, angular variability, and symmetry accounted for about 90% of response variance. The effect of symmetry in Attneave's experiment is worth noting: symmetric shapes were judged to be more complex than asymmetric ones when the number of independent turns was kept constant, but were judged to be less complex when the total number of turns was kept constant. Reflecting a shape symmetrically was found to be equivalent to an increase of about 19% in the number of independent turns in terms of judged complexity. The finding that symmetric shapes are intermediate between asymmetric shapes with equal number of independent turns and those with the same number of total turns was reported earlier by Attneave (1955). Houston, Garskof, and Silber (1965) have also reported an interactive effect of complexity and redundancy upon the judged complexity of cell matrices.

Stenson (1966) factor-analyzed the ratings of complexity of 20 method-4 forms, finding that a single factor accounted for most of the variance in complexity ratings. Four physical measures described this factor: number of turns in the form, length of the perimeter, perimeter-squared/area, and the variance of the internal angles of the form. Angular variability and compactness also appeared to influence judgments of complexity of random shapes in experiments by Goldstein and Andrews (1962) and by Sanders (1962).

While the rounding off of the corners of a polygon may affect its phenomenal appearance, information-wise, not much is changed since in both rectilinear and curvilinear shapes information is concentrated at points of maximum inflection in the contour. Neither Arnoult (1960) nor Attneave (1957) found that curvature affects complexity judgments in any way.

Of the subject variables, only the effects of familiarity on judged complexity have been investigated. The two existing studies, however, have yielded results that are exactly opposite. While Goldstein's (1961a) data show that familiar shapes are judged to be significantly less complex than unfamiliar shapes, Sanders' (1962) findings were that random shapes are judged to be more complex on second judgment, regardless of whether subjects have been through a familiarization procedure between the two judgments or not. One possible clue for this difference may be sought in the time interval between judgments: while Sanders' subjects made the second judgment soon after the first one, Goldstein's design called for a 48-hr. delay between pair-associates learning and the rating of the complexity of previously seen and new forms. Why this should reverse complexity judgments is not clear. Munsinger and Kessen (1964), in their study of preferences for random shapes as a function of complexity, report a similar phenomenon: a shift toward a different level of complexity took place in their experiment only after an intervening period of 24 hr. These authors do not refer either to Goldstein's or Sanders' work and do not present an explanation of this phenomenon of their own. Goldstein, to explain the decrease in complexity ratings that he found, reasons as follows. Both Goldstein (1961b) and Vanderplas and Garvin (1959) have found that complexity and association value are inversely related. If it is assumed that association value and familiarity are directly related and more-familiar shapes appear less complex (which is an everyday observation), shapes of high association value should be judged less complex. While this is a sound line of reasoning, more is involved in shifts of ratings of complexity and other attributes as a function of previous experience, as is evident from the work of Munsinger and Kessen (1964) presented in the next section.

C. PREFERENCE

The most extensive series of experiments on preference for random shapes as a function of their complexity has been undertaken by Munsinger and Kessen

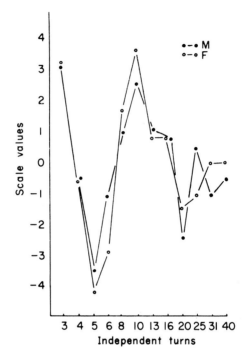

Fig. 6-8. Scale scores of preference for asymmetric random shapes varying in number of independent turns from 3 to 40. From Munsinger and Kessen (1964). Copyright 1964 by the American Psychological Association. Reproduced by permission.

(1964). In most of these experiments, scale values of preference and meaningfulness were derived from pair-comparison data, with number of turns, symmetry, and previous experience as the independent variables.

In one experiment, three series of random shapes ranging from 3 to 40 sides and logarithmically spaced on the number of turns yielded the preference function shown in Fig. 6-8. An inverted U-shaped function is evident for the middle range of the stimuli. The increase in preference for the most complex shapes is assumed by the authors to be the result of the emergence of meaningful configurations at this level of complexity. The abnormally high preference for the triangles and quadrilaterals was initially considered by the authors "troublesome," and additional experiments were performed which partially clarified the phenomenon. In one such experiment, only shapes of between 5 and 20 turns were scaled for complexity. The results of that experiment are shown in Fig. 6-9. They confirmed the authors' assumption that the

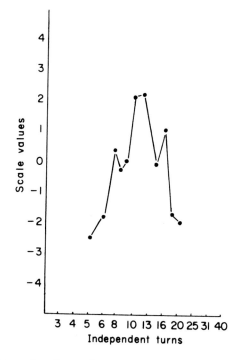

Fig. 6-9. Scale scores of preference for asymmetric random shapes varying in number of independent turns from 5 to 23. From Munsinger and Kessen (1964). Copyright 1964 by the American Psychological Association. Reproduced by permission.

exceptionally high preference for the extremes of the series of shapes produced an artifactual reduction in preference for the middle range of shapes. In addition, shapes in the 5-40-turn range were also scaled with respect to meaningfulness to correct complexity rating data for the influence of that variable. Meaningfulness was found to vary directly with the number of turns. When one-half the scale score of meaningfulness was subtracted from the scale scores of preference, the plotted difference scores yielded the function shown in Fig. 6-10, which was in excellent agreement with the prediction made about the relationship between the number of independent turns in random shapes and preference, and also confirms the assumption that the departure from prediction seen among shapes with many turns was due to meaningfulness.

Another experiment was performed to investigate the deviation from the predicted function at the lower end of the array of shapes. In this experiment, only an equilateral triangle, a square, a regular pentagon, and their irregular

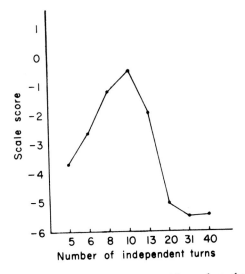

Fig. 6-10. Scale scores of preference of asymmetric random shapes corrected for meaningfulness. From Munsinger and Kessen (1964). Copyright 1964 by the American Psychological Association. Reproduced by permission.

counterparts were used. Both the regular and irregular quadrilaterals had almost identical scale values of preference. They were also the lowest. The regular pentagon was ranked highest, with both triangles in an intermediate position and also earning identical scale values. The only deviation was in the irregular five-sided figure, whose scaled preference was the same as that of the quadrilaterals. In view of the very limited number of stimuli used at each level of complexity, the results of this particular experiment are rather useless and the speculations of Munsinger and Kessen about the significance of the results not very helpful.

The results of preference scaling shown in Figs. 6-8, 6-9, and 6-10 were obtained with unselected college students. A very different picture was obtained when the subjects were art students (Fig. 6-11). An almost identical response was obtained from male college students when the asymmetric shapes used in the previously mentioned experiments were made symmetric by reflection (Fig. 6-12). Munsinger and Kessen explain the last two sets of results in terms of a reduction in cognitive uncertainty when stimulus variability is reduced either through past experience or through the introduction of symmetry.

In two of their experiments, Munsinger and Kessen studied the effect of experience on preference. In one experiment, the shapes used in the first

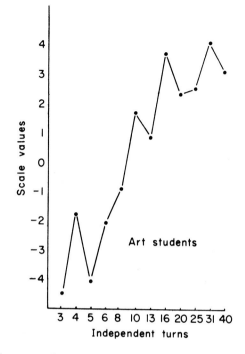

Fig. 6-11. Scale scores of preference of art students for asymmetric random shapes varying in number of independent turns from 3 to 40. From Munsinger and Kessen (1964). Copyright 1964 by the American Psychological Association. Reproduced by permission.

reported experiment were presented to subjects six times. While complexity judgments on the first trial were the same as before, by the sixth trial, preference for the simple shapes had dropped, preference for 16-40-sided shapes had increased, with preference for shapes in the middle range of turns remaining the same. In the last experiment, in addition to experience as such, type of experience was varied. Three groups of subjects were first given the task of pair-comparing 5-, 6-, 8-, 10-, 13-, 20-, 31-, and 40-sided random shapes with regard to preference. One group then made 112 pair-comparisons of 5-sided shapes, another was given the same task with ten-sided shapes, while the third group was exposed to 20-sided shapes. One-half of each group was retested immediately on the first set of shapes, while the other half was tested 24 hr. later. After a delay of 24 hr., the group exposed to ten-sided shapes showed an increase in preference for ten-sided shapes and a decrease in preference for shapes of 20 turns. Those exposed to shapes of 20 turns showed increased

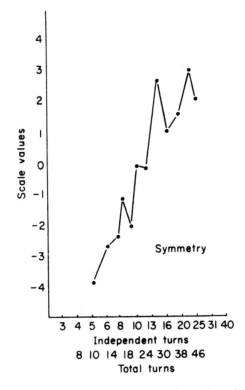

Fig. 6-12. Scale scores of preference for symmetric random shapes plotted against munber of independent and total number of turns. From Munsinger and Kessen (1964). Copyright 1964 by the American Psychological Association. Reproduced by permission.

preference for shapes of more turns and decreased preference for shapes of fewer turns. Other differences were not found to be statistically significant, and no differences showed up when subjects were retested immediately. While the effect of experience is suggestive, Munsinger and Kessen do not develop a very cogent account of the phenomena that were observed or of those that could or should have been observed but were not. Their discussion emphasizes the importance of cognitive uncertainty in preference judgments. Cognitive uncertainty is a combination of stimulus variability and the meaningfulness of stimuli (in terms of the observer's past experience). Preference varies with the subject's experience with variability since human beings can handle only a limited amount of cognitive uncertainty. Cognitive uncertainty may be modified by changing the stimulus, such as by making it symmetric, or by modifying the subject's cognitive structure, either during the course of the experiment or in the course of the educational process. This model, of course, is not novel, since similar ideas have been presented by Hebb, Dember, Osgood, and others (cf. Fiske & Maddi, 1961).

Some of the findings of Munsinger and Kessen have not been replicated. Dorfman and McKenna (1966) reported, e.g., that while they found a curvilinear relationship between stimulus uncertainty and preference for geometric patterns, both introductory psychology students (girls) and art students yielded this type of relationship. Taylor and Eisenman (1964) have produced data showing greater preference for the more complex (up to 24 sides) polygons in more-creative art students than in less-creative ones. In a comparison of the effects of complexity and symmetry, Eisenman (1967a) found that his subjects preferred symmetric shapes and rejected the more complex ones, although they did not necessarily prefer the simplest shapes. In another study (Eisenman & Rappaport, 1967), Eisenman found that symmetric shapes were reacted to favorably, regardless of whether they were high or low in complexity preference. In general, naive subjects in Eisenman's studies preferred simplicity. They preferred more complex figures only when these were also symmetric (Eisenman & Gellens, 1968).

To the list of factors that affect preference for random shapes can be added the factors of sex and birth order: in Eisenman's (1967b) group of subjects, girls tended to prefer complexity more than males, first-born males preferred complexity more than later-born males, but later-born females preferred complexity more than first-born females. It must be mentioned, though, that in all of Eisenman's studies, only 12 shapes have been used. Since, in addition, complexity, symmetry, and subject variables are occasionally confounded in Eisenman's studies, his results may be considered only as suggestive.

D. GOODNESS OF FORM

Only a few studies have been concerned with the scaling of shapes with respect to goodness of form. Zusne and Michels (1962a, 1962b) used systematic samples of 55 four-sided and 43 five-sided polygons in which every possible variant of such polygons was represented. Ratings on five-point scales of geometricity, regularity, and familiarity produced practically identical ordering of the forms, i.e., subjects considered these terms to be synonymous. A clear dichotomy was present in the ordering of the shapes, though. Shapes that were bilaterally symmetric were all ranked as being more geometric, etc., than asymmetric shapes. Within the symmetric group, shapes with more than one axis of symmetry were ranked above those with only one. Measured dispersion, elongation, and areal asymmetry did not predict the ranks of shapes in the symmetric subgroup; the weighted sum of these measures did predict ranking in the asymmetric subgroup, compactness being the best single predictor. Since in these experiments the instructions were varied in only one word ("geometric," "regular," "familiar"), a further test was made of the effects of instructions by substituting the term "pleasing." In an unpublished experiment, rated pleasantness of quadrilaterals correlated .41 with their rated geometricity and .47 with their rated familiarity, while a zero correlation was found between aesthetic value and measured geometricity (the weighted sum of compactness, elongation, and asymmetry). While bilateral symmetry did play a role in the ordering of shapes on pleasantness, its effect was a different one and not as pronounced as in the other experiments: the various V-shaped symmetric shapes resembling the Cadillac emblem all appeared ranked at the very top of the hierarchy of preference.

REFERENCES

Anastasi, A. The estimation of areas. *J. gen. Psychol.*, 1936, **14**, 201-225.

Andresen, H. Ueber die Auffassung diffus optischer Eindruecke; ein Beitrag zur Bedingungserforschung der Leistungsvollzuege beim Rorschachtest. *Z. Psychol.*, 1941, **150**, 6-91.

Andrews, M. H., & Brown, D. R. A multidimensional analysis of visual shape discrimination. Paper presented at Midwestern Psychological Association, Chicago, May, 1967.

Arnoult, M. D. Toward a psychophysics of form. In J. W. Wulfeck & J. H. Taylor (Eds.), *Form discrimination as related to military problems.* Washington, D. C.: Nat. Acad. Sci.-Nat. Res. Coun., 1957. Pp. 38-42.

Arnoult, M. D. Prediction of perceptual responses from structural characteristics of the stimulus. *Percept. mot. Skills*, 1960, **11**, 261-268.

Arnoult, M. D., & Price, C. W. Pattern matching in the presence of visual noise. *J. exp. Psychol.*, 1961, **62**, 372-376.

Arnoult, M. D., Gagne, R. M., & Vanderplas, J. M. A comparison of four measures of visual discrimination of shapes. *US Human Resources Res. Center Res. Bull.* No. 51-23, 1951.

Attneave, F. Dimensions of similarity. *Amer. J. Psychol.*, 1950, **63**, 516-556.

Attneave, F. Physical determinants of the judged complexity of shapes. *J. exp. Psychol.*, 1957, **53**, 221-227.

Attneave, F. Symmetry, information, and memory for patterns. *Amer. J. Psychol.*, 1955, **68**, 209-222.

Barden, H. P. Ueber die Schaetzung von Winkeln bei Knaben und Maedchen verschiedener Altersstufen. *Arch. ges. Psychol.*, 1927, **58**, 81-94.

Barskiǐ, B. V., & Guzeva, M. A. O zavisimosti prostranstvennykh porogov zreniya ot kharaktera vosprinimaemogo kontura. *Voprosy. Psikhol.*, 1962, 8(2), 101-114.

Battro, A. M., & Fraisse, P. Y a-t-il une relation entre la capacité d'apprehension visuelle et les mouvements des yeux? *Annee Psychol.*, 1961, **61**, 313-324.

Behrman, B. W., & Brown, D. R. Multidimensional scaling of form. *Percept. Psychophys.*, 1968, **4**, 19-25.

Blackwell, H. R. A literature survey of the effects of target size and shape upon visual detection. *J. Opt. Soc. Amer.*, 1957, **47**, 114. (Abstract)

Bolton, F. E. A contribution to the study of illusions. *Amer. J. Psychol.*, 1897-98, **9**, 167-182.

Boynton, R. M., Elworth, C. L., Onley, J. W., & Klingberg, C. L. Form discrimination as predicted by overlap and area. *USAF RADC TR* 60-158, 1960.

Boynton, R. M., Elworth, C. L., Monty, R. A., Onley, J. W., & Klingberg, C. L. Overlap as a predictor of form discrimination under suprathreshold conditions. *USAF RADC TR* 61-99, 1961.

Brandt, H. F. Study of ocular movements in the bi-dimensional plane and their physhological implications. Unpublished doctoral dissertation, Univ. of Iowa, 1937.

Brandt, H. F. Oscular patterns and their psychological implications. *Amer. J. Psychol.,* 1940, 53, 260-268.

Brandt, H. F. *The psychology of seeing.* New York: Philosophical Library, 1945.

Bridgen, R. L. A tachistoscopic study of the differentiation of perception. *Psychol. Monogr.,* 1933, 44, No. 197.

Brown, D. R., & LoSasso, J. S. Pattern degradation, discrimination difficulty, and quantified stimulus attributes. *Psychon. Sci.,* 1967, 9, 351-352.

Brown, D. R., & Owen, D. H. The metrics of visual form: Methodological dyspepsia. *Psychol. Bull.,* 1967, 68, 243-259.

Brown, D. R., Hitchcock, L., Jr., & Michels, K. M. Quantitative studies in form perception: An evaluation of the role of selected stimulus parameters in the visual discrimination performance of human subjects. *Percept. mot. Skills,* 1962. 14, 519-529.

Brown, R. H., & Niven, J. I. Relation between the foveal intensity threshold and length of an illuminated slit. *J. exp. Psychol.,* 1944, 34, 464-476.

Bryden, M. P. The role of post-exposural eye movements in tachistoscopic perception. *Can. J. Psychol.,* 1961, 15, 220-225.

Buehler, K. *Die Gestaltwahrnehmungen.* Stuttgart: Spemann, 1913.

Buswell, G. T. *How people look at pictures.* Chicago, Illinois: Chicago Univ. Press, 1935.

Butler, J. Visual discrimination of shape by humans. *Quart. J. exp. Psychol.,* 1964, 14, 272-276.

Carmichael, L., & Dearborn, W. F. *Reading and visual fatigue.* Boston, Massachusetts: Houghton, 1947.

Chambliss, D. J. The relation between judged similarity and the physical properties of plane figures. Unpublished doctoral dissertation, Univ of Wisconsin, 1957. *Diss. Abstr.,* 1957, 17, 2070.

Clark, W. C. Relation between the thresholds for single and multiple light pulses. Unpublished doctoral dissertation, Univ. of Michigan, 1958.

Coules, J., & Lekarczyk, M. A. Observer tolerance of form transformation as a function of form complexity. *USAF ESD Tech. Rep.* No. 63-135, 1963.

Crook, M. N. Facsimile-generated analogues for instrumental displays. In J. W. Wulfeck & J. H. Taylor (Eds.), *Form discrimination as related to military problems.* Washington, D.C.: Nat. Acad. Sci.-Nat. Res. Coun., 1957. Pp. 85-98.

Day, H. Brief note on the Berlyne-Heckhausen controversy. *Psychol. Rep.,* 1965, 17, 225-226.

Day, H. Evaluations of subjective complexity, pleasingness, and interestingness for a series of random polygons varying in complexity. *Percept. Psychophys.,* 1967, 2, 281-286.

Day, R. H. Application of the statistical theory to form perception. *Psychol. Rev.,* 1956, 63, 139-148.

Dayton, G. O., Jr., & Jones, M. H. Analysis of characteristics of fixation reflex in infants by use of direct current electrooculography. *Neurology,* 1964, 14, 1152-1156.

Della Valle, L., Andrews, T. G., & Ross, S. Perceptual thresholds of curvilinearity and angularity as functions of line length. *J. exp. Psychol.,* 1956, 51, 343-347.

Dember, W. N. *The psychology of perception.* New York: Holt, 1960.

Dodge, R., & Cline, T. S. The angle velocity of eye-movements. *Psychol. Rev.,* 1901, 8, 145-157.

Dorfman, D. D., & McKenna, H. Pattern preference as a function of pattern uncertainty. *Can. J. Psychol.,* 1966, **20**, 143-153.

Douglas, A. G. A tachistoscopic study of the order of emergence in the process of perception. *Psychol. Monogr.,* 1947, **61**(6), No. 287.

Edelman, S. K., Karas, G. G., & Cohen, B. J. The relative contributions of complexity and symmetry to the perception of form. Paper presented at Midwestern Psychological Association, Chicago, May, 1961.

Eisenman, R. Complexity-simplicity: I. Preference for symmetry and rejection of complexity. *Psychon. Sci.,* 1967, **8**, 169-170. (a)

Eisenman, R. Complexity-simplicity: II. Birth order and sex differences. *Psychon. Sci.,* 1967, **8**, 171-172. (b)

Eisenman, R., & Rappaport, J. Complexity preference and semantic differential ratings of complexity-simplicity and symmetry-asymmetry. *Psychon. Sci.,* 1967, **7**, 147-148.

Eisenman, R., & Gellens, H. K. Preference for complexity-simplicity and symmetry-asymmetry. *Percept. mot. Skills,* 1968, **26**, 888-890.

Enoch, J. M. Addendum. In A. Morris & E. P. Horne (Eds.), *Visual search techniques.* Washington, D.C.: Nat. Acad. Sci.-Nat. Res. Coun., 1960. Pp. 251-252.

Eriksen, C. W., & Hake, H. W. Multidimensional stimulus differences and accuracy of discrimination. *J. exp. Psychol.,* 1955. **50**, 153-160.

Falk, J. L. Theories of visual acuity and their physiological bases. *Psychol. Bull.,* 1956, **53**, 109-133.

Fiske, D. W., & Maddi, S. R. (Eds.) *Functions of varied experience.* Homewood, Illinois: Dorsey Press, 1961.

Ford, A., & Leonard, J. L. Techniques for the recording of surface bioelectric direct currents. *USN Electr. Lab. Res. Rep.* No. 839, 1958.

Ford, A., White, C. T., & Lichtenstein, M. Analysis of eye movements during free search. *J. Opt. Soc. Amer.,* 1959, **49**, 289-292.

Freeman, G. L. An experimental study of the perception of objects. *J. exp. Psychol.,* 1929, **12**, 340-358.

French, R. S. The accuracy of discrimination of dot patterns as a function of angular orientation of the stimuli. *USAF ATr Train. Command, HRRC, Res. Bull.* 53-3, 1953. (a)

French, R. S. The discrimination of dot patterns as a function of number and average separation of dots. *J. exp. Psychol.,* 1953, **46**, 1-9.

French, R. S. Pattern recognition in the presence of visual noise. *J. exp. Psychol.,* 1954, **47**, 27-31.

Fried, R. Monocular and binocular comparison of apparent size. *Amer. J. Psychol.,* 1964, **77**, 476-479.

Fry, G. A. The relation of the configuration of a brightness contrast border to its visibility. *J. Opt. Soc. Amer.,* 1947, **37**, 166-175.

Gaito, J. Visual discrimination of straight and curved lines. *Amer. J. Psychol.,* 1959, **72**, 236-242.

Galli, A. La percezione della forma nella visione periferica. *Pubbl. Univ. Cattol. S. Cuore,* 1931, **6**, 1-27.

Garner, W. R., Hake, H. W., & Eriksen, C. W. Operationism and the concept of perception. *Psychol. Rev.,* 1956, **63**, 149-159.

Gerjuoy, I. R., & Winters, J. J., Jr. Lateral preference for identical geometric forms: II. Retardates. *Percept. Psychophys.,* 1966, **1**, 104-106.

Goldstein, A. G. Familiarity and apparent complexity of random shapes. *J. exp. Psychol.,* 1961, **62**, 594-597. (a)

Goldstein, A. G. Spatial orientation as a factor in eliciting associative responses to random shapes. *Percept. mot. Skills,* 1961, **12**, 15-25. (b)

Goldstein, A. G., & Andrews, J. Perceptual uprightness and complexity of random shapes. *Amer. J. Psychol.,* 1962, **75**, 667-669.

Goodrick, C. L. A psychophysical analysis of the perception of difference in random shape pairs as a function of shape complexity. *Amer. Psychologists,* 1962, **17**, 351. (Abstract)

Graham, C. H., & Bartlett, N. R. The relation of size of stimulus and intensity in the human eye: II. Intensity thresholds for red and violet light. *J. exp. Psychol.,* 1939, **24**, 574-587.

Graham, C. H., Brown, R. H., & Mote, F. A. The relation of size of stimulus and intensity in the human eye: I. Intensity thresholds for white light. *J. exp. Psychol.,* 1939, **24**, 555-573.

Grunin, R., & Mostofsky, D. I. Eye movement: A bibliographic survey. *Percept. mot. Skills,* 1968, **26**, 623-639.

Gundlach, C., & Macoubry, C. The effect of color on apparent size. *Amer. J. Psychol.,* 1931, **43**, 109-111.

Hake, H. W. Contributions of psychology to the study of pattern vision. *WADC Tech. Rep.* 57-621, 1957.

Harlow, H. F. Learning set and error factor theory. In S. Koch (Ed.), *Psychology: A study of a science.* Vol. II. New York: McGraw-Hill, 1959. Pp. 492-537.

Hayami, H. The changes of the figure perception under the gradual increase of the illumination. *Jap. J. Psychol.,* 1935, **10**, 701-725.

Hayes, W. N. Shape recognition as a function of viewing time, eye movements, and orientation of the shape. Unpublished doctoral dissertation, Princeton Univ., 1961. *Diss. Abstr.,* 1962, **22**, 2474.

Heckhausen, H. Complexity in perception: Phenomenal criteria and information theoretical calculus—a note on D. E. Berlyne's "complexity effects." *Can. J. Psychol.,* 1964. **18**, 168-173.

Helson, H., & Fehrer, E. V. The role of form in perception. *Amer. J. Psychol.,* 1932, **44**, 79-102.

Hillix, W. A. Visual pattern identification as a function of fill and distortion. *J. exp. Psychol.,* 1960, **59**, 192-197.

Hitchcock, L., Jr., Brown, D. R., Michels, K. M., & Spiritoso, T. Stimulus complexity and the judgment of relative size. *Percept. mot. Skills,* 1962, **14**, 210.

Hochberg, J. In the mind's eye. In R. N. Haber (Ed.), *Contemporary theory and research in visual perception.* New York: Holt, 1968. Pp. 309-331.

Houston, J. P., Garskof, B. E., & Silber, D. E. The informational basis of judged complexity. *J. gen. Psychol.,* 1965, **72**, 277-284.

Ittelson, W. H. *Visual space perception.* New York: Springer, 1960.

Jasper, H. H., & Walker, R. Y. The Iowa eye-movement camera. *Science,* 1931, **74**, 291-294.

Karlslake, J. S. The Purdue eye-camera: A practical apparatus for studying the attention value of advertisements. *J. appl. Psychol.,* 1940, **24**, 417-440.

Kiesow, F. Ueber die Vergleichung linearer Strecken und ihre Beziehung zum Weberschen Gesetze. *Arch. ges. Psychol.,* 1926, **56**, 421-451.

Kincaid, W. M., Blackwell, H. R., & Kristofferson, A. B. Neural formulation of the effects of target size and shape upon visual detection. *J. Opt. Soc. Amer.,* 1960, **50**, 143-148.

Kristofferson, A. B. Foveal intensity discrimination as a function of area and shape. Unpublished doctoral dissertation, Univ. of Michigan, 1954.

Kristofferson, A. B. Visual detection as influenced by target form. In J. W. Wulfeck & J. H. Taylor (Eds.), *Form discrimination as related to military problems.* Washington, D.C.: Nat. Acad. Sci.-Nat. Res. Coun., 1957. Pp. 109-127.

Lamar, E. S., Hecht, S., Shlaer, S., & Hendley, C. D. Size, shape, and contrast in detection of targets by daylight vision. I. Data and analytical description. *J. Opt. Soc. Amer.,* 1947, **37**, 531-545.

Lamar, E. S., Hecht, S., Hendley, C. D., & Shlaer, S. Size, shape, and contrast in detection of targets by daylight vision. II. Frequency of seeing and the quantum theory of cone vision. *J. Opt. Soc. Amer.,* 1948, **38**, 741-755.

Landolt, E. Formsinn und Sehschaerfe. *Arch. Augenheilk.,* 1906, **55**, 219-223.

Lord, N. P., & Wright, W. D. Eye movements during monocular fixation. *Nature,* 1948, **162**, 25-26.

Mackworth, N. H., & Thomas, E. L. Head-mounted eye-marker camera. *J. Opt. Soc. Amer.,* 1962, **52**, 713-716.

Mansvelt, E. Over het schatten der grotte van figuren van verschillenden vorm. *Meded. u. h. Psychol. Lab. d. Rijksuniv. t. Utrecht,* 1928, **4**, II, 134-137.

Marg, E. Development of electro-oculography. *AMA Arch. Ophthalmol.,* 1951, **45**, 169-185.

McCullough, P. M. The perceptual discrimination of similarities. Unpublished doctoral dissertation, Univ. of Utah, 1957.

Michels, K. M., Pittman, G. G., Hitchcock, L., Jr., & Brown, D. R. Visual discrimination: tree squirrels and quantified stimulus dimensions. *Percept. mot. Skills,* 1962, **15**, 443-450.

Monty, R. A., & Boynton, R. M. Stimulus overlap and form similarity under suprathreshold conditions. *Percept. mot. Skills,* 1962, **14**, 487-498.

Mooney, C. M. Closure as affected by configural clarity and contextual consistency. *Can. J. Psychol.,* 1957, **11**, 80-88. (a)

Mooney, C. M. Closure as affected by viewing time and multiple visual fixation. *Can. J. Psychol.,* 1957, **11**, 21-28. (b)

Mooney, C. M. Recognition of novel visual configurations with and without eye movements. *J. exp. Psychol.,* 1958, **56**, 133-138.

Mooney, C. M. Recognition of symmetrical and non-symmetrical ink-blots with and without eye movements. *Can. J. Psychol.,* 1959, **13**, 11-19.

Mooney, C. M. Recognition of ambiguous and unambiguous visual configurations with short and longer exposures. *Brit. J. Psychol.,* 1960, **51**, 119-125.

Morris, A. Form discrimination in psychophysics. In J. W. Wulfeck & J. H. Taylor (Eds.), *Form discrimination as related to military problems.* Washington, D. C.: Nat. Acad. Sci.-Nat. Res. Coun., 1957. Pp. 12-15.

Munsinger, H., & Kessen, W. Uncertainty, structure, and preference. *Psychol. Monogr.,* 1964, **78**, No. 586.

Peters, W. Versuche ueber den Einfluss der Form auf die Wahrnehmung der Flaechengroesse. *Z. Psychol.,* 1933, **129**, 323-337.

Pfeiffer, H. E. Ueber die Wirksamkeit verschiedener Figuren gleicher geometrischer Flaechengroesse und ihre Beeinflussung durch Helligkeitsunterschiede. *Psychol. Forsch.,* 1932, **17**, 1-12.

Pheiffer, C. E., Eure, S. B., & Hamilton, C. B. Reversible figures and eye-movements. *Amer. J. Psychol.,* 1956, **69**, 452-455.

Pollack, I., & Klemmer, E. T. Visual noise filtering by the human operator. II. Linear dot patterns in noise. *AFCRC TR* 54-15. Bolling AFB, Washington, D.C., 1954.

Pratt, M. B. The visual estimation of angles. *J. exp. Psychol.,* 1926, **9**, 132-140.

Rabideau, G. F. Differences in visual acuity measurements obtained with different types of targets. *Psychol. Monogr.,* 1955, **69**(10), No. 395.

Rashbass, C. New method for recording eye movements. *J. Opt. Soc. Amer.,* 1960, **50**, 642-644.

Royer, F. L. Figural goodness and internal structure in perceptual discrimination. *Percept. Psychophys.*, 1966, 1, 311-314.

Salapatek, P., & Kessen, W. Visual scanning of triangles by the human newborn. *J. exp. child Psychol.*, 1966, 3, 155-167.

Sander, F. Experimentelle Ergebnisse der Gestaltpsychologie. In E. Becher (Ed.), *10. Kongr. Ber. exp. Psychol.*, Jena: Fischer, 1928. Pp. 23-88.

Sander, F. Structures, totality of experience, and gestalt. In C. Murchison (Ed.), *Psychologies of 1930*. Worcester, Massachusetts: Clark Univ. Press, 1930. P. 188-204.

Sanders, R. A. The effects of familiarization on the judged complexity of visual forms. Unpublished doctoral dissertation, Univ. of Arkansas, 1962. *Diss. Abstr.*, 1963, 23(9), 3503.

Scott, D. M. *An annotated bibliography of research on eye movements published during the period 1932-1961.* Canada: Department of National Defence, Defence Research Board, 1962.

Seiler, D. A., & Zusne, L. Judged complexity of tachistoscopically viewed random shapes. *Percept. mot. Skills*, 1967, 24, 884-886.

Sekuler, R. W., & Houlihan, K. Discrimination of mirror-images: Choice time analysis of human adult performance. *Quart. J. exp. Psychol.*, 1968, 20, 204-207.

Silver, C. A., Landis, D., & Messick, S. Multidimensional analysis of visual form: An analysis of individual differences. *Amer. J. Psychol.*, 1966, 79, 62-72.

Sleight, R. B. The relative discriminability of several geometric forms. *J. exp. Psychol.*, 1952, 43, 324-328.

Sleight, R. B., & Mowbray, G. H. Discriminability between geometric figures under complex conditions. *J. Psychol.*, 1951, 31, 121-127.

Small, V. H. Judged similarity of visual forms as functions of selected stimulus dimensions. Unpublished doctoral dissertation, Purdue Univ. 1961. *Diss. Abstr.*, 1962, 22, 2481.

Smith, J. P. The effects of figural shape on the perception of area. Unpublished doctoral dissertation, Fordham Univ., 1964. *Diss. Abstr.*, 1964, 25, 3712.

Smith, W. M., & Warter, P. J. Eye movement and stimulus movement. New photoelectric electromechanical system for recording and measuring tracking motions of the eye. *J. Opt. Soc. Amer.*, 1960, 50, 245-250.

Smith, W. M., & Gulick, W. L. A statistical theory of dynamic contour perception. *Psychol. Rev.*, 1962, 69, 91-108.

Stenson, H. H. The physical factor structure of random forms and their judged complexity. *Percept. Psychophys.*, 1966, 1, 303-310.

Stilson, D. W. A psychophysical investigation of triangular shape. Unpublished doctoral dissertation, Univ. of Illinois, 1956. *Diss. Abstr.*, 1957, 17, 905.

Stratton, G. M. Eye-movements and the aesthetics of visual form. *Phil. Stud.*, 1902, 20, 336-359.

Stratton, G. M. Symmetry, linear illusions, and the movements of the eye. *Psychol. Rev.*, 1906, 13, 82-96.

Takagi, K. On visual estimation of length of various curves. *Jap. J. Psychol.*, 1926, 1, 476-498.

Tanaka, Z. [The perception of figures based upon the exposure time.] *Jap. J. Psychol.*, 1939, 14, 71-88.

Taylor, R. E., & Eisenman, R. Perception and production of complexity by creative art students. *J. Psychol.*, 1964, 57, 239-242.

Thomas, H. Multidimensional analysis of similarities judgments to twenty visual forms. *Psychon. Bull.*, 1967, 1, 3.

Tinker, M. A. Apparatus for recording eye movements. *Amer. J. Psychol.*, 1931, **43**, 115-118.

Tomoda, Z. [The perception of figures based upon form and size.] *Jap. J. Psychol.*, 1937, **12**, 433-450.

Undeutsch, U. Die Aktualgenese in ihrer allgemein-philosophischen und ihrer charakterologischen Bedeutung. *Scientia*, 1942, **72**, 34-42, 95-98.

Vanderplas, J. M., & Garvin, E. A. The association value of random shapes. *J. exp. Psychol.*, 1959, **57**, 147-154.

Veniar, F. A. Difference thresholds for shape distortion of geometrical squares. *J. Psychol.*, 1948, **26**, 461-476.

Vladimirov, A. D., & Khomskaya, E. D. Fotoelektricheskiǐ metod registratsii dvizheniǐ glaz. *Voprosy Psikhol.*, 1961, **7**(2), 177-180.

Vladimirov, A. D., & Khomskaya, E. D. Fotoelektricheskiǐ metod registratsii dvizheniya glaz pri rassmatrivanii ob"ektov. *Voprosy Psikhol.*, 1962, **8**(5), 91-94.

Wagner, E. Das Abschaetzen von Flaechen. *Psychotech. Z.*, 1931, **6**, 140-148.

Warren, J. M., & Pinneau, S. R. Influence of form on judgment of apparent area. *Percept. mot. Skills*, 1955, **5**, 7-10.

Webster, R. B. Distortion, fill, and noise effects on pattern discrimination. *Human Factors*, 1966, **8**, 147-155.

Wendt, G. R., & Dodge, R. Practical directions for stimulating and for photographically recording eye movements of animals. *J. comp. physiol. Psychol.*, 1938, **25**, 9-49.

Winters, J. J., Jr., & Gerjuoy, I. R. Lateral preference for identical geometric forms: I. Normals. *Percept. Psychophys.*, 1966, **1**, 101-103.

Woodring, A. V., & Alluisi, E. A. Effects of choice-figure rotation on the visual perception of form. *Psychon. Sci.*, 1966, **4**, 403-404.

Woodworth, R. S., & Schlosberg, H. *Experimental psychology*. New York: Holt, 1954.

Yarbus, A. L. *Eye movements and vision*. New York: Plenum Press, 1967.

Zigler, M. J., Cook, B., Miller, D., & Wemple, L. The perception of form in peripheral vision. *Amer. J. Psychol.*, 1930, **42**, 246-259.

Zusne, L. Moments of area and of the perimeter of visual form as predictors of discrimination performance. *J. exp. Psychol.*, 1965, **69**, 213-220.

Zusne, L., & Michels, K. M. Geometricity of visual form. *Percept. mot. Skills*, 1962, **14**, 147-154.

Zusne, L., & Michels, K. M. More on the geometricity of visual form. *Percept. mot. Skills*, 1962, **15**, 55-58.

Zusne, L., & Michels, K. M. Nonrepresentational shapes and eye movements. *Percept. mot. Skills*, 1964, **18**, 11-20.

learning, memory, the process of recognition, and the various factors that affect these processes rather than the perception of form. Form to them is simply a convenient type of stimulus material to work with when studying learning.

There is no good agreement on the nature of memory. Gomulicki (1953), for instance, has listed some 250 trace theories of memory. A more recent review of the state of theory regarding form memory and recognition is given by Hake (1957, pp. 79-92). This lack of agreement on how meaning is attached to a pattern (by giving it a name or making a response) once it is clearly sensed is reflected in the loose usage of terms describing the tasks that subjects perform in experiments involving memory for form. Hake (1957) distinguishes between memory tasks in terms of (a) the type of response required of the subject and (b) the kind of decision required of the subject. According to the first classification, the tasks are recall and recognition. In the recall task, the form is typically reproduced or reconstructed after a shorter or longer delay. In the recognition task, "the subject's response is a judgment or decision about a presented stimulus in terms of his prior experience with it" (p. 79). In the second classification, the tasks are identification and familiarity tasks. In an identification task, the subject typically attaches a label to a form or gives it a name that he has learned previously. In the familiarity task, "the subject must indicate merely whether a form has occurred before in his experience" (p. 80). In terms of their definitions, there seems to be no difference between the recognition and familiarity tasks. In fact, the term "familiarity task" is seldom used. While there is no confusion between reproduction as an overt response and other tasks, recall as an intervening variable may be applied to identification, since the physical presence of the form at the time of the response is a matter of degree: copying is a type of reproduction with the model present, while tests for memory using the reproduction response may be given anywhere between the moment immediately following stimulus presentation and months or years later. On the other hand, identification may be called for after a tachistoscopic presentation of a stimulus, so that the naming response takes place without the stimulus being physically present. It is customary, though, to talk about recall as the process underlying the reproduction task.

While it should not be too difficult to distinguish between recognition and identification in terms of their definitions, in practice there is considerable confusion. If by recognition is meant the subjective feeling of familiarity and, overtly, the indication (a "yes" or a "no" response or the scale value of confidence of having seen a form before) that the form has been encountered in the subject's experience before, and by identification is meant a naming or labeling response, then these terms are certainly used in a confusing fashion in the literature. In the first place, an experiment in discrimination may have the word "recognition" in the title, while some studies labeled as discrimination studies actually involve recognition or even identification. A large number of identification studies have been labeled recognition studies; e.g., studies in which geometric forms have been used as stimuli. The triangle, the square, etc., are extremely well known shapes with well established names, so that any response above the point where merely the light coming through the interior of such shapes is reported is actually an identification response. Bona fide recognition tasks are only those in which the subject indicates that a nonrepresentational form, now being shown, has been presented before. Thus, Binder's (1955) theory of visual recognition is, in terms of his own definition, a theory of visual identification: ". . . a subject has recognized a visually presented object if he responds with an appropriate class name of the object" (p. 119), and "Recognition takes place when a visual experience becomes meaningful" (p. 125).

Recognition and identification as overt responses can be differentiated operationally. Whether recognition and identification are the two ends of the same continuum of subjective certainty is a question that has not been answered. A case may be made for the proposition that they are. A thoroughly familiar form, such as the face of a member of one's family, is normally identified, not recognized. Normal conditions, however, are those in which the appearance of the family member is very frequent and therefore expected or where the introduction of his facial features is gradual, even if it lasts only for a fraction of a second. When the person's face appears quite suddenly and its appearance is entirely unexpected, an initial period of uncertainty may intervene before the face is identified and labeled with the person's name. This period of uncertainty lasts very briefly, but it can be described as a moment of recognition: one feels that the face is familiar, but it cannot quite be "placed." As a result, there may even be a momentary feeling of anxiety. This moment of recognition, of a feeling of both familiarity and uncertainty, is followed by identification and a feeling of relief. In the case of casual acquaintances, there are certainly occasions on which the name that first comes to mind does not quite seem to fit the face, i.e., that is, there are degrees of certainty with which names are attached to forms. Recognition at its weakest would then be a vague sense of familiarity, something like identification at a threshold level.

1. Recognition and Identification

A. INTRODUCTION

The experimental conditions under which forms have been presented for recognition or identification vary considerably. Since recognition and identification under optimum viewing conditions take little time, the purpose of introducing conditions that make them more difficult is to slow down the recognition process. Under optimum viewing conditions, several stimuli may be presented simultaneously or succesively and the subject is asked to select or identify the one that he has seen before. The rest of recognition-identification studies employ some sort of "noise," to use this term very broadly. Representative "noisy" conditions that have been used are the following. (a) Nonrepresentational form, as in randomly constructed shapes or Rorschach inkblots. The recognition speed of such shapes can be controlled because all subjects start out with the same degree of familiarity. When applied to the associative task, the term "recognition" may be used in a figurative sense only, since it is not seriously expected that the testee will recognize, e.g., an inkblot as having actually been seen before. Rather, it is a "recognition" of certain similarities between certain details of the inkblot and real objects whose names are known. (b) Reversible figure-ground configurations. Depending on a variety of stimulus and observer variables, one or the other of two contiguous configurations may be "recognized" as the figure. The reversible figure-ground phenomenon has been discussed elsewhere in this book (Chap. 4). (c) Reversible-perspective figures. As in the case of the reversible figure-ground configurations, the term recognition is used here rather charitably. These figures have also been discussed elsewhere in this book (Chap. 2). (d) Visual noise. Both organized (embedded figures) and random visual noise have been used to obscure a previously clearly exposed figure, which in the recognition task must be found or recognized amidst the visual noise. (e) Peripheral vision. The presentation of geometric forms in the periphery of the visual field and their identification as they are moved closer to the fixation point has been a standard procedure in determining the extent of retinal form fields. (f) Tachistoscopic exposure. The tachistoscope is perhaps the most convenient device for slowing down the process of recognition without involving other processes. It is for this reason that the literature abounds in examples of its use. (g) Reduced levels of illumination, peripheral vision, and tachistoscopic exposure have been the three main methods employed in studies of form-recognition thresholds. (h) Incomplete closure. When the form stimuli are of the type used in Street's (1931) Gestalt Completion Test, the observer's task may be the recognition of the object represented by mentally completing the incomplete figure.

B. SOME EMPIRICAL GENERALIZATIONS

Judged familiarity of nonrepresentational shapes is a monotonic, negatively accelerated function of the frequency of previous exposure to the shapes (Arnoult, 1956b). This relationship was obtained when subjects rated the familiarity of 10 previously seen shapes presented among 20 new ones. Although the task was a scaling task, the study is mentioned here because the task can be considered an extension of a dichotomized judgment (familiar-unfamiliar) task of recognition. Previous experience was defined in terms of frequencies of exposure ranging from 0 to 25 times. Delays between familiarization and testing of 0, 1, 2, 3, and 5 hr. had no effect on recognition. Although Arnoult's appears to be the only such experiment, a generalization is formulated on its basis because additional supporting evidence has been obtained with visually presented words and syllables.

While familiarity and recognition are clearly related, Hake (1957) raises the question of whether rated familiarity would also predict recognition of forms under poor viewing conditions. He mentions experiments that support the hypothesis that recognition thresholds and frequency of exposure are related, but these are experiments in which words or nonsense syllables have been used, and the response has been the identification response. Unless the response is a simple yes or no, or even a forced-choice response that does not involve naming, the difference between familiarity and recognition is simply one of viewing conditions. Hence, the problem is not, as Hake has it, whether the relationship between recognition thresholds and frequency of prior seeing is identical to that between familiarity and frequency of prior seeing, but of whether recognition or familiarity thresholds are the same as identification thresholds. For form, this question has not been answered. Studies of verbal materials suggest that prior seeing and identification thresholds are related, as stated in the above generalization. When subjects are asked to rate their confidence in their recognition of verbal materials that contain items identical to those seen before and of others that resemble these to a greater or lesser extent, it is found that those factors that lead subjects to state that they have seen a previously unseen stimulus before are the same that evoke confidence in their judgment. Familiarity as a function of the degree of distortion of a previously exposed form (stimulus generalization) has never been studied.

The time to recognize incomplete or unstructured figures decreases, and the probability of response increases, as the frequency of exposure or its duration increase (Atkinson & Ammons, 1952; Gollin, 1965; Leeper, 1935). Leeper's figures were the Street Gestalt Completion Test figures. Whether recognition or identification is involved in the perception of such figures is a moot question. While the figure may eventually be named, the chief aspect of the perceptual process is similar to that of the sudden "recognition" of the alternate percept in a reversible-perspective figure, a reversible figure-ground design, or an inkblot.

Carlson and Eriksen (1966) have shown that there is dichopic summation of information: simultaneous stimulation of corresponding areas in the two eyes was equivalent to successive stimulation, i.e., the two presentations are like two trials whose effects are additive and help in the recognition of tachistoscopically presented forms.

Familiar forms, when presented in peripheral vision or tachistoscopically, are identified more readily than their less familiar transformations. Henle (1942) obtained this result using letters and numbers in their normal positions as well as their mirror-images. Although letters and numbers belong in a different category of visual stimuli than do nonrepresentational shapes, in Henle's experiment, they were used because of their identifiability, and their role was mainly that of forms, not of meaningful symbols.

Identification accuracy of metric figures is a decreasing function of the amount of visual noise (Alluisi, Hawkes, & Hall, 1964), while identification time of dot patterns increases as a linear function of relevant information load, being independent of the amount of irrelevant information (Archer, 1954). Recognition errors decrease as exposure time of visual forms is increased (Forsyth & Brown, 1967). This relationship was found for a series of exposure times of 4, 8, 12, 16, and 20 msec. and a presentation-test interval of 300 msec.

However defined, stimulus redundancy affects identification. Both the particular definition of redundancy and its interaction with complexity and the various experimental conditions determine whether redundancy will facilitate identification or make it more difficult. The effect of complexity on recognition has been studied mainly in metric figures. Since the complexity of metric figures has been measured as a sampling statistic and not as a single form measure, studies using metric figures and random polygons, for instance, are not readily comparable. This problem was discussed in detail in Chap. 5. Also in Chap. 5, a detailed exposition of the concept of redundancy as applied to visual form was given. Because of the complexity of the subject, generalizations more specific than the one appearing at the beginning of this paragraph cannot be given. The body of literature that relates redundancy and identification is substantial, and appears listed in the form-perception bibliography at the end of this book. Many of these studies have been discussed in detail by Garner (1962).

A shape rotated to a different position is less readily recognized than it is in the position in which it was originally learned; the angle of rotation, however, is not linearly related to recognition and identification difficulty: shapes are recognized better in some orientations than in others, depending on their configuration and on the relationship of the axis of rotation to the main dimensions of space. What Mach had demonstrated when he turned the square 45 degrees was that the square now looked different even though no change had occurred in the contours of the square. The earliest published study of the effects of rotation on recognition was performed by Dearborn (1899) with inkblots as stimuli. Presenting the inkblots in series, he repeated some of them in the original orientation and some rotated 90, 180, or 270 degrees. Stimuli presented in their original orientations were recognized most often; those rotated 180 degrees were recognized more often than when they were rotated 90 or 270 degrees. Since the original position of the inkblots had been determined by chance, it was not necessarily the position in which all of them would have been most readily recognized. Thus, Gibson and Robinson (1935) failed to replicate Dearborn's results. In addition, they established that recognition of forms seen in different orientations depends on whether these forms are normally seen in one position only (such as the outline of a country on a map) or in various different positions (such as keys, pencils, or books). Geographic forms and monooriented objects were recognized in this experiment much more readily in their normal position, the 180-degree rotation being the worst for recognition. Polyoriented objects, on the other hand, were recognized with equal facility in any position. Gibson and Robinson accepted the Gestalt interpretation of these results, namely that any perceived form is a form-in-relationship-to-the-spatial-framework, i.e., the phenomenal vertical and horizontal directions. What the "normal" orientation of any particular object is depends, however, on learning.

"Normal orientation" may be defined in two ways, either in terms of the customary orientation of the form in the environment or in terms of its customary orientation with regard to the observer's retina. This raises the question of how recognition is affected when (a) the form is tilted, but the observer's head remains upright; (b) the form remains in its normal position, but the observer's head is tilted; and (c) both the form and the observer's head are tilted (the same amount and in the same direction). In the first two cases, the result is disorientation with regard to the observer's retina. In the third case, there is no such disorientation, but both the form and the observer are disoriented with regard to their normal positions. The consequences of the two definitions of "normal orientation" were studied quite early by Oetjen (1915), who found that recognition was good only when forms maintained their customary orientation with regard to the observer's retina. Thouless (1947) similarly found that, when his observers were looking at pictures of the type illustrated in Fig. 4-3e, the majority of them saw the objectively inverted but phenomenally upright face.

While these studies show that retinal orientation is of primary importance in recognition, Irvin Rock (Rock, 1956; Rock & Heimer, 1957) has examined further the relationship between the two ways of changing orientation. With figures of the type illustrated in Fig. 4-3d, his conclusion is that, other things being equal, the phenomenal orientation of a form is determined by directions in the environment. These directions are supplied by the pull of gravity, the visual frame of reference, or instructions. The orientation of the image of the shape on the retina did not appear to play as great a role in Rock's experiments:

It is suggested that in those cases where a form is not recognized or looks strange and unfamiliar as a result only of retinal disorientation, it is not due to change in phenomenal shape but to inadequate communication with the appropriate [memory] trace. This, in turn, is due to difference in orientation of trace and process which for some as yet unexplained reason impairs acces to the trace. Generally, this only becomes of consequence in the case of complex or difficult forms and orientation changes of 90° or more. (Rock & Heimer, 1957, p. 511.)

Braine (1965), however, has found that establishing a phenomenal frame of reference by informing subjects of the exact orientation in which forms would appear does not facilitate recognition as compared with subjects who were only told that they would see disoriented forms.

Stimulus characteristics affect recognition, but the use of physical form parameters as recognition cues by subjects is selective (Forsyth & Brown, 1967; Goodnow, 1954; Weinstein, 1955). Goodnow, in his study, used airplane silhouettes and schematized faces that varied in three characteristics (wings, tail, air scoop; brow, nose, chin), but his subjects used only one or two, never all three of the characteristics to identify the planes or faces as belonging to one of two types, X or Y. Forsyth and Brown used a more sophisticated approach in which random quadrilaterals ranked with respect to three physical dimension factor scores were presented for recognition after exposure and a 300-msec. interval. Rather complex interactive effects were established in this experiment, which the authors interpret in terms of selective attention of subjects to some but not all physical shape cues.

Stimulus complexity has an effect on recognition that is a function of the heterogeneity of the stimulus sample (White, 1957). While Deese (1956) found that more complex patterns were more easily recognized, White obtained results showing that homogeneous sets of patterns are more difficult to recognize than heterogeneous ones, and that within homogeneous sets more complex patterns are more difficult to recognize than simple ones, which did not hold true for heterogeneous sets. White states that Deese's results can be attributed to the heterogeneity of Deese's patterns. If a sufficiently large sample of patterns is used and the sample is not divided into subsamples on the basis of homogeneity and heterogeneity, stimulus complexity and ease of identification appear to be related as a U-shaped function. As in the case of discriminability of random shapes, both the very simple and very complex patterns appear to be more difficult to identify than patterns consisting of between six and eight dots (French, 1954). Vanderplas and Garvin (1959b), however, obtained a simple inverse relationship between complexity of random shapes and ease of recognition.

Experience with patterns in one-half of the visual field interferes with the recognition of these patterns when presented in the other half. While Dees and Grindley (1947) found that there was 100% transfer of learning when dot patterns were presented in one portion of the visual field for learning and in another for recognition, subsequent research with words (Mishkin & Forgays, 1952; Orbach, 1952) and random shapes (Lordahl *et al.,* 1965) has shown that recognition is adversely affected by presenting a pattern for recognition in a retinal locus that is different from the one in which learning or familiarization take place.

The best training method for recognition of form involving familiarization with the critical form itself is one requiring the subject to copy the form (Arnoult, 1956a). Copying, i.e., reproduction, however, introduces systematic distortions in the copy. These distortions tend to persist in later attempts to draw the same form. This problem is discussed more fully in Section 2 of this chapter.

Subjects given predifferentiation training with forms of the type used in the recognition task perform better, in general, on the recognition task. This type of training is often verbal, and the formation of verbal associations to form has received considerable attention in the literature. The main ideas concerning the role of verbal associations to stimuli are either that naming increases the difference between stimuli (acquired distinctiveness of cues) or else that predifferentiation training results in an increase in the meaningfulness of stimuli, which, in turn, enhances transfer of learning. Increased meaningfulness in terms of an increased number of verbal associations is, of course, the result of having learned to attach a new name or names to a stimulus in the course of predifferentiation training. Fox (1935), in a well-known study, showed that there is a better-than-chance agreement among subjects as to which paralogs are best associated with certain nonrepresentational shapes. In other words, there is a consistent relation between language and form, which suggests that names assigned to forms may affect memory for these forms. This is the subject of some discussion later in this chapter in connection with the effects of labeling on the reproduction task. At this point, only those studies will be mentioned that have shown that, since associations are a matter of degree, recognition is also a function of the strength of verbal associations. Data that confirm this relationship are not plentiful, Hake and Eriksen (1956) producing some evidence that patterns whose names have been well learned are recognized more easily than patterns that can be remembered only with difficulty, and Ellis (1967) demonstrating that recognition performance with visual forms varies directly with their associativeness. Supporting data are also available from studies in which stimuli other than forms have been used. Hake (1957), however, is careful to emphasize that these experiments suggest only that, under certain conditions, the goodness of the association between a name and a form is helpful in predicting recognition performance. They do not suggest that the experimental conditions under which the associative learning takes place are related to the absolute number of these forms that may be recognized later. Vanderplas and Garvin (1959b), for instance, found no significant relationship between association value of random shapes and their recognizability.

The type of verbal label used in pretraining also has an effect on subsequent recognition of the forms to which these labels have been attached. Thus, Arnoult (1955), using as labels for random forms nonsense syllables, girls' names, modal names previously determined by 100 other subjects, and names of the subjects' own choosing, found that labels had no significant effect on recognition, but that they did differ in the ease with which they could be associated with the forms: modal names and names of the subjects' own choice were much superior to the other two types.

A number of recognition studies have dealt with the question of whether memory traces for form suffer systematic changes in time. In these studies, recognition has been used only to compare the results obtained in this task with those obtained with reproduction. Since reproduction is the task used in the majority of studies that have dealt with changes in traces of memory for form, these are discussed in Section 2.

Foveal Form-Identification Thresholds. The question of form thresholds was raised by the Gestalt school, resulting in a fairly large number of studies in the 1920s and especially in the 1930s. One assertion that came from that school was that good forms, such as the circle, should have the lowest detection thresholds (e.g., Koffka, 1935, p. 205). This assertion has never been definitely proved or disproved, in spite of all the studies in which the visibility of the circle has been compared with the visibility of other forms. It so happens that the threshold for the circle is not a fixed quantity but depends on a number of factors, some of which are the well-known ones that operate in any psychophysical experiment, and some of which are peculiar to form stimuli. All of these factors affect the recognition threshold of form, so that the following discussion applies to all forms, not the circle alone.

The most important difficulty, or rather, complex of difficulties, arises out of the fact that response to form in threshold experiments shows systematic biases. In brightness discrimination and acuity tests where the subject's responses are "yes" and "no" and where incorrect responses may be assumed, and have actually been shown (Hyman & Hake, 1954), to be randomly distributed among all available responses, correction for incorrect responses is a relatively simple matter. The assumption that guesses are independent of sensory discrimination underlies Abbott's formula for correction for chance that has been used in psychophysical experiments. In $P_k = (P_o - P_c)/(1 - P_c)$, P_k is the corrected proportion of responses, P_o the proportion of correct observed responses, and P_c an estimate of the proportion of correct responses obtained by chance. However, even for the light-threshold and acuity experiments involving only the yes-no response, this assumption was shown in the 1950s to be unwarranted. The relevant literature, which centers on the theory of signal detection, is ample.

When it comes to form-recognition thresholds, it can be taken for granted that incorrect responses will not be random but show some type of systematic bias. To begin with, any blurred form or form at a stage of visibility that is barely past the light-detection threshold tends to look roundish (e.g., Barskiǐ & Guzeva, 1962; Wilcox, 1932). This does not mean necessarily that a *circle* is seen (cf. Helson, 1933). Even so, since some of these experiences are reported as circles, a correction must be introduced to avoid spuriously low thresholds for the circle. Casperson (1950), for instance, used the following formula to effect this correction: $R_{c_x} = T_x - [W_x/(1 - P_x)]$, where R_{c_x} is the corrected number of right responses to form X, T_x the total number of form X presented, W_x the number of wrong responses to form X, and P_x the proportion of total errors made on all forms that were called form X. In a 1954 experiment by Hyman and Hake, the square, when incorrectly identified, was most often called a circle, while the diamond was most frequently mistaken for a cross or a circle rather than any other figure. In addition, the nature of the erroneous identifications changed depending on how many and which forms were used in the experiment. It stands to reason that, when the observer knows the range of the stimuli that he can expect and their identities, the mistaken identities must come from this range rather than anywhere else. Similar biases have been reported by other investigators (e.g., Bitterman, Krauskopf, & Hochberg, 1954; Casperson, 1950; Helson & Fehrer, 1932).

To this source of ambiguity must be added the apparent similarity between the light-detection task and the form-identification-threshold task. The recognition task, with its obligatory yes-no response, cannot be really applied to the measurement of form thresholds, unless the investigator is interested more in the phenomenology of form at threshold levels than in relating response probability and physical stimulus characteristics. If a single form is presented repeatedly using the method of limits (and therefore the yes-no response), as in the oft-cited experiment by Helson and Fehrer (1932), the conditions for a recognition-threshold task are satisfied, but the results are ambiguous since it is not known when the observer begins to see light (the L threshold of Helson and Fehrer), thinks that he is barely perceiving form (the $F1$ level of Helson and Fehrer), or is certain of the configuration of the form ($F2$ threshold of Helson and Fehrer). The large individual differences in thresholds found by Helson and Fehrer confirm this conjecture. Even disregarding individual differences, the criterion that the experimenter adopts for a threshold (L, $F1$, or $F2$, or some other) obviously determines what the form threshold will be. So does the observer's criterion for responding, which in turn is importantly determined by the type of response required, the yes-no response usually yielding higher thresholds than the forced-choice response, for instance. In other words, even less than for simple light and sound stimuli, there is no form threshold for any particular form, only sets of response thresholds. Of the six forms used by Helson and Fehrer, none could be said to be the "best" in terms of recognizability. By the measure of the number of presentations needed to obtain 50 correct responses, the "best" form was the chevron, the worst the rectangle, with the circle in the middle, but by other measures, the orders were quite different: the rectangle required the least amount of light and was less confused with other forms, while the triangle was the most frequently reported form, the circle being neither good nor bad by any of the criteria used.

Attempts to relate form-identification thresholds to the physical properties of forms have been made only for form complexity and compactness. Only a couple of studies have dealt with the complexity parameter. In an experiment by Kaneko (1938), perceptual development latencies were directly related to complexity, and the data of Barskiĭ and Guzeva (1962) showed the same relationship between thresholds and the information content of regular and irregular polygons and curved shapes.

Several investigators have made attempts to relate form compactness to identification thresholds, but the results are ambiguous. These studies sorely lack in generalizability. To facilitate identification, all of them have used a small number of well-known geometric shapes, with occasionally a single irregular shape mixed in with the others. The number of shapes in the stimulus sample has ranged from 3 to about 15. In most of these samples, complexity and compactness correlate very highly, and the results are therefore obscured by the confounding of these two variables.

Studies in which identification threshold has been found to vary directly with compactness, either estimated or actually measured, are those of Bitterman, Krauskopf, and Hochberg (1954), Engstrand and Moeller (1962), Hochberg, Gleitman, and McBride (1954), and Krauskopf, Duryea, and Bitterman (1954). Cheatham (1952) found no effect of compactness on identification thresholds, and Fox (1957) decided that, while form did affect form-identification thresholds, neither the length of the perimeter nor the P/A ratio predicted threshold responses. In Borg's (1964) study, the triangle and the rectangle had the lowest thresholds, the cross and the five-pointed star the highest, with the circle in an intermediate position. When crosses with varying arm widths were used as stimuli, light thresholds were lowest for the most compact crosses, while both the most and least compact crosses had the highest form thresholds, crosses of intermediate values of compactness having the lowest form-threshold values. Borg suggests that there are two kinds of shapes: for one, light and form thresholds decrease with increasing compactness, for the other, they decrease together up to a point, then form threshold begins to increase again while the light threshold continues decreasing. Unfortunately, Borg does not specify the physical characteristics of these two types of form. Casperson(1950), in his study, measured the maximum dimension, and the length of the perimeter of six geometric shapes, each of five different areas, finding that area was the best predictor of discriminability between the oval and the triangle; that the maximum dimension predicted the discriminability between the square and the diamond best; that the length of the perimeter was the best predictor of discriminability for the star and the cross; and that for the six forms as a group the best predictor was their maximum extent, while for all 30 shapes it was the length of the perimeter.

In the studies of Bitterman *et al.,* (1954), and of Krauskopf *et al.,* (1954), identification threshold was also found to vary inversely with the magnitude of what they called "critical detail." This term, used ocasionally by other investigators, has not been defined by them. While the idea appears to be that of a conspicuous feature of a form that most readily serves to discriminate the form from others and that may be pointed out in a specific form, it appears impossible to produce an operational definition of "critical detail" that would allow an unequivocal interpretation of experimental results in studies where this concept has been used.

It would appear from the above studies that in 30 or so years of studying form-identification thresholds for foveal vision we have learned very little that can be stated with any degree of certainty. Experimental designs involving large random samples of shapes, more subjects, and due consideration of the manifold factors that influence form thresholds are clearly called for.

Form Identification in Peripheral Vision. In Chap. 6, Day's (1956) theory of foveal form perception was mentioned. It is based upon the statistical theory of neurophysiological activity in area 17 of the brain. Day (1957) has also applied this theory to form perception in the peripheral retina. It follows the same line of reasoning as the first version. In an unpublished experiment, Day presented six nonrepresentational, right-angle figures on a campimeter to observers and asked them to both describe and draw what they saw. A number of predictions were made, based on the theory, regarding the apperance of the forms as they were moved closer to the point of fixation and before they became clearly visible. For instance, it was predicted that white spaces enclosed within a figure would be seen as filled in, that *L*- and *T*-shaped forms would be seen as roughly triangular, that the cross would look like a hazy rounded patch at first, then like a diamond, etc. Day's predictions were confirmed in all cases. Graefe (1964), while agreeing with Day that filling-in and blurring do take place, points out that additional phenomena observed in peripheral vision of form cannot be explained by Day's theory. For instance, while some corners of a figure may be seen as blurred, others are seen as sharpened; certain portions of a figure that are geometrically separated may be seen as joined and vice versa; that the degree of figure-ground separation is lowered; and that portions of the figure may experience shifts with regard to each other, as may differentiated portions of the ground with regard to the figure. Graefe's critique of Day's theory includes the suggestion that it is incomplete and should incorporate phenomenological aspects of form perception as well as give weight to the role of the surface of a form rather than emphasizing only the role of its contours. The critique is based on an extensive campimetric study of peripherally presented forms, performed in the Gestalt tradition.

The rest of the literature concerning form thresholds in peripheral vision is restricted to a single topic, namely the determination of form fields of the retina. Unlike the color fields, form fields have not been established with any degree of certainty. The reasons for this are the same as in the case of foveal form thresholds.

Some of the factors that affect the size of the field within which a form is visible are, in addition to form, area (or visual angle), brightness contrast, contrast-area interaction, location, visual defects, age of the subject, and experience. All investigators who have varied the visual angle of their stimuli report that for any given form the form field increases with increasing visual angle. Increasing contrast increases the size of the form field, but more so for the smaller-size stimuli (Ferree & Rand, 1931, 1932). The horizontal extent of a form field is greater than its vertical extent (Collier, 1931; Munn & Geil, 1931), emmetropes and hyperopes have wider form fields than persons with myopia or presbyopia, and form fields decrease in size after age 40 (Ferree, Rand, & Monroe, 1930), but increase with training for the same (but not other) stimuli (Crannel & Christensen, 1955).

The only consistent finding regarding the size of form fields of geometric shapes is that the triangle is seen best at the greatest peripheral eccentricities. There is also a good agreement on the hexagon and the octagon having the smallest form fields. The circle, as in the case of foveal thresholds, is usually found in an intermediate position between shapes with the largest and the smallest form fields. Collier's (1931) ordering of his shapes was: triangle with the largest form field, circle, hexagon, and octagon with the smallest, and the square and diamond in an intermediate position. The triangle, square, and the trapezoid had larger form fields than the hexagon and the octagon in Geissler's (1926) experiment. Kleitman and Bleier (1928) found that the triangle had the largest form field, the star the smallest, with the square and the circle in an intermediate position. Munn and Geil (1931) found that the triangle had a form-field boundary about 55 degrees from the fovea, the square and the diamond 46 degrees, the circle 44 degrees, the rectangle 35 degrees, and the hexagon 26 degrees. Whitmer (1931) ranked his forms from most to least discriminable as follows: triangle, diamond, square, rectangle, circle, hexagon. In a later experiment, the same author (Whitmer, 1933) found that the hexagon had a form field 10-20 degrees narrower than those of the square, rectangle, triangle, and the circle.

The above data hardly warrant the drawing of any conclusions regarding the physical shape determinants of identification thresholds in peripheral vision. Comparison of these studies among themselves as well as with foveal threshold experiments is made difficult both by experimental design inadequacies and the use of different methods of stimulus presentation. It is clear, e.g., that response should be differently affected by a form being briefly exposed in the periphery of vision as compared to a situation where it is moved slowly toward the center of vision and remains in sight all the time. It also makes a difference whether photopic or scotopic levels of illumination are used under these conditions, let alone whether the fovea or the periphery of the retina are stimulated. It seems reasonable to assume that a form seen briefly but in a flash of bright light in the fovea would be processed by the observer in a manner different from that employed when the same form is moved slowly toward the point of fixation under low levels of illumination. That set, false hypotheses, etc. would be operative under the latter condition is something that can be safely assumed, based on what is known about the perceptual process under such conditions (cf. Bruner & Potter, 1964), but neither this nor any of the other conditions just mentioned has ever been tested in the context of peripheral form-identification thresholds. In fact, the topic has exerted little attraction on investigators, and no studies of the type listed in the preceding paragraph can be found after 1933.

2. Reproduction

Experiments in which the reproduction of forms has been used as the perceptual task may be divided into two groups. One group consists of a very small number of studies in which the memory aspect of reproduction plays a subsidiary role. Instead, either immediate reproduction is used as just another means to study the perception of form, or else the influence of stimulus and subject factors upon reproduction are investigated. The rest of the reproduction studies, and their number is considerable, is concerned with a single problem, namely the distortions that may be observed in the reproduced form under certain conditions and the implications that this phenomenon has for the nature of the memory trace as conceived by Gestalt and non-Gestalt psychologists.

A. PAST EXPERIENCE, STIMULUS VARIABLES, AND ORGANIC FACTORS IN RE-PRODUCTION

There have been few investigations of the effect of past experience or practice upon reproduction, and they go back quite a number of years. For instance, Foster (1911) found that the ability to reproduce figures increased with practice, but that there was no relationship between this ability and the ability to visualize these figures, verbal description of the figures by the subjects themselves exercising a greater influence upon reproduction. Dallenbach (1914), upon undertaking to test the alleged improvement in perceptual abilities in school children as the result of training, found that practice in the rapid observation and reproduction of letters, digits, words, and geometric figures indeed improved their ability to perform this task as compared with untrained children. Upon retesting 50 weeks later, this effect was found to have persisted.

Fehrer, in her 1935 study, found that increasing exposure time from 40 to 680 msec. decreased the number of presentations needed for the correct reproduction of figures. Renshaw (1945), using tachistoscopic training,was able to bring college students to a level of skill in reproducing figures that, up to that time, had been considered the level of genius. Bevan and Zener (1952) were able to report the lowering of first-perception and incomplete-perception thresholds with repeated exposures of closed-contour shapes and connected and disconnected line patterns. The amount of change, however, depended upon the type of form used.

The effects of complexity and symmetry upon immediate reproduction have been studied in only three instances. Fehrer (1935) was first to find that the more-complex patterns required more presentations for correct reproduction. When the complexity of symmetric and asymmetric forms was equated, symmetric figures were still easier to reproduce than asymmetric ones. After information theory was introduced in psychology, Attneave (1955) undertook to test again the advantages that symmetric figures were alleged to have over asymmetric ones. Regardless of whether immediate reproduction, delayed reproduction, or identification tasks were used, symmetric dot patterns were in no instance easier to remember than asymmetric patterns of the same information content. Schnore and Partington (1967), while using 4×4 square cell patterns of varying degrees of symmetry, found that recall errors were a linear function of the degree of symmetry and the amount of information. This experiment differs from Attneave's in that information content and asymmetry varied together and the information content of the patterns was determined in statistical terms rather than as a single form parameter, which was the case in Attneave's experiment. Attneave's conclusion was that both simplicity and symmetry contribute to figural goodness. Hence, both Attneave and Schnore and Partington are in agreement that accuracy of memory in reproduction varies inversely with figural goodness.

Intelligence, age, mental disorders, and cerebral damage are among other subject factors that affect reproduction. Impaired ability to copy designs (construction dispraxia) is an important sign of brain damage, and the reproduction of forms is included in all brain-damage test batteries. The type of distortion, omissions, and other defects in the reproduction of forms are basic to the diagnosis of brain damage in the Bender-Gestalt Test. A detailed description of them may be found in Pascal and Suttell (1951).

The effects of other factors on the reproduction task have been given scarce attention, although they may be of potentially great importance in the interpretation of experimental results obtained with the reproduction task. Thus, Taylor (1961) investigated the constant errors that occur in the serial reproduction of form by using very simple stimuli: a dot, a line, or a rectangle placed on a blank card. The dot, for instance, when placed near the edge of the card, would tend to move away from the edge in successive reproductions, while moving toward an edge if placed in the center of the card. Anchor effects thus seem to play an important role in serial reproduction. No one, however, has undertaken the study of the combined effects of several anchors of different strengths upon more complex patterns as they would occur in the type of experiment described in the next section. Even when the memory span involved in reproduction is very short, such as when a figure is simply copied from a model, it makes a difference whether the subject looks at his drawing while copying or at the model. Wells (1917) discovered that fewer errors were made while looking at the model. His subjects complained that the sight of their own drawings interfered with their memory for what they had seen during the stimulus exposure.

B. MEMORY TRACES FOR FORM AND THEIR CHANGES IN REPRODUCTION

What happens to the reproduction of a visual form as the form is drawn from memory had been described in so many publications that they would make up a substantial volume if put together. Riley (1962) has written a monograph-length review on the subject. Although he refers to only about one-half of the existing studies, his very thorough review concentrates on the most important ones.

Changes in forms reproduced repeatedly after intervals of days or months have been studied since around the turn of the century (e.g., Philippe, 1897). Woodworth (1938) has summarized the results of the early experimental studies. It was at first hypothesized that the observed changes took place because of the weakening of the memory traces and because, with weakening memory, other factors assumed an increasingly important role in modifying memory traces. These factors were stated to be an increasing reliance on the verbal description of the figure when first seen, interference from similar forms seen between the original viewing and the test, lack of skill in drawing, differences in perceptual type of the subjects (in a 1913 study, e.g., Katz divided his subjects into peripheral and central types, depending on whether they were guided more by stimulus characteristics or their own central processes), and the like.

Wulf (1922), while performing a similar form-reproduction experiment, attached a new interpretation to the changes that he observed in his subjects' reproductions, an interpretation which aroused much subsequent experimental activity and theoretical speculation. Wulf, a Gestalt psychologist, asserted that not only did received stimulation determine perception, but that events in the central nervous system were just as important. These events were of such a nature as to render the perceived figures "better" than the proximal stimulus. Responsible for these events were forces inherent in the nature of the brain, the "autochtonous forces," which tended to simplify perception. Wulf showed six subjects 26 simple line drawings, then asked them to reproduce these drawings immediately, 24 hr. later, and a week later. Wulf decided that, of the 394 usable reproductions, 392 showed either exaggeration (sharpening) or underemphasis (leveling) of structural detail of the original figures. In addition, Wulf believed that both sharpening and leveling could be accomplished in three ways: by making the reproduced figure resemble some well-known shape (normalizing), by emphasizing a feature noted at the time of first viewing (pointing), and by making the reproduced figure a simpler, more regular, in short, a "better" figure (autonomous change). Wulf was able to refute effectively alternative explanations of these changes, such as the weakening of the memory trace or differential attention to the different parts of the figure. What followed was a series of studies that were either sympathetic to Wulf's position or else tried to refute him. As time went by, weaknesses in Wulf's experimental design were discovered and attempts were made to improve upon it. While few tried to deny that reproductions of figures showed changes away from the model, the main concern of the investigators who came after Wulf was to attach either a Gestalt or alternative interpretation to the experimental outcomes and to improve upon the experimental designs of others so as to make the interpretation of these outcomes less ambiguous.

Gibson (1928), while he classified the observed changes in the reproductions of his subjects in a manner similar to Wulf's, interpreted them not as the result of a single factor but as the consequence of perceptual habits—misperceptions and inaccurate drawing habits. Allport (1930) and Perkins (1932) both reported results that they believed supported the Gestalt hypothesis of autonomous changes toward greater simplicity, regularity, and symmetry.

The effect of verbal labels upon reproduction was first explored by Carmichael, Hogan, and Walter (1932). In their experiment, subjects were shown a series of figures. Before a figure was presented, the experimenter announced that it would resemble a certain object, after which the subject drew the figure he had just seen. The figures were sufficiently ambiguous to be called at least two different things. One group of subjects was given one of the two possible names, one was told to expect something resembling the second label, and a third group was given no labels. In the verbal label groups, 73 and 74% of the reproductions resembled the suggested objects, while in the uninfluenced group, only 45% of the reproductions showed a deviation toward the objects labeled in the two experimental groups. This experiment thus supported Gibson in his contention that the subject's interpretation of the stimulus determines his reproductions. In addition, by showing that the memory trace of a previously learned concept can influence a subsequently acquired trace, Carmichael, Hogan, and Walter actually confirmed Wulf's notion of "normalizing." The experiment, nevertheless, provided no information on the subject of autochtonous forces.

Beginning with 1937, investigators began to show awareness of the fact that the recognition and reproduction (recall) tasks were rather different. Zangwill (1937) had his subjects reproduce 10 nonsense forms after intervals ranging from

30 sec. to 18 days. While the reproductions did show certain changes away from the originals, Zangwill found no systematic changes in size, no clear-cut assimilation, and few instances of sharpening and leveling. In the recognition tests, subjects were shown the original figures, figures similar to them, and "cleaned-up" versions of their own reproductions. Typically, the figures recognized were more like the original stimulus figures than the last reproductions of them. Zangwill's results may be interpreted as either refuting the Gestalt theory or as demonstrating that either recognition or reproduction is an inadequate method for testing the hypothesis. Both interpretations were made of similar results after Zangwill's experiment. Hanawalt (1937), in comparing the recognition and reproduction methods, introduced a change in the experimental procedure by recognizing that repeated trials on the reproduction task cannot fail to affect the end result. He therefore used one group of subjects to make several reproductions after different intervals of time, and separate and different groups to make only one reproduction, each after one of the intervals used with the first group. When the drawings of different subjects over time were compared with those made by the same subjects, more loss in the memory trace was evident in the former, indicating that successive reproductions made by the same individuals help them to retain memory about the forms better. Recognition was still a more sensitive measure of retention, since the correct originals were recognized even when the reproductions deviated considerably from them. It also showed that successive reproductions had no effect on recognition. In addition, Hanawalt was able to establish that some 18% of the changes observed in and attributed to successive reproductions occurred while subjects were copying the figures during the inspection trials. Some of the changes were of the type described by Wulf, but not enough to lend any support to the Gestalt hypothesis. Hanawalt raised doubts about the adequacy of the reproduction method in measuring memory for form. It is a common assumption, though, that memory is a unitary process and that the different methods of measuring it may differ in their results simply because they are not complete by themselves and may partially overlap. The two methods differ in the stimulus situation (stimulus present in recognition, absent in reproduction), the nature of the response, as well as such things as the possibility that the subject might misinterpret the instructions in the reproduction task by being led to believe that an exact reproduction of the original is not possible and only an approximate sketch is required. Thus, while a sketch may show deviations from the original, recognition of the same form might show 100% retention. A theoretical interpretation of the difference between the two tasks has been given by Hake (1957) in the light of Bartlett's (1932) notion of "schema":

The reproductive task required of subjects in recall tests of memory for form places a unique strain on the subject. It looks as if the preservation of material which is required in recognizing is normally a preservation of schemes, of general settings, of order or form of arrangement; and as if the detailed reinstatement of individualized material is a special case. (P. 195.)

Unanticipated reproduction of a figure demands details of shape which are not retained and requires that the subject invent a figure of the type required. Thus, an unanticipated reproduction reveals not what the subject remembered of a particular figure but rather what his experience has been with a figure of a particular kind. (P. 90.)

Hanawalt and Demarest (1939) produced additional data on the effect of verbal labels on reproduction. While Carmichael *et al.* introduced the labels at the time of inspection, Hanawalt and Demarest did it at the time of the reproduction test. In addition, they also tested the effect of various inspection-test intervals (immediate recall, 2 days, 7 days). It was found that labeling affected reproduction in the direction of the label, and that this effect was the larger, the longer was the inspection-test interval. It was also found that in both the experimental and control groups there was a tendency for reproductions to follow the implicit labeling done at the time of inspection by the subjects themselves. This effect also increased with increasing delays between inspection and test.

An experiment by Hebb and Foord (1945) undermined the Gestalt hypothesis still further. They found no trends in any direction in the recognition of two inspection figures when these were presented among several similar ones either 5 min. or 24 hr. later. George (1952) replicated these results with the addition of a third recognition test 8 days after the original inspection. The conclusion of Hebb and Foord was that memory for form does not show consistent trends away from the inspection form in the course of time when the recognition method is used, and that such trends are solely the result of the use of the repeated reproduction method. The difference between the recognition and reproduction tasks was illuminated from still another angle by Prentice (1954), who performed an experiment along the lines of Carmichael *et al.*, but used a recognition test instead of reproduction. For recognition, the original stimuli were presented, plus two distorted versions of each figure made to resemble the objects suggested by the verbal labels used by Carmichael *et al.*, While many errors were made, they were symmetrically distributed about the basic figures. Prentice's conclusion was that verbal labels affect memory for form only when the perceptual task is one of reproduction.

In the 1950s, a number of studies continued with the task of correcting defects in the experimental designs of other investigators. For instance, Carlson and Duncan (1955) thought that Hebb and Foord had given their subjects too many figures to choose from in the memory test and that the inspection figures, by being symmetric, precluded a test of the Gestalt hypothesis that memory traces would tend to change in the direction of symmetry. They found that the number of stimuli presented for recognition did indeed affect the results: when presented in the form of a booklet, the subject's choice of the stimulus as the one presented for inspection depended on the page that he happened to open first. Crumbaugh (1954) and Karlin and Brennan (1957) exposed each subject to only one figure in both inspection and test trials. Using a procedure that combined discrimination with recognition, Crumbaugh, as well as Karlin and Brennan, either obtained no trends in the estimation of the size of gaps in circles and similar tasks or else reversals and even trends contrary to those suggested by the Gestalt theory. The task, however, did not involve reproduction but the comparison of two identical stimuli where one followed the other either immediately or after a few seconds. Walker and Veroff (1956) conducted an experiment similar to Hanawalt's (1937), except that only three figures were used: a circle with a gap (two sizes of the gap), an angle (acute and obtuse), and a quadrilateral (one with angles closer to 90 degrees than the other). Half the subjects drew the figures 15 sec. after inspection, the other half, 2 weeks later. The different figures yielded different results. For instance, the narrow gap in the circle was remembered as being larger, while the larger gap was drawn narrower in the immediate test for memory, a result that parallels those of Crumbaugh as well as of Karlin and Brennan. The larger gap was drawn even smaller after 2 weeks, but there was no further widening of the narrow gap. Thus, at least in some instances, changes in memory for form, although not necessarily progressive changes, may be observed with both the recognition and reproduction methods. There are two dozen or so studies of changes in the memory trace for the gapped circle. These have been reviewed by Holmes (1968), who concludes that in 19 of the 25 studies reviewed the predominant change in the memory trace has been in the direction of opening the gap rather than closing it, a result in direct opposition to the prediction made from the Gestalt theory.

The 1950s were an active decade in the study of changes in the memory for form, spurred by a general increase of interest in perception, and the advent of the "new look" in perception with its emphasis on set and past experience on perception. Studies of the effect of past experience upon form perception, however, had been made earlier (e.g., Braly, 1933). The effect of verbal labels (e.g., Bruner, Busiek, & Minturn, 1952; Herman, Lawless, & Marshall, 1957) continued to be investigated, and Postman (1954) showed that past experience in the form of artificial norms established during training period modify memory for form. von Wright's (1964) study, one of the very few conducted in the 1960s, showed that previously established norms may be changed in the course of training by interpolating appropriate stimuli, and that the effect shows up even in a recognition test.

As Riley (1962) points out, the two major trends in the development of research on memory for form are an increasing methodological sophistication and an increasing amount of evidence in favor of those who have offered interpretations of memory changes that were different from the Gestalt hypothesis. It is possible that the second development has been partially a result of the first. That changes in memory for form do occur is an established fact; it is also quite certain that they are more easily observed when the successive reproduction method is employed than when memory is tested by the recognition method. Whether these changes are systematic and progressive depends on a number of factors, which makes formulation of general principles difficult. That changes in memory, if progressive, follow the trends predicted by Gestalt theory is even less certain. As to the underlying cause of changes in memory for form, there is the question of whether the Gestalt hypothesis concerning autochthonous forces in the brain can be tested at all. This problem was discussed in Chap. 4 in connection with the Gestalt theory. Not only is it impossible to control the autochthonous forces in the brain at the present time, but also to separate their effects from the effects of the observer's past experience.

3. Association

Verbal associations to visual forms are ordinarily not considered a perceptual task. Since forms may suggest definite objects even when there has been no intention at representation, the question has been asked of whether a relationship might exist between physical stimulus characteristics and verbal responses to ambiguous or nonrepresentational forms. While the determinants of the associations that a person may form to an ambiguous shape reside mostly in the person himself and to a much lesser degree in the physical form, form does play a part. Hence, at least this aspect of the associative response is perceptual.

Attempts to relate form parameters to the associative response in a systematic way are a very late development. They begin with a 1959 study by Vanderplas and Garvin in which complexity of random shapes was related to measures of the associative response. Before that date, only the Rorschach inkblots and associations to them had been studied. While the Rorschach literature is enormous, there is little in it that is useful in the analysis of the relationship between the geometry of the inkblots and the nature of the response. It stands to reason, e.g., that the bilateral symmetry of the inkblots should produce more responses of animal and other biological forms than asymmetric shapes. While this has been recognized by some Rorschach workers, it is just as often asserted that psychological structure is the governing principle of the projective technique and that the similarity of responses to different types of inkblots indicates that a subject's projections are minimally dependent on the formal characteristics of the inkblots (e.g., Baughman, 1954; Dorken, 1956), or, at least, that the investigation of the stimulus aspect of the Rorschach test is a task for the future (Baughman, 1958).

The story of prediction of the associative response from stimulus characteristics, then, begins in 1959. If the introduction of random shapes by Attneave and Arnoult in 1956 may be considered the analog of the introduction of the nonsense syllable by Ebbinghaus, the measurement of the association value of random shapes by Vanderplas and Garvin parallels the measurement of the association value of nonsense syllables by Glaze and Noble. Vanderplas and Garvin (1959a) constructed 180 random shapes of 4, 6, 8, 12, 16, and 24 sides. Using a modified version of Glaze's (1928) procedure, they asked 50 subjects to either associate in a word or a phrase to these shapes when exposed for 3 sec., or else say "yes" if the shape reminded them of something but they could not immediately verbalize the association. They were to say "no" if a shape did not remind them of anything. The responses were tabulated in three ways. The association value of a shape was defined as the percentage of subjects who gave either a content or a "yes" response to it. The content value was the percentage of all subjects who gave a content response (all associative responses less the "yes" responses) to a shape. Heterogeneity of the associative response was computed by the entropy formula, $H = -\Sigma p_i \log p_i$, where p_i is the proportion of content responses of the ith class. The main finding of Vanderplas and Garvin was that of an inverse relationship between complexity and the number, content, and heterogeneity of associations. In addition, simple shapes produced more content responses, while shapes of greater complexity produced a greater variety of responses, reflecting lesser resemblance of the shapes to objects than did responses to the simpler shapes. The net result of this study was a pool of random shapes with known association values that could be used in other experiments where associations could be a variable affecting another response. Vanderplas (Vanderplas, Sanderson, & Vanderplas, 1965) has subsequently enlarged the pool of random shapes with known association values to 1100.

Since the percentage of subjects giving an associative response to a stimulus in a few seconds' time is only one of a number of definitions of meaning, some criticism concerning the use of this particular measure arose, as did proposals to use other methods of measuring the meaning of forms. Bartlett (1963) took exception to the idea that association value by itself is a sufficient measure and suggested that the less definite shapes, while yielding more associations than the more definite ones, should produce less appropriate or less univocal associations. She found in her experiment that the association value computed by Vanderplas and Garvin was actually inversely related to the mean scalar value of judged appropriateness of associations. Lewis and Boehnert (1965), in turn, decided to use the method of production proposed by Noble (1952), by which the average number of associations written down by a group of subjects during

60 sec. is taken as a measure of meaningfulness. Finding that highly meaningful shapes had very low values of meaningfulness because, to most subjects, they suggested only one or very few things, Lewis and Boehnert obtained a second index of meaning, called connotative strength. Connotative strength was defined as the average scaled value of judged appropriateness of the first associations given to the shape. This index and meaningfulness correlated practically zero. Lewis and Boehnert suggest that, tentatively at least, the connotative strength measure is a better measure of what shapes actually mean to untrained subjects.

Edelman, Karas, and Cohen (1961), without objecting to the association-value measure of Vanderplas and Garvin (1959a), hypothesized that latency of the first association might be directly related to the information content of a shape. Edelman *et al.* used as stimuli symmetric and asymmetric random shapes of two levels of complexity. The shapes were equated with respect to either their total number of points or the number of independent points. The results indicated that symmetric shapes had lower latencies than asymmetric shapes of the same number of independent turns and that the simpler shapes had lower latencies than the more-complex shapes, with no significant interaction between these two variables.

The rest of the relatively small number of studies in this area are concerned more directly with the effects of physical stimulus dimensions on the associative response. Edelman (1960), in his dissertation study, employed three types of forms: asymmetric portions from Rorschach inkblots, rectilinear transforma-tions of these inkblots, and random polygons, the last two types of forms containing 22 ±3 inflections. Edelman computed the association value of each shape and its content value in the same fashion as Vanderplas and Garvin (1959a) had computed them. The index of complex content value was the proportion of subjects responding with associations that transcended the stimulus, implying greater projection. These indices were computed on the basis of subjects' associations given within 3, 6, or 15 sec. While more associations were given in 6 than in 3 sec., 15 sec. did not produce a significantly larger number of responses than did 6 sec. The most significant finding was that, while the association values of the random shapes and the rectilinear transformations of the inkblots did not differ in association value, there was a significant difference between the untransformed (curvilinear) inkblots and their rectilinear transformations, curvilinear shapes eliciting more associations than the other two types of forms used. There was no difference in content value or complex content value among the three types of forms. The curvilinear shapes also had shorter first-association latencies than the other two types of shapes. Thus, curvilinearity appears to have a very definite effect on the associative response. This study also emphasizes the difference between measured and perceived information contents of shapes. While it is true that curvilinear shapes may be represented with rectilinear segments, curves, like poems, lose something in the process of this "translation." The associative response, at least, to curvilinear nonrepresentational shapes and their rectilinear transformations indicates that these two types of forms belong to very distinct stimulus domains.

Goldstein's (1961) aim was to test the effect of rotation on the association value of random shapes. Vanderplas and Garvin (1959a) had presented their shapes in one orientation only. It appears that, if rotated, a random shape may remind one of an entirely different object than it does in its original position. Goldstein took 10 shapes from each complexity class that had been used by Vanderplas and Garvin and presented them in their original positions, or else rotated 90, 180, and 270 degrees. Each rotation was shown to a separate group of subjects, the exposure time being 3 sec. It turned out that simple (4 and 6 points) and complex (16 and 24 points) shapes did not change their association value in comparison with the values obtained by Vanderplas and Garvin as much as did shapes of medium (8 and 12 points) complexity. Goldstein explains these results by stating that low-complexity shapes resemble simple, polyoriented objects, so that rotation does not affect their association value, because they keep resembling the same object. Complex shapes, on the other hand, are many-sided and elicit as many associations in one orientation as in any other, hence their association value does not change much with rotation either.

Aside from Edelman's (1960) study, only one other study has asked the question of how different populations of shapes might differ in association value. Karas, Edelman, Farrell, & DuBois (1961) compared the association values of 12 random shapes constructed by method 1 of Attneave and Arnoult (1956) and the same number of shapes constructed by method 2. Attneave and Arnoult had suggested that method 2 shapes probably contained less information than method 1 shapes. Since only 10 male and 10 female subjects were used and the number of stimuli was small also, their finding that method 2 shapes contained less information for females only must be taken only as provisional and suggestive, since other variables, not controlled in this experiment, apparently also play a role, as the authors themselves suggest.

Battig's (1962) was a large-scale study of the associative response, involving many variables. The 35 shapes, 7 on each level of complexity (4, 6, 8, 12, and 16 points) were presented either as constructed (method 1) or with either 50 or 100% of their contours made arbitrarily curvilinear. In addition to complexity and curvature, the length of the perimeter, area, perimeter squared over area, and angular variability were taken as form measures. Response was measured in terms of the percentage of subjects producing a written association to a shape when exposed for 8 sec. (%A); associative strength, defined as the mean rated strength of these associations on a 5-point scale; information uncertainty; and relative entropy. While the four association measures were highly intercorrelated, little or no relationship was found to exist between the physical form measures and association measures. Only for %A could as much as 10% of the variance in response be accounted for by the combined physical variables, including complexity. This is perhaps the most significant finding of this study. As indicated at the beginning of this chapter, if there is a hierarchy of perceptual tasks that ranges from those that are most perceptual to those that are less so and involve more learning factors, then it is reasonable to expect that, while the detection task would be substantially determined by the stimulus characteristics, the associative response would be least so determined. Battig's finding that association value and complexity were unrelated is in opposition to the findings of Vanderplas and Garvin's (1959a) as well as of Goldstein's (1961). Battig believes this discrepancy may have resulted from the significant interaction between complexity and curvature: for the 100% curved shapes, %A increased with complexity as compared with the 0 and 50% curved shapes. Since, however, Battig had only three discrete levels of curvature and five discrete levels of complexity, while all other variables varied continuously, product-moment correlations computed for such data must be taken very cautiously, especially since additional studies in which meaningfulness has been both scaled (Arnoult, 1960) and measured by the method of Vanderplas and Garvin (Eisenman, 1966) confirm its dependence on measured form complexity. Eisenman (1966), while using only three 4-sided, three 12-sided, and three 24-sided Vanderplas and Garvin shapes and three symmetric geometric figures, found that subjects tested in a classroom, as compared to a laboratory, produced more associations to form. The symmetric shapes produced more asociations than asymmetric ones, but, having only 4, 8, and 10 total points, they were considerably simpler than the asymmetric shapes. As Vanderplas and Garvin had demonstrated, the simpler forms do produce more associations.

The amount of work that has been dony in the area of the associative response to shapes is small. The matter of the meaning of forms, however, is one that has great importance for other areas of form perception. The relationship between measured information content and perceived meaning is a problem that appeared simultaneously with information theory and has been seeking a solution ever since. The associative technique offers one avenue toward its clarification, if not solution. The role of curved lines enters into this problem very prominently. The amount of research done on curves is again minimal, and it is on the associative response that curves produce the greatest effect in comparison with other perceptual tasks. Since a clear-cut phenomenon exists here, the study of curves should be most profitable using this particular perceptual task. Establishing reliable empirical relations connecting form, its physical characteristics, and meaning should also prove of great value to the study of memory processes for form.

REFERENCES

Allport, G. W. Change and decay in the visual memory image. *Brit. J. Psychol.*, 1930, **21**, 138-148.

Alluisi, E. A., Hawkes, G. R., & Hall, T. J. Effects of distortion on the identification of visual forms under two levels of multiple-task performance. *J. Eng. Psychol.*, 1964, **3**, 29-40.

Archer, E. J. Identification of visual patterns as a function of information load. *J. exp. Psychol.*, 1954, **48**, 313-317.

Arnoult, M. D. Recognition of shapes following paired-associates pre-training. *Air Force-NRC Science Symposium*, 1955.

Arnoult, M. D. A comparison of training methods in the recognition of spatial patterns. AFPTRC-TN-56-27, Lackland AFB, February, 1956. (a)

Arnoult, M. D. Familiarity and recognition of nonsense shapes. *J. exp. Psychol.*, 1956, **51**, 269-276. (b)

Arnoult, M. D. Prediction of perceptual response from structural characteristics of the stimulus. *Percept. mot. Skills*, 1960, **11**, 261-268.

Atkinson, R. C., & Ammons, R. B. Experiential factors in visual form perception: II. Latency as a function of repetition. *J. exp. Psychol.*, 1952, **43**, 173-178.

Attneave, F. Symmetry, information, and memory for patterns. *Amer. J. Psychol.*, 1955, **68**, 209-222.

Attneave, F., & Arnoult, M. D. The quantitative study of shape and pattern perception. *Psychol. Bull.*, 1956, **53**, 452-471.

Barskiĭ, B. V., & Guzeva, M. A. O zavisimosti prostranstvennykh porogov zreniya ot kharaktera vosprinimaemogo kontura. *Voprosy Psikhol.*, 1962, **8**(2), 101-114.

Bartlett, F. C. *Remembering.* London and New York: Cambridge Univ. Press, 1932.

Bartlett, J. A new approach to the assessment of the association values of random shapes. Paper read at Midwestern Psychological Association, Chicago, May, 1963.

Battig, W. F. Interrelationships between measures of association and structural characteristics of nonsense shapes. *Percept. mot. Skills*, 1962, **14**, 3-6.

Baughman, E. E. A comparative analysis of Rorschach forms with altered stimulus characteristics. *J. proj. Tech.*, 1954, **18**, 151-164.

Baughman, E. E. The role of the stimulus in Rorschach response. *Psychol. Bull.*, 1958, **55**, 121-147.

Bevan, W., & Zener, K. Some influences of past experience upon the perceptual threshold of visual form. *Amer. J. Psychol.*, 1952, **65**, 434-442.

Binder, A. A statistical method for the process of visual recognition. *Psychol. Rev.*, 1955, **62**, 119-129.

Bitterman, M. E., Krauskopf, J., & Hochberg, J. E. Threshold for visual form: A diffusion model. *Amer. J. Psychol.*, 1954, **67**, 205-219.

Borg, G. Studies of visual gestalt strength. Report, Dept. Educ., Umea Univ., Sweden, 1964. (Mimeographed)

Braine, L. G. Disorientation of forms: An examination of Rock's theory. *Psychon. Sci.*, 1965, **3**, 541-542.

Braly, K. W. The influence of past experience in visual perception. *J. exp. Psychol.*, 1933, **16**, 613-643.

Bruner, J. S., & Potter, M. C. Interference in visual recognition. *Science*, 1964, **144**, 424-425.

Bruner, J. S., Busiek, R. D., & Minturn, A. I. Assimilation in the immediate reproduction of visually perceived forms. *J. exp. Psychol.*, 1952, **44**, 151-155.

Carlson, J. B., & Duncan, C. P. A study of autonomous change in the memory trace by the method of recognition. *Amer. J. Psychol.*, 1955, **68**, 280-284.

Carlson, W. A., & Eriksen, C. W. Dichopic summation of information in the recognition of briefly presented forms. *Psychon. Sci.*, 1966, **5**, 67-68.

Carmichael, L., Hogan, H. P., & Walter, A. A. Experimental study of the effect of language on the reproduction of visually perceived form. *J. exp. Psychol.*, 1932, **15**, 73-86.

Casperson, R. C. The visual discrimination of geometric form. *J. exp. Psychol.*, 1950, **40**, 668-686.

Cheatham, P. G. Visual perceptual latency as a function of stimulus brightness and contour shape. *J. exp. Psychol.*, 1952, **43**, 369-380.

Collier, R. M. An experimental study of form perception in indirect vision. *J. comp. Psychol.*, 1931, **11**, 281-289.

Crannel, C. W., & Christensen, J. M. Expansion of the visual form field by perimeter training. *USAF, WADC TR 55-368*, 1955.

Crumbaugh, J. C. Temporal changes in the memory of visually perceived form. *Amer. J. Psychol.,*, 1954, **67**, 647-658.

Dallenbach, K. M. The effect of practice upon visual apprehension in school children. *J. educ. Psychol.*, 1914, **5**, 321-334, 387-404.

Day, R. H. Application of the statistical theory to form perception. *Psychol. Rev.*, 1956, **63**, 139-148.

Day, R. H. The physiological basis of form perception in the peripheral retina. *Psychol. Rev.*, 1957, **64**, 38-48.

Dearborn, G. V. N. Recognition under objective reversal. *Psychol. Rev.*, 1899, **6**, 395-406.

Dees, V., & Grindley, G. The transposition of visual patterns. *Brit. J. Psychol.*, 1947, **37**, 152-163.

Deese, J. Complexity of contour in the recognition of visual form. WADC, 1956.

Dorken, H. Psychological structure as the governing principle of projective techniques: Rorschach theory. *Can. J. Psychol.*, 1956, **10**, 101-106.

Edelman, S. K. Analysis of some stimulus factors involved in the associative response. Unpublished doctoral dissertation, Purdue Univ., 1960. *Diss. Abstr.*, 1960, **21**, 1630.

Edelman, S. K., Karas, G. G., & Cohen, B. J. The relative contributions of complexity and symmetry to the perception of form. Paper read at Midwestern Psychological Association, Chicago, May, 1961.

Eisenman, R. The association value of random shapes revisited. *Psychon. Sci.*, 1966, **6**, 397-398.

Ellis, H. C. Associative variables in visual form recognition. *Psychon. Bull.*, 1967, 1(2), 3.

Engstrand, R. D., & Moeller, G. The relative legibility of ten simple geometric figures. *Amer. Psychologist*, 1962, **17**, 386. (Abstract)

Fehrer, E. V. An investigation of learning of visually perceived forms. *Amer. J. Psychol.*, 1935, **47**, 187-221.

Ferree, C. E., & Rand, G. The effect of relation to background on the size and shape of the form field for stimuli of different sizes. *Amer. J. Ophthalmology.*, 1931, **14**, 1018-1029.

Ferree, C. E., & Rand, G. Two important factors in the size and shape of the form field and some of their relations to practical perimetry. *J. gen. Psychol.*, 1932, **6**, 414-428.

Ferree, C. E., Rand, G., & Monroe, M. M. A study of the factors which cause individual differences in the size of the form-field. *Amer. J. Psychol.*, 1930, **42**, 63-71.

Fox, C. W. An experimental study of naming. *Amer. J. Psychol.*, 1935, **47**, 545-579.

Fox, W. R. Visual discrimination as a function of stimulus size, shape, and edge gradient. In J. W. Wulfeck & J. H. Taylor (Eds.), *Form discrimination as related to military problems*. Washington, D.C.: Nat. Acad. Sci.-Nat. Res. Coun., 1957. Pp. 168-175.

Forsyth, G. A., & Brown, D. R. Recognition-discrimination performance as a function of stimulus characteristics to which subject attends. Paper read at Midwestern Psychological Association, Chicago, May, 1967.

Foster, W. S. The effect of practice upon visualizing and upon the reproduction of visual impressions. *J. educ. Psychol.*, 1911, **2**, 11-22.

French, R. S. Identification of dot patterns from memory as a function of complexity. *J. exp. Psychol.*, 1954, **47**, 22-26.

Garner, W. R. *Uncertainty and structure as psychological concepts.* New York: Wiley, 1962.

Geissler, L. R. Form perception in indirect vision. *Psychol. Bull.*, 1926, **23**, 135-136.

George, F. H. Errors in visual recognition. *J. exp. Psychol.*, 1952, **43**, 202-206.

Gibson, J. J. The reproduction of visually perceived forms. *J. exp. Psychol.*, 1928, **12**, 1-39.

Gibson, J. J., & Robinson, D. Orientation in visual perception: The recognition of familiar plane forms in differing orientations. *Psychol. Monog.*, 1935, **46**, No. 210.

Glaze, J. A. The association value of non-sense syllables. *J. genet. Psychol.*, 1928, **35**, 255-267.

Goldstein, A. G. Spatial orientation as a factor in eliciting associative responses to random shapes. *Percept. mot. Skills*, 1961, **12**, 15-25.

Gollin, E. S. Perceptual learning of incomplete pictures. *Percept. mot. Skills*, 1965, **21**, 439-445.

Gomulicki, B. The development and present status of the trace theory of memory. *Brit. J. Psychol., Monog. Suppl.*, 1953, No. 29.

Goodnow, R. E. The utilization of partially valid cues in perceptual identification. Unpublished doctoral dissertation, Harvard Univ., 1954.

Graefe, O. Qualitative Untersuchungen ueber Kontur und Flaeche in der optischen Warnehmung. *Psychol. Forsch.*, 1964, **27**, 260-306.

Hake, H. W. Contributions of psychology to the study of pattern vision. *WADC Tech. Rep.* 57-621, 1957.

Hake, H. W., & Eriksen, C. W. Role of response variables in recognition and identification of complex visual forms. *J. exp. Psychol.*, 1956, **52**, 235-243.

Hanawalt, N. G. Memory traces for figures in recall and recognition. *Arch. Psychol.*, 1937, **31**, No. 216.

Hanawalt, N. G., & Demarest, I. H. The effect of verbal suggestion in the recall period upon the reproduction of visually perceived forms. *J. exp. Psychol.*, 1939, **25**, 159-174.

Hebb, D. O., & Foord, E. N. Errors of visual recognition and the nature of the trace. *J. exp. Psychol.*, 1945, **35**, 335-348.

Helson, H. Dr. Wilcox on "The role of form in perception." *Amer. J. Psychol.*, 1933, **45**, 171-173.

Helson, H., & Fehrer, E. V. The role of form in perception. *Amer. J. Psychol.*, 1932, **44**, 79-102.

Henle, M. An experimental investigation of past experience as a determinant of visual form perception. *J. exp. Psychol.*, 1942, **30**, 1-22.

Herman, D. T., Lawless, R. H., & Marshall, R. W. Variables in the effect of language on the reproduction of visually perceived forms. *Percept. mot. Skills*, 1957, **7**, 171-186.

Hochberg, J. E., Gleitman, H., & McBride, P. D. Visual threshold as a function of simplicity of form. *Amer. Psychologist*, 1948, **3**, 341-342. (Abstract)

Holmes, D. S. Search for "closure" in a visually perceived pattern. *Psychol. Bull.*, 1968, **70**, 296-312.

Hyman, R., & Hake, H. W. Form recognition as a function of the number of forms which can be presented for recognition. *USAF WADC TR* 54-164, 1954.

Kaneko, H. [The perception time of different forms.] *Rep. 6th Congr. Jap. Psychol. Assoc.,* 1938, 78-82.

Karas, G. G., Edelman, S. K., Farrell, R. J., & DuBois, T. E. An experimental comparison of associative responses to two types of randomly derived stimuli. *Proc. Iowa Acad. Sci.,* 1961, **68**, 535-542.

Karlin, L., & Brennan, G. Memory for visual figures by the method of identical stimuli. *Amer. J. Psychol.,* 1957, **70**, 248-252.

Katz, D. Ueber individuelle Verschiedenheiten bei der Auffassung von Figuren. *Z. Psychol.,* 1913, **65**, 161-180.

Kleitman, N., & Blier, Z. A. Color and form discrimination in the periphery of the retina. *Amer. J. Physiol.,* 1928, **85**, 178-190.

Koffka, K. *Principles of Gestalt psychology.* New York: Harcourt Brace, 1935.

Krauskopf, J., Duryea, R., & Bitterman, M. E. Threshold for visual form: Further experiments. *Amer. J. Psychol.,* 1954, **67**, 427-440.

Leeper, R. A study of a neglected portion of the field of learning—the development of sensory organization. *J. genet. Psychol.,* 1935, **46**, 42-75.

Lewis, D., & Boehnert, J. B. Assessing the connotative strengths of random shapes. *Proc. Iowa Acad. Sci.,* 1965, **72**, 378-389.

Lordahl, D. S., *et al.* Deficits in recognition of random shapes with changed visual fields. *Psychon. Sci.,* 1965, **3**, 245-246.

Mishkin, M., & Forgays, D. C. Word recognition as a function of retinal locus. *J. exp. Psychol.,* 1952, **43**, 43-48.

Munn, N. L., & Geil, G. A. A note on peripheral form discrimination. *J. gen. Psychol.,* 1931, **5**, 78-88.

Noble, C. E. An analysis of meaning. *Psychol. Rev.,* 1952, **59**, 421-430.

Oetjen, F. Die Bedeutung der Orientierung des Lesestoffs fuer das Lesen und der Orientierung von sinnlosen Formen fuer das Wiedererkennen derselben. *Z. Psychol.,* 1915, **71**, 321-355.

Orbach, J. Retinal locus as a factor in the recognition of visually perceived words. *Amer. J. Psychol.,* 1952, **65**, 555-562.

Pascal, G. R., & Suttell, B. J. *The Bender-Gestalt test.* New York: Grune & Stratton, 1951.

Perkins, J. F. Symmetry in visual recall. *Amer. J. Psychol.,* 1932, **44**, 473-490.

Philippe, J. Sur les transformations de nos images mentales. *Rev. Phil.,* 1897, **43**, 481-493.

Postman, L. Learned principles of organization in memory. *Psychol. Monog.,* 1954, **68**, No. 374.

Prentice, W. C. H. Visual recognition of verbally labeled figures. *Amer. J. Psychol.,* 1954, **67**, 315-320.

Renshaw, S. The visual perception and reproduction of forms by tachistoscopic methods. *J. Psychol.,* 1945, **20**, 217-232.

Riley, D. A. Memory for form. In L. Postman (Ed.), *Psychology in the making.* New York: Knopf, 1962. Pp. 402-465.

Rock, I. The orientation of forms on the retina and in the environment. *Amer. J. Psychol.,* 1956, **69**, 513-528.

Rock, I., & Heimer, W. The effect of retinal and phenomenal orientation on the perception of form. *Amer. J. Psychol.,* 1957, **70**, 493-511.

Schnore, M. M., & Partington, J. T. Immediate memory for visual patterns: Symmetry and amount of information. *Psychon. Sci.,* 1967, **8**, 421-422.

Street, R. F. A gestalt completion test: A study of a cross section of intellect. In *Teachers College Contributions to Education,* No. 481. New York: Teachers College, Columbia Univ., 1931.

Taylor, M. M. Effect of anchoring and distance perception on the reproduction of forms. *Percept. mot. Skills,* 1961, **12**, 203-230.

Thouless, R. The experience of "upright" and "upside-down" in looking at pictures. *Miscell. Psychol. Albert Michotte,* 1947, 130.

Vanderplas, J. M., & Garvin, E. A. The association value of random shapes. *J. exp. Psychol.,* 1959, **57**, 147-154. (a)

Vanderplas, J. M., & Garvin, E. A. Complexity, association value, and practice as factors in shape recognition following paired associates training. *J. exp. Psychol.,* 1959, **57**, 155-163. (b)

Vanderplas, J. M., Sanderson, W. A., & Vanderplas, J. N. Statistical and associational characteristics of 1100 random shapes. *Percept. mot. Skills,* 1965, **21**, 414.

Walker, E. L., & Veroff, J. Changes in the memory-trace for perceived forms with successive reproduction. *Amer. J. Psychol.,* 1956, **69**, 395-402.

Weinstein, M. Stimulus complexity and the recognition of visual patterns. Unpublished doctoral dissertation, Ohio State Univ., 1955.

Wells, G. R. Some experiments in motor reproduction of visually perceived forms. *Psychol. Rev.,* 1917, **24**, 322-327.

White, B. W. Complexity and heterogeneity in the visual recognition of two-dimensional forms. In J. W. Wulfeck & J. H. Taylor (Eds.), *Form discrimination as related to military problems.* Washington, D.C.: Nat. Acad. Sci.-Nat. Res. Coun., 1957. Pp. 158-161.

Whitmer, C. A. Peripheral form and pattern discrimination under dark adaptation. *Univ. Pittsburgh Bull.,* 1931, **7**, 238-244.

Whitmer, C. A. Peripheral form discrimination under dark-adaptation. *J. gen. Psychol.,* 1933, **9**, 405-419.

Wilcox, W. W. Helson and Fehrer on the role of form in perception. *Amer. J. Psychol.,* 1932, **44**, 578-580.

Woodworth, R. S. *Experimental psychology.* New York: Holt, 1938.

Wright, J. M. von. On qualitative changes in the retention of forms. *Scand. J. Psychol.,* 1964, **5**(2), 65-70.

Wulf, F. Beitraege zur Psychologie der Gestalt: VI. Ueber die Veraenderung von Vorstellungen (Gedaechtnis und Gestalt). *Psychol. Forsch.,* 1922, **1**, 333-373.

Zangwill, O. L. An investigation of the relationship between the processes of reproducing and recognizing simple figures, with special reference to Koffka's trace theory. *Brit. J. Psychol.,* 1937, **27**, 250-276.

Chapter 8 / FORM DISCRIMINATION IN ANIMALS

Discrimination has been virtually the only task that animals have been trained to perform in form-perception experiments. Identification, reproduction, and the associative response are tasks that are within the capabilities of man alone. There are well-established procedures for determining light and color thresholds in animals, thus there is no reason why form-detection thresholds cannot be established in a similar manner. This seems to have never been done. Since learned discriminations in animals persist in time, as demonstrated in delayed reaction experiments, the basis is given for the recognition task: recognition would be demonstrated if the animal responded positively to the positive stimulus when presented among unfamiliar stimuli after period of delay. Form-recognition experiments with animals do not appear to have been recorded in the literature either. Scaling, being an extension of the discrimination task, is within the behavioral capacities of any animal that can discriminate form. This task, again, has not been given animals, except in the form of establishing dichotomized natural preferences.

The methodological problems that arise in experiments on form discrimination with animal subjects are caused by two related factors: animals cannot talk, and they must be therefore trained to perform a discrimination task before specific questions about how animals classify shapes may be asked. The need for prior training and the necessity of asking questions about perception in learning terms forces the psychologist interested in form perception in animals to take cognizance of much of learning theory and the very large body of literature that deals with the methodological issues involved in discrimination learning. Much of what appears to be experimental work in form perception in animals turns upon issues in learning, shapes being used merely for convenience and having no particular bearing on form perception. The number and variety of problems involved in discrimination learning are so large that volumes have been written on that subject. Sutherland (1961a), in his monograph on the visual discrimination of shape in animals, presents a survey of the problems in that context. Since these problems are ancillary to the main question of how animals classify patterns, only a brief resume of them will be given.

1. Methodology and Methodological Issues

A. SUBJECTS

As in learning experiments, the selection of animal species for form-perception experiments has been determined by a number of factors that have led to the overrepresentation of some and the neglect of other species. Of the hundreds of thousands of animal species, only a handful have been used as subjects in form-perception studies. The white rat has been by far the most preferred species, followed by the primates. As many studies have been done on chickens, pigeons, crows, and ducks together as on the octopus alone. Dogs, cats, squirrels, raccoons, half a dozen other species of quadrupeds, frogs, toads, turtles, lizards, some fifteen species of fish, the honeybee, and the housefly have each rated very few studies. Work on these animals constitutes the rest of the literature on form perception in animals, the white rat and the primates together accounting for as much of the literature as all other species taken together.

B. APPARATUS

A variety of test apparatus have been used in the past, most of which are still in use today, albeit with modifications. The specific form of the apparatus has been determined by two principal factors: the anatomical and behavioral characteristics of the species tested and attempts to control for the operation of factors other than visual discrimination, such as smell, kinesthesis, habits, and preferences.

Three basic types of apparatus have been used with quadrupeds: the jumping stand, the discrimination box, and the Wisconsin General Test Apparatus. In 1930, Lashley introduced the jumping stand to speed up discrimination learning in rats. While modifications have been introduced from time to time, the basic idea has remained the same (Fig. 8-1). The rat is placed on a platform from which he can jump against one of two visual stimuli. The stimuli are attached to doors. If the rat jumps against the correct stimulus, the door opens and the rat is fed behind the door on a feeding platform. If he jumps against the negative stimulus, the door does not open and the rat falls into a net below. Refusal to jump may be overcome by electric shock. The jumping stand is used with small animals that will jump willingly, notably the rat.

The discrimination box has undergone many variations since its first use early in this century (Yerkes & Watson, 1911). A contemporary version that has proved to be effective with rats, squirrels, raccoons, and small monkeys is the Purdue General Test Apparatus (Fig. 8-2). Before the discrimination experiment

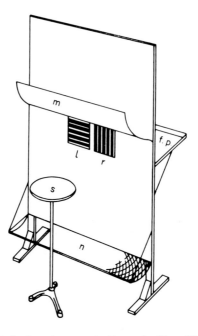

Fig. 8-1. Left: Lashley's jumping stand. From Lashley (1930). Reproduced by permission.

is performed, the animal is allowed to explore the box freely. In the course of this exploration, the animal finds that the doors located in one wall of the restraining cage have food wells behind them. Food is placed in all of them during the familiarization trials. In the course of the experiment, forms are attached to the doors and two screens lowered in front of the entire wall containing the stimuli: a transparent and an opaque one. At the beginning of each trial, the food-well behind the door with the positive stimulus is baited and the opaque screen is raised. The animal is allowed to look at the stimuli briefly before the transparent screen is raised. If the negative stimulus is approached, the opaque screen is lowered, which prevents the animal from making a second choice on the same trial. Automated versions of the discrimination box employ milk glass stimulus windows upon which the stimuli are back-projected. Pushing the windows activates microswitches that close the appropriate circuits, recording whether the response has been a correct or incorrect one and arranging for the presentation of the next stimulus.

The Wisconsin General Test Apparatus (Harlow & Bromer, 1938), shown in Fig. 8-3, is closely related to the discrimination box. It was designed for

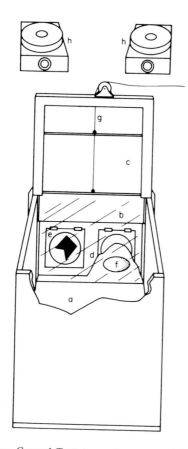

Fig. 8-2. Right: Purdue General Test Apparatus: *a* restraining box; *b* glass screen; *c* opaque screen; *d* stimulus display wall; *e* hinged door with round back-projection screen; *f* food well; *g* strings for raising and lowering glass and opaque screens; *h* slide projectors.

discrimination tests of three-dimensional objects in monkeys. The objects are placed on a tray so as to cover the food wells. The tray is moved toward the animal, who pushes aside the positive stimulus object and retrieves the bait.

Birds present no special problems in their apparatus requirements. The Yerkes-Watson discrimination apparatus has been used with pigeons and chickens. The pecking ability of these two species may be utilized to present the stimuli back-projected on small glass windows that are connected to microswitches. Pecking at the correct window produces a food reward in a food well. This arrangement has been used to measure brightness thresholds in birds.

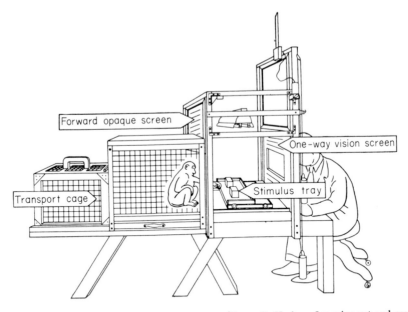

Fig. 8-3. Wisconsin General Test Apparatus. From H. Harlow. Learning set and error factor theory. In S. Koch (Ed.), *Psychology: a study of a science,* Vol. 2. Copyright 1959, New York: McGraw-Hill. Used by permission of McGraw-Hill Book Company.

Katz and Revesz (1908) were first to use edible shapes, the subjects being hens. This technique can be used with a variety of species: birds and fish, as well as quadrupeds. The negative stimulus is made inedible by making it immovable or unpalatable.

Herter's (1929, 1953) training-prong method of studying visual form discrimination in fish has been used by most researchers working with fish. In this method, the stimuli are inscribed on a plaque and lowered into one end of the water tank. Small pieces of bait are placed on the tips of a double prong, which is then held in front of the plaque so that each piece is in the middle of a shape. The bait in front of the negative shape is made inedible. In the few studies of form perception in amphibians and reptiles, variants of this technique have been employed.

The basic technique for use with the octopus was developed by Boycott and Young (Boycott, 1954; Boycott & Young, 1955). If a home made of rocks is built at one end of the tank, the octopus will usually stay in it. The shapes to be discriminated are attached to a clear plastic rod and lowered into the water at the other end of the tank. The octopus is trained to attack the positive shape. It is easier to elicit the attack if the shapes are moved back and forth at the rate of about 3 times per second. A correct response is rewarded with food, incorrect responses are discouraged by means of an electric prod.

With honeybees and other insect species that suck plant nectar, the basic technique is to place a container with sugar water on the positive pattern and a container with plain water or a glass-covered container on the negative pattern and to observe the relative frequency with which the insects alight on the patterns. Since bees also commonly enter vertical surfaces through holes in them, pairs of patterns with small holes drilled through their centers may be presented vertically for discrimination. The bee, after entering the hole in the positive pattern, is fed saccharose in a black box behind the pattern (Wehner, 1967).

C. EXPERIMENTAL PROCEDURE

Learning to discriminate among three different forms involves more than simply learning to approach one form and to avoid another: in addition to learning to classify stimuli, the animal has to learn to use three or more different responses whose connection to stimulus properties is arbitrary. Because of this, only apes and monkeys have been able to learn such discriminations. Since even in these species learning of this type of problem is slow, the multiple-choice discrimination procedure has been used in few studies and the two-choice discrimination procedure has been the preferred one.

There are several possible ways of presenting two stimuli simultaneously. The most commonly used method is to present a single instance of the positive shape and a single instance of the negative shape side by side. In the oddity method, while there is only a single instance of the positive shape, there are several identical negative shapes, and the animal's task is to select the odd shape. The advantage of this arrangement is that animals learn faster and that the reliability of the results increases considerably for the same amount of time spent training the animals. The fact that the rate of learning increases has been interpreted in different ways. One possibility is that, when only two shapes are present, the animal must learn not only that one of them means food, but also which particular one, i.e., the animal must remember the configuration that signifies food. In the oddity problem, there is less emphasis upon memory for form and more upon memory for simple oddity or difference, any difference, between one shape and a background of other shapes. Thus, the task is made to be less of a learning task and more a perceptual one. In addition, it seems that, at least in some species, such as fish (Meesters, 1940), there is an innate preference for the odd shape, which makes the oddity task even easier. Reliability is increased for the simple reason that, when there are only two shapes to choose from and the probability of choosing the correct one by chance on any given trial is .5, the probability of choosing the correct shape on two successive trials is .25. When the number of stimuli to choose from is increased to five, e.g., the probability of choosing the correct one by chance alone on any one trial is .2 and on two successive trials .04.

Another possibility is to present one positive stimulus and several different negative stimuli. This method has not been used, because the analysis of the stimulus properties that the animal is using in discriminating the positive shape from the negative ones is made difficult. The presentation of several identical or different positive stimuli and one negative stimulus has the disadvantage of decreased reliability, and for this reason, this method has not been employed.

In addition to presenting the two stimuli simultaneously, they may be presented successively, one on each trial. Sutherland's (1961a) analysis of the research done concerning the comparative efficiency of the two methods shows that, when the stimulus-response relationships are the same, there is nothing to favor one method over the other. In practice, researchers have mostly used simultaneous discrimination.

The control of discrimination cues other than configurational ones is much more of a problem in animal research than when subjects are humans. While two shapes may obviously be different to a human subject, it does not mean that an animal will know immediately what the difference is. Except for the primitive ability to distinguish figure from ground, one cannot assume that an animal will see the differences between two shapes that have been built into them by man. The animal will respond to that differential aspect of two shapes that is most readily accessible to it, or is familiar from previous experience, or that it is able to perceive by virtue of its sensory equipment. Some of the nonconfigurational cues connected with shapes that an animal may use are differences in brightness between the two shapes and differences in area. If the two shapes are close together or if the area of the background is small, figure-ground relationships may be responded to instead of the figure alone. This particular problem has already been discussed in Chap. 5. Two recent studies have provided specific information on optimum figure-ground ratios and on pattern spacing for the rat. In one (Elias, 1967), it was found that, of the pattern/background area ratios used, the ratio of 1 : 4 (1-sq. in. patterns on 4-sq. in. backgrounds) resulted in fastest learning. Elias concludes that a unique combination of optimum pattern and background areas may be more critical than pattern area, background area, or pattern-background ratio per se. A second study (Elias & Stein, 1968) led to the conclusion that decreased spacing in a pair of patterns improves learning and that this factor is more critical for difficult problems.

In addition to the immediately accessible and utilizable cues, animals respond to cues emanating from the apparatus, especially those that are associated with the experimental manipulation of the stimuli and the rewards. Sounds and sights accompanying these activities may become differentially associated with the stimuli, thus vitiating the experimental results. While auditory and visual cues may be detected and eliminated, kinesthetic, tactile, gustatory, and olfactory cues are often hard to identify. If proper controls are not instituted, however, animals will use such cues and confound the experimental results. One obvious precaution to be taken is the elimination of olfactory cues from the food reward or from the animal's own markings made on the stimuli and the walls of the apparatus. This can be done by allowing the animal to spend some time inside the apparatus before testing begins, by rubbing food over the entire surface where the stimuli are to appear, interposing a transparent screen between the animal and the stimuli while the animal decides which way to go, etc. When the stimuli themselves are edible, applying a bad-tasting substance to the negative stimulus does not automatically ensure that the stimulus will be avoided, since the animal may respond to olfactory cues. Chemical cues from edible targets are a problem in discrimination experiments with fish. It may be overcome by using real-looking but inedible bait over the negative stimulus or by introducing the food chemicals throughout the tank.

The problem of cues emanating from the experimenter is a well-known one. Animals with good daylight vision will pick up slight differences in the experimenter's movements and sounds made by him to improve their chances of obtaining food without necessarily learning to discriminate shapes. The best procedure is to keep the experimenter out of sight, either through the use of screens or automated apparatus.

Position habits and the tendency to alternate are best controlled for through the use of Gellerman's (1933a) sequences for right-left stimulus presentation. These sequences deviate from completely random sequences in that runs of several successive presentations of a stimulus on the same side are avoided. Such runs are bound to occur from time to time if sequences are selected from a table of random numbers. Preexisting preferences for particular shapes can be controlled for in this manner only up to a point. Further control may be achieved by using one shape as the positive stimulus with one-half of the subjects and as the negative shape with the other half.

In some instances, the animal's approach of a shape must be stimulated by the experimenter. While it may take a squirrel or a raccoon a relatively brief experience with the apparatus to learn to push against a door with a stationary shape on it, it is difficult to train an octopus, e.g., to approach a shape unless it is in motion. Good figure-ground contrast is another requisite for an animal to attend to the figure.

After having made an incorrect response, the animal can be prevented from making another response to the same stimulus pair and exposed to the next pair, or it can be allowed to make further responses to the same stimulus pair until the correct response is made. The first method, known as the noncorrection method, is easier to score; the correction method is useful in situations where position habits are likely to develop, such as on a jumping stand. By being forced to repeat a response without reinforcement, the animal is more likely to extinguish that response than when, in the extreme case, by continuing to go to the same side every time, the animal may still be able to obtain reward half the time in the long run. As far as teaching discrimination, there are no definitive data to indicate that one of these methods is better than the other.

As Sutherland (1961a) points out, it is difficult to state any general principles regarding the optimum strength of rewards and punishments in form-discrimination training. Rewards serve not only as reinforcers but also as modifiers of the hunger drive. While there is evidence that increasing the amount of reward may improve learning in the later stages of the experiment, it must be remembered that enough food may be consumed by an animal over the learning trials to reduce the level of its hunger drive and therefore of performance. The presentation of aversive stimulation contingent upon the emission of an incorrect response also affects drive level. Punishment, however, while it improves learning under certain conditions, is a complex phenomenon and its effects vary with the phylogenetic level of the animal, the strength of the aversive stimulus, discrimination difficulty, and other factors.

Poor discrimination learning observed in the earlier shape-discrimination experiments was due to the spatial and temporal dissociation between the stimuli and the reward. There is now no doubt that the closer together in time and space the positive stimulus and the reward are, the faster will the animal learn to make correct discriminations.

Research shows that, when trials are closely spaced, learning is slower than when some time is allowed between trials. The exact spacing depends on the particular species of animal used. In the white rat, the optimum spacing appears to be of the order of 3-4 min., whereas in the octopus, it makes little difference whether the trials are presented every 5 min. or every hour.

Transfer of training has been and still is the preferred method of determining which stimulus properties an animal is using in discriminating between two shapes. For instance, if in the triangle-circle pair the triangle is the positive stimulus and the animal keeps responding to it even when the triangle is turned upside down, the conclusion is that the animal discriminates triangularity as such, i.e., perceives the triangle as a triangle regardless of orientation. Failure to transfer, on the other hand, may be interpreted as the utilization of partial cues pertaining only to a particular orientation of the shape, such as an acute angle at the top or a horizontal line at the bottom of the figure. The transfer method, unfortunately, raises a host of methodological and theoretical problems, many of which are discussed by Sutherland (1961a). To mention just one, it is impossible to decide in the case of positive transfer whether the animal keeps giving a positive response to a rotated or otherwise transformed stimulus because it recognizes it as being the same or because it is simply perceived as the nonnegative stimulus, i.e., the shape-to-be-responded-to, regardless of what its particular configuration is.

Regardless of which particular method is used to answer the question of how animals classify shapes, the answer is bound to be ambiguous if the shapes themselves have no generalizability. The overwhelming majority of shape-discrimination studies with animal subjects have used, with little variation, the standard geometric shapes: the circle, equilateral triangle, square, diamond, rectangle, and the cross. The inadequacy of these shapes as stimulus material has been discussed in Chap. 5. Only a few, more recent studies show a movement away from the use of limited samples of extremely constrained stimuli as well as the abandonment of the transfer of learning paradigm. The combination of more-extensive samples of random shapes, quantified stimulus parameters, and factorial design promise a way out of decades of inconclusiveness, ambiguity, and contradiction in form-perception studies with animal subjects.

D. RESPONSE MEASURES

Some measure based on error scores is the common measure of discriminability between shapes used with animal subjects: number of errors made before reaching criterion performance, number of trials to criterion (which depends on the number of errors made), or the number of errors within blocks of trials. While it is possible to obtain reaction-time measures on animals as well as such other measures of discriminability as habituation (differences in the amount of exploratory activity as a function of novelty), these have either not been used at all or only in a few pilot studies.

2. Form-Discrimination Experiments with Animals

A. CHIMPANZEES AND MONKEYS

Transpositional Parameters. Apes and the higher monkeys have no difficulty in transferring learning to the same shape of a different area or in discriminating between identical shapes differing in area. Thus, Gellerman (1933b), in his well-known comparative study of children and chimpanzees, found transfer of discrimination to the same shapes of larger and smaller sizes. The range of size-reduction ratios within which transfer occurs without decrement is considerable. In Neet's (1933) study, the smallest ratio was 1/20. The absolute size of the shapes, however, is important. Discrimination improves in rhesus monkeys as the size of the shapes is increased from .9 sq. in. to 5.4 sq. in. (Warren, 1953a). Differences in area between two otherwise identical forms are also used by monkeys to discriminate between the positive and negative stimuli (Polidora, 1965, 1966; Polidora & Thompson, 1964, 1965).

Although in the primates different amounts of rotation affect the discriminability of identical shapes differently, neither rotation nor reflection present any special problems. Gellerman's (1933b) chimpanzees learned discriminations between a shape and its up-down reflection as readily as with any other pair of shapes. Forty-five-degree rotation did not upset the cimpanzees' discrimination performance, although the animals did tilt their heads while looking at the figure. Harlow's (1945a, 1945b) studies indicate that, while 180-degree-rotated and right-left-reflected figures are discriminated by rhesus monkeys, learning of the discriminations is made more difficult by these operations than in the case of just two different figures. Riopelle, Rahm, Itoigawa, & Draper (1964), however, rank right-left mirror-image problems as the most readily discriminable by rhesus monkeys, problems with one figure rotated 90 degrees as the least readily discriminable, and up-down mirror-image problems and problems with nonidentical stimuli as being of intermediate difficulty. It also makes a difference to the rhesus monkey whether it is the positive or the negative stimulus that is rotated. Hicks (1967) found that, if one of the two stimuli was rotated from trial to trial (90 degrees right or left, and 180 degrees), discrimination was best when only the negative stimulus was rotated, in contrast with the situations where the positive stimulus or both stimuli were rotated or even when both stimuli were kept in their original positions. Hicks explains this curious finding not in perceptual but learning terms, by referring to excitation as the basic feature of learning and the relative contrasts in excitation produced by variability in one of the stimulus or a lack of it.

Informational Parameters. The relationship between stimulus complexity and discrimination has been investigated in very few studies and by the same workers (Polidora, 1965, 1966; Polidora & Thompson, 1964, 1965). Although these studies suffer from a number of methodological problems (cf. Zusne, 1967), they definitely show that discrimination improves with increasing difference in complexity between the positive and negative stimuli. When random forms are used, difference in complexity is the most readily utilized discriminative clue in all animal species with which complexity has been used as an independent variable.

Configurational Parameters. The early studies of the use of configurational clues in discrimination by monkeys, as well as some that are more recent, suffer from an almost complete lack of stimulus generalizability (e.g., Gellerman, 1933b, 1933c; Kluever, 1933; Neet, 1933). These studies provide more information on concept formation than on form discrimination. Because of the type of stimuli used (circles, squares, triangles), it is often not clear what clues the animals actually used in discriminating among them. In the light of the few more-recent experiments with monkeys in which more generalizable patterns have been used, there is no doubt that monkeys can discriminate most any type of form. In Polidora's (e.g., Polidora, 1966) studies with rhesus monkeys using random patterns of lighted square cells in a 4 X 4 matrix, the "unique-elements" measure (cf. Chap. 5) determined the discriminant function, yielding the only significant correlation with response.

Although Warren (1953b) did not measure the parameters of the single forms save that of area, his study is interesting in that, in it, two populations of shapes were compared with regard to discriminability. In pair-comparing five regular geometric forms and five irregular curvilinear forms, rhesus monkeys made fewer errors when a pair consisted of a regular and an irregular shape than when two regular or two irregular shapes were paired. Three of the regular shapes had curves in them, and linearity differences therefore account for only a portion of the correct discriminations. Since complexity in the two stimulus samples was not equated, additional discriminations must have been made in terms of this parameter. The overall results, however, do indicate discrimination between the two samples on the basis of averaged stimulus dimensions.

Indirect evidence of the utilization of configurational clues comes from a study by Butter (1966) in which rhesus monkeys were able to find figures that were either hidden in an embedding context or else masked by lines that were not quite as inclusive of the masked figure. Butter's data indicate that, unlike human subjects, monkeys find both embedded and masked figures with equal ease. A technique to study the perception of embedded figures by monkeys has been described by Rosenblum, Witkin, Kaufman, & Brosgole (1965).

Rhesus, mangabey, and cebus monkeys show the horizontal-vertical illusion, its magnitude being approximately the same as in humans (Dominguez, 1954). This and only a few other studies have used the lower monkeys in form-perception tests. Woodburne (1965) demonstrated discrimination between members of pairs of slightly disparate geometric figures in the squirrel monkey. The import of a study by Nash and Michels (1966) is that, while squirrel monkeys discriminate random shapes with regard to complexity, sampling redundancy, and their relative spatial positions in two-choice discrimination tasks with varying numbers of the negative stimulus, the complexity of the interactions among these variables necessitates not only an analysis of the stimulus dimensions of the individual shapes, but also of the spatial dimensions and interactions in a plurality of shapes as they normally occur in the monkey's visual world.

B. DOGS

There is practically no information available on form discrimination in dogs. The few existing studies of dogs date back to about 1930, and their results are contradictory: while Williams (1926) found little ability to discriminate form (circles and squares, vertical and horizontal stripes) in the dog, Karn (1931; Karn & Munn, 1932) found that it possesses good pattern vision. Karn's subjects, for instance, learned to discriminate vertical from horizontal stripes and upright from inverted triangles (the former task was easier), and transferred learned discriminations to smaller-size figures.

C. CATS

K. U. Smith has provided most of the studies of form discrimination in the intact cat (Smith, 1933, 1934a, 1934b, 1934c, 1936). These studies, as well as those of McAllister and Berman (1931) and Sutherland (1963), show that the cat's ability to discriminate geometric forms is probably as good as that of the monkey's. It is not disturbed by changes in figure size, distortion of contours, rotation, and other transformations that call for concept formation.

D. SQUIRRELS

The squirrel as a subject in form-discrimination studies appears only in the 1960s. With the exception of a couple of papers (e.g., Dodwell, & Bessant, 1961), all studies on the squirrel have been done at Purdue University. Michels, Pittman, Hitchcock, & Brown (1962), using 4-, 5-, 6-, and 7-sided random shapes, demonstrated decreasing discrimination difficulty with increasing number of sides in the fox and gray squirrels, except for seven-sided figures, which were slightly more difficult than six-sided ones. When the number of sides were equal in the two figures, areal asymmetry and axial rotation (cf. Chap. 5) were used by the squirrels as discrimination clues. Hitchcock, Michels, & Brown (1963) compared form discrimination between two species of squirrels (fox and gray) and raccoons using random shapes and three measured form dimensions in a factorial design. The dimensions were number of sides (4, 5, 6, and 7), rotation, and areal asymmetry. In two-choice oddity problems, the performance of all animals remained at a chance level if there were no differences in these dimensions. In terms of increasing proficiency of performance, classes of problems containing clue differences could be ordered in this way: asymmetry; sidedness and asymmetry; sidedness, rotation, and asymmetry; rotation; rotation and asymmetry; and sidedness and rotation. While areal asymmetry did not have a statistically significant overall effect upon discrimination, it interacted with the other two clues to suppress their effect. This suppression was less pronounced in the case of the raccoon. While no difference was found between squirrels and raccoons in measures of overall performance, there were differences in the way the two species utilized available discriminative clues. When differences in areal asymmetry were present, squirrels, unlike raccoons, used this clue to the exclusion of all others.

E. RACOONS

After Munn (1930) had decided that raccoons could not discriminate forms unless they also differed in brightness, and Fields (1936b) had shown that raccoons both discriminated geometric forms and transferred learned discriminations to forms of other sizes as well as to rotated forms, no published studies appeared until the late 1950s and early 1960s. The only directly relevant study is that of Hitchcock *et al.* (1963), in which the performances of squirrels and raccoons in a form-discrimination task were compared. This study, described in the preceding section, establishes good form discrimination in the raccoon and the differential utilization of transpositional, informational, and configurational clues as a function of task conditions.

F. RATS

The white rat is not a very desirable subject in a number of respects: his form vision is not too good, he suffers from visual defects, he depends on other senses more than on vision, shows innate visual preferences, and does not learn too well. Still, the largest amount of work on visual form discrimination has been done using the laboratory rat as subject: he is the cheapest and most readily available animal subject that is easily and cheaply kept healthy in a laboratory.

Fields, Lashley, and Munn were the chief contributors to the literature on the rat in the 1930s. Munn reviewed the earlier studies on form perception in the rat in his 1950 handbook. Lately, the use of the rat as subject in visual form-discrimination studies has decreased, however, with a corresponding increase in the use of other species of animals.

Transpositional Parameters. All animals showing form discrimination also show transfer of learning to identical forms of larger or smaller size. By itself, such transfer is an equivocal test of the animal's ability to discriminate size: transfer to a different size may be interpreted either as the manifestation of size constancy or as the result of the animal's inability to discriminate size differences.

The absolute size of a form has been found to affect transfer: rats transfer discrimination learning more easily to larger than to smaller shapes (Dodwell, 1957; Fields, 1931b, 1932b, 1935, 1936a). Although this finding could be interpreted as a failure of the experimenters to provide the rat with large enough forms for optimum discrimination, the same trend has been observed in other species of animals, so that it cannot be dismissed simply as an experimental artifact.

Differences in size between two otherwise identical forms are discriminated by the rat. Not enough experimentation has been done, however, to answer questions about the size of the difference thresholds at various points within the range of sizes that the rat can discriminate.

While the rat learns to discriminate between a vertical and a horizontal rectangle or striation quite readily (e.g., Bitterman, Calvin, & Elam, 1953; Lashley, 1938; Sutherland, 1961b), he does so much less readily when the contours, while still forming a 90-degree angle between them, are each inclined 45 degrees to the horizontal (Lashley, 1938), a finding that is repeated in the octopus.

There seems to be little doubt that, to the rat, the bottom part of a shape is more important than its top (cf. Fields, 1929; Munn, 1950; Sutherland, 1961b). It is for this reason that, while the rat will learn to discriminate between an upright and an inverted triangle readily enough, discrimination between an upright triangle and any other shape that has a horizontal bottom line or even a curved one, like the circle, will be much more difficult. If the shape is a square with one side missing, it makes a difference whether the shape is reflected about its horizontal or vertical axes. Since the bottoms of the figures ⊏ and ⊐ are identical, they are more difficult to discriminate to the rat than the figures ⊓ and ⊔ (Lashley, 1938). Some reflections, such as of an S along its vertical axis, the rat fails to discriminate between (Lashley, 1938), whereas others, such as an F and its reflection about its vertical axis, present no special problem (Kirk, 1936). Sutherland's theory, which attempts to account for these differences, was presented in Chap. 3.

Configurational Parameters. The informational parameter of complexity as a factor in shape discrimination by rats has not been studied, although it has obviously played an uncontrolled role in many form-discrimination studies where "form" has been the intended independent variable. There are likewise no existing studies of the effects of single configurational parameters on form discrimination in the rat. In the older studies by Fields (1928, 1931a, 1932a, 1932b), Lashley (e.g., 1938), and Munn (1929, 1931a), variation in "form" is equivalent to the variation of several configurational parameters at the same time and in an uncontrolled fashion. In addition, the variety of forms has been limited to the equilateral triangle, the circle, square, cross, the H figure, and an assortment of other, haphazardly selected, contrained figures. As a result of these inadequacies of stimulus sampling, these experiments are not very informative. They have led to an undue amount of discussion and controversy among the investigators without shedding much light on what kinds of general stimulus properties the rat uses in discriminating forms. The only firm conclusions that can be drawn from the experiments of Fields, Lashley, and Munn are that (a) the rat pays more attention to the bottom part of stimulus figures than to their upper portions, hence finds it more difficult, e.g., to discriminate between figures which have horizontal lines at the bottom (e.g., the triangle and the square) and discriminates more easily between two figures whose bottom portions differ markedly (e.g., a triangle on its apex and a square); and (b) that conclusions regarding the ability of the rat to discriminate form details may range from very pessimistic ones (such as Munn's early conclusions) to quite optimistic ones, depending on whether the investigator has hit upon the right method to teach the rat a discrimination (cf. Dodwell, 1957).

There would be probably little exaggeration in saying that the combination of the jumping stand, geometric figures, and transfer of learning tests has done little to provide information about what the rat sees, how he classifies forms, or how fine his discriminations are. In the light of the results obtained in recent years with other animals, discrimination boxes, random shapes, and multivariate designs, it seems that, had the methodology been changed earlier, the large amount of effort expended in studying form discrimination in the rat would have produced a more commensurate yield of valid information.

G. OTHER MAMMALS

The Indian elephant (Rensch & Altevogt, 1953, 1955) discriminates between a cross and a square and transfers this discrimination to a rotated cross and a new shape. All other mammalian species that have been used in form-perception experiments have rated one study or so each. For this reason, the characteristics of form discrimination in the weasel (Herter, 1940), opossum (James, 1960), ferret (Pollard, Beale, Lysons, & Preston, 1967), sheep (Seitz, 1951), sea lion (Schusterman & Thomas, 1966), and the bottle-nose dolphin (Kellog & Rice, 1964) are little known, except that all of them show discrimination of form in terms of the available informational, configurational, or transpositional clues.

H. BIRDS

Except for the single studies of the crow (Coburn, 1914) and the duck (Pastore, 1958), the study of form discrimination in birds has been confined to only two species, the chicken and the pigeon. Some of the ethological investigations of the nature of various visual releasers, while not concerned with form-discrimination directly, provide some information on it. For instance, Tinbergen and Kuenen (1939) have shown that young thrushes must be discriminating size differences and responding to size ratios in flat, schematized cardboard models of an adult thrush. Although there is doubt as to whether the main hypothesis concerning the existence of perceptual templates of significant visual stimuli in young turkeys was adequately tested in an experiment by Tinbergen (1948), the existence of differential responses to a moving silhouette as a function of the direction of movement cannot be doubted. The silhouette was one that looked like a flying goose if moved in one direction or like a hawk if moved in the opposite direction. If nothing else, young turkeys may be credited with the ability to discriminate between a shape and its mirror image about a vertical axis.

The pigeon's ability to discriminate forms appears to be quite good. The pigeon has no difficulty in discriminating rectangles that are either in the vertical-horizontal, vertical-oblique, horizontal-oblique, or oblique-oblique positions with respect to each other (Zeigler & Schmerler, 1965), and transfers triangle-square discrimination to the same figures of different sizes, from solid to outline figures, and to figures with one side missing (Towe, 1954). Earlier, Warden and Baar (1929) had demonstrated the Mueller-Lyer illusion in the ring dove.

Some of the earliest form-discrimination experiments were performed with chickens. Katz and Revesz (1908) and Bingham (1913, 1922) trained chickens to discriminate between a triangle and a circle. Bingham found, however, that rotating the triangle or changing the size of the figures resulted in loss of discrimination. Munn (1931b) showed that transfer to other shapes occurred only when the bottom parts of the figures remained the same. Instances of transfer found by Menkhaus (1957) do not support the conclusion that chickens discriminate entirely in terms of the bottom part of a figure. Menkhaus also found that crosses were not treated as two bars crossing, since any shape consisting of two bars, such as an *L,* was treated the same by the chickens. Other findings, such as the loss of discrimination when the figure-ground brightness contrast is reversed, suggest that the goodness of form discrimination in chickens is similar to that of rats. At the same time, methodological problems in all of the chicken experiments make one wary of drawing any firm conclusions at all. In Menkhause's experiment, for instance, as in some of Lashley's rat experiments, the figure-ground ratio was so close to unity that the loss of ability to discriminate upon reversing the figure-ground brightness contrast is not surprising.

Innate form preferences have been demonstrated in chickens. These must be considered in form-discrimination experiments, especially if the forms to be presented for discrimination are small and have shapes resembling those of grains. Thus, Fantz (1957) demonstrated pecking preference for round over angular objects and the importance of both two-dimensional and three-dimensional clues in newborn chicks. Engelmann (1940a, 1940b, 1941) had earlier demonstrated size discrimination and preference for wheat grains over corn and peas, both with three-dimensional stimuli and their two-dimensional representations. Like the pigeon, the chicken is also susceptible to geometric illusions, such as the horizontal-vertical illusion, illusion of interrupted extent, the Mueller-Lyer illusion, and the illusion of the breadth of rectangles (Winslow, 1933).

I. AMPHIBIANS AND REPTILES

Frogs, toads, lizards, turtles, and tortoises have merited very few studies of their ability to perceive form, and no experiments have been performed with snakes as subjects. Tortoises and turtles appear to possess good color vision and the ability to discriminate differences in brightness and form. They learn to discriminate among circles, triangles, and squares in various combinations, and they respond to differences in rotation in these figures (Casteel, 1911; Kuroda, 1933). Frogs and toads learn to discriminate circles from triangles or squares, and between horizontally and vertically oriented rectangles (Parriss, 1963; Pache, 1932), but their ability to discriminate form does not appear to be as good as in the turtle. The only extant report on form discrimination in a lizard

(Ehrenhardt, 1937) speaks of strong innate responses to form which are difficult to modify through learning: *Lacerta agilis* appears to prefer compact to jagged forms, a preference which is not modified even when the preferred member in a stimulus pair is associated with the taste of quinine or with electric shock.

J. FISH

Of the 40,000 or so species of fish, only about 15 have been tested for form discrimination. Since most of them have rated only a single study and all of these studies suffer from the usual methodological problems, our knowledge of form perception in fish is very incomplete.

Transpositional Parameters. Schulte's (1957) experiments showed transfer to identical shapes of different sizes in the carp. Herter (1929) demonstrated ready discrimination learning between horizontal and vertical striations in the angel fish. Herter's gudgeons learned to discriminate between two identical triangles, one of which was rotated 180 degrees, reflected, or both, and transferred training to the discrimination between a square and a diamond, the apex-down triangle and the diamond being the positive shapes. Perch trained to discriminate between the letters *R* and *L* transferred training to situations where one of these letters was paired with its mirror image, 180-degree rotation, or inversion. Mackintosh and Sutherland (1963) showed discrimination between an upright and a horizontal rectangles in the goldfish, as well as discrimination between two rectangles, each slanted 45 degrees in the opposite directions. The latter discrimination, however, took more trials to learn. Following horizontal-vertical discrimination training, goldfish transferred training to shapes rotated as much as 35 degrees. With some shapes, however, 45-degree rotation represents an entirely new problem to some fish. For instance, carps show no transfer from a diamond-upright-rectangle discrimination to a square-horizontal-rectangle discrimination (Schulte, 1957). Different rotations of the triangle and of the square may be also treated as new problems, although training is transferred to a cross rotated 45 degrees (Meesters, 1940).

Sutherland (1961a) presents evidence that rats, octopuses, and fish discriminate better between pairs of shapes differing in their horizontal projections than when they differ in their vertical projections. Hager's (1938) finding that minnows did better discriminating a pair of striations differing in the number of lines if the striations were vertical than when they were horizontal constitutes an exception. There is no ready explanation for this finding or, for that matter, for the easier discrimination of shapes differing in their horizontal projections.

Meesters (1940) found discrimination between a triangle and a square in minnows and sticklebacks. Rotating both the positive and negative figures 10 or 20 degrees resulted in good transfer; it broke down with 30-degree rotations, while 45-degree rotation produced negative transfer, indicating the utilization of parts of the two shapes (a point and a horizontal line at the top) as clues.

Transitive Parameters. Herter (1949, 1950) demonstrated triangle-square discrimination in several species of fish, and square-circle discrimination in the pike. The latter discrimination was also established in three species of tropical fish by Hemmings (1965), but only after pretraining the fish on a circle-rectangle discrimination problem. The results of experiments in the discrimination of diamonds and crosses (Meesters, 1940) and circles and crosses (Herter, 1949, 1950) have been confounded by such factors as labile figure-ground configurations, high within-subject variability, and the usual failure to separate the effects of the different types of form parameters. Experiments with more complex shapes, such as pairs of letters (Fisher, 1940; Herter, 1929), also indicate that fish tend to discriminate partial, salient features, such as angles of a certain size, horizontal and vertical bars, etc. Unlike rats, fish learn to utilize clues from both top and bottom portions of a shape equally well (Schulte, 1957). Innate preferences have been studied only in the minnow (*Phoxinus laevis*), in which species Zunini (1937) found a preference for the star over both the circle and the square. There is also only a single study of the size of difference thresholds for the width of stripes and the diameter of circles in the goldfish (Rowley, 1934).

K. OCTOPUS

Besides the few species of insects, form discrimination has been studied in only one other invertebrate, the octopus (*Octopus vulgaris* Lamarck). It is nevertheless one of the most intensively studied animal species. This is due largely to the efforts of N. S. Sutherland and his co-workers at the University of Oxford.

Within limits, the octopus transfers discrimination training to smaller and larger shapes (Parriss & Young, 1962; Sutherland, 1957, 1960b), and can discriminate between identical shapes differing in area only (Boycott & Young, 1956). Shape discrimination in the octopus is very much orientation-bound. A consistent finding of Sutherland's (e.g., 1957, 1958a, 1960b) has been that, of all the many different discriminations that the octopus has been given, the discrimination between a vertical and a horizontal rectangle is the easiest, while it is almost impossible when the same rectangles are inclined 45 degrees to the horizontal and have a 90-degree angle between them. Discriminations between a vertical or horizontal rectangle and an oblique one are intermediate in difficulty. Sutherland's theory that the octopus discriminates between shapes by comparing their horizontal and vertical extents (cf. Chap. 3) was based on this and similar kinds of empirical evidence, e.g., that the octopus does not transfer training from a square to a diamond (Sutherland, 1959). Wells (1960) has shown that the elongated pupil of the octopus must be kept oriented invariantly with respect to the main dimensions of space. When this orientation is interfered with through the removal of the statocysts and the octopus no longer maintains its head and eyes in their proper orientation, perception of the orientation of shapes is affected.

Like the rat and the monkeys, the octopus also finds it easier to discriminate between a shape and its reflection about a horizontal axis than when reflection is made about a vertical axis. However, in the octopus, this relationship may be reversed if the pair $\wedge\vee$ is used instead of $\vee>$. Whereas the latter pair is readily discriminated, the former is not (Sutherland, 1960a). Sutherland explains this difference by pointing out the differences between the horizontal and vertical projections of the shapes in these two pairs. Extensive experiments (e.g., Sutherland, 1960b) show that the octopus does not discriminate in terms of the relative orientations of the contours in a pair of shapes.

Discrimination difficulty in the triangle-circle pair or the triangle-square pair is similar to that found with the square and the circle. The diamond-triangle pair, however, is more difficult for the octopus to discriminate, with the triangle in either the upright or inverted position (Sutherland, 1958b, 1959). Sutherland's experiments with closed and open shapes (Sutherland, 1960c) suggest to him that the octopus might also be using something like the P^2/A ratio as a clue in discrimination. Since, as discussed in Chaps. 3 and 5, this measure is related to the second moment of area of the one-dimensional projections of a shape, this conclusion is not surprising if the octopus is indeed guided by the horizontal and vertical projections of a shape.

Some of the peculiarities of form vision in the octopus are without doubt due to the presence either of receptive fields that respond to certain basic stimulus characteristics or some other pretuned neural mechanism. The above-mentioned radical difference between rectangles that are in alignment with the vertical and horizontal axes of space and those that are not is one item of indirect evidence. Others include the equivalence (in terms of transfer of discrimination) of large squares and horizontal rectangles and of small squares and vertical rectangles (Mackintosh, Mackintosh, & Sutherland, 1963), easier discrimination between large vertical and horizontal rectangles than between small ones and between duplicated patterns of small vertical and horizontal rectangles than between single small rectangles (Sutherland et al., 1963), and the preference for shapes moving in the direction of their long axes and their points to shapes moving across their long axes and across the direction of their points (Sutherland & Muntz, 1959).

L. INSECTS

The learning ability of insects is below that of the species discussed so far, while their innately determined preferences for specific forms are stronger. The training problems presented by insects have therefore restricted the investigation of their form vision to little more than their innate responses. The second major difference between the vertebrates and molluscs on the one hand and the insects on the other is the difference between the single-lens eye and the compound eye. Because the integrating function of a visual cortex is absent, the insect, instead of an uninterrupted visual field, probably sees a mosaic composed of as many elements as there are ommatidia.

The response of insects to the simpler aspects of visual stimulation, such as movement, is extremely good. There is also response to some aspects of form besides its color, brightness contrast, or movement. Even the larvae of a moth respond differently to different forms (Hundertmark, 1937). Flies (Buddenbrock, 1935) prefer to walk over that wall of a passage that has stripes painted on it as compared with a wall of homogeneous color, and prefer greater contrast between stripes (black-white over gray-white).

The single most investigated insect species has been the honeybee. Hertz (e.g., 1929) placed a sugar dish on top of one of two shapes and observed whether the bee returned to the rewarded figure. While the bee could not discriminate between a circle, square, triangle, or rectangle paired in any combination, it could discriminate between any member of this set of forms and the cross, an outline diamond, a pattern of four bars, and a Y shape. It was not able to discriminate between members of this second set of shapes. This and other experiments with the bee (e.g., Hertz, 1934) led Hertz to conclude that not only can the bee discriminate the more jagged figures from the more compact ones, but that it also prefers the former to the latter. This preference for forms that have a larger perimeter/area ratio has also been observed by Zerrahn (1933) and Autrum (1954) in the bee and by Ilse (1932) in two species of butterflies. Autrum, however, adds the observation that both the length of the contour and fragmentation of the pattern affect the bee's preference. Even if a pattern consisting of several adjacent but unconnected circles has a shorter total length of the contour, it will still be preferred by the bee over a pattern of concentric circles having a longer total contour.

Data obtained by Jander and Voss (1963) on the ant (*Formica rufa*) are somewhat different. They show, e.g., an innate preference for the less articulated of two figures. For instance, of two circles, it will prefer the one with no internal contours over one with pie-wedge contours inside it; it prefers the circle over a striation, and of two striations, it prefers the one that has fewer lines. The ant also shows a strong preference for vertical over horizontal striations. Attempts to reverse this preference proved unsuccessful, whereas its preference for the less articulated figures could be reversed. On the basis of additional experiments with the fly *Eristalis tenax* and the beetle *Stenus bipunctatus*, Jander and Voss conclude that the articulated-unarticulated and the vertical-horizontal variables are independent of each other, and that the vertical-horizontal preference constitutes an ecological adaptation whose direction is a function of species characteristics. Thus, while the *tenax*, like the ant, shows a strong preference for vertical striations, it completely ignores squares when these are paired with vertical striations. The *bipunctatus*, on the other hand, shows considerable preference for horizontal over vertical stripes.

More recent findings show higher levels of organization in the visual system of arthropods. Like the single eye of the octopus, the compound eyes of crabs (Waterman, Wiersma, & Bush, 1964), crayfish (e.g., Wiersma & Yamaguchi, 1966), and locusts (Horridge, Scholes, Shaw, & Tunstall, 1965) show the presence of receptive fields that respond selectively to the directionality of movement. Although direct evidence of the existence of such receptive fields in the eyes of the bee is lacking, the excellent ability of the bee to discriminate pairs of lines, patterns of parallel lines, and crosses differing in orientation is probably due to the existence of such receptive fields. Wehner and Lindauer (1966) report that the bee can discriminate between two single lines or sets of parallel lines inclined 10 degrees to each other, and differences in inclination as small as 4 degrees if the two figures are crosses. Wehner (1967) finds that, when the patterns are presented in the vertical plane, the bee measures angles with regard to the bounds of the visual field, but not when they are lying horizontally. The bee does not discriminate as accurately between lines in the horizontal plane as it does between lines in the vertical plane. There appears, however, to be no innate preference in the bee for horizontal or vertical stripes, whether they are located in the horizontal or the vertical plane.

REFERENCES

Autrum, H. Formensehen im menschlichen und tierischen Auge. *Umschau,* 1954, No. 1, 4-6.

Bingham, H. C. Size and form perception in *Gallus domesticus. J. Anim. Behav.,* 1913, **3,** 65-113.

Bingham, H. C. Visual perception in the chick. *Behav. Psychol. Monogr.,* 1922, **4.**

Bitterman, M. E., Calvin, A. D., & Elam, C. B. Perceptual differentiation in the course of non-differential reinforcement. *J. comp. physiol. Psychol.,* 1953, **46,** 393-397.

Boycott, B. B. Learning in *Octopus vulgaris* and other Cephalopods. *Pubbl. Sta. Zool. Napoli,* 1954, **25,** 67-93.

Boycott, B. B., & Young, J. Z. A memory system in *Octopus vulgaris* Lamarck. *Proc. Zool. Soc. London,* 1955, **143,** 449-480.

Boycott, B. B., & Young, J. Z. Reactions to shape in *Octopus vulgaris* Lamarck. *Proc. Roy. Soc. London,* 1956, **143,** 491-547.

Buddenbrock, W. v. Eine neue Methode zur Erforschung des Formensehens der Insekten. *Naturwissenschaften,* 1935, **23,** 98-100.

Butter, C. M. Detection of hidden figures by rhesus monkeys. *Percept. mot. Skills,* 1966, **23,** 979-986.

Casteel, D. B. The discriminative ability of the painted turtle. *J. Anim. Behav.,* 1911, **1,** 1-28.

Coburn, C. A. The behavior of the crow. *J. Anim. Behav.,* 1914, **4**, 185-201.

Dodwell, P. C. Shape recognition in rats. *Brit. J. Psychol.,* 1957, **48**, 221-229.

Dodwell, P. C., & Bessant, D. E. The squirrel as an experimental animal: Some tests of visual capacity. *Can. J. Psychol.,* 1961, **15**, 226-236.

Dominguez, K. E. A study of visual illusions in the monkey. *J. genet. Psychol.,* 1954, **85**, 105-127.

Ehrenhardt, H. Formensehen und Sehschaerfebestimmungen bei Eidechsen. *Z. vergl. Physiol.,* 1937, **24**, 258-304.

Elias, M. F. Relation of stimulus size to pattern discrimination training for the hooded rat. *Percept. mot. Skills,* 1967, **25**, 613-620.

Elias, M. F., & Stein, A. I. Relation of pattern spacing to pattern discrimination in the hooded rat. *Percept. mot. Skills,* 1968, **26**, 447-454.

Engelmann, C. Versuche ueber den Geschmackssinn des Huhnes. IV. Der Einfluss von Korngroesse und Koernerformen auf die Beliebtheit einiger Getreidearten bei Zwerghuehnern. *Z. Tierpsychol.,* 1940, **4**, 204-218. (a)

Engelmann, C. Versuche ueber den Geschmackssinn des Huhnes. V. Die Beliebtheit einzelner Koernerformen bei nur optischer Darbietung. *Z. Tierpsychol.,* 1940, **40**, 283-347. (b)

Engelmann, C. Versuche ueber den Geschmackssinn des Huhnes. VI. Ueber angeborenen Formvorlieben bei Huehnern. *Z. Tierpsychol.,* 1941, **5**, 42-59.

Fantz, R. L. Form preferences in newly hatched chicks. *J. comp. physiol. Psychol.,* 1957, **50**, 422-430.

Fields, P. E. Form discrimination in the white rat. *J. comp. physiol. Psychol.,* 1928, **8**, 143-158.

Fields, P. E. The white rat's use of visual stimuli in the discrimination of geometric figures. *J. comp. physiol. Psychol.,* 1929, **8**, 107-122.

Fields, P. E. Contributions to visual figure discrimination in the white rat. Part I. *J. comp. physiol. Psychol.,* 1931, **11**, 327-348. (a)

Fields, P. E. Contributions to visual figure discrimination in the white rat. Part II. *J. comp. physiol. Psychol.,* 1931, **11**, 349-366. (b)

Fields, P. E. Concerning the discrimination of geometrical figures by white rats. *J. comp. physiol. Psychol.,* 1932, **14**, 63-77. (a)

Fields, P. E. Studies in concept formation: I. The development of the concept of triangularity by the white rat. *Comp. Psychol. Monogr.,* 1932, **9**, 1-70. (b)

Fields, P. E. Studies in Concept formation: II. A new multiple stimulus jumping apparatus for visual figure discrimination. *J. comp. physiol. Psychol.,* 1935, **20**, 183-203.

Fields, P. E. Studies in concept formation: III. A note on the retention of visual figure discrimination. *J. comp. physiol. Psychol.,* 1936, **21**, 131-136. (a)

Fields, P. E. Studies in concept formation: IV. A comparison of white rats with raccoons with respect to their visual discrimination of geometric figures. *J. comp. physiol. Psychol.,* 1936, **21**, 341-355. (b)

Fisher, P. Untersuchungen ueber das Formsehen der Elritze. *Z. Tierpsychol.,* 1940, **4**, 797-876.

Gellerman, L. W. Chance orders of alternating stimuli in visual discrimination experiments. *J. genet. Psychol.,* 1933, **42**, 206-208. (a)

Gellerman, L. W. Form discrimination in chimpanzees and two-year-old children: I. Form (triangularity) per se. *J. genet. Psychol.,* 1933, **42**, 2-27. (b)

Gellerman, L. W. Form discrimination in chimpanzees and two-year-old children: II. Form versus background. *J. genet. Psychol.,* 1933, **42**, 28-50. (c)

Hager, H. J. Untersuchungen ueber das optische Differenzierungsvermoegen der Fische. *Z. vergl. Physiol.,* 1938, **26**, 282-302.

Harlow, H. F. Studies in discrimination learning by monkeys: III. *J. gen. Psychol.*, 1945, **32**, 213-227. (a)

Harlow, H. F. Studies in discrimination learning by monkeys: VI. *J. gen. Psychol.*, 1945, **33**, 225-235. (b)

Harlow, H. F., & Bromer, J. A. A test apparatus for monkeys. *Psychol. Rev.*, 1938, **22**, 434-436.

Hemmings, G. The effect of pretraining in the circle/square discrimination situation. *Anim. Behav.*, 1965, **13**, 212-216.

Herter, K. Dressurversuche an Fischen. *Z. vergl. Physiol.*, 1929, **10**, 688-711.

Herter, K. Psychologische Untersuchungen an einem Mauswiesel (*Mustela nivalis*). *Z. Tierpsychol.*, 1940, **3**, 249-263.

Herter, K. Zur Psychologie und Sinnesphysiologie der Zwergwelse (*Ameiurus nebulosus*). *Biol. Zbl.*, 1949, **68**, 77-95.

Herter, K. Vom Lernvermoegen der Fische. In *Moderne Biologie, Festschrift f. H. Nachtsheim*, 1950. Pp. 163-179.

Herter, K. *Die Fischdressur und ihre sinnesphysiologischen Grundlagen.* Berlin: Akademie-Verlag, 1953.

Hertz, M. Die Organisation des optischen Feldes bei der Biene. *Z. vergl. Physiol.*, 1929, **8**, 693-748.

Hertz, M. Zur Physiologie des Formen- und Bewegungssehens. III. Figurale Unterscheidung und reziproke Dressuren bei der Biene. *Z. vergl. Physiol.*, 1934, **21**, 604-615.

Hicks, L. H. Effects of stimulus rotation on discrimination learning by monkeys. *Psychon. Sci.*, 1967, **99**, 57-58.

Hitchcock, Jr., L., Michels, K. M., & Brown, D. R. Discrimination learning: squirrels vs raccoons. *Percept. mot. Skills,* 1963, **16**, 405-414.

Horridge, G. A., Scholes, J. H., Shaw, S., & Tunstall, J. Extracellular recordings from single neurones in the optical lobe and brain of the locust. In *The physiology of the insect central nervous system: Twelfth International Congress of Entomology,* London, July, 1964. New York: Academic Press, 1965. Pp. 165-202.

Hundertmark, A. Das Formenunterscheidungsvermoegen der Eiraupen der Nonne (*Lymantria monacha* L.). *Z. vergl. Physiol.*, 1937, **24**, 563-582.

Ilse, D. Zur "Formwahrnehmung" der Tagfalter. I. Spontane Bevorzugung von Formmerkmalen durch Vanessen. *Z. vergl. Physiol.*, 1932, **17**, 537-556.

James, W. T. A study of visual discrimination in the opossum. *J. genet. Psychol.*, 1960, **97**, 127-130.

Jander, R., & Voss, C. Die Bedeutung von Streifenmustern fuer das Formensehen der roten Waldameise (*Formica rufa*). *Z. Tierpsychol.*, 1963, **20**, 1-9.

Karn, H. W. Visual pattern discrimination in dogs. *Univ. Pittsburgh Bull.*, 1931, **7**, 391-392.

Karn, H. W., & Munn, N. L. Visual pattern discrimination in the dog. *J. genet. Psychol.*, 1932, **40**, 363-374.

Katz, D., & Revesz, G. Experimentell-psychologische Untersuchung mit Huehnern. *Z. Psychol.*, 1908, **50**, 59-116.

Kellog, W. N., & Rice, C. E. Visual problem-solving in a bottlenose dolphin. *Science,* 1964, **143**, 1052-1055.

Kirk, S. A. Extra-striate functions in the discrimination of complex visual patterns. *J. comp. Psychol.*, 1936, **21**, 145-159.

Kluever, H. *Behavior mechanisms in monkeys.* Chicago, Illinois: Univ. of Chicago Press, 1933.

Kuroda, R. Studies on visual discrimination in the tortoise *Clemmys japonica. Acta Psychol., Keijo,* 1933, **2**, 31-59.

Lashley, K. S. The mechanism of vision: I. A method for rapid analysis of pattern vision in the rat. *J. genet. Psychol.,* 1930, 37, 453-460.

Lashley, K. S. The mechanism of vision: XV. Preliminary studies of the rat's capacity for detail vision. *J. gen. Psychol.,* 1938, 18, 123-193.

Mackintosh, J., & Sutherland, N. S. Visual discrimination by the goldfish: The orientation of rectangles. *Anim. Behav.,* 1963, 11, 135-141.

Mackintosh, N. J., Mackintosh, J., & Sutherland, N. S. The relative importance of horizontal and vertical extents in shape discrimination by octopus. *Anim. Behav.,* 1963, 11, 355-358.

McAllister, W. G., & Berman, H. D. Visual form discrimination in the domestic cat. *J. comp. Psychol.,* 1931, 12, 207-242.

Meesters, A. Ueber die Organisation des Gesichtsfeldes der Fische. *Z. Tierpsychol.,* 1940, 4, 84-149.

Menkhaus, I. Versuche ueber einaeugiges Lernen und Transponieren beim Haushuhn. *Z. Tierpsychol.,* 1957, 14, 210-230.

Michels, K. M., Pittman, G. G., Hitchcock, Jr., L., & Brown, D. R. Visual discrimination: tree squirrels and quantified stimulus dimensions. *Percept. mot. Skills,* 1962, 15, 443-450.

Munn, N. L. Concerning visual form discrimination in the white rat. *J. genet. Psychol.,* 1929, 36, 291-302.

Munn, N. L. Pattern and brightness discrimination in raccoons. *J. genet. Psychol.,* 1930, 37, 3-34.

Munn, N. L. An apparatus for testing visual discrimination in animals. *J. genet. Psychol.,* 1931, 39, 343-358. (a)

Munn, N. L. The relative efficacy of form and background in the chick's discrimination of visual patterns. *J. comp. Psychol.,* 1931, 12, 41-75. (b)

Munn, N. L. *Handbook of psychological research on the rat.* Cambridge, Massachusetts: Riverside Press, 1950.

Nash, A. J., & Michels, K. M. Squirrel monkeys and discrimination learning: Figural interactions, redundancies, and random shapes. *J. exp. Psychol.,* 1966, 72, 132-137.

Neet, C. C. Visual pattern discrimination in the *Macacus rhesus* monkey. *J. genet. Psychol.,* 1933, 43, 163-196.

Pache, J. Formensehen bei Froeschen. *Z. vergl. Physiol.,* 1932, 17, 423-463.

Parriss, J. R. Retention of shape discrimination after regeneration of the optic nerves in the toad. *Quart. J. exp. Psychol.,* 1963, 15, 22-26.

Parriss, J. R., & Young, J. Z. The limits of transfer and of learned discrimination to figures of larger and smaller sizes. *Z. vergl. Physiol.,* 1962, 45, 618-635.

Pastore, N. Form perception and size constancy in the duckling. *J. Psychol.,* 1958, 45, 259-261.

Polidora, V. J. Stimulus correlates of visual pattern discrimination by monkeys: Sidedness. *Percept. mot. Skills,* 1965, 20, 461-469.

Polidora, V. J. Stimulus correlates of visual pattern discrimination by monkeys: Multidimensional analyses. *Percept. Psychophys.,* 1966, 1, 405-414.

Polidora, V. J., & Thompson, W. J. Stimulus correlates of visual pattern discrimination by monkeys: Area and contour. *J. comp. physiol. Psychol.,* 1964, 58, 264-269.

Polidora, V. J., & Thompson, W. J. Stimulus correlates of visual pattern discrimination by monkeys: Pattern complexity. *Percept. mot. Skills,* 1965, 21, 71-79.

Pollard, J. S., Beale, I. L., Lysons, A. M., & Preston, A. C. Visual discrimination in the ferret. *Percept. mot. Skills,* 1967, 24, 279-282.

Rensch, B., & Altevogt, R. Visuelles Lernvermoegen eines indischen Elefanten. *Z. Tierpsychol.*, 1953, **10**, 119-134.

Rensch, B., & Altevogt, R. Das Ausmass visueller Lernfaehigkeit eines indischen Elefanten. *Z. Tierpsychol.*, 1955, **12**, 68-76.

Riopelle, A. J., Rahm, U., Itoigawa, N., & Draper, W. A. Discrimination of mirror-image patterns by rhesus monkeys. *Percept. mot. Skills*, 1964, **19**, 383-389.

Rosenblum, L. A., Witkin, H., Kaufman, I. C., & Brosgole, L. Perceptual disembedding in monkeys: Note on method and preliminary findings. *Percept. mot. Skills*, 1965, **20**, 729-736.

Rowley, J. B. Discrimination limens of pattern and size in the goldfish *Carassius auratus*. *Genet. Psychol. Monogr.*, 1934, **15**, 245-302.

Schulte, A. Transfer- und Transpositionsversuche mit monokular dressierten Fischen. *Z. vergl. Physiol.*, 1957, **39**, 432-476.

Schusterman, R. J., Thomas, T. Shape discrimination and transfer in the California sea lion. *Psychon. Sci.*, 1966, **5**, 21-22.

Seitz, A. Untersuchungen ueber das Formensehen und optische Groessenunterscheidung bei der Skudde (ostpreussisches Landschaf). *Z. Tierpsychol.*, 1951, **8**, 423-441.

Smith, K. U. Form discrimination in the cat. *Psychol. Bull.*, 1933, **30**, 546-547. (Abstract)

Smith, K. U. The acuity of the cat's discrimination of visual form. *Psychol. Bull.*, 1934, **31**, 618-619. (Abstract) (a)

Smith, K. U. Visual discrimination in the cat: I. The capacity of the cat for visual form discrimination. *J. genet. Psychol.*, 1934, **44**, 301-320. (b)

Smith, K. U. Visual discrimination in the cat: II. A further study of the capacity of the cat for visual figure discrimination. *J. genet. Psychol.*, 1934, **45**, 336-357. (c)

Smith, K. U. Visual discrimination in the cat: III. The relative effect of paired and unpaired stimuli in the discriminative behavior of the cat. *J. genet. Psychol.*, 1936, **48**, 29-57.

Sutherland, N. S. Visual discrimination of orientation by *Octopus*. *Brit. J. Psychol.*, 1957, **48**, 55-71.

Sutherland, N. S. Visual discrimination of the orientation of rectangles by *Octopus vulgaris* Lamarck. *J. comp. physiol. Psychol.*, 1958, **51**, 452-458. (a)

Sutherland, N. S. Visual discrimination of shape by *Octopus*: Squares and triangles. *Quart. J. exp. Psychol.*, 1958, **10**, 40-47. (b)

Sutherland, N. S. Visual discrimination of shape by *Octopus*: Circles and squares, and circles and triangles. *Quart. J. exp. Psychol.*, 1959, **11**, 24-32.

Sutherland, N. S. Visual discrimination of orientation by *Octopus*: Mirror images. *Brit. J. Psychol.*, 1960, **51**, 9-18. (a)

Sutherland, N. S. The visual discrimination of shape by *Octopus*: Squares and rectangles. *J. comp. physiol. Psychol.*, 1960, **53**, 95-103. (b)

Sutherland, N. S. Visual discrimination of shape by *Octopus*: Open and closed forms. *J. comp. physiol. Psychol.*, 1960, **53**, 104-112. (c)

Sutherland, N. S. *The methods and findings of experiments on the visual discrimination of shape by animals*. Oxford, England: Experimental Psychology Society, 1961. (a)

Sutherland, N. S. Visual discrimination of horizontal and vertical rectangles by rats on a new discrimination training apparatus. *Quart. J. exp. Psychol.*, 1961, **13**, 117-121. (b)

Sutherland, N. S. Cat's ability to discriminate oblique rectangles. *Science*, 1963, **139**, 209-210.

Sutherland, N. S., & Muntz, W. R. A. Simultaneous discrimination training and preferred directions of motion in visual discrimination of shape in *Octopus vulgaris* Lamarck. *Pubbl. Sta. zool. Napoli*, 1959, **31**, 109-126.

Sutherland, N. S., Mackintosh, J., & Mackintosh, N. J. The visual discrimination of reduplicated patterns by octopus. *Anim. Behav.*, 1963, **11**, 106-110.

Tinbergen, N. Social releasers and the experimental method required for their study. *Wilson Bull.*, 1948, **60**, 6-51.

Tinbergen, N., & Kuenen, D. J. Ueber die ausloesenden und richtungsgebenden Reizsituationen der Sperrbewegung von jungen Drosseln (*Turdus m. merula* und *T. e. ericetorum*). *Z. Tierpsychol.*, 1939, **3**, 37-60.

Towe, A. L. A study of figural equivalence in the pigeon. *J. comp. physiol. Psychol.*, 1954, **47**, 283-287.

Warden, C. J., & Baar, J. The Mueller-Lyer illusion in the ring dove, *Turtur risorius. J. comp. Psychol.*, 1929, **9**, 275-292.

Warren, J. M. Additivity of cues in visual pattern discrimination by monkeys. *J. comp. physiol. Psychol.*, 1953, **46**, 484-486. (a)

Warren, J. M. Effect of geometrical regularity in visual form discrimination by monkeys. *J. comp. physiol. Psychol.*, 1953, **46**, 237-240. (b)

Waterman, T. H., Wiersma, C. A. G., & Bush, B. M. H. Afferent visual responses in the optic nerve of the crab, *Podophthalmus. J. Cell comp. Physiol.*, 1964, **63**, 135-155.

Wehner, R. Pattern recognition in bees. *Nature*, 1967, **215**, 1244-1248.

Wehner, R., & Lindauer, M. Zur Physiologie des Formensehens bei der Honigbiene. I. Winkelunterscheidung an vertikal orientierten Streifenmustern. *Z. vergl. Physiol.*, 1966, **52**, 290-324.

Wells, M. J. Proprioception and visual discrimination of orientation in *Octopus. J. exp. Biol.*, 1960, **37**, 489-499.

Wiersma, C. A. G., & Yamaguchi, T. The neuronal components of the optic nerve of the crayfish as studied by single unit analysis. *J. comp. Neurol.*, 1966, **128**, 333-358.

Williams, J. A. Experiments with form perception and learning in dogs. *Comp. Psychol. Monogr.*, 1926, **4**, No. 18.

Winslow, C. N. Visual illusions in the chick. *Arch. Psychol.*, 1933, No. 153. Geometrical shape discrimination by "Saimiri sciureus." *Psychon. Sci.*, 1965, **3**, 309-310.

Winslow, C. N. Visual illusions in the chick. *Arch. Psychol.*, 1933, No. 153.

Woodburne, L. S. Geometrical shape discrimination by "Saimiri sciureus." *Psychon. Sci.*, 1965, **3**, 309-310.

Yerkes, R. M., & Watson, J. B. Methods of studying vision in animals. *Behav. Monogr.*, 1911, **1**, No. 2.

Zeigler, H. P., & Schmerler, S. Visual discrimination of orientation by pigeons. *Anim. Behav.*, 1965, **13**, 475-477.

Zerrahn, G. Formdressur und Formunterscheidung bei der Honigbiene. *Z. vergl. Physiol.*, 1933, **20**, 117-150.

Zunini, G. Contributo allo studio dell'apprendimento dei pesci (*Phoxinus laevis* Agas). *Arch. Ital. Psicol.*, Fasc. II, E. III, 1937, **25**, 3-33.

Zusne, L. Stimulus correlates of visual pattern discrimination and the problem of grain. *Percept. Psychophys.*, 1967, **2**, 86-87.

Chapter 9 / DEVELOPMENT OF THE PERCEPTION OF VISUAL FORM

1. Development of the Visual Perception of Form in Children

While questions about form perception have often been asked independently of questions about perception in general, questions concerning the development of form perception have been less often asked outside the larger issue of how perception develops. Thus, there is only one theory that can be called a theory of the development of form perception, namely Hebb's (1949), but even in this case the issues concerning the development of form perception are subordinated to issues concerning perceptual development. Since the basic issues in perceptual development are still a matter of theoretical discussion and controversy and, in addition, have been fully treated in a number of volumes (e.g., Epstein, 1967; Piaget, 1967; Solley & Murphy, 1960) and numerous articles, they will only be indicated in this chapter, whose bulk is concerned with developmental trends in the perception of visual form as they emerge from observations made on human and animal experimental subjects and clinical studies.

Hershenson (1967), in his review of the development of the perception of visual form in human infants, points out that at least three different views of perceptual development have been expressed: "(a) Organization of the perceptual system manifest in an increasing ability to perceive; (b) elaboration of more distinctive percepts, as in learning to discriminate among wines; and (c) integration of perceptual and motor systems, as in acquiring motor skills" (p. 326). In the terminology of the Gibsons (Gibson & Gibson, 1955), the first view is the "enrichment" view of perceptual development, the other two representing the "differentiation" view. The basic difference between these two views is that, in one, perception is constructed from the ground up, or percepts grow as experience accrues to some initial core or seed, whereas in the other, perception develops as the original, given base is improved, differentiated, refined, or integrated with another perceptual system. A question related to this second point of view is whether improvement in discrimination can be attributed to the development of a "schema" or to learning to discriminate the "distinctive features" of stimuli (e.g., Pick, 1965), an issue that was encountered in Chap. 3

in connection with pattern-recognition programs for computers. Should studies of the development of form perception show that the newborn infant can perceive form, then, as Hershenson (1967) points out, from this angle at least, it can be argued strongly that perceptual development constitutes differentiation rather than enrichment. His review of the perceptual capacities of the newborn infant indicates that the prerequisites for the perception of form are present: both rods and cones are present in the retina of the fetus by the seventh month of prenatal life, and both the photopic and scotopic visual systems appear to be working at birth; although both EEG and histological data show that the central nervous system of the newborn infant is immature, there is no question but that all of the components of the visual system are in place, intact, and functioning; the newborn can orient their eyes toward single stimuli, i.e., convergence and conjugate eye movements are present; while accomodation is incomplete, even the observed locking of accomodation at the distance of about 8 in. (Haynes, White, & Held, 1965) in infants under 1 month of age makes it possible to present visual targets that would be visible, albeit blurred. It takes about 2 years for visual acuity to reach the adult level, and the acuity of infants under 1 month of age is about 20/200. The ability to resolve lines 1/8-in. thick at 10 in. (Fantz, Ordy, & Udelf, 1962) at least is there, however. Taken together, the evidence strongly favors at least the potential presence of form perception in newborn infants.

Granted that human infants perceive form, the next question concerns the effective dimensions of form that are utilized by infants in discriminating between them. Since discrimination-training techniques cannot be used with very young infants, other methods must be employed to answer this question. The most frequently used method consists in presenting forms singly or in pairs and recording either the duration or frequency of the infant's fixations. Differences in these measures are then taken to imply that differences in the magnitude or nature of form dimensions have produced differences in "attention" or "preference." In another method, the infant's eye movements are observed or recorded. The features of a shape that attract the infant's attention or are preferred by him may be identified directly by this method. While the recording of eye movements in newborn infants is a promising technique, it has been used in a few studies only and only in the past few years. Developmental trends in the perception of visual form in verbal children are assessed by the same means that are used with adult subjects.

A. FIGURE AND GROUND, EMBEDDED FIGURES, POLYFIGURATIONS, AND REVERSIBLE-PERSPECTIVE FIGURES

The ability to see figure on ground appears to be innate, although it has been argued (e.g., Hershenson, 1967) that the ability to see differences in brightness

increasing age the dominance of factors associated with the stimulus wanes while the influence of cognitive factors increases. Thus, if the punishment associated with the perception of one portion of the visual field is not too severe (e.g., losing money for seeing the "incorrect" face as the figure), it is likely to arouse the subject's curiosity rather than push it out of the focus of attention.

Developmental changes in the ability to alternate percepts in a labile figure-ground field are probably due to the same process that produces the change discussed in the preceding paragraph. Two opposite predictions as to the direction of this change may be made from two theories, however. The prediction from the Gestalt theory (Koehler & Wallach, 1944) is that figure-ground reversals should decrease with age: "permanent satiation" in stimulated brain tissue increases with age, and reversals take place more readily in nonsatiated tissue. Piaget (Piaget & Morf, 1958), on the other hand, predicts that reversals should increase in frequency because of the individual's increasing ability to perform intellectual operations. A test of these two predictions was made by Elkind and Scott (1962), who found in their data more support for Piaget than for the Gestalt theory. Their study, however, is not without its problems: the ability to see both percepts in a reversible figure-ground organization also increases with the child's I.Q., but since perceptual test scores, mental age, and chronological age are all positively intercorrelated, the interpretation of the results of this study is not unequivocal. A study by Elkind, Koegler, and Go (1962) also showed that, while training does increase the ability to alternate percepts in 6-, 7-, and 8-year-old children, the initial differences between the age groups were evident both immediately after training and one month later. Since at least one investigator (Farkas, 1959) has reported little change in the number of reversals in the Rubin figure in subjects aged 10-78, more work needs to be done in this area before firmer conclusions are made.

The dependence of the younger child upon the immediate context of the visual stimulus and the gradual shedding of this dependence with increasing age is also demonstrated in the change in performance on embedded-figure tasks. Only a couple of studies dealing with this development exist, but their results are in accord with the trends apparent in performance on other figure-ground tests. Performance on embedded-figure tests using a Gottschaldt design shows greatest improvement between the ages of 10 and 13 as well as further improvement through the age of about 17 in a study by Witkin, Lewis, Hertzman, Machover, Meissner, & Wapner (1954). Ghent (1956) compared overlapping and embedded figures with regard to the ease with which they are perceived. Overlapping figures, either realistic or geometric, caused no particular problem in children as young as 4. A similar finding is also reported by Piaget and Stettler-von Albertini (1954). Embedded figures, however, were much more difficult to see in Ghent's study. Their perception improved both with age (4-13 years) and practice. When a figure is masked by visual noise, older subjects are better able to separate the figure from low-density noise than from high-density noise, and children are better able to see the figure in systematic than in random noise (Munsinger & Gummerman, 1967).

Developmental changes have been noted in the perception of polyfigurations, such as Boring's "my wife and mother-in-law" drawing. Botwinick, Robin, & Brinley (1959) reported decreasing ability of older (65-81 years) people to reorganize the initial percept as compared with a younger (19-34 years) group of subjects, while Ramamurthi and Parmeswaran (1964) found more frequent alternations of the two percepts in younger than in older people.

In the case of reversible-perspective figures, the possibility at least exists that the developmental trend might not be linear but a U-shaped function. Farkas (1959) found that the number of fluctuations in reversible-perspective figures increased between the ages of 10 and 20-24, then decreased, the oldest subjects studied being 78 years of age.

B. GESTALT LAWS OF ORGANIZATION

Most investigators who have concerned themselves with the problem have shown that the Gestalt laws of organization play a role in perception that is a function of the perceiver's age. While this does not answer the question of whether the Gestalt principles of organization have an innate or learned basis or what the nature of the underlying mechanism might be, it does demonstrate that these principles are not a fixed, immutable affair but are subject to predictable changes.

Rush's (1937) study of developmental changes in the effectiveness of several Gestalt principles in the perceptual organization of dot patterns is still the major and most important source of information on the subject. Rush presented her subjects (N = 8589) with matrices of dots in which the dots were arranged in vertical and horizontal columns and asked them to draw straight lines through the dots to indicate the direction in which they appeared to be aligned. By varying the distances between adjacent dots in single columns and rows and those between adjacent rows or columns, Rush was both able to quantify the dimensions of her stimuli and to manipulate, singly or simultaneously, the variables of proximity, good continuation, and similarity. Rush observed no significant age-related changes in the role of the proximity factor in grade school subjects (the age range for all subjects was 6-22 years), a result also reported by Shroff (1928). This variable was more effective in older subjects. When proximity was opposed to continuation or similarity, its effectiveness decreased with age in comparison with that of continuation or similarity. Comparing the latter two, Rush found an increase in the effectiveness of continuation as an organizing factor, except in college-age subjects, in whom a reversal of this trend could be observed. Thus, at least up to college age, good continuation is an organizing principle whose effectiveness keeps increasing regardless of whether it is the only one present or pitted against others.

In 4-5-year-old children, continuation may not be effective at all. Piaget and Stettler-von Albertini (1954) found that, while children of this age had little or no difficulty in tracing overlapping figures when these were complete, children up to the age of 6 were practically unable to recognize figures presented singly but in the form of dashed contours. When several of these dashed contours were presented superimposed upon each other, subjects had to be at least 7 before they were able to recognize the objects represented. A more recent study (Bower, 1967), while confirming the finding of previous investigators that the effectiveness of the Gestalt principles of organization develops with age, was able to demonstrate their presence at an extremely early age, namely 36 days. Using an ingenious conditioning technique, Bower was able to establish that proximity is ineffective as an organizing principle at this age but that good continuation is. The technique used to assess the effectiveness of good continuation consisted in presenting an equilateral triangle interrupted by a black bar, reinforcing a sucking response to it by 10-sec. segments of a film showing an infant at play, then testing the effectiveness of triangles, with the top and bottom parts connected in different ways, in suppressing the sucking response. Response suppression was taken as evidence for novelty, hence dissimilarity between the conditioned stimulus and the test stimulus. Of the four test triangles presented, the one in which the top and bottom portions had been connected so as to form a complete, normal triangle, elicited significantly more responses than the other three. Bower concludes that, not only did the infants see phenomenal identity in the conditioned stimulus and the complete triangle, i.e., "knew" that the top and the bottom portions of the triangle were connected, but that they also knew the nature of this connection, i.e., they perceived form.

If a developmental trend exists for the several Gestalt principles and a "good" form incorporates all or several of them, then one might expect similar changes in the effectiveness of the role played by good forms in perception. The only relevant study shows increasing effectiveness of the goodness of form with increasing age. Piaget, Maire, and Privat (1954) attached the Mueller-Lyer arrowheads and feathers to the corners of a square, as illustrated in Fig. 9-2. The effect of the square was to reduce the magnitude of the Mueller-Lyer illusion. The magnitude of the reduction, however, was smallest in children and largest in adults. Piaget interprets this result as evidence for the growth of the effectiveness of good form with age.

C. GEOMETRIC ILLUSIONS

The most studied subject in the area of the development of visual form perception has been the geometric illusions. A book (Vurpillot, 1963), a monograph (Walters, 1942), and a review article (Wohlwill, 1960) have presented comprehensive overviews of theory and experimentation concerning developmental trends in the perception of geometric illusions.

Immergluck (1968) has shown that a relationship exists between figural aftereffects, geometric illusions, and field dependence-independence (cf. Chap. 2). If field independence increases with age and the geometric illusions are essentially a field-dependent phenomenon, it may be expected that the size of the illusions would also decrease with age. This, in fact, is the most common finding, although exceptions also exist. Jean Piaget has presented the only theory that attempts to account both for the general decrease in the magnitude of geometric illusions with age as well as for the occasional exceptions to this rule.

Piaget's theory of geometric illusions was presented in Chap. 4. His principal interest is in the development of behavior, hence the theory is essentially a developmental theory. According to Piaget, the basic reason for illusory perception is the phenomenon of "centering," which leads to the overestimation of those stimulus elements that, in the process of sampling the stimulus visually, happen to be fixated upon by the observer. With increasing age, "decentering" takes place, which results in an increased balance in the number of stimulus elements sampled from two lines, two angles, etc. that are being compared, hence a decrease in the absolute magnitude of the illusions takes place. Decentering is essentially the result of increased efficiency in visual exploratory behavior that comes with increasing experience. A decrease in the magnitude of illusions that comes with practice even over short periods of time (as in an experiment) has been observed in both children and adults and is due to the same process of decentering.

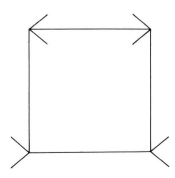

Fig. 9-2. The effect of a 'good' figure on the Mueller-Lyer illusion.

As visual exploration brings about increasing compensation for the effects of centering, a decrease in the magnitude of geometric illusions is not its only result. It also leads to relating stimulus elements that were previously not related and thus produces, again through the process of centering, illusions that Piaget calls secondary. For example, Piaget does not believe that the horizontal-vertical illusion is caused by anisotropy of space; rather, it is a secondary illusion since, instead of diminishing with age, it increases as a function of age, at least in the experiments performed by Piaget and his co-workers. This increase, according to Piaget, is due to the development of a spatial framework and the consequent fact that the vertical line, because of its asymmetry (while the horizontal line can be continued indefinitely in both directions, the vertical line can be visualized as extending only upwards), centers more of the observer's attention and is therefore overestimated. When the framework is unimportant, as when two vertical lines are aligned, the overestimation of the upper one decreases with age (Piaget & Morf, 1956).

Although other explanations of age-related changes in the magnitude of geometric illusions have been offered, none are as complete as Piaget's nor do they fit into larger theoretical schemes. Thus, e.g., Pollack (1963), finding that contour-detection thresholds increase from the age of 8 through 9, 10, 11, and 12, that the Mueller-Lyer illusion decreases with age, and that the Mueller-Lyer illusion appears to be related to figure-ground contrast, suggests that both detection thresholds and the magnitude of the illusion may change as a function of some aging process.

In developmental studies of the Mueller-Lyer illusion, subjects aged 4-77 years have been used. Most studies show a decrease in the magnitude of the illusion from the earliest age to anywhere between 10 and 15 years (Binet, 1895; Pollack, 1963; Sun Shih-luh, 1964; Walters, 1942; Wapner & Werner, 1957), others show a decrease between childhood and adulthood (Noelting, 1960; Piaget & von Albertini, 1950; Piaget et al., 1954; Pintner & Anderson, 1916; van Biervliet, 1896). In two studies at least (Walters, 1942; Wapner & Werner, 1957), a decrease was found to about 10 or 12, then an increase between 15 and 19, and in one study (Gajo, 1967), in which only adults were compared, the magnitude of the illusion was constant between the ages of 30 and 59, increasing to the age of 77 years. There is, then, the possibility that the illusion, while decreasing in magnitude through the early teens, may begin to increase slowly in the late teens, remain more or less constant through adulthood, then increase in old age.

The Ponzo illusion appears to increase in magnitude to the age of 7, remaining constant through the age of 28, which was the age of the oldest subject tested in one developmental study of this illusion (Leibowitz & Heisel, 1958). In another (Leibowitz & Judisch, 1967), the illusion was found to increase through the age of 13, remain constant through middle age, then decrease. Piaget and von Albertini (1950) point out that the Mueller-Lyer illusion may be converted into the parallel-line illusion by connecting the ends of the "arrowheads" or "feathers" and then eliminating the latter. The variables that affect the parallel-line illusion affect the Mueller-Lyer illusion also, and their developmental trends are very similar. Since the absolute magnitude of the Mueller-Lyer illusion is much greater, it is possible that, while a single factor may be operating in the case of the parallel-line illusion, the same factor plus some other factor, such as inappropriate constancy scaling, may be operating in the case of the Mueller-Lyer illusion, producing a stronger effect.

Piaget and von Albertini (1950) found, in general, a decrease in the parallel-line illusion between the ages of 5-9 years and adulthood. Giering (1905), in the only other developmental study of this illusion, found no change between subjects aged 6 and 14. Another contrast illusion, the Delboeuf illusion, has received more attention. The size and direction of the changes observed in this illusion, however, are such that it is diffiuclt to draw any firm conclusions. While Giering (1905) reported a decrease in the illusion between the ages of 6 and 14 and Piaget, Lambercier, Boesch, & von Albertini (1942) between 5 and 7, Ruessel (1934) found small, irregular changes between the ages of 4 and 6½, and Gajo's (1967) results show a statistically insignificant increase between the ages of 30 and 77. Santostefano's (1963) finding that the illusion increases between the ages of 6 and 9 and 9 and 12 if it is positive but decreases, albeit insignificantly, if it is negative, obscures the picture even further. If the Titchener circles are just another version of the concentric-circle illusion, then the findings of Ruessel (1934) and Wapner and Werner (1957) would lend support to the conclusion that, in general, contrast illusions of the three kinds just described would tend to decrease slightly early in childhood and to increase as slightly in adulthood, i.e., show changes analogous to those experienced with the Mueller-Lyer illusion. Since the changes are slight, differences in experimental design easily produce deviations from this trend.

Developmental data on intersecting-contour illusions are sparse and inconsistent. While Leibowitz and Gwozdecki (1957) reported an increase in the Poggendorff illusion between the ages of 5 and 10 and a constant effect from then on, Vurpillot (1957) showed a decrease from age 5 to ages above 9. In a variant of the checkerboard illusion, Piaget and Denis-Prinzhorn (1954) found an increase in the illusion up to the age of 10, followed by a decrease. Other illusions yield no useful data either, with Giering (1905) reporting an increase in the Jastrow illusion between the ages of 6 and 14 and Heiss (1930) a decrease in the Sanders parallelogram illusion with increasing age.

The amount of work done on the development of the horizontal-vertical illusion is appreciable but inconsistent, the various investigators reporting both an increase (Piaget & Morf, 1956; Wuersten, 1947) and a decrease (Griffin, 1962; Rivers, 1905; Soudkova & Riškova, 1966; Walters, 1942; Winch, 1907) with age in this illusion. Since both Piaget and Wuersten used noncontiguous line segments while in most cases the inverted T figure is used, the discrepancy may be attributed to this difference. Piaget and Morf (1956) explain the increase in the horizontal-vertical illusion observed by them in terms of the development of a stable system of spatial coordinates, which takes place by about the age of 9. Since in the inverted T figure the two intersecting lines provide their own coordinate system, as it were, the illusion operates immediately within it. The illusion is also stronger in this configuration than for the L figure or when the two lines are not connected.

D. FIGURAL AFTEREFFECTS

Although the literature on figural aftereffects is extensive, developmental studies of this phenomenon are very few. Testable hypotheses can be derived both from the Gestalt theory as well as other, competing theories of figural aftereffects. Thus, the postulated "permanent satiation" of brain tissue that increases with age (Koehler & Wallach, 1944) should decrease figural aftereffects as the individual grows older. The underlying mechanism is thought to be lowered metabolic rate which decreases the polarizability of brain tissue. Wertheimer (1955) has shown that correlation exists between measured metabolic rate and the size of figural aftereffects.

Immergluck's (1968) attempt to relate geometric illusions and figural aftereffects to the field dependence-independence phenomenon leads to the hypothesis, however, that figural aftereffects should increase with age: field dependence decreases with age and field-independent people show stronger figural aftereffects. Rich's (1958) study showed a decrease in figural aftereffects between the ages of 65 and 89, and Eisdorfer and Axelrod (1964) have presented evidence for its decrease between young adulthood and senescence. Thurner and Seyfried (1962), however, failed to note any significant changes in figural aftereffects with age. Pollack (1960) similarly found that, while a decrease in the number of subjects experiencing figural aftereffects may be observed between the ages of 4 and 12, this proportion increases again and reaches the original level at 13, remaining thereafter unchanged until the age of 24 (Fig. 9-3). Pollack hypothesizes that, while the dip in the curve may be due to a loss of sensitivity to prolonged visual stimulation as well as undeveloped cognitive capacity, the return of the curve to its previous level may be due to cognitive development, which brings about changes in the memory trace of the inspection figure. Following this line of reasoning, the results of Rich (1958) and Eisdorfer and Axelrod (1964) may be interpreted as a second manifestation of some physiological change, such as the increasing satiation postulated by the Gestalt psychologists.

E. DISCRIMINATION OF CONTOURS AND SHAPES

Informational Parameters. Differences in complexity are responded to soon after birth (e.g., Fantz, 1963b). This differentiation is usually inferred from a preference task and is therefore discussed in more detail below under that heading. Otherwise, the only pertinent study that needs to be mentioned here is that of Munsinger and Kessen (1966), in which it was found that estimation of the complexity of random polygons improves with age, the complexity of simple figures being estimated more accurately than that of more-complex figures by both children and adults.

Transpositional Parameters. In Estes' (1961) study, there were no age differences found in subjects from kindergarten through college level in the task of matching either identical or different shapes on size. The clues used to compare sizes (altitude, diameter, area, length of sides, and others) depended on the configuration of the stimuli (triangles, squares, and circles were used) and on which shape happened to be the standard and which the comparison shape. Children used areas as a cue in comparing sizes in only two of the six comparisons.

The commonly observed tendency of younger children to respond to mirror images (reflections) of shapes or to rotated shapes as if the difference in orientation did not matter has been the subject of an appreciable number of

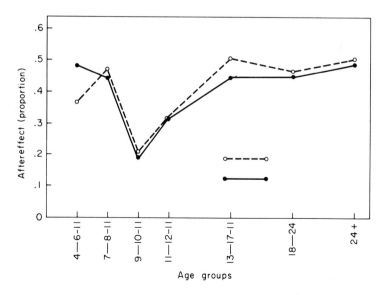

Fig. 9-3. Figural aftereffects as a function of age. From Pollack (1960). By permission of North-Holland Publishing Company, Amsterdam.

studies, both with the discrimination and the recognition tasks. Stern (1909) noted this phenomenon long ago. Ling (1941) found that discrimination of shapes by infants was little affected by changes in rotation, and Newhall (1937) found that discrimination in a matching task was not affected by either right-left or up-down reversals in children 3-5 years of age. He observed no age-related trends in that age range.

Both adult and child studies have shown repeatedly that there is a definite difference between right-left and up-down reversals, the latter kind making for easier discriminations than the former (Huttenlocher, 1967; Wohlwill & Wiener, 1964). Regardless of the type of reversal, confusion between mirror-image forms and inversions decreases with age (Davidson, 1934; Gibson, Gibson, Pick, & Osser, 1962; Rosenblith, 1965; Rudel & Teuber, 1963). Depending on the discrimination task used and the type of reversal, errors of reversal in letters are eliminated between the ages of 6 and 10.

The confusion of reflected shapes by young children may be due to the existence of orientation-specific receptive fields. Although direct electro-physiological data are lacking, Rudel and Teuber's (1963) essential replication, with children, of Sutherland's findings regarding the great difficulty experienced by the octopus in discriminating an oblique rectangle from its mirror image tends to support such a hypothesis. In Rudel and Teuber's experiment, no 3-year-old subject could make this discrimination, but the older the subjects were, the better were they able to perform, which suggests that learning overrode the innate determinants of perception.

An alternative explanation, which does not necessarily invalidate the receptive field hypothesis, is that it is not that the younger child cannot see the difference between, say, the letters *b* and *d* but that either he does not care whether there is a difference or that failure to discriminate is a result of the particular test procedure used. When Robinson and Higgins (1967) presented pairs of mirror-image shapes for "same-different" judgments, they found that many more subjects between the kindergarten and third-grade levels showed discrimination than had been previously reported. Even those who failed on this test showed that they actually saw the difference between the two figures by being able to point at the salient features of the figures that determined the difference in their directionality. Over and Over (1967) have provided analogous results. Young children who did not seem to be able to tell the difference between mirror-image obliques when asked to select the same one of a pair of such obliques over a series of trials, showed ready discrimination of orientation when asked whether the two shapes pointed in the same or different directions.

As shown by Huttenlocher (1967), the relative position of the two mirror-image figures in an array produce a difference in the degree of discrimination difficulty. If up-down reflections are presented side by side instead of one on top of the other, this relative position of the two figures is not equivalent to the side-by-side position of right-left reflected shapes. Reflecting a

$<$ in the vertical plane results in the pair $<$ $>$; however, reflecting $\wedge$ in the vertical plane does not result in $\wedge\vee$. To make relative positions comparable for right-left and up-down mirror images, the latter should be presented in an up-down relative position, either as $\begin{smallmatrix}\wedge\\\vee\end{smallmatrix}$ or $\begin{smallmatrix}\vee\\\wedge\end{smallmatrix}$. Huttenlocher's comparisons show that, while it is true that right-left mirror images are considerably more difficult for 5-year-old subjects to discriminate if they are presented side by side than are up-down mirror images, this difference is erased if both types of reflection are presented in the up-down relative position. Analogous results have been obtained by Sekuler and Rosenblith (1964) with first-graders using triangles and gapped circles as stimulus figures. A detailed review of perception of orientation by children and the effects of training upon it may be found in Fellows (1968).

Explanations of the difficulty that younger children have with forms and their orientation have been proposed in terms of developing cerebral dominance: younger children fail to discriminate between a form and its mirror image, for instance, because neither one of the cerebral hemispheres has as yet developed dominance. This explanation has been proposed by Mach (1914), Orton (e.g., 1937), and others. The existing evidence, however, fails to support it. Thus, lateralization does not seem to be related to any progress in reading; children of mixed laterality show no more reversal errors than children with unilateral development; the severance of the corpus callosum has no effect on the discrimination of mirror images; and animals with no hemispheric dominance show discrimination of mirror-imaged figures that is just as good or even better than in man.

Configurational Parameters. For reasons that were discussed in Chap. 5, developmental studies involving form discrimination based on configurational parameters have been sporadic and unsystematic, no two studies dealing with the same variables. Discrimination of differences in "shape" (i.e., several unspecified form parameters) improves with age, either as measured by the number of errors in a matching task (Gibson *et al.*, 1962, who used 167 4-8-year-old subjects) or by reaction time in oddity-type discrimination problems (Rajalakshmi & Jeeves, 1963, who used 163 subjects between the ages of 5½ and 74). Rajalakshmi and Jeeves also found that reaction time begins to increase after maturity is reached.

If preference for form implies discrimination of form, discrimination begins immediately after birth (Fantz, 1963b). At this point in development, discrimination is incomplete. Eye-movement recordings reveal that, while newborn infants do fixate salient points of a configuration, such as a corner of a triangle, other such points of the figure may be ignored, which suggests that not the entire form but only some of its parts are seen at any one time (Salapatek & Kessen, 1966). Even in preschool children and children in the first two grades, a tendency to be guided by cues in the bottom part of the figure has been recorded (Kerpelman & Pollack, 1964). As children grow older, a more equitable distribution of attention over the entire figure is observed and discrimination performance improves.

Imperfect discrimination, for whatever reason, is also the cause of poorer performance of younger children on tasks involving the estimation of the length of lines, size of angles, and the like. Welch (1939a, 1939b) has recorded considerable changes in children's ability to discriminate sizes, widths, and areas between the ages of 1 and 3-4 years. Data on the estimation of sizes (Estes, 1961) and of lengths by the method of reproduction (Giering, 1905) suggest that children may reach the adult level of accuracy of estimation by the time they are 4 or 5. In the case of illusion-producing contexts, however, further development and improvement may take place beyond that age, as was seen in the case of the geometric illusions and as is the case with such "building blocks" of the classical geometric illusions as angles and arcs of the circle. The overestimation of acute angles, the underestimation of obtuse angles, the underestimation of the sides of acute angles, and the overestimation of the sides of obtuse angles become less pronounced with age (Piaget, 1949), as does the overestimation of arcs of a circle (Piaget & Vurpillot, 1956).

F. PREFERENCE (SCALING)

Informational Parameters. While age trends in the perception of curves have not been studied at all, complexity has received considerable attention. One reason for this interest has been the influence of information theory on psychological theorizing in the field of perception. The other reason has been the recent revival of interest in the perceptual development of very young infants. Since figural complexity is easily measurable and in most cases constitutes the single most potent independent variable of form, complexity has been the main variable with whose help the development of form perception has been studied in human infants. The principal method of study is the method of preference, which was reintroduced in developmental research by Robert L. Fantz in the 1950s.

Fantz used the preference method first with chimpanzees (Fantz, 1956), then applied it to human infants (Fantz, 1958). The preference method had been used in developmental studies some time before Fantz. Staples (1932), for instance, used it to study the development of color preferences in infants. Her method consisted of holding a pair of differently colored circles in front of the infant, observing the infant's fixations through a hole between the two stimuli, and recording the time spent looking at each of them during a period of 2 min. Fantz has used essentially the same technique, except for the introduction of certain improvements. The experimenter, for instance, is kept out of sight by placing the infant in a partly covered crib. Pairs of stimuli are presented on the ceiling of the crib by raising a shield which conceals the stimuli between trials. A hole in the shield keeps the infant's attention in the general area of the stimuli, while another hole in the ceiling permits the experimenter to observe the infant's eye movements. Lighting in the crib is so arranged that the images of the stimuli may be seen reflected from the infant's corneas. The relative position of an image with regard to the pupil indicates which of the stimuli is being fixated. The experimenter records the total duration of fixations for each target during two 30-sec. periods. In the second period, the positions of the two targets are interchanged.

Defending an unpopular position, namely that perception precedes action, Fantz has produced a considerable amount of evidence in favor of that position. Of interest to the topic being discussed in this section is his consistent finding that from an early age infants prefer (i.e., look longer at) patterns to homogeneous stimuli and more complex patterns to simpler ones. Preference for patterns over plain stimuli, colored or achromatic, has been shown by Fantz to exist in infants under 5 days of age (Fantz, 1963b). Preference for the more complex of two patterns appears at the age of two months (Fantz, 1961, 1963a).

Other investigators have been able to confirm Fantz's results. Berlyne (1958), for instance, found preference for the more complex stimuli in infants 3-9-months old. Munsinger & Weir (1967) have extended Fantz's finding to infants and children between the ages of 9 and 41 months by showing preference to be an increasing linear function of complexity of random shapes. Cantor, Cantor, and Ditrichs (1963) showed that the same relationship exists in subjects aged 4-5½ years, while Thomas (1966) has covered the age range of 6-19 years. In the latter study, however, preference for complexity decreased between 17 and 19.

A discordant note has been injected by Maurice Hershenson, whose findings indicate that 2-, 3-, and 4-day-old infants do not necessarily prefer the more complex of two patterns. When the stimuli are checkerboard patterns of 4, 16, and 144 squares (the size of the smallest squares is still within the acuity range for this age level), infants look longer at the simplest pattern than at patterns of intermediate or high level of complexity, although the difference is statistically significant only between the 4- and 144-square patterns (Hershenson, 1964). When 5-, 10-, and 20-sided polygons are compared, however, ten-sided polygons are preferred over both five- and 20-sided ones (Hershenson, Munsinger, & Kessen, 1965), although here too the only statistically significant difference is between the five- and ten-sided polygons. Hershenson's conclusion that these two results are in "marked contrast" with Fantz's and that "complexity was not a contributing variable" in the polygon study (Hershenson, Munsinger, & Kessen, 1965) may be contested, however. If, instead of plotting the complexity of the checkerboard patterns as equally spaced points labeled "least," "medium," and "most" (Hershenson, Kessen, & Munsinger, 1967), the number of corners (9, 25, and 169) is taken as a measure of complexity and the results of both the checkerboard and the polygon studies are plotted together (Fig. 9-4), the results

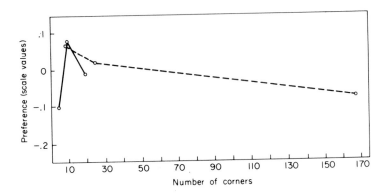

Fig. 9-4. Preference for polygons and checkerboards of varying complexity. Solid line represents data for polygons from Hershenson, Munsinger, and Kessen (1965); dashed line represents data for checkerboards from Hershenson, Kessen, and Munsinger (1964).

turn out to be rather consistent, indicating that the checkerboard study did not test response at the lowest levels of complexity. The preference for ten-sided polygons over five- and 20-sided ones, however, has been confirmed by others (McCall & Kagan, 1967).

Since Hershenon's subjects were infants less than a week old and preference for complexity has been most consistently demonstrated in infants 2-months old or older, a further examination of Hershenson's results was called for, especially for the purpose of testing response to complexity at age levels between birth and two months. Brennan, Ames, and Moore (1966) compared the preferences of infants 3-, 8-, and 14-weeks old to 2 × 2, 8 × 8, and 24 × 24 checkerboard patterns and homogeneous gray. Their results reconcile Hershenson's findings with those of Fantz and others in that the seeming preference for the simpler patterns shown by the younger (3-weeks old) subjects appears to be due to their inability to see the finer grain of the more complex patterns. In the 14-week-old infants, the preference pattern is diametrically opposite (Fig. 9-5). A confirmation of this trend for preference to change from less to more complex stimuli has been obtained in a developmental study of form perception in animals that involved neither visual deprivation nor enrichment (Sackett, 1966).

Learned preferences begin to influence the ranking of shapes of different complexities at later ages. Munsinger (1966) tested preference for random shapes ranging in complexity from 5 to 40 turns in over 800 subjects, children in grades 2-8 and adults. Although nonmonotonic functions were obtained at each age level, preference for the more complex shapes decreased with increasing age, the youngest children preferring the more complex figures while adults preferred

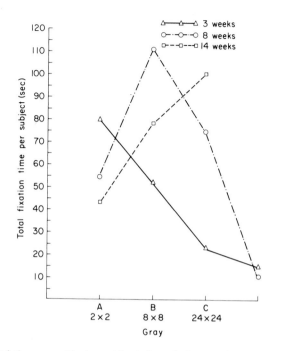

Fig. 9-5. Total time per subject spent by infants 3, 8, and 14 weeks of age looking at checkerboard patterns of varying complexity and a gray square. From Brennan, Ames, and Moore (1966). Copyright 1965 by the American Association for the Advancement of Science.

figures toward the simpler end of the complexity range. Munsinger was able to obtain evidence for the hypothesis that young children prefer high-complexity figures because they sample such figures instead of perceiving them as wholes. When adults were shown 5-, 10-, 20-, and 40-turn figures for 1 sec. only, their preference ranking of shapes was more like that of children, presumably because the short exposure time allowed only incomplete scanning of the shapes.

Transpositional Parameters. When Ghent, Bernstein, and Goldweber (1960) presented realistic and geometric figures to preschool children as they bent down looking between their legs, the children's classification of the stimuli into right-side-up and upside-down ones was guided mainly by their position with regard to the eye (in the case of pictures) or the direction of eye movements made in scanning the stimuli in a cephalo-caudal direction (in the case of geometric figures). In comparison with adult preferences, which dictate the labeling of the position of a figure in accordance with its relationship to the environment, the "egocentric" perception in children seems to take into account mainly the relationship of the observer to the perceived object and to disregard the relationship of the object to the rest of the objects in the immediate visual environment.

In a subsequent study, Ghent (1961) determined the stimulus characteristics of nonrepresentational shapes that correlate with the position that is called upright by preschool children. These were found to be the focal portion of the shape and its main axis. When the focal point was in the upper portion of the shape and the main axis in the vertical position, the figure was more apt to be called upright. Ghent attributed this finding to the tendency of children to scan figures in a downward direction. Because of this, figures in which the position of the focal point and of the main axis interfere with this tendency are apt to be called upside-down. Some studies have given support to Ghent's hypothesis about the direction of scanning movements in children, while others have failed to do so. Systematic studies of the direction and nature of eye movements as a function of age, however, have not been conducted.

Configurational Parameters. Age trends in preference for symmetry, compactness, and the like have not been studied directly. Investigators' attention has been drawn to these variables, however, in the process of investigating the development of response to complexity.

Several investigators have used two-dimensional schematized faces among their form stimuli. Although faces do attract more attention than other types of complex stimuli (Fantz, 1961; McCall & Kagan, 1967), even those who have supported the idea of an inborn preference for faces in human infants (Fantz, 1961) have changed their viewpoint after tests with faces in which the features were "scrambled" showed as much preference being given to the scrambled as to the unscrambled faces (Fantz, 1963a; Hershenson et al., 1967). Silbiger's (1968) study is the most recent and thorough comparative study of the relative importance of facedness and complexity as determiners of attention in the human infant. Using two-dimensional faces, simple, complex, abstract, and scrambled, and presenting various combinations of these to infants aged 2½-8 months, Silbiger established that (a) attentional preferences are a function of complexity; (b) attentional preferences based on complexity are a function of age; (c) when faces and abstracts of equal complexity are paired, faces elicit more attention; and (d) differential attention to faces, as compared with abstracts of equal complexity, increases with age.

Some investigators have hypothesized that even when complexity seems to be the chief determinant of preference, it may actually be some other variable or variables which, instead of or in addition to, complexity also determine preference (e.g., Spears, 1964). McCall and Kagan (1967) state outright that the number of fixations elicited by five-, ten-, and 20-sided polygons in 4-month-old infants is a function of mean contour length and unrelated to the number of turns. In random shapes, the number of turns and length of the perimeter are not independent of each other, however, since an increase in the number of sides or vertices of necessity leads to an increase in the length of the perimeter.

G. RECOGNITION AND IDENTIFICATION

Informational Parameters. Complexity was found by Wallace (1956) to decrease identification speed in older individuals in a situation where figures were displayed through a scanning aperture which permitted only a partial view of the figure at any one time. With simple figures, however, subjects ranging in age from under 30 to above 70 performed at about the same level. The difficulty experienced by older subjects with the more complex figures was attributed by Wallace to the decrease in the ability to integrate amounts of information that exceed a certain limit. Munsinger (1965) obtained analogous results using a tachistoscopic recognition task: both adults and children found 5-turn random shapes easier to recognize than 20-turn shapes.

Degrees of completeness or closure of a figure also represent different amounts of information. In comparison with high-school-age pupils, subjects aged 7-9 are more likely to recognize a closed figure than an open one (i.e., supply missing information), whereas subjects in the age range of 11-14 recognize either kind equally well (Tiernan, 1938).

Transpositional Parameters. Most developmental studies of recognition have been concerned with age differences in the ability to recognize shapes when these are reflected about a vertical or horizontal axis. As in the case of discrimination of mirror-image forms, there is always the question of whether a child actually fails to perceive the difference between them when no verbalization is made or whether the difference is perceived but no importance is attached to it. Thus, Rice's (1930) early study of the effect of rotation on recognition is equivocal because the failure of the subjects (children aged 4-5) to comment spontaneously on the shapes not being right-side-up is no indication that they did not perceive the difference. Rice, nevertheless, concluded that there is a sudden increase in the importance of form orientation between the ages of 5 and 6. Davidson's (1935) finding that confusion of up-down reflections and/or rotations of letters (*d-p, q-b, p-b*) is largely overcome by the time the child reaches the mental age of 6 is equivocal for the same reason. Davidson also found that right-left confusion of letters (*b-d, p-q*) continues until the mental age of about 7½. While the greater ease in identification of up-down reflections than of right-left reflections has also been shown by Newhall (1937), it must be remembered that the relative position of reflected shapes as they are presented to subjects plays a crucial role, as it did in Huttenlocher's (1967) discrimination experiment, mentioned above.

Shapes and objects presented in their upright position are recognized more often than when they are rotated to some other position. While in infants no verbal response of recognition may be obtained, smiling may be assumed to be a social response to familiar stimuli, i.e., a recognition response. Watson (1966) obtained more smiling responses from infants under 6 months of age to faces (those of the experimenter and of the subjects' mothers), pictures of faces, and a T when these were presented in $0°$ orientation than when rotated 90, 180, or 270 degrees. While the amount of smiling was not related to object familiarity, responses to rotated figures reached peaks at different ages and occurred earliest when the stimuli were not rotated. Subjects aged 3-4 recognize more representational (and monooriented) object pictures in the right-side-up than in any other position, but children 5-7-years old recognize them equally well in different orientations (Ghent, 1960). Ghent and Bernstein (1961) presented tachistoscopically various outline geometric figures that had been found to elicit strong preferences for orientation (Ghent, 1961) to 3-, 4-, and 5-year-old children. Recognition was found to be best when the forms were presented in the preferred right-side-up position. Ghent and Bernstein interpret this finding as evidence in support of the hypothesis that scanning of form starts with a focal point and continues in a downward direction, since the preferred orientation was one that had the focal point of a form in the upper portion of the shape and the main axis in a vertical position. In a subsequent study, Ghent (1964) concluded that the effect of preferred orientation on recognition is more immediately related to the speed of visual recognition than to mental or chronological ages. In addition, making a distinction between focal and distinguishing features of a form, Ghent (1965) found that recognition is enhanced in 3-year-old children if the focal point is at the top of the figure, whereas 5-year-old children were helped by the distinguishing feature's being in that position. Ghent interprets this finding as a developmental change in ocular scanning patterns.

Configurational Parameters. Developmental trends in the response to configurational parameters in recognition and identification tasks have practically not been studied at all. Crook, Alexander, Anderson, Coules, Hanson, & Jeffries (1958) conducted a large-scale (176 male subjects) study of discrimination, recognition, and identification of embedded, incomplete, familiar, and nonrepresentational but otherwise unquantified forms under conditions of tachistoscopic exposure, threshold luminance levels, and visual noise. The subjects' ages ranged from middle teens to the late fifties. Under optimum conditions, little difference in performance was noted as a function of age. Under less-than-optimum conditions, however, and especially at very low luminance levels, increasing losses as a function of increasing age were noted.

Munsinger and Forsman (1966), who studied the perception of symmetric and asymmetric random shapes of 5, 10, and 20 turns, noted that tachistoscopic recognition performance in their subjects (1st to 6th grades) improved with age. The results of this and the study just mentioned would indicate that tachistoscopic recognition performance and age between 5 and 50 are related by an inverted U function. As to symmetry, Munsinger and Forsman found that the addition of a symmetric half to the five- and ten-sided figures facilitated recognition but that a similar operation on the 20-sided shapes made recognition more difficult. These authors suggest that an explanation of this difference may lie in added symmetry acting like noise in the case of the more complex figures, while in figures that are at or near the subject's limit for processing information symmetry facilitates recognition.

H. REPRODUCTION

Age trends for the reproduction task have not been clearly established, because few studies have been conducted for that purpose. In an early study, Granit (1921) attempted to establish some of the determinants of reproduction in children and adults. His conclusion was that, when more or less ambiguous designs are presented tachistoscopically, children reproduce them more in accordance with what they know (i.e., by drawing familiar figures that resemble the stimulus figures) while adults draw them more in accordance with what they see. Beery (1968) found that form-reproduction scores of 1st-, 4th-, and 6th-graders were related primarily to mental age rather than chronological age.

As to accuracy, Osterrieth (1944) found that the accuracy of reproduction of complex nonrepresentational forms improves with age (4 years through adulthood) reaching a maximum at 9 years, while the time required to recall and to copy a figure decreases with age and with the goodness of the reproduction. Deviations from accuracy in children aged 5-10 were attributed by Slochower (1946) to a tendency to improve the figure in accordance with the Gestalt principles rather than simply a lack of dexterity in reproducing graphic models. Performance in a task involving the reproduction of designs made by a moving spot of light also improves with age, reaching the adult level at about the age of 16 (Johnson, Nilsson, & Weikert, 1968). As in Beery's (1968) study, goodness of reproduction was found by these investigators to correlate with intelligence-test scores. As far as the perception of configurations as wholes goes, the method used by Johnson *et al.* shows a slower rate of development than, e.g., the tachistoscopic method.

2. Clinical Data

In his celebrated query addressed to John Locke, Molyneux speculated that a man born blind but made seeing as an adult would not be able to distinguish between a cube and a sphere by sight alone even if he had learned this identification by touch while still blind. Molyneux was actually proposing an exploratory experiment long before psychological experimentation had begun.

For obvious reasons, no experiments of this nature have been performed on humans. Clinical cases of congenital blindness from which patients have recovered as adults, however, supply an answer to Molyneux's query, and the answer is very much like what Molyneux, Locke, and other empiricists thought it would be.

von Senden's 1932 monograph (von Senden, 1960), which Hebb (cf. Chap. 4) repeatedly refers to in his *Organization of Behavior,* reviewed all reports published up to that date on the vision of patients who, when operated upon for congenital blindness, were old enough to give a verbal report of what they saw. Most of the cases described were operated for cataracts, the clouding of the lens or the cornea. Cataracts admit diffuse light to the interior of the eye but do not allow pattern vision. The fact that diffuse light does illuminate the retina is important since animal experiments have demonstrated that in the absence of photic stimulation the retina degenerates, making vision impossible, whereas diffuse light, such as is allowed to enter the animal's eye through a ping-pong ball, for instance, permits normal maturation of the retina (e.g., Riesen, 1950).

The oldest of von Senden's 66 reports dates back to 1020 A.D. Even the more recent ones are incomplete at best, and many suffer from a lack of scientific rigor. In none of them was the physician primarily concerned with form perception. Since the postoperative tests were of necessity related to visual performance, they included tests of form vision and hence are relevant to the question of how form perception develops. The remarkable feature of these reports is that, in spite of the diversity of time, place, and testing method and the evident unawareness in at least some of the investigators of the work done by the others, considerable agreement exists concerning vision in cataract patients during the immediate postoperative period.

The unitary nature of figures and their distinctiveness from ground is perceived by all patients immediately upon acquiring vision. While in many patients vision is at first made difficult by nystagmus, dizziness, and other symptoms that interfere with vision, there is no doubt that patients respond to figures as wholes and that the figures are differentiated from ground. It must be concluded that the perception of figural unity is due to some innate mechanism requiring no previous experience for its existence.

von Senden's case histories are just as unequivocal in pointing out that the perception of figural unity and the identification of figures are two independent processes. The latter does depend on learning, and is therefore absent in an individual who sees for the first time. It is esspecially amazing to learn that, although the distinctive features of an object may be perceived, it takes a very long time for a patient to attach meaning to these features, to remember them, to generalize them, and thus to be able to tell an object, as an object, apart from another, i.e., to identify it. von Senden reports that the shortest time required to learn visual identification was 30 days. Before learning has taken place, while the patient may realize that there is a difference between two objects presented side by side, he cannot label this difference and may resort to such devices as, e.g., counting the number of inflections in a contour before being able to identify the shape. While correspondence between touch and vision in discrimination and recognition tasks is good in normal subjects (cf. Brown & Brumaghim, 1968; Brumaghim & Brown, 1968), such correspondence cannot be established in a blind person. In these, tactual identification may be prompt and precise, with no transfer to the visual modality taking place when the latter begins to function.

One important factor that must not be overlooked in von Senden's cases is that of individual differences. While many of the patients did show extremely slow perceptual learning, some did not. This can be attributed to variables pertaining to the subject (age, sex, intelligence, etc.), variables that are related to the operation (type of cataract, type of operation performed), or to both. The disturbances created by the operation itself cannot be overlooked. Thus, all of von Senden's earliest cases involved the removal of the lens, which results in a longer period of adjustment before normal vision is established. Operable opacity of the cornia leads to a lesser degree of damage to the eye. Corneal grafting was unknown in 1932. This method results in the most satisfactory restoration of vision in cases of corneal opacity. The most recent case of recovery from early blindness through a corneal transplant (Gregory & Wallace, 1963) shows that a combination of subject's intelligence and the corneal transplant technique may result in extremely rapid perceptual learning. The case of the patient S.B. is also unique in that it was investigated in detail by a psychologist whose main field of interest is vision.

After the bandages were removed, S.B. saw only a blur in the direction from which the surgeon's voice came. He did not at first see a world of objects, but was able to use his eyes well within a few days. This included the ability to tell time from a large wall clock, indicating rapid visual form-discrimination learning. S.B., however, had been acquainted with clocks by having used a pocket watch without a cover glass. Unlike von Senden's cases, S.B. apparently transferred meaningful information from the tactual to the visual modality without difficulty, being able to identify most objects that he had known previously by touch. This applied to the recognition of capital letters and numerals, which he had learned to recognize by touch, but it took him a long time to learn lowercase letters (which he had not touched in relief before), and he never learned to read by sight more than a few simple words. S.B. was able to make recognizable drawings of objects or models of objects he had touched before as early as 48 hr. after the operation and before having seen the objects. This included such things as buses and elephants. One type of visual form phenomenon that S.B. was unable to see was the geometric illusions (the Hering, Helmholtz, Zoellner, and Poggendorff illusions were used) and to experience reversals in reversible-perspective drawings (the Necker cube and the Schroeder staircase).

The case of S.B. is the best documented clinical case of vision gained in adulthood, and it does not confirm the slow identification learning rates reported by von Senden. It also throws doubt on the usefulness of adult clinical cases in making inferences about form perception in human infants. While some aspects of the initial stages of form perception may be similar, the differences between an immature and a mature nervous system, an intact and a damaged visual system, and, most important of all, between a totally inexperienced individual and an adult who has had all the experiences of adulthood with the exception of visual ones, are too great to allow anything but the simplest kind of analogy to be drawn.

3. Animal Studies

A. VISUAL-DEPRIVATION STUDIES

Following Hebb's (1949) suggestion, numerous studies of the effects of sensory deprivation have been performed with animal subjects. The number of studies in which the effects of deprivation on form perception have been tested deliberately and directly, however, is surprisingly small. Visual-deprivation experiments with different species show more or less marked impairment in the animal's visual function after removal to normal daylight conditions. It is also clear that there are profound interspecies differences in the severity of the effects of visual deprivation. It is probably true that the higher animals suffer more from deprivation than do lower animals. Unfortunately, the available data are confounded by the effects of the animal's life span and the duration of the deprivation period. Little attention has been paid to comparing the normal life spans of different species of animals and the relative duration of the deprivation period in research of the effects of deprivation on different species. The data are consistent, though, with the notion that lower animals are more resilient and suffer less from visual deprivation. Hebb (1937), in a study that started the present deprivation literature, found that dark-reared rats behaved in a practically normal fashion when given form-discrimination tasks upon being brought into light for the first time. Similar results were obtained later by Gibson, Walk, & Tighe (1959). Sixteen months of total darkness, however, made Riesen's (1947) two chimpanzees practically blind. In subsequent experiments, Riesen (1950) showed that the important factor was patterning of light, and that even as little as 1½ hr. of patterned light a day produced no adverse effects in any of the visual functions of a chimpanzee, whereas diffuse light led to initially inadequate performance on various visual tests, including the discrimination between vertical and horizontal stripes. This difficulty could be overcome only by training. Rhesus monkeys, on the other hand, deprived of pattern vision for up to 60 days differ little from normal controls in the rate of learning to discriminate forms and striations (Wilson & Riesen, 1966).

Hebb, in his *Organization of Behavior,* refers to both von Senden and Riesen for support of the hypothesis that experience is necessary for form discrimination. Some of Hebb's predictions concerning the effects of visual deprivation on pattern vision have not been borne out by subsequent research. Thus, his prediction of no interocular transfer of pattern-discrimination learning in visually deprived animals has been shown not to be true in the case of doves (Siegel, 1953a, 1953b) and cats (Meyers & McCleary, 1964). While in both species pattern-discrimination learning in deprived subjects was slower than in normal ones, pattern discrimination learned with one eye transferred to the other without too much difficulty. Visually-deprived rats tested by Michels, Bevan, and Strasel (1958) also behaved somewhat differently from Hebb's (1937) rats. Given three magnitude-discrimination tasks (brightness, size, height) and a form-discrimination task, the dark-reared animals showed progressive improvement in performance on the magnitude-discrimination task but performed more poorly on the form-discrimination task. Light-reared rats, by contrast, were superior to the dark-reared rats and performed uniformly on all four tasks. Both dark-reared and light-reared rats given the magnitude-discrimination problems before the form-discrimination problems were superior to rats given only the form problems. There was no difference in the performance of dark- and light-reared rats given only the form-discrimination problem: performance was much inferior to performance on this task after the magnitude-discrimination task learning. Evidence that the main types of form parameter may not be equivalent when testing post deprivation performance of animals is also provided by Tees (1968) in a study of the effects of visual deprivation on the discrimination of orientation and of patterns. While there was no significant difference between the visually deprived and normal rats in learning orientation problems with rectangles as stimuli, there was a highly significant difference between them in performance on pattern-discrimination tasks. Both area and rotation belong to the class of transpositional parameters, and their discrimination seems to be much easier than discrimination on tasks where the informational or configurational parameters are varied.

It does not appear that animal work has provided any firm conclusions regarding the genesis of form perception. There is no doubt that the experience of patterned light is necessary for the development of normal visual functioning, but this finding does not clarify the issue as to the precise mechanism that underlies normal form discrimination. While visual deprivation means lack of visual experience, it does not automatically mean that poorer visual performance after a period of deprivation is due to this lack of experience. As Teuber (1960) points out, it may be due to at least three other factors. One is that even after a relatively short period of deprivation some atrophy of structure takes place in the visual system, such as a decrease in nucleic proteins and acids and a loss of nerve fibers, which by itself may produce the poorer performance of visually-deprived animals on visual tasks. Another is that normal functions of a deprived visual system may be suppressed, as in the case of unilateral squint. Form perception may be lacking in a person with this defect while dark adaptation, spectral sensitivity, and other basic visual functions are present. A third factor is that, in addition to the specific impairment produced in the visual system proper, visual deprivation may lead to more general retardation which, in turn, would lead to lowered performance on postdeprivation visual tasks.

B. VISUAL-ENRICHMENT STUDIES

A seeing person's visual environment is so rich that studies of the effects of visual enrichment or differential exposure to form cannot be performed with human subjects. The visual environment of the typical laboratory animal, however, is sufficiently undifferentiated to make such studies possible using animal subjects.

As in the case of visual deprivation, the study of the effects of visual enrichment on visual perception was first suggested by Hebb (1949). Hebb described an informal experiment that demonstrated the superiority in visual discrimination of rats raised as pets over laboratory-raised animals. Of importance here is the variant of this type of study in which animals are exposed to specific forms for prolonged periods of time, then compared with control animals on their rate of discrimination learning. Without exception, the rat has been the only species used in enrichment and specific form preexposure studies.

Gibson and Walk (1956) performed the first experiment on the effects of specific form exposure upon subsequent discrimination performance, and all studies that have followed it have been attempts at replication or clarification of the Gibson and Walk study. Gibson and Walk split laboratory-born litters of rats into experimental and control groups, and raised the experimental group in cages that had black-painted metal forms (two equilateral triangles and two circles) handing from the cage walls, one on each wall, while the controls had no forms in their cages and could see only their cagemates, food, and water bottle. After 90 days under these conditions, the animals were given a discrimination-learning task. Figure 9-6 gives evidence of a clear-cut difference between the experimental and control subjects. This difference, according to Gibson and Walk, must be attributed to simple unreinforced visual experience with the forms to be discriminated.

In a subsequent experiment, Gibson, Walk, Pick, & Tighe (1968) examined the question of whether exposure to specific forms faciliated subsequent discrimination learning of these forms or whether such exposure generalized to other forms as well. It was found that, when the test forms were similar to the exposure forms (circle-ellipse, equilateral triangle-isosceles triangle), the experi-

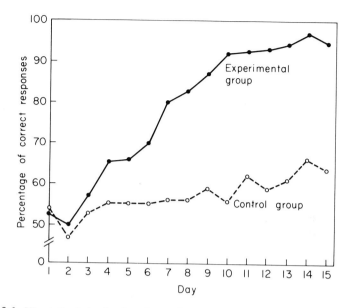

Fig. 9-6. Visual discrimination-learning performance in two groups of rats, one of which received prior exposure to the visual stimuli used in the experiment. From Gibson and Walk (1956). Copyright 1956 by the American Psychological Association. Reproduced by permission.

mental rats showed superiority in discrimination learning over control rats. In a second experiment, however, no significant difference was found between experimental and control groups that were preexposed to triangles and circles and irregular "rocks," respectively, and tested on either triangles and circles or horizontal and vertical striations. The only significant difference was found to exist between subjects in all of these conditions and a control group which had not been exposed to any forms and was tested on triangle-circle discrimination. Thus, the second experiment failed to clarify the issue and only confirmed the well-known fact that the discrimination between horizontal and vertical striations is the easiest one for a rat to learn. In the same study, it was also found that exposure to a single form facilitated subsequent discrimination between this and another form, but the question of whether exposures to single and to two forms were equivalent was not answered.

Forgus (1956) confirmed the finding of Gibson and Walk (1956) and also showed that exposure to forms between the ages of 16 and 41 days was more effective than exposure between the ages of 41 and 66 days. Gibson *et al.,* (1959), however, were not able to confirm Forgus' latter result. At the same time, it cannot be said Gibson *et al.* had tested the hypothesis of early versus late exposure adequately, since the early-exposure group had a nonexposure interval of 40 days before they were tested, along with the late-exposure group at the age of 90 days. Thus, the question about age and transfer effect remained unanswered.

Two subsequent studies by Forgus (1958a, 1958b) suggested that, when the forms are presented on cage walls next to each other (rather than each on a separate wall, as in the study done by Gibson and Walk), rats may learn to respond to this double configuration as a whole and therefore experience interference when required to discriminate between the two forms. Forgus also demonstrated that, when the exposure forms differ from the test forms (such as when only the angles or only the sides of a triangle are presented), discrimination is superior as compared to the condition when they are identical.

Further experiments were performed to answer questions about other conditions of preexposure. Gibson *et al.* (1959) found no transfer effect when the forms were painted on the walls of the cages, and suggested that the three-dimensionality of cutout shapes (that were used in the 1956 experiment by Gibson and Walk) was a facilitating factor. A study designed to test this hypothesis specifically (Walk, Gibson, Pick, & Tighe, 1959), however, showed a difference between painted and cutout figures at the .05 level of significance only. It must be mentioned, though, that Forgus (1958a, 1958b) did find positive transfer from exposure to painted forms.

As to reinforcement, a study (Walk, Gibson, Pick, & Tighe, 1958) conducted specifically to see whether it was food reinforcement that produced transfer showed that preexposure and not reinforcement was the decisive factor. Kerpelman (1965) has argued, nevertheless, that even nondifferential reinforcement may be expected to lead to faster discrimination learning, and has studied the effects of feeding and not feeding the rats in the presence of the forms. Kerpelman's evidence is equivocal, since the results from one of his experimental conditions favors the differentiation hypothesis while another condition favors the reinforcement hypothesis. In addition, Kerpelman also appears to have confounded reinforcement with attention (cf. Forgus, 1966). Bennett and Ellis (1968) have nevertheless produced evidence favoring Kerpelman. They allowed some rats to manipulate the forms (a triangle and a circle) during the preexposure period. Nondifferential reinforcement led to better performance in rats that had been allowed to manipulate the forms, whereas manipulation alone in the absence of nondifferential reinforcement produced no effect. Rats who had received nondifferential reinforcement performed better than rats who received differential experience alone. For this reason, Bennett and Ellis question the adequacy of both the "attention-getting" hypothesis and differentiation-alone hypothesis to account for the transfer effects.

In contrast to the early experiments, the later experimental evidence provided by both Gibson and Forgus attenuates the certainty of their earlier statements concerning the effects of form preexposure. There had also been at least one instance of a failure to replicate the results of the 1956 study by Gibson and Walk (Baird & Becknell, 1962). At the same time, the transfer effects of nonreinforced exposure to visual forms have been demonstrated so many times that the existence of the phenomenon cannot be doubted. The question of what accounts for the facilitation produced by form preexposure has been given several answers. One well-known answer has been provided by the Gibsons (Gibson & Gibson, 1955). It speaks of a sharpening of the organism's capacity for perceptual discrimination (differentiation) as the result of differential exposure to stimuli. Forgus (1966) favors the view that, as a result of preexposure, a disposition develops to base differential behavior on visual discrimination. Even though reinforcement is not contingent on the presence of specific forms, it is still possible that forms may come to serve as discriminative stimuli for other types of discriminatory behavior: if the discrimination-learning task involves learning the difference between two forms and also which of them is the positive one, then the experimental animals have an advantage because they have learned the first part of the task already. Another view is based on the concept of novelty and exploration. Animals preexposed to a set of stimuli are more likely to respond to the reward situation than animals not so exposed or exposed to one form only. For these subjects, the stimuli are equally novel or one is more novel than the other, and they will therefore engage in exploratory or alternation behavior before beginning to attend to the reward contingencies.

REFERENCES

Baird, J. C., & Becknell, J. C., Jr. Discrimination learning as a function of early form exposure. *Psychol. Rec.,* 1962, **12**, 309-313.

Beery, K. F. Geometric form reproduction: Relationship to chronological and mental age. *Percept. mot. Skills,* 1968, **26**, 247-250.

Bennett, T. L., & Ellis, H. C. Tactual-kinesthetic feedback from manipulation of visual forms and nondifferential reinforcement in transfer of perceptual learning. *J. exp. Psychol.,* 1968, **77**, 495-500.

Berlyne, D. E. The influence of the albedo and complexity of stimuli on visual fixation in the human infant. *Brit. J. Psychol.,* 1958, **49**, 315-318.

Binet, A. La mesure des illusions visuelles chez les enfants. *Rev. Phil.,* 1895, **40**, 11-25.

Botwinick, J., Robbin, J. S., & Brinley, J. F. Reorganization of perception with age. *J. Geront.,* 1959, **14**, 85-88.

Bower, T. G. Phenomenal identity and form perception in an infant. *Percept. Psychophys.,* 1967, **2**, 74-76.

Brennan, W. M., Ames, E. W., & Moore, R. W. Age differences in infants' attention to patterns of different complexities. *Science,* 1966, **151**, 354-356.

Brown, D. R., & Brumaghim, S. H. Perceptual equivalence, pattern perception, and multidimensional methods. *Percept. Psychophys.,* 1968, **4**, 253-256.

Brumaghim, S. H., & Brown, D. R. Perceptual equivalence between visual and tactual pattern perception: An anchoring study. *Percept. Psychophys.,* 1968, **4**, 175-179.

Cantor, G. N., Cantor, J. H., & Ditrichs, R. Observing behavior in preschool chidlren as a function of stimulus complexity. *Child Develop.,* 1963, **34**, 683-689.

Crook, M. N., Alexander, E. A., Anderson, E. M. S., Coules, J., Hanson, J. A., & Jeffries, N. T., Jr. Age and form perception. *USAF Sch. Aviat. Med. Rep.,* 1958, No. 57-124.

Davidson, H. P. A study of reversals in young children. *J. genet. Psychol.,* 1934, **45**, 452-465.

Davidson, H. P. A study of the confusing letters B, D, P, and Q. *J. genet. Psychol.,* 1935, **47**, 458-468.

Eisdorfer, C., & Axelrod, S. Senescence and figural aftereffects in two modalities: A correction. *J. genet. Psychol.,* 1964, **104**, 193-197.

Elkind, D., & Scott, L. Studies in perceptual development: I. The decentering of perception. *Child Develop.,* 1962, **33**, 619-630.

Elkind, D., Koegler, R. R., & Go, E. Effects of perceptual training at three age levels. *Science,* 1962, **137**, 755-756.

Epstein, W. *Varieties of perceptual learning.* New York: McGraw-Hill, 1967.

Estes, B. W. Judgment of size in relation to geometric shape. *Child Develop.,* 1961, **32**, 277-286.

Fantz, R. L. A method for studying early visual development. *Percept. mot. Skills,* 1956, **6**, 13-15.

Fantz, R. L. Pattern vision in young infants. *Psychol. Rec.,* 1958, **8**, 43-47.

Fantz, R. L. The origin of form perception. *Sci. Amer.,* 1961, **204**(5).

Fantz, R. L. Pattern discrimination and selective visual attention in the young infant as determinants of perceptual development. Paper read at AAAS symposium on "The development of perception during the first six months of life," at Cleveland, Ohio, December, 1963. (a)

Fantz, R. L. Pattern vision in newborn infants. *Science,* 1963, **140**, 296-297. (b)

Fantz, R. L., Ordy, J. M., & Udelf, M. S. Maturation of pattern vision in infants during the first six months. *J. comp. physiol. Psychol.,* 1962, **55**, 907-917.

Farkas, M. Fluctuatiile in perceperea figurilor reversibile la diferite virste. [Age differences in the perception of reversible figures.] *Stud. Univ. Babes-Bolyai,* 1959, 3(1, No. 4), 97-109.

Fellows, B. J. *The discrimination process and development.* New York: Pergamon Press, 1968.

Forgus, R. H. Advantage of early over late perceptual experience in improving form discrimination. *Can. J. Psychol.,* 1956, **10**, 147-155.

Forgus, R. H. The effect of different kinds of form preexposure on form discrimination learning. *J. comp. physiol. Psychol.,* 1958, **51**, 75-78. (a)

Forgus, R. H. The interaction between form preexposure and text requirements in determing form discrimination. *J. comp. physiol. Psychol.,* 1958, **51**, 588-591. (b)

Forgus, R. H. *Perception.* New York: McGraw-Hill, 1966.

Gajo, F. D. Adult age differences in the perception of visual illusions. Unpublished doctoral dissertation, Washington Univ., 1966. *Diss. Abstr.,* 1967, **27**(12-B), 4573.

Ghent Braine, L. Age changes in the mode of perceiving geometric forms. *Psychon. Sci.,* 1965, **2**, 155-156.

Ghent, L. Perception of overlapping and embedded figures by children of different ages. *Amer. J. Psychol.,* 1956, **69**, 575-587.

Ghent, L. Recognition by children of realistic figures presented in various orientations. *Can. J. Psychol.,* 1960, **14**, 249-256.

Ghent, L. Form and its orientation: A child's-eye view. *Amer. J. Psychol.*, 1961, **74**, 177-190.

Ghent, L. Effect of orientation on recognition of geometric forms by retarded children. *Child Develop.*, 1964, **35**, 1127-1136.

Ghent, L., & Bernstein, L. Influence of the orientation of geometric forms on their recognition by children. *Percept. mot. Skills*, 1961, **12**, 95-101.

Ghent, L., Bernstein, L., & Goldweber, A. M. Preferences for orientation of form under varying conditions. *Percept. mot. Skills*, 1960, **11**, 46.

Gibson, J. J., & Gibson, E. J. Perceptual learning: Differentiation or enrichment? *Psychol. Rev.*, 1955, **62**, 32-41.

Gibson, E. J., & Walk, R. D. The effect of prolonged exposure to visually presented patterns on learning to discriminate them. *J. comp. physiol. Psychol.*, 1956, **49**, 239-242.

Gibson, E. J., Walk, R. D., Pick, H. L., & Tighe, T. J. The effect of prolonged exposure to visual patterns on learning to discriminate similar and different patterns. *J. comp. physiol. Psychol.*, 1958, **51**, 584-587.

Gibson, E. J., Walk, R. D., & Tighe, T. J. Enhancement and deprivation of visual stimulation during rearing as factors in visual discrimination learning. *J. comp. physiol. Psychol.*, 1959, **52**, 74-81.

Gibson, E. J., Gibson, J. J., Pick, A. D., & Osser, H. A developmental study of the discrimination of letter-like forms. *J. comp. physiol. Psychol.*, 1962, **55**, 897-906.

Giering, H. Das Augenmass bei Schulkindern. *Z. Psychol.*, 1905, **39**, 42-87.

Granit, A. R. A study on the perception of form. *Brit. J. Psychol.*, 1921, **12**, 223-247.

Gregory, R. L., & Wallace, J. G. Recovery from early blindness. *Exp. Psychol. Soc. Monogr.*, 1963, No. 2.

Griffin, M. C. Effects of mental and chronological age upon the extent of the horizontal-vertical illusion. Unpublished doctoral dissertation, Univ. of Utah, 1961. *Diss. Abstr.*, 1962, **23**(1), 308.

Haynes, H., White, B. L., & Held, R. Visual accomodation in human infants. *Science*, 1965, **148**, 528-530.

Hebb, D. O. The innate organization of visual activity: I. Perception of figures by rats reared in total darkness. *J. genet. Psychol.*, 1937, **51**, 101-126.

Hebb, D. O. *The organization of behavior.* New York: Wiley, 1949.

Heiss, A. Zum Problem der isolierenden Abstraktion. *Neue psychol. Stud.*, 1930, **4**, 285-318.

Hershenson, M. Visual discrimination in the human newborn. *J. comp. physiol. Psychol.*, 1964, **58**, 270-276.

Hershenson, M. Development of the perception of form. *Psychol. Bull.*, 1967, **67**, 326-336.

Hershenson, M., Munsinger, H., & Kessen, W. Preference for shapes of intermediate variability in the newborn human. *Science*, 1965, **147**, 630-631.

Hershenson, M., Kessen, W., & Munsinger, H. Pattern perception in the human newborn: A close look at some positive and negative results. In W. Wathen-Dunn (Ed.), *Models for the perception of speech and visual forms.* Cambridge, Massachusetts: M.I.T. Press, 1967. Pp. 282-290.

Huttenlocher, J. Discrimination of figure orientation: Effects of relative position. *J. comp. physiol. Psychol.*, 1967, **63**, 359-361.

Immergluck, L. Further comments on "Is the figural aftereffect an *after*effect?" *Psychol. Bull.*, 1968, **70**, 198-200.

Jackson, D. N. A further examination of the role of autism in a visual figure-ground relationship. *J. Psychol.*, 1954, **38**, 339-357.

Johnson, G., Nilsson, I., & Weikert, C. Studies in Gestalt perception: Aspects on development from seven years to adult age. *Psychol. Res. Bull.*, 1968, 8(3).

Kerpelman, L. C. Preexposure to visually presented forms and nondifferential reinforcement in perceptual learning. *J. exp. Psychol.*, 1965, 69, 257-262.

Kerpelman, L. C., & Pollack, R. H. Developmental changes in the location of form discrimination cues. *Percept. mot. Skills*, 1964, 19, 375-382.

Koehler, W., & Wallach, H. Figural aftereffects; an investigation of visual processes. *Proc. Amer. Phil. Soc.*, 1944, 88, 269-357.

Leibowitz, H. W., & Gwozdecki, J. The magnitude of the Poggendorff illusion as a function of age. *Child Develop.*, 1957, 38, 573-580.

Leibowitz, H. W., & Heisel, M. A. L'evolution de l'illusion de Ponzo en function de l'âge. *Arch. Psychol., Genève*, 1958, 36, 328-331.

Leibowitz, H. W., & Judisch, J. M. The relation between age and the magnitude of the Ponzo illusion. *Amer. J. Psychol.*, 1967, 80, 105-109.

Ling, B. C. Form discrimination as a learning cue in infants. *Comp. Psychol. Monogr.*, 1941, 17, No. 2.

Mach, E. *The analysis of sensations.* Chicago: Open Court, 1914. (Republished: New York, Dover, 1959.)

McCall, R. B., & Kagan, J. Attention in the infant: Effects of complexity, contour, perimeter, and familiarity. *Child Develop.*, 1967, 38, 939-952.

Meyers, B., & McCleary, R. A. Interocular transfer of a pattern discrimination in pattern deprived cats. *J. comp. physiol. Psychol.*, 1964, 57, 16-21.

Michels, K. M., Bevan, W., & Strasel, H. C. Discrimination learning and interdimensional transfer under conditions of systematically controlled visual experience. *J. comp. physiol. Psychol.*, 1958, 51, 778-781.

Munsinger, H. Tachistoscopic recognition of stimulus variability. *J. exp. child Psychol.*, 1965, 2, 186-191.

Munsinger, H. Multivariate analysis of preference for variability. *J. exp. Psychol.*, 1966, 71, 889-895.

Munsinger, H., & Forsman, R. Symmetry, development, and tachistoscopic recognition. *J. exp. child Psychol.*, 1966, 3, 168-176.

Munsinger, H., & Kessen, W. Structure, variability, and development. *J. exp. child Psychol.*, 1966, 4, 20-49.

Munsinger, H., & Gummerman, K. Identification of form in patterns of visual noise. *J. exp. Psychol.*, 1967, 75, 81-87.

Munsinger, H., & Weir, M. W. Infants' and young children's preference for complexity. *J. exp. child Psychol.*, 1967, 5, 69-73.

Newhall, S. M. Identification by young children of differently oriented visual forms. *Child Develop.*, 1937, 8, 105-111.

Noelting, G. Recherches sur le développement des perceptions: XL. La structuration progressive de la figure Mueller-Lyer en fonction de la répétition chez l'enfant et l'adulte. *Arch. Psychol., Genève*, 1960, 37, 313-413.

Orton, S. T. *Reading, writing, and speech problems in children.* London: Chapman & Hall, 1937.

Osterrieth, P. A. Le test de copie d'une figure complexe; contribution à l'étude de la perception et de la mémoire. *Arch. Psychol., Genève*, 1944,

Over, R., & Over, J. Detection and recognition of mirror-image obliques by young children. *J. comp. physiol. Psychol.*, 1967, 64, 467-470.

Piaget, J. Recherches sur le développement des perceptions: X. Les illusions relatives aux angles et à la longeur de leurs côtés. *Arch. Psychol., Genève*, 1949, 32, 281-307.

Piaget, J. Le développement des perceptions en fonction de l'âge. In J. Piaget, P. Fraisse, E. Vurpillot, & R. Francès, Traité de psychologie expérimentale. Paris: Presses Universitaires de France. 1967. Pp. 1-62.

Piaget, J., & von Albertini, B. Recherches sur le développement des perceptions: XI. L'illusion de Mueller-Lyer. Arch. Psychol., Genève, 1950, 33, No. 129.

Piaget, J., & Denis-Prinzhorn, M. Recherches sur le développement des perceptions: XXI. L'illusion des quadrilatères partiallement superposés chez l'enfant et chez l'adulte. Arch. Psychol., Genève, 1954, 34, 289-321.

Piaget, J., & Morf, A. Recherches sur le développement des perceptions: XXX. Les comparaisons verticales à faible intervalle. Arch. Psychol., Genève, 1956, 35, 289-319.

Piaget, J., & Morf, A. Les isomorphismes partiels entre les structures logiques et les structures perceptives. In J. Piaget (Ed.), Logique et perception, Vol. 6. Paris: Presses Universitaires de France, 1958. Pp. 49-116.

Piaget, J., & Stettler-von Albertini, B. Recherches sur le développement des perceptions: XIX. Observations sur la perception des bonnes formes chez enfant par actualisation des lignes virtuelles. Arch. Psychol., Genève, 1954, 34, 203-242.

Piaget, J., & Vurpillot, E. Recherches sur le développement des perceptions: XXVII. La surestimation de la courbure des arcs de cercle. Arch. Psychol., Genève, 1956, 35, 215-232.

Piaget, J., Lambercier, M., Boesch, E., & von Albertini, B. Recherches sur le développement des perceptions: I. Introduction a l'étude des perceptions chez l'enfant et analyse d'une illusion relative à la perception visuelle de cercles concentriques (Delboeuf). Arch. Psychol., Genève, 1942, 29, No. 113.

Piaget, J., Maire, F., & Privat, F. Recherches sur le développement des perceptions: XVIII. La resistance des bonnes formes à l'illusion de Mueller-Lyer. Arch. Psychol., Genève, 1954, 34, 155-201.

Pick, A. D. Improvement of visual and tactual form discrimination. J. exp. Psychol., 1965, 69, 331-339.

Pintner, R., & Anderson, M. M. The Mueller-Lyer illusion with children and adults. J. exp. Psychol., 1916, 1, 200-210.

Pollack, R. H. Figural aftereffects as a function of age. Acta Psychol., Amst., 1960, 17, 417-423.

Pollack, R. H. Contour detectability threshold as a function of chronological age. Percept. mot. Skills, 1963, 17, 411-417.

Rajalakshmi, R., & Jeeves, M. A. Changes in tachistoscopic form perception as a function of age and intellectual status. J. Geront., 1963, 18, 275-278.

Ramamurthi, P. V., & Parmeswaran, E. G. A study of figure reversals in the old and the young. J. Psychol. Res., 1964, 8, 16-18.

Rice, C. The orientation of plane figures as a factor in their perception by children. Child Develop., 1930, 1, 111-143.

Rich, T. A. Perceptual aftereffects, learning, and memory in an aged group. Unpublished doctoral dissertation, Univ. of Florida, 1957. Diss. Abstr., 1958, 18, 311-312.

Riesen, A. H. The development of visual perception in man and chimpanzee. Science, 1947, 106, 107-108.

Riesen, A. H. Arrested vision. Sci. Amer., 1950, 183(7).

Rivers, W. H. R. Observations on the senses of the Todas. Brit. J. Psychol., 1905, 1, 321-396.

Robinson, J. S., & Higgins, K. E. The young child's ability to see a difference between mirror-image forms. Percept. mot. Skills, 1967, 25, 893-897.

Rosenblith, J. F. Judgments of simple geometric figures by children. *Percept. mot. Skills,* 1965, **21**, 947-990.

Rudel, R. G., & Teuber, H.-L. Discrimination of direction of line in children. *J. comp. physiol. Psychol.,* 1963, **56**, 892-898.

Ruessel, A. Ein entwicklungspsychologischer Beitrag zur Theorie der geometrisch-optischen Taeuschungen. *Arch. ges. Psychol.,* 1934, **91**, 289-304.

Rush, G. P. Visual grouping in relation to age. *Arch. Psychol.,* 1937, **31**, No. 217.

Sackett, G. P. Development of preference for differentially complex patterns by infant monkeys. *Psychon. Sci.,* 1966, **6**, 441-442.

Salapatek, P., & Kessen, W. Visual scanning of triangles by the human newborn. *J. exp. child Psychol.,* 1966, **3**, 155-167.

Santostefano, S. A developmental study of the Delboeuf illusion. *Percept. mot. Skills,* 1963, **17**, 23-29.

Schafer, R., & Murphy, G. The role of autism in a visual figure-ground relationship. *J. exp. Psychol.,* 1943, **32**, 335-343.

Sekuler, R. W., & Rosenblith, J. F. Discrimination of direction of line and the effect of stimulus alignment. *Psychon. Sci.,* 1964, **1**, 143-144.

Senden, M. von. *Space and sight.* Tr. P. Heath. London/New York: Methuen, 1960.

Shroff, E. Ueber Gestaltauffassung bei Kindern im Alter von 6 bis 14 Jahren. *Psychol. Forsch.,* 1928, **11**, 235-266.

Siegel, A. I. Deprivation of visual form definition in the ring dove. I. Discriminatory learning. *J. comp. physiol. Psychol.,* 1953, **46**, 115-119. (a)

Siegel, A. I. Deprivation of visual form definition in the ring dove. II. Perceptual-motor transfer. *J. comp. physiol. Psychol.,* 1953, **46**, 249-252. (b)

Silbiger, F. F. Facedness and complexity as determiners of attention in the human infant. Unpublished doctoral dissertation, Wayne State U., 1968. *Diss. Abstr.,* 1968, **28**(11-B), 4783.

Slochower, M. Z. Experiments on dimensional and figural problems in the clay and pencil reproductions of line figures by young children: II. Shape. *J. genet. Psychol.,* 1946, **69**, 77-95.

Solley, C. M., & Sommer, R. Perceptual autism in children. *J. gen. Psychol.,* 1957, **56**, 3-11.

Solley, C. M., & Engel, M. Perceptual autism in children: The effects of reward, punishment, and neutral conditions upon perceptual learning. *J. genet. Psychol.,* 1960, **97**, 77-91.

Solley, C. M., & Murphy, G. *Development of the perceptual world.* New York: Basic Books, 1960.

Soudkova, M., & Riškova, A. Vlijane vozrasta na pereocenku vertikalnoi linii v T-figure. *Stud. Psychologica,* 1966, **8**, 204-215.

Spears, W. C. Assessment of visual preference and discrimination in the four-month-old infant. *J. comp. physiol. Psychol.,* 1964, **57**, 381-386.

Staples, R. The responses of infants to color. *J. exp. Psychol.,* 1932, **15**, 119-141.

Stern, W. Ueber verlagerte Raumformen. *Z. Angew. Psychol.,* 1909, **2**, 498-526.

Sun Shih-luh. [Age differences in the Mueller-Lyer illusion.] *Acta Psychol. Sinica,* 1964, No. 3, 223-228.

Tees, R. C. Effect of early restriction on later form discrimination in the rat. *Can J. Psychol.,* 1968, **22**, 294-300.

Teuber, H.-L. Perception. In J. Field, H. W. Magoun, & V. E. Hall (Eds.), *Handbook of physiology,* Vol. 3. Washington, D. C.: American Physiological Soc., 1960. Pp. 1595-1668.

Thomas, H. Preference for random shapes: Ages six through nineteen years. *Child Develop.,* 1966, **37**, 843-859.

Thurner, F. K., & Seyfried, H. Are figural after-effects dependent upon age? *Acta psychol., Amsterdam,* 1962, **20**(1), 58-68.

Tiernan, J. J. The principle of closure in terms of recall and recognition. *Amer. J. Psychol.,* 1938, **51**, 97-108.

van Biervliet, J. J. Nouvelles mesures des illusions chez les adultes et les enfants. *Rev. Phil.,* 1896, **41**, 169-181.

Vurpillot, E. L'influence de la signification du matériel sur l'illusion de Poggendorff. *Ann. Psychol.,* 1957, **57**, 339-357.

Vurpillot, E. *L'organization perceptive: Son rôle dans l'evolution des illusions optico-geometriques.* Paris: Librairie Philosophique J. Vrin, 1963.

Walk, R. D., Gibson, E. J., Pick, H. L., Jr., & Tighe, T. J. Further experiments on prolonged exposure to visual forms: The effect of single stimuli and prior reinforcement. *J. comp. physiol. Psychol.,* 1958, **51**, 483-487.

Walk, R. D., Gibson, E. J., Pick, H. L., Jr., & Tighe, T. J. The effectiveness of prolonged exposure to cutouts vs. painted patterns for facilitation of discrimination. *J. comp. physiol. Psychol.,* 1959, **52**, 519-526.

Wallace, J. G. Some studies of perception in relation to age. *Brit. J. Psychol.,* 1956, **47**, 283-297.

Walters, A. A genetic study of geometrical-optical illusions. *Genet. Psychol. Monogr.,* 1942, **25**, 101-155.

Wapner, S., & Werner, H. *Perceptual development: An investigation within the framework of sensory-tonic field theory.* Worcester: Clark Univ. Press, 1957.

Watson, J. S. Perception of object orientation in infants. *Merrill-Palmer Quart.,* 1966, **12**, 73-94.

Welch, L. The development of discrimination of form and area. *J. Psychol.,* 1939, **7**, 37-54. (a)

Welch, L. The development of size discrimination between the ages of 12 and 40 months. *J. genet. Psychol.,* 1939, **55**, 243-268. (b)

Wertheimer, M. Figural aftereffects as a measure of metabolic efficiency. *J. Person.,* 1955, **24**, 56-73.

Wilson, P. D., & Riesen, A. H. Visual development in rhesus monkeys neonatally deprived of patterned light. *J. comp. physiol. Psychol.,* 1966, **61**, 87-95.

Winch, W. H. The vertical-horizontal illusion in school children. *Brit. J. Psychol.,* 1907, **2**, 220-225.

Witkin, H. A., Lewis, H. B., Hertzman, M., Machover, K., Meissner, P. B., & Wapner, S. *Personality through perception.* New York: Harper, 1954.

Wohlwill, J. F. Developmental studies in perception. *Psychol. Bull.,* 1960, **57**, 249-288.

Wohlwill, J. F., & Wiener, M. Discrimination of form orientation in young children. *Child Develop.,* 1964, **35**, 1113-1125.

Wuersten, H. Recherches sur le développement des perceptions: IX. L'evolution des comparaisons de longeurs de l'enfant à l'adulte avec variation d'angle entre la verticale et l'horizontale. *Arch. Psychol., Genève,* 1947, **32**, 1-144.

Chapter 10 / APPLICATIONS AND AESTHETICS

In many instances, it is inappropriate to speak of the "application" of visual-form-research findings to military, industrial, and other practical problems. For every instance in which laboratory findings have been applied to practical problems, there is one in which the problem has been solved or at least worked on within its own confines, with no reference to "pure" research.

Another characteristic of the applied aspect of visual form perception is that, while the number of specific problem areas is small and the areas are narrow and limited, they are always enmeshed with other problem areas. Thus, the problems of camouflage include not only the application of Gestalt laws to the structuring of the contours of the object to be camouflaged, but also the blending of its colors with the colors of the surround, as well as considerations concerning movement, illumination, shadows, paints to be used, hardware, etc. Likewise, reading performance depends not only on the configuration of the letters, their spacing, and other form characteristics, but also on the color of the paper, illumination, and a variety of other factors. In addition, reading is not chiefly a task of form detection or discrimination; it involves higher cognitive functions which normally need not be considered in form-perception experiments.

The main reason for the brevity of this chapter is that many of the basic principles and research findings that can and have been applied in practical situations have already been dealt with fully in the preceding chapters. In Chap. 3, pattern perception by computers was discussed. The ultimate purpose, expressed or implied, of every researcher writing a pattern-recognition program is to produce an automaton that will recognize patterns, and to put this automaton to work. In Chap. 4, the Gestalt theory of form was discussed, including the Gestalt laws of organization and the figure-ground phenomena. These form the basis of any successful effort to camouflage objects in a natural environment. The geometric illusions, also discussed in Chap. 4, may, on occasion, be a source of error in instrument reading and affect the legibility of alphanumeric characters. The entire Chap. 5 on the dimensions of form is basic to the design of visual displays that are to be perceived under less than optimum conditions of visibility, and some of the experimental findings described in Chap. 6 are directly translatable into recommendations for military and industrial applications. Those who wish to pursue any particular application problem further are referred to the various bibliographies and major works that survey each of the problem areas.

1. Military and Industrial Applications

Reviews of the requirements of the armed forces and of engineering psychology in the area of form perception (cf. Bersh, 1957; Fitts, 1951; Harker, 1957; Weisz, Licklider, Swets, & Wilson 1962; White, 1957) emphasize a relatively small number of restricted problem areas, some of which are specific to the armed forces only, such as comouflage, but most of which are equally relevant to both military interests and man-machine system designing in industrial settings.

The three major problem areas are detection, camouflage, and legibility. These areas may be thought of as concrete manifestations of the concepts associated with the three vertices of the triangle of figure-ground phenomena discussed in Chap. 4 and illustrated in Fig. 4-2. The detection of objects under less than optimum conditions corresponds to the detection of figures under conditions of random noise; the discrimination (or recognition, if the object is familiar) of camouflaged objects corresponds to the detection/discrimination tasks when noise is organized so that it incorporates the object's contours; and legibility concerns the relative discriminability of alphanumeric characters as a function of their shape and under conditions of no noise. The relationship between these tasks is illustrated in Fig. 10-1, which may be considered an "applied" version of Fig. 4-2. Other tasks, such as the discrimination of radar blips and visual search can also be located in this triangle in some relationship to its three cardinal points. Thus, it may be said that the bulk of applied problems in industrial and military psychology dealing with form perception concern some aspect of figure-ground discrimination.

A collection of papers concerning many aspects of form discrimination as applied to military problems resulted from a symposium on the subject held in 1957 (Wulfeck & Taylor, 1957), which appears to be the only book-size reference of this type. The annual US Army human factors research and development conference reports are a source of periodical information about ongoing research in human factors, including form perception. No book exists on form discrimination as related to industrial problems, although most texts in industrial psychology, engineering psychology, instrument and equipment design, etc. contain a chapter or section on the role of form discrimination in

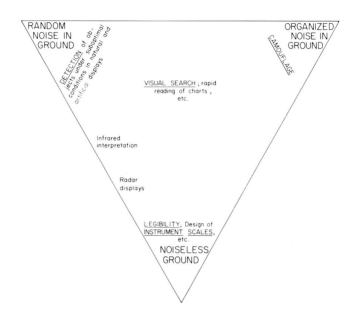

Fig. 10-1. Visual form-perception tasks in industrial and military settings conceived as instances of the discrimination of figure on noisy ground, with noise varying in amount and degree of organization.

man-machine systems, legibility, and the like (e.g., Chapanis, 1965; Fitts, 1967; Morgan, 1963).

In military operations, the problem of detecting or discriminating shape under conditions of reduced visibility takes a number of specific forms: the detection of ships in fog, at long distances, or in turbulent atmospheric conditions; the detection of enemy troops in haze, fog, or at night; the discrimination of significant targets by pilots of low-flying reconnaissance aircraft; the discrimination of enemy armor and aircraft silhouettes; interpretation of aerial photographs, and the like.

The pertinent literature is extensive; bibliographies and review articles, however, have been prepared for a few selected topics only: Blackwell's (1946) review of laboratory studies of the visibility of targets; a review of laboratory studies pertaining to visual air reconnaissance by Boynton, Elworth, and Palmer (1958); Duntley's (1948) article on the visibility of distant objects; Ireland's (1967) bibliography on the effects of surround illumination on visual performance; the visibility bibliography compiled by Leikind and Weiner (1952); and the detection, identification, and visual search bibliography compiled by Lyman (1968) are examples.

(a)   (b)

Fig. 10-2. In 1968, a cluster of silhouetted F–111A jet fighter planes [(a) from Wide World Photos] mimicked a six-choice discrimination problem used by the author three years earlier [(b) from Zusne (1965)].

While concern with form perception in connection with detection problems began with World War II, camouflage as an aspect of military operations arose early in this century. In September of 1914, Sir John Graham Kerr told the First Lord of the Admiralty about methods to render ships at sea less easily recognizable through the use of countershading and disruptive coloring, a method which later became known as "dazzle." Kerr's recommendations were based on camouflage principles observed in nature, hence lacked the systematicity and theoretical framework within which the Gestalt laws of organization were presented later. Although Schumann had defined all the main principles of organization as early as 1900, military authorities did not apply them until World War II. The early attempts at dazzle were naive and often unsuccessful. As late as 1940 (e.g., Anonymous, 1940), complaints were made about the sad state of affairs regarding camouflage in the Royal Armed Forces and the failure of military leaders to consult biologists and psychologists on the matter, even though the latter had all the necessary information for rendering camouflage more efficient. The state of camouflage after World War I is summarized in Luckiesh's (1922) book on visual illusions, from which it is clear that little systematic work had been done in that area. Even a World War II camouflage bibliography (Anonymous, 1942) lists only a total of 79 references.

In visual search tasks, the form factor is only one of the relevant variables. Concrete visual search situations include the searching of radar scopes for "blips" of a particular form, reading maps rapidly while alternating attention between the map and a primary visual target, and the like. These situations call for a coding of visual information so that its processing be optimum under conditions of blur, brief exposure, etc. The proceedings of a 1960 symposium on the subject (Morris & Horne, 1960) summarizes the problems and research results in this area, as does Neisser's (1964) article.

The interpretation of infrared images, a recent military development, involves aspects of form perception, but the subject has received little treatment. The designing of displays for cathode tube presentation, with the displays stored electronically for future use, involves the computation and manipulation of form parameters on the one hand and a combination of the tasks of visual search and of discrimination or legibility on the other. Relevant reference works are those of Baker and Grether (1954), NASA (1968), Department of the Navy (1967), and Sampson, Wade, et al. (1961).

Legibility is by far the most thoroughly researched topic in the area of applied visual form perception. It is of importance to both military and industrial applications. Under this heading may be subsumed the legibility of alphanumeric characters, of highway signs, and of instrument scales. The bulk of the literature is on the legibility of printed letters and numbers. In addition to Tinker's 1966 bibliography, the most thorough and most recent work on legibility has been done at the National Bureau of Standards (Cornog, Rose, & Walkowicz, 1964; Cornog & Rose, 1967). Of the 325 references listed in the 1964 bibliography, 203 are abstracted in the 1967 volume. A tabulation of these 203 studies by the variables investigated reveals the complexity of the topic. Of the 78 variables studied, 25 pertain to typography, i.e., some aspect of form perception. Six of these are character variables (alphabetic, numeric, upper case, lower case, etc.), 8 pertain to the type of face used (printed, handwritten, machine-generated), 9 describe the design of the face (height, width, etc.), and 8 refer to layout characteristics (spacing, line length, etc.). Given the large number of variables involved, it is not surprising the Cornog and Rose do not attempt any kind of summary of the research data. Tinker and Paterson, who have contributed a large number of systematic studies of the variables affecting legibility, stated some time ago that interaction between these variables is the rule rather than the exception. Thus, it seems that in each concrete instance of need for specification of variables a separate study must be made to produce such specifications. The existing literature is large enough, however, to be of considerable help in many cases of practical need.

2. Reading

Legibility is the connecting link between form perception and reading. Legibility affects to some extent any dependent variable measure of reading. Its contribution is larger in the beginning reader who, in general, is more stimulus-bound than the older individual. In the latter, cognitive development has progressed further and he now reads words and word groups as wholes. In the adult, the configuration of individual letters plays some role only when it radically differs from what he has been used to in the past, e.g., when encountering an unusual or scrawly handwriting, learning to read in some non-Roman alphabet, and the like. Past experience also plays an important role in that it facilitates the perception of reading material in the traditionally established direction in which lines of words or linguistic symbols run. Reading downward is considerably more difficult to one who has always read horizontally. Thus, Chen and Carr (1926) showed that Chinese students find it easier to read Chinese vertically and English horizontally than the other way around. Chinese students who have had considerable training in English, however, find it easier to read Chinese horizontally. Although native Hebrew readers recognize more English words in the right visual field, suggesting a similar effect of past experience, it is not impossible that such left-right recognition differentials may be due to some neurological factor, e.g., cerebral dominance (Orbach, 1967).

Aulhorn (1948) has derived an exact formula for predicting reading speed as a function of the orientation of letters and of rows of letters:

$$\frac{1}{T} = a + b \cos \gamma + C \cos^2 \gamma,$$

where T is reading time, γ the angle to which a row of letters is rotated about the fixation axis, and a, b, and C are reading times corresponding to the 0-, 90-, and 180-degree rotations of the row of letters. According to Aulhorn, the formula applies even when only the direction of the row changes but the letters remain vertical with respect to the reader. If only the letters are rotated, reading time depends on whether the letters are symmetric or not. If they are not symmetric about the axis of rotation, the equation still holds.

Information on additional aspects of perception involved in reading may be found in Carmichael and Dearborn (1947), Diack (1960), Fellows (1968), Goins (1958), Luckiesh and Moss (1942), Potter (1949), Vernon (1931), and Vernon and Pickford (1929).

3. Form-Perception Tests

The number of commercially available tests that center on the perception of visual form is small, and only very few of them test and predict form perception as such. While the Rorschach test stimuli are visual forms, the predicted behavior is twice removed from the stimuli, first by way of a response (the associative response) that is only "triggered" by the form (instead of being a direct response *to* form), and second by way of the inferences that are made from this response about a construct (personality) that is unrelated to form.

In still other tests, the perception of form is only a necessary intermediate step that precedes some behavior that is commonly taken to represent intelligence. These would include the various intelligence-test subtests that involve form, such as Koh's blocks, picture completion (e.g., Street figures), digit-symbol, spatial ability, perceptual speed (as in *Primary Mental Abilities* test), and formboard tests. Here, the response is used either to imply or predict form perception as one aspect of intellectual functioning.

In still another type of test, a perceptual score of a response to form is obtained, but the score is not a measure of sample behavior used to predict similar behavior in a life situation. Rather, it is used to predict whatever behavior happens to show consistent correlation with this score. This approach often leads one so far afield that all connection with the original stimulus-response situation is lost. Several tests that use embedded figures as test materials belong in this category. In 1944, Thurstone reported on the results of a factor analysis of 40 perceptual tests and tasks. Of the 11 primary perceptual factors obtained by him, four may be described as form factors: speed of closure, strength of closure, susceptibility to geometric illusions, and rate of reversals. The closure factors have no relation to the Gestalt concept of closure but refer to the ability to see embedded figures. The *Closure Flexibility* test is based on the second of the above-mentioned two closure factors and employs the same stimulus materials that Gottschaldt used in the 1920s. In this test, the task is to find a simple figure concealed in one of four complex designs. While the test manual states that closure flexibility is related to mechanical aptitude and certain kinds of reasoning, Leona Tyler, in her review of the test (Buros, 1965, p. 849), states that what this test needs more than anything else is evidence as to what it is valid for. The same is said (p. 850) about a second, similar test, the *Closure Speed* test, based on Thurstone's first closure factor. In this test, the testee is required to identify a picture from incomplete fragments, similar to those used in Street's *Gestalt Completion Test*. Again, the behavior predicted from performance on this test has no obvious relation to form perception: persons scoring above the mean on this test describe themselves as socially outgoing, confident, impulsive, artistic, etc.

Witkin's findings concerning the relationship between certain perceptual tests and the personality variable of field dependence-independence. One of these tests uses embedded figures derived from those employed by Gottschaldt. The *Embedded Figures Test* uses 24 of them. The time the testee takes to outline the simple figure in a complex embedding context after having seen the simple figure in isolation for 10 sec. is measured. As in the other two embedded-figure tests just described, the testee's score is not used to predict perceptual performance in a concrete situation involving embedded figures (although it could), but rather his field independence, cognitive clarity, perceptual mode (analytic or wholistic), and his general disposition to articulate and structure experience (Harrison Gough in Buros, 1965, p. 210).

In contrast to the intervening variable tests mentioned above, the *Bender-Gestalt* test diagnoses the existence of an independent variable, namely brain damage, on the basis of accumulated data on the effects of brain damage on the reproduction of figures. The main effect of brain damage is impaired ability to perceive Gestalten, such as two overlapping figures as two separate entities. Two other similar tests are the *Memory for Design Test* and the *Benton Visual Retention Test.*

Finally, there are those form-perception tests in which the task of the test represents a sample of the actual behavior that is being predicted. On *Graves Design Judgment Test,* used to measure artistic ability, the testee obtains a high score if he selects of two designs the one that shows dynamic rather than static symmetry. The designs are simple geometric forms placed in various relations to each other. A subscale of the *Welsh Figure Preference Test,* the *Barron-Welsh Art Scale,* is based on the finding that in a task requiring the sorting of various designs into preferred and nonpreferred categories artists and nonartists differ in that the former prefer complex designs while nonartists prefer the simpler shapes. Symmetry and asymmetry also influence the choices made by both artists and nonartists, but since this parameter has been defined by both Welsh and others (cf. Moyles, Tuddenham, & Block, 1965) in terms other than the simple presence or absence of bilateral symmetry, symmetry-asymmetry is confounded by simplicity-complexity as well as compactness-dispersion and its effects are therefore difficult to evaluate. The *Perceptual Speed Test,* by employing a form-matching task measures the testee's perceptual speed. Perceptual speed involving form discrimination is a component of certain jobs, performance on which may therefore be predicted from performance on this test. The *Perceptual Forms Test* requires the reproduction of seven geometric forms. The test is intended to diagnose underdeveloped eye-hand coordination in children aged 6-8½, i.e., at a time when they begin to read and write. The test also diagnoses insufficient visual development for other school tasks involving the visual perception and production or reproduction of forms. Two of the five subtests in the *Marianne Frostig Developmental Test of Visual Perception* involve visual form: one is a test of figure-ground perception in which overlapping and hidden figures are used, the other measures discrimination of rotated and reflected forms. The test is a diagnostic test intended to uncover deficiencies in visual perception that might affect learning of various school tasks that emphasize visual perception. The two tests are clearly pertinent to the reading and writing tasks. Some reading tests, such as the *Standard Reading Tests.* include subtests of the discrimination of rotated and reflected forms.

At least one psychologist, Newell C. Kephart, has made an effort to act upon the results of form-perception tests of the diagnostic variety and to remedy the deficiencies diagnosed. His ideas resemble in many respects those of K. U. Smith, D. O. Hebb, and J. Piaget. Kephart (cf. Kephart, 1960) proposes that the body image that the infant develops is based initially upon his learning to discriminate his right from his left side. This primitive system of spatial coordinates is later extended to include the world of surrounding objects, where laterality becomes directionality. Assuming that the perception of a form as a whole is based on the initial combination of visual elements and that this combination occurs within a spatial framework, the conclusion may be reached that failure to learn adequate right-left discrimination will result in an inadequately developed concept of a spatial coordinate system and hence in difficulties in form perception. Specifically, the child may experience difficulties on school tasks that involve form perception, e.g., reading. Remedial work prescribed by Kephart therefore consists in refining right-left discrimination by means of walking board exercises, jumping on a trampoline, and other activities that emphasize balance and laterality.

4. Experimental Aesthetics of Visual Form

In this section, the discussion of aesthetics will be limited to pleasingness of or preference for more or less simple nonrepresentational shapes. The terms "beauty" and "beautiful" are shunned in experiments of this kind. More often than not, the subject is asked whether he considers the stimulus object attractive or pleasing rather than whether he thinks it is beautiful. While people usually have a good idea of what they like, they are far from certain as to what beauty is and tend to disagree with each other widely. If the term "beautiful" is used, it is likely to produce a request for a definition of that term, reflecting the uncertainty that has surrounded the term since philosophers and aestheticians began discussing it some two thousand years ago.

The present discussion will also avoid the problem of relating beauty and art. This and associated problems in the psychology of aesthetics are fully discussed in the only book published on the subject since 1919, Valentine's (1962) *The Experimental Psychology of Beauty.*

Important psychological work has been done on the aesthetics of paintings and other complex objects of art. The significant thing about these studies is the low correlation between aesthetic response and the parameters of form. In fact, there are two separate bodies of literature, one on the aesthetics of simple, nonrepresentational forms and lines, the other on the aesthetics of complex visual materials and works of art. In experiments that constitute the former, the stimulus dimensions are manageable, and the response is often reliably linked to them—at least the relationship is no worse than in many other areas of psychology. The methodology in the experimental aesthetics of complex stimuli is either that of rating or ranking or the method of recording eye movements. Since in the rating method a work of art is judged as a whole, the response cannot be used to infer anything about the configurational properties that the judges may have been responding to. The eye-movement method, on the other hand, while giving exact information on the relationship between the oculomotor response and form parameters, indicates that this relationship, where it is present, is due not so much to the dimensions of form as such but rather to the occasional coincidence of contours with certain landmarks that attract attention and therefore control looking behavior: eyes, human figures in a landscape, columns and arches in Gothic cathedrals, and the like (Buswell, 1935; Yarbus, 1967).

A. LINES

Line segments have been presented to subjects for judgments of pleasingness or for their description by adjectives having emotional, evaluative, and aesthetic connotations. Valentine (1962) describes some experiments with lines performed by L. J. Martin. Most of Martin's subjects showed definite preferences in pair-comparing straight, curved, vertical, horizontal, and slanted lines. Valentine points out, however, that the reasons for preferring the same line may vary from person to person, and that large intersubject differences are observed: Valentine's own research shows that a line may be liked or disliked depending on whether it appears alone or paired with another, and whether in the latter case the line is to the left or to the right of the other line. The absolute size of the line also plays a role: the larger lines are generally preferred over the smaller ones, but not invariably so. Furthermore, the frame of reference with respect to which a line is judged plays a decisive role: if a person prefers vertical lines, an oblique line may be considered displeasing. However, if it is looked upon as a horizontal that rises itself to the vertical, it may be judged as pleasing. Thus, associations from the subject's past experience play a considerable role, and their effects are, of course, unpredictable unless one undertakes to examine each subject's past history for relevant influences.

One attractive and plausible hypothesis concerning the aesthetics of lines has been that the ease with which a line can be drawn determines its pleasingness, or that the smoothness, lack of effort, or symmetry in eye movements is what produces a feeling of aesthetic pleasure. This hypothesis in its various forms has been repeatedly and conclusively disproved. As early as 1902, Stratton showed that the eyes may or may not follow the contours of a shape, and that even when eye movements approximate the direction of the contours, they are never smooth and never follow a contour exactly. Rather, scanning eye movements consist of fixations and straight motion between fixations, even when a curve is examined. Backtracking is the rule rather than the exception. Because of the grossness, irregularity, and jerkiness of eye movements, it cannot be assumed that kinesthetic feedback from the smooth execution of a movement by the eye muscles is the basis of aesthetic enjoyment. Instead, eye movements are the mechanism whereby an impression of the various portions of the visual field is gained, and the cognitive and emotional responses take place on the basis of further transformation in the cortex of the information obtained by the perceptual mechanism. In a subsequent study, Stratton (1906) showed that symmetry has no particular effect on eye movements either, so that the assumption about a pleasurable effect produced by an even, bilateral distribution of eye movements about an axis of symmetry could not be supported. Analogous results were obtained by Buswell (1935) in an extensive study of the eye movements of subjects who examined simple lines, figures, ornamental borders, paintings, and photographs, both symmetric and asymmetric. The guiding effect supposedly exercised upon the eye by repetitive patterns, symmetry, and configuration in general was found to be either weak or completely absent.

When asked to draw a straight oblique line, more persons draw a right / oblique than a left \ oblique. The hypotheses that this is due to the greater ease with which a right oblique is drawn and that the right oblique would therefore be preferred to the left oblique have not been supported (L. J. Martin in Valentine, 1962, p. 75). Since most people are right-handed, the prevalence of the right slant as well as of left-facing human profiles in the drawings of naive subjects, children, and primitive peoples (Valentine, 1962, p. 76) is perhaps better attributed to the greater convenience in drawing in this fashion (the hand does not obscure that which is being drawn, etc.).

Studies of the physiognomic qualities of lines only partly belong with the studies on the aesthetics of visual form. In these studies, the most frequent approach has been that of having subjects describe various types of lines by certain adjectives. Such adjectives can be and have been used to describe more complex figurations as well, including works of art. Lundholm (1921) asked his subjects to describe curved, straight, wavy, and zig-zag lines using a list of supplied adjectives, such as sad, lazy, playful, gentle, powerful, etc. Lundholm concluded that the feeling tone of a line probably depends on the type of movement suggested by the line, especially the type of motor behavior and muscular responses observable in the various emotional states. Thus, slow and weak movement was suggested by lines with long and shallow waves, while rapid and intense movements seemed to be represented by lines with small waves and acute angles. To these particular types of lines were attached adjectives suggesting emotions with little motor expression in the former case and emotions with strong motor expression in the latter. Poffenberger and Barrow (1924) performed a similar experiment with the practical goal of establishing criteria for the use of different types of lines to suggest emotional moods in advertisements. Hevner (1935), setting himself a similar goal, found that curves were judged to be serene, graceful, and tender and sentimental while angles were described as robust, vigorous, and somewhat more dignified than curves.

B. THE "GOLDEN-SECTION" RECTANGLE

A line divided so that the whole is to the larger part as the larger part is to the smaller is divided in the ratio of .618, approximately. This is the so-called golden section of a line. A rectangle with sides in this proportion is a golden-section rectangle. Simplicity of ratios between dimensions in buildings, statues, etc. as a canon of beauty comes from Greek antiquity. The contemporary teacher of statistics still suggests to his students that they should prepare their graphs so that the ratio of the ordinate to the abscissa be 2:3 or 3:4. The golden section is by no means a simple ratio, but the idea of identical ratios between parts and between parts and the whole does bind the whole together in a unitary and simple fashion.

Fechner's first experiments on the aesthetics of rectangles were performed in the 1860s; he published monographs describing his work in the 1870s (cf. Fechner, 1871, 1876). Fechner's procedure consisted in placing 10 rectangles before a subject and asking him to select the most pleasing rectangle. The rectangles varied in their height/length ratios from 1.00 (square) to .40. Woodworth, who in his 1938 edition of *Experimental Psychology* devotes several pages to the experimental aesthetics of simple visual forms, points out that the important fact about Fechner's experiments was that nearly everyone was able to pick the most pleasing rectangle. The modal rectangle had a height/length ratio of .62, i.e., the golden section, with 76% of all choices centering on three rectangles having the ratios of .57, .62, and .67. While all other rectangles received less than 10% of the choices each, Fechner's results still indicated that many other rectangles besides the golden-section rectangle were considered the most pleasing by a fair number of subjects.

In Witmer's (1894) study, the mode for rated degree of pleasure extended from .57 to .65, with preferences tapering off gradually toward both extremes. Lalo (1908) in France also found that the .62-ratio rectangle was the modal choice (30.3%). The adjacent rectangles of the ratios .67 and .57, however, did not do nearly as well as in Fechner's study, all three rectangles accounting for only 48% of all choices. In addition, the square and the .40-ratio rectangle each showed an additional mode of choices (11.7 and 15.3%, respectively). Thorndike's (1917) study served to still further undermine the notion about the inherent aesthetic qualities of the golden-section rectangle. Of Thorndike's 12 rectangles, ranging in height/length ratio from .25 to .75, all were ranked in every position. The highest ranks were assigned to rectangles having ratios between .40 and .60, with higher- and lower-ratio rectangles receiving decreasingly lower ranks.

In the 1930s and 1940s, the effects of such factors as area of the rectangle, age of subjects, and practice in judging were explored. Weber's (1931) subjects pair-compared rectangles whose height/length ratios ranged from .40 to 1.00. The most preferred rectangles ranged in height/length ratio from .50 to .62, but the preference curve dropped only gradually toward the square. Weber gave the same task to the same subjects two weeks later. This produced a slight shift in the curve toward the flatter rectangles, a somewhat higher preference for the modal rectangles, and a faster-falling curve toward the square. It is likely that Weber's results were partly due to the fact that he presented the rectangles in the vertical position: it was Farnsworth's (1932) finding that the position in which the rectangles are presented has considerable effect on preference, as does color and size. Farnsworth concluded that the golden-section rectangle has a relatively high rating only under conditions that approximate Fechner's. One of Fechner's conditions was the selection of one, the most preferred rectangle, from a sample. Other investigators have used ranking, rating, and production methods, with results differing from those of Fechner. Thus, Haines and Davies (1904), instead of showing their subjects ready-made rectangles, had them produce the most pleasing rectangle by allowing them to manipulate the height of a variable rectangle. The results obtained were not unlike those of Weber (1931), more subjects producing rectangles ranging in height/length ratio between .44 and .64, there being several modes and the most preferred rectangles ranging from very flat ones all the way to the square. Similar results were obtained by Davis (1933) in a rectangle-drawing task that was repeated with the same subjects 40 min. later. On the second trial, some of the subjects changed the height/length ratio of their preferred rectangle very markedly while some did not change it at all. Like Haines and Davies, Davis obtained a multimodal distribution of perferences. Based on the results obtained with more than 600 subjects, Davis' conclusion was that to establish *a* most preferred rectangle or even a golden section on the basis of averaged group or individual data is an erroneous procedure.

There is thus no doubt that the discrepancies in the results obtained by the various investigators may be attributed to differences in experimental design and procedure. One important design-related factor has received scant mention. In a given series of rectangles, the modal rectangle is not only the result of its aesthetic value but also of the range of variation in the height/length ratios of the series of rectangles presented to the subjects for judgment, and especially of the size of this ratio at the extremes of the series, i.e., anchor effects. Fillenbaum (1963) has clearly demonstrated that the judged slimness of rectangles varies depending on whether the judged series includes a slim anchor, a broad anchor, a double anchor, or no anchor at all. Although the range of variation in the height/length ratios has varied from investigator to investigator, the question of how this might have affected the subjects' adaptation level has hardly been raised.

The effect of age on preference for rectangles has been studied by several researchers. Thompson (1946) found no pattern of preference in preschool children, a mode of .55 for college students, with third- and sixth-graders moving toward the adult standard. Shipley, Dattman, and Steele (1947) had both children and adults rank rectangles ranging in height/length ratio from .25 to .75 and having either a constant area or constant length. The constant-length series of rectangles produced a preference curve similar to that of Thompson (1946). While children's preferences increased steadily for the wider rectangles as their age increased, the adult mode was the ratio of .65, with preferences for the wider rectangles decreasing markedly. The constant-area rectangles showed the same trends, but to a much lesser extent. The effect of area was such that children tended to prefer the larger rectangles while adults preferred medium-sized ones. While Nienstadt and Ross (1951) obtained the same mode for adults aged 18-27 as Shipley et al. (1947), namely .65, they found a shift toward the less elongated rectangles in individuals aged 61-91, their most preferred ratio being .75.

There is no doubt that the reasons for which a particular rectangle may be preferred by a given individual vary widely and that his criteria may not be specifically aesthetic. Thus, people prefer certain rectangles because they have the proportions of a postal card, an envelope, a notebook, painter's canvas, or some other often-used object. Granted that these objects do vary in the ratio of their sides, one must also admit that the range of variation is not very wide and that squares or near-squares and very elongated rectangles are not a common format for books, note pads, cards, envelopes, paintings, and the like. The height/length ratios of these objects are very nearly the same that turn out to be the most preferred ones in the golden-section rectangle experiments. One explanation for these particular ratios is that of practical considerations: for many purposes, very narrow strips of paper, etc. would not be very practical. This, however, does not explain the avoidance of squares and near-squares. A suggestive finding comes from Stone and Collins (1965). If internal and external rectangles are constructed inside and around the binocular visual field and the heights and lengths of these two rectangles averaged, the average height/length ratio turns out to be .665, or close to the golden-section ratio. The area within the average rectangle is more than 90% of the area within the outlines of the visual field. Stone and Collins leave open the question of how the dimensions of the averaged rectangle became connected with aesthetic appreciation. As Schiffman (1966) points out, these authors failed to show that the orientation of the preferred rectangle also coincides with the orientation of the rectangle that fits the visual field, namely the horizontal orientation. While Schiffman was able to show that the overwhelming majority of subjects do orient their most preferred rectangle horizontally, the modal rectangle drawn by Schiffman's subjects had its height/length ratio between .459 and .560, which is consistent with the general finding that American subjects tend to lean toward the slenderer rectangles.

Since the peripheral hypothesis seems to have considerable merit, it would be worthwhile exploring it further, e.g., by relating the exact shape of the visual field of each subject to his preferred rectangle, as well as comparing the shape and size of visual fields in subjects from different continents.

C. AESTHETIC PREFERENCE FOR POLYGONS

In addition to rectangles, Fechner had subjects choose the most preferred one of other shapes, such as the ellipse. According to Witmer (1894), who published Fechner's data, the modal ellipse had a minor/major axis ratio of .67. The most preferred ellipse had a range of ratios between .57 and .75. These ellipses accounted for 86.9% of all choices. Although the circle was included in the sample, it rated only 1.2% of first choices, a rather unexpected result.

With the exception of the equilateral triangle, which is a special case of the isosceles triangle, all isosceles triangles have only one axis of symmetry. The isosceles triangle, which may be considered the triangular counterpart of the rectangle, is therefore more variable than the rectangle, and different results may be expected when judges are presented a series of such triangles and asked to select the most pleasing one. For one thing, varying the equilateral triangle produces two distinct types of triangles at the extremes of variation instead of one as in the case of the rectangle: a thin, peaked one and a thin, flat one. Witmer (1894), who used isosceles triangles that were wider than they were high, obtained a modal preferred ratio of .41. Thorndike (1917), on the other hand, found that for peaked triangles preferences centered around the height/base ratios of 1.6 and 1.7. Austin and Sleight (1951) had their subjects pair-compare both Witmer's and Thorndike's triangles. While all 12 isosceles triangles used by Austin and Sleight had the same base, their height/base ratios ranged from .25 to 3.00. Although the modal triangles ranged between 1.00 and 2.00 in their height/base ratios, most-liked triangles were found at the extremes of the height/base ratio, i.e., while triangles in the modal range were disliked the least, they were not liked the best.

Birkhoff (1933) is known for his formula of aesthetic measure of polygonal forms. Birkhoff, along with Fechner (1876), believed that the feeling of value or aesthetic measure (M) could be predicted from the complexity (C) of the polygon and its degree of order (O). While Fechner expected complexity and aesthetic feeling to be directly related, Birkhoff related them inversely, thus:

$$M = O/C.$$

Birkhoff proposed as a measure of complexity of a polygon the number of its sides, and vertical symmetry, equal sides, equal angles, rotational symmetry, relation to a horizontal-vertical coordinate system, and the like, as measures of order. These properties were assigned the values of +1, +2, or +3 when present, 0 when absent, and −1 when they had a negative associative value. In general, Birkhoff's rules for measuring O, especially in complex, figures, are quite arbitrary and vary depending on the particular form being measured.

While Birkhoff did not attempt to correlate his M with actual ratings of preference, his book contains 90 polygons for which the values of M are given. Others have taken these and have had subjects rate them as well as other polygons on aesthetic preference. Davis (1936), for instance, found that for 10 of Birkhoff's polygons ranging in M from 1.50 to −.17 the correlation between M and preference ratings by art students was .05, unspecialized students producing a correlation of .11. While both correlations were statistically insignificant, the greater tendency for subjects with no artistic background to agree with Birkhoff than for subjects with artistic background (e.g., art students) to do so has been noted by others. The reason is the same as the reason for which artists score higher on the *Barron-Welsh Art Scale,* for instance: Birkhoff's M varies inversely with complexity, and artistic individuals prefer more complex forms in comparison with nonartistic individuals. In Davis' experiment, an additional factor contributing to the negative results could have been the freedom allowed the subjects to rotate the figures, since Birkhoff's O measure depends largely on the orientation of the polygon.

The Beebe-Center studies of Birkhoff's aesthetic measure (Beebe-Center & Pratt, 1937; Harsh, Beebe-Center, & Beebe-Center, 1939) emphasize the very substantial individual differences in correlations between Birkhoff's M and ratings or rankings of polygons on aesthetic appeal: they ranged all the way from −.26 to .85. Since a factor analysis revealed four factors—smoothness of contour, tall and upward-reaching figures, simplicity, and symmetry—and only the latter two are represented in the M measure, this measure, according to Beebe-Center, is at least incomplete.

Barnhart (1940) had 50 female students rank 16 of Birkhoff's polygons on preference, and again obtained a low correlation (.21) between rankings and M. A novel feature of Barnhart's experiment was to ask the subjects for their reasons for ranking the polygons as they did. Barnhart's analysis revealed three main factors: the shape of the polygons, the associations evoked by them, and their potentialities for use in designs. The first reason was given by 90% of the subjects, the second by 57%, and the third by 16%, 78% of the subjects advancing more than one criterion for their choices.

The rather unpredictable experiential and connotative factors that vary from individual to individual and from one population of subjects to another can often be seen as influencing aesthetic judgment as strongly as the configurational factor. In an unpublished experiment by the author, the instructions used in a previous scaling experiment (Zusne & Michels, 1962) were modified by substituting the term "aesthetic value" for "familiarity" and "geometricity"— the attributes that had been rated in a sample of quadrilaterals before—and the experiment was replicated. While the last-mentioned three labels produced practically identical rank orders of the stimuli (the correlations ranged from .91 to .97), the rank orders of the 55 stimuli under the instructions to judge their aesthetic value and under the instructions to judge their familiarity or geometricity correlated only .47 and .41, respectively. The physical measures of elongation, compactness, and areal asymmetry that had predicted rated geometricity and familiarity quite well showed zero correlation with rated aesthetic value. One of the factors contributing to the shift in judgment could have been an associative or value factor: all four of the symmetric, V-shaped quadrilaterals that resembled the V-shaped emblems used on Cadillac automobiles every year since 1946 were ranked among the top eight shapes, the other four shapes having single or twofold symmetry and a general configuration that is typically used for emblems on automobiles and appliances.

The latest attempt to come to grips with Birkhoff's M comes from Eysenck (1968) who, like Harsh et al. (1939) before him, factor-analyzed preference ratings of Birkhoff's polygons. Eysenck used all 90 of Birkhoff's polygons instead of only 26, however, which may have been one reason for his finding 13 different factors instead of just 4. In addition, Eysenck was able to extract a single third-order bipolar factor characterized by complexity and order, the two variables on which Birkhoff's measure is based.

Eysenck's analysis suffers from a certain confusion among the main variables involved. Thus, e.g., in two adjacent paragraphs (Eysenck, 1968, p. 11) Eysenck refers to the bipolarity of his third-order factor both as simplicity versus complexity and as O versus C. The 16 polygons in Fig. 10-3a had the highest positive factor loading on the third-order factor, while those shown in Fig. 10-3b had the highest negative factor loadings. Eysenck calls the first group of polygons "simple," the second "complex." Yet, in terms of both independent and total turns the first sample is clearly more complex than the second (4.7 versus 3.4 independent turns per figure and 9.4 versus 6.3 total turns). The inconsistency is probably due to the fact that Eysenck included in his complexity measure a score of 20 for each polygon having angles that deviated from 90 degrees. Eysenck gives no explanation for this procedure, and it is hard to understand how deviation from the right angle would contribute to complexity; still, since in the second sample no shape has a right angle, the complexity of the sample turns out to be higher by Eysenck's reckoning. In addition to greater complexity, 11 sample A polygons have two or more axes of symmetry, whereas only 5 in sample B do (Eysenck does not mention this fact); sample A figures have predominantly right angles, whereas none in sample B do; and the A figures are more likely to be encountered in everyday situations since most of them resemble letters, signs, emblems, and other familiar objects. Symmetry and repeated elements are aspects of redundancy or order, and familiarity is synonymous with internal or subjective redundancy. Thus, sample

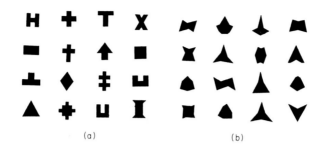

(a)   (b)

Fig. 10-3. Two groups of polygons from Eysenck's (1968) study. The polygons are from G. D. Birkhoff. *Aesthetic measure.* Harvard University Press, 1933. Reproduced by permission.

A in Fig. 10-3 is characterized by a high degree of order and complexity, while sample *B* is characterized by simplicity and a lower degree of order. The 16 polygons that were liked best by Eysenck's subjects also show a higher degree of symmetry and complexity than the 16 polygons that were liked the least. Because of the confusion among variables just indicated, Eysenck goes through some unnecessary additional steps to show that his proposed modification of Birkhoff's formula, namely $M = O \times C$, is a better predictor of preference ratings than Birkhoff's original measure. It is, as is evident from a simple examination of Fig. 10-3.

Rashevsky (e.g., Rashevsky, 1938, 1942a, 1942b, 1945; Rashevsky & Brown, 1944a, 1944b) has theorized about the visual aesthetics of both simple geometric patterns and more complex works of art, such as paintings, and has formulated mathematical models of aesthetic response to these stimuli. Since Rashevsky is not too much concerned with actual behavior, and his efforts, more than anything else, are a high-level intellectual exercise, they have failed to produce any experimental studies or even follow-up work, either in the field of mathematical biophysics or psychology.

REFERENCES

Anonymous. Camouflage in modern warfare. *Nature,* 1940, **145**, 949-951.

Anonymous. Camouflage bibliography. *Pratt. Inst. Libr. Quart. Bklist,* 1942, **6**, No. 8, 3-11.

Aulhorn, O. Die Lesegeschwindigkeit als Funktion von Buchstaben- und Zeilenlage. *Pflueg. Arch. ges. Physiol.,* 1948, **250**, 12-25.

Austin, T. R., & Sleight, R. B. Aesthetic preference for isosceles triangles. *J. appl. Psychol.,* 1951, **35**, 430-431.

Baker, C. A., & Grether, W. A. Visual presentation of information. WADC Tech. Rep. 54-160, 1954.

Barnhart, E. N. The criteria used in preferential judgments of geometrical forms. *Amer. J. Psychol.*, 1940, **53**, 354-370.

Beebe-Center, J. G., & Pratt, C. C. A test of Birkhoff's aesthetic measure. *J. gen. Psychol.*, 1937, **17**, 339-353.

Bersh, P. J. Air Force requirements for forms research. In J. W. Wulfeck & J. H. Taylor (Eds.), *Form discrimination as related to military problems*. Washington, D.C.: Nat. Acad. Sci.-Nat. Res. Coun., 1957, Pp. 8-12.

Birkhoff, G. D. *Aesthetic measure*. Cambridge, Massachusetts: Harvard Univ. Press, 1933.

Blackwell, H. R. *Laboratory studies of the visibility of targets*. Washington, D.C.: U.S. Dept. Commerce, 1946.

Boynton, R. M., Elworth, C., & Palmer, R. M. Laboratory studies pertaining to visual air reconnaissance. WADC Tech. Rep. 55-304, Part III, 1958.

Buros, O. K. (Ed.) *The sixth mental measurements yearbook*. Highland Park, New Jersey: Gryphon Press, 1965.

Buswell, G. T. *How people look at pictures*. Chicago, Illinois: Chicago Univ. Press, 1935.

Carmichael, L., & Dearborn, W. F. *Reading and visual fatigue*. Boston, Massachusetts: Houghton, 1947.

Chapanis, A. *Man-machine engineering*. Belmont, California: Wadsworth Publ., 1965.

Chen, L. K., & Carr, H. A. The ability of Chinese students to read in vertical and horizontal directions. *J. exp. Psychol.*, 1926, **9**, 110-117.

Cornog, D. Y., & Rose, F. C. Legibility of alphanumeric characters and other symbols: II. A reference handbook. *Nat. Bur. Std. Miscell. Publ.*, 1967, No. 262-2.

Cornog, D. Y., Rose, F. C., & Walkowicz, J. L. (Eds.) Legibility of alphanumeric characters and other symbols: I. A permuted title index and bibliography. *Nat. Bur. Std. Miscell. Publ.*, 1964, No. 262-1.

Davis, F. Aesthetic proportion. *Amer. J. Psychol.*, 1933, **45**, 298-302.

Davis, R. C. An evaluation and test of Birkhoff's aesthetic measure formula. *J. gen. Psychol.*, 1936, **15**, 231-240.

Dept. of the Navy. Naval Reconnaissance and Technical Support Center. *Image interpretation*. Vol. I. Washington, D.C.: Departments of the Army, Navy, and the Air Force, 1967.

Diack, H. *Reading and the psychology of perception*. New York: Philosophical Library, 1960.

Duntley, S. Q. The visibility of distant objects. *J. Opt. Soc. Amer.*, 1948, **38**, 237-249.

Eysenck, H. J. An experimental study of aesthetic preference for polygonal figures. *J. gen. Psychol.*, 1968, **79**, 3-17.

Farnsworth, P. R. Preferences for rectangles. *J. gen. Psychol.*, 1932, **7**, 479-481.

Fechner, G. T. *Zur experimentellen Aesthetik*. Leipzig: S. Hirzel, 1871.

Fechner, G. T. *Vorschule der Aesthetik*. Leipzig: Breitkopf & Haertel, 1876.

Fellows, B. J. *The discrimination process and development*. New York: Pergamon Press, 1968.

Fillenbaum, S. Contextual effects in judgment as a function of restriction in response-language. *Amer. J. Psychol.*, 1963, **76**, 103-109.

Fitts, P. M. Engineering psychology and equipment design. In S. S. Stevens (Ed.), *Handbook of experimental psychology*. New York: Wiley, 1951. Pp. 1287-1340.

Fitts, P. M. *Human performance*. New York: Brooks-Cole, 1967.

Goins, J. T. *Visual perceptual ability and early reading progress*. Chicago, Illinois: Chicago Univ. Press, 1958.

Haines, T. H., & Davies, A. E. The psychology of aesthetic reaction to reactangular form. *Psychol. Rev.,* 1904, **11**, 249-281.

Harker, G. S. The significance of form discrimination to current Army problems. In J. W. Wulfeck & J. H. Taylor (Eds.), *Form discrimination as related to military problems.* Washington, D.C.: Nat. Acad. Sci.-Nat. Res. Coun., 1957. Pp. 6-8.

Harsh, C. M., Beebe-Center, J. G., & Beebe-Center, R. Further evidence regarding preferential judgment of polygonal forms. *J. Psychol.,* 1939, **7**, 343-350.

Hevner, K. Experimental studies of the affective value of colors and lines. *J. appl. Psychol.,* 1935, **19**, 385-398.

Ireland, F. H. Effects of surround illumination on visual performance. An annotated bibliography. Aerospace Med. Res. Lab., Wright-Patterson AFB, TR-67-103, 1967.

Kephart, N. C. *The slow learner in the classroom.* Columbus, Ohio: Charles E. Merrill, 1960.

Lalo, C. *L'esthétique expérimentale contemporaine.* Paris: Alcan, 1908.

Leikind, M., & Weiner, J. (Eds.) *Visibility: A bibliography.* Washington, D.C.: Library of Congress, 1952.

Luckiesh, M. *Visual illusions.* Princeton, New Jersey: Van Nostrand, 1922. (Republished: New York: Dover, 1965.)

Luckiesh, M., & Moss, F. K. *Reading as a visual task.* Princeton, New Jersey: Van Nostrand, 1942.

Lundholm, H. The affective tone of lines: Experimental researches. *Psychol. Rev.,* 1921, **28**, 43-60.

Lyman, B. *Visual detection, identification, and localization: An annotated bibliography.* Alexandria, Virginia: Geo. Washington Univ., HumRRO, 1968.

Morgan, C. T. *Human engineering guide to equipment design.* New York: McGraw-Hill, 1963.

Morris, A., & Horne, E. P. (Eds.) *Visual search techniques.* Washington, D.C.: Nat. Acad. Sci.-Nat. Res. Coun., 1960.

Moyles, E. W., Tuddenham, R. D., & Block, J. Simplicity/complexity or symmetry/ asymmetry? A re-analysis of the Barron-Welsh scales. *Percept. mot. Skills,* 1965, **20**, 685-690.

National Aeronautics and Space Administration. Visual information display systems. A survey. NASA, 1968.

Neisser, U. Visual search. *Sci. Amer.,* 1964, **210**(6).

Nienstedt, C. W., Jr., & Ross, S. Preferences for rectangular proportions in college students and the aged. *J. genet. Psychol.,* 1951, **78**, 153-158.

Orbach, J. Differential recognition of Hebrew and English words in right and left visual fields as a function of cerebral dominance and reading habits. *Neuropsychologia,* 1967, **5**(2), 127-134.

Pemberton, C. L. A study of the speed and flexibility of closure factors. Unpublished doctoral dissertation, Univ. of Chicago, 1951.

Poffenberger, A. T., & Barrows, B. E. The feeling value of lines. *J. appl. Psychol.,* 1924, **8**, 187-205.

Potter, M. C. *Perception of symbol orientation and early reading success.* New York: Columbia Univ., 1949.

Rashevsky, N. Contribution to the mathematical biophysics of visual perception with special reference to the theory of aesthetic values of geometric patterns. *Psychometrika,* 1938, **3**, 253-271.

Rashevsky, N. Further contributions to the mathematical biophysics of visual aesthetics. *Bull. Math. Biophys.,* 1942, **4**, 117-120. (a)

Rashevsky, N. Some problems in mathematical biophysics of visual perception and aesthetics. *Bull. Math. Biophys.,* 1942, **4**, 177-191. (b)

Rashevsky, N. A contribution to the mathematical biophysics of visual aesthetics. *Bull. Math. Biophys.,* 1945, **7**, 41-45.

Rashevsky, N., & Brown, V. A contribution to the mathematical biophysics of visual perception and aesthetics. *Bull. Math. Biophys.,* 1944, **6**, 119-124. (a)

Rashevsky, N., & Brown, V. Contributions to the mathematical biophysics of visual aesthetics. *Bull. Math. Biophys.,* 1944, **6**, 163-168. (b)

Sampson, P. B., Wade, E. A., *et al. Literature survey on human factors in visual displays.* Medford, Massachusetts: Institute for Psychol. Res., Tufts Univ., 1961.

Schiffman, H. R. Golden section: Preferred figural orientation. *Percept. Psychophys.,* 1966, **1**, 193-194.

Shipley, W. C., Dattman, P. E., & Steele, B. A. The influence of size on preferences for rectangular proportion in children and adults. *J. exp. Psychol.,* 1947, **37**, 333-336.

Stone, L. A., & Collins, L. G. The golden section revisited: A perimetric explanation. *Amer. J. Psychol.,* 1965, **78**, 503-506.

Stratton, G. M. Eye-movements and the aesthetics of visual form. *Phil. Stud.,* 1902, **20**, 336-359.

Stratton, G. M. Symmetry, linear illusions, and the movements of the eye. *Psychol. Rev.,* 1906, **13**, 82-96.

Thompson, G. G. The effect of chronological age on aesthetic preferences for rectangles of different proportions. *J. exp. Psychol.,* 1946, **36**, 50-58.

Thorndike, E. L. Individual differences in judgments of the beauty of simple forms. *Psychol. Rev.,* 1917, **24**, 147-153.

Thurstone, L. L. *A factorial study of perception.* Chicago, Illinois: Univ. of Chicago Press, 1944.

Tinker, M. A. Experimental studies of the legibility of print: An annotated bibliography. *Reading Res. Quart.,* 1966, **1**(4), 67-118.

Valentine, C. W. *The experimental psychology of beauty.* London: Methuen, 1962.

Vernon, M. D. *The experimental study of reading.* London and New York: Cambridge Univ. Press, 1931.

Vernon, M. D., & Pickford, R. W. *Studies in the psychology of reading.* London: Her Majesty's Stationery Office, 1929.

Weisz, A. Z., Licklider, J. C., Swets, J. A., & Wilson, J. P. Human pattern recognition procedures as related to military recognition problems. Cambridge, Massachusetts: Bolt, Report No. 939, 1962.

Weber, C. O. The aesthetics of rectangles and theories of affection. *J. appl. Psychol.,* 1931, **15**, 310-318.

White, C. T. The significance of form discrimination in Navy operations. In J. W. Wulfeck & J. H. Taylor (Eds.), *Form discrimination as related to military problems.* Washington, D. C.: Nat. Acad. Sci.-Nat. Res. Coun., 1957.

Witmer, L. Zur experimentellen Aesthetic einfacher raeumlicher Formverhaeltnisse. *Phil. Stud.,* 1894, **9**, 96-144, 209-263.

Woodworth, R. S. *Experimental psychology.* New York: Holt, 1938.

Wulfeck, J. W., & Taylor, J. H. (Eds.) *Form discrimination as related to military problems.* Washington, D.C.: Nat. Acad. Sci.-Nat. Res. Coun., 1957.

Yarbus, A. L. *Eye movements and vision.* New York: Plenum Press, 1967.

Zusne, L. Moments of area and of the perimeter of visual form as predictors of discrimination performance. *J. exp. Psychol.,* 1965, **69**, 213-220.

Zusne, L., & Michels, K. M. Geometricity of visual form. *Percept. mot. Skills,* 1962, **14**, 147-154.

BIBLIOGRAPHY

The 2583 items of this bibliography pertain to the same topics as are discussed in the body of the present volume. The bibliography represents most of the published psychological literature on these topics as well as unpublished American doctoral dissertations, with the following limitations. Only those items were included that dealt directly with two-dimensional visual form. For instance, of the very substantial Gestalt literature, only those references were included that in their entirety had a more or less direct bearing on the visual perception of form. The body of literature on pattern recognition by machines is also very large; to keep the bibliography manageable, only books and articles dealing with psychologically interesting issues were included: articles on optical readers, for instance, and other electromechanical devices that respond to only one specific set of characters were excluded, as were articles in foreign languages. To prevent the bibliography from becoming too amorphous, the sections on clinical studies of the development of form perception, industrial and military applications, and legibility list only bibliographies, review articles, and handbooks. The literature on the psychology of aesthetics is also very large; the present bibliography contains mostly references concerning experimental work on the aesthetics of lines and polygons, i.e., the topics discussed in the text.

Although all pertinent items in the *Psychological Index* and *Psychological Abstracts* were included (the review of *Psychological Abstracts* ended with the last issue of 1968), as well as a considerable number of items not listed there (such as references concerning pattern recognition by computers abstracted in *Computer Reviews*), there must be a number of references which should have been included but managed to escape my attention. Since it is impossible to attain completeness in a bibliography of this size, the noninclusion of these items can only be regretted. It is hoped that with help from the readers a more complete bibliography may be prepared in the future.

Arranging a bibliography by topics raises the problem of cross-referencing. Since complete cross-referencing would have increased the size of the bibliography excessively without a commensurate yield in additional useful information, the following policy was followed instead. In some sections, users are referred to other headings under which the topic is covered from some additional point of view. Most of the entries are journal articles, and since most journal articles deal with only one central topic, this topic determined the location of the item in the bibliography. Titles being often misleading or ambiguous, the location of a publication in the bibliography was determined by its actual contents rather than its title. Since obviously not every item in the bibliography could be examined, items that were not actually seen are classified by their titles. Publications that emphasize two or more topics equally are classified by the first-mentioned topic in the title of the publication. Since the number of such publications is not too large and the topics are usually closely related, users of the bibliography should find no difficulty in locating a given reference of this type.

I. GENERAL REFERENCES; VISUAL FORM IN GENERAL

A. Texts of visual perception of form; selected chapters and sections (pages) in representative textbooks; general articles (see also Section VI,A)

Andreas, B. G. *Experimental psychology.* New York: Wiley, 1960. (Pp. 273–282, 298–301.)

Attneave, F. Criteria for a tenable theory of form perception. In W. Wathen-Dunn (Ed.), *Models for the perception of speech and visual forms.* Cambridge, Massachusetts: M. I. T. Press, 1967. Pp. 56–57.

Boring, E. G. *Sensation and perception in the history of experimental psychology.* New York: Appleton, 1942. (Pp. 221–262, 268–270.)

Boynton, R. M. Spatial vision. *Annu. Rev. Psychol.,* 1962, **13**, 171–200.

Dember, W. N. *The psychology of perception.* New York: Holt, 1960. (Pp. 115–361 passim.)

Duret, R. *Les aspects de l'image visuelle.* Paris: Boivin, 1935.

Epstein, W. *Varieties of perceptual learning.* New York: McGraw-Hill, 1967. (Pp. 93–106, 107–116, 125–140, 144–157, 272–278.)

Forgus, R. H. *Perception.* New York: McGraw-Hill, 1966. (Pp. 108–111, 117–131, 147–157, 165–168, 175–181.)

Francès, R. La perception des formes et des objets. In J. Piaget, E. Vurpillot, & R. Francès, *Traité de psychologie expérimentale,* Vol. VI. Paris: Presses Universitaires de France, 1967. Pp. 187–239.

Garner, W. R. *Uncertainty and structure as psychological concepts.* New York: Wiley, 1962. (Chapter 6.)

Graham, C. H. Form perception and sensory processes. In J. W. Wulfeck & J. H. Taylor (Eds.), *Form discrimination as related to military problems.* Washington, D. C.: Nat. Acad. Sci.-Nat. Res. Coun., 1957. Pp. 25–27.

Graham, C. H., Bartlett, N. R., Brown, J. L., Hsia, Y., Mueller, C. G., & Riggs, L. A. *Vision and visual perception.* New York: Wiley, 1965. (Chapter 19; pp. 549–552, 555–562.)

Hake, H. W. Contributions of psychology to the study of pattern vision. *WADC Tech. Rep.* 57–621, 1957.

Hochberg, J. The psychophysics of pictorial perception. *Audio-Visual Commun. Rev.,* 1962, **10**(5), 22–54.

Hochberg, J. In the mind's eye. In R. N. Haber (Ed.), *Contemporary theory and research in visual perception.* New York: Holt, 1968. Pp. 309-331.

Julesz, B. Some recent studies in vision relevant to form. In W. Wathen-Dunn, (Ed.), *Models for the perception of speech and visual forms.* Cambridge, Massachusetts: M. I. T. Press, 1967. Pp. 136–154.

Kolers, P. A. Some psychological aspects of pattern recognition. In P. A. Kolers & M. Eden (Eds.), *Recognizing patterns.* Cambridge, Massachusetts: M. I. T. Press, 1968. Pp. 4–61.

Krech, D., Crutchfield, R. S., & Livson, N. *Elements of psychology.* New York: Knopf, 1969. (Units 10, 11.)

Le Grand, Y. *Form and space vision.* Bloomington, Indiana: Indiana Univ. Press, 1967. (Chapters 5, 7.)

Metzger, W. *Gesetze des Sehens.* Frankfurt a. M.: Verlag von Waldemar Kramer, 1953. (Passim.)

Myers, C. M. Phenomenological idiom and perceptual form. *Phil. Sci.,* 1958, **25**, 71–81.

Obonai, T. [*Visual perception.*] Tokyo: Nakayama Shoten, 1955.

Osgood, C. E. *Method and theory in experimental psychology.* London and New York: Oxford Univ. Press, 1953. (Chapters 5, 6.)

Reese, H. W. *The perception of stimulus relations.* New York; Academic Press, 1968. (Chapter 7.)

Robinson, E. J. The problem of form in visual perception. *Amer. J. Optom.,* 1955, **32**, 599–615.

Selety, F. Die Wahrenhmung der geometrischen Figuren. *Arch. Syst. Phil,* 1915, **21**, 49–58.

Sleight, R. B., & Duvoisin, G. An annotated bibliography of form perception. The Johns Hopkins Univ. Inst. of Coop. Res., Report 166–I–153, August, 1952.

Smith, O. W. The significance of form discrimination for psychology in general. In J. W. Wulfeck & J. H. Taylor (Eds.), *Form discrimination as related to military problems.* Washington, D. C.,: Nat. Acad. Sci.-Nat. Res. Coun., 1957. Pp. 28–32.

Taylor, J. G. The behavioural basis of the visual perception of shape. *Proc. S. Afr. Psychol. Ass.* , 1951, No. 2, 19–20. (Abstract)

Teuber, H.-L. Perception. In J. Field, H. W. Magoun, & V. E. Hall (Eds.), *Handbook of physiology.* Vol. 3 Washington, D. C.: Amer. Physiol. Soc. 1960. Pp. 1595–1668. (Pp. 1613–1623, 1654–1660.)

Underwood, B. J. *Experimental psychology.* New York: Appleton, 1966. (Chapter 3.)

Vernon, M. D. *Visual perception.* New York: Macmillan, 1937. (Chapters 6, 8, 9.)

Vernon, M. D. *A further study of visual perception.* London and New York: Cambridge Univer. Press, 1962. (Pp. 41–45; Chapter 3.)

Vernon, M. D. *The psychology of perception.* Baltimore, Maryland: Penguin Books, 1962. (Chapters 4, 6.)

Woodworth, R. S., & Schlosberg, H. *Experimental psychology.* New York: Holt, 1954. (Chapters 14, 17; pp. 591–593, 714–717, 773–776.)

Yakose, Z. [*Psychology of visual perception.*] Tokyo: Kyoritsu-Shuppan, 1956.

B. History and historical references

Ackerknecht, H. Ueber Anfang und Wert des Begriffes, "Gestaltqualitaet." *Z. Psychol.,* 1913, **67**, 289ff.

Bentley, I. M. The psychology of mental arrangement. *Amer. J. Psychol.* 1902, **13**, 269–293.

Benussi, V. Zur Psychologie des Gestalterfassens. In A. Meinong (Ed.), *Gegenstandstheorie und Psychologie.* Leipzig: Barth, 1904.

Benussi, V. Die Gestaltwahrnehmungen. *Z. Psychol.*, 1914, **69**, 256–292.

Bingham, H. C. A definition of form. *J. Anim. Behav.*, 1914, **4**, 136-141.

Boring, E. G. A *history of experimental psychology*. New York: Appleton, 1950. (Chapters 19, 23.)

Cornelius, H. Ueber Verschmelzung und Analyse. *Vtljsch. Wiss. Phil.*, 1892, **16**, 404–446.

Cornelius, H. Ueber Verschmelzung und Analyse. *Vtljsch. Wiss. Phil.*, 1893, **17**, 30–75.

Cornelius, H. Ueber Gestaltqualitaeten. *Z. Psychol.*, 1899, **22**, 101–121.

Ehrenfels, C. von. Ueber Gestaltqualitaeten. *Vtljsch. Wiss. Phil.*, 1890, **14**, 249–292.

Ehrenfels, C. von. On Gestalt-qualities. *Psychol. Rev.*, 1937, **44**, 521–525.

Gelb, A. Theoretisches ueber "Gestaltqualitaeten." *Z. Psychol.*, 1910, **58**, 1–58.

Helson, H. H. The psychology of Gestalt. *Amer. J. Psychol.*, 1926, **37**, 25–62, 189–216.

Hempstead, L. The perception of visual form. *Amer. J. Psychol.*, 1901, **12**, 185–192.

Hoefler, A. Gestalt und Beziehung–Gestalt and Anschauung. *Z. Psychol.*, 1911, **60**, 161–228.

Hutchins, R. M. (Ed.) *Great books of the western world*, Vol. 2, The great ideas: I, Chapter 28. Form. Chicago, Illinois: Encyclopedia Britannica, 1952.

James, W. *The principles of psychology*. New York: Holt, 1890. (Republished: New York: Dover, 1950.) (Pp. 149–150, 270–282.)

Lipps, T. Zu den "Gestaltqualitaeten." *Z. Psychol.*, 1900, **22**, 383–385.

Mach, E. *The analysis of sensations*. Chicago: Open Court, 1914. (Republished: New York: Dover, 1959.) (Chapters 6, 10.)

Meinong, A. Zur Psychologie der Komplexionen and Relationen. *Z. Psychol.*, 1891, **2**, 245–265.

Meinong, A. Ueber Gegenstaende hoeherer Ordnung und deren Verhaeltnis zur inneren Wahrnehmung. *Z. Psychol.*, 1899, **11**, 180–272.

Rubin, E. Die visuelle Wahrnehmung von Figuren. In F. Schumann (Ed.), *Ber. VI. Kongr. exp. Psychol.* Leipzig: Barth, 1914. Pp. 60–63.

Schumann, F. Beitraege zur Analyse der Gesichtswahrnehmungen. I. *Z. Psychol.*, 1900, **23**, 1–32.

Schumann, F. Beitraege zur Analyse der Gesichtswahrnehmungen. II. *Z. Psychol.*, 1900, **24**, 1–33.

Schumann, F. Beitraege zur Analyse der Gesichtswahrnehmungen, III. *Z. Psychol.*, 1902, **30**, 241–291.

Schumann, F. Beitraege zur Analyse der Gesichtswahrnehmungen. IV. *Z. Psychol.*, 1904, **36**, 161–185.

Witasek, S. *Psychologie der Raumwahrnehmung des Auges*. Heidelberg: Winter, 1910.

C. Form as figure on ground; embedded figures

1. The figure-ground phenomenon (see also Section II,C,1)

Bahnsen, P. Eine Untersuchung ueber Symmetrie and Asymmetrie bei visuellen Wahrnehmungen, *Z. Psychol.* 1928, **108**, 129–154.

Berliner, A., Crabtree, D., & Garfield, L. H. Observations on dominance in reversible figures. Optom. Weekly, 1956, **47**, 2315-2317.

Carmichael, L. Another 'hidden-figure' picture. *Amer. J. Psychol.*, 1951, **64**, 137–138.

Dalla Volta, A. Contributi allo studio della percezione con particulare riferimento alla psicologia differenziale. II. Forma e significato nel processo di inversione del rapporto di figura e sfondo. *Arch. Psicol. Neurol. Psichiat.*, 1948, **9**, 307–328, 403–442.

Dalla Volta, A. Contributi allo studio della percezione con particolare riferimento alla psicologia differenziale. II. Forma e significato nel processo di inversione del rapparto di figura e sfondo. *Arch. Psicol. Neurol. Psichiat.*, 1949, **10**, 19–69.

Dallenbach, K. M. A puzzle-picture with a new principle of concealment. *Amer. J. Psychol.*, 1951, **64**, 431-433.

Dana, R. H., & Goocher, B. Embedded figures and personality. *Percept. mot Skills*, 1959, **9**, 99–102.

Ehrenstein, W. Untersuchungen ueber Figur-Grund Fragen. *Z. Psychol.*, 1930, **117**, 339–412.

Ehrenstein, W. The region of the vision-field within which arbitrary reversion of ambivalent figure-ground patterns is possible. *J. exp. Psychol.*, 1940, **27**, 699-702.

Ekman, G., & Lindman, R. Measurement of the underlying process in perceptual fluctuations. *Vision Res.*, 1962, **2**, 253–260.

Fernberger, S. W. An early example of a 'hidden-figure' picture. *Amer. J. Psychol.*, **63**, 448–449.

Frisch, H. L., & Julesz, B. Figure-ground perception and random geometry. *Percept. Psychophys.*, 1966, **1**, 389–398.

Fry, G. A., & Robertson, V. M. The physiological basis of the periodic merging of area into background. *Amer. J. Psychol.*, 1935, **47**, 644-655.

Galli, A. La percezione di "figura" e di "fondo." *Scritti Onore Kiesow*, 1933, 99–116.

Galli, A., & Zama, A. Contributi allo studio della percezione della forma. *Atti VII. Convegno di Psicol. Sper. e Psicotecn.*, 1929.

Galli, A., & Zama, A. Ricerche sulla percezione di configurazioni geometriche piane mascherate in tutto o in parte de ultra configurazioni. *Pubbl. Univ. Catt. S. Cuore*, 1931, **6**, 29–76.

Galli, A., & Zama, A. Untersuchungen ueber die Wahrnehmung ebener geometricher Figuren, die ganz oder teilweise von anderen geometrischen Figuren verkeckt sind. *Z. Psychol.*, 1931, **123**. 308–348.

Galli, G. Contiguità e continuità fenomenica. *Riv. Psicol.*, 1964, **58**, 325–339.

Goldhammer, H. The influence of area, position, and brightness in the visual perception of a reversible configuration. *Amer. J. Psychol.*, 1934, **46**, 189–206.

Gordon, O. J., Brayer, R., & Tikofsky., R. Personality variables and the perception of embedded figures. *Percept. mot. Skills*, 1961, **12**, 195–202.

Graham, C. H. Area, color, and brightness difference in a reversible configuration. *J. gen. Psychol.*, 1929, **2**, 470–483.

Granit, R. Die Bedeutung von Figur und Grund fuer bei univeraenderter Schwarzinduktion bestimmte Helligkeitsschwellen. *Skand. Arch. Physiol.*, 1924, **45**, 43–57.

Harrower, M. R. Some factors determining figure-ground articulation. *Brit. J. Psychol.*, 1936, **26**, 407–424.

Hoffeditz, E. L., & Guilford, J. P. The factors present in the fluctuation of fifteen ambiguous phenomena. *Psychol. Bull.*, 1935, **32**, 726–727. (Abstract)

Kahneman, D. Exposure duration and effective figure-ground contrast. *Quart. J. exp. Psychol.*, 1965, **17**, 308–314.

Karp. S. A. A factorial study of overcoming embeddedness in perceptual and intellectual functioning. Unpublished doctoral dissertation, New York Univ., 1962.

Kuennapas, T. Experiments on figural dominance. *J. exp. Psychol.*, 1957, **53**, 31–39.

Kuennapas, T. Measurement of the intensity of an underlying figural process. *Scand. J. Psychol.*, 1961, **2**, 174–184.

Kuennapas, T. Intensity of the underlying figural process. *Percept. Psychophys.*, 1966, **1**, 288–292.

Lapi, L. Contributo allo studio del processo di inversione del rapporto figura-sfondo. *Riv. Psicol.*, 1949, **45**, 125–130.

Longnecker, E. D. Form perception as a function of anxiety, motivation, and the testing situation. Unpublished doctoral dissertation, Univ. of Texas, 1956.

Metelli, F. Oggettualità, stratificazione e risalto nell'organizzazione percettiva di figura e sfondo. *Arch. Psicol. Neurol. Psichiat.,* 1941, **2**, 831–841.

Meux, M. O. The role of reasoning and spatial abilities in performance at three different levels of the embedded figures task. Unpublished doctoral dissertation, Univ. of Illinois, 1960. *Diss. Abstr.,* 1960, **21**, 1625.

Newbigging, P. L. The relationship between reversible perspective and imbedded figures. *Can. J. Psychol.,* 1954, **8**, 204–208.

Newhall, S. M. Hidden cow puzzle-picture. *Amer. J. Psychol.,* 1952, **65**, 110.

Oyama, T. Figure-ground dominance as a function of sector angle, brightness, hue, and orientation. *J. exp. Psychol.,* 1960, **60**, 299–305.

Oyama, T., & Sasamoto, S. [Experimental studies of figure-ground reversal: II. The effects of brightness, brightness gradient, and area under tachistoscopic exposure.] *Jap. J. Psychol.,* 1957, **28**, 18–27.

Oyama, T., Torii, S., & Hamamoto, N. Experimental studies of figure-ground reversal: III. The influence of size, brightness gradient, illuminance, and the number of sectors upon the rate of reversal. *Jap. J. Psychol.,* 1957, **28**, 210–222.

Pemberton, C. L. A study of the speed and flexibility of closure factors. Unpublished doctoral dissertation, Univ. of Chicago, 1951.

Pikler, J. Grund and Figur bei schwacher Beleuchtung. *Z. Psychol.,* 1928, **106**, 316–326.

Porter, E. L. H. Factors in the fluctuation of fifteen ambiguous phenomena. *Psychol. Rec.,* 1938, **2**, 231–253.

Porter, P. B. Another puzzle-picture. *Amer. J. Psychol.,* 1954, **67**, 550–551.

Rubin, E. *Synoplevede figurer.* Copenhagen: Gyldendalske, 1915.

Rubin, E. *Visuell wahrgenomenne Figuren.* Copenhagen: Gyldendalske, 1921.

Sato, S., & Ohwaki, Y. Function of the ground as "framework" in the perception of size. (II). *Tohoku Psychol. Folia,* 1955, **14**, 83–104.

Sayanagi. T. [On the influence of the contour figure upon the surrounding ground.] *Jap. J. Psychol.,* 1942, **17**, 406–423.

Sayanagi, T. [On the influence of the contour figure upon the surrounding ground.] *Jap. J. Psychol.,* 1943, **18**, 33–44.

Torii, S. Figure-ground reversals under successively repeated observations. *Jap. Psychol. Res.,* 1960, No. 9, 25–37.

Torii, S. Effect of unequality in color upon figure-ground dominance. *Percept. mot. Skills,* 1963, **16**, 10.

Traylor, T. Nuns and nudes. In R. Prelisser, Vision in engineering. *Int. Sci. Technol.,* 1965, **46**, 61–66.

Weigle, E. Untersuchungen zur psychischen Umstellbarkeit auf Grund normal psychologischer und klinischer Befunde. *Report on 12th Psychol. Cong.,* Jena, 1932.

Weitz, J. The effect of stereoscopic presentation on a reversible configuration. *Psychol. Bull.,* 1949, **39**, 584. (Abstract)

Weitzman, B. A threshold difference produced by a figure-ground dichotomy. *J. exp. Psychol.,* 1963, **66**, 201–205.

Wever, E. G. Figure and ground in the visual perception of form. *Amer. J. Psychol.,* 1927, **38**, 194–226.

Wever, E. G. Attention and clearness in the perception of figure and ground. *Amer. J. Psychol.,* 1928, **40**, 51–74.

Witkin, H. A. Individual differences in ease of perception of embedded figures. *J. Person.,* 1950, **19**, 1–15.

Witkin, H. A. "Embedded figures and personality": A reply. *Percept. mot Skills,* 1960, **11**, 15–20.

2. Figure-ground and experience

Ammons, R., Ammons, C., Dubbe, A., Techida, A., & Preuninger, C. Preliminary report of studies of perspective and figure-ground reversals as learned responses to depth perception. *Proc. Mont. Acad. Sci.,* 1958, **18**, 81.

Botha, E. Past experience and figure-ground perception. *Percept. mot. Skills,* 1963, **16**, 283–288.

Braly, K.W. The influence of past experience in visual perception. *J. exp. Psychol.,* 1933, **16**, 613–643.

Cesarec, Z. Figure-ground reversal as related to stimulus exposure, observation time, and some personality dimensions. *Psychol. Res. Bull.,* 1963, 3(5), 1–17.

Cornwell, H. G. Prior experience as a determinant of figure-ground organization. *J. exp. Psychol.,* 1963, **65**, 156–162.

Cornwell, H. G. Effect of training on figure-ground organization. *J. exp. Psychol.,* 1964, **68**, 108–109.

Djang, S. The role of past experience in the visual perception of the masked forms. *J. exp. Psychol.,* 1937, **20**, 29–59.

Dutton, M. B., & Traill, P. M. A repetition of Rubin's figure-ground experiment. *Brit. J. Psychol.,* 1933, **23**, 389–400.

Epstein, W., & De Shazo, D. Recency as a function of perceptual oscillation. *Amer. J. Psychol.,* 1961, **74**, 215–223.

Francès, R. L'apprentisage de la ségrégation perceptive. *Psychol. Franc.,* 1963, 8, 16–27.

Goldstein, A. G., & Chance, J. E. Effects of practice on sex-related differences in performance on Embedded Figures. *Psychon. Sci.,* 1965, 3, 361–362.

Gottschaldt, K. Ueber den Einfluss der Erfahrung auf die Wahrnehmung von Figuren. *Psychol. Forsch.,* 1926, 8, 261–317.

Gottschaldt, K. Ueber den Einfluss der Erfahrung auf die Wahrnehmung von Figuren. II. Vergleichende Untersuchungen ueber die Wirkung figuraler Einpraegung und den Einfluss spezifischer Geschehensverlaeufe auf die Auffassung optischer Komplexe. *Psychol. Forsch.,* 1929, **12**, 1–87.

Hanawalt, N. G. The effect of practice upon the perception of simple designs masked by more complex designs. *J. exp. Psychol.,* 1942, **31**, 134–148.

Hochberg, J. E. Figure-ground reversal as a function of visual satiation. *J. exp. Psychol.,* 1950, **40**, 682–686.

Kolers, P. A., & Zink, D. L. Some aspects of problem solving: Sequential analysis of the detection of embedded patterns. Aerospace Med. Res. Lab. Tech. Doc. Rep. No. AMRL-TDR-62-148, December, 1962.

Podell, J. E. Shape recognition as a function of context structure. *Amer. Psychologist,* 1963, **18**, 425. (Abstract)

Rock, I., & Kremen, I. A re-examination of Rubin's figural after-effect. *J. exp. Psychol.,* 1957, **53**, 23–30.

Schwartz, C. B. Visual discrimination of camouflaged figures. Unpublished doctoral dissertation, Univ. of California at Berkeley, 1961.

Vetter, R. J. Perception of ambiguous figure-ground patterns as a function of past experience. *Percept. mot. Skills,* 1965, **20**, 183–188.

3. Figure-ground and motivation

Ayllon, T., & Sommer, R. Autism, emphasis, and figure-ground perception. *J. Psychol.*, 1956, **41**, 163–176.

Hochberg, J. E., & Brooks, V. Effects of previously associated annoying stimuli (auditory) on visual recognition thresholds. *J. exp. Psychol.*, 1958, **55**, 490–491.

Jackson, D. N. A further examination of the rôle of autism in a visual figure-ground relationship. *J. Psychol.*, 1954, **38**, 339–357.

Lie, I. Reward and punishment: A determinant in figure-ground perception? *Scand. J. Psychol.*, 1965, **6**(3), 186–194.

Mangan, G. L. The role of punishment in figure-ground reorganization. *J. exp. Psychol.*, 1959, **58**, 369–375.

Page, M. Modification of figure-ground perception as a function of awareness of demand characteristics. *J. Pers. Soc. Psychol.*, 1968, 9, 59–66.

Postman, L. The experimental analysis of motivational factors in perception. In J. S. Brown *et al., Current theory and research in motivation: a symposium.* Lincoln, Nebraska: Univ. of Nebraska Press, 1953. Pp. 58–108.

Rock, I., & Fleck, F. S. A re-examination of the effect of monetary reward and punishment on figure-ground perception. *J. exp. Psychol.*, 1950, **40**, 766–776.

Saugstad, P. Effect of reward and punishment on visual perception of figure-ground. *Scand. J. Psychol.*, 1965, **6**(4), 225–236.

Schafer, R., & Murphy, G. The role of autism in a visual figure-ground relationship. *J. exp. Psychol.*, 1943, **32**, 335–343.

Smith, D. E. P., & Hochberg, J. E. The effect of "punishment" (electric shock) on figure-ground perception. *J. Psychol.*, 1954, **38**, 83–87.

Solley, C. M., & Long, J. Affect, fantasy, and figure-ground organization. *J. gen. Psychol.*, 1960, **62**, 75–82.

Sommer, R. The effects of rewards and punishments during perceptual organization. *J. Pers.*, 1957, **25**, 550–558.

D. Polyfigurations

Boring, E. G. A new ambiguous figure. *Amer. J. Psychol.*, 1930, **42**, 444–445.

Botwinick, J. Husband and father-in-law: A reversible figure. *Amer. J. Psychol.*, 1961, **74**, 312–313.

Crowley, M. E. A puzzle-picture in silhouette. *Amer. J. Psychol.*, 1952, **65**, 302–304.

Epstein, W., & Rock, I. Perceptual set as an artifact of recency. *Amer. J. Psychol.*, 1960, **73**, 214–228.

Fisher, G. H. Ambiguous figure treatments in the art of Salvador Dali. *Percept. Psychophys.*, 1967, **2**, 328–330.

Fisher, G. H. Measuring ambiguity. *Amer. J. Psychol.*, 1967, **80**, 541–557.

Fisher, G. H. Preparation of ambiguous stimulus materials. *Percept. Psychophys.*, 1967, **2**, 421–422.

Fisher, G. H. Ambiguity of form: Old and new. *Percept. Psychophys.*, 1968, 4, 189–192.

Kolers, P. A. The boys from Syracuse: Another ambiguous figure. *Amer. J. Psychol.*, 1964, **77**, 671–672.

Leeper, R. A study of neglected portion of the field of learning – the development of sensory organization. *J. genet. Psychol.*, 1935, **46**, 42–75.

Newell, P. *Topsys and Turvys.* New York: Dover, 1964.

Steinfeld, G. S. Concepts of set and availability and their relation to the reorganization of ambiguous pictorial stimuli. *Psychol. Rev.*, 1967, **74**, 505–522.

E. Impossible objects

Escher, M. C. *The graphic work of M. C. Escher.* New York: Duell, 1960.

Penrose, L., & Penrose, R. Impossible objects: a special type of visual illusion. *Brit. J. Psychol.,* 1958, **49**, 31–33.

Schuster, D. H. A new ambiguous figure: A three-stick clevis. *Amer. J. Psychol.,* 1964, **77**, 673.

F. Geometric illusions

Anonymous. The Mueller-Lyer illusion. *Amer. J. Psychol.,* 1896, **7**, 305.

Andrews, T.G. & Robinson, I. P. Time-error and the Mueller-Lyer illusion. *Amer. J. Psychol.,* 1948, **61**, 229–235.

Aubert, H. *Grundzuege der physiologischen Optik.* Leipzig: Engelmann, 1876. (P. 630 ff.)

Auerbach, F. Erklaerung der Brentano'schen optischen Taeuschung. *Z. Psychol.,* 1894, **7**, 152-160.

Azuna, H. [The effect of experience on the amount of the Mueller-Lyer illusion.] *Jap. J. Psychol.,* 1952, **22**, 111–123.

Bader, P. *Augentaeuschungen.* Leipzig: Duerr, 1907.

Baldwin, J. M. Studies from the Princeton Laboratory. III. The effect of size-contrast upon judgments of position in the retinal field. *Psychol. Rev.,* 1895, **2**, 244–259.

Baldwin, J. M. An optical illusion. *Science,* 1896, **4**, 774.

Balser, M. Untersuchungen zu Kristofs Zweikomponententheorie der geometrischoptischen Taeuschungen. *Arch. ges. Psvchol.,* 1963, **115**, 307–329.

Bates, M. A study of Mueller-Lyer illusion, with special reference to paradoxical movement and the effect of attitude. *Amer. J. Psychol.,* 1923, **34**, 46–72.

Battelli, F. Di olciene illusioni ottiche. *Rev. Venet. Sci. Med.,* 1897, **26**, 369–380.

Beeler, N. F., & Branley, F. M. *Experiments in optical illusion.* New York: Crowell, 1951.

Benussi, V. Ueber den Einfluss der Farbe auf die Groesse der Zoellner'schen Taeuschung. *Z. Psychol.,* 1902, **29**, 264–351, 385–433.

Benussi, V. Zur Psychologie des Gestalterfassens. *Untersuch. Gegenstandstheorie,* 1904, 303–448.

Benussi, V. Stroboskopische Scheinbewegungen und geometrisch-optische Gestalt-taeuschungen. *Arch. ges. Psychol.,* 1912, **24**, 31–62.

Benussi, V. Gesetze der inadequaten Gestaltauffassung. *Arch. ges. Psychol.,* 1914, **32**, 396–419.

Berenda, C. W., & Moskowitz, B. Visual illusions on television. *Amer. Psychologist,* 1955, **10**, 87–88.

Berliner, A. Spatial displacement of straight and curved lines. *Amer. J. Psychol.,* 1949, **62**, 20–31.

Berliner, A., & Berliner, S. The distortion of straight and curved lines in geometric fields. *Amer. J. Psychol.,* 1948, **61**, 153–166.

Berry, J. W. Ecology, perceptual development and the Mueller-Lyer illusion. *Brit. J. Psychol.,* 1968, **59**, 205–210.

Beucke, K. *Ueber die optischen Taeuschungen.* Berlin: 1900.

Bidwell, S. *Curiosities of light and sight.* London: Sonnenschein, 1899.

Bidwell, S. Some curiosities of vision. In Smithsonian Institute, Annual Report 1898. Washington. D. C.: 1899.

Biervliet, J. J. van. Nouvelles mesures des illusions visuelles chez les adultes et chez les enfants. *Rev. Phil.,* 1896, **41**, 169–181.

Binet, A. Reverse illusions of orientation. *Psychol Rev.*, 1894, **1**, 337–350.

Blatt, P. Optische Taeuschungen und Metakontrast. *Arch. ges. Physiol.*, 1911, **142**, 396–402.

Blix, M. Die sogenannte Poggendorff'sche Taeuschung. *Skand. Arch. Physiol.*, *1902*, **13**, 193–228.

Bonaventura, E. Le illusioni ottico-geometriche. *Riv. Psicol.*, 1920, **16**, 220–236.

Boring. E. G. Letter to editor. *Sci. Amer.*, 1961, **204**(6).

Botti, L. Ein Beitrag zur Kenntniss der variabeln geometrisch-optischen Streckentaeuschungen. *Arch. ges. Psychol.*, 1905, **6**, 306–315.

Botti, L. Ricerche sperimentali sulle illusioni otticogemetriche. *Memorie della R. Accad. delle Scienze di Torino*, 1909, Ser. II, 60.

Botti, L. Sur les illusions optico-geometriques. *Arch. Ital. Biol.*, 1910, **53**, 165–182.

Botti, L. Di alcune illusioni ottico-geometriche. *Riv. Psicol.*, 1912, **8**, 331–347.

Bourdon, B. Une illusion d'optique. *Rev. Phil.*, 1893, **35**, 507–509.

Bracken, H. v. Wahrnehmungstaeuschungen und scheinbare Nachbildgroesse bei Zwillingen. *Arch. ges. Psychol.*, 1939, **103**, 203–230.

Brentano, F. Ueber ein optisches Paradoxon. *Z. Psychol.*, 1892, **3**, 349–358

Brentano, F. Ueber ein optisches Paradoxon. *Z. Psychol.*, *1893*, **5**, 61–82.

Brentano, F. Zur Lehre von den optischen Tauschungen. *Z. Psychol.*, 1893, **6**, 1–7.

Bressler, J. Illusion in the case of subliminal visual stimulation. *J. gen. Psychol.*, 1931, **5**, 244–250.

Bruecke, E.T.V. Ueber eine neue optische Taeuschung. *Zentbl. Physiol.*, 1906, **20**, 737–738.

Brunot. Les illusions d'optique. *Rev. Sci.*, 1893, **52**, 210–212.

Burmester, E. Beitrag zur experimentellen Bestimmung geometrisch-optischer Tauschungen. *Z. Psychol.*, 1896, **12**, 355-394.

Burmester, L. Theorie der geometrisch-optischen Gestalt-Taeuschungen. *Z. Psychol.*, 1906, **41**, 321–348.

Burmester, L. Theorie der geometrisch-optischen Gestalttaeuschungen. *Z. Psychol.*, 1908, **50**, 219–274.

Burnham, C. A. Decrement of the Mueller-Lyer illusion with saccadic and tracking eye movements. *Percept. Psychophys.*, 1968, **3**, 424–426.

Calvin, A. D., & Youniss, J. The enclosing contour effect: Some additional remarks. *Percept. mot. Skills*, 1962, **14**, 132.

Cameron, E. H., & Steele, W. M. The Poggendorff illusion. *Psychol. Rev.*, *Monogr. Suppl.*, 1905, No. 29, 83–111.

Carlson, J. A. The effect of instructions and perspective drawing ability on perceptual constancies and geometrical illusions. Unpublished doctoral dissertation, Univ. of Iowa. *Diss. Abstr.*, 1966, **26**, 6177–6178.

Carlson, J. A. Effect of instructions and perspective-drawing ability on perceptual constancies and geometrical illusions. *J. exp. Psychol.*, 1966, **72**, 874–879.

Carnegie, D. Optical illusions. *Nature*, 1906, **74**, 610.

Carr, H. Space illusions. *Psychol. Bull.*, 1911, **8**, 235–239.

Carr, H. Space illusions. *Psychol. Bull.*, 1912, **9**, 257–260.

Carr, H. Space illusions. *Psychol. Bull.*, 1913, **10**, 261–264.

Carr, H. Space illusions, *Psychol. Bull.*, 1914, **11**, 241–245.

Carr, H. Space illusions. *Psychol. Bull.*, 1915, **12**, 216–218.

Carr, H. Space illusions. *Psychol. Bull.*, 1916, **13**, 265–266.

Carr, H. Space illusions. *Psychol. Bull.*, 1917, **14**, 233–234.

Carr, H. Space illusions. *Psychol. Bull.*, 1918, **15**, 170–172.

Carr, H. Space illusions. *Psychol. Bull.*, 1919, **16**, 249–250.

Carr, H. *An introduction to space perception.* New York: Longmans, Green, 1935. (Passim)

Carraher, R. G., & Thurston, J. B. *Optical illusions and the visual arts.* New York: Reinhold, 1966.

Chiang, C. A new theory to explain geometrical illusions produced by crossing lines. *Percept. Psychophys.,* 1968, **3,** 174–176.

Cibrario, M. Andamento dell' errore nella illusione di Poggendorff. *Arch. Ital. Psicol.,* 1932, **10,** 57–59.

Cleary, A. A binocular parallax theory of the geometric illusions. *Psychon. Sci.,* 1966, **5,** 241–242.

Coillie, R. van. Illusion d'optique. *Rev. Sci.,* 1902, **18,** 76–83.

Crosland, H. R., Taylor, H. R., & Newsom, S. J. Intelligence and susceptibility to the Mueller-Lyer illusion. *J. exp. Psychol.,* 1927, **10,** 40–51.

Day, R. H. On the stereoscopic observation of geometric illusions. *Percept. mot. Skills.* 1961, **13,** 247–258.

Day, R. H. The effects of repeated trials and prolonged fixation on error in the Mueller-Lyer figure. *Psychol. Monogr.,* 1962, **76,** No. 14 (Whole No. 533).

Delabarre, E. B. Influence of surrounding objects upon the apparent direction of a line. *German Stud. Phil. Psychol.,* 1906, 239–296.

Delacey, E. A. An alternative method of presenting the Mueller-Lyer illusion. *Percept. mot. Skills,* 1965, **21,** 943–946.

Delboeuf, J. Une nouvelle illusion d'optique. *Rev. Sci.,* 1893, **51,** 237–241.

Delboeuf, J. Sur une nouvelle illusion d'optique. *Bull. Acad. Roy. Belg.,* 1893, **24,** 545–558.

De Marchi, S. Percezione della forma e impressione di quantita: spora un caso particolare della figura di Mueller-Lyer. *Atti VII. convegno psicol. sper. e psicotecn.,* Torino, 1929. Pp. 72–73.

Desai, K. G, The "in" and "out" method in M-L illusion. *J. gen. Psychol.,* 1964, **71,** 125–129.

Deshayes, M. L. L'eventail magique. *J. Psychol.,* 1932, **29,** 310–318.

Dewar, R. E. The effect of angle between the oblique lines on the decrement of the Mueller-Lyer illusion with extended practice. *Percept. Psychophys.,* 1967, **2,** 426–428.

Dewar, R. E. Effect of length of oblique lines and prominence of the horizontal line on the decrement of the Mueller-Lyer illusion with extended practice. *Psychon. Sci.,* 1967, **8,** 509–510.

Dewar, R. E. Sex differences in the magnitude and practice decrement in the Mueller-Lyer illusion. *Psychon. Sci.,* 1967, **9,** 345–346.

Dewar, R. E. Stimulus determinants of the magnitude of the Mueller-Lyer illusion. *Percept. mot. Skills,* 1967, **24,** 708–710.

Dewar, R. E. Stimulus determinants of the practice decrement of the Mueller-Lyer illusion. *Can. J. Psychol.,* 1967, **21,** 504–520.

Dewar, R. E. Distribution of practice and the Mueller-Lyer illusion. *Percept. Psychophys.,* 1968, **3,** 246–248.

Dreistadt, R. The effect of figural after-effects on geometrical illusions. *J. Psychol.,* 1968, **69,** 63–73.

Dresslar, F. B. A new illusion for touch and an explanation for the illusion of displacement of certain cross lines in vision. *Amer. J. Psychol.,* 1893–5, **6,** 275–276.

Duboisson, M. La vision monoculaire du relief et les illusions d'optique. In *Notes Mem. Congr. Ass. Fr. Avanc. Sci.,* 1914, 1915, **43,** 600–605.

Dufour, M. Une illusion optique due à l'irradiation. *C. R. Soc. Biol.,* 1928, **99,** 411.

Dufour, M. Illusions d'optique observées en regardant un damier à travers une fente. *C. R. Soc. Biol.,* 1931, **107,** 716–717.

Dunlap, K. The effect of imperceptible shadows on the judgment of distance. *Psychol. Rev.,* 1900, **7,** 435–453.

Eldridge-Green, F. W. An optical illusion. *Nature*, 1914, **93**, 214.

Egger, V. Sur quelques illusions visuelles. *Rev. Phil.*, 1885, **20**, 485–498.

Ehrenstein, V. Versuche ueber Beziehungen zwischen Bewegungs– und Gestaltwahrnehmung. *Z. Psychol.*, 1924, **95**, 305–352.

Einthoven, W. Eine einfache physiologische Erklaerung fuer verschiedene geometrisch-optische Taeuschungen. *Arch. ges. Physiol.* 1898, **71**, 1–43.

Elworth, C. L. A study of distortion in the perception of the square. Unpublished doctoral dissertation, Univ. of Rochester, 1963. *Diss. Abstr.*, 1963, **24**, 2133.

Emmert, E. *Gesichtswahrnehmungen und Sinnestaeuschungen.* Bern, 1873.

Eriksson, E. S. Field effects and two-dimensional form perception. *Scand. J. Psychol.*, 1967, **8**, 218–242.

Eysenck, H. J. Susceptibility to a visual illusion, as related to primary and secondary suggestibility and other functions. *Brit. J. Psychol.*, 1943, **34**, 32–36.

Eysenck, H. J., & Slater, P. Effects of practice and rest on fluctuations in the Mueller-Lyer illusion. *Brit. J. Psychol.*, 1958, **49**, 246–256.

Fauser, A. Aus der Psychologie der Sinnestaeuschungen. *Arch. Psychiat. Nervenk.*, 1912, **49**, 253–264.

Fellows, B. J. Reversal of the Mueller-Lyer illusion with changes in the length of the inter-fins line. *Quart. J. exp. Psychol.*, 1967, **19**, 208–214.

Ferree, C. E., & Rand, G. The effect of relation to background on the size and shape of the form field for stimuli of different sizes. *Amer. J. Ophthal.*, 1931, **14**, 1018–1029.

Festinger, L., White, C. W., & Allyn, M. R. Eye movements and decrement in the Mueller-Lyer illusion. *Percept. Psychophys.*, 1968, **3**, 376–382.

Fick, A. *De errore quodam optico asymmetria bulbi effecto.* Marburg: Koch, 1851.

Filehne, W. . Die geometrisch-optischen Taeuschungen als Nachwirkungen der im koerperlichen Sehen erworbenen Erfahrung. *Z. Psychol.*, 1898, **17**, 15–61.

Filehne, W. Ueber eine dem Brentano-Mueller-Lyerschen Paradoxen analoge Taeuschung im raumlichen Sehen. *Arch. Physiol.*, 1911, **34**, 273–286.

Fischer, M. H. Sinnesempfindung (sensation), Sinneswahrnehmung (perception) und Sinnestaeuschung (illusion). *Pflueg. Arch.*, 1952, **255**, 68–74.

Fisher, G. H. An experimental comparison of rectilinear and curvilinear illusions. *Brit. J. Psychol.*, 1968, **59**, 23–28.

Fisher, G. H. Gradients of distortion seen in the context of the Ponzo illusion and other contours. *Quart. J. exp. Psychol.*, 1968, **20**, 212–217.

Foley, J. P. The effect of context upon perceptual differentiation. *Arch. Psychol.*, 1935, No. 184, 5–67.

Fornasari, G. Errori ed illusioni nella determinazione di angoli. *Arch. Ital. Psicol.*, 1923, **2**, 195–199.

Franklin, C. L. A method for the experimental determination of the horporter. *Amer. J. Psychol.*, 1887, **1**, 99–111.

Franklin, C. L. An optical illusion. *Science*, 1896, **3**, 274–275.

Fraser, J. A new visual illusion of direction. *Brit. J. Psychol.*, 1908, **2**, 297–320.

Froehlich, F. W. Die geometrisch-optischen Taeuschungen als Zeit-Raum-Phaenomen. *Stzber. Abh. Naturforsch. Ges. Rostock*, 1930, **2**, 13–16.

Galperin, P. J. Neue verstaerkte Form der Poggendorfschen Figur: Zur Theorie der geometrisch-optischen Illusionen. *Z. Psychol.*, 1931, **122**, 84–97.

Gardner, R. W., & Long, R. I. Selective attention and the Mueller-Lyer illusion. *Psychol. Rec.*, 1961, **11**, 317–320.

Gatti, A. Contributo allo studio dell' illusione di Poggendorff. *Pubbl. Univ. Catt. Milano*, 1925, Serie I, **1**, fasc. iv, 319–332.

Gatti, A. Di alcune nuove illusioni ottiche in rapporto alla percezione dei complessi rappresentativi. *Arch. Ital. Psicol.*, 1926, **4**, 208–225.

Gatti, A. La percezione dei rapporti spaziali nei complessi visivi. *Pubbl. Univ. Catt. Milano*, Serie I, 1926, **11**, 81–191.

Gatti, A. Analisi di una illusione ottico-geometrica. *Arch. Ital. Psicol.*, 1931, **9**, No. 4.

Gatti, A. L'illusione di Poggendorff e il principio del minimo mezzo. *Arch. Ital. Psicol.*, 1932, **10**, 29–56.

Gatti, A.Ricerche sperimentali sopra la soglia di rettilineità. *Arch. Ital. Psicol.*, 1933, **11**, 89–112.

Gandreau, J., Lavoie, G., & Delorme, A. La perception des illusions de Mueller-Lyer et d'Opell-Kundt chez les deficients mentaux. *Can. J. Psychol.*, 1963, **17**, 259–263.

Gerhards, K. Zum optischen Verformungskontrast. *Naturwissenschaften*, 1937, **25**, 493.

Gertz, H. Untersuchungen ueber Zoellners anorthoskopische Taeuschung. *Skand. Arch. Physiol.*, 1899, **10**, 53–73.

Giese, F. Untersuchungen ueber die Zoellnersche Taeuschung. *Psychol. Stud.*, 1914, **9**, 405–435.

Giltay, J. W., & Edrige-Green, F. W. An optical illusion. *Nature*, 1914, **93**, 189–214.

Goldstein, M. E. An experimental investigation of subliminal perception with optical illusions. Unpublished doctoral dissertation, Yeshiva Univ., 1958. *Diss. Abstr.*, 1959, **19**, 2145.

Goto, T. An experimental study of perception of parallel lines of identical size. Especially in relation to the filled-unfilled illusion. *Jap. J. Psychol.*, 1964, **35**, 227–234.

Goudge, T. A. Some realist theories of illusion. *Monist*, 1934, **44**, 108–125.

Graham, J. L. Illusory trends in the observations of bar graphs. *J. exp. Psychol.*, 1937, **20**, 597–608.

Grahmann, B. Verlagerungen bei der Auffassung optischer Gestalten im geographischen Anschauungsbilde. *Z. paed. Psychol.*, 1931, **32**, 92–98.

Gramss, K. *Gesichts-Taeuschungen.* Lepzig: Paul, 1911.

Grant, V. W. *Psychological optics.* Chicago: Professional Press, 1938. (Chapter 8.)

Green, R. I., & Hoyle, E. M. The Poggendorff illusion as a constancy phenomenon. *Nature*, 1963, **200**, 611–612.

Green, R. I., & Hoyle, E. M. The influence of spatial orientation on the Poggendorff Illusion. *Acta Psychol. Amsterdam*, 1965, **22**, 348–366.

Gregor, A. J., & McPherson, D. A. A study of susceptibility to geometric illusion among cultural subgroups of Australian aborigines. *Psychol. Afr.*, 1965, **11**, 1–13.

Gregory, R. L. Distortion of visual space as inappropriate constancy scaling. *Nature*, 1963, **199**, 678–680.

Gregory, R. L. Inappropriate constancy explanation of spatial distortions. *Nature*, 1965, **207**, 891–893.

Gregory, R. L. Comment on Dr. Vernon Hamilton's paper. *Quart J. exp. Psychol.*, 1966, **18**, 73–74.

Gregory, R. L. *Eye and brain.* New York: McGraw-Hill, 1966. (Chapter 9.)

Gregory, R. L. Comments on the inappropriate constancy scaling of the illusions and its implications. *Quart. J. exp. Psychol.*, 1967, **19**, 219–223.

Guillaume, C. E. Une illusion optique. *Bull. Soc. Franc. Phys.*, Nr. 125, Seance du 6. jan. 1899.

Hamilton, V. Susceptibility to the Mueller-Lyer illusion and its relationship to differences in size constancy. *Quart, J. exp. Psychol.*, 1966, **18**, 63–72.

Hasserodt, W. Gesichtspunkte zu einer experimentellen Analyse geometrischoptischer Taeuschungen. *Arch. ges Psychol.*, 1913, **28**, 336–347.

Hayami, H., & Miya, K. [On the Gestalt apprenhension of the Mueller-Lyer figure.] *Jap. J. Psychol.*, 1937, **12**, 525–552.

Haythornthwaite, B. F. An optical illusion. *Brit. J. Ophthal.*, 1925, **9**, 68.

Hecht, H. Neue Untersuchungen ueber die Zoellnerschen anorthoskopischen Zerrbilder: Die simultane Erfassung der Figuren. *Z. Psychol.*, 1924, **94**, 153.

Helmholtz, H. v. *Treatise on psychological optics.* Vol. III. Rochester, New York: American Optical Society, 1925. (Republished: New York, Dover, 1962.)(Pp. 191–204,234–242.)

Henning, R. Eine unerklaerte optische Taeuschung. *Z. Psychol.*, 1915, **72**, 383–386.

Henry, C. Sur les variations de grandeur apparente des lignes et des angles, dans la vision directe. *C. R. Acad. Sci.*, 1894, **119**, 449–450.

Hering, E. *Beitraege zur Physiologie.* Vol. I Leipzig: Englemann, 1861–1864. Pp. 66–69.

Heuven, J. A. v. Ueber das Schaetzen von Kreisscheiben. *Z. Psychol.*, 1942, **152**, 332–338.

Heymans, G. Quantitative Untersuchungen ueber das "optische Paradoxon." *Z. Psychol.*, 1896, **9**, 221–255.

Heymans, G. Quantitative Untersuchungen ueber die Zoellnersche und Loebsche Taeuschung. *Z. Psychol.*, 1897, **14**, 101–139.

Higginson, G. D. A new explanation of some so-called illusory patterns. *J. Psychol.*, 1936, **1**, 295–311.

Hofmann, F. B. Der Einfluss schraeger Konturen auf die scheinbare Horizontale und Vertikale. *Ber. IV Kongr. exp. Psychol.*, 1911, 236–239.

Holt-Hansen, K. Hering's illusion. *Brit. J. Psychol.*, 1961, **52**, 317–321.

Hoppe, J. I. *Psychologisch-physiologische Optik.* Leipzig: Wigand, 1881.

Hotopf, W. H. The size-constancy theory of visual illusions. *Brit. J. Psychol.*, 1966, **57**, 307–318.

Houssay, F. Une curieux illusion d'optique. *J. Psychol. norm. Pathol.*, 1904, **1**, 460–461.

Houssiadas, L. The visual slant in the perception of illusions. *Acta Psychol.*, Amsterdam, 1963, **21**, 35–39.

Huguenin, G. Ueber Sinnestaeuschungen. Basel: Schweighauserische Verlagsbuchhandlung. 1874.

Hyde, W. F. A varient of the chessboard illusion. *Amer. J. Psychol.*, 1929, **41**, 296–297.

Imai, S. A review of recent studies on geometrical optical illusion. *Jap. J. Psychol.*, 1960, **30**, 366–375.

Imai, S. Experiments on Lipps illusion of direction: I. Exploration of optimum conditions. *Jap. J. Psychol.*, 1963, **34**, 218–229.

Imai, S. Experiments on Lipps illusion of direction: II. An analysis of interaction between refracting lines. *Jap. J. Psychol.*, 1964, **35**, 235–247.

Imbert, A. Sur une illusion d'optique. *C. R. Soc. Biol.*, 1897, **4**, 673.

Immergluck, L. Resistance to an optical illusion, figural aftereffects, and field dependence. *Psychon. Sci.*, 1966, **6**, 281–282.

Indow, T., & Koyazu, T. Experiments in induction in a binocular field composed of independent monocular fields. *Jap. Psychol. Res.*, 1960, **2**, 142–151.

Indow, T., & Koyazu, T. Experiments in induction in a binocular field composed of independent monocular fields: II. *Jap. Psychol. Res.*, 1961, **3**, 42–56.

Indow, T., Kuno, U., & Yoshida, T. (Studies of induction in the visual process, using electrical phosphenes as an indicator: II.] *Psychologia*, 1958, **1**, 175–181.

Indow, T., Kuno, U., Yoshida, T., & Kozaki, T. [Studies of induction in the visual process using electrical phosphenes as an indicator: I] *Jap. J. Psychol.*, 1958, **29**, 29–39.

Indow, T., Kuno, U., Yoshida, T., & Kozaki, T. [Studies of induction in the visual process using electrical phosphenes as an indicator: III.] *Jap. J. Psychol.*, 1958, **29**, 295–301.

Indow, T., Kuno, U., Yoshida, T., & Kozaki, T. [Studies of induction in the visual process using electrical phosphenes as an indicator: IV.] *Jap. J. Psychol.*, 1959, **30**, 1–7.

Ipsen, G. Ueber Gestaltauffassung. (Eroerterung des Sandersschen Parallelograms.) *Neue Psychol. Stud.*, 1926, **1**, 167–279.

Ito, M. [Measurement of field-forces in visual perception by flicker method.] *Jap. J. Psychol.*, 1956, **27**, 209–217.

Jahoda, G. Geometric illusions and environment: A study in Ghana. *Brit. J. Psychol.*, 1966, **57**, 193–199.

Janet, P. Une illusion d'optique interne. *Rev. Phil.*, 1877, 3, 497–502.

Jastrow, J. On the judgment of angles and position of lines. *Amer. J. Psychol.*, 1893, **5**, 214–248.

Jastrow, J. The mind's eye. *Pop. Sci. Monthly*, 1899, **54**, 299–312.

Jastrow, J., & West, H. A study of Zoellner's figures and other related illusions. *Amer. J. Psychol.*, 1892, **4**, 382–398.

Jenkin, N., & West, N. I. Perception in organic mental defectives: An exploratory study. II. The Mueller-Lyer illusion. *Train. Sch. Bull.*, 1959, **55**, 67–70.

Johnson, G. L. Two curious optical illusions. *Arch. Ophthal.*, 1927, **56**, 465–468.

Judd, C. H. An optical illusion. *Psychol. Rev.*, 1898, **5**, 286–294.

Judd, C. H. A study of geometrical illusions. *Psychol. Rev.*, 1899, **6**, 241–261.

Judd, C. H. Practice and its effects on the perception of illusions. *Psychol. Rev.*, 1902, **9**, 27, 39.

Judd, C. H. The Mueller-Lyer illusion. *Psychol. Rev., Monogr. Suppl.*, 1905, No. 29, 55–82.

Judd, C. H., & Courten, H. C. The Zoellner illusion. *Psychol. Rev., Monogr. Suppl.*, 1905, No. 29, 112–141.

Juhasz, A., & Katona, G. Experimentelle Beitraege zum Problem der geometrisch-optischen Taeuschungen auf Linienfiguren. *Z. Psychol.*, 1925, **97**, 252–262.

Kaneko, T., & Obonai, T. [Factors of intensity, quantity, and distance in psychophysiological induction.] *Jap. J. Psychol.*, 1952, **23**, 73–79.

Keats, J. A. An application of the method of paired comparisons to the study of the Delboeuf illusion. *Aust. J. Psychol.*, 1964, **16**, 169–174.

Kennett, J. R. Influence of subliminal stimuli on comparative judgments of length. *Percept. mot. Skills*, 1962, **14**, 383–389.

Kido, M. [Awareness of shape and estimate of relation in the perception.] *Jap. J. Psychol.*, 1927, **1**, 262–282.

Kiesow, F. Ueber einige geometrisch-optische Taeuschungen. *Arch. ges. Psychol.*, 1905, **6**, 289–305.

Kiesow, F. Demonstrationen einiger optischen Taeuschungen. In *Ber. Kongr. exp. Psychol.* Leipzig: Barth, 1912. Pp. 162–163.

Kiesow, F. Di una illusione ottico-geometrica. *Arch. Ital. Psicol.*, 1924, **3**, 180–184.

Kiesow, F. La percezione della forma. *Atti VII. convegno psicol. sper. psicotecn.*, Torino, 1929, Pp. 41–46.

Kiesow, F. L'illusione di Sander. *Arch. Ital. Psicol.*, 1931, **9**, No. 4.

Kleining, G. Die optischen Taeuschungen. *Z. Exp. Angew. Psychol.*, 1953, **1**, 501–523.

Knox, H. W. On the quantitative determination of an optical illusion. *Amer. J. Psychol.*, 1893, **6**, 413–421.

Kobayashi, T. Analytical study of displacement in visual perception. *Jap. Psychol. Res.*, 1956, **3**, 37–44.

Koehler, W., & Fishback, J. The destruction of the Mueller-Lyer illusion in repeated trials: I. An examination of two theories. *J. exp. Psychol.*, 1950, **40**, 267–281.

Koehler, W., & Fishback, J. The destruction of the Mueller-Lyer illusion in repeated trials: II. Satiation patterns and memory trace. *J. exp. Psychol.*, 1950, **40**, 938–410.

Korn, *Ueber Sinneswahrnehmungen und Sinnestaeuschungen.* Leipzig, 1901.

Kreibig, K. Ueber den Begriff der "Sinnestaeuschung." *Z. Phil.,* 1902, **120**, 197–202.

Kristof, W. Ueber die Einordnung geometrisch-optischer Taeuschungen in die Gesetzmaessigkeit der visuellen Wahrnehmung. Teil I. *Arch. ges. Psychol.,* 1961, **113**, 1–48.

Kristof, W. Bemerkungen zu Balsers Kritik an der "Zweikomponententheorie" der geometrisch-optischen Taeuschungen. *Arch. ges. Psychol.,* 1963, **115**, 330–333.

Kristof, W. Eine Faktorenanalyse geometrisch-optischer Taeuschungen. *Z. Exp. Angew. Psychol.,* 1963, **10**, 583–596.

Krus, D., & Wapner, S. Effect of lysergic acid diethylamide (LSD-25) on perception of part-whole relationships. *J. Psychol.,* 1959, **48**, 87–95.

Kundt. Untersuchungen ueber Augenmass und optische Taeuschungen. *Pogg. Ann. Phys. Chem.,* 1863, **196**, 118–158.

Láska, W. Ueber einige optische Urteiltaeuschungen. *Arch. Physiol.,* 1890, 326–328.

Lau, E. Versuche ueber das stereoskopisches Sehen. *Psychol. Forsch.,* 1923, **2**, 1–4.

Lau, Ueber das stereoskopisches Sehen. *Psychol. Forsch.,* 1924, **6**, 121–126.

Lautenbach, R. Die geometrisch-optischen Taeuschungen und ihre psychologische Bedeutung. *Z. Hypnot.,* 1898, 8, 28–39, 292–295.

Lechelas, G. Une illusion optique. *Rev. Sci.,* 1896, **5**, 346.

Lehmann, A. Die Irradiation als Ursache geometrisch-optischen Taeuschungen. *Pflueg. Arch. ges. Physiol.,* 1904, **101**, 103.

Lehmann, G. Die Analyse geometrisch-optischer Taeuschungen durch Vektorfelder. *Z. Exp. Angew. Psychol.,* 1967, **14**, 442–462.

Lehrer, L. [Characteristics of visual perception and their relation to some geometric optical illusions.] *Shr. Psychol. Pedag.,* 1933, **1**, 275–294.

Leibowitz, H. W. *Visual perception.* New York: Macmillan, 1965. (Chapter 6.)

Lewis, E. O. The effect of practice on the perception of the Mueller-Lyer illusion. *Brit. J. Psychol.,* 1908, **2**, 294–306.

Lewis, E. O. Confluxion and contrast effects in the Mueller-Lyer illusion. *Brit. J. Psychol.,* 1909, **3**, 21–41.

Lewis, E. O. The illusion of filled and unfilled space. *Brit. J. Psychol.,* 1912, **5**, 36–50.

Lindworsky, J. Zum Problem der Gestalttaeuschungen. *Arch. ges. Psychol.,* 1929, **71**, 391–408.

Lipps, T. Aesthetische Faktoren der Raumanschauung. *Helmholtz-Festschrift,* 1891, 217.

Lipps. T. Optische Streitfragen. *Z. Psychol.,* 1892, **3**, 493–504.

Lipps, T. Die geometrisch-optischen Taeuschungen. *Z. Psychol.,* 1896, **12**, 39–61, 275.

Lipps, T. Bemerkung zu Heymans Artikel 'Quantiative Untersuchungen ueber die Zoellnersche und die Loebsche Taeuschung.' *Z. Psychol.,* 1897, **15**, 132–138.

Lipps, T. Raumaesthetik und geometrisch-optische Taeuschungen. *Z. Psychol.,* 1897, **16**, 234-256.

Lipps, T. *Raumaesthetik und geometrisch-optische Taeuschungen.* Leipzig: Barth, 1897.

Lipps, T. Raumaesthetik und geometrisch-optische Taeuschungen. *Z. Psychol.,* 1898, **18**, 405–441.

Lipps, T. Zur Verstaendingung ueber die geometrisch-optischen Taeuschungen. *Z. Psychol.,* 1905, **38**, 241–295.

Loeb, J. Ueber den Nachweis von Contrasterscheinungen im Gebiete der Raumempfindungen des Auges. *Arch. ges. Physiol.,* 1895, **40**, 509–518.

Lotze, R. *Medicinische Psychologie.* Leipzig: Weidmann, 1852. (Pp. 435–452.)

Luckiesh, M. *Visual illusions.* Princeton, New Jersey: Van Nostrand, 1922. (Republished: New York: Dover, 1965.)

Lung, S-H. [Concerning a general theory of illusions and the explanation and control of them.] *Acta Psychol. Sinica,* 1962, No. 4, 282–291.

McGurk, E. L. N. Determinants of differential susceptibility to visual illusions. Unpublished doctoral dissertation, Univ. of California, 1965. *Diss. Abstr.,* 1965, **25**, 7382–7383.

McGurk, E. Susceptibility to visual illusions. *J. Psychol.,* 1965, **61**, 127–143.

Maheux, M., Townsend, J. C., & Gresock, C. J. Geometric factors in illusions of direction. *Amer. J. Psychol.,* 1960, **73**, 535–543.

Mann, J. W., & Murray, C. O. Relational distortions in a simple illusion. *Psychol. Afr.* 1963, **10**, 73–88.

Marshall, A. J., & Di Lollo, V. Hering's illusion with impoverishment of the stimulus in scotopic and photopic vision. *Amer. J. Psychol.,* 1963, **76**, 644–652.

Marshal, A. J., & Di Lollo, V. Distortion of parallel lines in geometrical fields as a function of size of the display. *Psychon. Sci.,* 1966, **4**, 405–406.

Mayer, A. *Die Sinnestaeuschungen.* Wien, 1869.

Mayer-Hillebrand, F. Die geometrischen Taeuschungen als Auswirkungen allgemein geltender Wahrnehmungsgesetze. *Z. Psychol.,* 1942, **152**, 126–210, 293–331.

Mercado, S. J., Ribes I., E., & Barrera R., F. Depth cues effects on the perception of visual illusions. *Rev. Interamer. psicol.,* 1967, 1(2), 137–142.

Meumann, E. Ueber einige optische Taeuschungen. *Arch. ges. Psychol.,* 1910, **15**, 401–408.

Meyer, G. H. *Ueber Sinnestaeuschungen,* Berlin: Luederitz, 1871.

Mitsui, T. [Minor studies from the psychological laboratory of Hosei University.] *Jap. J. Psychol.,* 1927, **2**, 856–872.

Miya, K., & Hayami, H. [On the Gestalt apprehension of the Mueller-Lyer figure.] *Rep. 6th Congr. Jap. Psychol. Ass.,* 1938, 119–125.

Moed, G. Satiation theory and the Mueller-Lyer illusion. Unpublished doctoral dissertation, Univ. of Pennsylvania, 1958, *Diss. Abstr.,* 1958, **18**, 2230.

Moed, G. Satiation theory and the Mueller-Lyer illusion. *Amer. J. Psychol.,* 1959, **72**, 609–611.

Morgan, P. A study in perceptual differences among cultural groups in Southern Africa using tests of geometric illusions. *J. Nat. Inst. Personnel, Johannesburg,* 1959, 8(9), 39–43.

Mori, T., & Obonai, T. [Studies on the process of decay of the induction by the method of utilization time.] *Proc. 20th Annu. Meeting Jap. Psychol. Ass.,* 1956, 40.

Morinaga, S. [Experimental study in Ebbinghaus' illusion. II.] *Jap. J. Psychol.,* 1932, 7, 253–266.

Morinaga, S. Untersuchungen ueber die Zoellnersche Taeuschung. *Jap. J. Psychol.,* 1933, 8, 195–243.

Morinaga, S. [Some conditions of contrast-assimilation illusion.] *Saikin Shinrigaku Ronbunshu,* 1935, 28–48.

Morinaga, S. [Some considerations on the Mueller-Lyer figure.] *Jap. J. Psychol.,* 1941, **16**, 26–39.

Morinaga, S. [Optical illusions and figural after-effects.] *Jap. J. Psychol.,* 1952, **23**, 57–58. (Abstract)

Morinaga, S., & Ikeda, H. [Paradox of displacement in geometric illusions and the problem of dimensions: A contribution to the study of space perception.] *Jap. J. Psychol.,* 1965, **36**, 231–238.

Morinaga, S., & Kansaku, H. [A study of the influence of figural brightness on the ilusion of concentric circles.] *Jap. J. Psychol.,* 1961, **32**, 148–159.

Motokawa, K. Field of retinal induction and optical illusion. *J. Neurophysiol.,* 1950, **13**, 413–426.

Motokawa, K., & Akita, M. [Electrophysiological studies of the field of retinal induction.] *Psychologia,* 1957, 1, 10–16.

Mountjoy, P. T. The effects of exposure time and intertrial interval upon rates of decrement in the Mueller-Lyer illusion. Unpublished doctoral dissertation, Indiana Univ., 1957, *Diss. Abstr.,* 1957, **17**, 2322.

Mountjoy, P. T. Spontaneous recovery following response decrement to the Mueller-Lyer illusion. *J. Sci. Lab. Denison Univ.*, 1957–58, **44**, 229–238.

Mountjoy, P. T. Fixation and decrement to the Mueller-Lyer figure. *Psychol. Rec.*, 1960, **10**, 219–223.

Mountjoy, P. T. Monocular regard and decrement to the Mueller-Lyer illusion. *Psychol. Rec.*, 1960, **10**, 141–143.

Mountjoy, P. T. Mueller-Lyer decrement as a function of number of adjustment trials and configurations of the illusion figure. *Psychol. Rec.*, 1963, **13**, 471–481.

Mountjoy, P. T. Effects of self-instruction, information, and misinformation upon decrement to the Mueller-Lyer figure. *Psychol. Rec.*, 1965, **15**, 7–14.

Mountjoy, P. T. New illusory effect of the Mueller-Lyer figure. *J. exp. Psychol.*, 1966, **71**, 119–123.

Mouren, P., & Tatossian, A. Les illusions visuo-spatiales: Étude clinique. *Encéphale*, 1963, **52**, 517–573.

Mukerji, N. Is 'illusion' illusion? *J. gen. Psychol.*, 1957, **57**, 209–212.

Mueller-Freienfels, R. Ueber Illusionen und andere pathologische Formen der Wahrnehmung. *Z. Psychother. med. Psychol*, 1914, **6**, 15–32.

Mueller-Lyer, F. C. Optische Urteilstaeuschungen. *Arch. Physiol., Suppl. Ed.*, 1889, 263–270.

Mueller-Lyer, F. C. Zur Lehre von den optischen Taeuschungen, *Z. Psychol.*, 1894, **9**, 1–16.

Mueller-Lyer, F. C. Ueber Kontrast und Konfluxion. *Z. Psychol.*, 1896, **9**, 1–16.

Mueller-Lyer, F. C. Ueber Kontrast und Konfluxion. *Z. Psychol.*, 1896, **10**, 421–431.

Muensterberg, H. Die verschobene Schachbrettfigur. *Z. Psychol.*, 1897, **15**, 184–188.

Nagel, W. A. Zwei optische Taeuschungen. *Z. Psychol.*, 1901, **27**, 277–281.

Nakagawara, M. [An experimental study of divided space.] *Rep. 6th Congr. Jap. Psychol. Ass.*, 1938, 149–157.

Ni, C.-F. The effect of combining some geometrical optical illusions. *J. gen. Psychol.*, 1934, **10**, 472–476.

Novak, S. Effects of free inspection and fixation on the magnitude of the Poggendorff illusion. *Percept. mot. Skills*, 1966, **23**, 663–670.

Nozawa, S. [The influence of so-called subliminal stimulus upon the perception of shape.] *Proc. 24th Annu. Meeting Jap. Psychol. Ass.*, 1960, 77.

Obonai, T. [Experimental investigations on the structure of visual space.] *Proc. Imp. Acad. (Tokyo)*, 1931, **7**, 19–22.

Obonai, T. [Contributions to the study of psychophysical induction. I. Experiments on the illusion of contrast and confluence.] *Jap. J. Psychol.*, 1933, **8**, 1–21.

Obonai, T. [Contributions to the study of psychophysical induction. III. Experiments on the illusion of filled space.] *Jap. J. Psychol.*, 1933, **8**, 699–721.

Obonai, T. [Contributions to the study of psychophysical induction. IV. General law of psychophysical induction.] *Jap. J. Psychol.*, 1934, **9**, 53–65.

Obonai, T. [Contributions to the study of psychophysical induction. VI. Experiments on the Mueller-Lyer illusion.] *Jap. J. Psychol.*, 1935, **10**, 205–224.

Obonai, T. Induction effects in estimates of extent. *J. exp. Psychol.*, 1954, **47**, 57–60.

Obonai, T. [The concept of psychophysical induction: A review of experimental works.] *Psychologia*, 1957, **1**, 3–9.

Obonai, T. [Some analytical studies of the induction field.] *Psychol. Beitraege*, 1962, **6**, 620–629.

Obonai, T. [An overview of Japanese studies of perceptual induction.] *Annu. Rep. Tokyo Univ. Educ.*, 1963, **9**, 39–76.

Obonai, T., & Suzumura, K. Contribution to the study of psychophysical induction. XLIII. The characteristic of successive induction during periods immediately following retinal stimulation. *Jap. Psychol. Res.*, 1954, **1**, 45–54.

Obonai, T., & Kuzuhara, S. [An explanation of directional illusion in terms of retinal curvature.] *Jap. J. Psychol.*, 1956, **27**, 87–93.

Oesterreich, T. K. Zum Problem der geometrisch-optischen Taeuschungen. *Z. Psychol.*, 1928, **105**, 371–385.

Ogasawara, J. [Displacement effect of concentric circles.] *Jap. J. Psychol.*, 1952, **22**, 224–234.

Ogasawara, J. Motokawa's induction-field theory and form perception. *Psychologia*, 1958, **1**, 182–183.

Ogasawara, J. [Problem of the "field." In M. Sagara (Ed.), *Problems in the current psychology.*], 1961, 35–62.

Ohkawa, N. The effect of various figures upon critical fusion frequency of a flickering small patch. *Jap. Psychol. Res.*, 1954, No. 1, 34–44.

Ohshima, M. [On induction phenomena of retina.] *J. Sci. Labour*, 1950, **26**, 416–423.

Ohwaki, S. On the destruction of geometrical illusions in stereoscopic observation. *Tohoku Psychol. Folia*, 1960, **19**, 30–36.

Ohwaki, Y., & Onizawa, T. Function of the ground as "frame-work" in the perception of size. *Tohoku Psychol. Folia*, 1951, **12**, 53–66.

Oppel, J. J. Ueber geometrisch-optische Taeuschungen. *Jber. Phys. Ver. Frankfurt*, 1854–1855, 37–47.

Oppel, J. J. Nachlese zu den geometrisch-optischen Taeuschungen. *Jber. Phys. Ver. Frankfurt*, 1856–1857, 47–45.

Oppel, J. J. Nachlese zu den geometrisch-optischen Taeuschungen. *Jber. Phys. Ver. Frankfurt*, 1860–1861, 26–37.

Opperman, A. *Experimentelle Untersuchungen ueber den Einfluss von Stoerungslinien auf das Nachzeichnen einer Normalstrecke*, Hamburg, 1910.

Orbison, W. D. Shape as a function of the vector field. *Amer. J. Psychol.*, 1939, **52**, 31–45.

Orbison, W. D. The correction of an omission in *Shape as a Function of the Vector Field. Amer. J. Psychol.*, 1939, **52**, 309.

Over, R. Explanations of geometrical illusions. *Psychol. Bull*, 1968, **70**, 545–562.

Oyama, T. Japanese studies on the so-called geometrical-optical illusions. *Psychologia*, 1960, **3**, 7–20.

Oyama, T. The effect of hue and brightness on the size-illusion of concentric circles. *Amer. J. Psychol.*, 1962, **75**, 45–55.

Oyama, T., & Imai, S. [The effect of color upon the illusion of concentric circles and figural after-effects.] *Proc. 23rd Annu. Meet. Jap. Psychol. Ass.*, 1959, III, 53.

Oyama, T., & Akatsuka, R. Effect of color-similarity on the size-illusion of triple circles. *Percept. mot. Skills*, 1965, **20**, 14.

Parker, N. I., & Newbigging, P. L. Magnitude and decrement of the Mueller-Lyer illusion as a function of pre-training. *Can. J. Psychol.*, 1963, **17**, 134–140.

Parrish, M., Lundy, R. M., & Leibowitz, H. W. Hypnotic age-regression and magnitudes of the Ponzo and Poggendorff illusions. *Science*, 1968, **159**, 1375–1376.

Pauli, R. Eine neuse geometrisch-optische Taeuschung (Sektorentaeuschung). *Arch. Ges. Psychol.*, 1939, **103**, 151–159.

Pearce, H. J. The law of attraction in relation to some visual and tactual illusions. *Psychol. Rev.*, 1904, **11**, 143–178.

Peterson, J. Illusion of direct orientation. *J. Philos. Psychol.*, 1916, **13**, 222–236.

Piaget, J. Quelques illusions géométriques renversées. *Schweiz. Z. Psychol. Anwend.*, 1952, **11**, 19–25.

Piaget, J. Recherches sur le développement des perceptions. XXII. Essai d'une nouvelle interprétation probabiliste des effets du centration de la loi de Weber et de celle des centrations relatives. *Arch. Psychol., Genève*, 1955, **35**, 1–24.

Piaget, J., & Morf, A. Recherches sur le développement des perceptions. XXIV. Note sur l'illusion des droits inclinées. *Arch. Psychol., Genève*, 1955, **35**, 65–76.

Piaget, J., & Vinh-Bang. L'enregistrement des mouvements oculaires en jeu chez l'adulte dans la comparaison de lignes verticales, horizontales ou obliques et dans les perceptions de la figure en équerre. *Arch. Psychol., Genève*, 1961, **38**, 89–141.

Piaget, J., Vinh-Bang, & Matalon, B. Note on the law of the temporal maximum of some optico-geometric illusions. *Amer. J. Psychol.*, 1958, **71**, 277–282.

Pierce, A. H. Geometrical optical illusions. *Science*, 1898, **8**, 814–829.

Pierce, A. H. A new explanation for the illusory movement seen by Helmholtz on the Zoellner diagram. *Psychol. Rev.*, 1900, **7**, 356–376.

Pieron, H. L'illusion de Mueller-Lyer et son double mecanisme. *Rev. Phil.*, 1911, **71**, 245–284.

Pietarinen, J., & Virsu, V. Geometric illusions: II. Features of the method of magnitude estimation of length differences. *Scand. J. Psychol.*, 1967, **8**, 172–176.

Pike, A. R. & Stacey, B. G. The perception of luminous Mueller-Lyer figures and its implications for the misapplied constancy theory. *Life Sci.*, 1968, **7**, 355–362.

Polimanti, O. Étude de quelques nouvelles illusions optiques géometriques. *J. Psychol. norm. pathol.*, 1913, **10**, 43–47.

Pollack, R. H. Simultaneous and successive presentation of elements of the Mueller-Lyer figure and chronological age. *Percept. mot. Skills*, 1964, **19**, 303–310.

Pollack, R. H., & Chaplin, M. R. Effects of prolonged stimulation by components of the Mueller-Lyer figure upon the magnitude of illusion. *Percept. mot. Skills*, 1964, **18**, 377–383.

Pollack, R. H., & Zetland, F. K. Translation of "New Measurements of Visual Illusions in Adults and Children" by Jean-Jacques van Biervliet. *J. Hist. Behav. Sci.*, 1966, **2**, 148–158.

Ponzo, M. Rapports de contraste angulaire et l'appréciation de grandeur des astres à l'horizon. *Arch. Ital. Biol.*, 1912, **58**, 327–329.

Ponzo, M. Deviation de la ligne horizontale dans les dessins de series de lignes droites obliques. *Arch. Ital. Biol.*, 1913, **58**, 321–326.

Pressey, A. W. Field dependence and susceptibility to the Poggendorff illusion. *Percept. mot. Skills*, 1967, **24**, 309–310.

Pressey, A. W. A theory of the Mueller-Lyer illusion. *Percept. mot. Skills*, 1967, **25**, 569–572.

Pritchard, R. M. Visual illusions viewed as stabilized retinal images. *Quart. J. exp. Psychol.*, 1958, **10**, 77–81.

Quercy. Les illusions geometriques. *Congr. Ass. Fr. Avan. Sci.*, 1922, 1246–1251.

Rausch, E. *Struktur und Metrik figural-optischer Wahrnehmung.* Frankfurt am Main: Waldemar Kramer, 1952.

Reuss, A. V. Ueber eine optische Taeuschung. *Z. Sinnesphysiol.*, 1907, **42**, 101–108.

Richet, C. Une illusion optique. *C. R. Acad. Sci.*, 1921, **173**, 805–806.

Reimann, H. Ueber Messungen des Taeuschungsbetrages bei geometrisch-optischen Taeuschungen und deren Verwendbarkeit als Mittel der typologische Diagnose des Grades der Ganzheitlichkeit der Bewustseinsstruktur. Unpublished dissertation, Technische Hochscule, Danzig, 1933.

Robinson, E. S. Space illusions. *Psychol. Bull.*, 1920, **17**, 243.

Rodriguez Etchart, C. *La ilusión.* Buenos Aires: Imp. de Coni Hnos., 1912.

Ronchi, V. "Ciò che si vede" coincide con "ciò che c'è"? *Atti Fond. Giorgio Ronchi*, 1957, **12**, 350–360.

Rosenbach, O. Zur Lehre von den Urtheilstaeuschungen. *Z. Psychol.*, 1902, **29**, 434–448.

Rothschild, H. Untersuchungen ueber die sogenannten Zoellnerschen anorthoskopischen Zerrbilder. *Z. Psychol.*, 1922, **90**, 137ff.

Rubin, E. Nogle geometrisk-optiske figurer. *Nord. Psykol.*, 1949, **1**, 77–78.

Rubin, E. Visual figures apparently incompatible with geometry. *Acta Psychol.*, 1950, **7**, 365–387.

Ruckmick, C. A. Illusions in printed matter. *Science*, 1941, **93**, 236

Rudel, R. G., & Teuber, H.-L. Decrement of visual and haptic Mueller-Lyer illusion on repeated trials: A study of crossmodal transfer. *Quart. J. exp. Psychol.*, 1963, **15**, 125–131.

Rutten, F. J. T. *Psychologie der waarneming. Een studie over gezichtsbedrog.* Nijmegen: N. V. Dekker & Van de Vegt en J. W. Van Leeuwen, 1929.

Sander, F. Optische Taeuschungen und Psychologie. *Neue Psychol. Stud.*, 1926, **1**, 159–167.

Sanford, E. C. *A course in experimental psychology.* Boston: Heath, 1898. (Pp. 212–260.)

Sato, K. [The framework and the Poggendorff illusion.] *Jap. J. Exp. Psychol.*, 1936, **3**, 135–145.

Sato, K. Symposium on the structure of the induction field in visual form perception. *Psychologia*, 1957, **1**, 2.

Schiller, P., & Wechsler, D. The illusion of the oblique intercept. *J. exp. Psychol.*, 1936, **19**, 747–757.

Schiller, P., & Wiener, M. Binocular and stereoscopic viewing of geometric illusions. *Percept. mot. Skills*, 1962, **15**, 739–747.

Schroeder, P. Die Lokalisation von Sinnestaeuschungen. *Arch. Psychiat. Nervenkr.*, 1925, **76**, 784–789.

Schroeder, P. Sinnestaeuschungen und Hirnlokalisation. *Z. ges. Neurol. Psychiat.*, 1937, **158**, 261–264.

Schumann, F. Neue Untersuchungen ueber die Zoellnerschen anorthoskopischen Zerrbilder. *Z. Psychol.*, 1924, **94**, 146–152.

Schumann, F., & Volk, J. Neue Untersuchungen ueber die Zoellnerschen anorthoskopischen Zerrbilder, III. Tachistoskopische Untersuchungen. *Z. Psychol.*, 1927, **102**, 57–106.

Schwirtz, P. Das Mueller-Lyersche Paradoxon in der Hypnose. *Arch. ges. Psychol.*, 1914, **32**, 339, 395.

Seashore, C. E. Measurements of illusions and hallucinations in normal life. *Stud. Fr. Yale Psychol. Lab.*, 1895, **3**, 1–67.

Seashore, C. E. Weber's law in illusions. *Stud. fr. Yale Psychol. Lab.*, 1896, **4**, 62–68.

Seashore, C. E., & Williams, M. C. An illusion of length. *Psychol. Rev.*, 1900, **7**, 592–599.

Seashore, C. E., & Williams, M. C. An illusion of length. *Univ. Iowa Stud. Psychol.*, 1902, **3**, 29–37.

Seashore, C. E., Carter, E. A., Farnum, E. C., & Sies, R. W. The effect of practice on normal illusions. *Psychol. Rev., Monogr. Suppl.*, 1908, No. 38, **9**, 103–148.

Segall, M. H., Campbell, D. T., & Herskovits, M. J. Cultural differences in the perception of geometric illusions. *Science*, 1963, **139**, 769–771.

Segal, M. H., Campbell, D. T., & Herskovits, M. J. *The influence of culture on visual perception.* Indianapolis, Indiana: Bobbs-Merrill, 1966.

Selkin, J., & Wertheimer, M. Disappearance of the Mueller-Lyer illusion under prolonged inspection. *Percept. mot. Skills*, 1957, **7**, 265–266.

Sickles. W. R. Experimental evidence for the electrical character of visual fields derived from a quantitative analysis of the Ponzo illusion. *J. exp. Psychol.*, 1942, **30**, 84–91.

Simchowitz, H. Ueber die Zoellnerschen anorthoskopischen Zerrbilder. *Arch. ges. Psychol.*, 1926, **56**, 1–54.

Sinha, A. K. P., & Sinha, S. N. Mueller-Lyer illusion in subjects high and low in anxiety. *Percept. mot. Skills,* 1967, **24**, 194.

Skramlik, E. v. Lebensgewohnheiten als Grundlage von Sinnestaeuschungen. *Naturwissenschaften,* 1925, **13**, 117–122, 134–142.

Skramlik, E. v. Ueber irrtuemliche Wahrnehmungen. *Ergebnisse Physiol.,* 1925, **24**, 648–662.

Smith, G. Twin differences with reference to the Mueller-Lyer illusion. *Lunds Univ. Arsskr.,* 1953, **50**(3), 1–27.

Smith, O. W., & Smith, P. C. An illusion of parallelism. *Percept. mot. Skills,* 1962, **15**, 455–461.

Smith, O. W., & Smith, P. C. A developmental study of the illusion of parallelism. *Percept. mot. Skills,* 1963, **16**, 871–878.

Smith, O. W., & Smith, P. C. Some stimuli and aptitudes determining apparent parallelism. *Percept. mot. Skills,* 1963, **16**, 813–829.

Smith, W. G. A study of some correlations of the Mueller-Lyer visual illusion and allied phenomena. *Brit. J. Psychol.,* 1906, **2**, 16–51.

Smith, W. G. The prevalence of spatial contrast in visual perception. *Brit. J. Psychol.,* 1919, **8**, 317–326.

Smith, W. G., & Milne, J. C. R. The influence of margins on the bisection of a line. *Brit. J. Psychol.,* 1909, **3**, 78–93.

Smith, W. G., Kennedy-Fraser, D., & Nicolson, W. The influence of margins on the process of bisection: additional experiments with observations on the affective character of the determinations. *Brit. J. Psychol.,* 1912, **5**, 331–353.

Springbett, B. M. Some stereoscopic phenomena and their implications. *Brit. J. Psychol,* 1961, **52**, 105–109.

Stevens, R. F. When believing is seeing–an optical illusion. *Science,* 1930, **71**, 439.

Stewart, C. C. Zoellner's anorthoscopic illusion. *Amer. J. Psychol.,* 1900, **11**, 240–243.

Sully, J. *Illusion.* New York: Appleton, 1881.

Suto, Y. [Comparative study of assimilation-contrast illusion, figural aftereffect, and time error for extents of circle and line stimuli.] *Jap. Psychol. Res.,* 1961, **3**, 1–16.

Suzuki, Y., Fujiii, K., & Onizawa, T. Studies on sensory deprivation: IV, Part 6. Effect of sensory deprivation upon perceptual function. *Tohoku Psycholog. Folia,* 1965, **24**, 24–29.

Swindle, P. F. A physiological explanation of certain optical illusions. *Amer. J. Physiol. Opt.,* 1922, **3**, 238–255.

Szewezuk, W. Les illusions optico-geometriques. *Trav. Lab. Psychol. Exp. Univ. Cracovie,* 1938, **2**, 89–140.

Takagi, K. [Effect of figure lines on the structure of visual field.] *Jap. J. Psychol.,* 1927, **2**, 217–261.

Tamaika, J. [On the change of the phenomenal size of figure in correspondence with the structure of the visual field.] *Jap. J. Psychol.,* 1933, **8**, 579–587.

Tausch, R. Optische Taeuschungen als artifizielle Effekte der Gestaltungsprozesse von Groessen- und Formenkonstanz in der natuerlichen Raumwahrnehmung. *Psychol. Forsch.,* 1954, **24**, 299–348.

Tausch, R. Ueber gestaltpsychologische Wahrnehmungserklaeurungen. *Z. Psychol,* 1962, **166**, 26–61.

Taylor, M. M. Geometry of a visual illusion. *J. Opt. Soc. Amer.,* 1962, **52**, 565–569.

Taylor, M. M. Non-additivity of perceived distance with the Mueller-Lyer figure. *Percept. mot. Skills,* 1965, **20**, 1964.

Terstenjak, A. Geometrisch-optische Taeuschungen als dynamischer Vorgang. *Cont. Lab. Psicol. Univ. Sacro Cuore, Milano,* 1952, Ser. 15, 243–309.

Thiery, A. Ueber geometrisch-optischen Taeuschungen. *Phil. Stud.,* 1895, **11**, 307–370.

Thiery, A. Ueber geometrisch-optische Taeuschungen. *Phil. Stud.,* 1896, **12**, 67–126.

Tichy, G. Ueber eine vermeintliche optische Taeuschung. *Z, Psychol.,* 1912, **60**, 267–279.

Tinker, M. A. Susceptibility to optical illusions: specific or general? *J. exp. Psychol.,* 1938, **22**, 593–598.

Titchener, E. B. *Experimental psychology,* Vol. 1, Pt. I. New York: Macmillan, 1901. (Pp. 151–170.)

Titchener, E. B. *Experimental psychology,* Vol. 1, Pt. II. New York: Macmillan, 1901. (Pp. 303–328.).

Titchener, E. B., & Pyle, W. H. The effect of imperceptible shadows on the judgment of distance. *Proc. Amer. Phil. Soc.,* 1907, **46**, 94–109.

Tolansky, S. *Optical illusions.* New York: Pergamon Press, 1964.

Trimble, R., & Eriksen, C. W. "Subliminal cues" and the Mueller-type illusion. *Percept. Psychophys.,* 1966, **1**, 401–404.

Tsuzuki, A. [On nearness.] *Jap. J. Psychol.,* 1939, **14**, 271–278.

Tsuzuki, A. [On nearness. (Addendum)] *Jap. J. Psychol.,* 1940, **15**, 455–461.

Ueberhorst, K. Eine neue Theorie der Gesichtswahrnehmung. *Z. Psychol.,* 1896, **13**, 54–65.

Velinsky, S. Explication physiologique de l'illusion Poggendorff. *Année Psychol.,* 1925, **26**, 107–116.

Vinoda, K. S. Analysis of factors contributing to illusions involving straight lines. *Pratibha,* 1959, **2**(2), 77–80.

Virsu, V. Systematic error of estimation as a function of stimulus magnitude: An experiment with Oppel's illusion. *Rep. fr. Psychol. Inst.,* Univ. Helsinki, 1965, No. 4.

Virsu, V. Contrast and confluxion as components in geometric illusions. *Quart. J. exp. Psychol.,* 1967, **19**, 198–207.

Virsu, V. Geometric illusions: I. Effects of figure type, instruction, and pre- and intertrial training on magnitude and decrement of illusion. *Scand. J. Psychol.,* 1967, **8**, 161–171.

Virsu, V. Geometric illusions as categorization effects: A system of interpretation. *Ann. Acad. Sci. Fenn.,* Helsinki, B 154, 1968, **2**, 1–73.

Vurpillot, É. L'influence de la signification du matériel sur l'illusion de Poggendorff. *Année Psychol.,* 1957, **57**, 339–357.

Vurpillot, É. L'aspect fonctionnel de la signification et son influence sur l'illusion de Delboeuf. *Psychol. Franc.,* 1959, **4**, 127–132.

Vurpillot, É. La distinction entre illusions primaires et secondaires se justifie-t-elle? In *Psychologie et épistémologie génétiques, thémes piagétiens.* Paris: Dunod, 1965. Pp. 285–299.

Wallace, G. K. Measurements of the Zoellner illusion. *Acta Psychol., Amsterdam,* 1965, **22**, 407–412.

Wallace, G. K. The effect of background on the Zoellner illusion. *Acta Psychol., Amsterdam,* 1966, **25**, 373–380.

Wallin, J. E. W. The size illusion of the depressed letter P. *Sci. Amer.,* 1905, **93**, 315.

Watanabe, R. On the quantitative determination of an optical illusion. *Amer. J. Psychol.,* 1893, **6**, 509–514.

Waters, C. E. Illusions in printed matter. *Science,* 1941, **94**, 136–137.

Webster, H. The distortion of straight and curved lines in geometrical fields. *Amer. J. Psychol.,* 1948, **61**, 573–575.

Weinland, J. D. Illusions and error. *J. Psychol.,* 1951, **31**, 73–79.

Wenzel, E. L. Neue Untersuchungen ueber die Zoellnerschen anorthoskopischen Zerrbilder: II. Die sukzessive Erfassung der Figuren. *Z. Psychol.,* 1926, **100**, 289–324.

Williams, M. C. Normal illusions in representative geometrical forms. *Univ. Iowa Stud. Psychol.*, 1902, **3**, 38–139.

Wingender, P. Beitraege zur Lehre von den geometrisch-optischen Taeuschungen. *Z. Psychol.*, 1919, **82**, 21–66.

Winkler, F. *Studien ueber Wahrnehmungstaeuschungen.* Wien: Breitenstein, 1915.

Witasek, S. Ueber die Natur der geometrisch-optischen Taeuschungen. *Z. Psychol*, 1898, **19**, 81–174.

Wundt, W. *Grundzuege der physiologischen Psychologie.* 4th ed. Leipzig: Engelmann, 1893. (P. 58ff.)

Wundt, W. Zur Theorie der raeumlichen Gesichswahrnehmungen. *Phil. Stud.*, 1898, **14**, 1–118.

Wundt, W. Die geometrisch-optischen Taeuschungen. *Abh. K. Saechs, Ges. Wiss., Math.-Phys. Cl.*, 1898, **24**, 53–178.

Wundt, W. *Die geometrisch-optischen Taeuschungen.* Leipzig: Teubner, 1898.

Wundt, W. Die Projektionsmethode und die geometrisch-optischen Taeuschungen. *Phil. Stud.*, 1907, **2**, 493–498.

Wyczolkowska, A. [On optical illusions.] *Bull. Int. Acad. Sci. Cracovie*, Jan., 1900.

Yacorzynski, G. K. Brain dynamism as reflected in illusions. *Genet. Psychol. Monogr.*, 1963, **68**(1), 3–47.

Yakose, Z. The law of the "field" in visual form perception. I. A theoretical formula to seek the field strength of the form and its experimental proof. *Jap. Psychol. Res.*, 1954, No. 1, 55–64.

Yakose, Z. Theoretical formula of vector-field and its experimental proof. *Psychologia*, 1957, **1**, 17–21.

Yakose, Z., & Goto, T. the measurement of the magnitude of the field-force of a circle and circular arcs. *Jap. Psychol. Res.*, 1965, 7(3), 101–109.

Yakose, Z., & Ichikawa, N. [A study of the direction of the field force in shape perception.] *Jap. J. Psychol.*, 1953, **23**, 261–274.

Yakose, Z., & Kawamura, H. [A study of the direction of the field force in shape perception.] *Jap. J. Psychol.*, 1952, **23**, 133–143.

Yakose, Z., & Uchiyama, M. [The measurement of the field forces in visual perception.] *Jap. J. Psychol.*, 1952, **22**, 41–56.

Yanagisawa, N. [An experimental study on a modified Mueller-Lyer figure.] *Jap. J. Psychol.*, 1939, **14**, 321–326.

Yarbus, A. L. O nekotorykh illyuziyakh v otsenke vidimykh rasstoyanii mezhdu krayami predmetov. In *Issledovaniya po psikhologii vospriyatiya.* Moscow: Izdatel'stvo AN SSSR, 1948.

Yarbus, A. L. O nekotorykh illyuziyakh v otsenke vidimykh chastei i summ otrezkov rasstoyanii. *Prob. Fiz. Opt.*, 1950, **9**, 179–190.

Yarbus, A. L. Pereotsenka verkhnei chasti figury. *Prob. Fiz. Opt.*, 1952, **10**.

Yarbus, A. L. K voprosu o zritel'noi otsenki rasstoyanii. In *Sbornik posvyashchennyi pamyati akad. P. P. Lazareva.* Moscow: Izdatel'stvo AN SSSR, 1956.

Zajac, J. L. Some investigations on the so-called "geometrico optical illusions." *Acta Psychol.*, 1957, **13**, 140–150.

Zanforlin, M. Some observations on Gregory's theory of perceptual illusions. *Quart. J. exp. Psychol.*, 1967, **19**, 193–197.

Zehender, W. Die geometrisch-optischen Taeuschungen. *Abh. K. Saechs. Ges. Wiss., Math.-Phys. Cl.*, 1898, **24**, 53–178.

Zehender, W. Die geometrisch-optischen Taeuschungen. *Klin. Monatsbl. Augenh.*, 1898, **36**, 410–412.

Zehender, W. Ueber geometrisch-optische Taeuschunge *Z. Psychol.*, 1899, **20**, 65–117.

Zehender, W. *Ueber optische Taeuschungen.* Leipzig: Barth, 1902.

Zigler, E. Size estimates of circles as a function of size of adjacent circles. *Percept. mot. Skills,* 1960, **11,** 47–53.

Zoellner, F. Ueber eine neue Art von Pseudoskopie und ihre Beziehung zu den von Plateau und Oppel beschriebenen Bewegungsphaenomenen. *Ann. Phys. Chem.,* 1860, **186,** 500–525.

Zusne, L. Visual illusions: publication trends. *Percept. mot. Skills,* 1968, **27,** 175–177.

G. Anisotropy of space; the horizontal-vertical illusion

Ames, A. J., Proctor, C. A., & Ames, B. Vision and the techniques of art. *Proc. Amer. Acad. Arts Sci.,* 1923, **58,** 36.

Attneave, F. Perception of place in a circular field. *Amer. J. Psychol.,* 1955, **68,** 69–82.

Attneave, F., & Olson, R. K. Discriminability of stimuli varying in physical and retinal orientation. *J. exp. Psychol.,* 1967, **74,** 149–157.

Bartley, S. H. Localization of a simple form in an unstructured field. *Percept. mot. Skills,* 1959, **9,** 44.

Bartley, S. H., & Thompson, R. A further study of horizontal asymmetry in the perception of pictures. *Percept. mot. Skills,* 1959, **9,** 135–138.

Begelman, D. A., & Steinfeld, G. An investigation of several parameters of the horizontal-vertical illusion. *Percept. Psychophys.,* 1967, **2,** 539–543.

Brown, K. T. Factors affecting differences in apparent size between opposite halves of a visual meridian. *J. Opt. Soc. Amer.,* 1953, **43,** 464–472.

Buck, A. F. Observations on the overestimation of vertical as compared with horizontal lines. *Univ. Chicago Contrib. Philos.,* 1899, **2**(2), 7–11.

Carlson, W. S., & Tinker, M. A. Visual reaction-time as a function of variations in the stimulus figure. *Amer. J. Psychol.,* 1946, **59,** 450–457.

Chapanis, A., & Mankin, D. A. The horizontal-vertical illusion in a visually rich environment. *Percept. Psychophys.,* 1967, **2,** 249–255.

Craig, E. A., & Lichtenstein, M. Visibility-invisibility cycles as a function of stimulus-orientation. *Amer. J. Psychol.,* 1953, **66,** 554–563.

Finger, F. W., & Spelt, D. K. The illustration of the horizontal-vertical illusion. *J. exp. Psychol.,* 1947, **37,** 243–250.

G., C. E. Les illusions de la verticale. *Nature,* 1897, **25**(II), 99–100.

Ganguli, M. L. Visual perception of geometrical figures. *Indian J. Psychol.,* 1928, **3,** 142–147.

Gardner, R. W., & Long, R. I. Errors of the standard and illusion effects with the inverted T. *Percept. mot. Skills,* 1960, **10,** 47–54.

Gardner, R. W., & Long, R. I. Errors of the standard and illusion effects with L-shaped figures. *Percept. mot. Skills,* 1960, **10,** 107–109.

Ghent Braine, L. Asymmetries of pattern perception observed in Israelis. *Neuropsychologia,* 1968, **6,** 73–88.

Gibson, J. J. Vertical and horizontal orientation in visual perception. *Psychol. Bull.,* 1934, **31,** 739–740.

Harcum, E. R. Three inferred factors in the visual recognition of binary targets. In J. W. Wulfeck & J. H. Taylor (Eds.), *Form discrimination as related to military problems.* Washington, D. C.: Nat. Acad. Sci.-Nat. Res. Coun., 1957. Pp. 32–37.

Harcum, E. R. Visual recognition along various meridians of the visual field: XII. Acuity for open and blackened circles presented eccentrically. Univ. of Michigan Eng. Res. Inst., Proj. Mich. Rep., No. 2144–315–T, 1958.

Harcum, E. R. Detection versus localization errors on various radii of the visual field. In A. Morris & E. P. Horne (Eds.), *Visual search techniques.* Washington, D. C.: Nat. Acad. Sci.-Nat. Res. Coun., 1960. Pp. 99–111.

Harcum, E. R. Reproduction of linear visual patterns tachistoscopically exposed in various orientations. *College of William & Mary Monogr.*, 1964.

Harcum, E. R., & Blackwell, H. R. Visual recognition along various meridians of the visual field: II. Identification of the number of blackened circles presented. Univ. of Michigan Eng. Res. Inst., Proj. Mich. Rep., No. 2144–314–T, 1958.

Harcum, E. R., & Rabe, A. Visual recognition along various meridians of the visual field: III. Patterns of blackened circles in an eight-circle template. Univ. of Michigan Eng. Res. Inst., Proj. Mich. Rep., No. 2144–294–T, 1958.

Harcum, E. R., & Rabe, A. Visual recognition along various meridians of the visual field: VIII. Patterns of solid circles and squares. Univ. of Michigan Eng. Res. Inst., Proj. Mich. Rep., No. 2144–306–T, 1958.

Hayes, J. W. Horizontal-vertical illusion in foveal vision apparent in astronomical observations of the relative luminosity of twin stars. *Psychol. Mongr.*, 1915, **20**, Whole No. 85.

Hicks, G. D., & Rivers, W. H. R. The illusion of compared horizontal and vertical lines. *Brit. J. Psychol.*, 1908, **2**, 243–260.

Higgins, G. C., & Stultz, K. Visual acuity as measured with various orientations of a parallel-line test object. *J. Opt. Soc. Amer.*, 1948, **38**, 756–758.

Hofmann, F. B. Der Einfluss schraeger Konturen auf die scheinbare Horizontal und Vertikal. *Ber. IV Kongr.,exp. Psychol.*, 1911, 236–239.

Hofmann, F. F., & Bielschowsky, A. Ueber die Einstellung der scheinbaren Horizontalen und Vertikalen bei Betrachtung eines von schraegen Konturen erfuellten Gesichtsfeldes. *Arch. ges. Physiol.*, 1909, **126**, 453–475.

Jastrow, J. The perception of horizontal and of vertical lines. *Science*, 1899, **10**, 579–580.

Kuennapas, T. M. An analysis of the "vertical-horizontal illusion." *J. exp. Psychol.*, 1955, **49**, 134–140.

Kuennapas, T. M. Influence of frame size on apparent length of a line. *J. exp. Psychol.*, 1955, **50**, 168–170.

Kuennapas, T. M. Interocular differences in the vertical-horizontal illusion. *Acta Psychol.*, 1957, **13**, 253–259.

Kuennapas, T. M. Interocular differences in the vertical-horizontal illusion. *Nord. Psykol.*, 1957, **9**, 195–201.

Kuennapas, T. M. Vertical-horizontal illusion and surrounding field. *Acta Psychol.*, 1957, **13**, 35–42.

Kuennapas, T. M. Vertical-horizontal illusions and surrounding field. *Nord. Psykol*, 1957, **9**, 35–42.

Kuennapas, T. M. The vertical-horizontal illusion and the visual field. *J. exp. Psychol.*, 1957, **53**, 405–407.

Kuennapas, T. M. Fixation and the vertical-horizontal illusion. *Acta Psychol.*, 1958, **14**, 131–136.

Kuennapas, T. M. Fixation and the vertical-horizontal illusion. *Nord. Psykol.*, 1958, **10**, 87–92.

Kuennapas, T.M. Influence of head inclination on the vertical-horizontal illusion. *J. Psychol.*, 1958, **46**, 179–185.

Kuennapas, T. M. Measurements of subjective length in the vertical-horizontal illusion. *Acta Psychol.*, 1958, **14**, 371–374.

Kuennapas, T. M. Measurements of subjective length in the vertical-horizontal illusion. *Nord. Psykol.*, 1958, **10**, 203–206.

Kuennapas, T. M. The vertical-horizontal illusion in artificial visual fields. *J. Psychol.*, 1959, **47**, 41–48.

Kuennapas, T. M. Visual field and subjective center of a diamond. *J. Psychol.*, 1959, **47**, 305–316.

Kuennapas, T. M. *Visual field as a frame of reference: With special regard to the vertical-horizontal illusion.* Uppsala: Almquist & Wiksells, 1959.

Kuennapas, T. M. The frame illusion: A rectification. *Percept. mot. Skills,* 1963, **17**, 369–370.

Leibowitz, H. Some observations and theory on the variation of visual acuity with the orientation of the test object. *J. Opt. Soc. Amer.,* 1953, **43**, 902–905.

Leibowitz, H., Myers, N. A., and Grant, D. A. Frequency of seeing and radial localization of single and multiple visual stimuli. *J. exp. Psychol.,* 1955, **50**, 369–373.

Leibowitz, H., Myers, N. A., & Grant, D. A. Radial localization of a single stimulus as a function of luminance and duration of exposure. *J. Opt. Soc. Amer.,* 1955, **45**, 76–78.

Michaels, R. M. Anisotropy and interaction of fields of spatial induction. *J. exp. Psychol.,* 1960, **60**, 235–241.

Morinaga, S., Noguchi, K., & Ohishi, A. The horizontal-vertical illusion and the relation of spatial and retinal orientations. *Jap. Psychol. Res.,* 1962, **4**(1), 25–29.

Mountjoy, P. T., & Cordes, C. K. Decrement to the vertical-horizontal illusion. *J. Sci. Lab. Denison Univ.,* 1957–58, **44**, 239–242.

Muller, P. F., Sidovsky, R. C., Slivinske, A. J., Alluisi, E. A., & Fitts, P. M. The symbolic coding of information on cathode ray tubes and similar displays. USAF WADC TR 55–375, October, 1955.

Nagel, W. A. Ueber das Aubertsche Phaenomen und verwandte Taeuschungen ueber die vertikale Richtung. *Z. Psychol.,* 1898, **16**, 373–398.

Ohwaki, S. On the destruction of geometrical illusions in stereoscopic observation. *Tohoku Psychol. Folia,* 1960, **19**, 29–36.

Ono, S. A study on the horizontal-vertical illusion. *Jinbunkenkya* (Osaka City Univ.), 1959, **10**, 41–60.

Pan, S. [The vertical-horizontal illusion.] *N. C. J. Psychol. Nat. Cent. U.,* 1934, **1**, No. 1, 125–128.

Piaget, J., & Morf, A. Note sur la comparaison de lignes perpendiculaires égales. *Arch. Psychol., Genève,* 1956, **35**, 233–255.

Pierce, B. O. The perception of horizontal and of vertical lines. *Science,* 1899, **10**, 425–429.

Pollack, W. T., & Chapanis, A. The apparent length of a line as a function of its inclination. *Quart. J. exp. Psychol.,* 1952, **4**, 170–178.

Ritter, S. M. The vertical-horizontal illusion: An experimental study of meridional disparities in the visual field. *Psychol. Monogr.,* 1917, **23**, No. 4 (Whole No. 101.)

Rock, I., & Leaman, R. An experimental analysis of visual symmetry. *Acta Psychol.,* 1963, **21**, 171–183.

Shipley, W. C., Mann, B. M., & Penfield, M. J. The apparent length of tilted lines. *J. exp. Psychol.,* 1949, **39**, 548–551.

Sleight, R. B., & Austin, T. R. The horizontal-vertical illusion in plane geometric figures. *J. Psychol.,* 1952, **33**, 279–287.

Stavrianos, B. K. Relation of shape perception to explicit judgments of inclination. *Arch. Psychol.,* 1945, **42**, 1–94.

Thouless, R. H. The experience of 'upright' and 'upside-down' in looking at pictures. In *Miscellanea psychologica Albert Michotte.* Paris: Librairie Philosophique, 1947. Pp. 130–137.

Valentine, C. W. The effect of astigmatism on the horizontal-vertical illusion, and a suggested theory of the illusion. *Brit. J. Psychol.,* 1912, **5**, 308–330.

Valentine, C. W. Psychological theories of the horizontal-vertical illusion. *Brit. J. Psychol.,* 1912, **5**, 8–35.

II. PHYSIOLOGY OF FORM PERCEPTION

A. Eye tremor

Bennet-Clark, H. C., & Evans, C. R. Fragmentation of patterned targets when viewed as prolonged after-images. *Nature,* 1963, **199,** 1215–1216.

Bowling, L., & Klein, G. S. Fragmentation phenomena in luminous designs. *Percept. mot. Skills,* 1966, **23,** 143–152.

Campbell, F. W., & Robson, J. G. A fresh approach to stabilized retinal images. *J. Physiol.,* 1961, **158,** 1–11.

Clarke, F. J. J. Rapid light adaptation of localized areas of the extra-foveal retina. *Opt. Acta,* 1957, **4,** 69–77.

Clarke, F. J. J., & Evans, C. R. Luminous design phenomena. *Science,* 1964, **144,** 1359.

Clowes, M. B. Some factors in brightness discrimination with constraint of retinal image movement. *Opt. Acta,* 1961, **8,** 81–91.

Clowes, M. B., & Ditchburn, R. W. An improved apparatus for producing a stabilized retinal image. *Opt. Acta,* 1961, **8,** 81.

Cohen, H. B. The effect of contralateral visual stimulation on visibility with stabilized retinal images. *Can. J. Psychol.,* 1961, **15,** 212–219.

Cornsweet, T. N. Determination of the stimuli for involuntary drifts and saccadic eye movements. *J. Opt. Soc. Amer.,* 1956, **46,** 987–993.

Cornsweet, T. N. A stabilized image requiring no attachments to the eye. *Amer. J. Psychol.,* 1962, **75,** 653–656.

Craig, E. A., & Lichtenstein, M. Visibility-invisibility cycles as a function of stimulus-orientation. *Amer. J. Psychol.,* 1953, **66,** 554–563.

Ditchburn, R. W., & Fender, D. H. The stabilized retinal image. *Opt. Acta,* 1955, **2,** 128–133.

Ditchburn, R. W., & Ginsborg, B. L. Vision with a stabilized retinal image. *Nature,* 1952, **170,** 36–37.

Ditchburn, R. W., & Pritchard, R. M. Stabilized interference fringes on the retina. *Nature,* 1956, **177,** 434.

Ditchburn, R. W., & Pritchard, R. M. Binocular vision with two stabilized retinal images. *Quart. J. exp. Psychol.,* 1960, **12,** 26–32.

Ditchburn, R. W., Fender, D. H., & Mayne, S. Vision with controlled movements of the retinal image. *J. Physiol.,* 1959, **145,** 98–107.

Doesschate, J. T. A new form of physiological nystagmus. *Ophthalmologica,* 1954, **127,** 65–73.

Donderi, D. C. Visual disappearances caused by form similarity. *Science,* 1966, **152,** 99–100.

Evans, C. R. Some studies of pattern perception using a stabilized retinal image. *Brit. J. Psychol.,* 1965, **56,** 121–133.

Evans, C. R. New approach to pattern perception. *Discovery,* 1966, **27,** 17–21.

Evans, C. R. Studies of pattern perception using an afterimage as the method of retinal stabilization. *Amer. Psychologist,* 1966, **21,** 646. (Abstract)

Evans, C. R. Further studies of pattern perception and a stabilized retinal image: The use of prolonged after-images to achieve perfect stabilization. *Brit. J. Psychol.,* 1967, **58,** 315–327.

Ferree, C. E. An experimental examination of the phenomenon usually attributed to fluctuation of attention. *Amer. J. Psychol.,* 1906, **17,** 81–120.

Fry, G. A., & Robertson, V. M. The physiological basis of the periodic merging of area into background. *Amer. J. Psychol.,* 1935, **47,** 644–655.

Gippenreĭter, Y. B., Vergiles, H. Y., & Shchedrovitskiĭ, L. P. Novoe o metodike registratsii tremora glaz. *Voprosy Psikhol.*, 1964, **10**(5), 118–121.

Heckenmueller, E. G. Stabilization of the retinal image: A review of method, effects, and theory. *Psychol. Bull.*, 1965, **63**, 157–169.

Heinrich, W., & Chiwistek, L. Ueber das periodische Verschwinden kleiner Punkte. *Z. Sinnesphysiol.*, 1906, **41**, 59–73.

Honisett, J., & Oldfield, R. C. Movement and distortion in visual patterns during prolonged fixation. *Scand. J. Psychol.*, 1961, **2**, 49–55.

Junge, K. The moving radii illusion. *Scand. J. Psychol.*, 1963, **4**(1), 14–16.

Junge, K. Final note on the moving radii illusion. *Scand. J. Psychol.*, 1963, **4**(3), 134.

Krauskopf, J. Effects of retinal image motion on contrast thresholds for maintained vision. *J. Opt. Soc. Amer.*, 1957, **47**, 740–747.

Krauskopf, J., & Riggs, L. A. Interocular transfer in the disappearance of stabilized images. *Amer. J. Psychol.*, 1959, **72**, 248–252.

MacKay, D. M. Moving visual images produced by regular stationary patterns, II. *Nature*, 1958, **181**, 362, 363.

MacKay, D. M. Monocular 'rivalry' between stabilized and unstabilized retinal images. *Nature*, 1960, **185**, 834.

MacKay, D. M. Interactive processes in visual perception. In W. A. Rosenblith (Ed.), *Sensory communication*. Cambridge, Massachusetts: M.I.T. Press, 1961, Pp. 339–355.

MacKay, D. M. Visual effects of non-redundant stimulation. *Nature*, 1961, **192**, 739–740.

McFarland, J. H. "Parts" of perceived visual forms: New evidence. *Percept. Psychophys.*, 1968, **3**, 118–120.

McKinney, J. P. Disappearance of luminous designs. *Science*, 1963, **140**, 403–404.

Monahan, J. B. The effect of stimulus form in disappearance phenomena in the visual after-image. *Papers Psychol.*, 1967, **1**(1), 32–33.

Oster, G. *The science of moiré patterns*. Barrington, New Jersey: Edmund Sci. Co., 1964.

Pirenne, M. H. Light-adaptation. In H. Davson (Ed.), *The eye*. Vol, 2, New York: Academic Press, 1962. Pp. 197–204.

Pritchard, R. M. A collimator stabilizing system. *Quart. J. exp. Psychol.*, 1961, **13**, 181–183.

Pritchard, R. M. Stabilized images on the retina. *Sci. Amer.*, 1961, **204**(6), 72–77.

Pritchard, R. M., Heron W., & Hebb, D. Visual perception approached by the method of stabilized images. *Can. J. Psychol.*, 1960, **14**, 67–77.

Ratliff, F. The role of physiological nystagmus in monocular acuity. *J. exp. Psychol.*, 1952, **43**, 163–172.

Ratliff, F. Stationary retinal images requiring no attachments to the eye. *J. Opt. Soc. Amer.*, 1958, **48**, 274–275.

Ratliff, F. & Riggs, L. A. Involuntary motions of the eye during monocular fixation. *J. exp. Psychol.*, 1950, **40**, 687–701.

Reiff, H. J. Zur Erklaerung der Thompsonschen optischen Taeuschung. *Arch. ges. Physiol.*, 1907, **119**, 580–581.

Riggs, L. A., & Ratliff, F. Visual acuity and the normal tremor of the eyes. *Science*, 1951, **114**, 17–18.

Riggs, L. A., & Tulaney, S. U. Visual effects of varying the extent of compensation for eye movements. *J. Opt. Soc. Amer.*, 1959, **9**, 741–745.

Riggs, L. A., Armington, J. C., & Ratliff, F. Motions of the retinal image during fixation. *J. Opt. Soc. Amer.*, 1954, **44**, 315–321.

Riggs, L. A., Ratliff, F., Cornsweet, J. C., & Cornsweet, T. N. The disappearance of steadily fixated visual test objects. *J. Opt. Soc. Amer.*, 1953, **43**, 495–501.

Roessel, F. P., Jr. Disappearances of semi-stabilized retinal images as a function of cell assemblies, field effects, and angle of orientation. Unpublished doctoral dissertation, Univ. of Minnesota, 1965. *Diss. Abstr.,* 1966, **27**(4–B), 1312–1313.

Sommer, W. *Zerfall optischer Gestalten.* Muenchen: Beck, 1937.

Stratton, G. M. The illusory undulation and shimmer of straight lines. *Psychol. Rev., Monogr. Suppl.,* 1909, No. 40, **10**, 63–84.

Tees, R. C. The role of field effects in visual perception. *Undergrad. Res. Proj. Psychol., McGill Univ.,* 1961, **3**, 87–96.

Thompson, S. P. Optical illusions of motion. *Brain,* 1880, **3**, 289–298.

Thompson, S. P. Optical illusions of motion. *Pop. Sci. Monthly,* 1881, **18**, 519–526.

Troxler. Ueber das Verschwinden gegebener Gegenstaende innerhalb unsers Gesichtskreises. In K. Himly & J. A. Schmidt (Eds.), *Ophthalmologische Bibliothek,* Vol. 2, 1804. Pp. 51–53.

Vergiles, N. Y. Metod uvelicheniya vremeni vospriyatiya stabilizirovannogo obraza. *Voprosy Psikhol.,* 1966, **12**(2), 166–169.

Yarbus, A. L. Novyĭ metod izucheniya deyatel'nosti razlichnykh chasteĭ setchatki. *Biofizika,* 1957, **2**, 165–167.

Zinchenko, V. P. Dvizheniya glaz i formirovaniya obraza. *Voprosy Psikhol.,* 1958, **4**(5), 63–76.

B. Neural correlates of form (see also Section IV,A)

Berger, C., & Buchthal. F. [Function of the fovea and perception of form.] *Skand. Arch. Physiol.,* 1938, **79**, 15–26.

Broca, A., & Sulzer, D. Inertie rétinienne relative au sens des formes. Sa variation suivant le criterium adopté. Formation d'une onde de sensibilité sur la rétine. *C. R. Acad. Sci.,* 1903, **136**, 1287–1290.

Broca, A., & Sulzer, D. Inertie du sens visuel des formes. *J. Physiol. Path. Gen.,* 1903, **15**, 293–307, 637–643.

Burns, B. D., Heron, W., & Pritchard, R. Physiological excitation of visual cortex in cat's unanesthetized isolated retina. *J. Neurophysiol.,* 1962, **25**, 165–181.

Coker, C. Optical memory. *Optom. Weekly.,* 1940, **31**, 1308.

Cramer, V. V. Uchenie o vospriyatii zritel'noĭ formy. *Sov. nevropatol.,* 1934, **3**, No. 2–3, 126–131.

Glezer, V. D. O fiziologicheskom soderzhanii ponyatiya "zritel'noĭ obraz." *Zh. Vyssh. Ner. Deyat.,* 1965, **15**, 869–877.

Guillery. Einiges ueber den Formsinn. *Arch. f. Augenhk.,* 1894, **38**, 263–276.

Guillery. Messende Untersuchungen ueber den Formsinn. *Arch. ges. Physiol.,* 1899, **75**, 466–522.

Guillery. Weitere Untersuchungen zur Physiologie des Formensinnes. *Arch. Augenheilk.,* 1905, **51**, 209–226.

John, R. E., Herrington, R. N., & Sutton, S. Effects of visual form on the evoked response. *Science,* 1967, **155**, 1439–1442.

Lashley, K. S. Patterns of cerebral integration indicated by the scotomas of migraine. *Arch. Neurol. Psychiat.,* 1941, **46**, 331–339.

Lashley, K. S. The problem of cerebral organization in vision. In J. Cattell (Ed.), *Biological symposia.* Vol. VII: Visual mechanisms (H. Kluever, Ed.). Lancaster, Pennsylvania: Jacques Cattell Press, 1942. Pp. 301–322.

Platt, J. R. How we see straight lines. *Sci. Amer.,* 1960, **202**(6), 121–129.

Platt, J. R. How a random array of cells can learn to tell whether a straight line is straight. In H. von Foerster & G. W. Zopf (Eds.), *Principles of self-organization.* New York: Pergamon Press, 1962. Pp. 315–323.

C. Contour as gradient

Bartley, S. H. *Vision.* Princeton, New Jersey: Van Nostrand, 1941. (Chapter 10.)

Flom, M. C., Weymouth, F. W., & Kahneman, D. Visual resolution and contour interaction. *J. Opt. Soc. Amer.,* 1963, 53, 1026–1032.

Fry, G. A., & Bartley, S. H. The effect of one border in the visual field upon the threshold of another. *Amer. J. Physiol.,* 1935, 112, 414–421.

Fry, G. A., & Cobb, P. W. Visual discrimination of two parallel bright bars in a dark field. *Amer. J. Psychol.,* 1937, 49, 76–81.

Holt-Hansen, K. Kinds of experiences in the perception of a circle. *Percept. mot. Skills,* 1967, 24, 3–32.

Koppitz, W. J. Mach bands and retinal interaction. Unpublished doctoral dissertation, Ohio State Univ., 1958. *Diss. Abstr.,* 1958, 19, 885.

Kravkov, S. V. Illumination and visual acuity. *Acta Ophthal.,* 1938, 16, 385–395.

Ludvigh, E. Perception of contour: I. Introduction. *US Naval Sch. Aviat. Med. Res. Rep.,* 1953, Rep. No. NM 001 075.01.04, Joint Rep. No. 4.

Ludvigh, E. Perception of contour: II. Effect of rate of change on retinal intensity gradient. *US Naval Sch. Aviat. Med. Res. Rep.,* 1953, No. 001 075.01.05, Joint Rep. No. 5.

Marshall, W. H., & Talbot, S. A. Recent evidence for neural mechanisms in vision leading to a general theory of sensory acuity. In J. Cattell (Ed.), *Biological symposia.* Vol. VII: Visual mechanisms (H. Kluever, Ed.). Lancaster, Pennsylvania: Jacques Cattell Press, 1942, Pp. 117–164.

O'Brien, V. Contour perception, illusion, and reality. *J. Opt. Soc. Amer.,* 1958, 48, 112–119.

Ratliff, F. *Mach bands.* San Francisco, California: Holden-Day, 1965.

Riggs, L. A., Ratliff, F., & Keesey, U. T. Appearance of Mach bands with a motionless retinal image. *J. Opt. Soc. Amer.,* 1961, 51, 702–703.

Selety, F. Die Wahrnehmung der geometrischen Figuren. *Arch. Syst. Phil.,* 1915, 21, 49–58.

Springbett, B. M. The subjective edge. *Amer. J. Psychol.,* 1961, 74, 101–103.

Weston, H. C., Bridgers, D. J., & Ledger, J. A study of the effect of pattern on the detection of detail at different levels of illumination. *Ergonomics,* 1963, 6, 367–377.

Wilcox, W. W. The basis of the dependence of visual acuity on illumination. *Proc. Nat. Acad. Sci.,* 1932, 18, 47–56.

D. Metacontrast

Alpern, M. The effect of luminance, exposure, asynchrony, and spatial separation of stimuli on the magnitude of metacontrast. *J. Opt. Soc. Amer.,* 1950, 40, 796. (Abstract)

Alpern, M. Metacontrast; historical introduction. *Amer. J. Optom.,* 1952, 29, 631–646.

Alpern, M. Metacontrast. *J. Opt. Soc. Amer.,* 1953, 43, 648–657.

Alpern, M. The effect of luminance of the contrast-inducing flashes on the spatial range of metacontrast. *Amer. J. Optom. Arch.,* 1954, 31, 363–369.

Baroncz, Z. Versuche ueber den sogenannten Metakontrast. *Arch. ges. Physiol.,* 1911, 140, 491–508.

Blanc-Garin, J. Quelques problemes posées par l'étude du métacontraste visuel. *Psychol. Franc.,* 1965, 65, 147–154.

Blanc-Garin, J. Les relations temporelles dans le masquage latéral visuel. *Année Psychol.,* 1966, **66**, 365–381.

Cheatham, P. G. Visual perceptual latency as a function of stimulus brightness and contour shape. *J. exp. Psychol.,* 1952, **43**, 369–380.

Dember, W. N., & Purcell, D. G. Recovery of masked visual targets by inhibition of the masking stimulus. *Science,* 1967, **157**, 1335–1336.

Eriksen, C. W., & Collins, J. F. Backward masking in vision. *Psychon. Sci.,* 1964, **1**, 101–102.

Eriksen, C. W., & Collins, J. F. Reinterpretation of one form of backward and forward masking in visual perception. *J. exp. Psychol.,* 1965, **70**, 343–351.

Fehrer, E. Contribution of perceptual segregation to the relationship between stimulus similarity and backward masking. *Percept. mot. Skills,* 1965, **21**, 27–33.

Fehrer, E., & Raab, D. H. Reaction time to stimuli masked by metacontrast. *J. exp. Psychol.,* 1962, **63**, 143–147.

Fitzgerald, R. E., & Kirkham, R. Backward visual masking as a function of average uncertainty of the masking pattern. *Psychon. Sci.,* 1966, **6**, 469–470.

Flom, M. C., Heath, G. G., & Takahashi, E. Contour interaction and visual resolution: Contralateral effects. *Science,* 1963, **142**, 979–980.

Fraisse, P. Visual perceptive simultaneity and masking of letters successively presented. *Percept. Psychophys.,* 1966, **1**, 285–287.

Fry, G. A. Depression of the activity aroused by a flash of light by applying a second flash immediately afterwards to adjacent areas of the retina. *Amer. J. Physiol.,* 1934, **108**, 701–707.

Heckenmueller, E. G., & Dember, W. N. Paradoxical brightening of a masked black disc. *Psychon. Sci.,* 1965, **3**, 457–458.

Kahneman, D. Temporal effects in the perception of light and form. In W. Wathen-Dunn (Ed.), *Models for the perception of speech and visual forms.* Cambridge, Massachusetts: M.I.T. Press, 1967, Pp. 157–170.

Kahneman, D. Method, findings, and theory in studies of visual masking. *Psychol. Bull.,* 1968, **70**, 404–425.

Kinsbourne, M., & Warrington, E. K. The effect of an after-coming random pattern on the perception of brief visual stimuli. *Quart. J. exp. Psychol.,* 1962, **14**, 223–234.

Kinsbourne, M., & Warrington, E. K. Further studies on the masking of brief visual stimuli by a random pattern. *Quart. J. exp. Psychol.,* 1962, **14**, 235–245.

Kolers, P. A. Intensity and contour effects in visual masking. *Vision Res.,* 1962, **2**, 277–294.

Kolers, P. A., & Rosner, B. S. On visual masking (metacontrast): Dichoptic observation. *Amer. J. Psychol.,* 1960, **73**, 1–21.

Levine, R., Didner, R., & Tobenkin, N. Backward masking as a function of interstimulus distance. *Psychon. Sci.,* 1967, **9**, 185–186.

Mayzner, M. S., Blatt, M. H., Buchsbaum, W. H., Friedel, R. T., Goodwin, D. K., Keleman, A., & Nilsson, W. D. A U-shaped backward masking function in vision: A partial replication of the Weisstein and Haber study with two ring sizes. *Psychon. Sci.,* 1965, **3**, 79–80.

Okata, T. [Studies on contour effect in successive exposition of figures.] *Jap. J. Psychol.,* 1937, **12**, 335–359.

Piéron, H. Le métacontraste. *J. Psychol. norm. Pathol.,* 1935, **32**, 651–652.

Piéron, H. Le processus du métacontraste. *J. Psychol. norm. pathol.,* 1935, **32**, 1–24.

Pollack, R. H. Backward figural masking as a function of chronological age and intelligence. *Psychon. Sci.,* 1965, **3**, 65–66.

Pollack, R. H. Effects of figure-ground contrast and contour orientation on figural masking. *Psychon. Sci.,* 1965, **2**, 369–370.

Raab, D. H. Backward masking. *Psychol. Bull.*, 1963, 60, 118–129.

Schiller, P. H. Metacontrast interference as determined by a method of comparisons. *Percept. mot. Skills*, 1965, 20, 279–285.

Schiller, P. H. Monoptic and dichoptic visual masking by patterns and flashes. *J. exp. Psychol.*, 1965, 69, 193–199.

Schiller, P. H. Forward and backward masking as a function of relative overlap and intensity of test and masking stimuli. *Percept. Psychophys.*, 1966, 1, 161–164.

Schiller, P. H., & Chorover, S. L. Metacontrast: Its relation to evoked potentials. *Science*, 1966, 153, 1398–1400.

Schiller, P. H., & Wiener, M. Monoptic and dichoptic visual masking. *J. exp. Psychol.*, 1963, 66, 386–393.

Schiller, P. H., & Smith, M. C. A comparison of forward and backward masking. *Psychon. Sci.*, 1965, 3, 77–78.

Schiller, P. H., & Smith, M. C. Detection in metacontrast. *J. exp. Psychol.*, 1966, 71, 32–39.

Sekuler, R. W. Spatial and temporal determinants of visual backward masking. *J. exp. Psychol.*, 1965, 70, 401–406.

Smith, G. J. W., & Henriksson, M. The effect on an established percept of a perceptual process beyond awareness. *Acta Psychol.*, 1955, 11, 346–355.

Smith, M. C., & Schiller, P. H. Forward and backward masking: A comparison. *Can. J. Psychol.*, 1966, 20, 191–197.

Sperling, G. What visual masking can tell us about temporal factors in perception. In *Proc. 17th Int. Congr. Psychol.*, Washington, D. C., 1963. Amsterdam: North Holland Publ., 1964.

Stein, W. Tachistoskopische Untersuchung ueber das Lesen. *Arch. ges. Psychol.*, 1928, 64, 301–346.

Stigler, R. Chronophotische Studien ueber den Umgebungskontrast. *Arch. ges. Physiol.*, 1910, 134, 365–435.

Streicher, H. W., & Pollack, R. H. Backward figural masking as a function of intercontour distance. *Psychon. Sci.*, 1967, 7, 69–70.

Toch, H. H. The perceptual elaboration of a stroboscopic presentation of three contiguous squares. Unpublished doctoral dissertation, Princeton Univ., 1955, *Diss. Abstr.*, 1955, 15, 2316–2317.

Vreuls, D., & Schmidt, J. F. Model for effect of a second visual stimulus upon reaction time to the first. *Percept. mot. Skills*, 1966, 23, 323–328.

Wake, T. The effect of separation and overlap between the disk and the ring upon the contour effect. *Jap. Psychol. Res.*, 1967, 9, 35–41.

Weisstein, N., & Haber, R. N. A U-shaped backward masking function in vision. *Psychon. Sci.*, 1965, 2, 75–76.

Werner, H. Studies on contour: I. Qualitative analyses. *Amer. J. Psychol.*, 1935, 47, 40–64.

E. Figural aftereffects

Adachi, M. [Studying figural aftereffects by the CFF method. II.] *Proc. 22nd Annu. Meet., Jap. Psychol. Ass.*, 1958. P. 29.

Adachi, M. [Studying figural aftereffects by the CFF method. III.] *Proc. 24th Annu. Meet., Jap. Psychol. Ass.*, 1960, P. 51.

Adam, J. A note on visual illusions of direction. *Aust. J. Psychol.*, 1964, 16, 53–56.

Brown, K. T. Methodology for studying figural aftereffects and practice effects in the Mueller-Lyer illusion. *Amer. J. Psychol.*, 1953, 66, 629–634.

Bzhalava, I. T. Kontrastnaya illyuziya ili effekt posledstviya figury. *Voprosy Psikhol.,* 1962, 8(5), 57–69.

Chkhartishvili, S. N. K voprosu o lokalizatsii opticheskikh illyuzii ustanovki. *Voprosy Psikhol.,* 1964, 10(5), 94–102.

Christman, R. J. Figural aftereffects utilizing apparent movement as inspection figure. *Amer. J. Psychol.,* 1953, 66, 66–72.

Crawford, F. T., & Klingman, R. L. Figural aftereffects as a function of hue. *J. exp. Psychol.,* 1966, 72, 916–918.

Crawford, F. T., & Kubala, A. L. Displacement of figural aftereffects as a function of hue. *Psychol. Rec.,* 1964, 14, 427–432.

Day, R. H. On interocular transfer and the central origin of visual aftereffects. *Amer. J. Psychol.,* 1958, 71, 784–789.

Day, R. H. Excitatory and inhibitory processes as the basis of contour shift and negative aftereffect. *Psychologia,* 1962, 5(4), 185–193.

Day, R. H., & Logan, J. A. A further investigation of apparent size and retinal size as determinants of the figural aftereffect. *Quart. J. exp. Psychol.,* 1961, 13, 193–203.

Day, R. H., Pollack, R. H., & Seagrim, G. N. Figural aftereffects: A critical review. *Aust. J. Psychol.,* 1959, 11, 15–45.

Deutsch, J. A. The statistical theory of figural aftereffects and acuity. *Brit. J. Psychol.,* 1956, 47, 208–215.

Deutsch, J. A. Neurophysiological contrast phenomena and figural aftereffects. *Psychol. Rev.,* 1964, 71, 19–26.

Dodwell, P. C., & Gaze, L. The role of experience without set in figural aftereffects. *Psychon. Sci.,* 1965, 2, 277–278.

Duncan, C. P. Figural displacement with quasi-circular stimuli. *Percept. mot. Skills,* 1958, 8, 295–305.

Duncan, C. P. Effect of self-satiation on perceived size of a visual figure. *J. exp. Psychol.,* 1960, 60, 130–136.

Duncan, C. P. Amount and rate of decay of visual figural aftereffect as functions of type of inspection stimulus and inspection time. *Amer. J. Psychol.,* 1962, 75, 242–250.

Eysenck, H. J. Cortical inhibition, figural aftereffect, and the theory of personality. *Bull. Brit. Psychol. Soc.,* 1954, 23 (Inset), 10–11. (Abstract)

Eysenck, H. J. Cortical inhibition, figural aftereffect, and theory of personality. *J. Abnorm. Soc. Psychol.,* 1955, 51, 94–106.

Eysenck, H. J. Figural aftereffects, personality, and intersensory comparisons. *Percept. mot. Skills,* 1962, 15, 405–406.

Eysenck, H. J., & Holland, H. Two measures of figural aftereffect. *Indian J. Psychol.,* 1958, 33, 85–92.

Farnè, M. Ulteriore contributo allo studio degli stimoli marginali. *Arch. Psicol. Neurol. Psichiat.,* 1964, 25, 444–463.

Farnè, M. Figural aftereffects with short exposure time. *Psychol. Forsch.,* 1965, 28, 519–534.

Fehrer, E., & Ganchrow, D. Effects of exposure variables on figural aftereffects under tachistoscopic presentation. *J. exp. Psychol.,* 1963, 66, 506–513.

Flamant, F. Étude de la repartition de lumière dans l'image rétinienne d'une fente. *Rev. Opt.,* 1955, 34, 433–459.

Fox, B. H. Figural aftereffects: the influence of certain variables on the Koehler effect and adaptation. Unpublished doctoral dissertation, Univ. of Rochester, 1949.

Fox, B. H. Figural aftereffects: "satiation" and adaptation. *J. exp. Psychol.,* 1951, 42, 317–326.

Freeburne, C. M. A study of the relationship between figural aftereffect and reading test performance. *J. educ. Psychol.,* 1952, **43**, 309–312.

Freeburne, C. M., & Hamilton, C. E. The effect of brightness on figural aftereffect. *Amer. J. Psychol.,* 1949, **62**, 567–569.

Freeman, R. B. Figural aftereffects: Displacement or contrast? *Amer. J. Psychol.,* 1964, **77**, 607–613.

Fujiwara, K., & Obonai, T. [Quantitative analysis of figural aftereffect. II. Effects of inspection time and intensity of light stimulus upon the amount of figural aftereffect.] *Jap. J. Psychol.,* 1953, **24**, 114–120.

Ganz, L. Lateral inhibition and the location of visual contours: An analysis of figural aftereffects. *Vision Res.,* 1965, **4**, 465–481.

Ganz, L. Is the figural aftereffect an *after*effect? *Psychol. Bull.,* 1966, **66**, 151–165.

Ganz, L. Mechanism of the figural aftereffects. *Psychol. Rev.,* 1966, **73**, 128–150.

Ganz, L., & Day, R. H. An analysis of the satiation-fatigue mechanism of figural aftereffects. *Amer. J. Psychol.,* 1965, **78**, 345–361.

Gardner, R. A. A note on theory and methodology in the study of figural aftereffects. *Psychol. Rev.,* 1960, **67**, 272–276.

Gardner, R. W. Individual differences in figural aftereffects and response to reversible figures. *Brit. J. Psychol.,* 1961, **52**, 269–272.

Gaze, L., & Dodwell, P. C. The role of induced set in figural aftereffects. *Psychon. Sci.,* 1965, **2**, 275–276.

George, F. H. On the theory of the figural aftereffect. *Can. J. Psychol.,* 1953, **7**, 167–171.

George, F. H. Acuity and the statistical theory of figural aftereffects. *J. exp. Psychol.,* 1962, **63**, 423–425.

Gibb, M., Freeman, I., & Adam, J. Effects of luminance contrast factors upon figural aftereffects induced by short fixation periods. *Percept. mot. Skills,* 1966, **22**, 535–541.

Graham, E. H. Figural aftereffects as functions of contrast area and luminance of the inspection figure. *Psychologia,* 1961, **4**(4), 201–207.

Hammer, E. R. Temporal factors in figural aftereffects. *Amer. J. Psychol.,* 1949, **62**, 337–354.

Harvey, W. M. Magnitude of the figural aftereffect as a function of the degree of similarity between test and inspection figures. Unpublished doctoral dissertation, Washington Univ., 1966. *Diss. Abstr.,* 1966, **27**(6–B), 2120.

Hochberg, J. E., & Bitterman, M. E. Figural aftereffects as a function of the retinal size of the inspection figure. *Amer. J. Psychol.,* 1951, **64**, 99–102.

Hochberg, J. E., & Triebel, W. Figural aftereffects with colored stimuli. *Amer. J. Psychol.,* 1955, **68**, 133–135.

Hochberg, J. E., & Hay, J. Figural aftereffect, afterimage, and physiological nystagmus. *Amer. J. Psychol.,* 1956, **69**, 480–482.

Hochberg, J. E., Day, R. H., & Hardy, D. Hue and brightness differences, contours, and figural aftereffects. *Amer. J. Psychol.,* 1960, **73**, 638–639.

Ikeda, H. [Studies in figural aftereffects.] Unpublished doctoral dissertation, Tokyo Bunrika Univ., 1951.

Ikeda. H. [On the cancellation of two opposing figural aftereffects.] *Jap. J. Psychol.,* 1956, **26**, 407–410.

Ikeda, H., & Obonai, T. [The quantitative analysis of figural aftereffects. I. The process of growth and decay of figural aftereffects.] *Jap. J. Psychol.,* 1953, **24**, 59–66.

Ikeda, H., & Obonai, T. [The quantitative analysis of figural aftereffects. II. On "self-satiation."] *Jap. J. Psychol.,* 1953, **24**, 179–192.

Ikeda, H., & Obonai, T. The studies of figural aftereffects. IV. The contrast-confluence illusion of concentric circles and the figural after-effect. *Jap. Psychol. Res.*, 1955, **2**, 17–23.

Ikeda, H., & Obonai, T. [Figural aftereffect, retroactive effect, and simultaneous illusion.] *Jap. J. Psychol.*, 1955, **26**, 235–246.

Ikuta, H. [Displacement in figural aftereffect and simultaneous illusions.] *Jap. J. Psychol.*, 1956, **27**, 218–226.

Ikuta, H. [Displacement in figural aftereffect and simultaneous illusion. II. Temporal factors.] *Jap. J. Psychol.*, 1960, **31**, 173–180.

Immergluck, L. Figural aftereffects, rate of "figure-ground" reversal, and field dependence. *Psychon. Sci.*, 1966, **6**, 45–46.

Immergluck, L. Resistance to an optical illusion, figural aftereffects, and field-dependence. *Psychon. Sci.*, 1966, **6**, 281–282.

Immergluck, L. Visual figural aftereffects and field-dependence. *Psychon. Sci.*, 1966, **6**, 219–220.

Immergluck, L. Comment on "Figural aftereffects, illusions, and the dimension of field dependence." *Psychon. Sci.*, 1968, **11**, 363.

Immergluck, L. Further comments on "Is the figural aftereffect an *after*effect?" *Psychol. Bull.*, 1968, **70**, 198–200.

Immergluck, L. Individual differences in figural aftereffect potency: Aftereffect trace versus immediate stimulus context as a determiner of perception. *Psychon. Sci.*, 1968, **10**, 203–204.

Jahnke, J. C. A group method for the study of figural aftereffects. *Amer. J. Psychol.*, 1957, **70**, 319–320.

Kaneko, T., & Obonai, T. [Studies on figural aftereffects by the method of threshold of light spot.] *Proc. 21st Annu. Meet. Jap Psychol. Ass.*, 1957, P. 23.

Kelm, H. Koehler's satiation theory and Deutsch's neurophysiological model of figural aftereffects. Unpublished doctoral dissertation, Univ. of Saskatchewan, 1966. *Diss. Abstr.*, 1966, **27**(5–B), 1939.

Kietzman, M. L. The perceptual interference of successively presented visual stimuli. Unpublished doctoral dissertation, Univ. of California at Los Angeles, 1962.

Koffman, G., & Pressey, A. W. Sex differences on a group test of figural aftereffects. *Psychon. Sci.*, 1967, **8**, 511–512.

Kogiso, I. [An experiment on the displacement in figural aftereffects.] *Jap. J. Psychol.*, 1956, **26**, 405–407.

Koehler, W. Unsolved problems in the field of figural aftereffects. *Psychol. Rec.*, 1964, **15**, 63–83.

Koehler, W. Movement aftereffects and figural aftereffects. *Percept. mot. Skills*, 1965, **20**, 591–595.

Koehler, W., & Wallach, H. Figural aftereffects; an investigation of visual processes. *Proc. Amer. Phil. Soc.*, 1944, **88**, 269–357.

Koehler, W., & Emery, D. A. Figural aftereffects in the third dimension of visual space. *Amer. J. Psychol.*, 1947, **60**, 159–201.

Krauskopf, J. The magnitude of figural aftereffects as a function of the duration of the test period. *Amer. J. Psychol.*, 1954, **67**, 684–690.

Krauskopf, J. Figural aftereffects with a stabilized image. *Amer. J. Psychol.*, 1960, **73**, 294–297.

Luchins, A. S., & Luchins, E. H. On the relationship between figural aftereffects and the principle of Praegnanz. *Amer. J. Psychol.*, 1952, **65**, 16–26.

Luchins, A. S., & Luchins, E. H. The satiation theory of figural aftereffects and Gestalt principles of perception. *J. gen. Psychol.*, 1953, 49, 3–29.

Luchins, A. S., & Luchins, E. H. The satiation theory of figural aftereffects and the principle of Praegnanz. *J. gen. Psychol.*, 1953, 49, 185–199.

Madison, H. L. A statistical learning analysis of figural aftereffects. Unpublished doctoral dissertation, Indiana Univ., 1959, *Diss. Abstr.*, 1959, 20, 1451–1452.

Malhotra, M. K. Figural aftereffects: An examination of Koehler's theory. *Acta Psychol.*, 1958, 14, 161–199.

Malhotra, M. K. The dependence of the figural aftereffect on the location of the stimuli in the visual field. *Acta Psychol.*, 1960, 17, 253–259.

Malhotra, M. K. Supplement to "Figural aftereffects: An examination of Koehler's theory." *Acta Psychol.*, 1960, 17, 148–154.

Malhotra, M. K. Figurale Nachwirkungen. *Psychol. Forsch.*, 1966, 30, 1–104.

Marks, M. R. A study of figural aftereffects: The Koehler effect. *Amer. Psychologist*, 1948, 3, 334. (Abstract)

Marquart, D. I. The satiational theory of figural aftereffects. *J. gen. Psychol.*, 1954, 51, 83–91.

Mathews, T., & Wertheimer, M. An experimental test of the Koehler-Wallach and the Osgood-Heyer theories of figural aftereffects. *Amer. J. Psychol.*, 1958, 71, 611–612.

McEwen, P. Figural aftereffects. *Brit. J. Psychol., Monogr. Suppl.*, 1958, No. 31.

McEwen, P. *Figural aftereffects.* London and New York: Cambridge Univ. Press, 1958.

McEwen, P. Figural aftereffects, retinal size. *Brit. J. Psychol.*, 1959, 50, 41–47.

Meyer, D. R., Sukemune, S., & Myers, R. Local variations in the magnitude of a figural aftereffect. *J. exp. Psychol.*, 1960, 60, 314–317.

Mori, T. Figural aftereffects and stimulus organization. *Jap. Psychol. Res.*, 1956, No. 3, 8–14.

Mori, T. [The influence of the field of illusion upon the figural aftereffects.] *Proc. 23rd Annu. Meet. Jap. Psychol. Ass.*, 1959, III-56.

Mori, T., & Nagashima, K. The effects of the organization of the total patterns upon figural aftereffects. *Essays & Stud. by Members of Tokyo Women's Christ. Coll.*, 1953, 87–107.

Mori, T., & Obonai, T. [Studies on figural aftereffects by the measurement of threshold of light spot.] *Proc. 21st Annu. Meet. Jap. Psychol. Ass.*, 1957, p. 24.

Morikawa, Y. Successive comparison of a visual size: III. Effects of prolonged stimulus. *J. child Develop.* (Japan), 1966, 2, 27–40.

Moseley, D. V. A tachistoscopic study of figural aftereffect. *Percept. mot. Skills*, 1964, 18, 882.

Motokawa, K., Nakagawa, D., & Kohata, T. Figural aftereffects and retinal induction. *J. gen. Psychol.*, 1957, 57, 121–135.

Nozawa, S. [Prolonged inspection of a figure and the aftereffect thereof.] *Jap. J. Psychol.*, 1953, 23, 217–234.

Nozawa, S. [Prolonged inspection of a figure and the aftereffect thereof.] *Jap. J. Psychol.*, 1953, 24, 47–58.

Nozawa, S. On the aftereffect by intermittent presentation of inspection figure. *Jap. Psychol. Res.*, 1955, No. 2, 9–15.

Nozawa, S. An experimental study on figural aftereffect by the measurement of field strength. *Jap. Psychol. Res.*, 1956, No. 3, 15–24.

Nozawa, S. An experimental study on figural aftereffect by the measurement of field strength. II. *Jap. Psychol. Res.*, 1958, No. 5, 22–27.

Nozawa, S. [Studies on figural aftereffects by the measurement of the threshold of small spots.] *Proc. 22nd Annu. Meet. Jap. Psychol. Ass.*, 1958, p. 29.

Nozawa, S. [Studies on figural aftereffects by the measurement of field strength.] *Proc. 25th Annu. Meet. Jap. Psychol. Ass.*, 1961, p. 91.

Nozawa, S. Studies on figural aftereffects by the measurement of field strength and the factor of spatial distance. *Seishin Stud. (Univ. of the Sacred Heart, Tokyo)*, 1961, 16, 111–140.

Obonai, T., & Suto, Y. [Studies of figural aftereffects by the inspection of short time.] *Jap. J. Psychol.*, 1952, 22, 248. (Abstract)

Obonai, T., & Ikeda, H. [The quantitative analysis of figural aftereffects. I. The process of growth and decay of figural aftereffects.] *Jap. J. Psychol.*, 1953, 23, 246–260.

Osgood, C. E. Kendon Smith's comments on "A new interpretation of figural aftereffects." *Psychol. Rev.*, 1953, 60, 211–212.

Osgood, C. E., & Heyer, A. W., Jr. A new interpretation of figural aftereffects. *Psychol. Rev.*, 1952, 59, 98–118.

Oyama, T. [Figural aftereffects and reversible figures.] *Chiwa Sensei Kanreki Kinen Ronbunshu*, 1952, 47–55.

Oyama, T. [Experimental studies of figural aftereffects. I. Temporal factors.] *Jap. J. Psychol.*, 1953, 23, 239–245.

Oyama, T. [Experimental studies on figural aftereffects. II. Spatial factors.] *Jap. J. Psychol.*, 1954, 25, 195–206.

Oyama, T. [Experimental studies of figural aftereffects. III. Displacement effect.] *Jap. J. Psychol.*, 1956, 26, 365–375.

Oyama, T. Temporal and spatial factors in figural aftereffects. *Jap. Psychol. Res.*, 1956, No. 3, 25–36.

Oyama, T. [Aftereffects of two inspection figures.] *Jap. J. Psychol.*, 1957, 26, 202–203.

Oyama, T. Figural aftereffects as a function of hue and brightness. *Jap. Psychol., Res.*, 1960, No. 2, 74–80.

Parducci, A., & Brookshire, K. Figural aftereffects with tachistoscopic presentation. *Amer. J. Psychol.*, 1956, 69, 635–639.

Paul, S. K. A note on sex differences in figural aftereffects. *Psychol. Stud.*, 1965, 10(2), 143–144.

Pollack, R. H. Figural aftereffects: Quantitative studies of displacement. *Aust. J. Psychol.*, 1958, 10, 269–277.

Pollack, R. H. Application of the sensory-tonic theory of perception to figural aftereffect. *Acta Psychol.*, 1963, 21, 1–16.

Pollack, R. H. Effects of temporal order of stimulus presentation on the direction of figural aftereffects. *Percept. mot. Skills*, 1963, 17, 875–880.

Pollack, R. H. Comment on "Is the figural aftereffect and *after*effect?" *Psychol. Bull.*, 1967, 68, 59–61.

Prentice, W. C. H. On the size of the figural aftereffect with varying distances. *Amer. J. Psychol.*, 1950, 63, 589–593.

Prentice, W. C. H. Aftereffects in perception. *Sci. Amer.*, 1962, 206(1), 44–50.

Pressey, A. W. A reply to comments on "Figural aftereffects, illusions, and the dimension of field dependence." *Psychon. Sci.*, 1968, 11, 364.

Pressey, A. W., & Kelm, H. Effects of sleep deprivation on a visual figural aftereffect. *Percept. mot. Skills*, 1966, 23, 795–800.

Prysiazniuk, A. W., & Kelm, H. Visual figural aftereffects in retarded adults. *J. abnorm. soc. Psychol.*, 1963, 67, 505–509.

Prysiazniuk, A. W., & Kelm, H. Counter displacement in the visual figural aftereffect. *Quart. J. exp. Psychol.*, 1965, 17, 69–74.

Sagara, M., & Oyama, T. Experimental studies on figural aftereffects in Japan. *Psychol. Bull.*, 1957, 54, 327–338.

Seagrim, G. N. A further examination of non-satiational figural aftereffects. *Aust. J. Psychol.,* 1957, 9, 20–30.

Seagrim, G. N. Non-satiational figural aftereffects: Supplementary report. *Aust. J. Psychol.,* 1958, 10, 364–365.

Seltzer, W. J., & Sheridan, C. L. Effects of inspection figure persistence on a figural aftereffect. *Psychon. Sci.,* 1965, 2, 279–280.

Shibata, T. [The influence of contour figure upon the negative afterimage.] *Jap. J. Psychol.,* 1936, 11, 223–241.

Shinjo, M. [An experimental study on figural aftereffects: Measurement of aftereffect by CFF.] *Proc. 21st Annu. Meet. Jap. Psychol. Ass.,* 1957, p. 22.

Smith, K. The statistical theory of the figural aftereffect. *Psychol. Rev.,* 1952, 59, 401–402.

Smith, K. "Attraction" in figural aftereffects. *Amer. J. Psychol.,* 1954, 67, 174–176.

Smith, K. R. The satiational theory of the figural aftereffect. *Amer. J. Psychol.,* 1948, 61, 282–286.

Spitz, H. H., & Blackman, L. S. A comparison of mental retardates and normals on visual figural aftereffects and reversible figures. *J. abnorm. soc. Psychol.,* 1959, 58, 105–110.

Story, A. Figural aftereffects as a function of the perceived characteristics of the inspection figure. *Amer. J. Psychol.,* 1959, 72, 46–56.

Story, A. W. Has apparent size been tested as a factor in figural aftereffects? *Quart. J. exp. Psychol.,* 1961, 13, 204–208.

Summerfield, A., & Miller, K. M. Visual illusion and figural aftereffect, with and without fixation. *Quart. J. exp. Psychol.,* 1955, 7, 149–158.

Sutherland, N. S. Figural aftereffects, retinal size, and apparent size. *Quart. J. exp. Psychol.,* 1954, 6, 35–44.

Sutherland, N. S. Figural aftereffects and apparent size. *Quart. J. Exp. Psychol.,* 1961, 13, 222–228.

Suto, Y., & Ikeda, H. [An examination of the relationship between the inspection time and the figural aftereffects.] *Jap. J. Psychol.,* 1957, 27, 377–380.

Takagi, K., & Ishikawa, M. [Experimental study on figural aftereffects.] *Proc. 21st Annu. Meet. Jap. Psychol. Ass.,* 1957, p. 21.

Taylor, M. M. Figural aftereffects: A psychophysical theory of the displacement effect. *Can. J. Psychol.,* 1962, 16, 247–277.

Taylor, M. M. Numerical prediction of a simple figural aftereffect as a function of the contrast of the inspection figure. *Psychol. Rev.,* 1963, 70, 357–360.

Taylor, M. M. "Adaptation and repulsion in the figural aftereffect" and the psychophysical theory. *Quart. J. exp. Psychol.,* 1966, 18, 175–177.

Terwilliger, R. F. Studies in visual aftereffects. Unpublished doctoral dissertation, Stanford Univ., 1960. *Diss. Abstr.,* 1960, 21, 1266.

Terwilliger, R. F. Retinal size as a determiner of the direction of size distortion in figural aftereffects. *Quart. J. exp. Psychol.,* 1961, 13, 209–217.

Terwilliger, R. F. Evidence for a relationship between figural aftereffects and afterimages. *Amer. J. Psychol.,* 1963, 76, 306–310.

Uchiyama, M. [Visual field in the successive stimulus situation. I.] *Proc. 24th Annu. Meet. Jap. Psychol. Ass.,* 1960, p. 53.

Uchiyama, M. Experimental study on the declining process of the form field: The field after figure disappearance. *Psychologia,* 1960, 3, 41–49.

Weiskrantz, L. Figural aftereffects in stroboscopic motion. *Quart. J. exp. Psychol.,* 1950, 2, 113–118.

Weitz, J., & Compton, B. A further stereoscopic study of figural aftereffects. *Amer. J. Psychol.,* 1950, 63, 78–83.

Weitz, J., & Post, D. A stereoscopic study of figural aftereffects. *Amer. J. Psychol.,* 1948, **61,** 59–65.

Weitzman, B. A figural aftereffect produced by a phenomenal dichotomy in a uniform contour. *J. exp. Psychol.,* 1963, **66,** 195–200.

Weitzman, B. Figural aftereffect produced by a phenomenal dichotomy in a uniform contour. *J. exp. Psychol.,* 1966, **71,** 781–783.

Wertheimer, M. Constant errors in the measurement of figural aftereffects. *Amer. J. Psychol.,* 1954, **67,** 543-546.

Wertheimer, M. The differential satiability of schizophrenic and normal subjects: A test of a deduction from the theory of figural aftereffects. *J. gen. Psychol.,* 1954, **51,** 291–299.

Wertheimer, M., & Jackson, C. W., Jr. Figural aftereffects, "brain modifiability," and schizophrenia: A further study. *J. gen. Psychol.,* 1957, **57,** 45–54.

Wertheimer, M., & Wertheimer, N. A metabolic interpretation of individual differences in figural aftereffects. *Psychol. Rev.,* 1954, **61,** 279–280.

Willems, E. P. Nonstimulus and nonretinal mechanisms in figural aftereffects. *J. exp. Psychol.,* 1967, **74,** 452–454.

Wilson, J. An apparatus for recording figural aftereffects. *Quart. J. exp. Psychol.,* 1962, **14,** 119–121.

Wilson, J. Adaptation and repulsion in the figural aftereffect. *Quart. J. exp. Psychol.,* 1965, **17,** 1–13.

Yokoyama. A. [Measurement of figural aftereffects: Examination of measurement of decaying process.] *Proc. 21st Annu. Meet. Jap. Psychol. Ass.,* 1957, p. 24.

Yoshida, T. [An experimental study of figural aftereffect.] *Jap. J. Psychol.,* 1953, **23,** 235–238.

Yoshida, T. [On the wave motion in decaying process of figural aftereffects.] *Proc. 21st Annu. Meet. Jap. Psychol. Ass.,* 1957, 25–26.

Yoshida, T. [On the wave motion in growing process of figural aftereffects.] *Proc. 23rd Annu. Meet. Jap. Psychol. Ass.,* 1959, III–55.

Yoshida, T. Figural aftereffects as a function of the brightness ratio between the inspection figure and its surrounding field. In *Studies in psychology in commemoration of Prof. Matsusaburo Yokoyama's birthday.* Tokyo: Kei Univ., 1960. Pp. 99–114.

F. Theories

1. J. A. Deutsch (see also Section II,F,2)

Deutsch, J. A. A theory of shape recognition. *Brit. J. Psychol.,* 1955, **46,** 30–37.

Deutsch, J. A. Shape recognition: A reply to Dodwell. *Brit. J. Psychol.,* 1958, **49,** 70–71.

Deutsch, J. A. The plexiform zone and shape recognition in the octopus. *Nature,* 1960, **188,** 443–446.

Deutsch, J. A. Theories of shape discrimination in the *Octopus. Nature,* 1960, **188,** 1090–1092.

Deutsch, J. A. A system for shape recognition. *Psychol. Rev.,* 1962, **69,** 492–500.

Deutsch, J. A., & Traister, L. Lateral inhibition as a mechanism of shape recognition. In W. Wathen-Dunn (Ed.), *Models for the perception of speech and visual forms.* Cambridge, Massachusetts: M.I.T. Press, 1967. Pp. 380–387.

Dodwell, P. C. Shape recognition in rats. *Brit. J. Psychol.,* 1957, **48,** 221–229.

Dodwell, P. C. Shape recognition: A reply to Deutsch. *Brit. J. Psychol.,* 1958, **49,** 158–159.

2. P.C. Dodwell (see also Section V,B,7)

Dodwell, P. C. Visual discrimination of shape in animals and men. Unpublished doctoral dissertation, Oxford Univ., 1958.

Dodwell, P. C. Discrimination of small shapes by the rat. *Quart. J. exp. Psychol.,* 1960, **12,** 237–241.

Dodwell, P. C. Coding and learning in shape discrimination. *Psychol. Rev.,* 1961, **68,** 373–382.

Dodwell, P. C. Facts and theories of shape discrimination. *Nature,* 1961, **191,** 578–581.

Dodwell, P. C. A test of two theories of shape discrimination. *Quart. J. exp. Psychol.,* 1962, **14,** 65–70.

Dodwell, P. C. A coupled system for coding and learning in shape discrimination. *Psychol. Rev.,* 1964, **71.** 148–159.

Dodwell, P. C., & Niemi, R. R. Contour separation and orientation in shape discrimination by rats. *Psychon. Sci.,* 1967, **9,** 519–520.

3. N. S. Sutherland (see also Sections V,B,7 and 12)

Dodwell, P. C. Shape discrimination in the octopus and the rat. *Nature,* 1957, **179,** 1088.

Sutherland, N. S. Shape discrimination in the *Octopus. Nature,* 1957, **179,** 1310.

Sutherland, N. S. Visual discrimination of orientation and shape by *Octopus. Nature,* 1957, **179,** 11–13.

Sutherland, N. S. Stimulus analysing mechanisms. In National Physical Laboratory Symposium No. 10: *Mechanisation of thought processes.* Vol. II. London: Her Majesty's Stationery Office, 1959, Pp. 575–609.

Sutherland, N. S. A test of a theory of shape discrimination in *Octopus vulgaris Lamarck. J. comp. physiol. Psychol.,* 1959, **52,** 135–141.

Sutherland, N. S. Theories of shape discrimination in *Octopus. Nature,* 1960, **186,** 840–844.

Sutherland, N. S. Theories of shape discrimination in the *Octopus. Nature,* 1960, **188,** 1092–1094.

Sutherland, N. S. Facts and theories of shape discrimination. *Nature,* 1961, **191,** 581–583.

Sutherland, N. S. Shape discrimination and receptive fields. *Nature,* 1963, **197,** 118–122.

4. Neurohistology and form perception

Barlow, H. B., & Hill, R. M. Selective sensitivity to direction of movement in ganglion cells of the rabbit retina. *Science,* 1963, **139,** 412–414.

Baumgartner, G., Brown, J. L., & Schultz, A. Visual motion detection in the cat. *Science,* 1964, **146,** 1070–1071.

Hubel, D. H. The visual cortex of the brain. *Sci. Amer.,* 1963, **209**(11).

Hubel, D. H., & Wiesel, T. N. Receptive fields of single neurones in the cat's striate cortex. *J. Physiol.,* 1959, **148,** 574–591.

Hubel, D. H., & Wiesel, T. N. Receptive fields of optic nerve fibres in the spider monkey. *J. Physiol.,* 1960, **154,** 572–580.

Hubel, D. H., & Wiesel, T. N. Receptive fields, binocular interaction, and functional architecture in the cat's visual cortex. *J. Physiol.,* 1962, **160,** 106–123.

Hubel, D. H., & Wiesel, T. N. Receptive fields of cells in striate cortex of very young, visually inexperienced kittens. *J. Neurophysiol.,* 1963, **26,** 994–1002.

Hubel, D. H., & Wiesel, T. N. Receptive fields and functional architecture in two non-striate visual areas (18 & 19) of the cat. *J. Neurophysiol.,* 1965, **28,** 229–289.

Lettvin, J. Y., Maturana, H. R., McCulloch, W. S., & Pitts, W. H. What the frog's eye tells the frog's brain. *Proc. IRE,* 1959, **47**, 1940–1951.

Lettvin, J. Y., Maturana, H. R., Pitts, W. H., & McCulloch, W. S. Two remarks on the visual system of the frog. In W. A. Rosenblith (Ed.), *Sensory communication,* Cambridge, Massachusetts: M.I.T. Press, 1961, Pp. 757–776.

Maturana, H. R., & Frenk, S. Directional movement and horizontal edge detectors in the pigeon retina. *Science,* 1963, **142**, 977–979.

Maturana, H. R., Lettvin, J. Y., McCulloch, W. S., & Pitts, W. H. Anatomy and physiology of vision in the frog *(Rana pipiens). J. gen. Physiol.,* 1960, **43**, Part 2, 129–176.

Michael, C. R. Receptive fields of directionally selective units in the optic nerve of the ground squirrel. *Science,* 1966, **152**, 1092–1095.

Michael, C. R. Receptive fields of single optic nerve fibers in a mammal with an all-cone retina. *J. Neurophysiol.,* 1968, **31**, 249–282.

Michael, C. R. Retinal processing of visual images. *Sci. Amer.,* 1969, **220**(5).

Muntz, W. R. A. Mechanisms of visual form recognition in animals. In W. Wathen-Dunn (Ed.), *Models for the perception of speech and visual forms.* Cambridge, Massachusetts: M.I.T. Press, 1967, Pp. 126–136.

Oyster, C. W., & Barlow, H. B. Direction-selective units in rabbit retina: Distribution of preferred directions. *Science,* 1967, **155**, 841–842.

Rodieck, R. W. Receptive fields in the cat retina: A new type. *Science,* 1967, **157**, 90–92.

Spinelli, D. N. Visual receptive fields in the cat's retina: Complications. *Science,* 1966, **152**, 1768–1769.

Stone, J., & Fabian, M. Specialized receptive fields of the cat's retina. *Science,* 1966, **152**, 1277–1279.

G. Brain lesions and form preception

1. Case histories

Baldó, M., Malbran, J., & Franke, E. Doble incongruencia hemianópsica de orígen cortical (estudio anatómico-clínico). *Arch. Argent. Neurol.,* 1934, **10**, 201–212.

Battersby, W.S., Krieger, H. P., Pollack, M., & Bender, M. B. Figure-ground discrimination and the "abstract attitude" in patients with cerebral neoplasm. *Arch. Neurol. Psychiat.,* 1953, **70**, 703–712.

Bender, L. A visual motor Gestalt test and its clinical use. *Amer. Orthopsychiat. Ass., Res. Monogr.* No. 3, 1938.

Bender, M. B. Phenomena of fluctuation, extinction, and completion in visual perception. *Arch. Neurol. Psychiat.,* 1946, **55**, 627–658.

Bender, M. B. *Disorders of perception.* Springfield, Illinois: Thomas, 1952.

Bender, M. B., & Battersby, W. S. Homonymous macular scotomata in cases of occipital lobe tumor. *Arch. Ophthal.,* 1958, **60**, 928–938.

Bender, M. B., & Kanzer, M. Dynamics of homonymous hemianopias and preservation of central vision. *Brain,* 1939, **62**, 404–421.

Bender, M. B., & Furlow, L. T. Phenomenon of visual extinction in homonymous fields and psychological principles involved. *Arch. Neurol. Psychiat.,* 1945, **53**, 29–33.

Bender, M. B., & Furlow, L. T. Visual disturbances produced by bilateral lesions of the occipital lobes with central scotomas. *Arch. Neurol. Psychiat.,* 1945, **53**, 165–170.

Bender, M. B., & Teuber, H.-L. Spatial organization of visual perception following injury to the brain. *Arch. Neurol. Psychiat.,* 1947, **58**, 721–739.

Bender, M. B., & Teuber, H.-L. Spatial organization of visual perception following injury to the brain. *Arch. Neurol. Psychiat.,* 1948, **59**, 39–62.

Bender, M. B., & Teuber, H.-L. Disturbances in visual perception following cerebral lesions. *J. Psychol,* 1949, **28**, 223–233.

Brain, R. Visual disorientation with special reference to lesions of the right cerebral hemisphere. *Brain,* 1941, **64**, 244–272.

Cohen, L. Perception of reversible figures by normal and brain-injured subjects. *Arch. Neurol. Psychiat.,* 1959, **81**, 765–775.

Critchley, M. Types of visual perseveration: "paliopsia" and "illusory visual spread." *Brain,* 1951, **74**, 267–299.

Critchley, M. *The parietal lobes.* London: Arnold, 1953.

Cushing, H. The field defects produced by temporal lobe lesions. *Brain,* 1922, **44**, 341–396.

Faust, C. Ueber Gestaltzerfall als Symptom des parieto-occipitalen Uebergangsgebietes bei doppelseitiger Verletzung nach Hirnschuss. *Nervenarzt,* 1947, **18**, 103–115.

Franz, S. I. On the functions of the cerebrum: The occipital lobes. *Psychol. Rev. Monogr.,* 1911, **13**(56).

Gazzaniga, M. S., Bogen, J. E., & Perry, R. W. Observations on visual perception after disconnexion of the cerebral hemispheres in man. *Brain,* 1965, **88** (Part 2), 221–236.

Gelb, A., & Goldstein, K. *Psychologische Analysen hirnpathologischer Faelle.* Leipzig: Barth, 1920.

Gneisse, K. Die Entstehung der Gestaltvorstellungen unter besonderer Beruecksichtigung neuerer Untersuchungen von kriegsbeschaedigten Seelenblinded. *Arch. ges. Psychol.,* 1921, **41**, 295–334.

Gordon, O. J., & Tikofsky, R. S. Performance of brain-damaged subjects on Gottschaldt's Embedded Figures. *Percept. mot. Skills,* 1961, **12**, 179–185.

Graham, F. K., & Kendall, B. S. Performance of brain-damaged cases on a memory-for-designs test. *J. abnorm. soc. Psychol,* 1946, **41**, 303–314.

Harrower, M. R. Changes in figure-ground perception in patients with cortical lesions. *Brit. J. Psychol,* 1939, **30**, 47–51.

Hécaen, H., Penfield, W., Bertrand, C., & Malmo, R. The syndrome of apractognosia due to lesions of the minor cerebral hemispheres. *Arch. Neurol. Psychiat.,* 1956, **75**, 400–434.

Holmes, G. Disturbances of vision by cerebral lesions. *Brit. J. Ophthal.,* 1918, **2**, 353–384.

Holmes, G. Disturbances of visual space perception. *Brit. Med. J.,* 1919, **2**, 230–233.

Holmes, G. A contribution to the cortical representation of vision. *Brain,* 1931, **54**, 470–479.

Holmes, G., & Lister, W. T. Disturbances of vision from cerebral lesions with special reference to the macula. *Brain,* 1916, **39**, 34–73.

Jablonski, W. Ricerche sulla percezione delle forme nei miopi. *Arch. Ital. Psicol.,* 1937, **15**, 70–81.

Loeb, J. Sehstoerungen nach Verletzung der Grosshirnrinde. *Arch. ges. Physiol.,* 1884, **34**, 67–172.

Marie, P., & Chatelin, C. Les troubles visuels dus aux lésions des voies optiques intracérébrales et de la sphère visuelle corticale dans les blessures du crâne par coup de feu. *Rev. Neurol.,* 1914–15, **28**, 882–925.

Milian, G. Cécité morphologique. *Bull. Acad. Méd.,* 1932, **107**, 664–666.

Orton, S. T. "Word-blindness" in school children. *Arch. Neurol. Psychiat.,* 1925, **14**, 581–615.

Pascal, G. R., & Suttell, B. J. *The Bender-Gestalt test.* New York: Grune & Stratton, 1951.

Paterson, A., & Zangwill, O. L. Disorders of visual space perception associated with lesions of the right cerebral hemisphere. *Brain,* 1944, **67**, 331–358.

Poppelreuter, W. *Die psychischen Schaedigungen durch Kopfschuss im Kriege 1914–16; die Stoerungen der niederen und hoeheren Sehleistungen durch Verletzung des Okzipitalhirns.* Vol. I. Leipzig: Voss, 1917.

Poppelreuter, W. Zur Psychologie der optischen Wahrnehmung. *Z. ges. Neurol. Psychiat.,* 1923, **83**, 26 ff.

Renfrew, S. The regional variations of extrafoveal perception of form in the central visual fields (photopic vision). *Brit. J. Ophthal.,* 1950, **34**, 577–593.

Saenger, A. Ueber die durch die Kriegsverletzungen bedingten Veraenderungen im optischen Zentralapparat. *Deut. Z. Nervenhk.,* 1918, **59**, 192 ff.

Shapiro, M. B. An experimental investigation of the block design rotation effect: An analysis of a psychological effect of brain damage. *Brit. J. Med. Psychol.,* 1954, **27**, 84–88.

Teuber, H.-L., & Bender, M. B. The significance of changes in pattern vision following occipital lobe injury. *Amer. Psychol.,* 1946, **1**, 255. (Abstract)

Teuber, H.-L., & Weinstein, S. Ability to discover hidden figures after cerebral lesions. *Arch. Neurol. Psychiat.,* 1956, **76**, 369–379.

Teuber, H.-L., Battersby, W. S., & Bender, M. B. *Visual field defects after penetrating missile wounds of the brain.* Cambridge, Massachusetts: Harvard Univ. Press, 1960.

Werner, H., & Strauss, A. A. Pathology of the figure-background relation in the child. *Psychol. Bull.,* 1940, **37**, 440. (Abstract)

Werner, H., & Strauss, A. A. Pathology of figure-background relation in the child. *J. abnorm. Soc. Psychol.,* 1941, **36**, 236–248.

Werner, H., & Weir, A. The figure-ground syndrome in the brain-injured child. *Int. Rec. Med.,* 1956, **169**, 362–367.

Wilbrand, H. Ueber die wissenschaftliche Bedeutung der Kongruenz und Inkongruenz der Gesichtsfelddefekte. *J. Psychol. Neurol.,* 1930, **40**, 133–146.

Zollinger, R. Removal of left cerebral hemisphere: Report of a case. *Arch. Neurol. Psychiat.,* 1935, **34**, 1055–1064.

2. Animal studies

Ades, H. W. Effect of extirpation of parastriate cortex on learned visual discrimination in monkeys. *J. Neuropathol. exp. Neurol.,* 1946, **5**, 60–65.

Ades, H. W., & Raab, D. H. Effect of preoccipital and temporal decortication on learned visual discrimination in monkeys. *J. Neurophysiol.,* 1949, **12**, 101–108.

Blake, L. The effect of lesions of the superior colliculus on brightness and pattern discrimination in the cat. *J. comp. physiol. Psychol.,* 1959, **52**, 272–278.

Blake, L. The effect of lesions of the composite gyrus on visual pattern discrimination in the cat. Unpublished doctoral dissertation, Univ. of Kansas, 1964. *Diss. Abstr.,* 1965, **26**, 498–499.

Blum, J. S., Chow, K. L., & Pribram, K. H. A behavioral analysis of the organization of the parieto-temporo-pre-occipital cortex. *J. Comp. Neurol.,* 1950, **93**, 53–100.

Bridgman, C. S., & Smith, K. U. Bilateral neural integration in visual perception after section of the corpus callosum. *J. comp. Neurol.,* 1945, **83**, 57–68.

Brush, E. S., Mishkin, M., & Rosvold, H. E. Effects of object preferences and aversions on discrimination learning in monkeys with frontal lesions. *J. comp. Physiol.,* 1961, **54**, 319–325.

Butter, C. M., & Gekoski, W. L. Alterations in pattern equivalence following infero-temporal and lateral striate lesions in rhesus monkeys. *J. comp. Physiol., Psychol.,* 1966, **61**, 309–312.

Chang, M. C. Neural mechanism of monocular vision: I. Disturbance of monocular pattern discrimination in the albino rat after destruction of the cerebral visual area. *Chin. J. Psychol.,* 1936, **1**, 10–20.

Chang, M. C Neural mechanism of monocular vision: II. Pattern discrimination in the monocular rat before and after destruction of the visual area and in the rat deprived of the visual area on one side before and after severance of the contralateral optic nerve. *Chin. J. Psychol.,* 1936, 1, 91–100.

Chang, M. C. Neural mechanism of monocular vision: III. Disturbance of monocular size discrimination in the albino rat after destruction of the cerebral visual area. *Chin. J. Psychol.,* 1937, 1, 221–229.

Chow, K. L. Conditions influencing the recovery of visual discriminative habits in monkeys following temporal neocortical ablations. *J. comp. physiol. Psychol.,* 1952, 45, 430–437.

Chow, K. L. Further studies on selective ablation of associative cortex in relation to visually mediated behavior. *J. comp. physiol. Psychol.,* 1952, 45, 109–118.

Chow, K. L. Lack of behavioral effects following destruction of some thalamic association nuclei in monkeys. *Arch. Neurol. Psychiat.,* 1954, 71, 762–771.

Clark, G., & Lashley, K. S. Visual disturbances following frontal ablations in the monkey. *Anat. Rec.,* 1947, 97, 326.

Cushing, H. Distortion of the visual fields in cases of brain tumor. VI. The field defects produced by temporal lobe lesions. *Brain,* 1922, 44, 341–396.

Diamond, I. T., & Chow, K. L. Biological psychology. In S. Koch (Ed.), *Psychology: A study of a science,* Vol. 4. New York: McGraw-Hill, 1962. Pp. 158–241. (Passim.)

Dodwell, P. C., & Freedman, N. L. Visual form discrimination after removal of the visual cortex in cats. *Science,* 1968, 160, 559–560.

Doty, R. W. *Neurophysiologie und Psychophysik des visuellen Systems.* Berlin: Springer, 1961. (Pp. 228–246.)

Ettlinger, G. Visual discrimination with a single manipulandum following temporal abalations in the monkey. *Quart. J. exp. Psychol.,* 1959, 11, 164–174.

Evarts, E. V. Effects of ablation of prestriate cortex on auditory-visual association in monkeys. *J. Neurophysiol.,* 1952, 15, 191–200.

Freeman, G. L., & Papez, J. W. The effects of subcortical lesions on the visual discrimination of rats. *J. comp. Psychol.,* 1930, 11, 185–192.

Galambos, R., Norton, T. T., & Frommer, G. P. Optic tract lesions sparing pattern vision in cats. *Exp. Neurol.,* 1967, 18, 8–25.

Gualtierotti, T. Changes of visual pattern discrimination in adult cats after removal of an aspecific area of cerebral cortex. *Amer. J. Physiol.,* 1961, 200, 1215–1218.

Harlow, H. F. Recovery of pattern discrimination in monkeys following unilateral occipital lobectomy. *J. Comp. Psychol.,* 1939, 27, 467–489.

Harlow, H. F., Davis, R. T., Settlage, P. H., & Meyer, D. R. Analysis of frontal and posterior association syndromes in brain-damaged monkeys. *J. comp. physiol. Psychol.,* 1952, 45, 419–429.

Hebb, D. O. The innate organization of visual activity. III. Discrimination of brightness after removal of the striate cortex in the rat. *J. comp. Psychol.,* 1938, 25, 427–437.

Jameson, H. D., Settlage, P. H., & Bogumill, G. P. The effect of lesions in the amygdaloid area in monkeys. *J. gen. Psychol.,* 1957, 57, 91–102.

Kennard, M. A. Alterations in response to visual stimuli following lesions of frontal lobe in monkeys. *Arch. Neurol. Psychiat.,* 1939, 41, 1153–1165.

Klebanoff, S. G. Psychological changes in organic brain lesions and ablations. *Psychol. Bull.,* 1945, 42, 585–623.

Kluever, H. Visual disturbances after cerebral lesions. *Psychol. Bull.,* 1927, 24, 316.

Kluever, H. Certain effects of lesions of the occipital lobes in macaques. *J. Psychol.,* 1937, 4, 383–401.

Kluever, H. Visual functions after removal of the occipital lobes. *J. Psychol.*, 1941, **11**, 23–45.

Kluever, H., & Bucy, P. C. An analysis of certain effects of bilateral temporal lobectomy in the rhesus monkey, with special reference to "psychic blindness." *J. Psychol.*, 1938, **5**, 33–54.

Kluever, H., & Bucy, P. C. Preliminary analysis of functions of the temporal lobes in monkeys. *Arch. Neurol. Psychiat.*, 1939, **42**, 979–1000.

Lashley, K. S. Studies of cerebral function in learning: IV. Vicarious function after destruction of the visual area. *Amer. J. Physiol.*, 1922, **59**, 44–71.

Lashley, K. S. The mechanism of vision: IV. The cerebral areas necessary for pattern vision in the rat. *J. comp. Neurol.*, 1931, **53**, 419–478.

Lashley, K. S. The mechanism of vision: XVI. The functioning of small remnants of the visual cortex. *J. comp. Neurol.*, 1939, **70**, 45–67.

Lashley, K. S. The mechanism of vision: XVII. Anatomy of the visual cortex. *J. genet. Psychol.*, 1942, **60**, 197–221.

Lashley, K. S. The mechanism of vision: XVIII. Effects of destroying the visual "associative areas" of the monkey. *Genet. Psychol. Monogr.*, 1948, **37**, 107–166.

Lashley, K. S., & Frank, M. The mechanism of vision. VI. The lateral portion of the area striata in the rat: a correction. *J. comp. Neurol.*, 1932, **55**, 525–529.

Lashley, K. S., & Frank, M. The mechanism of vision: X. Postoperative disturbances of habits based on detail vision in the rat after lesions in the cerebral visual areas. *J. comp. Psychol.*, 1934, **17**, 355–391.

Layman, J. D. The avian visual system. I. Cerebral function of the domestic fowl in pattern vision. *Comp. Psychol. Monogr.*, 1936, **12**.

Lukaszewska, I., & Thompson, R. Retention of an overtrained pattern discrimination following pretectal lesions in rats. *Psychon. Sci.*, 1967, **8**, 121–122.

McFie, J., Piercy, M. F., & Zangwill, O. L. Visual-spatial agnosia associated with lesions of the right cerebral hemisphere. *Brain*, 1950, **73**, 167–190.

Meyer, P. M. Analysis of visual behavior in cats with extensive neocortical ablations. *J. comp. physiol. Psychol.*, 1963, **56**, 397–401.

Milner, B. Intellectual function of the temporal lobes. *Psychol. Bull.*, 1954, **51**, 42–62.

Mishkin, M. Effects of selective ablations of the temporal lobes on the visually guided behavior in monkeys and baboons. Unpublished doctoral dissertation, McGill Univ., 1951.

Mishkin, M. Visual discrimination performance following partial ablations of the temporal lobe: II. Ventral surface vs. hippocampus. *J. comp. physiol. Psychol.*, 1954, **47**, 187–193.

Mishkin, M., & Hall, M. Discrimination along a size continuum following ablation of the inferior temporal convexity in monkeys. *J. comp. physiol. Psychol.*, 1955, **48**, 97–101.

Mishkin, M., & Pribram, K. H. Visual discrimination performance following partial ablations of the temporal lobe: I. Ventral vs. lateral. *J. comp. physiol. Psychol.*, 1954, **47**, 14–20.

Myers, R. E., & Sperry, R. W. Contralateral mnemonic effect with ipsilateral sensory inflow. *Fed. Proc.*, 1956, **15**, 134.

Orbach, J., & Fantz, R. L. Differential effects of temporal neocortical resections on over-trained and non-overtrained visual habits in monkeys. *J. comp. physiol. Psychol.*, 1958, **51**, 126–129.

Parriss, J. R. Retention of shape discrimination after regeneration of the optic nerves in the toad. *Quart. J. Exp. Psychol.*, 1963, **15**, 22–26.

Pasik, P., Pasik, T., Battersby, W. S., & Bender, M. B. Target size and visual form discrimination in monkeys with bitemporal lesions. *Fed. Proc.*, 1958, **17**, 122.

Pasik, P., Pasik, T., Battersby, W. S., & Bender, M. B. Visual and tactual discriminations by macaques with serial temporal and parietal lesions. *J. comp. physiol. Psychol.,* 1958, 51, 427–436.

Riopelle, A. J., & Ades, H. W. Visual discrimination performance in rhesus monkeys following extirpation of prestriate and temporal cortex. *J. genet. Psychol.,* 1953, 83, 63–77.

Riopelle, A. J., Harlow, H. F., Settlage, P. H., & Ades, H. W. Performance of normal and operated monkeys on visual learning tests. *J. comp. physiol. Psychol.,* 1951, 44, 283–289.

Schneider, G. E. Two visual systems. *Science,* 1969, 163, 895–902.

Sechzer, J. A. Successful interocular transfer of pattern discrimination in "split-brain" cats with shock avoidance motivation. Unpublished doctoral dissertation, Univ. of Pennsylvania, 1962. *Diss. Abstr.,* 1962, 23, 1427–1428.

Settlage, P. H. The effect of occipital lesions on visually-guided behavior in the monkey: I. Influence of the lesions on final capacities in a variety of problem situations. *J. comp. Psychol.,* 1939, 27, 93–131.

Smith, K. U. Visual discrimination in the cat: VI. The relation between pattern vision and visual acuity and the optic projection centers of the nervous system. *J. genet. Psychol.,* 1938, 53, 251–272.

Snide, J. D. The effects of simultaneous and successive cortical lesions and postoperative pretraining upon pattern vision in the rat. Unpublished doctoral dissertation, Ohio State Univ., 1957. *Diss. Abstr.,* 1957, 17, 1609–1610.

Snyder, M., Hall, W. C., & Diamond, I. T. Vision in tree shrews (*Tupia glis*) after removal of striate cortex. *Psychon. Sci.,* 1966, 6, 243–244.

Sperry, R. W., & Miner, N. Pattern perception following insertion of mica plates into visual cortex. *J. comp. physiol. Psychol.,* 1955, 48, 463–469.

Sperry, R. W., Miner, N., & Myers, R. E. Visual pattern perception following subpial slicing and tantalum wire implanatations in the visual cortex. *J. comp. physiol. Psychol.,* 1955, 48, 50–58.

Tsang, Yue-Chuean. Visual sensitivity in rats deprived of visual cortex in infancy. *J. comp. Psychol.,* 1937, 24, 255–262.

Vitzou, A. N. Récuperation de la vue perdue à la suite d'une première ablation totale des lobes occipitaux chez les singes. *J. Physiol.,* 1898, 23, 57 ff.

Warren, J. M., & Harlow, H. F. Discrimination learning by normal and brain operated monkeys. *J. genet. Psychol.,* 1952, 81, 45–52.

Weiskrantz, L. Behavioral changes associated with ablation of the amygdaloid complex in monkeys. *J. comp. physiol. Psychol.,* 1956, 49, 381–391.

Wells, M. J. Proprioception and visual discrimination of orientation in *Octopus. J. exp. Biol.,* 1960, 37, 489–499.

Wetzel, A. B., Thompson, V. E., Horel, J. A., & Meyer, P. M. Some consequences of perinatal lesions of the visual cortex in the cat. *Psychon. Sci.,* 1965, 3, 381–382.

Wilson, M. Effects of circumscribed cortical lesions upon somesthetic and visual discrimination in the monkey. *J. comp. physiol. Psychol.,* 1957, 50, 630–635.

Wilson, M., Wilson, W. A., Jr., & Sunenshine, H. S. Perception, learning, and retention of visual stimuli by monkeys with inferotemporal lesions. *J. comp. physiol. Psychol.,* 1968, 65, 404–412.

Wilson, W. A., & Mishkin, M. Comparison of the effects of inferotemporal and lateral occipital lesions on visually guided behavior in monkeys. *J. comp. physiol. Psychol.,* 1959, 52, 10–17.

Winans, S. S. Visual form discrimination after removal of the visual cortex in cats. *Science,* 1967, 158, 944–946.

Young, J. Z. The failure of discrimination learning following removal of the vertical lobes in *Octopus. Proc. Roy. Soc. B.,* 1960, **153**, 18–46.

III. FORM DETECTION AND DISCRIMINATION THEORIES

A. Cybernetics, information theory, and form perception (see also Section V,A,2)

Alluisi, E. A. On the use of information measures in studies of form perception. *Percept. mot. Skills,* 1960, **11**, 195–203.

Attneave, F. Some informational aspects of visual perception. *Psychol. Rev.,* 1954, **61**, 183–193.

Attneave, F. *Applications of information theory to psychology.* New York: Holt, 1959.

Culbertson, J. T. A mechanism for optic nerve conduction and form perception. I. *Bull. Math. Biophys.,* 1948, **10**, 31–39.

Culbertson, J. T. A mechanism for optic nerve conduction and form perception. II. *Bull. Math. Biophys.,* 1948, **10**, 97–102.

Green, R. T., & Courtis, M. C. Information theory and figure perception: The metaphor that failed. *Acta Psychol.,* 1966, **25**, 12–35.

Harpur, J. G. The information content of visual patterns. *Papers Psychol.,* 1967, 1(1), 27.

Hochberg, J. E., & McAlister, E. A quantitative approach to figural "goodness." *J. exp. Psychol.,* 1953, **46**, 361–364.

Hoffman, W. C. The Lie algebra of visual perception. *J. Math. Psychol.,* 1966, **3**, 65–98.

Kilmartin, L. A. Perception of geometric shapes: The application of information theory to form perception. *Aust. Psychologist,* 1967, 2(1).

Murphree, O. D. Maximum rates of form perception and the alpha rhythm: An investigation and test of current nerve net theory. *J. exp. Psychol.,* 1954, **48**, 57–61.

Musatti, C. L. Forma e assimilazione. *Arch. Ital. Psicol.,* 1931, **9**, 61–156.

Nieder, P. Statistical codes for geometrical figures. *Science,* 1960, **131**, 934–935.

Novikoff, A. B. J. Integral geometry as a tool in pattern perception. In H. von Foerster & G. W. Zopf, Jr. (Eds.), *Principles of self-organization.* New York: Pergamon Press, 1962. Pp. 347–368.

Pitts, W., & McCulloch, W. S. How we know universals; the perception of auditory and visual forms. *Bull. Math. Biophys.,* 1947, **9**, 127–147.

Platt, J. R. Functional geometry and the determination of pattern is mosaic receptors. *Gen. Syst.,* 1962, **7**, 103–119.

Tanner, W. P., Jr. Information theory and form discrimination. In J. W. Wulfeck & J. H. Taylor (Eds.), *Form discrimination as related to military problems.* Washington, D. C.: Nat. Acad. Sci.-Nat. Res. Coun., 1957. Pp. 18–22.

Wiener, N. *Cybernetics.* New York: Wiley, 1948. (Chapter 6.)

Zeeman, E. C. The topology of the brain and visual perception. In M. K. Fort, Jr. (Ed.), *Topology of 3-manifolds.* Englewood Cliffs, New Jersey: Prentice-Hall, 1962. Pp. 240–256.

B. Machine models of form perception

Abramson, N., & Braverman, D. Learning to recognize patterns in a random environment. *IRE Trans.,* 1962, **IT**–8(5), 558–563.

Abramson, N., Braverman, N., & Sebestyen, G. Pattern recognition and machine learning. *IEEE Trans.,* 1963, IT–9(4), 257–261.

Aizerman, M. A., Braverman, E. M., & Razonoer, L. I. The probability problem of pattern recognition learning and the method of potential functions. *Automat. Remote Contr.,* 1964, 25, 1175–1193.

Aizerman, M. A., Braverman, E. M., & Razonoer, L. I. Theoretical principles of potential functions method in the problem of teaching automata to recognize classes. *Automat. Remote Contr.,* 1964, 25, 821–837.

Akers, S. B., Jr., & Rutter, B. H. The use of threshold logic in character recognition. *Proc. IRE,* 1964, 52(8), 931–938.

Albert, A. A mathematical theory of pattern recognition. *Ann. Math. Stat.,* 1963, 34, 282–299.

Amari, S. A theory of adaptive pattern classifiers. *IEEE Trans.,* 1967, EC–16, 299–307.

Arbib, M. *Brains, machines, and mathematics.* New York: McGraw-Hill, 1964. (Chapter 2.)

Arkadev, A. G., & Braverman, E. M. *Computers and pattern recognition.* Washington, D. C.: Thompson Book Co., 1967.

Baran, P., & Estrin, G. An adaptive character reader. *IRE WESCON Conv. Rec.,* 1960, 4(Pt. 4), 29–36.

Basharinov, A. E. On designs for automatic recognition of patterns in noise. *IRE Trans.,* 1962, IT–8(5), 5291–5292.

Bashkirov, O. A., Braverman, E. M., & Muchnik, I. B. Potential function algorithms for pattern recognition learning machines. *Automat. Remote Contr.,* 1964, 25, 629–631.

Bernhard, R. On visual perception and retinal motions. *Proc. IRE,* 1962, 50, 2133.

Blaydon, C. C. On a pattern classification result of Aizerman, Braverman, and Razonoer. *IEEE Trans.,* 1966, IT–12, 82–83.

Bledsoe, W. W. Further results on the n-tuple pattern recognition method. *IRE Trans.,* 1961, EC–10, 1–96.

Bledsoe, W. W., & Browning, I. Pattern recognition and reading by machine. *Proc. East. Joint Comp. Conf. 1959.* Pp. 225–232.

Block, R. H. A method of pattern recognition by machine. Unpublished doctoral dissertation, Univ. of Wisconsin, 1963.

Blum, H. An associative machine for dealing with the visual field and some of its biological implications. In E. E. Bernard & M. R. Kare (Eds.), *Biological prototypes and synthetic systems.* Vol. 1. New York: Plenum Press, 1962.

Bomba, J. S. Alpha-numeric character recognition using local operations. *Proc. East. Joint Comp. Conf. 1959,* 16, 218–224.

Bonner, R. E. A "logical pattern" recognition program. *IBM J. Res. Develop.,* 1962, 6, 353–360.

Borsellino, A., & Gamba, A. An outline of a mathematical theory of PAPA. *Nuovo Cimento,* 1961, 20, Suppl. No. 2, 221–231.

Bradshaw, J. A. Letter recognition using a captive scan. *IEEE Trans.* 1963, EC–12, 26.

Brailovskiĭ, V. L. On a method of recognizing objects which are described by several parameters, and its possible applications. *Automat. Remote Contr.,* 1962, 23, 1542–1551.

Braverman, D. J. Machine learning and automatic pattern recognition. Tech. Rep. No. 2003–1, Stanford Electronics Labs., Stanford Univ., Feb. 17, 1961.

Braverman, D. J. A decision theoretic approach to machine learning and pattern recognition. *IRE WESCON,* August, 1961.

Braverman, E. M. Experiments on machine learning to recognize visual patterns. *Automat. Remote Contr.,* 1962, 23, 315–327.

Braverman, E. M. Experiments in training a machine to recognize visual images, pts. 1 and 2. *Automat. Exp.,* 1962, **4**, 31–33, 34–40.

Brousil, J. K., & Smith, D. R. A threshold logic network for shape invariance. *IEEE Trans.,* 1967, **EC–16**, 818–828.

Brown, D. W. Recognition of typed letters in noise. *Informat. Control,* 1963, **6**, 301–305.

Brown, R. M. On-line computer recognition of handprinted characters. *IEEE Trans.,* 1964, **EC–13**, 750–752.

Buell, D. N. Chrysler Optical Processing Scanner (COPS): a character recognition system which is independent of character, translation, size, or orientation. *Proc. East. Joint Comp. Conf. 1961.* Pp. 352–370.

Bush, W. R., Kelly, R. B., & Donahue, V. M. Pattern recognition and display characteristics. *IRE Trans. Human Factors Electron.,* 1960, 11–21.

Bushor, W. E. The Perceptron–an experiment in learning. *Electronics,* 1960, **33**, 56–59.

Capon, J. Hilbert space methods for detection theory and pattern recognition. *IEEE Trans.,* 1965, **IT–11**, 247–259.

Casey, R., & Nagy, G. Recognition of printed Chinese characters. *IEEE Trans.,* 1966, **EC–15**, 91–101.

Chien, Y. T., & Fu, K. S. A modified sequential recognition machine using time-varying stopping boundaries. *IEEE Trans.,* 1966, **IT–12**, 206–214.

Chow, C. K. Optimum character recognition system using decision function. *IRE WESCON Conv. Rec.,* 1957, **1**(Pt. 4), 121–129.

Chow, C. K. A recognition method using neighbor dependence. *IRE Trans.,* 1962, **EC–11**, 683–690.

Chow, C. K. An experimental result in character recognition. *IEEE Trans.,* 1963, **EC–12**, 25.

Chu, J. T. Optimal decision functions for computer character recognition. *J. ACM,* 1965, **12**(2), 213–226.

Clark, W. A., & Farley, B. G. Generalization of pattern recognition in a self-organizing system. *Proc. West. Joint Comp. Conf. 1955.* Pp. 86–91.

Clavier, P. A. Self-educating machine for recognition and classification of patterns. *Proc. IRE,* 1961, **49**(8), 1335.

Clowes, M. B. Character recognition. EDP Symposium, London, October, 1961. New York: Pitman, 1964. Pp. 558–575.

Cooper, D. B., & Cooper, P. W. Non-supervised adaptive signal detection and pattern recognition. *Informat. Control,* 1964, **7**, 416–444.

Cooper, P. W. The hyperplane in pattern recognition. *Cybernetica,* 1962, **5**, 215–238.

Cover, T. M. Geometrical and statistical properties of systems of linear inequalities with applications in pattern recognition. *IEEE Trans.,* 1965, **EC–14**, 326–334.

Cover, T. M., & Hart, P. E. Nearest neighbor pattern classification. *IEEE Trans.,* 1967, **IT–13**, 21–27.

Dickinson, W. E. A character-recognition study. *IBM J. Res. Develop.,* 1960, **4**, 335–348.

Dimond, T. L. Devices for reading handwritten characters. *Proc. East. Joint Comp. Conf. 1957,* **T–92**, 232–237.

Dineen, G. Y. Programming pattern recognition. *Proc. West. Joint Comp. Conf. 1955.* Pp. 94–100.

Doyle, W. Recognition of sloppy hand-printed characters. *Proc. West. Joint Comp. Conf. 1960* Pp. 133–142.

Doyle, W. Operations useful for similarity-invariant pattern recognition. *J. ACM,* 1962, **9**, 259–267.

Dressler, R. F. Error rates for two methods of statistical pattern recognition. *J. ACM,* 1964, **11**(4), 471–480.

Duda, R. O., & Fossum, H. Pattern classification by iteratively determined linear and piecewise linear discriminant functions. *IEEE Trans.,* 1966, **EC–15**, 220–232.

Earnest, L. D. Machine recognition of cursive writing. *Proc. IFIP Congr. 62.* Amsterdam: North Holland Publ., 1962.

Eden, M. Handwriting and pattern recognition. *IRE Trans.,* 1962, **IT–8**, 160–166.

Eden, M., & Halle, M. The characterization of cursive writing. In C. Cherry (Ed.), *Fourth London symposium on information theory.* London and Washington, D. C.: Butterworth, 1961. Pp. 287–299.

Edwards, A. W., & Chambers, R. L. Can *a priori* probabilities help in character recognition? *J. ACM,* 1964, **11**, 465–470.

Eldredge, K. R., Kamphoefner, F. J., & Wendt, P. H. Teaching machines to read. *Stanford Res. Inst. J.,* 1957, **1**, 18–23.

Evey, R. J. Use of a computer to design character recognition logic. *Proc. East. Joint Comp. Conf. 1959,* **16**, 205–211.

Farley, B. G. Self-organizing models for learned perception. In M. C. Yovits & S. Cameron (Eds.), *Self-organizing systems.* New York: Pergamon Press, 1960.

Farley, B. G., & Clark, W. A. Simulation of self-organizing systems by digital computer. *IRE Trans.,* 1954, **IT–4**, 76–84.

Farley, B. G., & Clark W. A. Generalization of pattern recognition in a self-organizing system. *Proc. West. Joint Comp. Conf. 1955.*

Fischer, G. L. et al. (Eds.), *Optical character recognition.* Washington, D. C.: Spartan Books, 1962.

Fischler, M. A. Hyperplane techniques in pattern recognition. *Proc. IRE,* 1963, **51**, 497–498.

Fischler, M., Mattson, R. L., Firschein, O., & Healy, L. D. An approach to general pattern recognition. *IRE Trans.,* 1962, **IT–8**, 64–73.

Foulkes, J. D. A class of machines which determine the statistical structure of a sequence of characters. *IRE WESCON Conv. Rec.,* 1959, **3**(Pt. 4), 66–73.

Fralick, S. C. Learning to recognize patterns without a teacher. *IEEE Trans.,* 1967, **IT–13**, 57–64.

Frankel, S. On the design of automata and the interpretation of cerebral behavior. *Psychometrika,* 1955, **20**, 148–162.

Frankel, S. Information-theoretic aspects of character reading. In *Information processing.* Paris: UNESCO, 1960, Pp. 248–251.

Frishkopf, L. S., & Harmon, L. D. Machine-reading of cursive script. In C. Cherry (Ed.), *Fourth London symposium on information theory.* London and Washington, D. C.: 1961. Pp. 300–316.

Funkunaga, K., & Ito, T. A design theory of recognition functions in self-organizing systems. *IEEE Trans.,* 1965, **EC–14**, 44–52.

Gagliardo, E. On the evaluation of a formula for the errors of a learning machine. *Nuovo Cimento,* 1961, **20**, Suppl. No. 2, 232–238.

Gamba, A., Gamberini, L., Palmieri, G., & Sanna, R. Further experiments with PAPA. *Nuova Cimento,* 1961, **20**, Suppl. No. 2, 112–115.

Gamba, A., Palmieri, G., & Sanna, R. Preliminary experimental results with PAPA. *Nuovo Cimento,* 1962, **23**, Suppl. No. 2, 280–284.

Gill, A. Minimum-scan pattern recognition. *IRE Trans.,* 1959, **IT–5**, 52–58.

Gill, A. A note on a pattern recognition scheme. *IRE Proc.,* 1960, **48**, 1912.

Gliklikh, M. O., Drisilov. A. D., & Poddubnyǐ, G. V. Analysis of the reliability of character recognition based on statistical analysis. *Automat. Remote Contr.*, 1964, **24**, 995–1002.

Glucksman, H. A. A parapropagation pattern classifier. *IEEE Trans.*, 1965, **EC–14**, 434–443.

Golay, M. J. E. Theoretical considerations anent pattern recognition by means of random masks. *Proc. IRE*, 1963, **51**, 629–630.

Golovin, N. E. Reading printed data electronically. *Automation*, 1961, 8(12), 60–64.

Greanias, B. C., Hoppel, C. J., Kloomok, M., & Osborne, J. S. The design of the logic for the recognition of printed characters by simulation. *IBM J. Res. Develop.*, 1957, **1**, 8–18.

Greanias, E. C., Meagher, P. F., Norman, R. J., & Essinger, P. The recognition of handwritten numerals by contour analysis. *IBM J. Res. Develop.*, 1963, 7(1), 14–22.

Green, B. F., Jr. Using computers to study human perception. *Educ. Psychol. Meas.*, 1961, **21**, 227–233.

Greene, P. H. A suggested model for information representation in a computer that perceives, learns, and reasons. *Proc. West. Joint Comp. Conf. 1960*, **17**, 151–164.

Grimsdale, R. L., & Bullingham, J. M. Character recognition by digital computer using a special flying-spot scanner. *Comput. J.*, 1961, 4(2), 129–136.

Grimsdale, R. L., Sumner, F. H., Tunis, C. J., & Kilburn, T. A system for the automatic recognition of patterns. *Proc. IEE*, 1959(3), **106**(B), No. 26, 210–221.

Groner, G. F. Real-time recognition of handprinted text. RAND Corp., Santa Monica, Cal., RM-5016-ARPA, Oct. 1966.

Guiliano, V. E., Jones, P. E., Kimball, G. E., Meyer, R. F., & Stein, B. A. Automatic pattern recognition by a Gestalt method. *Informat. Control*, 1961, **4**, 332–345.

Gyr, J. W., Brown, J. S., Willey, R., & Zivian, A. Computer simulation and psychological theories of perception. *Psychol. Bull.*, 1966, **65**, 174–192.

Harmon, L. D. A line-drawing pattern recognizer. *Proc. West. Joint Comp. Conf.*, 1960, **17**, 351–364.

Hart, R. D. An information processing model of the detection and use of form properties. Unpublished doctoral dissertation, Univ. of Texas, 1964. *Diss. Abstr.*, 1965, **25**, 5400.

Hassenstein, B. A cross correlation process in the nervous system of an insect eye. *Nuovo Cimento*, 1959, **13**(Suppl. 2), 617–619.

Hay, J. C., Martin, F. C., & Wightman, C. W. The Mark I Perceptron: Design and performance. *IRE Int. Conv. Rec.*, 1960, 8(Pt. 2), 78–87.

Hayward, H. L., & Hilton, A. M. Pattern recognition for diagnosis of facial characteristics. *Data Process. Sci. Eng.*, 1963, 1(1), 31–34.

Highleyman, W. H. Linear decision functions with application to pattern recognition. Unpublished doctoral dissertation, Polytechnic Institute of Brooklyn, 1961.

Highleyman, W. H. An analog method for character recognition. *IRE Trans.*, 1961, **EC–10**, 502–512.

Highleyman, W. H. A note on optimum pattern recognition systems. *IRE Trans.*, 1961, **EC–10**, 287–288.

Highleyman, W. H. The design and analysis of pattern recognition experiments. *Bell Syst. Tech. J.*, 1962, **41**, 723–744.

Highleyman, W. H. Linear decision functions, with application to pattern recognition. *Proc. IRE*, 1962, 6, 1501–1515.

Highleyman, W. H., & Kamentsky, L. A. A generalized scanner for pattern and character recognition studies. *Proc. West. Joint Comp. Conf. 1959*. Pp. 291–294.

Highleyman, W. H., & Kamentsky, L. A. Comments on a character recognition method of Bledsoe and Browning. *IRE Trans.*, 1960, **EC–9**, 263.

Hilgrad, E. R., & Bower, G. H. *Theories of learning.* New York: Appleton, 1966. (Pp. 390–397.)

Hoffman, W. C. Pattern recognition by the method of isoclines: A mathematical model for the visual integrative process. Seattle, Washington: Boeing Sci. Res. Labs. Math. Note No. 351, 1964. Pp. 27–28.

Horwitz, L. P., & Shelton, G. L., Jr. Pattern recognition using autocorrelation. *Proc. IRE,* 1961, 49, 175–184.

Hough, P. V. C. General purpose visual input for a computer. *Ann. N. Y. Acad. Sci.,* 1962, 99, 323–334.

Hu, M.-K. Pattern recognition by moment invariants. *Proc. IRE,* 1961, 49, 1428.

Innes, D. Filter: A topological pattern separation computer program. *Proc. East. Joint Comp. Conf. 1960,* 18, 25–37.

Joseph, R. D. On predicting Perceptron performance. *IRE Int. Conv. Rec.,* 1960, 8(Pt. 2), 71–77.

Julesz, B. Visual pattern discrimination. *IRE Trans.,* 1962, IT–8, 84–91.

Kabrisky, M. *A proposed model for visual information processing in the human brain.* Urbana, Illinois: Univ. of Illinois Press, 1966.

Kain, R. Y. Autocorrelation pattern recognition. *Proc. IRE,* 1961, 49, 1085–1086.

Kalin, T. A. Some metric considerations in pattern recognition. Bedford, Massachusetts: AF Cambridge Res. Labs., July 1961. AFCRL 327.

Kamentsky, L. A. Pattern and character recognition systems: Picture processing by nets of neuron-like elements. *Proc. West. Joint Comp. Conf. 1959.* Pp. 304–309.

Kamentsky, L. A. Simulation of three machines which read rows of handwritten Arabic numbers. *IRE Trans.,* 1961, EC–10, 489–501.

Kamentsky, L. A., & Liu, C. N. Computer-automated design of multifont print recognition logic. *IBM J. Res. Develop.,* 1963, 7(1), 2–13.

Kazmierczak, H. The potential field as an aid to character recognition. *Proc. Int. Conf. Infomat. Process.,* UNESCO, Paris, 1959, 244–247.

Keller, H. B. Finite automata, pattern recognition and perceptrons. *J. ACM,* 1961, 8, 1–20.

Kesten, H. Asymptotic behavior of a perceptron. Report No. RC-135, 1959, IBM Res. Center, Yorktown Heights, New York.

Koford, J. S., & Groner, G. F. The use of an adaptive threshold element to design a linear optimal pattern classifier. *IEEE Trans.,* 1966, IT–12, 42–50.

Kolers, P. A., & Eden, M. (Eds.), *Recognizing patterns.* Cambridge, Massachusetts: M.I.T. Press, 1968.

Kotelly, J. C. A mathematical model of Blum's theory of pattern recognition. AFCRL-TR-63-164, USAF Cambr. Res. Lab., 1963.

Kovalevskiĭ, V. A. Present and future of pattern recognition theory. *Proc. IFIP Congr. 65,* Vol. 1. Washington, D. C.: Spartan Books, 1965. Pp. 37–43.

Kovalevsky, V. A. Character readers and pattern recognition. Washington, D. C.: Spartan Books, 1968.

Kovasznay, L. S. G., & Joseph, H. M. Processing of two-dimensional patterns by scanning techniques. *Science,* 1953, 118, 475–477.

Kovasznay, L. S. G., & Joseph, H. M. Image processing. *Proc. IRE,* 1955, 43, 560–570.

Ledley, R. S., & Ruddle, F. H. Chromosome analysis by computer. *Sci. Amer.,* 1966, 214(6), 40–46.

Lewis, P. M. The characteristic selection problem in recognition systems. *IRE Trans.,* 1962, IT–8, 171–178.

Liu, C. N. A programmed algorithm for designing multifont character recognition logics. *IEEE Trans.,* 1964, EC–13, 586–593.

Lodwick, G. S., Haun, C. L., Smith, W. E., Keller, R. F., & Robertson, E. D. Computer diagnosis of primary bone tumors. *Radiology,* 1963, 80, 273–275.

Lodwick, G. S., Keats, T. E., & Dorst, J. P. The coding of roentgen images for computer analysis as applied to lung cancer. *Radiology,* 1963, 81, 185–200.

Loebner, E. E. Image processing and functional retinal analysis. In *Bionics symposium,* Sept. 1960, PB 171258 (Dec. 1960). Washington, D.C.: Office Tech. Serv., 1960.

Londe, D. L., & Simmons, R. F. NAMER: a pattern recognition system for generating sentences about relations between line drawings. In *Proc. ACM 20th Nat. Conf., Aug., 1965,* New York: ACM, 1965. Pp. 162–175.

Lower, W. M., & Buck, J. D. Character recognition systems. *Proc. Comp. Data Process. Soc. Canada,* 1960, 346–355.

McCormick, B. H. The Illinois pattern recognition computer–ILLIAC III. *IEEE Trans.,* 1963, EC–12, 791–813.

Marill, T. A note on pattern recognition techniques and game-playing programs. *Infomat. Control,* 1963, 6, 213–217.

Marill, T., & Green, D. M. Statistical recognition functions and the design of pattern recognizers. *IRE Trans.,* 1960, EC–9, 472–477.

Marill, T., & Green, D. M. On the effectiveness of receptors in recognition systems. *IEEE Trans.,* 1963, IT–9, 11–17.

Marzocco, F. N. Computer recognition of handwritten first names. *IEEE Trans.,* 1965, EC–14, 210–217.

Mays, C. H. Comments on learning and adaptive mechanisms for pattern recognition. *Proc. AFIPS,* 1964 Fall Joint Comp. Conf., 623–630.

Mazmierczak, H., & Steinbuch, K. Adaptive system in pattern recognition. *IEEE Trans.,* 1963, EC–12, 822–835.

Mermelstein, P., & Eden, M. Experiments on computer recognition of connected handwritten words. *Infomat. Control,* 1964, 7, 255–270.

Metzelaar, P. Mechanical realization of pattern recognition. In *Bionics symposium,* Sept. 1960. PB 171258 (Dec. 1960). Washington, D. C.: Office Tech. Ser., 1960.

Minneman, M. J. Handwritten character recognition employing topology, cross correlation, and decision theory. *IEEE Trans.,* 1966, SSC–2, 86–96.

Minot, O. N. Automatic devices for recognition of visible two-dimensional patterns: A survey of the field. *USN Electr. Lab. Rep.,* No. TM364, 1959.

Minsky, M. L., Pryor, C. N., & Clavier, P. A. "Self-educating" pattern recognition schemes. *Proc. IRE,* 1962, 50, 1707–1708.

Muntz, W. R. A., Kalin, T. A., Talland, G. A., Ervin, F., & Julesz, B. Symposium on biological and psychological aspects of pattern recognition. *Proc. IFIP Congr. 62.* Amsterdam: North Holland Publ. Pp. 471–477.

Murray, A. E. A review of the perceptron program. *Proc. Nat. Electron. Conv.,* 1959, 15, 346–356.

Narasimhan, R. Syntactic descriptions of pictures and Gestalt phenomena of visual perception. Univ. of Illinois Digital Comp. Lab., Rep. No. 142, July 1963.

Neisser, U., & Weene, P. A note on human recognition of hand-printed characters. *Infomat. Control,* 1960, 3, 191–196.

Newman, E. A. Some comments on character recognition. *Compt. J.,* 1961, 4(2), 114–120.

Nisnevich, L. B. Perceptron-type models for recognition of continuous patterns. Foreign Develop. Mach. Transl. Infomat. Proc., No. 148 SPRS, 22484 (Dec. 1963). Washington, D. C.: Office Tech. Ser. Pp. 12–23.

Novikoff, A. B. J. Integral geometry as a tool in pattern perception. In *Bionics symposium,* Sept. 1960, PB 171258 (Dec. 1960). Washington, D. C.: Office Tech. Serv., 1960.

Palmieri, G., & Sanna, R. Automatic probabilistic programmer/analyzer for pattern recognition. *Methodos* **48**, 1960, 12.

Palmieri, G., & Wanke, E. A pattern recognition machine. *Kybernetik,* 1968, 4(3), 69–80.

Patrick, E. A., & Hancock, J. C. Non-supervised sequential classification and recognition of patterns. *IEEE Trans.,* 1966, **IT–12**, 362–372.

Pay, B. E. A display unit for computer generated patterns. *Quart. J. exp. Psychol.,* 1965, **17**, 79–83.

Perotto, P. G. A new method for automatic character recognition. *IEEE Trans.,* 1963, **EC–12**, 521–526.

Prather, R. C., & Uhr, L. M. Discovery and learning techniques for pattern recognition. *Proc. ACM 19th Nat. Conf., 1964.* New York: ACM, 1964.

Roberts, L. G. Pattern recognition with an adaptive network. *IRE 1960 Int. Conv. Rec.* Pp. 66–70.

Rosen, C. A., & Hall, D. J. A pattern recognition experiment with near optimum results. *IEEE Trans.,* 1966, **EC–15**, 666–667.

Rosenblatt, F. The perceptron: A probabilistic model for information storage and organization in the brain. *Psychol. Rev.,* 1958, **65**, 386–408.

Rosenblatt, F. Perceptron simulation experiments. *Proc. IRE,* 1960, **48**, 301–309.

Rosenblatt, F. Perceptual generalization over transformation groups. In M. C. Yovits & S. Cameron (Eds.), *Self-organizing systems.* New York: Pergamon Press, 1960. Pp. 63–100.

Rosenblatt, F. Comparison of a five-layer Perceptron with human visual performance. In L. Fein & A. B. Callahan (Eds.), *Natural automata and useful simulations.* Washington, D. C.: Spartan Books, 1966. Pp. 139–148.

Rosenfeld, A. Perceptrons as "figure" detectors. *IEEE Trans.,* 1965, **IT–11**, 304–305.

Saaty, T. L. A discrete search problem in pattern recognition. *IEEE Trans.,* 1966, **IT–12**, 69–70.

Sayre, K. M. *Recognition: a study in the philosophy of artificial intelligence.* Notre Dame, Indiana: Univ. of Notre Dame Press, 1965.

Schade, O. H. Optical and photoelectric analog of the eye. *J. Opt. Soc. Amer.,* 1956, **46**, 721–739.

Scudder, H. J. Probability of error of some adaptive pattern-recognition machines. *IEEE Trans.,* 1965, **IT–11**, 363–371.

Sebestyen, G. S. Categorization in pattern recognition. Unpublished doctoral dissertation, M.I.T., 1960.

Sebestyen, G. S. *Decision-making processes in pattern recognition.* New York: Macmillan, 1962.

Sebestyen, G. S. Pattern recognition by an adaptive process of sample set construction. *IRE Trans.,* 1962, **IT–8**, 582–591.

Selfridge, O. G. *Pattern recognition and learning.* Cambridge, Massachusetts: M.I.T. Lincoln Lab., 1955.

Selfridge, O. G. Pattern recognition and modern computers. *Proc. West. Joint Comp. Conf. 1955.* Pp. 91–93.

Selfridge, O. G. Pattern recognition and learning. In C. Cherry (Ed.), *Information theory.* London and Washington, D. C.: Butterworth, 1956. Pp. 345–353.

Selfridge, O. G. Pandemonium: A paradigm for learning. In *Mechanization of thought processes.* London: Her Majesty's Stationery Office, 1959. Pp. 513–526.

Selfridge, O. G., & Neisser, U. Pattern recognition by machines. *Sci. Amer.,* 1960, **203**(8), 60–68.

Sezaki, N., & Katagiri, H. Pattern recognition by follow method. *Proc. IEEE,* 1965, **53**, 510.

Sherman, H. A quasi-topological method for the recognition of line patterns. In *Information processing.* Paris: UNESCO, 1960. Pp. 232–238.

Shimbel, A. A logical program for the simulation of visual pattern recognition. In H. von Foerster & G. W. Zopf (Eds.), *Principles of self-organization.* New York: Pergamon Press, 1962. Pp. 521–526.

Sholl, D. A., & Uttley, A. M. Pattern discrimination and the visual cortex. *Nature,* 1953, 171, 387–388.

Singer, J. R. Electronic analog of the human recognition system. *J. Opt. Soc. Amer.,* 1961, 51, 61–69.

Singer, J. R. A self-organizing recognition system. *Proc. West. Joint Comp. Conf. 1961,* 19, 545–554.

Sneath, P. H. A. A method for curve seeking from scattered points. *Comput. J.,* 1966, 8, 383–391.

Specht, D. F. Generation of polynomial discriminant functions for pattern recognition. *IEEE Trans.,* 1967, EC–16, 308–319.

Specht, D. F. Vectorcardiographic diagnosis using the polynomial discriminant method of pattern recognition. *IEEE Trans.,* 1967, BME–14, 90–95.

Spinrad, R. J. Machine recognition of hand printing. *Infomat. Control.,* 1965, 8(2), 124–142.

Sprick, W., & Ganzhorn, K. An analogous method for pattern recognition by following the boundary. In *Information processing.* Paris: UNESCO, 1960. Pp. 238–244.

Stearns, S. D. Method for design of pattern recognition logic. *IRE Trans.,* 1960, EC–9, 48–53.

Steck, G. P. Stochastic model for the Browning-Bledsoe pattern recognition scheme. *IRE Trans.,* 1962, EC–11, 274–282.

Sternberg, S. Two operations in character recognition: Some evidence from reaction time experiments. *Percept. Psychophys.,* 1967, 2, 45–53.

Stevens, M. E. Abstract shape recognition by machine. *Proc. East. Joint Comp. Conf. 1961,* 332–351.

Sublette, I. H., & Tults, J. Character recognition by digital feature detection. *RCA Rev.,* 1962(3), 60–80.

Swerling, P. Statistical properties of the contours of random surfaces. *IRE Trans.,* 1962, IT–8, 315–320.

Taylor, W. K. Electrical simulation of nervous system functional activities. In C. Cherry (Ed.), *Information theory.* London and Washington, D. C.: Butterworth, 1956. P. 314.

Taylor, W. K. Automatic pattern recognition. In *Mechanization of thought processes.* London: Her Majesty's Stationery Office, 1959. Pp. 951–952.

Taylor, W. K. Pattern recognition by means of automatic analogue apparatus. *Proc. IRE,* 1959, 106(Pt. B), 198–204.

Teitelman, W. Real time recognition of hand-drawn characters. *Proc. AFIPS 1964 Fall Joint Comput. Conf.* Pp. 559–575.

Townsend, R. Geometry of automatic character recognition. *Electro-Technol.,* 1964, 73(5), 54–57.

Uhr, L. Machine perception of forms by means of assessment and recognition of gestalts. University of Michigan, Preprint No. 34, Oct. 1959.

Uhr, L. Intelligence in computers: The psychology of perception in people and in machines. *Behav. Sci.,* 1960, 5, 177–182.

Uhr, L. A possibly misleading conclusion as to the inferiority of one method for pattern recognition to a second method to which it is guaranteed to be superior. *IRE Trans.,* 1961, EC–10, 96–97.

Uhr, L. "Pattern recognition" computers as models for form perception. *Psychol. Bull.,* 1963, 60, 40–73.

Uhr, L. Pattern recognition. In A. Kent & O. E. Taulbee (Eds.), *Electronic information handling.* Washington, D. C.: Spartan Books, 1965. Pp. 51–72.

Uhr, L. (Ed.) *Pattern recognition.* New York: Wiley, 1966.

Uhr, L., & Vossler, C. Suggestions for self-adapting computer model of brain functions. *Behav. Sci.,* 1961, 6, 91–97.

Uhr, L., & Vossler, C. A pattern recognition program that generates, evaluates, and adjusts its own operators. In E. A. Feigenbaum & J. Feldman (Eds.), *Computers and thought.* New York: McGraw-Hill, 1963. Pp. 251–268.

Uhr, L., Vossler, & Uleman, J. Pattern recognition over distortion, by human subjects and by a computer simulation of a model for human form perception. *J. exp. Psychol.,* 1962, 63, 227–234.

Ullman, J. R. A consistency technique for pattern association. *IRE Trans.,* 1962, IT–8, 574–581.

Unger, S. H. A computer oriented toward spatial problems. *Proc. IRE,* 1958, 46, 1744–1750.

Unger, S. H. Pattern detection and recognition. *Proc. IRE,* 1959, 47, 1737–1752.

Uttley, A. M. Temporal and spatial patterns in a conditional probability machine. In C. E. Shannon & J. McCarthy (Eds.), *Automata studies.* Princeton, New Jersey: Princeton Univ. Press, 1956. Pp. 277–285.

Vossler, C., & Uhr, L. Computer simulation of a perceptual learning model for sensory pattern recognition, concept formation, and symbol transformation. Proc. IFIP, Munich, 1962. Amsterdam: North Holland Publ., 1962. Pp. 181–184.

Wada, H., Takahashi, S., Iijima, T., Okumuru, Y., & Imoto, K. An electronic reading machine. In *Information processing.* Paris: UNESCO, 1960. Pp. 227–232.

Wathen-Dunn, W. (Ed.), *Models for the perception of speech and visual forms.* Cambridge, Massachusetts: M.I.T. Press, 1967.

Weeks, R. W. Rotating raster character recognition system. *Commun. Electron.,* 1961, 56, 353–359.

White, B. W. Studies of perception. In H. Borko (Ed.), *Computer applications in the behavioral sciences.* Englewood Cliffs, New Jersey: Prentice–Hall, 1962. Pp. 280–307.

Widrow, B. Pattern recognition and adaptive control. *IEEE Trans.,* 1964, AI–83, 74, 269–277.

Wurtele, Z. S. A problem in pattern recognition. *SIAM J.,* 1965, 13(1), 60–67.

Young, D. A. Automatic character recognition. *Electron. Eng.,* 1960, 32, 2–10.

IV. GLOBAL THEORIES

A. Gestalt theory (see also Sections I,C,1,2, and 3; I,F; I,G; II,E; II,G,1; V,A,4a,b; V,A,7 and 8; VI,A,1c)

Beck, J. Effect of orientation and of shape similarity on perceptual grouping. *Percept. Psychophys.,* 1966, 1, 300–302.

Beck, J. Perceptual grouping produced by changes in orientation and shape. *Scinece,* 1966, 154, 538–540.

Beck, J. Perceptual grouping produced by line figures. *Percept. Psychophys.,* 1967, 2, 491–495.

Bell, R. A. An analysis of Gestalt principles of perceptual organization. Unpublished doctoral dissertation, Kansas State Univ., 1967. *Diss. Abstr.,* 1967, 28, 2153.

Bender, L. Gestalt principles in sidewalk drawings. *J. gen. Psychol.*, 1932, 41, 192–210.

Bender, L. Principles of Gestalt in copied form in mentally defective and schizophrenic persons. *Arch. Neurol. Psychiat.*, 1932, 28, 661–673.

Bobbitt, J. M. An experimental study of the phenomenon of closure as a threshold function. *J. exp. Psychol.*, 1942, 30, 273–294.

Buehler, K. *Die Gestaltwahrnehmungen.* Stuttgart: Spemann, 1913.

Campbell, I. G. A quantitative study of the effect which a visual whole has upon its membral parts. *Psychol. Forsch.*, 1937, 21, 290–310.

Clement, D. E. Uncertainty and latency of verbal naming responses as correlates of pattern goodness. *J. Verb. Learn. Verb. Behav.*, 1964, 3, 150–157.

Corbin, H. H. Perception of grouping in visual displays. In J. W. Wulfeck & J. H. Taylor (Eds.), *Form discrimination as related to military problems.* Washington, D. C.: Nat. Acad. Sci.-Nat. Res. Coun., 1957. Pp. 217–222.

Cowan, R. F., & Bliss, W. D. Resistance to distortion as a metric for pattern goodness. *Psychon. Sci.,* 1967, 9, 481–482.

Dinnerstein, D. Previous and concurrent visual experience as determinants of phenomenal shape. *Amer. J. Psychol.,* 1965, 78, 235–242.

Ehrenstein, W. Untersuchungen zur Bewegungs- und Gestaltwahrnehmung. *Arch. ges. Psychol.,* 1928, 61, 155–202.

Feinberg, N., & Koffka, K. Experimentelle Untersuchungen ueber die Wahrnehmung im Gabiet des blinded Flecks. *Psychol. Forsch.,* 1925, 7, 16 ff.

Fraisse, P. Recherches sur les lois de la perception des formes. *J. Psychol. norm. path.,* 1938, 35, 414–424.

Frank, H. Ueber die Beeinflussung von Nachbildern durch die Gestalteigenschaften der Projektionsflaeche. *Psychol. Forsch.,* 1923, 4, 33–41.

Fuchs, P. Experimentelle Untersuchungen zum Problem der Auffassung. *Arch. ges. Psychol.,* 1929, 73, 257–368.

Fuchs, W. Untersuchungen ueber das Sehen der Hemianopiker und Hemiamblyopiker. I. Verlagerungserscheinungen. *Z. Psychol.,* 1920, 84, 67–169.

Fuchs, W. Untersuchungen ueber das Sehen der Hemianopiker und Hemiamblyopiker. II. Die totalisierende Gestaltauffassung. *Z. Psychol.,* 1921, 86, 1–143.

Fuchs, W. Eine Pseudofovea bei Hemianopikern. *Psychol. Forsch.,* 1922, 1, 157–186.

Fuchs, W. Experimentelle Untersuchungen ueber das Hintereinandersehen auf derselben Sehrichtung. *Z. Psychol.,* 1923, 91, 145–235.

Gelb, A., & Granit, R. Farbenpsychologische Untersuchungen. I. Die Bedeutung von "Figur" und "Grund" fuer die Farbenschwelle. *Z. Psychol.,* 1923, 93, 83–118.

Giorgi, A. P., & Colaizzi, P. F. Simple geometric figures and the part-whole problem. *Percept. mot. Skills,* 1967, 25, 880.

Glueck, G. La buona forma matematica: contributo alla psicologia della forma. *Riv. Psicol. Norm. Pat.,* 1939, 35, 209–254.

Glueck, G. Psicopatologia della percezione della forma: principi della forma nei disegni copiati di malati mentali. *Arch. Psicol. Neurol. Psichiat.,* 1940, 1, 603–664.

Goldstein, A. G. Gestalt similarity principle, difference thresholds, and pattern discriminability. *Percept. Psychophys.,* 1967, 2, 377–382.

Granit, R. Bedeutung von Figur und Grund fuer bei unveraenderter Schwarz-Induktion bestimmte Helligkeitsschwellen. *Skand. Arch. Physiol.,* 1924, 45, 43–57.

Guillaume, P. La théorie de la forme. *J. Psychol.,* 1925, 22, 768–800.

Guillaume, P. L'appréhension des figures géométriques. *J. Psychol. norm. path.,* 1937, 34, 675–710.

Guillaume, P. *La psychologie de la forme.* Paris: Flammarion, 1937.

Gurwitch, A. Quelques aspects et quelques développements de la psychologie de la forme. *J. Psychol. norm. path.,* 1936, **33**, 413–471.

Hallett, W. N. A psychophysical study of visual Gestalten. *Amer. J. Psychol.,* 1933, **45**, 691–700.

Hartgenbusch, H. G. Beitraege zur Psychologie der Gestalt. XIV. Ueber die Messung von Wahrnehmungsbildern. *Psychol. Forsch.,* 1926, **8**, 28–75.

Helson, H. H. The psychology of Gestalt. *Amer. J. Psychol.,* 1925, **36**, 342–370, 494–526.

Helson, H. H. The fundamental propositions of Gestalt psychology. *Psychol. Rev.,* 1933, **40**, 13–32.

Henriquez, G. K. Ueber die Aenderungsempfindlichkeit fuer optische Gestalten. *Neue Psychol. Stud.,* 1937, **10**, 45–102.

Holmes, D. S. Search for "closure" in a visually perceived pattern. *Psychol. Bull.,* 1968, **70**, 296–312.

Hsiao, H. H. [Determinants in the formation of perceptual units. II.] *Monogr. Psychol. Educ., Nat. Cent. Univ.,* 1936, **3**, No. 2.

Hubbell, M. B. Naive subjects' attempts to produce 'good' configurations. *Psychol. Bull.,* 1938, **35**, 698–699.

Hubbell, M. B. Configurational properties considered "good" by naive subjects. *Amer. J. Psychol.,* 1940, **53**, 46–69.

Kainz, F. Gestaltgesetzlichkeit und Ornamententstehung. *Z. angew. Psychol.,* 1927, **28**, 267–327.

Ketzner, E. Subjective Kraefte figuraler Formung bei optischer Gestaltauffassung. *Arch. ges. Psychol.,* 1936, **96**, 277–310.

Klemm, O. Ueber die Aenderungsempfindlichkeit fuer optische Gestalten. *Ber. Kongr. Dtsch. Ges. Psychol., Tuebingen,* 1935, **14**, 297–298.

Koffka, K. Beitraege zur Psychologie der Gestalt- und Bewegungserlebnisse. *Z. Psychol.,* 1913, **67**, 353–358.

Koffka, K. Beitraege zur Psychologie der Gestalt- und Bewegungserlebnisse. III. Zur Grundlegung der Wahrnehmungspsychologie; Eine Auseinandersetzung mit V. Benussi. *Z. Psychol.,* 1915, **73**, 11–90.

Koffka, K. Perception: An introduction to the Gestalt-Theorie. *Psychol. Bull.,* 1922, **19**, 531–585.

Koffka, K. Beitraege zur Psychologie der Gestalt; Experimentelle Untersuchungen ueber das Entstehen und Vergehen von Gestalten. *Psychol. Forsch.,* 1923, **2**, 5–60.

Koffka, K. *Principles of Gestalt psychology.* New York: Harcourt, Brace, 1935. (Chapters III, IV, V, VI, VII.)

Koehler, W. *Die physischen Gestalten in Ruhe und im stationaeren Zustand.* Erlangen: Philosophische Akademie, 1920.

Koehler, W. Gestaltprobleme und Anfaenge einer Gestalttheorie. *Jahresb. ges. Physiol.,* 1922.

Koehler, W. The problem of form in perception. *Brit. J. Psychol.,* 1924, **14**, 262–268.

Koehler, W. *Gestalt psychology.* New York: Liveright, 1929. (Chapter V, VI.)

Koehler, W., & Held, R. The cortical correlate of pattern vision. *Science,* 1949, **110**, 414–419.

Kopfermann, H. Psychologische Untersuchungen ueber die Wirkung zweidimensionaler Darstellungen koerperlicher Gebilde. *Psychol. Forsch.,* 1930, **13**, 293–364.

Korte, W. Ueber die Gestaltauffassung im indirekten Sehen. *Z. Psychol.,* 1923, **93**, 17–82.

Lashley, K. S., Chow, K. L., & Semmes, J. An examination of the electrical field theory of cerebral integration. *Psychol. Rev.,* 1951, **58**, 123–136.

Lauenstein, O. Sukzessivvergleich von gebogenen Linien. *Psychol. Forsch.,* 1938, **22**, 343–371.

Lenk, E. Ueber die optische Auffassung geometrisch regelmaessiger Gestalten. *Neue Psychol. Stud.*, 1926, 1, 573–613.

Liebmann, S. Ueber das Verhalten farbiger Formen bei Helligkeitsgleichheit von Figur und Grund. *Psychol. Forsch.*, 1927, 9, 300–353.

Lindemann, E., & Koffka, K. Experimentelle Untersuchungen ueber das Entstehen und Vergehen von Gestalten. *Psychol. Forsch.*, 1922, 2, 5–60.

Linke, P. Das paradoxe Bewegungsphaenomen und die "neue" Wahrnehmungslehre. *Arch. ges. Psychol.*, 1915, 33, 261–265.

Luchins, A. S. An evaluation of some current criticisms of Gestalt psychological work on perception. *Psychol. Rev.*, 1951, 58, 69–95.

Metzger, W. Optische Untersuchungen am Ganzfeld. II. Zur Phaenomenologie des homogenen Ganzfelds. *Psychol. Forsch.*, 1930, 13, 6–29.

Michael, D. N. A cross-cultural investigation of closure. *J. abnorm. soc. Psychol.*, 1953, 48, 225–230.

Michotte, A., & De Clerk, J. Structures perceptives circulaires correspondant à des formes géométriques angulaires. *Année psychol.*, 1951, 50, 305–326.

Mooney, C. M. A factorial study of closure. *Can. J. Psychol.*, 1954, 8, 51–60.

Moore, M. G. Gestalt vs. experience. *Amer. J. Psychol.*, 1930, 42, 453–455.

Nozawa, S., & Iritani, T. A review of Gestalt studies in Japan: Development of studies on form perception. *Psychologia*, 1963, 6(1–2), 22–45.

Petermann, B. *The gestalt theory and the problem of configuration.* New York: Harcourt, Brace, 1932. (Pt. 2, Chapters I, II.)

Postman, L., & Bruner, J. S. Hypothesis and the principle of closure: the effect of frequency and recency. *J. Psychol.*, 1952, 33, 113–125.

Prentice, W. C. H. The systematic psychology of Wolfgang Koehler. In S. Koch (Ed.), *Psychology: A study of a science*, Vol. I. New York: McGraw-Hill, 1959. Pp. 427–455.

Rashevsky, N. Physico-mathematical aspects of the Gestalt problem. *Phil. Sci.*, 1934, 1, 409–419.

Rignano, E. La teoria della forma della nuova scuola psicologica inglese. La "Gestalt." I, II, III. *Scientia*, 1927, 21, 145–158, 215–228, 280–290.

Rignano, E. The psychological theory of form. *Psychol. Rev.*, 1928, 35, 118–135.

Rignano, E. La théorie psychologique de la forme. *Rev. Phil.*, 1928, 53, 33–49.

Rothschild, H. Ueber den Einfluss der Gestalt auf das negative Nachbild ruhender visueller Figuren. *Arch. Ophthal.*, 1923, 112, 1–128.

Rubin, E. Die Psychophysic der Geradtheit. *Z. Psychol.*, 1922, 90, 67ff.

Schoenfeld, N. The metaphor of 'closure.' *Psychol. Rev.*, 1941, 48, 487–497.

Sickles, W. R. Psycho-geometry of order. *Psychol. Rev.*, 1944, 51, 189–199.

Street, R. F. The Gestalt completion test and mental disorder. *J. abnorm. soc. Psychol.*, 1934, 9, 38–52.

Tresselt, M. E., & Simberg, A. L. A quantitative experimental investigation of the phenomenon of closure. *J. gen. Psychol.*, 1953, 48, 21–27.

Warrington, E. K. The effect of stimulus configuration on the incidence of the completion phenomenon. *Brit. J. Psychol.*, 1965, 56, 447–454.

Werner, H. Rhythmik, eine mehrwertige Gestaltverkettung. *Z. Psychol.*, 1919, 82, 189–218.

Wertheimer, M. Experimentelle Studien ueber das Sehen von Bewegungen. *Z. Psychol.*, 1912, 61, 161–265.

Wertheimer, M. Untersuchung zur Lehre von der Gestalt. I. *Psychol. Forsch.*, 1922, 1, 47–58.

Wertheimer, M. Untersuchungen zur Lehre von der Gestalt. II. *Psychol. Forsch.*, 1923, 4, 301–350.

Wertheimer, M. Ueber Gestalttheorie. *Symposion*, 1925, 1, 39–60.

Wertheimer, M. *Ueber Gestalttheorie.* Erlangen: Philosophische Akademie, 1925.
Yagi, B. [The influence of form upon the Liebmann effect.] *Jap. J. Psychol.,* 1938, **13,** 213–235.
Zigler, M. J. An experimental study of visual form. *Amer. J. Psychol.,* 1920, **31,** 273–300.
Zuckerman, C. B., & Rock, I. A reappraisal of the role of past experience and innate organizing processes in visual perception. *Psychol. Bull.,* 1957, **54,** 269–296.

B. D. O. Hebb

Ganz, L., & Wilson, P. D. Innate generalization of a form discrimination without contouring eye movements. *J. comp. physiol. Psychol.,* 1967, **63,** 258–269.
Hazen, R. C. Intraocular transfer of pattern perception. Unpublished doctoral dissertation, Florida State Univ., 1961. *Diss. Abstr.,* 1962, **23,** 721.
Hebb, D. O. *The organization of behavior.* New York: Wiley, 1949. (Chapters 1, 2, 3, 4, 5.)
Hebb, D. O. A neuropsychological theory. In S. Koch (Ed.) *Psychology: A study of a science,* Vol. I. New York: McGraw-Hill, 1959. Pp. 622–643.
McFarland, J. H. The effect of different sequences of part presentation on perception of a form's parts as simultaneous. *Proc. 73rd Annu. Conv. APA,* 1965, 43–44.
McFarland, J. H. Sequential part presentation: A method of studying visual form perception. *Brit. J. Psychol.,* 1965, **56,** 439–446.
McFarland, J. H. Some evidence bearing on operations of "analysis" and "integration" in visual form perception by humans. In W. Wathen-Dunn (Ed.), *Models for the perception of speech and visual forms.* Cambridge, Massachusetts: M.I.T. Press, 1967. Pp. 212–219.
Parks, A. Post-retinal visual storage. *Amer. J. Psychol.,* 1965, **78,** 145–147.
Shontz, W. D. Factors affecting the processing of sequentially presented form parts. Unpublished doctoral dissertation, Iowa State Univ., 1968. *Diss. Abstr.,* 1968, **28**(9–B), 3907.

C. J.J. Gibson

Gibson, J. J. Adaptation with negative aftereffect. *Psychol. Rev.,* 1937, **44,** 222–244.
Gibson, J. J. The perception of visual surfaces. *Amer. J. Psychol.,* 1950, **63,** 367–384.
Gibson, J. J. *The perception of the visual world.* Boston, Massachusetts: Houghton, 1950.
Gibson, J. J. What is form? *Psychol. Rev.,* 1951, **58,** 403–412.
Gibson, J. J. Optical motions and transformations as stimuli for visual perception. *Psychol. Rev.,* 1957, **64,** 288–295.
Gibson, J. J. *The senses considered as perceptual systems.* Boston, Massachusetts: Houghton, 1966. (Pp. 246–249, 312–313.)

V. FORM PERCEPTION EXPERIMENTS

A. Human subjects

1. Methodology

Bechtoldt, H. P., & Mager, R. F. Stimulus presentation devices for use in studies of discrimination ability. *USAF Human Resources Res. Cent. Res. Bull.,* 1953, No. 53–23.
Behar, I. A new tachistoscope for animals and man. *Amer. J. Psychol.,* 1960, **73,** 305–306.

Ferree, C. E., & Rand, G. A multiple-exposure tachistoscope. *J. exp. Psychol.*, 1937, **21**, 240–259.

Geratewohl, S. J. Target appearance and identification thresholds on the radar PPI using various electrical parameters, filters, and sweep characteristics. In J. W. Wulfeck & J. H. Taylor (Eds.), *Form discrimination as related to military problems.* Washington, D. C.: Nat. Acad. Sci.-Nat. Res. Coun., 1957. Pp. 192–207.

Goldiamond, I. A multi-purpose perceptual device. *J. Exp. Anal. Behav.*, 1963, **6**, 291–292.

Hanson, J. A. Two optical systems for controlling chromatic and achromatic contrast in forms research. In J. W. Wulfeck & J. H. Taylor (Eds.), *Form discrimination as related to military problems.* Washington, D. C.: Nat. Acad. Sci.-Nat. Res. Coun., 1957. Pp. 98–101.

Haralson, J. V. An apparatus for varying size of rectangles continuously and proportionally. *Percept. mot. Skills*, 1965, **21**, 313–314.

Horowitz, M. Efficient use of a picture correlator. *J. Opt. Soc. Amer.*, 1957, **47**, 327.

Humphrey, G., Dawe, P. G. M., & Mandell, B. New high-speed electronic tachistoscope. *Nature*, 1955, **176**, 231–234.

Kretzmer, E. R. Statistics of television signals. *Bell Syst. Tech. J.*, 1952, **31**, 751–763.

Pay, B. E. A display unit for computer generated patterns. *Quart. J. exp. Psychol.*, 1965, **17**, 79–83.

Ponzo, M. Demonstration einer Einrichtung fuer die Analyse von Erkennungs- und Benennungszeiten. In F. Schumann (Ed.), *Ber. VI Kongr. exp. Psychol*, Leipzig: Barth, 1914. P. 58.

Thomas, H. A flexible apparatus for presenting pairs of visual stimuli to children. *J. Exp. Anal. Behav.*, 1966, **9**, 119–120.

2. *Stimulus variables (see also Section III,B)*

Alexander, C., & Carey, S. Subsymmetries. *Percept. Psychophys.*, 1968, **4**, 73–77.

Anderson, N. S. Pattern recognition: A probability approach. In J. W. Wulfeck & J. H. Taylor (Eds.), *Form discrimination as related to military problems.* Washington, D. C.: Nat. Acad. Sci.-Nat. Res. Coun., 1957. Pp. 45–49.

Arnoult, M. D. Toward a psychophysics of form. In J. W. Wulfeck & J. H. Taylor (Eds.), *Form discrimination as related to military problems.* Washington, D. C.: Nat. Acad. Sci.-Nat. Res. Coun., 1957. Pp. 38–42.

Attneave, F. The relative importance of parts of a contour. US Human Resources Res. Cent. Res. Note P&MS No. 51–8, 1951.

Attneave, F. The verbal description of shapes. Staff Res. Memo, Skill Components Res. Lab., AFPTRC, Lackland AFB, April 21, 1954.

Attneave, F. Perception and related areas. In S. Koch (Ed.), *Psychology: A study of a science,* Vol. IV. New York: McGraw-Hill, 1962. Pp. 619–659.

Attneave, F., & Arnoult, M. D. The quantitative study of shape and pattern perception. *Psychol. Bull.*, 1956, **53**, 452–471.

Baughman, E. E. A comparative analysis of Rorschach forms with altered stimulus characteristics. *J. proj. Tech.*, 1954, **18**, 151–164.

Baughman, E. E. The role of the stimulus in Rorschach response. *Psychol. Bull.*, 1958, **55**, 121–147.

Blum, H. A transformation for extracting new descriptors of shape. In W. Wathen-Dunn (Ed.), *Models for the perception of speech and visual forms.* Cambridge, Massachusetts: M.I.T. Press, 1967. Pp. 362–380.

Brown, D. R., & Michels, K. M. Quantification procedures, stimulus domains, and discrimination difficulty. *Percept. mot. Skills*, 1966, **22**, 421–422.

Brown, D. R., & Owen, D. H. The metrics of visual form: Methodological dyspepsia. *Psychol. Bull.,* 1967, **68**, 243–259.

Brown, L. T. Quantitative description of visual pattern: Some methodological suggestions. *Percept. mot. Skills,* 1964, **19**, 771–774.

Chou, S. K. Reading and legibility of Chinese characters: IV. An analysis of judgments of position of Chinese characters by American subjects. *J. exp. Psychol.,* 1935, **18**, 318–347.

Crook, M. Facsimile-generated analogues for instrumental form displays. In J. W. Wulfeck & J. H. Taylor (Eds.), *Form discrimination as related to military problems.* Washington, D. C.: Nat. Acad. Sci.-Nat. Res. Coun., 1957. Pp. 85–98.

Dearborn, G. V. Blots of ink in experimental psychology. *Psychol. Rev.,* 1897, **4**, 390–391.

Debons, A. Target identification in radar presentation. In J. W. Wulfeck & J. H. Taylor (Eds.), *Form discrimination as related to military problems.* Washington, D. C.: Nat. Acad. Sci.-Nat. Res. Coun., 1957. Pp. 141–144.

Duke, J. A. Noise methods in pattern perception. *Percept. Psychophys.,* 1967, **2**, 338–340.

Edmonston, N. E., & Griffith, R. M. Rorschach content and ink blot structure. *J. Proj. Technol.,* 1958, **22**, 394–397.

Evans, S. H. Redundancy as a variable in pattern perception. *Psychol. Bull.,* 1967, **67**, 104–113.

Evans, S. H., Hoffman, A. A., & Arnoult, M. D. Vargus 6D: A simple system for producing "noisy" patterns (for IBM 1620 and IBM 1401). *Behav. Sci.,* 1967, **12**, 268.

Freeman, H. On the encoding of arbitrary geometric configurations. *IRE Trans.,* 1961, EC–10, 260–268.

Freeman, H. Techniques for the digital-computer analysis of chain-encoded arbitrary plane curves. *Proc. Nat. Electron. Conf.,* 1961, **17**, 421–432.

Freeman, H. On the digital computer classification of geometric line patterns. *Proc. Nat. Electron. Conf.,* 1962, **18**, 312–324.

Freeman, H. On the classification of line drawing data. In W. Wathen-Dunn (Ed.), *Models for the perception of speech and visual forms.* Cambridge, Massachusetts: M.I.T. Press, 1967. Pp. 408–412.

Fry, G. A. Blur as a factor in form discrimination. In J. W. Wulfeck & J. H. Taylor (Eds.), *Form discrimination as related to military problems.* Washington, D. C.: Nat. Acad. Sci.-Nat. Res. Coun., 1957. Pp. 75–82.

Garner, W. R., & Clement, D. E. Goodness of pattern and pattern uncertainty. *J. Verb. Lrng. Verb. Behav.,* 1963, **2**, 446–452.

Garner, W. R., & Lee, W. An analysis of redundancy in perceptual discrimination. *Percept. mot. Skills,* 1962, **15**, 367–388.

Goldstein, M. A comment concerning stimuli in discrimination learning experiments. *Percept. mot. Skills,* 1966, **22**, 533–534.

Green, B. F., Jr. The use of high-speed digital computers in studies of form perception. In J. W. Wulfeck & J. H. Taylor (Eds.), *Form discrimination as related to military problems.* Washington, D. C.: Nat. Acad. Sci.-Nat. Res. Coun., 1957. Pp. 65–75.

Handel, S., & Garner, W. R. The structure of visual pattern associates and pattern goodness. *Percept. Psychophys.,* 1966, **1**, 33–38.

Hochberg, J., & Silverstein, A. A quantitative index of stimulus similarity proximity vs. differences in brightness. *Amer. J. Psychol.,* 1956, **69**, 456–458.

Hu, M.-K. Visual pattern recognition by moment invariants. *IRE Trans.,* 1962, IT–8, 179–187.

Knoll, R. L., & Stenson, H. H. A computer program to generate and measure random forms. *Percept. Psychophys.,* 1968, **3**, 311–316.

Kovaszany, L. S. G., & Joseph, H. M. Processing of two-dimensional patterns by scanning techniques. *Science,* 1953, 118, 475–477.

LaBerge, D. L. A method of generating and scaling random visual forms of graded similarity. Unpublished doctoral dissertation, Stanford Univ., 1955. *Diss. Abstr.,* 1956, 16, 164.

LaBerge, D. L., & Lawrence, D. H. Two methods for generating matrices of forms of graded similarity. *J. Psychol.,* 1957, 43, 77–100.

Michels, K. M., & Zusne, L. Metrics of visual form. *Psychol. Bull.,* 1965, 63, 74–86.

Polidora, V. J. Reply to Zusne. *Percept. Psychophys.,* 1967, 2, 87–88.

Somnapan, R. Development of sets of mutually equally discriminable visual stimuli. Unpublished doctoral dissertation, Univ. of Iowa, 1962. *Diss. Abstr.,* 1963, 23, 2997.

Somnapan, R. Development of sets of mutually equally discriminable random shapes. *J. exp. Psychol.,* 1968, 76, 303–308.

Staniland, A. C. Redundancy as an experimental variable. *Quart. J. exp. Psychol.,* 1960, 12, 149–161.

Staniland, A. C. *Patterns of redundancy.* London and New York: Cambridge Univ. Press, 1966.

Thurmond, J. B., & Alluisi, E. A. An extension of the information-deductive analysis of form. *Psychon. Sci.,* 1967, 7, 157–158.

Vanderplas, J. M., Sanderson, W. A., & Vanderplas, J. N. Statistical and associational characteristics of 1100 random shapes. *Percept. mot. Skills,* 1965, 21, 414.

Vurpillot, E. Vers une psychophysique de la forme. *Année Psychol.,* 1959, 59, 117–142.

Webster, R. B. Stimulus characteristics and effects of fill, distortion, and noise on pattern perception. *Percept. mot. Skills,* 1966, 23, 19–33.

Weisz, A. The use of facsimile equipment and controlled visual noise in forms research. In J. W. Wulfeck & J. H. Taylor (Eds.), *Form discrimination as related to military problems.* Washington, D. C.: Nat. Acad. Sci.-Nat. Res. Coun., 1957. Pp. 83–84.

Zusne, L. Stimulus correlates of visual pattern discrimination and the problem of grain. *Percept. Psychophys.,* 1967, 2, 86–87.

3. Response and task variables

Arnoult, M. D. Accuracy of shape discrimination as a function of the range of exposure intervals. US Human Resources Res. Cent. Res. Bull. 51–32, 1951.

Arnoult, M. D., & Lewis, J. T. Form discrimination during brief exposures. *Percept. mot. Skills,* 1960, 11, 259–260.

Blackwell, H. R. General comments on the psychophysical study of form discrimination. In J. W. Wulfeck & J. H. Taylor (Eds.), *Form discrimination as related to military problems.* Washington, D. C.: Nat. Acad. Sci.-Nat. Res. Coun., 1957. Pp. 15–17.

Brown, J. H. Frequency of occurrence and identification of ambiguous perceptual forms. *Percept. mot. Skills,* 1964, 19, 119–129.

Eriksen, C. W., & Wechsler, H. Some effects of experimentally induced anxiety upon discrimination behavior. *J. abnorm. soc. Psychol.,* 1955, 51, 458–463.

Gerjuoy, I. R., & Winters, J. J., Jr. Lateral preference for identical geometric forms: II. Retardates. *Percept. Psychophys.,* 1966, 1, 104–106.

Morris, A. Form discrimination in psychophysics. In J. W. Wulfeck & J. H. Taylor (Eds.), *Form discrimination as related to military problems.* Washington, D. C.: Nat. Acad. Sci.-Nat. Res. Coun., 1957. Pp. 12–15.

Winters, J. J., Jr., & Gerjuoy, I. R. Lateral preference for identical geometric forms: I. Normals. *Percept. Psychophys.,* 1966, 1, 101–103.

a. Form and eye movements

Battro, A. M., & Fraisse, P. Y a-t-il une relation entre la capacité d'apprehénsion visuelle et les mouvements des yeux? *Année psychol.,* 1961, 61, 313–324.

Brandt, H. F. Study of ocular movements in the bi-dimensional plane and their psychological implications. Unpublished doctoral dissertation, Univ. of Iowa, 1937.

Brandt, H. F. Ocular patterns and their psychological implications. *Amer. J. Psychol.,* 1940, 53, 260–268.

Brandt, H. F. *The psychology of seeing.* New York: Philosophical Library, 1945.

Bryden, M. P. The role of post-exposural eye movements in tachistoscopic perception. *Can. J. Psychol.,* 1961, 15, 220–225.

Buswell, G. T. *How people look at pictures.* Chicago, Illinois: Univ. of Chicago Press. 1935.

Carlson, V. R. Eye movements and perceptual adaptation to curvature. *Scand. J. Psychol.,* 1964, 5, 262–270.

Chamber, E. G. Mouvements oculaires et perception visuelle. *Bull. Étud. Rech. Psychol.,* 1962, 11, 343–354.

Granovskaya, R. M., & Ganzen, V. A. Oroli motornogo zvena zritel'noĭ sistemy pri opoznaniĭ ob"ekta po vneshnemu konturu. *Voprosy Psikhol.,* 1965, 11(1), 66–82.

Grunin, R., & Mostofsky, D. I. Eye movement: A bibliographic survey. *Percept. mot. Skills,* 1968, 26, 623–639.

Harsh, C. M., & Craig, E. *Exposure time and pattern complexity as factors affecting form discrimination.* San Diego, California: USN Electronics Lab., 1956.

Hayes, W. N. Shape recognition as a function of viewing time, eye movements, and orientation of the shape. Unpublished doctoral dissertation, Princeton Univ., 1961. *Diss. Abstr.,* 1962, 22, 2474.

Judd, C. H. Movement and consciousness. *Psychol. Monogr.,* 1905, No. 29.

Langford, R. C. Ocular behavior and the principle of pictorial balance. *J. gen. Psychol.,* 1936, 15, 292–325.

Mackworth, N. H., & Morandi, A. J. The gaze selects informative details within pictures. *Percept. Psychophys.,* 1967, 2, 547–552.

Mooney, C. M. Closure with negative afterimages under flickering light. *Can. J. Psychol.,* 1956, 10, 191–199.

Mooney, C. M. Closure as affected by configural clarity and contextual consistency. *Can. J. Psychol.,* 1957, 11, 80–88.

Mooney, C. M. Closure as affected by viewing time and multiple visual fixation. *Can. J. Psychol.,* 1957, 11, 21–28.

Mooney, C. M. Recognition of novel visual configurations with and without eye movements. *J. exp. Psychol.,* 1958, 56, 133–138.

Mooney, C. M. Recognition of symmetrical and non-symmetrical ink blots with and without eye movements. *Can. J. Psychol.,* 1959, 13, 11–19.

Mooney, C. M. Recognition of ambiguous and unambiguous visual configurations with short and longer exposures. *Brit. J. Psychol.,* 1960, 51, 119–125.

Sakano, N. The role of eye movements in the various forms of perception. *Psychologia,* 1963, 6, 215–227.

Sanders, A. F. (Ed.) *Attention and performance.* Amsterdam: North Holland Publ., 1967. (Pp. 335–370.)

Scott, D. M. *An annotated bibliography of research on eye movements published during the period 1932–1961.* Canada Dept. Nat. Defence, Defence Res. Board, 1962.

Stratton, G. M. Eye movements and the aesthetics of visual form. *Phil. Stud.,* 1902, 20, 336–359.

Stratton, G. M. Symmetry, linear illusions, and the movements of the eye. *Psychol. Rev.,* 13, 82–96.

Thomas, E. L. Eye movements and fixations during initial viewing of Rorschach cards. *J. Proj. Tech. Pers. Assess.,* 1963, 27, 345–353.

Woodworth, R. S., & Schlosberg, H. *Experimental psychology.* New York: Holt, 1954. (Chapter 17.)

Yarbus, A. L. Zapisi dvizheniǐ glaza v protsesse chteniya i rassmatrivaniya izobrazheniǐ na ploskosti. *In Sbornik posvyashchennyǐ pamyati akad. P. P. Lazareva.* Moscow: Izdatel'stvo AN SSSR, 1956.

Yarbus, A. L. Dvizheniya glaz pri rassmatrivaniya slozhnykh ob"ektov. *Biofizika,* 1961, 6(2), 207–212.

Yarbus, A. L. *Eye movements and vision.* New York: Plenum Press, 1967.

Zinchenko, V. P. Dvizheniya glaz i formirovanie obraza. *Voprosy Psikhol.,* 1958, 4(5), 63–76.

Zusne, L., & Michels, K. M. Nonrepresentational shapes and eye movements. *Percept. mot. Skills,* 1964, 18, 11–20.

4. Detection

a. Light thresholds and form

Bevan, W., Jr. The influence of figural aftereffects upon visual intensity threshold. *J. gen. Psychol.,* 1951, 45, 189–207.

Blackwell, H. R. A literature survey of the effects of target size and shape upon visual detection. *J. Opt. Soc. Amer.,* 1957, 47, 114. (Abstract)

Blackwell, H. R. Neural theories of simple visual discriminations. *J. Opt. Soc. Amer.,* 1963, 53, 129–160.

Blackwell, H. R., & Smith, S. W. Report of Project MICHIGAN, the effects of target size and shape on visual detection: II. Continuous foveal targets at zero background luminance. Rep. No. 2144-334-T, 1959.

Brown, R. H., & Niven, J. I. Relation between the foveal intensity threshold and length of an illuminated slit. *J. exp. Psychol.,* 1944, 34, 464–476.

Craik, K. J. W., & Zangwill, O. L. Observations relating to the threshold of a small figure within the contour of a closed-line figure. *Brit. J. Psychol.,* 1939, 30, 139–149.

Fry, G. A. The relation of the length of a border to its visibility. *J. Opt. Soc. Amer.,* 1946, 36, 713. (Abstract)

Fry, G. A. The relation of the configuration of a brightness contrast border to its visibility. *J. Opt. Soc. Amer.,* 1947, 37, 166–175.

Graham, C. H., & Bartlett, N. R. The relation of size of stimulus and intensity in the human eye: II. Intensity thresholds for red and violet light. *J. exp. Psychol.,* 1939, 24, 574–587.

Graham, C. H., Brown, R. H., & Mote, F. A. The relation of size of stimulus and intensity in the human eye. I. Intensity thresholds for white light. *J. exp. Psychol.,* 1939, 24, 555–573.

Graham, C. H., & Margaria, R. Area and the intensity-time relation in the peripheral retina. *Amer. J. Physiol.,* 1935, 113, 299–305.

Hanes, R. M. Some effects of shape on apparent brightness. *J. exp. Psychol.,* 1950, 40, 650–654.

Kincaid, W. M., Blackwell, H. R., & Kristofferson, A. B. Neural formulation of the effects of target size and shape upon visual detection. *J. Opt. Soc. Amer.,* 1960, 50, 141–148.

Kristofferson, A. B. Foveal intensity discrimination as a function of area and shape. Unpublished doctoral dissertation, Univ. of Michigan, 1954.

Kristofferson, A. B. Visual detection as influenced by target form. In J. W. Wulfeck & J. H. Taylor (Eds.), *Form discrimination as related to military problems.* Washington, D. C.: Nat. Acad. Sci.-Nat. Res. Coun., 1957. Pp. 109–127.

Kristofferson, A. B., & Blackwell, H. R. Effects of target size and shape on visual detection: I. Continuous foveal targets at moderate background luminance. *J. Opt. Soc. Amer.,* 1957, **47**, 114. (Abstract)

Lamar, E. S., Hecht, S., Shlaer, S., & Hendley, C. D. Size, shape, and contrast in detection of targets by daylight vision. I. Data and analytical description. *J. Opt. Soc. Amer.,* 1947, **37**, 531–545.

Lamar, E. S., Hecht, S., Hendley, C. D., & Shlaer, S. Size, shape, and contrast in detection of targets by daylight vision. II. Frequency of seeing and the quantum theory of cone vision. *J. Opt. Soc. Amer.,* 1948, **38**, 741–755.

Machman, M. The influence of size and shape on the visual threshold of the detectability of targets. Boston U., Optical Res. Lab., Tech. Note 109, 1953.

Machman, M. The influence of size and shape on the discrimination of visual intensity. *Amer. J. Psychol.,* 1957, **70**, 211–218.

Naruse, G. [The influence of form upon the visual-perception-threshold.] *Jap. J. Psychol.,* 1951, **21**(3/4), 26–35.

Smith, S. W., & Blackwell, H. R. Effects of target size and shape on visual detection: II. Continuous foveal targets at zero background luminance. *J. Opt. Soc. Amer.,* 1957, **47**, 114. (Abstract)

Tanaka, F. [The effect of the figure on the light stimulus threshold.] *Jap. J. Psychol.,* 1956, **27**, 55–57.

b. Form at threshold

Andresen, H. Ueber die Auffassung diffus optischer Eindruecke; ein Beitrag zur Bedingungserforschung der Leistungsvollzuege beim Rorschachtest. *Z. Psychol.,* 1941, **150**, 6–91.

Baranski, L. J. Temporal characteristics of dynamic contour perception. Unpublished doctoral dissertation, Princeton Univ., 1960. *Diss. Abstr.,* 1960, **20**, 4432.

Berger, C., & Buchthal, F. Formwahrnehmung und Funktion der Fovea. *Skand. Arch. Physiol.,* 1938, **79**, 15–26.

Bridgen, R. L. A tachistoscopic study of the differentiation of perception. *Psychol. Monogr.,* 1933, **44**, (Whole No. 197), 153–166.

Butzmann, K. Aktualgenese im indirekten Sehen. *Arch. ges. Psychol.,* 1940, **106**, 137–193.

Carl, H. Versuche ueber tachistoskopisches Bilderkennen. *Z. Psychol.,* 1933, **129**, 1–42.

Day, R. H. Application of the statistical theory to form perception. *Psychol. Rev.,* 1956, **63**, 139–148.

Douglas, A. G. A tachistoscopic study of the order of emergence in the process of perception. *Psychol. Monogr.,* 1947, **61**(6).

Drury, M. B. Progressive changes in non-foveal perception of line patterns. *Amer. J. Psychol.,* 1933, **45**, 628–646.

Dun, F. T. Aktualgenetische Untersuchung des Auffassungsvorganges chinesischer Schriftzeichen. *Arch. ges. Psychol.,* 1939, **104**, 131–174.

Flavell, J. H., & Draguns, J. A microgenetic approach to the perception and thought. *Psychol. Bull.,* 1957, **54**, 197–217.

Freeman, G. L. An experimental study of the perception of objects. *J. exp. Psychol.,* 1929, **12**, 340–358.

Galli, A. La percezione della forma nella visione periferica. *Arch. Ital. Psicol.*, 1931, 9, 31–60.

Galli, A. La percezione della forma nella visione periferica. *Pubbl. Univ. Cat. S. Cuore*, 1931, 6, 1–27.

Galli, A. Percezione totalizzatrice della forma attraverso alla fovea centrale nella luce crepuscolare. *Arch. Ital. Psicol.*, 1934, 12, 137–240.

Gemelli, A. Ueber das Entstehen von Gestalten. Beitrag zur Phaenomenologie der Wahrnehmung. *Arch. ges. Psychol.*, 1928, 65, 207–268.

Gulick, W. L. Monocular contour perception under the influence of prior stimulation of the contralateral eye. *Psychol. Rec.*, 1960, 10, 123–130.

Hayami, H. [The changes of the figure perception under the gradual increase of the illumination.] *Jap. J. Psychol.*, 1935, 10, 701–725.

Hempstead, L. The perception of visual form. *Amer. J. Psychol.*, 1901, 12, 185–192.

Johannes, T. Der Einfluss der Gestaltbildung auf das Behalten. *Arch. ges. Psychol.*, 1932, 85, 411–457.

Johannes, T. Der Einfluss der Gestaltbildung auf das Behalten. 2. Teil. *Arch. ges. Psychol.*, 1939, 104, 74–130.

Mantell, U. Aktualgenetische Untersuchungen an Situationsdarstellung. *Neue Psychol. Stud.*, 1936, 13, 1–96.

Moore, T. V. The process of abstraction. *Univ. Cal. Publ. Psychol.*, 1910, 1, 73–197.

Pikler, J. Grund und Figur bei schwacher Beleuchtung. *Z. Psychol.*, 1928, 106, 316–326.

Rogers, A. S. An analytical study of visual perception. *Amer. J. Psychol.*, 1917, 28, 521–538.

Sander, F. Experimentelle Ergebnisse der Gestaltpsychologie. In E. Becher (Ed.), *Ber. 10. Kongr. exp. Psychol.* Jena: Fischer, 1928. Pp. 23–88.

Sander, F. Structures, totality of experience, and gestalt. In C. Murchison (Ed.), *Psychologies of 1930.* Worcester, Massachusetts: Clark Univ. Press, 1930. Pp. 188–204.

Smith, W. M., & Gulick, W. L. Visual contour and movement perception. *Science*, 1956, 124, 316–317.

Smith, W. M., & Gulick, W. L. Dynamic contour perception. *J. exp. Psychol.*, 1957, 53, 145–152.

Smith, W. M., & Gulick, W. L. A statistical theory of dynamic contour perception. *Psychol. Rev.*, 1962, 69, 91–108.

Sommer, W. Zerfall optischer Gestalten, Erlebnisformen, und Strukturzusammenhaenge. *Neue Psychol. Stud.*, 1937, 10, 1–66.

Sperling. G. The information available in brief visual presentations. *Psychol. Monogr.*, 1960, 74(11).

Tanaka, Z. [The perception of figures based upon the exposure time.] *Jap. J. Psychol.*, 1939, 14, 71–88.

Tomoda, Z. [The perception of figures based upon form and size.] *Jap. J. Psychol.*, 1937, 12, 433–450.

Tomoda, Z. [The perception of figures based upon form and size.] *Rep. 6th Congr. Jap. Psychol. Ass.*, 1938, 235–239.

Undeutsch, U. Die Aktualgenese in ihrer allgemein-psychologischen und ihrer charakterologischen Bedeutung. *Scientia*, 1942, 72, 34–42, 95–98.

Wever, E. G. Figure and ground in the visual perception of form. *Amer. J. Psychol.*, 1927, 38, 194–226.

Wohlfahrt, E. Der Auffassungsvorgang an kleinen Gestalten. Ein Beitrag zur Psychologie des Vorgestalterlebnisses. *Neue Psychol. Stud.*, 1932, 4, 347–414.

Zigler, M. J., Cook, B., Miller, D., & Wemple, L. The perception of form in peripheral vision. *Amer. J. Psychol.*, 1930, 42, 246–259.

5. Discrimination

Adams, O. S., Fitts, P. M., Rappaport, M., & Weinstein, M. Relations among some measures of pattern discriminability. *J. exp. Psychol.*, 1954, 48, 81–88.

Alluisi, E. A., & Hall, T. J. Effects of a transphenomenal parameter on the visual perception of form. *Psychon. Sci.*, 1965, 3, 543–544.

Amano, T. [On distance between two objects in simultaneous comparison.] *Rep. 6th Congr. Jap. Psychol. Ass.*, 1938, 20–33.

Amano, T., & Shiegeno, M. Preliminary study on the perception of visual size. *Acta Psychol., Keijo*, 1933, 2, 1–12.

Anastasi, A. The estimation of areas. *J. gen. Psychol.*, 1936, 14, 201–225.

Arnoult, M. D. Measures of shape discrimination performance in a study of the effects of angular orientation of the stimulus. US Human Resources Res. Cent. Res. Note P&MS 51–10, November, 1951.

Arnoult, M. D. Shape discrimination as a function of the angular orientation of the stimuli. *J. exp. Psychol.*, 1954, 47, 323–328.

Arnoult, M., Gagne, R. M., & Vanderplas, J. M. A comparison of four measures of visual discrimination of shapes. US Human Resources Res. Cent. Res. Bull. No. 51–23, 1951.

Arnoult, M. D., & Price, C. W. Pattern matching in the presence of visual noise. *J. exp. Psychol.*, 1961, 62, 372–376.

Augenstine, L., Blank, A. A., Quastler, H., & Wayner, M. Human performance in information transmission. Part IV. Flash recognition of familiar displays. Control Syst. Lab., Univ. of Illinois, Report No. R–69, 1956.

Baker, E. J., & Alluisi, E. A. Effects of complexity, noise, and sampling rules on visual and auditory form perception. *Amer. Psychologist,* 1962, 17, 387. (Abstract)

Baker, E. J., & Alluisi, E. A. Information handling aspects of visual and auditory form perception. *J. Eng. Psychol.*, 1963, 1, 159–179.

Barden, H. P. Ueber die Schaetzung von Winkeln bei Knaben und Maedchen verschiedener Altersstufen. *Arch. ges. Psychol.*, 1927, 58, 81–94.

Beery, K. E. Estimation of angles. *Percept. mot. Skills,* 1968, 26, 11–14.

Berlyne, D. E. Objective and phenomenal complexity—comments on Heckhausen's note. *Can. J. Psychol.*, 1964, 18, 245–247.

Bobbitt, J. M. Determinants of the threshold of closure in simple geometric forms. *Psychol. Bull.*, 1937, 34, 712–713.

Bobbitt, J. M. An experimental study of the phenomenon of closure as a threshold function. *J. exp. Psychol.*, 1942, 30, 273–294.

Bolton, F. E. A contribution to the study of illusions. *Amer. J. Psychol.*, 1898, 9, 167–182.

Boynton, R. M., Elworth, C. L., Onley, J. W., & Klingberg, C. L. Form discrimination as predicted by overlap and area. USAF RADC TR 60–158, 1960.

Boynton, R. M., Elworth, C. L., Monty, R. A., Onley, J. W., & Klingberg, C. L. Overlap as a predictor of form discrimination under suprathreshold conditions. USAF RADC TR 61–99, 1961.

Brown, D. R. An evaluation of the role of selected stimulus parameters in the visual discrimination of human subjects. Unpublished doctoral dissertation, Purdue Univ., 1961. *Diss. Abstr.*, 1962, 22, 2472.

Brown, D. R., & Andrews, M. H. Visual form discrimination: Multidimensional analyses. *Percept. Psychophys.*, 1968, 3, 401–406.

Brown, D. R., & LoSasso, J. S. Pattern degradation, discrimination difficulty, and quantified stimulus attributes. *Psychon. Sci.*, 1967, 9, 351–352.

Brown, D. R., Hitchcock, L., Jr., & Michels, K. M. Quantitative studies in form perception: an evaluation of the role of selected stimulus parameters in the visual discrimination performance of human subjects. *Percept. mot. Skills*, 1962, **14**, 519–529.

Butler, J. Visual discrimination of shape by humans. *Quart. J. exp. Psychol.*, 1964, **14**, 272–276.

Carver, L. E., & Marshall, M. E. The relative discriminability of twelve random shapes. *Proc. Iowa Acad. Sci.*, 1961, **68**, 522–528.

Chou, S. K. Reading and legibility of Chinese characters: III. Judging the position of Chinese characters by American subjects. *J. exp. Psychol.*, 1930, **13**, 438–452.

Colardeau, E. L'evaluation sensorielle des longeurs. *Rev. Sci.*, 1898, **10**, 97–104.

Colegrove, F. W. Notes on mental standards of length. *Amer. J. Psychol.*, 1899, **10**, 292–295.

Coules, J., & Lekarczyk, M. A. Observer tolerance of form transformation as a function of form complexity. *USAF ESD Tech. Rep.*, 1963, No. 63–135.

Crook, M. N., Gray, F. E., Hanson, J. A., & Weisz, A. The effect of noise on the perception of forms in electro-visual display systems: A set of irregular forms. Tufts Univ., Inst. Appl. Exp. Psychol., 1959.

Crumbaugh, J. C. Temporal changes in the memory of visually perceived form. *Amer. J. Psychol.*, 1954, **67**, 647–658.

Day, H. Brief note on the Berlyne-Heckhausen controversy. *Psychol. Rep.*, 1965, **17**, 225–226.

Deese, J. The ability of untrained observers to match visual forms that are slightly disparate in contour. USAF WADC Tech. Rep. No. 56–570, 1956.

de Lacey, P. R. Form discrimination in European and part-aboriginal children. *Aust. Psychologist*, 1967, **2**(1).

Della Valle, L., Andrews, T. G., & Ross, S. Perceptual thresholds of curvilinearity and angularity as functions of line length. *J. exp. Psychol.*, 1956, **51**, 343–347.

Dunlap, K. A new measure of visual discrimination. *Psychol. Rev.*, 1915, **22**, 28–35.

Eriksen, C. W., & Hake, H. W. Multidimensional stimulus differences and accuracy of discrimination. *J. exp. Psychol.*, 1955, **50**, 153–160.

Fitts, P. M. Stimulus characteristics determining speed of classifying visual patterns. Minutes 35th Meet. Armed Forces-Nat. Res. Coun. Vision Committee, November, 1954.

Fitts, P. M. Stimulus determinants of speed in classifying visual patterns. ONR Symp. on Physiol. Psychol., March, 1955, Rep. ACR–1. Pp. 102–116.

Fitts, P. M., & Leonard, J. A. *Stimulus correlates of visual pattern recognition.* Columbus, Ohio: Ohio State Univ., 1957.

Forsyth, G. A., & Brown, D. R. Stimulus correlates of tachistoscopic discrimination-recognition performance: Compactness, jaggedness, and areal asymmetry. *Percept. Psychophys.*, 1967, **2**, 597–600.

French, R. S. The accuracy of discrimination of dot patterns as a function of angular orientation of the stimuli. USAF ATr Trng. Command, HRRC, Res. Bull. 53–3, March, 1953.

French, R. S. The discrimination of dot patterns as a function of number and average separation of dots. *J. exp. Psychol.*, 1953, **46**, 1–9.

French, R. S. Pattern recognition in the presence of visual noise. *J. exp. Psychol.*, 1954, **47**, 27–31.

Fried, R. Monocular and binocular comparison of apparent size. *Amer. J. Psychol.*, 1964, **77**, 476–479.

Gaito, J. Visual discrimination of straight and curved lines. *Amer. J. Psychol.*, 1959, **72**, 236–242.

Gatti, A. Nuove ricerche sopra l'apprezzamento del centro nelle figure piane geometriche. *Pubbl. Univ. Catt. Milano*, 1925, Ser. I, **1**, fasc. iv, 69–112.

Gerard, R. Untersuchungen ueber Groessenempfindungen bei binokularem und monokularem Sehen. *Z. Sinnesphysiol.*, 1936, 67, 80–90.

Goldmeier, E. Ueber Aehnlichkeit bei gesehenen Figuren. *Psychol. Forsch.*, 1937, 21, 146–209.

Goodrick, G. L. A psychophysical analysis of the perception of difference in random shape pairs as a function of shape complexity. *Amer. Psychologist*, 1962, 17, 351–352. (Abstract)

Gundlach, C., & Macoubry, C. The effect of color on apparent size. *Amer. J. Psychol.*, 1931, 43, 109–111.

Hecht, I. H. Die simultane Erfassung der Figuren. *Z. Psychol.*, 1924, 94, 153–194.

Heckhausen, H. Complexity in perception: phenomenal criteria and information theoretical calculus—a note on D. E. Berlyne's "complexity effects." *Can. J. Psychol.*, 1964, 18, 168–173.

Henriquez, G. K. Ueber die Aenderungsempfindlichkeit fuer optische Gestalten. *Neue Psychol. Stud.*, 1937, 10, 45–102.

Hillix, W. A. Visual pattern identification as a function of fill and distortion. *J. exp. Psychol.*, 1960, 59, 192–197.

Hitchcock, L., Jr., Brown, D. R., Michels, K. M., & Spiritoso, T. Stimulus complexity and the judgment of relative size. *Percept. mot. Skills*, 1962, 14, 210.

Irwin, F. W., & Seidenfeld, M. A. The application of the method of comparison to the problem of memory change. *J. exp. Psychol.*, 1937, 21, 363–381.

James, H. Guessing, expectancy, and autonomous change. *Quart. J. exp. Psychol.*, 1958, 10, 107–110.

Karlin, L., & Brennan, G. Memory for visual figures by the method of identical stimuli. *Amer. J. Psychol.*, 1957, 70, 248–252.

Kiesow, F. Ueber die Vergleichung linearer Strecken und ihre Beziehung zum Weberschen Gesetze. *Arch. ges. Psychol.*, 1926, 56, 421–451.

Křivohlavy, J. [Discrimination and equivalence of visible stimuli of various shapes.] *Československá psychologie*, 1967, 11(5), 450–457.

Krulee, G. K. Some informational aspects of form discrimination. *J. exp. Psychol.*, 1958, 55, 143–149.

Kuennapas, T., Maelhammer, G., & Svensson, O. Multidimensional ratio scaling and multi-dimensional similarity of simple geometric figures. *Scand. J. Psychol.*, 1964, 5, 249–256.

Landolt, E. Formsinn und Sehschaerfe. *Arch. Augenhk.*, 1906, 55, 219–223.

Lesser, O. Ueber Linien- und Flaechenvergleichung. *Z. Psychol.*, 1915, 74, 1–127.

Mansvelt, E. Over het schatten der grotte van figuren van verschillenden vorm. *Meded. Psychol. Lab. Rijksuniv. Utrecht*, 1928, 4, II, 134–137.

McNamara, H. J. Nonveridical perception as a function of rewards and punishments. *Percept. mot. Skills*, 1959, 9, 67–80.

McNamara, H. J. The development of form constancy as a function of reward. Unpublished doctoral dissertation, Univ. of Kansas, 1960. *Diss. Abstr.*, 1960, 21, 1262.

Miles, W. R. Light sensitivity and form perception in dark adaptation. *J. Opt. Soc. Amer.*, 1953, 43, 560–566.

Miller, E. F., II. Evaluation of certain visual and related tests: III. Form fields. USN Sch. Aviat. Med. Res. Rep., 1958, Proj. No. NM 1401 11, Sub. 6, No. 3.

Mitra, S. A report on some experiments on the indirect perception of forms. *Indian J. Psychol.*, 1927, 2, 15–22.

Monty, R. A., & Boynton, R. M. Stimulus overlap and form similarity under supra-threshold conditions. *Percept. mot. Skills*, 1962, 14, 487–498.

Moody, J. A. An experimental investigation of sensitivity to increments and decrements in continuous frontal plane transformations of visual forms. Unpublished doctoral dissertation, Ohio State Univ., 1956. *Diss. Abstr.*, 1956, **16**, 2223.

Nesmith, R., & Rodwan, A. S. Effect of duration of viewing on form and size judgments. *J. exp. Psychol.*, 1967, **74**, 26–30.

Ogilvie, J., & Daicar, E. The perception of curvature. *Can. J. Psychol.*, 1967, **21**, 521–525.

Peters, W. Versuche ueber den Einfluss der Form auf die Wahrnehmung der Flaechengroesse. *Z. Psychol.*, 1933, **129**, 323–337.

Pfeiffer, H. E. Ueber die Wirksamkeit verschiedener Figuren gleicher geometrischer Flaechengroesse und ihre Beeinflussung durch Helligkeitsunterschiede. *Psychol. Forsch.*, 1932, **17**, 1–12.

Philip, B. R. Proactive and retroactive effects in the recognition of form. *J. exp. Psychol.*, 1940, **26**, 502–513.

Piaget, J., & Morf, A. L'action des facteurs spatiaux et temporels de centration dans estimation visuelle des longeurs. *Arch. Psychol., Genève*, 1954, **34**, 243–288.

Polidora, V. J. Stimulus correlates of visual pattern discrimination by humans: area and contour. *J. exp. Psychol.*, 1965, **69**, 221–223.

Pollack, I., & Klemmer, E. T. Visual noise filtering by the human operator. II. Linear dot patterns in noise. AFCRC TR 54–15, Bolling AFB, Washington, D. C., July, 1954.

Rappaport, M. Redundancy as a stimulus parameter in form discrimination. In J. W. Wulfeck & J. H. Taylor (Eds.), *Form discrimination as related to military problems.* Washington, D. C.: Nat. Acad. Sci.-Nat. Res. Coun., 1957. Pp. 161–168.

Rappaport, M. The role of redundancy in the discrimination of visual forms. *J. exp. Psychol.*, 1957, **53**, 3–10.

Rappaport, M. The role of redundancy in the discrimination of visual forms. Unpublished doctoral dissertation, Ohio State Univ., 1959. *Diss. Abstr.*, 1959, **20**, 2403.

Robinson, J. S. The effect of learning verbal labels for stimuli on their later discrimination. *J. exp. Psychol.*, 1955, **49**, 112–115.

Rodwan, A. S. Primacy of a form criterion in perceptual judgments. *J. exp. Psychol.*, 1965, **70**, 231–232.

Rommetveit, R., & Svalheim, R. Some halo effects in perception of geometrical patterns. *Acta Psychol.*, 1959, **16**, 1–24.

Rommetveit, R., & Svalheim, R. Some halo effects in perception of geometrical patterns. *Nord. Psykol.*, 1959, **11**, 11–24.

Samanta, M. N. Visual estimation of angles. *Indian J. Psychol.*, 1928, **3**, 185–188.

Samanta, M. N. Visual perception of areas. *Indian J. Psychol.*, 1932, **7**, 67–74.

Seiler, D. A., & Zusne, L. Judged complexity of tachistoscopically viewed random shapes. *Percept. mot. Skills*, 1967, **24**, 884–886.

Sekuler, R. W., & Houlihan, K. Discrimination of mirror-images: Choice time analysis of human adult performance. *Quart. J. exp. Psychol.*, 1968, **20**, 204–207.

Sleight, R. B., & Mowbray, G. H. Discriminability between geometric figures under complex conditions. *J. Psychol.*, 1951, **31**. 121–127.

Smith, J. P. The effects of figural shape on the perception of area. Unpublished doctoral dissertation, Fordham Univ., 1964. *Diss. Abstr.*, 1964, **25**, 3712.

Stenson, H. H. The psychophysical dimensions of similarity among random shapes. *Percept. Psychophys.*, 1968, **3**, 201–214.

Takagi, K. [On visual estimation of length of various curves.] *Jap. J. Psychol.*, 1926, **1**, 476–498.

Veniar, F. A. Difference thresholds for shape distortion of geometrical squares. *J. Psychol.*, 1948, **26**, 461–476.

Wagner, E. Das Abschaetzen von Flaechen. *Psychotech. Z.,* 1931, **6,** 140–148.

Warden, C. J., & Brown, H. C. A preliminary investigation of form and motion acuity at low levels of illumination. *J. exp. Psychol.,* 1944, **34,** 437–449.

Warden, C. J., & Flynn, E. L. The effect of color on apparent size. *Amer. J. Psychol.,* 1926, **37,** 398–401.

Warren, H. C., & Shaw, W. J. Studies from the Princeton Laboratory. II. Further experiments on memory for square size. *Psychol. Rev.,* 1895, **2,** 239–244.

Warren, J. M., & Pinneau, S. R. Influence of form on judgment of apparent area. *Percept. mot. Skills,* 1955, **5,** 7–10.

Webster, R. B. Distortion, fill, and noise effects on pattern discrimination. *Human Factors,* 1966, **8,** 147–155.

Woodring, A. V., & Alluisi, E. A. Effects of choice-figure rotation on the visual perception of form. *Psychon. Sci.,* 1966, **4,** 403–404.

Yamane, K. [On the perception of curves.] *Jap. J. Psychol.,* 1937, **12,** 223–252.

Zusne, L. Behavioral correlates of visual form quantified by moments of area. Unpublished doctoral dissertation, Purdue Univ., 1964. *Diss. Abstr.,* 1964, **25,** 2632.

Zusne, L. Moments of area and of the perimeter of visual form as predictors of discrimination performance. *J. exp. Psychol.,* 1965, **69,** 213–220.

6. Scaling

Arnoult, M. D. Prediction of perceptual response from structural characteristics of the stimulus. *Percept. mot. Skills,* 1960, **11,** 261–268.

Attneave, F. Dimensions of similarity. *Amer. J. Psychol.,* 1950, **63,** 516–556.

Attneave, F. Physical determinants of the judged complexity of shapes. *J. exp. Psychol.,* 1957, **53,** 221–227.

Behrman, B. W. Multidimensional scaling of form: A psychophysical analysis. Unpublished doctoral dissertation, Purdue Univ., 1968. *Diss. Abstr.,* 1968, **28**(11–B), 4555.

Behrman, B. W., & Brown, D. R. Multidimensional scaling of form. *Percept. Psychophys.,* 1968, **4,** 19–25.

Berlyne, D. E., & Peckham, S. The semantic differential and other measures of reaction to visual complexity. *Can. J. Psychol.,* 1966, **20,** 125–135.

Brown, L. T. Further studies of the attentional response of humans and squirrel monkeys to visual patterns. *Percept. mot. Skills,* 1967, **25,** 397–406.

Brown, L. T., & Farha, W. Some physical determinants of viewing time under three instructional sets. *Percept. Psychophys.,* 1966, **1,** 1–4.

Brown, L. T., & Lucas, J. H. Supplementary report: Attentional effects of five physical properties of visual patterns. *Percept. mot. Skills,* 1966, **23,** 343–346.

Brown, L. T., & O'Donnell, C. R. Attentional response of humans and squirrel monkeys to visual patterns varying in three physical dimensions. *Percept. mot. Skills,* 1966, **22,** 707–717.

Cabe, P. A. Magnitude estimation of line pattern complexity: Preliminary report. *Percept. mot. Skills,* 1968, **26,** 614.

Chambliss, D. J. The relation between judged similarity and the physical properties of plane figures. Unpublished doctoral dissertation, Univ. of Wisconsin, 1957. *Diss. Abstr.,* 1957, **17,** 2070.

Chambliss, D. J., & Attneave, F. The relation between judged similarity and the physical properties of plane polygons. *Amer. Psychologist,* 1958, **13,** 384. (Abstract)

Coules, J., Duva, J. S., & Ganem, G. Effect of visual noise on the judgment of complex forms. *USAF CCDD Tech. Rep.,* 1960, No. 60–40.

Day, H. Evaluations of subjective complexity, pleasingness, and interestingness for a series of random polygons varying in complexity. *Percept. Psychophys.,* 1967, **2**, 281–286.

Day, H. The importance of symmetry and complexity in the evaluation of complexity, interest, and pleasingness. *Psychon. Sci.,* 1968, **10**, 339–340.

Dorfman, D. D., & McKenna, H. Pattern preference as a function of pattern uncertainty. *Can. J. Psychol.,* 1966, **20**, 143–153.

Eisenman, R. Complexity-simplicity: I. Preference for symmetry and rejection of complexity. Psychon. Sci., 1967, **8**, 169–170.

Eisenman, R. Complexity-simplicity: II. Birth order and sex differences. *Psychon. Sci.,* 1967, **8**, 171–172.

Eisenman, R. Novelty ratings of simple and complex shapes. *J. gen. Psychol.,* 1968, **78**, 275–278.

Eisenman, R. Semantic differential ratings of polygons varying in complexity-simplicity and symmetry-asymmetry. *Percept. mot. Skills,* 1968, **26**, 1243–1248.

Eisenman, R., & Gellens, H. K. Preference for complexity-simplicity and symmetry-asymmetry. *Percept. mot. Skills,* 1968, **26**, 888–890.

Eisenman, R., & Rappaport, J. Complexity preference and semantic differential ratings of complexity-simplicity and symmetry-asymmetry. *Psychon. Sci.,* 1967, **7**, 147–148.

Eisenman, R., & Jones, D. Complexity-simplicity: Random vs. non-random arrangement of shapes. *Percept. mot. Skills,* 1968, **26**, 682.

Elliott, L. L. Reliability of judgments of figural complexity. *J. exp. Psychol.,* 1958, **56**, 335–338.

Elliot, L. L. Factor structures and semantic differential responses to visual forms and prediction of factor scores from structural characteristics of the stimuli. *Amer. Psychologist,* 1961, **16**, 420. (Abstract)

Elliott, L. L., & Tannenbaum, P. H. Factor structure of semantic differential responses to visual forms and prediction of factor scores from structural characteristics of the stimuli. USAF Sch. Aerospace Med. Rep., 1961, No. 62–8.

Fritzky, F. J. Aesthetic preference for abstract designs as a function of their perceived complexity. *Educ. Test. Serv. Res. Bull.,* 1963, **27**, 1–41.

Goldstein, A. G. Familiarity and apparent complexity of random shapes. *J. exp. Psychol.,* 1961, **62**, 594–597.

Goldstein, A. G., & Andrews, J. Perceptual uprightness and complexity of random shapes. *Amer. J. Psychol.,* 1962, **75**, 667–669.

Houston, J. P., Garskof, B. E., & Silber, D. E. The informational basis of judged complexity. *J. gen. Psychol.,* 1965, **72**, 277–284.

Leckart, B. T. Looking time: The effects of stimulus complexity and familiarity. *Percept. Psychophys.,* 1966, **1**, 142–144.

McCullough, P. M. The perceptual discrimination of similarities. Unpublished doctoral dissertation, Univ. of Utah, 1957. *Diss. Abstr.,* 1958, **18**, 1866.

Munsinger, H., & Kessen, W. Uncertainty, structure, and preference. *Psychol. Monogr.,* 1964(9), **78**, No. 586.

Payne, B. R. The relationship between judged complexity and amount of descriptive information for visual patterns generated from binary and ternary sequences. Unpublished doctoral dissertation, Univ. of Washington, 1962. *Diss. Abstr.,* 1963, **23**(11), 4436.

Royer, F. L. Figural goodness and internal structure in perceptual discrimination. *Percept. Psychophys.,* 1966, **1**, 311–314.

Rump, E. E. Is there a general factor of preference for complexity? *Percept. Psychophys.,* 1968, **3**, 346–348.

Sanders, R. A. The effects of familiarization on the judged complexity of visual forms. Unpublished doctoral dissertation, Univ. of Arkansas. *Diss. Abstr.,* 1963, **23**(9), 3503.

Silver, C. A., Landis, D., & Messick, S. Multidimensional analysis of visual form: An analysis of individual differences. *Amer. J. Psychol.,* 1966, **79**, 62–72.

Sleight, R. B. The relative discriminability of several geometric forms. *J. exp. Psychol.,* 1952, **43**, 324–328.

Small, V. H. Judged similarity of visual forms as functions of selected stimulus dimensions. Unpublished doctoral dissertation, Purdue Univ., 1961. *Diss. Abstr.,* 1962, **22**(3), 2481.

Stenson, H. H. The physical factor structure of random forms and their judged complexity. *Percept. Psychophys.,* 1966, **1**, 303–310.

Stilson, D. W. A psychophysical investigation of triangular shape. Unpublished doctoral dissertation, Univ. of Illinois, 1956. *Diss. Abstr.,* 1957, **17**, 905.

Stilson, D. W. A multidimensional psychophysical method for investigating visual form. In J. W. Wulfeck & J. H. Taylor (Eds.), *Form discrimination as related to military problems.* Washington, D. C.: Nat. Acad. Sci.-Nat. Res. Coun., 1957. Pp. 54–64.

Taylor, R. E., & Eisenman, R. Perception and production of complexity by creative art students. *J. Psychol.,* 1964, **57**, 239–242.

Taylor, R. E., & Eisenman, R. Birth order and sex differences in complexity-simplicity, color-form preference, and personality. *J. Proj. Tech. Pers. Assess.,* 1968, **32**, 383–387.

Thomas, H. Multidimensional analysis of similarities judgments to twenty visual forms. *Psychon. Bull.,* 1967, **1**, 3.

Vitz, P. Preference for different amounts of visual complexity. *Behav. Sci.,* 1966, **11**, 105–114.

Woods, W. A., & Boudreau, J. C. Design complexity as a determiner of visual attention among artists and non-artists. *J. appl. Psychol.,* 1950, **34**, 355–362.

Zusne, L., & Michels, K. M. Geometricity of visual form. *Percept. mot. Skills,* 1962, **14**, 147–154.

Zusne, L., & Michels, K. M. More on the geometricity of visual form. *Percept. mot. Skills,* 1962, **15**, 55–58.

7. Recognition and identification

Alluisi, E. A., Hawkes, G. R., & Hall, T. J. Effects of distortion on the identification of visual forms under two levels of multiple-task performance. *J. Eng. Psychol.,* 1964, **3**, 29–40.

Ammons, R. B. Experiential factors in visual form perception. I. Review and formulation of problems. *J. genet. Psychol.,* 1954, **84**, 3–25.

Anderson, N. S., & Leonard, J. A. The recognition, naming, and reconstruction of visual figures as a function of contour redundancy. *J. exp. Psychol.,* 1958, **56**, 262–270.

Archer, S. J. Identification of visual patterns as a function of information load. *J. exp. Psychol.,* 1954, **48**, 313–317.

Arnoult, M. D. A comparison of training methods in the recognition of spatial patterns. AFPTRC-TN-56-27, Lackland AFB, February, 1956.

Aroult, M. D. Familiarity and recognition of nonsense shapes. *J. exp. Psychol.,* 1956, **51**, 269–276.

Attneave, F., & Olson, R. K. Discriminability of stimuli varying in physical and retinal orientation. *J. exp. Psychol.,* 1967, **74**, 149–157.

Baldwin, J. M., & Shaw, W. J. Memory for square size. *Psychol. Rev.,* 1895, **2**, 236–239.

Binder, A. A statistical model for the process of visual recognition. *Psychol. Rev.,* 1955, **62**, 119–129.

Bricker, P. D. The identification of redundant stimulus patterns. *J. Exp. Psychol.*, 1955, 49, 73–81.

Brown, J. Distortions in immediate memory. *Quart. J. exp. Psychol.*, 1956, 8, 134–139.

Brown, J. H. The influence of frequency on the identification of forms rendered ambiguous by two-dimensional similarity. Unpublished doctoral dissertation, Univ. of Virginia, 1963. *Diss. Abstr.*, 1963, 23(8), 2989–2990.

Bryden, M. P. Tachistoscopic recognition of non-alphabetical material. *Can. J. Psychol.*, 1960, 14, 78–86.

Carl, H. Versuche ueber tachistoskopisches Bilderkennen. *Z. Psychol.*, 1933, 129, 1–42.

Carlson, J. B., & Duncan, C. P. A study of autonomous change in the memory trace by the method of recognition. *Amer. J. Psychol.*, 1955, 68, 280–284.

Carlson, W. A., & Eriksen, C. W. Dichopic summation of information in the recognition of briefly presented forms. *Psychon. Sci.*, 1966, 5, 67–68.

Dearborn, G. V. N. Recognition under objective reversal. *Psychol. Rev.*, 1899, 6, 395–406.

Dees, V., & Grindley, G. The transposition of visual patterns. *Brit. J. Psychol.*, 1947, 37, 152–163.

Deese, J. Complexity of contour in the recognition of visual form. USAF WADC Tech. Rep. 56–60, 1956.

Dwelshauvers, G. Recherches sur la memoire des formes. *Année Psychol.*, 1923, 23, 125–143.

Elliott, F. R. Memory for visual, auditory, and visual-auditory material. *Arch. Psychol., N. Y.,* 1936, No. 199.

Ellis, H. C. Associative variables in visual form recognition. *Psychon. Bull.*, 1967, 1, 3.

Eriksen, C. W., & Hoffman, M. Form recognition at brief durations as a function of adapting field and interval between stimulations. *J. exp. Psychol.*, 1963, 66, 485–499.

Eriksen, C. W., & Lappin, J. S. Selective attention and very short-term recognition memory for nonsense forms. *J. exp. Psychol.*, 1967, 73, 358–364.

Filozof, J. [Test of memory for forms. Material for a monograph of the test and a contribution to the study of the methodology of psychotechnical notation.] *Psikhotekhnika,* 1933, 8, 122–134.

Fitts, P. M., Weinstein, M., Rappaport, M., Anderson, N. S., & Leonard, J. A. Stimulus correlates of visual pattern recognition: A probability approach. *J. exp. Psychol.*, 1956, 51, 1–11.

Forsyth, G. A., & Brown, D. R. Stimulus recognizability judgments as a function of the utility of physical dimensions in recognition-discrimination problems. *Percept. Psychophys.*, 1968, 3, 85–88.

French, R. S. Identification of dot patterns from memory as a function of complexity. *J. exp. Psychol.*, 1954, 47, 22–26.

George, F. H. Errors of visual recognition. *J. exp. Psychol.*, 1952, 43, 202–206.

Ghent Braine, L. Disorientation of forms: An examination of Rock's theory. *Psychon. Sci.*, 1965, 3, 541–542.

Gibson, J. J., & Robinson, D. Orientation in visual perception; the recognition of familiar plane forms in differing orientations. *Psychol. Monogr.*, 1935, 46(6), (Whole No. 210).

Goldberg, S. The problem of form recognition in the uniform visual field. Unpublished doctoral dissertation, Univ. of Buffalo, 1960. *Diss. Abstr.*, 1960, 21, 238.

Goldstein, A. G. On the use of the term "recognition." *Amer. J. Psychol.*, 1958, 71, 790–791.

Gollin, E. S. Perceptual learning of incomplete pictures. *Percept. mot. Skills,* 1965, 21, 439–445.

Goodnow, R. E. The utilization of partially valid cues in perceptual identification. Unpublished doctoral dissertation, Harvard Univ., 1954.

Guillery. Messende Versuche ueber die Schnelligkeit der Formenwahrnehmung. *Arch. Augenhk.*, 1909, **62**, 227–232.

Gurnee, H. The effect of mild annoyance upon the learning of visual forms. *J. exp. Psychol.*, 1939, **25**, 215–220.

Gurnee, H. Comparative retention of open and closed visual patterns. *Psychol. Bull.*, 1940, **37**, 568. (Abstract)

Gurnee, H., Witzeman, B. E., & Heller, M. Comparative retention of open and closed visual forms. *J. exp. Psychol.*, 1940, **27**, 66–70.

Hake, H. W., & Eriksen, C. W. Role of response variables in recognition and identification of complex visual forms. *J. exp. Psychol.*, 1956, **52**, 235–243.

Hanawalt, N. G. The method of comparison applied to the problem of memory change. *J. exp. Psychol.*, 1952, **43**, 37–42.

Hebb, D. O., & Foord, E. N. Errors of visual recognition and the nature of the trace. *J. exp. Psychol.*, 1945, **35**, 335–348.

Henneman, R. H. Factors determining the identification of ambiguous visual stimuli. In A. Morris & E. P. Horne (Eds.), *Visual search techniques.* Washington, D. C.: Nat. Acad. Sci.-Nat. Res. Coun., 1960. Pp. 112–118.

Henneman, R. H., & Mathews, J. R. The role of training in the identification of ambiguous visual forms. In W. Wathen-Dunn (Ed.), *Models for the perception of speech and visual forms.* Cambridge, Massachusetts: M.I.T. Press, 1967. Pp. 274–278.

Holmes, D. S. "Closure" in a gapped circle figure. *Amer. J. Psychol.*, 1967, **80**, 1967, 80, 614–618.

Hufschmidt, H. J., & del Castillo, N. J. Contribución al estudio de la estructura temporal de la percepción visual de las formas. *Act. Luso–Esp. Neurol. Psiquiat.*, 1951, **10**, 75–84.

Irwin, F. W., & Rovner, H. Further study of the method of comparison applied to the problem of memory change. *J. exp. Psychol.*, 1937, **21**, 533–544.

Johnson, R. E. Qualitative changes in the memory traces of incomplete circles. *Amer. J. Psychol.*, 1962, **75**, 629–633.

Knight, O. D. The role of the figure-ground relation in perceiving and memorizing visual forms. Unpublished doctoral dissertation, Ohio State Univ., 1936.

Lewin, K. Ueber die Umkehrung der Raumlage auf dem Kopf stehender Worte und Figuren in der Wahrnehmung. *Psychol. Forsch.*, 1923, **4**, 210–261.

Lordahl, D. S., Kleinman, K. M., Levy, B., Massoth, N. A., Pessin, M. S., Storandt, M., Tucker, R., & Vanderplas, J. M. Deficits in recognition of random shapes with changed visual fields. *Psychon. Sci.*, 1965, **3**, 245–246.

Mayer, S. R. The effect of induced tension during training on visual form recognition. *J. educ. Psychol.*, 1957, **48**, 11–17.

Moroz, M. J. Verbal coding as a factor in the recognition of random shapes. Unpublished doctoral dissertation, Univ. of Oregon, 1967. *Diss. Abstr.*, 1967, **27**, 3315.

Orbach, J. Retinal locus as a factor in the recognition of visually perceived words. *Amer. J. Psychol.*, 1952, **65**, 555–562.

Prentice, W. C. H. Visual recognition of verbally labeled figures. *Amer. J. Psychol.*, 1954, **67**, 315–320.

Rock, I. The orientation of forms on the retina and in the environment. *Amer. J. Psychol.*, 1956, **69**, 513–528.

Rock, I., & Heimer, W. The effect of retinal and phenomenal orientation on the perception of form. *Amer. J. Psychol.*, 1957, **70**, 493–511.

Rose, D. W. Some stimulus variables in the identification of incomplete pictures. Unpublished doctoral dissertation, Univ. of Oregon, 1964. *Diss. Abstr.*, 1964, **25**, 3126–3127.

Saha, G. B. Memory for visual forms. *Indian J. Psychol.*, 1961, **36**(4), 155–160.

Saul, E. V. Immediate and delayed recognition of geometric form. *J. gen. Psychol.*, 1956, **55**, 163–171.

Seidenfeld, M. A. The temporal interval as a factor in the recognition of visually perceived figures. *Psychol. Bull.*, 1937, **34**, 731. (Abstract)

Seidenfeld, M. A. Time as a factor in the recognition of visually perceived figures. *Amer. J. Psychol.*, 1938, **51**, 64–82.

Soltz, D. F., & Wertheimer, M. The retention of "good" and "bad" figures. *Amer. J. Psychol.*, 1959, **72**, 450–452.

Suzuki, S. [The influence of experience on the visual perception of figures.] *Jap. J. Psychol.*, 1931, **6**, 305–368.

Thouless, R. The experience of "upright" and "upside-down" in looking at pictures. *Misc. Psychol. Albert Michotte*, 1947, 130.

Tsao, J. C. A study in the recognition of figures. *Brit. J. Psychol.*, 1949, **40**, 57–67.

Tsujimura, Y. [On the recognition of the displaced figure.] *Jap. J. Psychol.*, 1935, **10**, 601–651.

Van De Geer, J. P., & Levelt, W. J. M. Detection of visual pattern disturbed by noise. *Quart. J. exp. Psychol.*, 1963, **15**, 192–204.

Vanderplas, J. M., & Garvin, E. A. Complexity, association value, and practice as factors in shape recognition following paired associates training. *J. exp. Psychol.*, 1959, **57**, 155–163.

Vernon, M. D. Different types of perceptual ability. *Brit. J. Psychol.*, 1947, **38**, 79–89.

Weigl, E. Zur Psychologie sogenannter Abstraktionsprozesse: Wiedererkennungsversuche mit Umrissfiguren. *Z. Psychol.*, 1927, **103**, 257–322.

Weinstein, M. Stimulus complexity and the recognition of visual patterns. Unpublished doctoral dissertation, Ohio State Univ., 1955. *Diss. Abstr.*, 1955, **15**, 1127.

Weinstein, M., & Fitts, P. M. A quantitative study of the role of stimulus complexity in visual pattern discrimination. *Amer. Psychologist*, 1954, **9**, 490. (Abstract)

White, B. W. Complexity and heterogeneity in the visual recognition of two-dimensional form. In J. W. Wulfeck & J. H. Taylor (Eds.), *Form discrimination as related to military problems.* Washington, D. C.: Nat. Acad. Sci.-Nat. Res. Coun., 1957. Pp. 158–161.

White, B. W. Recognition of familiar characters under an unfamiliar transformation. *Percept. mot. Skills,* 1962, **15**, 107–116.

Wright, J. M. v. On qualitative changes in the retention of forms. *Scand. J. Psychol.*, 1964, **5**(2), 65–70.

Wylie, M. Recognition of Chinese symbols. *Amer. J. Psychol.*, 1926, **37**, 224–232.

a. Training and recognition

Arnoult, M. D. Transfer of predifferentiation training in simple and multiple shape discrimination. *J. exp. Psychol.*, 1953, **45**, 401–409.

Arnoult, M. D. Recognition of shapes following paired-associates pre-training. *Air Force-Nat. Res. Coun. Sci. Symp.*, 1955.

Arnoult, M. D. Recognition of shapes following paired-associates pretraining. In F. Finch & C. Cameron (Eds.), *Symposium on Air Force human engineering, personnel, and training research.* Washington, D. C.: Nat. Res. Coun., 1956.

Atkinson, R. C., & Ammons, R. B. Experiential factors in visual form perception. II. Latency as a function of repetion. *J. exp. Psychol.*, 1952, **43**, 173–178.

Attneave, F. Transfer of experience with a class-schema to identification learning of patterns and shapes. *J. exp. Psychol.*, 1957, **54**, 81–88.

Marx, M. H., Murphy, W. W., & Brownstein, A. J. Recognition of complex visual stimuli as a function of training with abstracted patterns. *J. exp. Psychol.*, 1961, **62**, 456–460.

Vanderplas, J. M. Theoretical mediators of form perception following verbal training. In J. W. Wulfeck & J. H. Taylor (Eds.), *Form discrimination as related to military problems.* Washington, D. C.: Nat. Acad. Sci.-Nat. Res. Coun., 1957. Pp. 211–217.

b. Form thresholds: foveal vision

Barskiĭ, B. V., & Guzeva, M. A. O zavisimosti prostranstvennykh porogov zreniya ot kharaktera vosprinimaemogo kontura. *Voprosy psikhol.*, 1962, **8**(2), 101–114.

Bitterman, M. E., Krauskopf, J., & Hochberg, J. E. Threshold for visual form: a diffusion model. *Amer. J. Psychol.*, 1954, **67**, 205–219.

Blumenfeld, W. Untersuchungen ueber die Formvisualitaet. *Z. Psychol.*, 1922, **91**, 1–82.

Blumenfeld, W. Untersuchungen ueber die Formvisualitaet II. *Z. Psychol.*, 1923, **91**, 236–292.

Borg, G. Studies of visual gestalt strength. Report, Dept. Educ., Umeå U., Sweden, 1964. (Mimeographed)

Bowen, H. M., Andreassi, J., Truax, S., & Orlansky, J. Optimum symbols for radar displays. *Human Factors,* 1960, **2**, 28–33.

Casperson, R. C. The visual discrimination of geometric forms. Unpublished doctoral dissertation, Johns Hopkins Univ., 1950.

Casperson, R. C. The visual discrimination of geometric forms. *J. exp. Psychol.*, 1950, **40**, 668–686.

Cheatham, P. G. Visual perceptual latency as a function of stimulus brightness and contour shapes. *J. exp. Psychol.*, 1952, **43**, 369–380.

Engstrand, R. D., & Moeller, G. The relative legibility of ten simple geometric figures. *Amer. Psychologist,* 1962, **17**, 386. (Abstract)

Fox, W. R. Visual discrimination as a function of stimulus size, shape, and edge gradient. In J. W. Wulfeck & J. H. Taylor (Eds.), *Form discrimination as related to military problems.* Washington, D. C.: Nat. Acad. Sci.-Nat. Res. Coun., 1957. Pp. 168–175.

Fox, W. R. Visual discrimination as a function of stimulus size, shape, and edge gradient. Boston Univ., Physical Res. Labs., Tech. Note No. 132, 1957.

Helson, H. Dr. Wilcox on "The role of form in perception." *Amer. J. Psychol.*, 1933, **45**, 171–173.

Helson, H., & Fehrer, E. V. The role of form in perception. *Amer. J. Psychol.*, 1932, **44**, 79–102.

Hochberg, J. E. Form and visual detection. In J. W. Wulfeck & J. H. Taylor (Eds.), *Form discrimination as related to military problems.* Washington, D. C.: Nat. Acad. Sci.-Nat. Res. Coun., 1957. Pp. 129–133.

Hochberg, J. E., Gleitman, H., & McBride, P. D. Visual threshold as a function of simplicity of form. *Amer. Psychologist,* 1948, **3**, 341–342. (Abstract)

Hyman, R., & Hake, H. W. Form recognition as a function of the number of forms which can be presented for recognition. USAF WADC TR 54–164, May, 1954.

Kaneko, H. [The perception time of different forms.] *Rep. 6th Congr. Jap. Psychol. Ass.,* 1938, 78–82.

Krauskopf, J., Duryea, R., & Bitterman, M. E. Threshold for visual form: further experiments. *Amer. J. Psychol.*, 1954, **67**, 427–440.

Low, F. N. Effect of suprathreshold changes in brightness on form perception. *Amer. J. Physiol.*, 1948, **155**, 409–419.

Pierce, J. R. Determinants of threshold for form. *Psychol. Bull.*, 1963, **60**, 391–407.

Ross, S. Scotopic form perception at various distances. *Bull. Can. Psychol. Ass.*, 1945, **5**, 81. (Abstract)

Semeonoff, B. Form perception in dark-adapted vision. *Brit. Psychol. Soc. Quart. Bull.*, 1950, **1**(7), 281–282.

Shevarev, P. [The noticing and identifying of the simple geometric figures.] *Psikhol.*, 1932, No. 4, 101–117.

Shevarev, P. A. [Comparative visibility of simple geometrical figures.] In [*Visual sensation and perception*, Vol. II.] Moscow: Gosekgiz, 1935. Pp. 243–246.

Smith, S. W., & Louttit, R. T. Some effects of target microstructure on visual detection. In A. Morris & E. P. Horne (Eds.), *Visual search techniques.* Washington, D. C.: Nat. Acad. Sci.-Nat. Res. Coun., 1960. Pp. 94–98.

Strauss, H. Untersuchungen ueber das Erloeschen und Herauspringen von Gestalten. *Psychol. Forsch.*, 1927, **10**, 57–83.

Wilcox, W. W. Helson and Fehrer on the role of form in perception. *Amer. J. Psychol.*, 1932, **44**, 578–580.

c. Form thresholds: peripheral vision

Aulhorn, E., & Voges, W. Parafoveale Gesichtsfeldgrenzen in Abhaengigkeit von der Lage der dargebotenen Konturen. *Arch. ges. Physiol.*, 1953, **257**, 329–342.

Bartz, A. E. Recognition time for symbols in peripheral vision. Unpublished doctoral dissertation, Univ. of Arizona, 1960. *Diss. Abstr.*, 1961, **22**, 648–649.

Christensen, J. M., & Crannell, C. W. The effect of selected visual training procedures on the visual form field. WADC Tech. Rep. 54–239, 1955.

Collier, R. M. An experimental study of form perception in indirect vision. *J. comp. Psychol.*, 1931, **11**, 281–289.

Crannell, C. W., & Christensen, J. M. Expansion of the visual form field by perimeter training. USAF WADC Tech. Rep. 55–368, 1955.

Day, R. H. The physiological basis of form perception in the peripheral retina. *Psychol. Rev.*, 1957, **64**, 38–48.

Delgado, J. M. R. Ueber extramakulares Sehen der Form. *Ophthalmologica*, 1945, **10**, 170–190.

Ferree, C. E., & Rand, G. The effect of relation to background on the size and shape of the form field for stimuli of different sizes. *Amer. J. Ophthal.*, 1931, **14**, 1018–1029.

Ferree, C. E., & Rand, G. Two important factors in the size and shape of the form field and some of their relations to practical perimetry. *J. gen. Psychol.*, 1932, **6**, 414–428.

Ferree, C. E., Rand, G., & Monroe, M. M. A study of the factors which cause individual differences in the size of the form field. *Amer. J. Psychol.*, 1930, **42**, 63–71.

Ferree, C. E., Rand, G., & Sloan, L. L. The effect of size of pupil on the form and color fields. *J. gen. Psychol.*, 1934, **10**, 83–99.

Ganguli, M. Studies on the visual perception of geometrical figures: indirect vision. *Indian J. Psychol.*, 1939, **14**, 27–36.

Geissler, L. R. Form perception in indirect vision. *Psychol. Bull.*, 1926, **23**, 135–136.

Gordon, D. A. The relation between the threshold of form, motion, and displacement in parafoveal and peripheral vision at a scotopic level of illumination. *Amer. J. Psychol.*, 1947, **60**, 202–225.

Graefe, O. Qualitative Untersuchungen ueber Kontur und Flaeche in der optischen Wahrehmung. *Psychol. Forsch.*, 1964, **27**, 260–306.

Granger, G. W. Light and form thresholds during dark adaptation. *Acta Ophthal., Kbh.,* 1957, **35**, 361–371.

Grindley, G. C. Psychological factors in peripheral vision. *Med. Res. Coun. Spec. Rep. Ser.* 163, 1931.

Hofmann, F. B. Ueber den Einfluss schraeger Konturen auf die optische Lokalisation bei seitlicher Kopfneigung; einleitende Versuche. *Arch. ges. Physiol.,* 1910, **136**, 724–740.

Kirschmann, A. Ueber die Erkennbarkeit geometrischer Figuren und Schriftzeichen im indirekten Sehen. *Arch. ges. Psychol.,* 1908, **13**, 352–388.

Kleitman, N., & Blier, Z. A. Color and form discrimination in the periphery of the retina. *Amer. J. Physiol.,* 1928, **85**, 178–190.

Low, F. N. The development of peripheral visual acuity during the process of dark adaptation. *Amer. J. Physiol.,* 1946, **146**, 622–629.

Low, F. N. Some characteristics of peripheral visual performance. *Amer. J. Physiol.,* 1946, **146**, 573–584.

Meisenheimer, J. Experimente in peripherem Sehen von Gestalten, Untersuchungen zur Lehre vom Sehfeld, von der Vorstellungsproduktion und der Aufmerksamkeit. *Arch. ges. Psychol.,* 1928, **67**, 1–130.

Mitra, S. A report on some experiments on the indirect perception of form. *Indian J. Psychol.,* 1927, **2**, 15–22.

Munn, N. L., & Geil, G. A. A note on peripheral form discrimination. *J. gen. Psychol.,* 1931, **5**, 78–88.

Whitmer, C. A. Peripheral form and pattern discrimination under dark adaptation. *Univ. of Pittsburgh Bull.,* 1931, **7**, 238–244.

Whitmer, C. A. Peripheral form discrimination under dark adaptation. *J. gen. Psychol.,* 1933, **9**, 405–419.

Whitmer, C. A. Peripheral form discrimination under dark adaptation—erratum. *J. gen. Psychol.,* 1934, **10**, 237.

8. Reproduction

Abe, K. [An investigation of the law of memory trace deviation. I. Reproduction method and its verification.] *Jap. J. Psychol.,* 1951, **21**, 33–46.

Albien, G. *Der Anteil der nachkonstruierenden Taetigkeit des Auges und der Apperzeption an dem Behalten und der Wiedergabe einfacher Formen.* Leipzig: Nemnich, 1907.

Allport, G. W. Change and decay in the visual memory image. *Brit. J. Psychol.,* 1930, **21**, 138–148.

Amano, T. [Perception of visual forms and its reproduction. III.] *Jap. J. Psychol.,* 1931, **6**, 369–400.

Attneave, F. Symmetry, information, and memory for patterns. *Amer. J. Psychol.,* 1955, **68**, 209–222.

Baddeley, A. D. Closure and response bias in short-term memory for form. *Brit. J. Psychol.,* 1968, **59**, 139–145.

Bartel, H. Ueber die Abhaengigkeit spontaner Reproducktionen von Feldbedingungen. *Psychol. Forsch.,* 1937, **22**, 1–25.

Bartlett, F. C. *Remembering.* London and New York: Cambridge Univ. Press, 1932. (Pp. 16–33, 177–185.)

Berry, K. E. Form reproduction as a function of angularity, orientation of brightness contrast, and hue. *Percept. mot. Skills,* 1968, **26**, 235–243.

Berry, K. E. Form reproduction as a function of complexity. *Percept. mot. Skills,* 1968, **26**, 219–222.

Bevan, W., Jr., & Zener, K. Some influences of past experience upon the perceptual threshold of visual form. *Amer. J. Psychol.,* 1952, **65,** 434–442.

Braly, K. W. The influence of past experience in visual perception. *J. exp. Psychol.,* 1933, **16,** 613–643.

Brand, H., & Cohen, B. H. 'Figural goodness,' stimulus dimensions, and accuracy of recall. *Percept. mot. Skills,* 1956, **6,** 143–146.

Bresson, F., & Vurpillot, E. Contribution a une psychophysique des formes. *Psychol. Franc.,* 1960, **5,** 29–45.

Brown, W. Growth of memory images. *Amer. J. Psychol.,* 1935, **47,** 90–102.

Bruner, J. S., & Wechsler, H. Sequential probability as a determinant of perceptual closure. *J. Psychol.,* 1958, **71,** 604–606.

Bruner, J. S., Busiek, R. D., & Minturn, A. I. Assimilation in the immediate reproduction of visually perceived forms. *J. exp. Psychol.,* 1952, **44,** 151–155.

Burton, A., & Tueller, R. Successive reproductions of visually perceived forms. *J. genet. Psychol.,* 1941, **58,** 71–82.

Carmichael, L., Hogan, H. P., & Walter, A. A. Experimental study of the effect of language on the reproduction of visually perceived form. *J. exp. Psychol.,* 1932, **15,** 73–86.

Dallenbach, K. M. The effect of practice upon visual apprehension in school children. *J. educ. Psychol.,* 1914, **5,** 321–334, 387–404.

Eilks, H. Gestalttheorie, Gestaltpsychologie und Typologie, *Z. Psychol.,* 1938, **143,** 19–79.

Fehrer, E. V. An investigation of learning of visually perceived forms. *Amer. J. Psychol,* 1935, **47,** 187–221.

Foley, J. P., Jr. The effect of context upon perceptual differentiation. *Arch. Psychol., N. Y.,* 1935, No. 184.

Foster, W. S. The effect of practice upon visualizing and upon the reproduction of visual impressions. *J. educ. Psychol.,* 1911, **2,** 11–22.

Galli, A. Osservazioni sulla riproduzione di profili a più significati. *Arch. Ital. Psicol.,* 1934, **12,** 165–240.

Galli, A., & Hochheimer, W. Beobachtungen an Nachzeichnungen mehrdeutiger Feldkonturen. *Z. Psychol.,* 1934, **132,** 304–334.

Gibson, J. J. The reproduction of visually perceived forms. *J. exp. Psychol.,* 1928, **12,** 1–39.

Giese, F. Ein Versuch ueber Gestaltgedaechtnis. *Z. Paed. Psychol.,* 1915, **16,** 127–131.

Goldmeier, E. Progressive changes in memory trace. *Amer. J. Psychol.,* 1941, **54,** 490–503.

Graefe, O. Analyse des inneren Aufbaus einer im peripheren Gesichtsfeld wahrgenommenen Figur. *Z. exp. angew. Psychol.,* 1957, **4,** 104–138.

Granit, A. R. A study on the perception of form. *Brit. J. Psychol.,* 1921, **12,** 223–247.

Hanawalt, N. G. Memory traces for figures in recall and recognition. *Arch. Psychol., N. Y.,* 1937, **31,** No. 216.

Hanawalt, N. G., & Demarest, I. H. The effect of verbal suggestion in the recall period upon the reproduction of visually perceived forms. *J. exp. Psychol.,* 1939, **25,** 159–174.

Henle, M. An experimental investigation of past experience as a determinant of visual form perception. *J. exp. Psychol.,* 1942, **30,** 1–22.

Herman, D. T., Lawless, R. H., & Marshall, R. W. Variables in the effect of language on the reproduction of visually perceived forms. *Percept. mot. Skills,* 1957, **7,** 171–186.

Homma, T. [The law of Praegnanz in the process of drawing figures.] *Jap. J. Psychol.,* 1937, **12,** 112–153.

Irwin, F. W., & Seidenfeld, M. A. Asymmetries in judgment of visually perceived figures. *Psychol. Bull.,* 1936, **33,** 595–596. (Abstract)

Johannes, T. Der Einfluss der Gestaltbindung auf das Behalten. *Arch. ges. Psychol.,* 1932, **85,** 411–466.

Johannes, T. Der Einfluss der Gestaltbindung auf das Behalten. 2. Der Formenwandel von Einzelfiguren beim Einpraegungsvorgang. *Arch. ges. Psychol.,* 1939, **104**, 74–130.

Katz, D. Ueber individuelle Verschiedenheiten bei der Auffassung von Figuren. *Z. Psychol.,* 1913, **65**, 161–180.

Kern, G. Motorische Umreissung optischer Gestalten. *Neue Psychol. Stud.,* 1933, **9**, 69–108.

Koehler, W., & Restorff, H. v. Analyse von Vorgaengen im Spurenfeld: II. Zur Theorie der Reproduktion. *Psychol. Forsch.,* 1935, **21**, 56–112.

Kuhlmann, F. On the analysis of the memory consciousness: A study of mental imagery and memory of meaningless visual forms. *Psychol. Rev.,* 1906, **13**, 316–348.

Kuhlmann, F. On the analysis of memory consciousness for pictures of familiar objects. *Amer. J. Psychol.,* 1907, **18**, 389–420.

Lony, G. *Ueber die beim Nachzeichnen von Streckenteilungen auftretenden Groessenfehler.* Hamburg, 1907.

Lovibond, S. H. A further test of the hypothesis of autonomous memory trace change. *J. exp. Psychol.,* 1958, **55**, 412–415.

Meisenheimer, J. Experimente im peripheren Sehen von Gestalten. *Arch. ges. Psychol.,* 1929, **67**, 1–130.

Meyer, P. Weitere Versuche ueber die Reproduktion raeumlicher Lagen frueher wahrgenommener Figuren. *Z. Psychol.,* 1919, **82**, 1–20.

Michel, O. Experimentelle Untersuchungen ueber das Gedaechtnis: Reproduktion und Wiedererkennen von optischen Eindruecken. *Arch. ges. Psychol.,* 1923, **44**, 244–271.

Obonai, T., & Katsui, A. [Characteristics of errors in the recognition and reproduction of geometrical figures.] *Jap. J. Psychol.,* 1957, **27**, 352–361.

Perkins, J. F. Symmetry in visual recall. *Amer. J. Psychol.,* 1932, **44**, 473–490.

Philippe, J. Sur les transformations de nos images mentales. *Rev. Phil.,* 1897, **43**, 481–493.

Piéron, H. Recherches comparatives sur la mémoire des formes et celle des chiffres. *Année Psychol.,* 1920, **21**, 119–148.

Postman, L. Learned principles of organization in memory. *Psychol. Monogr.,* 1954, **68**, No. 374.

Pratt, M. B. The visual estimation of angles. *J. exp. Psychol.,* 1926, **9**, 132–140.

Radner, M., & Gibson, J. J. Orientation in visual perception; the perception of tip-character in forms. *Psychol. Monogr.,* 1935, **46**, No. 210, 48–65.

Rensch, B. Zur Psychologie des Abzeichnens einfacher geometrischer Figuren. *Z. Psychol.,* 1936, **138**, 309–328.

Renshaw, S. The visual perception and reproduction of forms by tachistoscopic methods. *J. Psychol.,* 1945, **20**, 217–232.

Richter, J., & Wamser, H. Experimentelle Untersuchung der beim Nachzeichnen von Strecken und Winkeln entstehenden Groessenfehler. *Z. Psychol.,* 1904, **35**, 321–339.

Riley, D. A. Memory for form. In L. Postman (Ed.), *Psychology in the making.* New York: Knopf, 1962. Pp. 402–465.

Rock, I., & Englestein, P. A study of memory for visual form. *Amer. J. Psychol.,* 1959, **72**, 221–229.

Sato, K. [Studies on the structure of perception in the insane: I. On the drawing of schizophrenics when reproducing an object and when copying from a pattern.] *Jap. J. Psychol.,* 1933, **8**, 91–107.

Saul, E. V. Immediate and delayed recognition of geometric form. *J. gen. Psychol.,* 1956, **55**, 163–171.

Schnore, M. M., & Partington, J. T. Immediate memory for visual patterns: Symmetry and amount of information. *Psychon. Sci.*, 1967, 8, 421–422.

Stoer, L., Corotto, L. V., & Curnutt, R. H. The role of visual perception in the reproduction of Bender-Gestalt designs. *J. Proj. Technol. Pers. Assess.*, 1965, 29, 473–478.

Sugimonto, Y. [The disintegration of content of Gestalt perception in the memory process.] *Jap. J. Psychol.*, 1934, 9, 38–52.

Taylor, M. M. Effect of anchoring and distance perception on the reproduction of forms. *Percept. mot. Skills*, 1961, 12, 203–230.

Tsao, J. C. A study in the recognition of figures. *Brit. J. Psychol.*, 1949, 40, 57–67.

Tsuji, S. [The function of "vector of situation" in memory.] *Jap. J. Psychol.*, 1935, 10, 567–599.

Turner, M. B. The relation of preference to figural reproductions. *Amer. J. Psychol.*, 1952, 65, 161–176.

Turner, M. B., & Craig, E. A. The effect of figural reproduction on recognition. *J. Psychol.*, 1954, 38, 265–270.

Walker, E. L., & Veroff, J. Changes in the memory trace for perceived forms with successive reproduction. *Amer. J. Psychol.*, 1956, 69, 395–402.

Wallen, R. Size changes in remembered figures. *J. exp. Psychol.*, 1943, 32, 464–472.

Ward, T. H. G. An experiment on serial reproduction with special reference to the changes in the design of early coin types. *Brit. J. Psychol.*, 1949, 39, 142–147.

Wells, G. R. Some experiments in motor reproduction of visually perceived forms. *Psychol. Rev.*, 1917, 24, 322–327.

Witwicki, T. [*On representation or the relation between the image and the reproduced object.*] Lwow: Nakladem Towarzystwa Naukowego, 1935.

Wright, J. v. On qualitative changes in the retention of forms. *Scand. J. Psychol.*, 1964, 5, 65–70.

Wulf, F. Beitraege zur Psychologie der Gestalt: VI. Ueber die Veraenderung von Vorstellungen (Gedaechtnis und Gestalt). *Psychol. Forsch.*, 1922, 1, 333–373.

Zangwill, O. L. An investigation of the relationship between the processes of reproducing and recognizing simple figures, with special reference to Koffka's trace theory. *Brit. J. Psychol.*, 1937, 27, 250–276.

Zoll, M. Die Fehler bei der graphischen Interpolation einer vorher gezeigten Kurve. *Arch. ges. Psychol.*, 1939, 105, 58–100.

9. Associative response

Battig, W. F. Interrelationships between measures of association and structural characteristics of nonsense shapes. *Percept. mot. Skills*, 1962, 14, 3–6.

Edelman, S. K. Analysis of some stimulus factors involved in the associative response. Unpublished doctoral dissertation. Purdue Univ. 1960. *Diss. Abstr.*, 1960, 21, 1630.

Eisenman, R. The association value of random shapes revisited. *Psychon. Sci.*, 1966, 6, 397–398.

Goldstein, A. G. Spatial orientation as a factor in eliciting associative responses to random shapes. *Percept. mot. Skills,*, 1961, 12, 15–25.

Karas, G. G., Edelman, S. K., Farrell, R. J., & DuBois, T. E. An experimental comparison of associative responses to two types of randomly derived stimuli. *Proc. Iowa Acad. Sci.*, 1961, 68, 535–542.

Karas, G. G., Edelman, S. K., Zyzanski, S., & Goodrich, D. An analysis of the content of perceptual responses to randomly derived stimuli. *Proc. Iowa Acad. Sci.*, 1961, 68, 529–534.

Lewis, D., & Boehnert, J. B. Assessing the connotative strengths of random shapes. *Proc. Iowa Acad. Sci.,* 1965, 72, 378–389.

Vanderplas, J. M., & Garvin, E. A. The association value of random shapes. *J. exp. Psychol.,* 1959, 57, 147–154.

B. Animal subjects

1. General

Falk, J. L., & D'Amato, C. J. Automation of pattern discrimination in the rat. *Psychol. Rep.,* 1962, 10, 24.

Gellerman, L. W. Chance orders of alternating stimuli in visual discrimination experiments. *J. genet. Psychol.,* 1933, 42, 206–208.

Hinde, R. A. *Animal behavior.* New York: McGraw-Hill, 1966. (Pp. 66–74.)

Howarth, C. I., The methodology of experiments in pattern recognition. In W. Wathen-Dunn (Ed.), *Models for the perception of speech and visual forms.* Cambridge, Massachusetts: The M.I.T. Press, 1967. Pp. 290–295.

Hunter, W. S. The question of form perception. *J. Anim. Behav.,* 1913, 3, 329–333.

Johnson, H. M. Hunter on the question of form perception in animals. *J. Anim. Behav.,* 1914, 4, 134–135.

Johnson, H. M. Visual pattern discrimination in the vertebrates. I. Problems and methods. *J. Anim. Behav.,* 1914, 4, 319–339.

Sutherland, N. S. *The methods and findings of experiments on the visual discrimination of shape by animals.* Oxford, England: Exp. Psychol. Soc., 1961.

Sutherland, N. S. Visual discrimination in animals. *Brit. Med. Bull.,* 1964, 20(1), 54–59.

Yerkes, R. M., & Watson, J. B. Methods of studying vision in animals. *Behav. Monogr.,* 1911, 1, No. 2.

2. Apes and monkeys

Andrew, G., & Harlow, H. F. Performance of macaque monkeys on a test of the concept of generalized triangularity. *Comp. Psychol. Monogr.,* 1948, 19, No. 3.

Butter, C. M. Detection of hidden figures by rhesus monkeys. *Percept. mot. Skills,* 1966, 23, 979–986.

Cole, J. The relative importance of color and form in discrimination learning in monkeys. *J. comp. physiol. Psychol.,* 1953, 46, 16–18.

Dominguez, K. E. A study of visual illusions in the monkey. *J. genet. Psychol.,* 1954, 85, 105–127.

Farrer, D. N., & Craver, G. P. Picture memory in chimpanzees. USAF Arl. Tech. Rep. No. 65–7, 1965.

Gellerman, L. W. Form discrimination in chimpanzees and two-year-old children: I. Form (triangularity) per se. *J. genet. Psychol.,* 1933, 42, 2–27.

Gellerman, L. W. Form discrimination in chimpanzees and two-year-old children: II. Form versus background. *J. genet. Psychol.,* 1933, 42, 28–50.

Hicks, L. H. Effects of stimulus rotation on discrimination learning by monkeys. *Psychon. Sci.,* 1967, 9, 57–58.

Hunton, V. D., & Hicks, L. H. Discrimination of figural orientation by monkeys and children. *Percept. mot. Skills,* 1965, 21, 55–59.

Johnson, H. M. Visual pattern discrimination in the vertebrates. III. Effective differences in width of visible stria for the monkey and the chick. *J. Anim. Behav.,* 1916, 6, 169–188.

Kluever, H. *Behavior mechanisms in monkeys.* Chicago, Illinois: Univ. of chicago Press, 1933.

Nash, A. J., & Michels, K. M. Squirrel monkeys and discrimination learning: Figural interaction, redundancies, and random shapes. *J. exp. Psychol.,* 1966, **72**, 132–137.

Neet, C. C. Visual pattern discrimination in the *Macacus rhesus* monkey. *J. genet. Psychol.,*
1933, **43**, 163–196.

Nissen, H. W., & McCulloch, T. L. Equated and non-equated stimulus conditions in discrimination learning by chimpanzees: I. Comparison with unlimited response. *J. comp.
Psychol.,* 1937, **23**, 165–189.

Polidora, V. J. Stimulus correlates of visual pattern discrimination by monkeys: sidedness.
Percept. mot. Skills, 1965, **20**, 461–469.

Polidora, V. J. Stimulus correlates of visual pattern discrimination by monkeys: Multidimensional analyses. *Percept. Psychophys.,* 1966, **1**, 405–414.

Polidora, V. J., & Thompson, W. J. Stimulus correlates of visual pattern discrimination by
monkeys: area and contour. *J. comp. physiol. Psychol.,* 1964, **58**, 264–269.

Polidora, V. J., & Thompson, W. J. Stimulus correlates of visual pattern discrimination by
monkeys: pattern complexity. *Percept. mot. Skills,* 1965, **21**, 71–79.

Riopelle, A. J., Rahm, U., Itoigawa, N., & Draper, W. A. Discrimination of mirror image
patterns by rhesus monkeys. *Percept. mot. Skills,* 1964, **19**, 383–389.

Rosenblum, L. A., Witkin, H., Kaufman, J. C., & Brosgole, L. Perceptual disembedding in
monkeys: note on method and preliminary findings. *Percept. mot. Skills,* 1965, **20**,
729–736.

Tellier, M. L'intelligence des singes inférieurs. La vision des formes et la généralisation. *Mém.
Soc. Sci. Liége,* 1933, **19**, 1–76.

Verlaine, L. L'analyse et la synthèse dans la perception des formes chez le macaque. *Ann.
Soc. Zool. Belg.,* 1935, **66**, 57–66.

Warren, J. M. Additivity of cues in visual pattern discrimination by monkeys. *J. comp.
physiol. Psychol.,* 1953, **46**, 484–486.

Warren, J. M. Effect of geometrical regularity in visual form discrimination by monkeys. *J.
comp. physiol. Psychol.,* 1953, **46**, 237–240.

Warren, J. M. The influence of area and arrangement on visual pattern discrimination by
monkeys. *J. comp. physiol. Psychol.,* 1953, **46**, 231–236.

Warren, J. M. Perceptual dominance in discrimination learning by monkeys. *J. comp.
physiol. Psychol.,* 1954, **47**, 290–292.

Woodburne, L. S. Geometrical shape discrimination by "Saimiri sciureus." *Psychon. Sci.,*
1965. **3**, 309–310.

3. Dogs

Karn, H. W. Visual pattern discrimination in dogs. *Univ. Pittsburgh Bull.,* 1931, **7**, 391–392.

Karn, H. W., & Munn, N. L. Visual pattern discrimination in the dog. *J. genet. Psychol.,*
1932, **40**, 363–374.

Williams, J. A. Experiments with form perception and learning in dogs. *Comp. Psychol.
Monog.,* 1926, **4**, No. 18.

4. Cats

McAllister, W. G., & Berman, H. D. Visual form discrimination in the domestic cat. *J. comp.
Psychol.,* 1931, **12**, 207–242.

Robinson, J. S., Metzger, D. R., & Voneida, T. J. Same-different discrimination of
horizontal and vertical stripe patterns in cats. *Psychon. Sci.,* 1968, **11**, 331–332.

Smith, K. U. Form discrimination in the cat. *Psychol. Bull.,* 1933, **30**, 546–547. (Abstract)

Smith, K. U. The acuity of the cat's discrimination of visual form. *Psychol. Bull.,* 1934, **31**, 618–619. (Abstract)

Smith, K. U. Visual discrimination in the cat: I. The capacity of the cat for visual figure discrimination. *J. genet. Psychol.,* 1934, **44**, 301–320.

Smith, K. U. Visual discrimination in the cat: II. A further study of the capacity of the cat for visual figure discrimination. *J. genet. Psychol.,* 1934, **45**, 336–357.

Smith, K. U. Visual discrimination in the cat: III. The relative effect of paired and unpaired stimuli in the discriminative behavior of the cat. *J. genet. Psychol.,* 1936, **48**, 29–57.

Sutherland, N. S. Cat's ability to discriminate oblique rectangles. *Science,* 1963, **139**, 209–210.

5. Squirrels

Dodwell, P. C., & Bessant, D. E. The squirrel as an experimental animal: Some tests of visual capacity. *Can. J. Psychol.,* 1961, **15**, 226–236.

Hitchcock, L., Jr. Comparative studies of the contribution of areal asymmetry, rotation, and sidedness to form discrimination. Unpublished doctoral dissertation, Purdue Univ., 1961. *Diss. Abstr.,* 1962, **22**, 2476.

Hitchcock, L., Jr., Michels, K. M., & Brown, D. R. Discrimination learning: squirrels vs. raccoons. *Percept. mot. Skills,* 1963, **16**, 405–414.

Michels, K. M., Pittman, G. G., Hitchcock, L., Jr., & Brown, D. R. Visual discrimination: tree squirrels and quantified stimulus dimensions. *Percept. mot. Skills,* 1962, **15**, 443–450.

Pittman, G. G. Form discrimination and learning set formation by two species of *Sciurus* as a function of quantitatively controlled stimulus parameters. Unpublished doctoral dissertation, Purdue Univ., 1959. *Diss. Abstr.,* 1960, **20**, 2924.

6. Raccoons (see also Section V, B, 5)

Johnson, J. I., Jr. Studies of visual discrimination by raccoons. Unpublished doctoral dissertation, Purdue Univ., 1957. *Diss. Abstr.,* 1957, **17**, 1608.

Johnson, J. I., Jr., & Michels, K. M. Learning sets and object size effects in visual discrimination by raccoons. *J. comp. physiol. Psychol.,* 1958, **51**, 376–379.

Munn, N. L. Pattern and brightness discrimination in raccoons. *J. genet. Psychol.,* 1930, **37**, 3–34.

7. Rats and mice (see also Sections II, F, 1, 2, and 3)

Bitterman, M. E., Calvin, A. D., & Elam, C. B. Perceptual differentiation in the course of non-differential reinforcement. *J. comp. physiol. Psychol.,* 1953, **46**, 393–397.

Brown, L. T. Some properties of stimulus complexity related to exploratory behavior in rats. Unpublished doctoral dissertation, Princeton Univ., 1961. *Diss. Abstr.,* 1962, **23**, 1790.

Dodwell, P. C. Some effects of pre-training on subsequent shape discrimination in rats. *Brit. J. Anim. Behav.,* 1956, **4**, 81. (Abstract)

Dodwell, P. C. Visual orientation preferences in the rat. *Quart. J. exp. Psychol.,* 1961, **13**, 40–47.

Dodwell, P. C. Anomalous transfer effects after shape discrimination training in the rat. *Psychon. Sci.,* 1965, **3**, 97–98.

Elias, M. F. Relation of stimulus size to pattern discrimination training for the hooded rat. *Percept. mot. Skills,* 1967, **25**, 613–620.

Elias, M. F., & Stein, A. I. Relation of pattern spacing to pattern discrimination in the hooded rat. *Percept. mot. Skills,* 1968, **26**, 447–454.

Fields, P. E. Form discrimination in the white rat. *J. comp. Psychol.,* 1928, **8**, 143–158.

Fields, P. E. The white rat's use of visual stimuli in the discrimination of geometric figures. *J. comp. Psychol.,* 1929, **8**, 107–122.

Fields, P. E. A reply to Munn concerning form discrimination. *J. genet. Psychol.,* 1930, **37**, 546–552.

Fields, P. E. Contributions to visual figure discrimination in the white rat, Part I. *J. comp. Psychol.,* 1931, **11**, 327–348.

Fields, P. E. Contributions to visual figure discrimination in the white rat, Part II. *J. comp. Psychol.,* 1931, **11**, 349–366.

Fields, P. E. Concerning the discrimination of geometrical figures by white rats. *J. comp. Psychol.,* 1932, **14**, 63–77.

Fields, P. E. Studies in concept formation. I. The development of the concept of triangularity by the white rat. *Comp. Psychol. Monogr.,* 1932, **9**, 1–70.

Fields, P. E. Studies in concept formation: II. A new multiple stimulus jumping apparatus for visual figure discrimination. *J. comp. Psychol.,* 1935, **20**, 183–203.

Fields, P. E. Studies in concept formation: III. A note on the retention of visual figure discrimination. *J. comp. Psychol.,* 1936, **21**, 131–136.

Fields, P. E. Studies in concept formation: IV. A comparison of white rats with raccoons with respect to their visual discrimination of geometric figures. *J. comp. Psychol.,* 1936, **21**, 341–355.

Fields, P. E. The efficiency of the serial multiple visual discrimination apparatus and method with white rats. *J. comp. physiol. Psychol.,* 1953, **46**, 69–76.

Hunter, I. M. L. The visual world of rats. *Brit. J. Anim. Behav.,* 1953, **1**, 160–161. (Abstract)

Karmel, B. Z. Randomness, complexity, and visual preference behavior in the hooded rat and domestic chick. *J. comp. physiol. Psychol.,* 1966, **61**, 487–489.

Karmel, B. Z. The effect of complexity, amount of contour, element size, and element arrangement on visual preference behavior in the hooded rat, domestic chick, and human infant. Unpublished doctoral dissertation, George Washington Univ., 1966. *Diss. Abstr.,* 1967, **27**(8–B), 2894.

Kirk, S. A. Extra-striate functions in the discrimination of complex visual patterns. *J. comp. Psychol.,* 1936, **21**, 145–159.

Krechevsky, I. An experimental investigation of the principle of proximity in the visual perception of the rat. *Arch. Neurol. Psychiat.,* 1938, **22**, 497–523.

Krechevsky, I. A note on the perception of linear gestalten in the rat. *J. genet. Psychol.,* 1938, **52**, 241–246.

Lashley, K. S. Visual discrimination of size and form in the albino rat. *J. Anim. Behav.,* 1912, **2**, 329ff.

Lashley, K. S. The mechanism of vision: I. A method for rapid analysis of pattern vision in the rat. *J. genet. Psychol.,* 1930, **37**, 453–460.

Lashley, K. S. The mechanism of vision: VIII. The projection of the retina upon the cerebral cortex of the rat. *J. comp. Neurol.,* 1934, **60**, 57–79.

Lashley, K. S. Conditional reactions in the rat. *J. Psychol.,* 1938, **6**, 311–324.

Lashley, K. S. The mechanism of vision: XV. Preliminary studies of the rat's capacity for detail vision. *J. gen. Psychol.,* 1938, **18**, 123–193.

Law, O. I. Preference in the rat for vertical or horizontal stripes after training on a white-black discrimination. *Amer. J. Psychol.,* 1954, **67**, 714–716.

Libaw, F. B. The effects of prior part-experiences on visual form perception in the albino rat. Unpublished doctoral dissertation, Univ. of Southern California, 1960. *Diss. Abstr.,* 1961, **22**, 1724.

Munn, N. L. Concerning visual form discrimination in the white rat. *J. genet. Psychol.,* 1929, **36**, 291–302.

Munn, N. L. A note on Lashley's method for studying vision in the rat. *J. genet. Psychol.,* 1930, **37**, 528–530.

Munn, N. L. An answer to Fields concerning form discrimination. *J. genet. Psychol.,* 1930, **37**, 552–553.

Munn, N. L. Visual pattern discrimination in the white rat. *J. comp. Psychol.,* 1930, **10**, 145–166.

Munn, N. L. An apparatus for testing visual discrimination in animals. *J. genet. Psychol.,* 1931, **39**, 342–358.

Munn, N. L. *Handbook of psychological research on the rat.* Cambridge, Massachusetts: Riverside Press, 1950.

North, A. J., Maller, O., & Hughes, C. Conditional discrimination and stimulus patterning. *J. comp. physiol. Psychol.,* 1958, **51**, 711–715.

Reetz, W. Unterschiedliches visuelles Lernvermoegen von Ratten und Maeusen. *Z. Tierpsychol.,* 1957, **14**, 347–361.

Rowley, J. B., & Bolles, M. M. Form discrimination in white mice. *J. comp. Psychol.,* 1935, **20**, 205–210.

Sutherland, N. S. Visual discrimination of horizontal and vertical rectangles by rats on a new discrimination training apparatus. *Quart. J. exp. Psychol.,* 1961, **13**, 117–121.

Sutherland, N. S. A further experiment on the discrimination of open and closed shapes by rats. *Quart. J. exp. Psychol.,* 1964, **16**, 268–271.

Sutherland, N. S., & Carr, A. E. Visual discrimination of open and closed shapes by rats: II. Transfer tests. *Quart. J. exp. Psychol.,* 1962, **14**, 140–156.

Sutherland, N. S., & Carr, A. E. Shape discrimination by rats: Squares and rectangles. *Brit. J. Psychol.,* 1964, **55**, 39–48.

Sutherland, N. S., Carr, A. R., & Mackintosh, J. A. Visual discrimination of open and closed shapes by rats: I. Training. *Quart. J. exp. Psychol.,* 1962, **14**, 129–139.

Thompson, W. R., & Solomon, L. M. Spontaneous pattern discrimination in the rat. *J. comp. physiol. Psychol.,* 1954, **47**, 104–107.

Woerner, R. Ueber die Leistungsgrenze beim Auffassen figuraler Gestalten durch Maeuse. *Biol. Zbl.,* 1936, **56**, 2–27.

Zimmerling, H. Die Orientierung von Maeusen durch unselbststaendige transponierte Teilinhalte des optischen Wahrnehmungsfeldes. *Biol. Zbl.,* 1934, **54**, 226–250.

8. Other mammals

Herter, K. Psychologische Untersuchungen an einem Mauswiesel (*Mustela nivalis*). *Z. Tierpsychol.,* 1940, **3**, 249–263.

James, W. T. A study of visual discrimination in the opossum. *J. genet. Psychol.,* 1960, **97**, 127–130.

Kellog, W. N., & Rice, C. E. Visual problem-solving in a bottlenose dolphin. *Science,* 1964, **143**, 1052–1055.

Pollard, J. S., Beale, I. L., Lysons, A. M., & Preston, A. C. Visual discrimination in the ferret. *Percept. mot. Skills,* 1967, **24**, 279–282.

Rensch, B. The intelligence of elephants. *Sci. Amer.,* 1957, **196**(2), 44–49.

Rensch, B., & Altevogt, R. Visuelles Lernvermoegen eines indischen Elefanten. *Z. Tierpsychol.,* 1953, **10**, 119–134.

Rensch, B., & Altevogt, R. Das Ausmass visueller Lernfaehigkeit indischer Elefanten. *Z. Tierpsychol.,* 1955, **12**, 68–76.

Schusterman, R. J., & Thomas, T. Shape discrimination and transfer in the California sea lion. *Psychon. Sci.,* 1966, **5**, 21–22.

Seitz, A. Untersuchungen ueber das Formensehen und optische Groessenunterscheidung bei der Skudde (ostpreussisches Landschaf). *Z. Tierpsychol.,* 1951, **8**, 423–441.

9. Birds

Bingham, H. C. Size and form perception in *Gallus domesticus. J. Anim. Behav.,* 1913, **3**, 65–113.

Bingham, H. C. Visual perception of the chick. *Beh. Psychol. Monogr.,* 1922, **4**.

Coburn, C. A. The behavior of the crow. *J. Anim. Behav.,* 1914, **4**, 185–201.

Englemann, C. Versuche ueber den Geschmacksinn des Huhnes. IV. Der Einfluss von Korngroesse und Koernerformen auf die Beliebtheit einiger Getreidearten bei Zwerg-huehnern. *Z. Tierpsychol.,* 1940, **4**, 204–218.

Engelmann, C. Versuche ueber den Geschmacksinn des Huhnes. V. Die Beliebtheit einzelner Koernerformen bei nur optischer Darbietung. *Z. Tierpsychol.,* 1940, **4**, 283–347.

Engelmann, C. Versuche ueber den Geschmacksinn des Huhnes. VI. Ueber angeborenen Formvorlieben bei Huehnern. *Z. Tierpsychol.,* 1941, **5**, 42–59.

Fantz, R. L. Form preferences in newly hatched chicks. *J. comp. physiol. Psychol.,* 1957, **50**, 422–430.

Katz, D., & Revesz, G. Experimentell-psychologische Untersuchung mit Huehnern. *Z. Psychol.,* 1908, **50**, 59–116.

Menkhaus, I. Versuche ueber einaeugiges Lernen und Transponieren beim Haushuhn. *Z. Tierpsychol.,* 1957, **14**, 210–230.

Munn, N. L. The relative efficacy of form and background in the chick's discrimination of visual patterns. *J. comp. Psychol.,* 1931, **12**, 41–75.

Pastore, N. Form perception and size constancy in the duckling. *J. Psychol.,* 1958, **45**, 259–261.

Revesz, G. Experiments on animal space perception. II. Investigation of illusory space perception in hens. *Brit. J. Psychol.,* 1924, **14**, 399–414.

Stichmann, W. Transpositionsversuche mit Haushuhnrassen stark verschiedener Koerper-groesse. *Z. Tierpsychol.,* 1962, **19**, 290–320.

Towe, A. L. A study of figural equivalence in the pigeon. Unpublished doctoral dissertation, Univ. of Washington, 1953. *Diss. Abstr.,* 1954, **14**, 559.

Towe, A. L. A study of figural equivalence in the pigeon. *J. comp. physiol. Psychol.,* 1954, **47**, 283–287.

Warden, C. J., & Baar, J. The Mueller-Lyer illusion in the ring dove. *J. comp. Psychol.,* 1929, **9**, 275–292.

Winslow, C. N. Visual illusions in the chick. *Arch. Psychol., N. Y.,* 1933, No. 153.

Zeigler, H. P., & Schmerler, S. Visual discrimination by pigeons. *Anim. Behav.,* 1965, **13**, 475–477.

10. Amphibians and reptiles

Casteel, D. B. The discriminative ability of the painted turtle. *J. Anim. Behav.,* 1911, **1**, 1–28.

Ehrenhardt, H. Formensehen und Sehschaerfebestimmungen bei Eidechsen. *Z. vergl. Physiol.*, 1937, **24**, 258–304.

Kuroda, R. Studies on visual discrimination in the tortoise *Clemmys Japonica. Acta Psychol., Keijo*, 1933, **2**, 31–59.

Meng, M. Untersuchungen zum Farben- und Formensehen der Erdkroete (*Bufo bufo). Zool. Beitr.*, 1957, **3**, 313–364.

Pache, J. Formensehen bei Froeschen. *Z. vergl. Physiol.*, 1932, **17**, 423–463.

Parriss, J. R. Retention of shape discrimination after regeneration of the optic nerves in the toad. *Quart. J. exp. Psychol.*, 1963, **15**, 22–26.

11. Fish

Braddock, J. C., Braddock, Z. I., & Richter, H. Form discrimination in the Siamese fighting fish, *Betta splendens. Amer. Zoologist,* 1961, **1**, 345. (Abstract)

Fisher, P. Untersuchungen ueber das Formsehen der Elritze. *Z. Tierpsychol.*, 1940, **4**, 797–876.

Hager, H. J. Untersuchungen ueber das optische Differenzierungsvermoegen der Fische. *Z. vergl. Physiol.*, 1938, **26**, 282–302.

Hemmings, G. The effect of pretraining in the circle/square discrimination situation. *Anim. Behav.*, 1965, **13**, 212–216.

Hemmings, G., & Matthews, W. A. Shape discrimination in tropical fish. *Quart. J. exp. Psychol.*, 1963, **15**, 272–278.

Herter, K. Dressurversuche an Fischen. *Z. vergl. Physiol.*, 1929, **10**, 699–711.

Herter, K. Weitere Dressurversuche an Fischen. *Z. vergl. Physiol.*, 1930, **11**, 730–748.

Herter, K. Zur Psychologie und Sinnesphysiologie der Zwergwelse (*Ameiurus nebulosus). Biol. Zbl.*, 1949, **68**, 77–95.

Herter, K. Vom Lernvermoegen der Fische. In *Moderne Biologie, Festschrift f. H. Nachtsheim.* Berlin, 1950. Pp. 163–179.

Herter, K. *Die Fischdressuren und ihre sinnesphysiologische Grundlagen.* Berlin: Akademie-Verlag, 1953.

Macintosh, J., & Sutherland, N. S. Visual discrimination by the goldfish: The orientation of rectangles. *Anim. Behav.*, 1963, **11**, 135–141.

Maes, R. La vision des formes chez les poissons. *Ann. Soc. Zool. Belg.*, 1929, **60**, 103–129.

Matthews, W. A. Shape discrimination in tropical fish. *Anim. Behav.*, 1964, **12**, 111–115.

Meesters, A. Ueber die Organisation des Gesichtsfeldes der Fische. *Z. Tierpsychol.*, 1940, **4**, 84–149.

Perkins, F. T. A further study of configurational learning in the goldfish. *J. exp. Psychol.*, 1931, **14**, 508–538.

Perkins, F. T., & Wheeler, R. H. Configurational learning in the goldfish. *Comp. Psychol. Monogr.*, 1930, **7**, No. 31.

Rowley, J. B. Discrimination limens of pattern and size in the goldfish *Carassius auratus. Genet. Psychol. Monogr.*, 1934, **15**, 245–302.

Saxena, A. Lernkapazitaet, Gedaechtnis und Transpositionsvermoegen bei Forellen. *Zool. Jahrb.*, 1960, **69**, 63–94.

Schaller, A. Sinnesphysiologische und psychologische Untersuchungen an Wasserkaefern und Fischen. *Z. vergl. Physiol.*, 1926, **4**, 1–38.

Schulte, A. Transfer- und Transpositionsversuche mit monokular dressierten Fischen. *Z. vergl. Physiol.*, 1957, **39**, 432–476.

Zunini, G. Contributo allo studio dell'apprendimento dei pesci (*Phoxinus laevis* Agas). *Arch. Ital. Psicol.*, Fasc. II, E. III, 1937, **25**, 3–33.

12. Octopus (see also Sections II, F, 1, 2, and 3)

Boycott, B. B. Learning in *Octopus vulgaris* and other Cephalopods. *Pubbl. Staz. Zool. Napoli,* 1954, **25**, 67–93.

Boycott, B. B., & Young, J. Z. A memory system in *Octopus vulgaris* Lamarck. *Proc. Zool. Soc. London,* 1955, **143**, 449–480.

Boycott, B. B., & Young, J. Z. Reactions to shape in *Octopus vulgaris* Lamarck. *Proc. Royal Soc.,* 1956, **126**, 491–547.

Cate, J. ten, & Cate-Kazeewa, B. ten. Les octopus vulgaris peuvent-ils discerner les formes? *Arch. Néerl. Physiol.,* 1938, **23**, 541–551.

Mackintosh, N. J., Mackintosh, J., & Sutherland, N. S. The relative importance of horizontal and vertical extents in shape discrimination by octopus. *Anim. Behav.,* 1963, **11**, 355–358.

Parriss, J. R., & Young, J. Z. The limits of transfer and of learned discrimination to figures of larger and smaller sizes. *Z. vergl. Physiol.,* 1962, **45**, 618–635.

Sutherland, N. S. Visual discrimination in octopuses. *Bull. Brit. Psychol. Soc.,* 1956, **29**, 38. (Abstract)

Sutherland, N. S. Visual discrimination of orientation by *Octopus. Brit. J. Psychol.,* 1957, **48**, 55–71.

Sutherland, N. S. Visual discrimination of orientation and shape by *Octopus. Nature,* 1957, **179**, 11–13.

Sutherland, N. S. Visual discrimination of the orientation of rectangles by *Octopus vulgaris* Lamarck. *J. comp. physiol. Psychol.,* 1958, **51**, 452–458.

Sutherland, N. S. Visual discrimination of shape by *Octopus:* Squares and triangles. *Quart. J. exp. Psychol.,* 1958, **10**, 40–47.

Sutherland, N. S. Visual discrimination of shape by *Octopus:* Circles and squares, and circles and triangles. *Quart. J. exp. Psychol.,* 1959, **11**, 24–32.

Sutherland, N. S. Visual discrimination of orientation by *Octopus:* Mirror images. *Brit. J. Psychol.* 1960, **51**, 9–18.

Sutherland, N. S. Visual discrimination of shape by *Octopus:* Open and closed forms. *J. comp. physiol. Psychol.,* 1960, **53**, 104–112.

Sutherland, N. S. The visual discrimination of shape by *Octopus:* Squares and rectangles. *J. comp. physiol. Psychol.,* 1960, **53**, 95–103.

Sutherland, N. S. Discrimination of horizontal and vertical extents by *Octopus. J. comp. physiol. Psychol.,* 1961, **54**, 43–48.

Sutherland, N. S. Visual discrimination of shape by *Octopus:* Squares and crosses. *J. comp. physiol. Psychol.,* 1962, **55**, 939–943.

Sutherland, N. S. The shape discrimination of stationary shapes by octopuses. *Amer. J. Psychol.,* 1963, **76**, 177–190.

Sutherland, N. S., & Carr, A. E. The visual discrimination of shape by *Octopus:* The effects of stimulus size. *Quart. J. exp. Psychol.,* 1963, **15**, 225–235.

Sutherland, N. S., Mackintosh, J., & Mackintosh, N. J. The visual discrimination of reduplicated patterns by octopus. *Anim. Behav.,* 1963, **11**, 106–110.

Sutherland, N. S., & Muntz, W. R. A. Simultaneous discrimination training and preferred direction of motion in visual discrimination of shape in *Octopus vulgaris* Lamarck. *Pubbl. Staz. Zool. Napoli,* 1959, **31**, 109–126.

Young, J. Z. The visual system of *Octopus:* I. Regularities in the retina and optic lobes of *Octopus* in relation to form discrimination. *Nature,* 1960, **186**, 836–839.

13. Insects

Autrum, H. Formensehen in menschlichen und tierischen Augen. *Umschau,* 1954, No. 1, 4–6.

Baumgaertner, H. Der Formensinn und die Sehschaerfe der Bienen. *Z. vergl. Physiol.,* 1928, 7, 56–143.

Buddenbrock, W. v. Eine neue Methode zur Erforschung des Formensehens der Insekten. *Naturwissenschaften,* 1935, 23, 98–100.

Hertz, M. Die Organisation des optischen Feldes bei der Biene. *Z. vergl. Physiol.,* 1929, 8, 693–748.

Hertz, M. Die organisation des optischen Feldes bei der Biene. III. *Z. vergl. Physiol.,* 1931, 14, 629–674.

Hertz, M. Ueber figurale Intensitaeten und Qualitaeten in der optischen Wahrnehmung der Biene. *Biol. Zentbl.,* 1933, 53, 10–40.

Hertz, M. Zur Physiologie des Formen- und Bewegungssehens. III. Figurale Unterscheidung und reziproke Dressuren bei der Biene. *Z. vergl. Physiol.,* 1934, 21, 604–615.

Hertz, M. Die Organisation des optischen Feldes bei der Biene. II. *Z. vergl. Physiol.,* 1936, 11, 107–145.

Hertz, M. Beitrag zum Farbensinn und Formensinn der Biene. *Z. vergl. Physiol.,* 1937, 24, 413–421.

Hundertmark, A. Das Formenunterscheidungsvermoegen der Eiraupen der Nonne (*Lymantria monacha* L.). *Z. vergl. Physiol.,* 1937, 24, 563–582.

Ilse, D. Zur "Formwahrnehmung" der Tagfalter. I. Spontane Bevorzugung von Formmerkmalen durch Vanessen. *Z. vergl. Physiol.,* 1932, 17, 537–556.

Jander, R., & Voss, C. Die Bedeutung von Streifenmustern fuer das Formensehen der roten Waldameise (*Formica rufa*). *Z. Tierpsychol.,* 1963, 20, 1–9.

Tischler, W. Ein Beitrag zum Formensehen der Insekten. *Zool. Jahrb., Allg. Zool. Physiol.,* 1936, 57, 157–202.

Turner, C. H. Experiments on pattern vision of the honey bee. *Biol. Bull.,* 1911, 21, 249–264.

Verlaine-Gos, M. La théorie de la forme. Le problème de la prégnance. *Bull. Soc. sci. Liége,* 1937, 2–3.

Verlaine-Gos, M. La théorie de la forme. La perception des formes géométriques simples. *Bull. Soc. Sci. Liége,* 1937, 5, 186–193.

Verlaine-Gos, M. La théorie de la forme. Perception des formes et passé psychologique du sujet. *Bull. Soc. Sci. Liége,* 1937, 8–10, 287–291.

Wallace, G. K. Some experiments on form perception in the nymphs of the desert locust, *Schistocerca gregaria* Forskal. *J. exp. Biol.,* 1958, 35, 765–775.

Wallace, G. K. Visual perception and behavior in the desert locust. *Anim. Behav.,* 1958, 6, 242–243.

Wehner, R. Pattern recognition in bees. *Nature,* 1967, 215, 1244–1248.

Wehner, R., & Lindauer, M. Zur Physiologie des Formensehens bei der Honigbiene. I. Winkelunterscheidung an vertikal orientierten Streifenmustern. *Z. vergl. Physiol.,* 1966, 52, 290–324.

Zerrahn, G. Formdressur und Formunterscheidung bei der Honigbiene. *Z. vergl. Physiol.,* 1933, 20, 117–150.

VI. DEVELOPMENT OF FORM PERCEPTION

A. In man

1. Ontogenetic studies

Fellows, B. J. *The discrimination process and development*. New York: Pergamon Press, 1968. (Chapters 16, 17, 18.)

Fantz, R. L. A method for studying early visual development. *Percept. mot. Skills,* 1956, 6, 13–15.

Francès, R. *Le développement perceptif.* Paris: Presses Universitaires de France, 1962.

Held, R., & Hein, A. On the modifiability of form perception. In W. Wathen-Dunn (Ed.), *Models for the perception of speech and visual forms.* Cambridge, Massachusetts: M.I.T. Press, 1967. Pp. 296–304.

Hershenson, M. Development of the perception of form. *Psychol. Bull.,* 1967, 67, 326–336.

Nelson, T. M., & Bartley, S. H. Various factors playing a role in children's response to flat copy. *J. genet. Psychol.,* 1962, **100**, 289–308.

Piaget, J. *Les mécanismes perceptifs.* Paris: Presses Universitaires de France, 1961.

Pick, A. D. Improvement of visual and tactual form discrimination. *J. exp. Psychol.,* 1965, 69, 331–339.

Rosenblith, J. F. Judgments of simple geometric figures by children. *Percept. mot. Skills,* 1965, 21, 947–990.

Ruessel, A. Ueber Formauffassung zwei- bis fuenfjaehriger Kinder. *Neue Psychol. Stud.,* 1931, 7, 1–108

Shabalin, S. N. [The objective-gnostic moments in the perception of form in preschool children.] *Sci. Mem. Herzen Pedag. Inst.,* 1939, 18, 59–106.

Solley, C. M., & Murphy, G. *Development of the perceptual world.* New York: Basic Books, 1960. (Chapters 7, 13.)

Wohlwill, J. F. Developmental studies in perception. *Psychol. Bull.,* 1960, 57, 249–288.

a. Eye movements

Piaget, J., & Vinh-Bang. Comparaison des mouvements oculaires et des centrations du regard chez l'enfant et chez l'adulte. *Arch. Psychol., Genève,* 1961, 38, 167–200.

Salapatek, P. H. Visual scanning of geometric forms by the human newborn. *Amer. Psychologist,* 1966, 21, 609. (Abstract)

Salaptek, P. H. Visual scanning of geometric figures by the human newborn. Unpublished doctoral dissertation, Yale Univ., 1966. *Diss. Abstr.,* 1967, 28(1–B), 368.

Salaptek, P., & Kessen, W. Visual scanning of triangles by the human newborn. *J. exp. Child Psychol.,* 1966, 3, 155–167.

Zinchenko, V. P., Ruzshaya, A. G., & Tarakanov, V. V. Sravnitel'nyĭ analiz osyazaniya i zreniya. Soobshchenie IX. Kharakteristiki dvizheniĭ glaz v fiksatsii u deteĭ doshkol'nogo vozrasta. *Dokl. Akad. Pedagog. Nauk RSFSR,* 1961, 6, 81–84.

b. Figure and ground; polyfigurations

Botha, E. Practice without reward and figure-ground perceptions of adults and children. *Percept. mot. Skills,* 1963, 16, 271–273.

Botwinick, J., Robbin, J. S., & Brinley, J. F. Reorganization of perceptions with age. *J. Geront.*, 1959, **14**, 85–88.

Elkind, D., Koegler, R. R., & Go, E. Effects of perceptual training at three age levels. *Science*, 1962, **137**, 755–756.

Elkind, D., & Scott, L. Studies in perceptual development. I. The decentering of perception. *Child Develop.*, 1962, **33**, 619–630.

Farkas, M. [Age differences in the perception of reversible figures.] *Stud. Univ. Babes-Bolyai*, 1959, **3**(1, No. 4), 97–109.

Ghent, L. Perception of overlapping and embedded figures by children of different ages. *Amer. J. Psychol.*, 1956, **69**, 575–587.

Karagianis, L. D., & Olson, D. R. Children's learning to respond to the ground of a figure-ground stimulus. *Ontario J. educ. Res.*, 1966, **9**(1), 33–41.

Meister, D. A comparative study of figure-ground discrimination in preschool children and adults. *J. genet. Psychol.*, 1949, **74**, 311–323.

Munsinger, H., & Gummerman, K. Identification of form in patterns of visual noise. *J. exp. Psychol.*, 1967, **75**, 81–87.

Ramamurthi, P. V., & Parmeswaran, E. G. A study of figure reversals in the old and the young. *J. Psychol. Res.*, 1964, **8**(1), 16–18.

Sokhina, V. P. O vydelenii figury iz fona doshkol'nikami: Soobshchenie III. Vydelenie formy v protsesse konstruirovaniya. *Dokl. Akad. Pedag. Nauk RSFSR*, 1962, No. 3, 91–95.

Solley, C. M., & Engel, M. Perceptual autism in children: The effect of reward, punishment, and neutral conditions upon perceptual learning. *J. genet. Psychol.*, 1960, **97**, 77–91.

Solley, C. M., & Sommer, R. Perceptual autism in children. *J. gen. Psychol.*, 1957, **56**, 3–11.

c. Gestalt laws

Bower, T. G. R. The determinants of perceptual unity in infancy. *Psychon. Sci.*, 1965, **3**, 323–324.

Bower, T. G. R. Phenomenal identity and form perception in an infant. *Percept. Psychophys.*, 1967, **2**, 74–76.

Crudden, C. H. Symmetry and asymmetry in form abstraction by children. *Microfilm Abstracts*, 1939, **2**, No. 1.

Furth, H. G., & Mendez, R. A. The influence of language and age on Gestalt laws of perception. *Amer. J. Psychol.*, 1963, **76**, 74–81.

Koffka, K. Théorie de la forme et psychologie de l'enfant. *J. Psychol.*, 1924, **21**, 102–112.

Koffka, K. *The growth of mind*. New York: Harcourt, Brace, 1927.

Mooney, C. M. Age in the development of closure ability in children. *Can. J. Psychol.*, 1957, **11**, 219–226.

Piaget, J., Maire, F., & Privat, F. Recherches sur le développement des perceptions. XVIII. La résistance des bonnes formes a l'illusion de Mueller-Lyer. *Arch. Psychol.*, Genève, 1954, **34**, 155–201.

Piaget, J., & Stettler-von Albertini, B. Recherches sur le développement des perceptions. XIX. Observations sur la perception des bonnes formes chez enfant par actualisation des lignes virtuelles. *Arch. Psychol.*, Genève, 1954, **34**, 203–242.

Rabbitt, P. M. A. Grouping of stimuli in pattern recognition as a function of age. *Quart. J. exp. Psychol.*, 1964, **16**, 172–176.

Rush, G. P. Visual grouping in relation to age. *Arch. Psychol.*, N. Y., 1937, **31**, No. 217.

Shroff, E. Ueber Gestaltauffassung bei Kindern im Alter von 6 bis 14 Jahren. *Psychol. Forsch.,* 1928, **11**, 235–266.

Usnadze, D. Gruppenbildungsversuche bei vorschulpflichtigen Kindern. *Arch. ges. Psychol.,* 1929, **73**, 216–248.

d. Geometric illusions

Binet, A. La mesure des illusions visuelles chez les enfants. *Rev Phil.,* 1895, **40**, 11–25.

Fraisse, P., & Vautrey, P. The influence of age, sex, and specialized training on the vertical-horizontal illusion. *Quart. J. exp. Psychol.,* 1956, **8**, 114–120.

Gajo, F. D. Adult age differences in the presence of visual illusions. Unpublished doctoral dissertation, Washington Univ., 1966. *Diss. Abstr.,* 1967, **27**(12–B), 4573.

Galli, A. Di Alcune illusioni ottiche per associazione nei bambini normali e negli anormali. *Pubbl. Univ. Catt. Milano,* Serie prima, 1926, **11**, 61–76.

Giering, H. Das Augenmass bei Schulkindern. *Z. Psychol.,* 1905, **39**, 42–87.

Griffin, M. C. Effects of mental and chronological age upon the extent of the horizontal-vertical illusion. Unpublished doctoral dissertation, Univ. of Utah, 1961. *Diss. Abstr.,* 1962, **23**, 308.

Hartmann, G. W., & Triche, A. Differential susceptibility of children and adults to standard illusions. *J. genet. Psychol.,* 1933, **42**, 493–498.

Knapp, B. W. Age trends in susceptibility to geometric illusions. *Amer. Psychologist,* 1964, **19**, 514. (Abstract)

Leibowitz, H. W., & Heisel, M. A. L'évolution de l'illusion de Ponzo en fonction de l'âge. *Arch. Psychol., Genève,* 1958, **36**, 328–331.

Leibowitz, H. W., & Gwozdecki, J. The magnitude of the Poggendorff illusion as a function of age. *Child Develop.,* 1967, **38**, 573–580.

Leibowitz, H. W., & Judisch, J. M. The relation between age and the magnitude of the Ponzo illusion. *Amer. J. Psychol.,* 1967, **80**, 105–109.

Noelting, G. Recherches sur le développement des perceptions. XL. La structuration progressive de la figure Mueller-Lyer en fonction de la répétition chez l'enfant et l'adulte. *Arch. Psychol., Genève,* 1960, **37**, 313–413.

Piaget, J. Le développement des perceptions en fonction de l'âge. In J. Piaget, P. Fraisse, E. Vurpillot, & R. Francès, *Traité de psychologie experimentale.* Paris: Presses Universitaires de France, 1967. Pp. 1–62.

Piaget, J., & von Albertini, B. Recherches sur le développement des perceptions. XI. L'illusion de Mueller-Lyer. *Arch. Psychol., Genève,* 1950, **33**, No. 129, 1–48.

Piaget, J., & Denis-Prinzhorn, M. Recherches sur le développement des perceptions. XVI. L'estimation perceptive des cotés du rectangle. *Arch. Psychol., Genève,* 1953, **34**, 109–131.

Piaget, J., & Osterrieth, P. A. Recherches sur le développement des perceptions. XVII. L'évolution de l'illusion d'Oppel-Kundt en fonction de l'âge. *Arch. Psychol., Genève,* 1953, **34**, 1–38.

Piaget, J., & Denis-Prinzhorn, M. Recherches sur le développement des perceptions. XXI. L'illusion des quadrilatères partiallment superposés chez l'enfant et chez l'adulte. *Arch. Psychol., Genève,* 1954, **34**, 289–321.

Piaget, J., & Morf, A. Recherches sur le développement des perceptions. XXVIII. Note sur la comparaison de lignes perpendiculaires égales. *Arch. Psychol., Genève,* 1955, **35**, 233–255.

Piaget, J., & Lambercier, M. Recherches sur le développement des perceptions. XXXI. Les comparaisons verticales à intervalles croissants. *Arch. Psychol., Genève,* 1956, **35,** 321–367.

Piaget, J., & Morf, A. Recherches sur le développement des perceptions. XXX. Les comparaisons verticales à faible intervalle. *Arch. Psychol., Genève,* 1956, **35,** 289–319.

Piaget, J., & Taponier, S. Recherches sur le développement des perceptions. XXXII. L'estimation des longeurs de deux droites horizontales et parallèles à extrémités décalées. *Arch. Psychol., Genève,* 1956, **35,** 369–400.

Piaget, J., & Morf, A. Recherches sur le développement des perceptions. XLIII. La comparaison des verticales et de horizontales dans la figure en équerre. *Arch. Psychol., Genève,* 1961, **38** (Whole No. 149), 69–88.

Piaget, J., Lambercier, M., Boesch, E., & von Albertini, B. Recherches sur le développement des perceptions. I. Introduction à l'étude des perceptions chez l'enfant et analyse d'une illusion relative à la perception visuelle de cercles concentriques (Delboeuf). *Arch. Psychol., Genève,* 1942, **29.** No. 113.

Pintner, R., & Anderson, M. M. The Mueller-Lyer illusion with children and adults. *J. exp. Psychol.,* 1916, **1,** 200–210.

Pollack, R. H., & Silver, S. D. Magnitude of the Mueller-Lyer illusion in children as a function of pigmentation of the Fundus oculi. *Psychon. Sci.,* 1967, **8,** 83–84.

Pollack, R. H., & Zetland, F. K. A translation of "the measurement of visual illusions in children" by Alfred Binet. *Percept. mot. Skills,* 1965, **20,** 917–930.

Ruessel, A. Ein entwicklungspsychologischer Beitrag zur Theorie der geometrisch-optischen Taeuschungen. *Arch. ges. Psychol.,* 1934, **91,** 289–304.

Santostefano, S. A developmental study of the Delboeuf illusion. *Percept. mot. Skills,* 1963, **17,** 23–29.

Soudková, M., & Rišková, A. [Effect of age on overestimation of the vertical line in the T-figure.] *Stud. Psychol.,* 1966, **8,** 204–215.

Spitz, H. H., & Blackman, L. S. The Mueller-Lyer illusion in retardates and normals. *Percept. mot. Skills,* 1956, **6,** 219–225.

Sun Shih-luh. [Age differences in the Mueller-Lyer illusion.] *Acta Psychol. Sinica,* 1964, No. 3, 223–228.

Vurpillot, É. L'influence de la signification du matériel sur l'illusion de Poggendorff. *Année Psychol.,* 1957, **57,** 339–357.

Vurpillot, E. *L'organisation perceptive: Son rôle dans l'évolution des illusions optico-géométriques.* Paris: Librairie Philosophique J. Vrin, 1963.

Walters, A. A genetic study of geometrical-optical illusions. *Genet. Psychol. Monogr.,* 1942, **25,** 101–155.

Winch, W. H. The vertical-horizontal illusion in school-children. *Brit. J. Psychol.,* 1907, **2,** 220–225.

Wuersten, H. Recherches sur le développement des perceptions. IX. L'évolution des comparaisons de longeurs de l'enfant à l'adulte avec variation d'angle entre la verticale et l'horizontale. *Arch. Psychol., Genève,* 1947, **32,** 1–144.

e. Figural aftereffects

Axelrod, S., & Eisdorfer, C. Senescence and figural aftereffects in two modalities. *J. genet. Psychol.,* 1962, **100,** 85–91.

Eisdorfer, C., & Axelrod, S. Senescence and figural aftereffects in two modalities: A correction. *J. genet. Psychol.,* 1964, **104,** 193–197.

Pollack, R. H. Figural aftereffects as a function of age. *Acta Psychol.,* 1960, **17,** 417–423.

Rich, T. A. Perceptual aftereffects, learning and memory in an aged group. Unpublished doctoral dissertation, Univ. of Florida, 1957. *Diss. Abstr.,* 1958, **18**, 311–312.

Thurner, F. K., & Seyfried, H. Are figural aftereffects dependent upon age? *Acta Psychol.,* 1962, **20**, 58–68.

Wertheimer, M. Figural aftereffects as a measure of metabolic efficiency. *J. Pers.,* 1955, **24**, 56–73.

f. Detection and discrimination

Davidson, H. P. A study of reversals in young children. *J. genet. Psychol.,* 1934, **45**, 452–465.

Dodd, J. M., & Strang, H. Conformity of perception of figure inversion in children. *Percept. mot. Skills,* 1966, **22**, 703–706.

Estes, B. W. Judgment of size in relation to geometric shape. *Child Develop.,* 1961, **32**, 277–286.

Huttenlocher, J. Discrimination of figure orientation: Effects of relative position. *J. comp. physiol. Psychol.,* 1967, **63**, 359–361.

Kerpelman, L. C., & Pollack, R. H. Developmental changes in the location of form discrimination cues. *Percept. mot. Skills,* 1964, **19**, 375–382.

Knoblauch, E. Vergleichende Untersuchungen zur optischen Auffassung hochgradig schwachsinniger und normaler Kinder. *Z. Angew. Psychol.,* 1934, **47**, 305–375.

Ling, B. C. Form discrimination as a learning cue in infants. *Comp. Psychol. Monogr.,* 1941, **17**, No. 2.

Loebenstein, R. *Formunterscheidung im ersten Lebensjahre.* Borna-Leipzig: Noske, 1936.

Long, L. Size discrimination in children. *Child Develop.,* 1941, **12**, 247–254.

Munn, N. L., & Steining, B. R. The relative efficacy of form and background in a child's discrimination of visual patterns. *J. genet. Psychol.,* 1931, **39**, 73–90.

Munsinger, H., & Kessen, W. Structure, variability, and development. *J. exp. child Psychol.,* 1966, **4**, 20–49.

Newhall, S. M. Identification by young children of differently oriented visual forms. *Child Develop.,* 1937, **8**, 105–111.

Newson, E. The development of line figure discrimination in pre-school children. Unpublished doctoral dissertation, Univ. of Nottingham, 1955.

Over, R., & Over, J. Detection and recognition of mirror-image obliques by young children. *J. comp. physiol. Psychol.,* 1967, **64**, 467–470.

Piaget, J. Recherches sur le développement des perceptions. X. Les illusions relatives aux angles et à la longeur de leurs côtes. *Arch. Psychol., Genève,* 1949, **32**, 281–307.

Piaget, J., & Morf, A. Recherches sur le développement des perceptions. XX. L'action des facteurs spatiaux et temporels de centration dans l'estimation visuelle des longeurs. *Arch. Psychol., Genève,* 1954, **34**, 243–288.

Piaget, J., & Pène, F. Recherches sur le développement des perceptions. XXV. Essai sur l'illusion de la médiane des angles en tant que mesure de l'illusion des angles. *Arch. Psychol., Genève,* 1955, **35**, 77–92.

Piaget, J., & Vurpillot, E. Recherches sur le développement des perceptions. XXVIII. La surestimation de la courbure des arcs de cercle. *Arch. Psychol., Genève,* 1956, **35**, 215–232.

Pollack, R. H. Contour detectability threshold as a function of chronological age. *Percept. mot. Skills,* 1963, **17**, 411–417.

Rajalakshmi, R., & Jeeves, M. A. Changes in tachistoscopic form perception as a function of age and intellectual status. *J. Gerontol.,* 1963, **18**, 275–278.

Robinson, J. S., & Higgins, K. E. The young child's ability to see a difference between mirror-image forms. *Percept. mot. Skills,* 1967, **25**, 893–897.

Rudel, R. G., & Teuber, H.-L. Discrimination of direction of line in children. *J. comp. physiol. Psychol.,* 1963, **56**, 892–898.

Sekuler, R. W., & Rosenblith, J. F. Discrimination of direction of line and the effect of stimulus alignment. *Psychon. Sci.,* 1964, **1**, 143–144.

Skeels, H. M. The use of conditioning techniques in the study of form discrimination of young children. *J. exp. Educ.,* 1933, **2**, 127–137.

Steggerda, M. Form discrimination tests as given to Navajo, Negro, and white school children. *Hum. Biol.,* 1941, **13**, 239–246.

Stern, W. Ueber verlagerte Raumformen. *Z. Angew. Psychol.,* 1909, **2**, 498–526.

Tanaka, T. [A developmental study of the comparison of figures varying in direction and arrangement of elements. III.] *Jap. J. Psychol.,* 1958, **28**, 344–349.

Tanaka, T. [A developmental study of the comparison of similarity of figures which change in direction and arrangement of elements. IV.] *Jap. J. Psychol.,* 1959, **30**, 97–102.

Welch, L. The development of discrimination of form and area. *J. Psychol.,* 1939, **7**, 37–54.

Welch, L. The development of size discrimination between the ages of 12 and 40 months. *J. genet. Psychol.,* 1939, **55**, 243–268.

Wohlwill, J. F., & Wiener, M. Discrimination of form orientation in young children. *Child Develop.,* 1964, **35**, 1113–1125.

g. Scaling

Berlyne, D. E. The influence of the albedo and complexity of stimuli on visual fixation in the human infant. *Brit. J. Psychol.,* 1958, **49**, 315–318.

Brennan, W. M., Ames, E. W., & Moore, R. W. Age differences in infants' attention to patterns of different complexities. *Science,* 1966, **151**, 354–356.

Cantor, G. N., Cantor, J. H., & Ditrichs, R. Observing behavior in preschool children as a function of stimulus complexity. *Child Develop.,* 1963, **34**, 683–689.

Fantz, R. L. Pattern vision in young infants. *Psychol. Rec.,* 1958, **8**, 43–47.

Fantz, R. L. The origin of form perception. *Sci. Amer.,* 1961, **204**(5), 66–72.

Fantz, R. L. Pattern vision in newborn infants. *Science,* 1963, **140**, 296–297.

Fantz, R. L. Visual perception and experience in early infancy: A look at the hidden side of behavior development. In H. W. Stevenson (Ed.), *Early behavior: Comparative and developmental approaches.* New York: Wiley, 1967. Pp. 181–224.

Fantz, R. L., & Nevis, S. Pattern preferences and perceptual-cognitive development in early infancy. *Merrill-Palmer Quart.,* 1967, **13**, 77–108.

Fantz, R. L., & Ordy, J. M. A visual acuity test for infants under six months of age. *Psychol. Rec.,* 1959, **9**, 159–164.

Fantz, R. L., Ordy, J. M., & Udelf, M. S. Maturation of pattern vision in infants during the first six months. *J. comp. physiol. Psychol.,* 1962, **55**, 907–917.

Ghent, L. Form and its orientation: A child's-eye view. *Amer. J. Psychol.,* 1961, **74**, 177–190.

Ghent, L., Bernstein, L., & Goldweber, A. M. Preferences for orientation of form under varying conditions. *Percept. mot. Skills,* 1960, **11**, 46.

Hershenson, M. Visual discrimination in the human newborn. Unpublished doctoral dissertation, Yale Univ., 1964. *Diss. Abstr.,* 1965, **26**, 1793.

Hershenson, M. Visual discrimination in the human newborn. *J. comp. physiol. Psychol.,* 1964, **58**, 270–276.

Hershenson, M., Kessen, W., & Munsinger, H. Pattern perception in the human newborn: A close look at some positive and negative results. In W. Wathen-Dunn (Ed.), *Models for the perception of speech and visual forms.* Cambridge, Massachusetts: M.I.T. Press, 1967. Pp. 282–290.

Hershenson, M., Munsinger, H., & Kessen, W. Preference for shapes of intermediate variability in the newborn human. *Science,* 1965, **147**, 630–631.

McCall, R. B., & Kagan, J. Attention in the infant: Effects of complexity, contour, perimeter, and familiarity. *Child Develop.,* 1967, **38**, 939–952.

Munsinger, H. Multivariate analysis of preference for variability. *J. exp. Psychol.,* 1966, **71**, 889–895.

Munsinger, H., & Weir, M. W. Infants' and young children's preference for complexity. *J. exp. Child Psychol.,* 1967, **5**, 69–73.

Silbiger, F. F. Facedness and complexity as determiners of attention in the human infant. Unpublished doctoral dissertation, Wayne State Univ., 1968. *Diss. Abstr.,* 1968, **28**(11–B), 4783.

Spears, W. C. The assessment of visual discrimination and preferences in the human infant. Unpublished doctoral dissertation, Brown Univ., 1962. *Diss. Abstr.,* 1963, **23**, 2998.

Spears, W. C. Assessment of visual preference and discrimination in the four-month-old infant. *J. comp. physiol. Psychol.,* 1964, **57**, 381–386.

Thomas, H. Preference for random shapes: Ages six through nineteen years. *Child Develop.,* 1966, **37**, 843–859.

Willis, E. J., & Dornbush, R. L. Preference for visual complexity. *Child Develop.,* 1968, **39**, 639–646.

h. Recognition and identification

Binet, A., & Henri, V. Le développement de la memoire visuelle chez les enfants. *Rev. Phil.,* 1894, **37**, 348–350.

Blair, F. X. A study of the visual memory of deaf and hearing children. Unpublished doctoral dissertation, Northwestern Univ., 1955. *Diss. Abstr.,* 1955, **15**, 2304.

Crook, M. N., Alexander, E. A., Anderson, E. M. S., Coules, J., Hanson, J. A., & Jeffries, N. T., Jr. Age and form perception. USAF Sch. Aviat. Med. Rep., 1958, No. 57–124.

Davidson, H. P. A study of the confusing letters B, D, P, and Q. *J. genet. Psychol.,* 1935, **47**, 458–468.

Fukuda, K. [Space perception in children and inverted letters.] *Nipon Seiri. Zasshi.,* 1937, **1**, 197–202.

Ghent, L. Recognition by children of realistic figures presented in various orientations. *Can. J. Psychol.,* 1960, **14**, 249–256.

Ghent, L. Effect of orientation on recognition of geometric forms by retarded children. *Child Develop.,* 1964, **35**, 1127–1136.

Ghent Braine, L. Age changes in the mode of perceiving geometric forms. *Psychon. Sci.,* 1965, **2**, 155–156.

Ghent, L., & Bernstein, L. Influence of the orientation of geometric forms on their recognition by children. *Percept. mot. Skills,* 1961, **12**, 95–101.

Hunter, I. M. L., & Duthie, J. H. The effect of interpolated experience on visual recognition. *Quart. J. exp. Psychol.,* 1957, **9**, 21–27.

Hunton, V. D. The recognition of inverted pictures by children. *J. genet. Psychol.,* 1955, **86**, 281–288.

Munsinger, H. Tachistoscopic recognition of stimulus variability. *J. exp. Child Psychol.,* 1965, **2**, 186–191.

Munsinger, H., & Forsman, R. Symmetry, development, and tachistoscopic recognition. *J. exp. Child Psychol.*, 1966, 3, 168–176.

Oetjen, F. Die Bedeutung der Orientierung des Lesestoffs fuer das Lesen und der Orientierung von sinnlosen Figuren fuer das Wiedererkennen derselben. *Z. Psychol.*, 1915, 71, 321–355.

Rice, C. The orientation of plane figures as a factor in their perception by children. *Child Develop.*, 1930, 1, 111–143.

Tanaka, T. [Developmental study on the comparison of similarity of figures which change in direction and arrangement of elements. VIII. Through the recognition method.] *Jap. J. Psychol.*, 1962, 32, 388–394.

Tiernan, J. J. The principle of closure in terms of recall and recognition. *Amer. J. Psychol.*, 1938, 51, 97–108.

Wallace, J. G. Some studies of perception in relation to age. *Brit. J. Psychol.*, 1956, 47, 283–297.

Watson, J. S. Perception of object orientation in infants. *Merrill-Palmer Quart.*, 1966, 12, 73–94.

i. Reproduction

Beery, K. E. Geometric form reproduction: Relationship to chronological and mental age. *Percept. mot. Skills*, 1968, 26, 247–250.

Burkhardt, H. Veraenderungen der Raumlage in Kinderzeichnungen. *Z. Paedag. Psychol.*, 1925, 26, 352–371.

Granit, A. R. A study on the perception of form. *Brit. J. Psychol.*, 1921, 12, 223–247.

Hanfmann, E. Some experiments on spacial position as a factor in children's perception and reproduction of simple figures. *Psychol. Forsch.*, 1933, 17, 319–329.

Johnson, G., Nilsson, I., & Weikert, C. Studies in Gestalt perception: Aspects on development from seven years to adult age. *Psychol. Res. Bull.*, 1968, 8(3).

Kroeber, W. Ueber das Aufzeichnen von Formen aus dem Gedaechtnis. *Z. angew. Psychol.*, 1938, 54, 273–327.

Osterrieth, P. A. Le test de copie d'une figure complexe; contribution à l'étude de la perception et de la mémoire. *Arch. Psychol., Genève*, 1944, 30, 206–356.

Slochower, M. Z. Experiments on dimensional and figural problems in the clay and pencil reproductions of line figures by young children. I. Dimension. *J. genet. Psychol.*, 1946, 69, 57–75.

Slochower, M. Z. Experiments on dimensional and figural problems in the clay and pencil reproductions of line figures by young children. II. Shape. *J. genet. Psychol.*, 1946, 69, 77–95.

Vedder, R. *Over het copieren van eenvoudige geometrische figuren door oligophrenen en jonge kinderen.* Amsterdam: N. V. Noord-Hollandsche Uitgevers Maatschappi, 1939.

Vurpillot, É., & Florés, A. La genèse de l'organisation perceptive. I. Rôle du contour et de la surface enclose dans la perception des figures. *Année Psychol.*, 1964, 64, 375–395.

2. Clinical studies

Gregory, R. L., & Wallace, J. G. Recovery from early blindness. *Exp. Psychol. Soc. Monogr.*, 1963, No. 2.

Senden, M. v. *Raum- und Gaestaltauffassung bei operierten Blindgeborernen vor und nach der Operation.* Leipzig: Barth, 1932.

Senden, M. v. *Space and sight.* London and New York: Methuen, 1960.

B. In animals

1. Deprivation studies

Hebb, D. O. The innate organization of visual activity: I. Perception of figures by rats reared in total darkness. *J. genet. Psychol.,* 1937, 51, 101–126.

Meyers, B., & McCleary, R. A. Interocular transfer of a pattern discrimination in pattern-deprived cats. *J. comp. physiol, Psychol.,* 1964, 57, 16–21.

Michels, K. M., Bevan, W., & Strasel, H. C. Discrimination learning and interdimensional transfer under conditions of systematically controlled visual experience. *J. Comp. Physiol. Psychol.,* 1958, 51, 778–781.

Riesen, A. H. The development of visual perception in man and chimpanzee. *Science,* 1947, 106, 107–108.

Riesen, A. H. Arrested vision. *Sci. Amer.,* 1950, 183(7).

Riesen, A. H., Chow, K. L., Semmes, J., & Nissen, H. W. Chimpanzee vision after four conditions of light deprivation. *Amer. Psychologist,* 1951, 5, 282. (Abstract.)

Siegel, A. I. Deprivation of visual form definition in the ring dove. I. Discriminatroy learning. *J. comp. physiol. Psychol.,* 1953, 46, 115–119.

Siegel, A. I. Deprivation of visual form definition in the ring dove. II. Perceptual-motor transfer, *J. comp. physiol. Psychol.,* 1953, 46. 249–252.

Tees, R. C. Effect of early restriction on later form discrimination in the rat. *Can. J. Psychol.,* 1968, 22, 294–301.

Wilson, P. D., & Riesen, A. H. Visual development in rhesus monkeys neonatally deprived of patterned light. *J. comp. physiol. Psychol.,* 1966, 61, 87–95.

2. Enrichment studies

Baird, J. C., & Becknell, J. C., Jr. Discrimination learning as a function of early form exposure. *Psychol. Rec.,* 1962, 12, 309–313.

Bennett, T. L., & Ellis, H. C. Tactual-kinesthetic feedback from manipulation of visual forms and nondifferential reinforcement in transfer of perceptual learning. *J. exp. Psychol.,* 1968, 77, 495–500.

Forgus, R. H. Advantage of early over late perceptual experience in improving form discrimination. *Can. J. Psychol.,* 1956, 10, 147–155.

Forgus, R. H. The effect of different kinds of form pre-exposure on form discrimination learning. *J. comp. physiol. Psychol.,* 1958, 51, 75–78.

Forgus, R. H. The interaction between form pre-exposure and test requirements in determining form discrimination. *J. comp. physiol. Psychol.,* 1958, 51, 588–591.

Gibson, E. J., & Walk, R. D. The effect of prolonged exposure to visually presented patterns on learning to discriminate them. *J. comp. physiol. Psychol.,* 1956, 49, 239–242.

Gibson, E. J., Walk, R. D., Pick, H. L., & Tighe, T. J. The effect of prolonged exposure to visual pattern on learning to discriminate similar and different patterns. *J. comp. Physiol. Psychol.,* 1958, 51, 584–587.

Gibson, E. J., Walk, R. D., & Tighe, T. J. Enhancement and deprivation of visual stimulation during rearing as factors in visual discrimination learning. *J. comp. physiol. Psychol.,* 1959, 52, 74–81.

Kerpelman, L. C. Pre-exposure to visually presented forms and nondifferential reinforcement in perceptual learning. *J. exp. Psychol.,* 1965, 69, 257–262.

Sackett, G. P. Development of preference for differentially complex patterns by infant monkeys. *Psychon. Sci.,* 1966, 6, 441–442.

Walk, R. D., Gibson, E. J., Pick, H. L., Jr., & Tighe, T. J. Further experiments on prolonged exposure to visual forms: the effect of single stimuli and prior reinforcement. *J. comp. Physiol. Psychol.,* 1958, 51, 483–487.

Walk, R. D., Gibson, E. J., Pick, H. L., Jr., & Tighe, T. J. The effectiveness of prolonged exposure to cutouts vs. painted patterns for facilitation of discrimination. *J. comp. Physiol. Psychol.,* 1959, 52, 519–526.

VII. APPLICATIONS

A. Military and industrial applications

Baker, C. A., & Grether, W. A. Visual presentation of information. WADC Tech. Rep. 54–160, August, 1954.

Bersh, P. J. Air Force requirements for forms research. In J. W. Wulfeck & J. H. Taylor (Eds.), *Form discrimination as related to military problems.* Washington, D. C.: Nat. Acad. Sci.-Nat. Res. Coun., 1957. Pp. 8–12.

Blackwell, H. R. *Laboratory studies of the visibility of targets.* Washington, D. C.: US Dept. Commerce, 1946.

Boynton, R. M., Elworth, C., & Palmer, R. M. Laboratory studies pertaining to visual air reconnaissance. WADC Tech. Rep. 55–304, Part III, 1958.

Dept. US Navy, Naval Reconn. Tech. Support Center. *Image interpretation handbook.* Vol. 1. Washington, D.C.: Depts. of the Army, Navy, and the Air Force, Dec. 1967.

Duntley, S. Q. The visibility of distant objects. *J. Opt. Soc. Amer.,* 1948, 38, 237–249.

Fitts, P. M. Engineering psychology and equipment design. In S. S. Stevens (Ed.), *Handbook of experimental psychology.* New York: Wiley, 1951. Pp. 1287–1340.

Goldstein, A. G. Two proposed studies on configuration perception. In J. W. Wulfeck & J. H. Taylor (Eds.), *Form discrimination as related to military problems.* Washington, D.C.: Nat. Acad. Sci.-Nat. Res. Coun., 1957. Pp. 184–189.

Gordon, D. A. Visual detection and identification: Military applications. Memo. of Proj. MICHIGAN 2144-397-R, Univ. of Michigan, Willow Run Lab., Ann Arbor, Michigan, 1959.

Harker, G. S. The significance of form discrimination to current army problems. In J. W. Wulfeck & J. H. Taylor (Eds.), *Form discrimination as related to military problems.* Washington, D. C.: Nat. Acad. Sci.-Nat. Res. Coun., 1957. Pp. 6–8.

Ireland, F. H. Effects of surround illumination on visual performance. An annotated bibliography. Aerosp. Med. Res. Labs., Wright-Patterson AFB, TR-67-103, 1967.

Leikind, M., & Weiner, J. (Comps.) *Visibility: A bibliography* (1925–1950). Washington, D. C.: Library of Congress, 1952.

Lyman, B. Visual detection, identification, and localization: An annotated bibliography HumRRO Tech. Rep., 1968, No. 68–2.

Morgan, C. T. *Human engineering guide to equipment design.* New York: McGraw-Hill, 1963.

Morris, A., & Horne, E. P. (Eds.), *Visual search techniques.* Washington, D. C.: Nat. Acad. Sci.-Nat. Res. Coun., 1960.

National Aeronautics and Space Administration. Visual information display systems. A survey. NASA, 1968.

Neisser, U. Visual search. *Sci. Amer.,* 1964, 210(6).

Sampson, P. B., Wade, E. A., et al. Literature survey on human factors in visual displays. RADC TR 61–95, 1961.

Sleight, R. B. Psychological factors in form discrimination studies. In J. W. Wulfeck & J. H. Taylor (Eds.), *Form discrimination as related to military problems.* Washington, D. C.: Nat. Acad. Sci.-Nat. Res. Coun., 1957. Pp. 42–45.

Weisz, A. Z., Licklider, J. C., Swets, J. A., & Wilson, J. P. Human pattern recognition procedures as related to military recognition problems. Cambridge, Massachusetts: Bolt, Rep. No. 939, 15 June 1962 (AFCRL–62–387).

White, C. T. The significance of form discrimination in Navy operations. In J. W. Wulfeck & J. H. Taylor (Eds.), *Form discrimination as related to military problems.* Washington, D. C.: Nat. Acad. Sci.-Nat. Res. Coun., 1957. Pp. 3–5.

Wulfeck, J. W., & Taylor, J. H. (Eds.), *Form discrimination as related to military problems.* Washington, D. C.: Nat. Acad. Sci.-Nat. Res. Coun., 1957.

1. Camouflage bibliographies

Anonymous. Camouflage. *Archit. Forum,* 1940, Nov.

Anonymous. Camouflage in modern warfare. *Nature,* 1940, **145**, 949–951.

Anonymous. Camouflage. *Pencil Points,* 1941, **22**, 288.

Anonymous. Camouflage bibliography. *Pratt Inst. Libr. Quart. Bklist,* 1942, **6**, No. 8, 3–11.

Cott, H. B. Camouflage in nature and in war. *Roy. Eng. J.,* 1938, Dec., 501–517.

Hill, W. P. T. Review of camouflage literature. *Marine Corps Gazette,* 1939, Nov., 22–26, 66–72.

Hill, W. P. T. Review of camouflage literature. *Marine Corps Gazette,* 1940, March, 40–48; Nov., 16, 70–80.

Hill, W. P. T. Review of camouflage literature. *Marine Corps Gazett,* 1941, March, 21, 52–64.

Library of Congress, Division of Bibliography. List of references on camouflage. Comp. G. H. Fuller, 1940, Nov. 13.

B. Legibility

Cornog, D. Y., & Rose, F. C. Legibility of alphanumeric characters and other symbols: II. A reference handbook. *Nat. Bur. Std. Misc. Publ.,* 1967, No. 262–2.

Cornog, D. Y., Rose, F. C., & Walkowicz, J. L. (Comps.) Legibility of alphanumeric characters and other symbols: I. A permuted title index and bibliography. *Nat. Bur. Std. Misc. Publ.,* 1964, No. 262–1.

Tinker, M. A. Experimental studies on the legibility of print: An annotated bibliography. *Reading Res. Quart.,* 1966, 1(4), 67–118.

C. Reading

Aulhorn, O. Die Lesegeschwindigkeit als Funktion von Buchstaben- un Zeilenlage. *Arch. ges. Physiol.,* 1948, **250**, 12–25.

Burtt, H. E. Typography and readability. *Elem. Engl.,* 1949, **26**, 212–221.

Carmichael, L., & Dearborn, W. F. *Reading and visual fatigue.* Boston, Massachusetts: Houghton, 1947.

Diack, H. *Reading and the psychology of perception.* New York: Philosophical Library, 1960.

Gibson, E. J. Development of perception: Discrimination of depth compared with discrimination of graphic symbols. In J. C. Wright & J. Kagan (Eds.), Basic cognitive processes in children. *Monogr. Soc. Res. Child Develop.,* 1963, 28, No. 2. Pp. 5–24.

Gibson, E. J., Gibson, J. J., Pick, A. D., & Osser, H. A developmental study of the discrimination of letter-like forms. *J. comp. physiol. Psychol.,* 1962, 55, 897–906.

Goins, J. T. *Visual perceptual ability and early reading progress.* Chicago, Illinois: Univ. of Chicago Press, 1958.

Luckiesh, M., & Moss, F. K. *Reading as a visual task.* Princeton, New Jersey: Van Nostrand, 1942.

Pierro, P. S. An investigation of visual form perception and eidetic imagery in students who read well and spell poorly. Unpublished doctoral dissertation, Northern Illinois Univ., 1966. *Diss. Abstr.,* 1967, 27, 2894–2895.

Potter, M. C. *Perception of symbol orientation and early reading success.* New York: Columbia Univ. Press, 1949.

Vernon, M. D. *The experimental study of reading.* London and New York: Cambridge Univ. Press, 1931.

Vernon, M. D., & Pickford, R. W. *Studies in the psychology of reading.* London: Her Majesty's Stationery Office, 1929.

VIII. THE AESTHETICS OF VISUAL FORM

Alexander, C. A result in visual aesthetics. *Brit. J. Psychol.,* 1960, 51, 357–371.

Angier, R. P. The aesthetics of unequal division. *Psychol. Rev., Monogr. Suppl.,* 1905, 4(17), 541–561.

Austin, T. R., & Sleight, R. B. Aesthetic preference for isosceles triangles. *J. appl. Psychol.,* 1951, 35, 430–431.

Barnhart, E. N. The criteria used in preferential judgments of geometrical forms. *Amer. J. Psychol.,* 1940, 53, 354–370.

Barron, F., & Welsh, G. F. Artistic perception as a possible factor in personality style. Its measurement by a figure preference test. *J. Psychol.,* 1952, 33, 199–203.

Beebe-Center, J. G., & Pratt, C. C. A test of Birkhoff's aesthetic measure. *J. gen. Psychol.,* 1937, 17, 339–353.

Berliner, A. Geometrischaesthetische Untersuchungen mit Japanern und an japanischem Material. *Arch. ges. Psychol.,* 1924, 49, 433–450.

Birkhoff, G. D. *Aesthetic measure.* Cambridge, Massachusetts: Harvard Univ. Press, 1933.

Buswell, G. T. *How people look at pictures.* Chicago, Illinois: Univ. of Chicago Press, 1935.

Calkins, M. W. An attempted experiment in psychological aesthetics. *Psychol. Rev.,* 1900, 7, 580–591.

Chandler, A. R., & Barnhart, E. N. *A bibliography of psychological and experimental aesthetics, 1864–1937.* Berkeley, California: Univ. of California Press, 1938. (Pp. 8–18, 47–70.)

Davis, F. C. Aesthetic proportion. *Amer. J. Psychol.,* 1933, 45, 298–302.

Davis, R. C. An evaluation and test of Birkhoff's aesthetic measure formula. *J. gen. Psychol.,* 1936, 15, 231–240.

Emch, A. Mathematical principles of aesthetic form. *The Monist,* October, 1900.

Eysenck, H. The empirical determination of an aesthetic formula. *Psychol. Rev.,* 1941, 48, 83–92.

Eysenck, H. J. An experimental study of aesthetic preference for polygonal figures. *J. gen. Psychol.,* 1968, 79, 3–17.

Farnsworth, P. R. Preferences for rectangles. *J. gen. Psychol.,* 1932, 7, 479–481.

Fechner, G. T. *Zur experimentalen Aesthetik.* Leipzig: S. Hirzel, 1871.

Fechner, G. T. *Vorschule der Aesthetik.* Leipzig: Breitkopf & Haertel, 1876.

Fere, C. Sentiment agreable produit par la vue de formes geometriques simples. *C. R. Soc. Biol.,* 1906, **61**, 269ff.

Goetz, K. O. Was ist am Bilde messbar? *SYN,* No. 2, 1966. Baden-Baden: Agis-Verlag.

Goetz, K. O. Bildmessung und Bildwahrnehmung: Untersuchungen ueber subjektive Redundanz. *Nachrichten, Bilder, Berichte* (Staatliche Kunstakademie Duesseldorf), No. 3. Sommersemester 1967.

Haines, T. H., & Davies, A. E. The psychology of aesthetic reaction to rectangular form. *Psychol. Rev.,* 1904, **11**, 249–281.

Harsh, C. M., Beebe-Center, J. G., & Beebe-Center, R. Further evidence regarding preferential judgment of polygonal forms. *J. Psychol.,* 1939, **7**, 343–350.

Heckel, R. Optische Formen und aesthetisches Erleben. In O. Kroh (Ed.), *Untersuchungen ueber das aesthetische Erleben,* Heft 1. Goettingen: Vandenhoek & Ruprecht, 1927.

Hevner, K. Experimental studies of the effective value of colors and lines. *J. appl. Psychol.,* 1935, **19**, 385–398.

Jennings, F. Preferences of pre-school children for specific geometric figures. *Child Develop.,* 1936, **7**, 227–235.

Kato, M. [An experimental study on esthetic proportion in simple forms.] *Jap. J. Exp. Psychol.,* 1938, **5**, 57–61.

Lalo, C. *L'esthetique expérimentale contemporaine.* Paris: Alcan, 1908.

Legowski, L. W. Beitraege zur experimentellen Aesthetik. *Arch. ges. Psychol.,* 1908, **12**, 236–311.

Lundholm, H. The affective tone of lines. *Psychol. Rev.,* 1921, **28**, 43–60.

Martin, L. J. An experimental study of Fechner's principles of aesthetics. *Psychol. Rev.,* 1906, **13**, 142–188.

McWhinnie, H. J. Effects of learning experience on preference for complexity and asymmetry. *Percept. mot. Skills,* 1966, **23**, 119–122.

Nienstedt, C. W., Jr., & Ross, S. Preferences for rectangular proportions in college students and the aged. *J. genet. Psychol.,* 1951, **78**, 153–158.

Ogden, R. M. Naive geometry in the psychology of art. *Amer. J. Psychol.,* 1937, **49**, 198–216.

Pierce, E. Aesthetics of simple form. *Psychol. Rev.,* 1894, **1**, 483–495.

Pierce, E. The aesthetics of simple forms. *Psychol. Rev.,* 1896, **3**, 270–282.

Poffenberger, A. T., & Barrows, B. E. The feeling value of lines. *J. appl. Psychol.,* 1924, **8**, 187–205.

Rashevsky, N. Contribution to the mathematical biophysics of visual perception with special reference to the theory of aesthetic values of geometric patterns. *Psychometrika,* 1938, **3**, 253–271.

Rashevsky, N. Further contributions to the mathematical biophysics of visual aesthetics. *Bull. Math. Biophys.,* 1942, **4**, 117–120.

Rashevsky, N. Some problems in mathematical biophysics of visual perception and aesthetics. *Bull. Math. Biophys.,* 1942, **4**, 177–191.

Rashevsky, N. A contribution to the mathematical biophysics of visual aesthetics. *Bull. Math. Biophys.,* 1945, **7**, 41–45.

Rashevsky, N., & Brown, V. A contribution to the mathematical biophysics of visual perception and aesthetics. *Bull. Math. Biophys.,* 1944, **6**, 119–124.

Rashevsky, N., & Brown, V. Contributions to the mathematical biophysics of visual aesthetics. *Bull. Math. Biophys.,* 1944, **6**, 163–168.

Rashkis, H. A., & Kahn, L. An apparatus for the study of form-preference. *Amer. J. Psychol.*, 1949, **62**, 421–423.

Rowland, E. H. The aesthetics of repeated space forms. *Harvard Psychol. Stud.*, 1906, **2**, 193–268.

Rowland, E. H. A study in vertical symmetry. *Psychol. Rev.*, 1907, **14**, 391–394.

Sander, F. Elementar-aesthetische Wirkungen zusammengesetzter geometrischer Figuren. *Psychol. Stud.*, 1913, **9**, 1–34.

Schiffman, H. R. Golden section: Preferred figural orientation. *Percept. Psychophys.*, 1966, **1**, 193–194.

Segal, J. Beitraege zur experimentellen Aesthetik: I. Ueber die Wohlgefaelligkeit einfacher raeumlicher Formen. *Arch. ges. Psychol.*, 1906, **7**, 53–124.

Shipley, W. C., Dattman, P. E., & Steele, B. A. The influence of size on preference for rectangular proportion in children and adults. *J. exp. Psychol.*, 1947, **37**, 333–336.

Stone, L. A., & Collins, L. G. The golden section revisited: a perimetric explanation. *Amer. J. Psychol.*, 1965, **78**, 503–506.

Terwilliger, R. F. Pattern complexity and affective arousal. *Percept. mot. Skills*, 1963, **17**, 387–395.

Thompson, G. G. The effect of chronological age on aesthetic preferences for rectangles of different proportions. *J. exp. Psychol.*, 1946, **36**, 50–58.

Thorndike, E. L. Individual differences in judgments of the beauty of simple forms. *Psychol. Rev.*, 1917, **24**, 147–153.

Valentine, C. W. *The experimental psychology of beauty.* London: Methuen, 1962.

Weber, C. O. The aesthetics of rectangles and theories of affection. *J. appl. Psychol.*, 1931, **15**, 310–318.

Witmer, L. Zur experimentellen Aesthetik einfacher raeumlicher Formverhaeltnisse. *Phil. Stud.*, 1894, **9**, 96–144, 209–263.

Woodworth, R. S. *Experimental psychology.* New York: Holt, 1938. Pp. 384–391.

AUTHOR INDEX

Numbers in italics refer to the pages on which the complete references are listed.

517

SUBJECT INDEX